A REPRESENT...

of some of America...
Colonial times to the present day

In this compact anthology Oscar Williams
and Edwin Honig have gathered
together the work of 20 major poets. The
selections—more than 370
poems in all—are large enough and
diverse enough to encompass the range and
individuality of each poet's genius.
To round out their volume
the editors have contributed biographical
notes on each poet's life and
Edwin Honig has written
a comprehensive introduction on the
role of the poet and of poetry
in a nation's history,
self-realization, and growth.

The Mentor Book of Major American Poets
features, in full, such long poems as:
Walt Whitman's *Song of Myself*
Vachel Lindsay's *The Congo*
Hart Crane's *The Bridge*
Ezra Pound's *Hugh Selwyn Mauberley*
Wallace Stevens's *Esthétique du Mal*
and up to 25 poems each
by such poets as
E. E. Cummings, Robert Frost,
W. H. Auden

The
MENTOR BOOK
of
MAJOR AMERICAN POETS

FROM
EDWARD TAYLOR AND WALT WHITMAN
TO
HART CRANE AND W. H. AUDEN

Edited by
OSCAR WILLIAMS
and
EDWIN HONIG

**WITH AN INTRODUCTION
AND NOTES ON THE POETS**

A MENTOR BOOK

MENTOR
Published by the Penguin Group
Penguin Books USA Inc , 375 Hudson Street,
New York, New York 10014, U.S.A.
Penguin Books Ltd, 27 Wrights Lane, London W8 5TZ, England
Penguin Books Australia Ltd, Ringwood, Victoria, Australia
Penguin Books Canada Ltd, 10 Alcorn Avenue, Toronto, Ontario, Canada
M4V 3B2
Penguin Books (N.Z.) Ltd, 182–190 Wairau Road, Auckland 10, New Zealand

Penguin Books Ltd, Registered Offices: Harmondsworth, Middlesex, England

Published by Mentor, an imprint of Dutton Signet a division of Penguin Books
USA Inc

First Mentor Printing, July, 1962
37 36 35 34 33

The editors wish to thank the following for permission to reprint the poems listed:
The Belknap Press of Harvard University Press, Cambridge Massachusetts, for
selections from *The Poems of Emily Dickinson*, edited by Thomas H Johnson,
copyright, 1951, 1955, by The President and Fellows of Harvard College.
Faber & Faber Ltd., London, for poems by W H Auden from *Collected Shorter
Poems, 1930–1944, Another Time, For the Time Being, Nones*, and *Homage
to Clio*.
Harcourt, Brace & World, Inc , New York, for the following selections from
Poems 1923-1954 by e e cummings: SPRING IS LIKE A PERFECT HAND, Copyright
1925, by e. e. cummings. A MAN WHO HAD FALLEN AMONG THIEVES and "NEXT
TO, OF COURSE GOD AMERICA I," Copyright 1926, by Horace Liveright; renewed,
1954, by e e cummings. IF THERE ARE ANY HEAVENS MY MOTHER WILL (ALL
BY HERSELF) HAVE and I SING OF OLAF GLAD AND BIG, Copyright, 1931, © 1959,
by e e cummings, MOUSE)WON, Copyright, 1935, by e e cummings, ANYONE
LIVED IN A PRETTY HOW TOWN and MY FATHER MOVED THROUGH DOOMS OF
LOVE, Copyright, 1940, by e e cummings, PITY THIS BUSY MONSTER, MANUN-
KIND, NO MAN, IF MEN ARE GODS; BUT IF GODS MUST, ALL IGNORANCE TOBOG-
GANS INTO KNOWN, DARLING! BECAUSE MY BLOOD CAN SING, and WHAT IF A
MUCH OF A WHICH OF A WIND Copyright, 1944, by e. e. cummings, WHEN SER-
PENTS BARGAIN FOR THE RIGHT TO SQUIRM and I THANK YOU GOD FOR MOST
THIS AMAZING, Copyright, 1950, by e e cummings; from *95 Poems* by e e
cummings: MAGGIE AND MILLY AND MOLLY AND MAY, © 1956, by e e cum-
mings, SO SHY SHY SHY AND WITH A, IN TIME OF DAFFODILS) WHO KNOW, and
STAND WITH YOUR LOVER ON THE ENDING EARTH, © 1958, by e. e. cummings,
THAT MELANCHOLY and I CARRY YOUR HEART WITH ME (I CARRY IT IN, Copy-
right, 1952, by e e cummings, THANKSGIVING (1956), and I AM A LITTLE
CHURCH (NO GREAT CATHEDRAL), © 1957, by e. e. cummings, WHATEVER'S
MERELY WILFUL, Copyright, 1950, by e. e. cummings, IF UP'S THE WORLD; AND
A WORLD GROWS GREENER, © 1958, by e. e. cummings
Holt, Rinehart and Winston, Inc., New York, for selections from *Complete Poems
of Robert Frost*, Copyright, 1930, 1949 by Holt, Rinehart and Winston, Inc.;
and for POLE STAR FOR THIS YEAR from *Public Speech· Poems by Archibald
MacLeish*, copyright 1936 by Archibald MacLeish
Houghton Mifflin Company, Boston, Massachusetts, for the following selections
from *Streets in the Moon* by Archibald MacLeish, copyright 1926, 1954 by
Archibald MacLeish: THE SILENT SLAIN, ELEVEN, ARS POETICA, THE END OF

(The two pages following constitute an extension of this copyright page)

The New England 'Quarterly, Burnswick, Maine, for STUPENDOUS LOVE: ALL SAINTS' ASTONISHMENT! and STILL I COMPLAIN; I AM COMPLAINING STILL by Edward Taylor, first published in *The New England Quarterly*.

Princeton University Press, Princeton, New Jersey, for selections (except for STUPENDOUS LOVE! ALL SAINTS' ASTONISHMENT! and STILL I COMPLAIN; I AM COMPLAINING STILL) from *Poetical Works of Edward Taylor*, edited by T. H. Johnson, Copyright 1939 by Rockland Editions, Copyright 1943 by Princeton University Press.

Random House, Inc., New York, for the following selections from *The Collected Poetry of W. H. Auden:* PETITION, O WHERE YOU GOING?, and SOMETHING IS BOUND TO HAPPEN, Copyright 1934 and renewed 1961 by W.H. Auden, O WHAT IS THAT SOUND, Copyright 1937 by Wystan Hugh Auden, MUSEE DES BEAUX ARTS, THE UNKNOWN CITIZEN, THE COMPOSER, IN MEMORY OF W. B. YEATS, HERMAN MELVILLE, THE NOVELIST, and EPITAPH ON A TYRANT, Copyright 1940 by W. H. Auden, MUNDUS ET INFANS, Copyright 1942 by W. H. Auden, NARRATOR ("Well, so that is that."), Copyright 1944 by W. H. Auden, ANOTHER TIME, WHO'S WHO, THE DIASPORA, THE CLIMBERS, and MACAO, Copyright 1945 by W. H. Auden; from *Nones:* THE CHIMERAS, Copyright 1951 by W. H. Auden; from *Homage to Clio:* WORDS, Copyright 1960 by W. H. Auden; and for POEM IN PROSE from *Act Five and Other Poems* by Archibald MacLeish, Copyright 1948 by Archibald MacLeish.

Edwin Honig's introduction (pp. xiii-xxix) was published in substantially the same form in *The Virginia Quarterly Review*, Summer, 1960 (Vol. 36, No. 3), pp. 416–429, under the title "American Poetry and the Rationalist Critic."

(M) REGISTERED TRADEMARK—MARCA REGISTRADA

Library of Congress Catalog Card Number: 62-14316

Printed in the United States of America

CONTENTS

EDWIN ARLINGTON ROBINSON (*1869-1935*)

STEPHEN CRANE (*1871-1900*)

ROBERT FROST (*b. 1874*)

VACHEL LINDSAY (*1879-1931*)

WALLACE STEVENS (1879-1955)

WILLIAM CARLOS WILLIAMS (b. 1883)

EZRA POUND (b. 1885)

MARIANNE MOORE (b. 1887)

JOHN CROWE RANSOM (b. 1888)

EDNA ST. VINCENT MILLAY (1892-1950)

ARCHIBALD MacLEISH (b. 1892)

E. E. CUMMINGS (*b. 1894*)

HART CRANE (*1899-1932*)

W. H. AUDEN (*b. 1907*)

INTRODUCTION

There are several useful anthologies representing American poetry from Colonial times to the present. But they invariably include much secondary material, for where the aim is comprehensiveness anywhere between sixty and a hundred poets must be exhibited. The same thing often happens when the anthologist limits himself to American poetry of the past hundred years: too many poets are included, so that the bulk of those barely in mid-career tend to crowd out the few older poets who really count. Profusion brings confusion, and the reader who makes his way through such a book feels like the circus spectator who has been distracted from the superb high-diving acrobats by the white mice or the lewd mandrills: he goes off wondering what the cheering was all about. There is some need, then, for a compact anthology restricted to sizable selections from the works of only the proven and best American poets.

To make such a collection, the editors had free range, at least hypothetically, over a period of three centuries. In English literature this is the period from 1660, which began as the metaphysical poets and the taste for their flamboyant style were being displaced by the makers of the boxed couplet and the rule of decorum. After a hundred years of the Augustan age, a renewed interest in landscapes and external nature emerged, leading to the Romantic revival. Then came the long Victorian age with its incredible appetite for didactic, historical, and sentimental verse. Around 1900 this was succeeded by a movement of reaction and revolt—soon dominated by the young transplanted Americans, Eliot and Pound, and by a middle-aging Irishman, W. B. Yeats—which introduced a new poetry, stripped of pieties, rhetoric, and rhyme, that we have been calling the modern style for sixty years. In Puritan America there was little time and less occasion for the practice of poetry, so that during Colonial times and for several decades after the Revolution not much first-rate poetry was or could be written. Until Whitman, in fact, what was thought to be of any merit usually reflected the prevailing tastes in London—or Boston, which looked to London for approval. Consequently one cannot expect to distribute equally among the centuries major poets who did not begin to appear in force until rather recently. And so to give a true picture of the best poetry in America means to put the emphasis where it belongs: on the steadier and more vital work produced since Whitman.

American poetry burst through its provincial shell with the publication of *Leaves of Grass* in 1855. But it took Americans a full century to recognize the fact, and to understand that Whitman was our first significant major poet. Not till quite recently was it possible to see that the emergence of Whitman's book—grown to four times its original length by the time he died in 1892—showed how a genuine poetic voice could find its full range and subject on native grounds.

By 1855 Poe's work was done; almost unnoticed at home, it was soon to undergo a surprising transformation through Baudelaire's translations, which made it the sacred cow of the French Symbolists. Meanwhile Longfellow's poetry was already being overrated. Dickinson had just begun to write, and the poetry of Edward Taylor was unknown; neither was to be conclusively discovered till the next century. In Emerson, Hawthorne, Thoreau, and Melville we had a distinguished group of imaginative writers who had much to do with releasing Whitman's voice. As Whitman put it in a famous acknowledgment, "I was simmering, simmering, simmering; Emerson brought me to a boil." But if he was liberated by Emerson, Whitman himself was to have little direct influence on the extraordinary poetry to come a decade or so after his death. Actually the immediate effect of *Leaves of Grass* was to stimulate both good and bad poets to a garrulous, often insipid expressionism wherever it was taken as a guide. Yet it was Whitman who first made poetry interesting as the full-time concern of an American concentrating on a native and contemporaneous subject matter. And as we have learned to assess his accomplishment, we have begun to understand the type of vision, with all its exaltation based on common but minutely observed instances, which had to establish itself before a major poetry could flourish in America. This is why Whitman is crucial to the history of American poetry. By his example we discover how to recognize our major poets and how to estimate the expense of imagination that has had to work against the difficult conditions of nurture in American life. Whitman's real influence has been cumulative, inundant, but underground, having indirectly fed a number of excellent and very different poets of our era—Hopkins, Laforgue, Perse, Yeats, Eliot, Frost, and Pound. Though rejecting his "democratic vistas," they sought through him the courage and sustenance by which to work out their own experiments in idiomatic language and "the prose tradition." "It was you that broke the new wood," Pound acknowledges. "We have one sap and one root—Let there be commerce between us."

These comments will turn on the common inheritance and aims of the major American poets which have made their activity significant. Occasionally the presence of a stubborn intruder will be detected in the foreground. He is the ubiquitous type of popular critic (more stony-headed preacher than critic) who somehow gets in whenever poetry is discussed nowadays and presents his anachronistic cause by misrepresenting the nature of poetry. He must be reckoned with because his is the voice of the confusionmonger magnified by the traditional solemnity of the rationalist and the intensity of the man with fixed ideas. Though he thinks himself on the side of the angels, he serves here as the devil's advocate; by consciously opposing him we get to know what we value and believe, and to make such things intelligible to ourselves.

Against such an antagonist stand the major poets, and they are harder to characterize because they differ so much from one another. Certain traits, nevertheless, they do have in common. A major poet contributes to the development of the art of poetry by the magnitude or the implacable center of gravity of his vision and craft. The energy of his expression withstands close scrutiny, sustaining its power and effect over the years. Just as everyone owns his particular face and voice, so the major poet owns his particular style and makes it do what he wishes it to do in a way that is rarely mistakable. For his manner of treating a subject invariably remakes it so that it appears to be presented for the first time.

But, having said this much, we must quickly add that such qualifications are ideal. Though the major poet often fulfills them, he sometimes loses rank by failing to do so in one poem or another—particularly, among more ambitious poets, in the longer poem. In defense of such lapses, it may be agreed that when Whitman nods we *know* that it is Whitman nodding and not Eddie Guest. And if he falls short of the mark, it is often because poetic exuberance requires a prolonged exhibition before some special excellence can emerge. In the greatest imaginative works, manner frequently succumbs to matter. And where such diverse interests and ambitions are at work as in American poetry, one expects many lapses.

2.

The technical diversity of our poetry is so prodigious it is bewildering. The free rhythms and long cadenced lines of Whitman, Jeffers, and Lindsay confront the intricate formal stanzas of Taylor, Poe, and Ransom. Millay's conventional sonnetry opposes the openhanded, deceptively free sonnetry of Robinson and Frost. Dickinson's light but sinewy quatrains have little in common with Auden's heavily freighted ballads where a traditional English measure often merges with the American cowboy song. The dense, eccentric linear developments of Marianne Moore's stanzas convert essayistic prose rhythms into original verse patterns; though starting from documentary and other prose interests she shares with William Carlos Williams, her style is completely opposed to his loose-jointed lines that are dyed in the colloquialisms of modern speech. Both the exultant formalist and the word-splitting, jargonish, tough-guy informalist are united in E. E. Cummings, who finds his models in Pound and Joyce as well as in Whitman's swelling line and Poe's echolalia. Pound's linguistic obsessions in the *Cantos,* his ragpicking accumulations of historical "exhibits" and his celebration of autocrats, cranks, and bigots nearly swamp one's patience just at the point where a good lyrical sail, urged on by a nice rhythmic wind, quickens it again. Whitman's sense-withering catalogues are just as trying; they show a similar need to embrace the reader's total sympathies with what barely escapes becoming a death grip but for some beguiling sense, emerging at the last moment, of the poet's sheer beneficences. No poetry is better finished than Wallace Stevens'; his elegant diction conventionalizes the unpredictable adjective or noun and shuns rhyme for verbal texture and intricate sound patterns until each poem becomes an airy, clean, and self-fulfilling structure, like a house by Frank Lloyd Wright. MacLeish's gift for euphony is strengthened by what he borrows from Pound, Eliot, and Perse, though at times suggesting a closer temperamental affinity with the nostalgias of Longfellow and the *longueur* of Swinburne. Gene Derwood and Hart Crane respect the hard resilient line of the English Metaphysicals and the French Symbolists; but as a result their language often suffers from overcompression— Derwood's on the side of archaisms and Crane's on the side of technical modernisms; still, no other contemporary poets have written so magnificently of the raw pity of death.

Even more striking than their technical and temperamental diversity is the coherence of aim that links poets of different sensibilities and periods. This is most pronounced in their addiction to the realistic portrayal of objects and the language of common speech. English poetry, which experienced a sharp break between the Metaphysicals and the Romantics because of the intervening rule of Neoclassical tastes and the formidable prose masters of the eighteenth century, had to struggle into the present century with the burden of a deteriorated poetic style. American poetry, which was still unrooted, fared better; its problem was not to shake off an unpromising manner, but to discover its own matter. One thing in its favor was that the source of the vivid, inventive common language of the seventeenth century, which it shared with England, was never too far below the surface in America. (This may be one reason why Eliot's campaign to redirect poetry to that source eventually succeeded so well.) Another favorable condition was America's free perceptiveness in coping with reality, its sense of necessity and its resourcefulness in dealing with the country's gigantic physical possibilities. De Tocqueville's well-known observation about the American imagination is apropos: "Its chief function is to devise what may be useful, and to represent what is real." Such needs and capacities brought Whitman "to a boil," and still challenge and perplex the imaginative energies of American poets.

"The fact," as Robert Frost says, "is the sweetest dream that labor knows." The statement refines Whitman's lines on the arrival of the Muse in America:

Bluffed not a bit by drainpipe, gasometer, artificial fertilizers,
Smiling and pleased with palpable intent to stay,
She's here installed amid the kitchenware.

This need for a realistic diet was what Yeats had remarked at the turn of the century about poets who are "full of an unsatisfied hunger for the commonplace." Surely the hunger—appetite rather than hunger—was more than satisfied in Whitman and Dickinson. But the same appetite is expressed as early as Edward Taylor:

> Who laced and filleted the earth so fine,
> With rivers like green ribbons smaragdine?
> Who made the seas its selvage, and it locks
> Like a quilt ball within a silver box?
> . . . .
> Who in this bowling alley bowled the sun?

It recurs when Taylor writes to God of his "damask web of velvet verse" in "Sacramental Meditations LVI" ("should I with silver tools delve through the hill"):

> To deck thy works up, all my web would run
> To rags and jags: so snick-snarled to the thrum.

The sharp flavor of the commonplace appears in Williams' description of peasants dancing in a Breughel painting:

> . . . the squeal and the blare
> and the tweedle of bagpipes, a bugle
> and fiddles tipping their bellies (round
> as the thick-sided glasses whose wash
> they impound) their hips and their
> bellies off balance to turn them. Kicking
> and rolling about the Fair Grounds,
> swinging their butts . . .

It is close at hand and slowly heightens in the opening stanza of Stevens' beautifully speculative "Sunday Morning":

> . . . late
> Coffee and oranges in a sunny chair,
> . . . .
> The pungent oranges and bright, green wings
> Seem things in some procession of the dead,
> Winding across wide water, without sound.

It is evident at the end of Marianne Moore's "Nevertheless" in the direct statement which sums up a world of fastidious observation:

> . . . What sap
> went through that little thread
> to make the cherry red!

The addiction to realism and common speech is so persistently exploited that one is inclined to regard it as characteristic of American poetry. The point needs stressing because single-minded critics often claim the opposite is true: that most American poetry is obscure and that all its practitioners, save those whose language and intent are absolutely obvious, commit something like treason against the nation. The charge only reveals a mistrust of poetry in those who cannot read it except as some rose-tinctured adulteration of prose or prose-sense. No poetry worthy of the name can be called treasonable; on the contrary, the cultural historian looks to the poetry of the past to discover how and what people felt most strongly about. The conscience and sensitivity of a nation are rarely expressed more keenly than by its poets—by those still living as well as those long dead. Yet the poet's role in society is poorly understood.

3.

Poets like MacLeish, Millay, and Cummings have written verse about the social scene, though not always in their most effective poetry. It is not the poet's job to speak merely of what he sees, but rather of that through which he sees and most realizes his consciousness as a man. "I am not anxious to give you the truth," wrote Whitman. "But I am very anxious to have you understand that all truth and power are feeble to you except your own. —Can I beget a child for you?" And again: "The universal and fluid soul impounds within itself not only all good characters and heroes but the distorted characters, murderers, thieves." And further, of the delegates to political conventions in the eighteen-fifties, Whitman observed, "the politicians . . . gaudy with gold chains made from the people's money and harlot's money twisted together; crawling, serpentine men, the lousy combings and born freedom sellers of the earth." Whitman's imagination thrived on a developing view of selfhood, which he identified with the evolving self-consciousness of America as a nation. At its best this view of selfhood irritates, not because it is egotistical, but because it challenges the deep uneasiness all men feel who have given their allegiance to high-sounding abstractions in the name of something bigger than themselves.

With nothing more or less than himself at stake, the poet is intricately engaged to the society of his time, which he serves as the voice that transcends impersonal authority—the self-possessed voice of one man speaking for every man. No larger voice can break the spell of the abstract, televised, antihuman, institutionalized, big-brother, mass-man voice that is built into us all, inhibiting the grave, silent, multifarious birth of the individual self. One may assume that this has always been the poet's role, at least among the greatest poets, where it is most consciously and consistently adhered to. But in our age, and typically in a large, mobile industrial society, with all its spectacular inventiveness, disruptions, and anxieties (and where "public opinion" is often a simulacrum for right thinking created by those who hold or seek power), people tend to become indifferent about their ability to think or feel for themselves. As recent history has made so terrifyingly evident, civilized men and women easily relinquish their liberty of action and belief to disciplined madmen incarnating some abstract notion of national or racial supremacy. If the tragic meaning of this harrowing event were fully understood, it would become clear that the poet's voice is needed now more than ever before—that voice which celebrates the difficult, joyous, imaginative process by which the individual man discovers and enacts his selfhood. Without this voice there is a real danger that future generations will have no conception of what it means to be an individual, so that some future poet may have to create man again because man will no longer really exist.

Solemn and well-respected critics often accuse poets occupied with the idea of selfhood of creating a "romantic impasse" which has alienated them from the life of a well-ordered society. The society these critics have in mind is a cherished dream of the English eighteenth-century world or the Southern agrarian world of pre-Civil War America. There, gentlemen in their country houses and adjoining chapels surround themselves with bevies of retainers or slaves, read Horace or Virgil on one day, James Thomson and Pope on the next, and are conveyed by carriage to the capital the following day to confer about their investments in the overseas trade before subsiding in their clubs for a long weekend. Since there are no clues that such a society, based on the country squire's prerogatives, any longer exists, these critics dream that some reversely triggered spring of time will one day shoot history back into the desired social order. Meanwhile, they speak about and write about the poetry of the past hundred and fifty years like a keeper fleaing an underbred dog that is only half the dog its sire was.

This polemical note would be irrelevant if their anachronistic prejudices were not taken seriously and if they were not using the "impasse" blamed on the poets as a text for denouncing modern poetry and modern life. They are lay preachers disguised as literary critics, propagating the dream of a buried status quo when poets dutifully heeled behind patrons, wrote occasional verse in their honor, and extolled the moral philosopher, the hegemony of the church, and the divine right of the ruling class to rule. The "orthodoxy" and "well-ordered society" these critics revere are blander forms of the modern authoritarian state, with its glorification of five-year plans, "objective" facts, extrovert behavior, and its class of petty managers "protecting the interests" of the "communal life" against the free-thinking individual. People who take these critics seriously are too confused, angry, or tired to concern themselves with a poetry they cannot easily (or dare not) understand and with the burdens of individual freedom they cannot bear. When a critic seems to share their grievance and to formulate their intolerable uneasiness, they swallow his prescription of "orthodoxy" with his diagnosis of "impasse." Beguiled by his single-mindedness, they accept the opposition he establishes between "serious" or "religious" poets, in whose work is read a clear-cut message, and the word-juggling "hedonistic" poets, who are labeled obscure. Thus Taylor is crudely set against Whitman and Eliot against Stevens, as if the religiosity of one poet were more trustworthy than the hedonism of the other. The truth is that such critics do not care much for Taylor or Eliot; moral dicta and political ideology interest them more than poetry. And they are not really concerned about a "romantic impasse," nor even about the modern age. They are the cultural salesmen of an estate that was liquidated by the Napoleonic Wars in Europe and the Civil War in the United States.

4.

The poem of the mind in the act of finding
What will suffice.   It has not always had
To find: the scene was set; it repeated what
Was in the script.

Then the theatre was changed
To something else.   Its past was a souvenir.

It has to be living, to learn the speech of the place.
It has to face the men of the time and to meet
The women of the time.   It has to think about war
And it has to find what will suffice.   It has
To construct a new stage. It has to be on that stage.
And, like an insatiable actor, slowly and
With meditation, speak words that in the ear,
In the delicatest ear of the mind, repeat,
Exactly, that which it wants to hear, at the sound
Of which, an invisible audience listens,
Not to the play, but to itself, expressed
In an emotion as of two people, as of two
Emotions becoming one.

Wallace Stevens is the poet; "Of Modern Poetry," the poem.
The excerpt describes the poet's role in revealing the source of
exchange between himself and the reader. It says that this
mutual educative process is a slow one, assuming that there is
a place for the poet and another for an audience that can listen
to itself through the words of the poet. But the poem is not
merely about modern poetry; it is also about the difficult busi-
ness of becoming an individual.

The greatest poverty is not to live
In a physical world, to feel that one's desire
Is too difficult to tell from despair. Perhaps,
After death, the non-physical people, in paradise,
Itself nonphysical, may, by chance, observe
The green corn gleaming and experience
The minor of what we feel. The adventurer
In humanity has not conceived of a race
Completely physical in a physical world.
The green corn gleams and the metaphysicals
Lie sprawling in majors of the August heat,
The rotund emotions, paradise unknown.

This is the thesis scrivened in delight,
The reverberating psalm, the right chorale.

One might have thought of sight, but who could think
Of what it sees, for all the ill it sees?
Speech found the ear, for all the evil sound,
But the dark italics it could not propound.
And out of what one sees and hears and out
Of what one feels, who could have thought to make
So many selves, so many sensuous worlds,
As if the air, the mid-day air, was swarming
With the metaphysical changes that occur,
Merely in living as and where we live.

The poet is Stevens again; the excerpt, the final section of "Esthétique du Mal," written during the last war. Its message would not comfort stubborn rationalists, rigid metaphysicians, or proponents of the orthodoxy of a well-ordered society. The message, however, is basically religious: it celebrates the virtues of existence, the only life man can experience totally, "in a physical world." The message is of course also hedonistic, for the same reason.

When, in "Hurt Hawks," Robinson Jeffers writes, "I'd sooner, except the penalties, kill a man than a hawk," he appears to be opposed to the humanism of poets like Whitman and Stevens. But if one reads the whole poem, and then reads his other poems in which the same indignant cry of the "inhumanist" persists, one sees that the poet's outraged denunciations of mankind are another means of propounding the principles of the good life in a world that has been devastated by the prime instruments of modern rationalism—industrialization and war. The same may be said of the sharply ironical attitude in Williams' "These" and in the many of Cummings' poems, but especially "pity this busy monster,manunkind" and the fierce "I sing of Olaf." There is indignation in the outspoken political poems of Stephen Crane, particularly in "War is Kind," in the poems of Edna Millay; in those of MacLeish, Hart Crane, Gene Derwood, Moore, Pound, and Robinson; in Whitman, even in Emily Dickinson.

The counterpart to these expressions of moral indignation— which the rationalist critic often misnames pessimism—is the search in American poetry for an island of promise, a spiritual garden, a personal refuge enclosed in reality. The place is not to be confused with a never-never land, since it must exist in some relation to the physical world; for the poets are not fantasists but, in Marianne Moore's words, " 'literalists of/ the imagination'—above/ insolence and triviality and can present/ for inspection, imaginary gardens with real toads in them . . ." Such a place is described on the road to the lost house and town in Frost's "Directive":

> Back out of all this now too much for us,
> Back in a time made simple by the loss
> Of detail, burned, dissolved, and broken off
> Like graveyard marble sculpture in the weather,
> There is a house that is no more a house
> Upon a farm that is no more a farm
> And in a town that is no more a town.
> The road there, if you'll let a guide direct you
> Who only has at heart your getting lost . . . .

The place is strongly associated with the poet's past life, but it evokes, at the same time, the symbol of a national or cultural past. In "Four Quartets" Eliot continually alternates the symbol and the reality, thereby suggesting the peculiar sense in which all of time is always present in human existence. (His rhythms and imagery are startlingly like Frost's, the more conventional poet whose "Directive" was published later than the "Quartets.")

> In succession
> Houses rise and fall, crumble, are extended,
> Are removed, destroyed, restored, or in their place
> Is an open field, or a factory, or a by-pass....
>
> Now the light falls
> Across the open field, leaving the deep lane
> Shuttered with branches, dark in the afternoon,
> Where you lean against a bank while a van passes,
> And the deep lane insists on the direction
> Into the village, in the electric heat
> Hypnotized. In a warm haze the sultry light
> Is absorbed, not refracted, by gray stone.
> The dahlias sleep in the empty silence.

In Eliot's rose garden, the world of a past that is always present wakens the poet's perception of the lost childhood of both one man and all mankind:

> Through the first gate,
> Into our first world, shall we follow
> The deception of the thrush? Into our first world.
> There they were, dignified, invisible,
> Moving without pressure, over the dead leaves,
> In the autumn heat, through the vibrant air,
> And the bird called, in response to
> The unheard music hidden in the shrubbery,
> And the unseen eyebeam crossed, for the roses
> Had the look of flowers that are looked at.
> There they were as our guests, accepted and accepting.
> So we moved, and they, in a formal pattern,
> Along the empty alley, into the box circle,
> To look down into the drained pool.
> Dry the pool, dry concrete, brown edged,
> And the pool was filled with water out of sunlight,
> And the lotus rose, quietly, quietly,
> The surface glittered out of heart of light,
> And they were behind us, reflected in the pool.
> Then a cloud passed, and the pool was empty.
> Go, said the bird, for the leaves were full of children,
> Hidden excitedly, containing laughter.
> Go, go, go, said the bird: human kind
> Cannot bear very much reality.

Here the trick is to find oneself when one is most lost and has no hope of discovering anything, least of all oneself. And this is precisely Frost's message in "Directive."

As for the woods' excitement over you
That sends light rustle rushes to their leaves,
Charge that to upstart inexperience.
Where were they all not twenty years ago?
. . . .
Make yourself up a cheering song of how
Someone's road home from work this once was,
. . . .
And if you're lost enough to find yourself
By now, pull in your ladder road behind you
And put a sign up CLOSED to all but me.
Then make yourself at home . . . .
. . . .
Your destination and your destiny's
A brook that was the water of the house,
Cold as a spring as yet so near its source,
. . . .
I have kept hidden in the instep arch
Of an old cedar at the waterside
A broken drinking goblet like the Grail
. . . .
(I stole the goblet from the children's playhouse.)
Here are your waters and your watering place.
Drink and be whole again beyond confusion.

This private place where the poetic vision rediscovers its source
and from which it goes forth to do its work is associated with
the sea in Crane's "Voyages"; with a landscape of underground
streams and rock in Auden's "Praise of Limestone"; with a for-
gotten birdsong in Whitman's "Out of the Cradle Endlessly
Rocking"; and with her father's garden in most of Dickinson's
poems. The visionary movement toward such a place and con-
dition is not a retreat from reality; it is a journey to recover
the buried heart of the poet's and the culture's identity, and
to bring it back into reality. Here there can be no question of
hedonism, willful obscurity or romantic impasse; it is a matter
of the simple necessity of the poetic imagination, which is to
restore man's belief in his own image and self, in his own
mortal continuity.

Often working under the necessity of believing "without
belief, beyond belief," as Wallace Stevens puts it, American
poets have constructed worlds where the human actor speaks
with all the modulations of which his voice is capable when it
is most conscious of being not merely a doctor, professor,
librarian, hermit, executive, clerk, or even poet, but of being a
full-time individual. In this most significant sense, American
poetry is unsurpassed by that of any other modern nation.

—Edwin Honig

The
MENTOR BOOK
of
MAJOR AMERICAN POETS

EDWARD TAYLOR
(1645–1729)

THE PREFACE

Infinity, when all things it beheld,
In nothing, and of nothing all did build,
Upon what base was fixed the lath, wherein
He turned this globe, and riggalled it so trim?
Who blew the bellows of his furnace vast?
Or held the mold wherein the world was cast?
Who laid its cornerstone? Or whose command?
Where stand the pillars upon which it stands?
Who laced and filleted the earth so fine,
With rivers like green ribbons smaragdine?
Who made the seas its selvage, and it locks
Like a quilt ball within a silver box?
Who spread its canopy? Or curtains spun?
Who in this bowling alley bowled the sun?
Who made it always when it rises set:
To go at once both down, and up to get?
Who the curtain rods made for this tapestry?
Who hung the twinkling lanthorns in the sky?
Who? who did this? or who is he? Why, know
It's only Might Almighty this did do.
His hand hath made this noble work which stands
His glorious handiwork not made by hands.
Who spake all things from nothing; and with ease
Can speak all things to nothing, if he please.
Whose little finger at his pleasure can
Out mete ten thousand worlds with half a span:
Whose might almighty can by half a looks
Root up the rocks and rock the hills by the roots.
Can take this mighty world up in his hand,
And shake it like a squitchen or a wand.
Whose single frown will make the heavens shake
Like as an aspen leaf the wind makes quake.
Oh! what a might is this! Whose single frown
Doth shake the world as it would shake it down?
Which all from nothing fet, from nothing, all:
Hath all on nothing set, lets nothing fall.
Gave all to nothing man indeed, whereby

Through nothing man all might him glorify,
In nothing is embossed the brightest gem
More precious than all preciousness in them.
But nothing man did throw down all by sin:
And darkened that lightsome gem in him,
   That now his brightest diamond is grown
   Darker by far than any coalpit stone.

OUR INSUFFICIENCY TO PRAISE GOD SUITABLY FOR HIS MERCY

Should all the world so wide to atoms fall,
   Should th' air be shred to motes; should we
  See all the earth hacked here so small
    That none could smaller be?
Should heaven and earth be atomized, we guess
The number of these motes were numberless.

But should we then a world each atom deem,
   Where dwell as many pious men
  As all these motes the world could teem,
    Were it shred into them?
Each atom would the world surmount, we guess,
Whose men in number would be numberless.

But had each pious man as many tongues
   At singing all together then
  The praise that to the Lord belongs,
    As all these atoms men?
Each man would sing a world of praise, we guess,
Whose tongues in number would be numberless.

And had each tongue, as many songs of praise
   To sing to the Almighty All;
  As all these men have tongues to raise
    To him their holy call?
Each tongue would tune a world of praise, we guess,
Whose songs in number would be numberless.

Nay, had each song as many tunes most sweet,
   Or one intwisting in't as many,
  As all these tongues have songs most meet
    Unparalleled by any?
Each song a world of music makes, we guess,
Whose tunes in number would be numberless.

Now should all these conspire in us, that we
  Could breathe such praise to thee, Most High:
    Should we thy sounding organs be
      To ring such melody?
Our music would the world of worlds outring,
Yet be unfit within thine ears to ting.

Thou didst us mold, and us new-mold when we
  Were worse than mold we tread upon.
    Nay, nettles made by sin we be:
      Yet hadst compassion.
Thou hast plucked out our stings; and by degrees
Hast of us, lately wasps, made lady bees.

Though e'er our tongues thy praises due can fan,
  A weevil with the world may fly,
    Yea fly away: and with a span
      We may out mete the sky.
Though what we can is but a lisp, we pray
Accent thereof. We have no better pay.

HOUSEWIFERY

Make me, O Lord, thy spinning wheel complete;
  Thy holy word my distaff make for me.
Make mine affections thy swift fliers neat,
  And make my soul thy holy spool to be.
    My conversation make to be thy reel,
    And reel the yarn thereon spun of thy wheel.

Make me thy loom then, knit therein this twine:
  And make thy holy spirit, Lord, wind quills:
Then weave the web thyself. The yarn is fine.
  Thine ordinances make my fulling mills.
    Then dye the same in heavenly colors choice,
    All pinked with varnished flowers of paradise.

Then clothe therewith mine understanding, will,
  Affections, judgment, conscience, memory;
My words and actions, that their shine may fill
  My ways with glory and thee glorify.
    Then mine apparel shall display before ye
    That I am clothed in holy robes for glory.

AM I THY GOLD? OR PURSE, LORD, FOR THY WEALTH

CANTICLES II : 1 : *I am . . . the lily of the valleys.*

Am I thy gold? Or purse, Lord, for thy wealth;
 Whether in mine or mint refined for thee?
I'm counted so, but count me o'er thyself,
 Lest gold-washed face, and brass in heart I be.
 I fear my touchstone touches when I try
 Me, and my counted gold too overly.

Am I new-minted by thy stamp indeed?
 Mine eyes are dim; I cannot clearly see.
Be thou my spectacles that I may read
 Thine image and inscription stamped on me.
 If thy bright image do upon me stand,
 I am a golden angel in thy hand.

Lord, make my soul thy plate: thine image bright
 Within the circle of the same enfoil.
And on its brims in golden letters write
 Thy superscription in an holy style.
 Then I shall be thy money, thou my hoard:
 Let me thy angel be, be thou my Lord.

THY HUMAN FRAME, MY GLORIOUS LORD, I SPY

Thy human frame, my glorious Lord, I spy,
 A golden still with heavenly choice drugs filled:
Thy holy love, the glowing heat whereby
 The spirit of grace is graciously distilled.
 Thy mouth the neck through which these spirits still;
 My soul thy vial make, and therewith fill.

Thy speech the liquor in thy vessel stands,
 Well tinged with grace, a blessed tincture, lo,
Thy words distilled grace in thy lips poured, and
 Give grace's tincture in them where they go.
 Thy words in grace's tincture still, Lord, may
 The tincture of thy grace in me convey.

That golden mint of words thy mouth divine
 Doth tip these words, which by my fall were spoiled:
And dub with gold dug out of grace's mine,

That they thine image might have in them foiled.
Grace in thy lips poured out's as liquid gold:
Thy bottle make my soul, Lord, it to hold.

I KENNING THROUGH ASTRONOMY DIVINE

I kenning through astronomy divine
  The world's bright battlement, wherein I spy
A golden path my pencil cannot line
  From that bright throne unto my threshold lie.
  And while my puzzled thoughts about it pore,
  I find the bread of life in't at my door.

When that this bird of paradise put in
  This wicker cage (my corpse) to tweedle praise
Had pecked the fruit forbid: and so did fling
  Away its food, and lost its golden days,
  It fell into celestial famine sore,
  And never could attain a morsel more.

Alas! alas! poor bird, what wilt thou do?
  This creature's field no food for souls e'er gave:
And if thou knock at angels' doors, they show
  An empty barrel: they no soul bread have.
  Alas! poor bird, the world s white loaf is done,
  And cannot yield thee here the smallest crumb.

In this sad state, God's tender bowels run
  Out streams of grace: and he to end all strife,
The purest wheat in heaven, his dear-dear Son
  Grinds, and kneads up into this bread of life:
  Which bread of life from heaven down came and stands
  Dished in thy table up by angels' hands.

Did God mold up this bread in heaven, and bake,
  Which from his table came, and to thine goeth?
Doth he bespeak thee thus: this soul bread take;
  Come, eat thy fill of this, thy God's white loaf?
  It's food too fine for angels; yet come, take
  And eat thy fill! it's heaven's sugar cake.

What grace is this knead in this loaf? This thing
  Souls are but petty things it to admire.
Ye angels, help: this fill would be to the brim
  Heaven's whelmed-down crystal meal bowl, yea and higher.
  This bread of life dropped in thy mouth doth cry:
  Eat, eat me, soul, and thou shalt never die.

THE ACCUSATION OF THE INWARD MAN

You want clear spectacles: your eyes are dim:
Turn inside out, and turn your eyes within.
Your sins like motes in the sun do swim: nay, see
Your mites are molehills, molehills mountains be.
Your mountain sins do magnitude transcend:
Whose number's numberless, and doth want end.
The understanding's dark, and therefore will
Account of ill for good, and good for ill.
As to a purblind man men oft appear
Like walking trees within the hemisphere,
So in the judgment carnal things excel:
Pleasures and profits bear away the bell.
The will is hereupon perverted so,
It lackeys after ill; doth good forgo.
The reasonable soul doth much delight
A pickpack t' ride o' the sensual appetite.
And hence the heart is hardened, and toys
With love, delight, and joy, yea vanities.

Make but a thorough search, and you may spy
Your soul a trudging hard, though secretly
Upon the feet of your affections mute,
And hankering after all forbidden fruit.
Ask but yourself in secret, laying near
Thy head thereto: 'twill whisper in thine ear
That it is tickled much, though secretly.
And greatly itches after villainy.
'Twill mock thee in thy face, and though it say
It must not tell, it scorns to tell thee nay.
But slack the reins, and come a loophole lower:
You'll find it was but pen-cooped up before.
Nay, muster up your thoughts, and take the pole
Of what walk in the entry of your soul:
Which if you do, you certainly will find
With robbers, cutthroats, thieves it's mostly lined.
And hundred rogues you'll find lie gaming there:
For one true man, that in that path appears.
Your true man too's oft footsore, seldom is
Sound wind and limb: and still to add to this,
He's but a traveler within that way:
Whereas the rest there pitch their tents, and stay.
Nay, nay, what thoughts unclean? lascivious?
Blasphemous? murderous? and malicious?
Tyrannic? wrathful? atheistic rise

Of evils new and old, of every size?
These bed and board here; make the heart a sty
Of all abominable brothelry.
    Then is it pure? is this the fruit of grace?
    If so, how do ye: you and I embrace!

UPON A SPIDER CATCHING A FLY

Thou sorrow, venom elf;
    Is this thy play,
To spin a web out of thyself
    To catch a fly?
        For why?

I saw a pettish wasp
    Fall foul therein:
Whom yet thy whorl pins did
        not hasp
    Lest he should fling
        His sting

But as afraid, remote
    Didst stand hereat,
And with thy little fingers
        stroke
    And gently tap
        His back.

Thus gently him didst treat
    Lest he should pet,
And in a froppish, aspish heat
    Should greatly fret
        Thy net.

Whereas the silly fly,
    Caught by its leg,
Thou by the throat tookst
        hastily,
    And 'hind the head
        Bite dead.

This goes to pot, that not
    Nature doth call.
Strive not above what
        strength hath got,
    Lest in the brawl
        Thou fall.

This fray seems thus to us:
    Hell's spider gets
His entrails spun to whipcords
        thus,
    And wove to nets,
        And sets.

To tangle Adam s race
    In's stratagems
To their destructions, spoiled,
        made base
    By venom things,
        Damned sins.

But mighty, gracious Lord,
    Communicate
Thy grace to break the cord;
        afford
    Us glory's gate
        And state

We'll nightingale sing like,
    When perched on high
In glory's cage, thy glory,
        bright:
    Yea, thankfully,
        For joy.

THE OUTWARD MAN ACCUSED

Turn o'er thy outward man, and judge aright.
Doth not a pagan's life outshine thy light?
Thy fleering looks, thy wanton eyes, each part
Are painted signpost of a wanton heart.
If thou art weighed in golden scales, dost do
To others as thou wouldst be done unto?
Weigh, weigh thy words: thy untruths, all which came
Out of thy mouth, and thou confessed the same.
Why did thy tongue detract from anyone,
Whisper such tales thou wouldst not have be known?
When thou wast got in such a merry vein,
How far didst thou exceed the golden mean?
When that thou wast at such a boon or feast,
Why didst thou rather lie than lose thy jest?
How wast thou tickled when thy droughty ears
Allayed their thirst with filthy squibs and jeers?
Why did thou glaver[1] men of place? And why
Scowl, gloat, and frown on honest poverty?
Why didst thou spend thy state in foolish pranks?
And peacock up thyself above thy ranks?
Why thoughtest thyself out of the world as shut,
When not with others in the cony cut?[2]
Hold up thy head; is't thus or no? if yea,
How then is all thy folly purged away?
  If no, thy tongue belies itself, for lo
Thou saidst thy heart was dressed from sin also.

THE JOY OF CHURCH FELLOWSHIP
RIGHTLY ATTENDED

In heaven soaring up, I dropped an ear
    On earth: and oh! sweet melody!
And listening, found it was the saints who were
    Encroached for heaven that sang for joy.
    For in Christ's coach they sweetly sing,
    As they to glory ride therein.

Oh! joyous hearts! Enfired with holy flame!
    Is speech thus tasseled with praise?
Will not your inward fire of joy contain,
    That it in open flames doth blaze?
    For in Christ's coach saints sweetly sing,
    As they to glory ride therein.

[1] *wheedle*   [2] *pony catching, swindling*

And if a string do slip by chance, they soon
   Do screw it up again: whereby
They set it in a more melodious tune
   And a diviner harmony.
     For in Christ's coach they sweetly sing,
     As they to glory ride therein.

In all their acts, public and private, nay,
   And secret too, they praise impart.
But in their acts divine, and worship, they
   With hymns do offer up their heart.
     Thus in Christ's coach they sweetly sing,
     As they to glory ride therein.

Some few not in; and some whose time and place
   Block up this coach's way, do go
As travelers afoot; and so do trace
   The road that gives them right thereto;
     While in this coach these sweetly sing,
     As they to glory ride therein.

AN ADDRESS TO THE SOUL OCCASIONED
BY A RAIN

Ye flippering Soul,
   Why dost between the nippers dwell?
Not stay, nor go. Not yea, nor yet contro'
   Doth this do well?
     Rise journeying when the skies fall weeping showers,
     Not o'er nor under the clouds and cloudy powers.

Not yea, nor no:
   On tiptoes thus? Why sit on thorns?
Resolve the matter: Stay thyself or go:
   Ben't both ways born.
     Wager thyself against thy surpliced see,
     And win thy coat, or let thy coat win thee.

Is this th' effect
   To leaven thus my spirits all?
To make my heart a crabtree cask direct?
   A verjuiced hall?
     As bottle ale, whose spirits prisoned must
     When jogged, the bung with violence doth burst?

Shall I be made
  A sparkling wildfire shop,
Where my dull spirits at the fireball trade
  Do frisk and hop?
      And while the hammer doth the anvil pay,
      The fireball matter sparkles ev'ry way.

One sorry fret,
  An anvil spark, rose higher,
And in thy temple falling, almost set
  The house on fire.
      Such fireballs dropping in the temple flame
      Burns up the building: Lord, forbid the same.

STUPENDOUS LOVE! ALL SAINTS' ASTONISHMENT!

JOHN VI: 55: *For my flesh is meat indeed, and my blood
is drink indeed.*

Stupendous love! All saints' astonishment!
  Bright angels are black motes in this sun's light.
Heaven's canopy, the pantile to God's tent,
  Can't cover't neither with its breadth nor height.
      Its glory doth all glory else outrun,
      Beams of bright glory to't are motes i'the sun.

My soul had caught an ague, and like hell
  Her thirst did burn: she to each spring did fly,
But this bright blazing love did spring a well
  Of aqua vigae in the Deity,
      Which on the top of heaven's high hill outburst
      And down came running thence t'allay my thirst.

But how it came, amazeth all communion.
  God's only Son doth hug humanity
Into his very person. By which union
  His human veins its golden gutters lie.
      And rather than my soul should die by thirst,
      These golden pipes, to give me drink, did burst.

This liquor brewed, thy sparkling art divine,
  Lord, in thy crystal vessels did up tun,
(Thine ordinances) which all earth o'ershine,
  Set in thy rich wine cellars out to run.

Lord, make thy butler draw, and fill with speed
My beaker full: for this is drink indeed.

Whole butts of this blest nectar shining stand
  Locked up with sapph'rine taps, whose splendid flame
Too bright do shine for brightest angels' hands
  To touch, my Lord. Do thou untap the same.
  Oh! make thy crystal butts of red wine bleed
  Into my crystal glass this drink indeed.

How shall I praise thee then? My blottings jar
  And wrack my rhymes to pieces in thy praise.
Thou breath'st thy vein still in my porringer,
  To lay my thirst, and fainting spirits raise.
  Thou makest glory's chiefest grape to bleed
  Into my cup: And this is drink indeed.

Nay, though I make no pay for this red wine,
  And scarce do say I thank ye for't; strange thing!
Yet were thy silver skies my beer bowl fine,
  I find my Lord would fill it to the brim.
  Then make my life, Lord, to thy praise proceed
  For thy rich blood, which is my drink indeed.

OH! WHAT A THING IS MAN? LORD, WHO AM I?

I JOHN II: 1: *And if any man sin, we have an advocate with the Father.*

Oh! What a thing is man? Lord, who am I?
  That thou shouldst give him law (Oh! golden line)
To regulate his thoughts, words, life thereby:
  And judge him wilt thereby too in thy time.
  A court of justice thou in heaven holdst,
  To try his case while he's here housed on mold.

How do thy angels lay before thine eye
  My deeds both white and black I daily do?
How doth thy court thou panelst there them try?
  But flesh complains. What right for this? let's know!
  For right or wrong, I can't appear unto't.
  And shall a sentence pass on such a suite?

Soft blemish not this golden bench, or place.
  Here is no bribe, nor colorings to hide,

Nor pettifogger to befog the case;
But justice hath her glory here well tried:
Her spotless law all spotted cases tends;
Without respect or disrespect them ends.

God's judge himself, and Christ attorney is;
The Holy Ghost registerer is found.
Angels the sergeants are, all creatures kiss
The book, and do as evidence abound.
All cases pass according to pure law,
And in the sentence is no fret nor flaw.

What saith, my soul? Here all thy deeds are tried.
Is Christ thy advocate to plead thy cause?
Art thou his client? Such shall never slide.
He never lost his case: he pleads such laws
As carry do the same, nor doth refuse
The vilest sinner's case that doth him choose.

This is his honor, not dishonor: nay,
No habeas corpus 'gainst his clients came;
For all their fines his purse doth make down pay.
He non-suites Satan's suite or casts the same.
He'll plead thy case, and not accept a fee.
He'll plead sub forma pauperis for thee.

My case is bad. Lord, be my advocate.
My sin is red: I'm under God's arrest.
Thou has the hit of pleading; plead my state.
Although it's bad, thy plea will make it best.
If thou wilt plead my case before the King,
I'll wagonloads of love and glory bring.

STILL I COMPLAIN, I AM COMPLAINING STILL

I JOHN II: 21: *And he is the propitiation for our sins; and not for ours only, but also for the sins of the whole world.*

Still I complain; I am complaining still.
O woe is me! Was ever heart like mine?
A sty of filth, a trough of washing swill,
A dunghill pit, a puddle of mere slime,
A nest of vipers, hive of hornets' stings,
A bag of poison, civet box of sins.

Was ever heart like mine? So bad? black? vile?
  Is any devil blacker? Or can hell
Produce its match? It is the very soil
  Where Satan reads his charms and sets his spell;
  His bowling alley where he shears his fleece
  At ninepins, nine holes, morris, fox and geese.

His palace garden where his courtiers walk;
  His jewel cabinet. Here his cabal
Do sham it and truss up their privy talk
  In fardels of consults and bundles all.
  His shambles and his butchers' stalls herein.
  It is the fuddling school of every sin.

Was ever heart like mine? Pride, passion fell,
  Ath'ism, blasphemy pot, pipe it, dance,
Play barleybreaks, and at last couple in hell:
  At cudgels, kit-cat, cards and dice here prance:
  At noddy, ruff and trump, fink, post and pair,
  Put, one-and-thirty, and such other ware.

Grace shuffled is away; Patience oft sticks
  Too soon, or draws itself out, and's out put.
Faith's overtrumped, and oft doth lose her tricks.
  Repentance's chalked up noddy, and out shut.
  They post and pare off grace thus, and its shine.
  Alas! alas! was ever heart like mine?

Sometimes methinks the serpent's head I maul:
  Now all is still: my spirits do recruit.
But ere my harp can tune sweet praise, they fall
  On me afresh and tear me at my root.
  They bite like badgers now: nay worse, although
  I took them toothless skulls, rot long ago.

My reason now's more than my sense, I feel
  I have more sight than sense: which seems to be
A rod of sunbeams t'whip me for my steel.
  My spirit's spiritless and dull in me
  For my dead prayerless prayers: the spirit's wind
  Scarce blows my mill about. I little grind.

Was ever heart like mine? My Lord, declare
  I know not what to do: What shall I do?
I wonder, split I don't upon despair.
  It's grace's wonder that I wrack not so.

I faintly shun't, although I see this case
Would say my sin is greater than thy grace.

Hope's day-peep down hence through this chink, Christ's name,
Propitiation is for sins. Lord, take
It so for mine. Thus quench thy burning flame
In that clear stream that from his side forth brake.
I can no comfort take while thus I see
Hell's cursed imps thus jetting strut in me.

Lord, take thy sword: these Anakims destroy;
Then soak my soul in Zion's bucking-tub
With holy soap, and niter, and rich lye.
From all defilement me cleanse, wash, and rub.
Then rinse, and wring me out till the water fall
As pure as in the well: not foul at all.

And let thy sun shine on my head out clear.
And bathe my heart within its radiant beams:
Thy Christ make my propitiation dear:
Thy praise shall from my heart break forth in streams.
This reaching virtue of Christ's blood will quench
Thy wrath, slay sin, and in thy love me bench.

SHOULD I WITH SILVER TOOLS DELVE THROUGH THE HILL

JOHN XV: 24: *If I had not done among them the works which none other man did, they had not had sin: but now have they both seen and hated both me and my Father.*

Should I with silver tools delve through the hill
Of Cordilera for rich thoughts, that I
My Lord, might weave with an angelic skill
A damask web of velvet verse, thereby
To deck thy works up, all my web would run
To rags and jags: so snick-snarled to the thrum.

Thine are so rich: within, without refined:
No work like thine. No fruits so sweet that grow
On the trees of righteousness of angel kind,
And saints, whose limbs reeved with them bow down low.
Should I search ore the nutmeg gardens shine,
Its fruits in flourish are but skegs to thine.

The clove, when in its white-greened blossoms shoots,
  Some call the pleasantst scent the world doth show,
None eye e'er saw, nor nose e'er smelt such fruits,
  My Lord, as thine, thou tree of life in'ts blow.
  Thou rose of Sharon, valleys lily true,
  Thy fruits most sweet and glorious ever grew.

Thou art a tree of perfect nature trim,
  Whose golden lining is of perfect grace,
Perfumed with deity unto the brim,
  Whose fruits, of the perfection, grow, of grace.
  Thy buds, thy blossoms, and thy fruits adorn
  Thyself and works, more shining than the morn.

Art, nature's ape, hath many brave things done:
  As the Pyramids, the Lake of Meris vast,
The pensile orchards built in Babylon,
  Psammitich's labyrinth (art's cramping task),
  Archimedes his engines made for war,
  Rome's golden house, Titus his theater.

The clock of Strasbourg, Dresden's table sight,
  Regsamont's fly of steel about that flew,
Turrian's wooden sparrows in a flight,
  And th' artificial man Aquinas slew,
  Mark Scaliota's lock and key and chain
  Drawn by a flea, in our Queen Bettie's reign.

Might but my pen in nature's inventory
  Its progress make, 't might make such things to jump,
All which are but invention's vents or glory:
  Wit's wantonings, and fancy's frolics plump:
Within whose maws lies buried times, and treasures,
  Embalmed up in thick-daubed sinful pleasures.

Nature doth better work than art, yet thine
  Outvie both works of nature and of art.
Nature's perfection and the perfect shine
  Of grace attend thy deed in ev'ry part.
  A thought, a word, and work of thine, will kill
Sin, Satan. and the curse: and law fulfill.

Thou art the tree of life in paradise,
  Whose lively branches are with clusters hung
Of lovely fruits, and flowers more sweet than spice.
  Bend down to us, and do outshine the sun.

Delightful unto God, do man rejoice
The pleasantest fruits in all God's paradise.

Lord, feed mine eyes then with thy doings rare,
  And fat my heart with these ripe fruits thou bear'st
Adorn my life well with thy works; make fair
  My person with apparel thou prepar'st.
  My boughs shall loaded be with fruits that spring
  Up from thy works, while to thy praise I sing.

THE REFLECTION

Lord, art thou at the table head above
  Meat, med'cine, sweetness, sparkling beauties, to
Enamor souls with flaming flakes of love,
  And not my trencher, nor my cup o'erflow?
  Ben't I a bidden guest? Oh! sweat mine eye:
  O'erflow with tears: Oh! draw thy fountains dry.

Shall I not smell thy sweet, oh! Sharon's rose?
  Shall not mine eye salute thy beauty? Why?
Shall thy sweet leaves their beauteous sweets upclose?
  As half ashamed my sight should on them lie?
  Woe's me! For this my sighs shall be in grain,
  Offered on sorrow's altar for the same.

Had not my soul's, thy conduit, pipes stopped been
  With mud, what ravishment would'st thou convey?
Let grace's golden spade dig till the spring
  Of tears arise, and clears this filth away.
  Lord, let thy spirit raise my sighings till
  These pipes my soul do with thy sweetness fill.

Earth once was paradise of heaven below,
  Till ink-faced sin had it with poison stocked;
And chased this paradise away into
  Heaven's upmost loft, and it in glory locked.
  But thou, sweet Lord, has with thy golden key
  Unlocked the door, and made a golden day.

Once at thy feast, I saw thee pearl-like stand
  'Tween heaven and earth, where heaven's bright glory all
In streams fell on thee, as a floodgate and
  Like sunbeams through thee on the world to fall.
  Oh! Sugar-sweet then! My dear sweet Lord, I see
  Saints' heaven-lost happiness restored by thee.

Shall heaven and earth's bright glory all up lie,
  Like sunbeams bundled in the sun in thee?
Dost thou sit rose at table head, where I
  Do sit, and carv'st no morsel sweet for me?
  So much before, so little now! Sprindge, Lord,
  Thy rosy leaves, and me their glee afford.

Shall not thy rose my garden fresh perfume?
  Shall not thy beauty my dull heart assail?
Shall not thy golden gleams run through this gloom?
  Shall my black velvet mask thy fair face veil?
  Pass o'er my faults: shine forth, bright sun; arise!
  Enthrone thy rosy self within mine eyes.

RALPH WALDO EMERSON
(1803–1882)

CONCORD HYMN

Sung at the completion of the Battle Monument, July 4, 1837

By the rude bridge that arched the flood,
  Their flag to April's breeze unfurled,
Here once the embattled farmers stood
  And fired the shot heard round the world.

The foe long since in silence slept;
  Alike the conqueror silent sleeps;
And Time the ruined bridge has swept
  Down the dark stream which seaward creeps.

On this green bank, by this soft stream,
  We set today a votive stone;
That memory may their deed redeem,
  When, like our sires, our sons are gone.

Spirit, that made those heroes dare,
  To die, and leave their children free,
Bid Time and Nature gently spare
  The shaft we raise to them and thee.

BRAHMA

If the red slayer think he slays,
  Or if the slain think he is slain,
They know not well the subtle ways
  I keep, and pass, and turn again.

Far or forgot to me is near;
  Shadow and sunlight are the same;
The vanquished gods to me appear;
  And one to me are shame and fame.

They reckon ill who leave me out;
    When me they fly, I am the wings;
I am the doubter and the doubt,
    And I the hymn the Brahmin sings.

The strong gods pine for my abode,
    And pine in vain the sacred Seven;
But thou, meek lover of the good!
    Find me, and turn thy back on heaven.

THE RHODORA

On Being Asked, Whence Is The Flower?

In May, when sea winds pierced our solitudes,
I found the fresh rhodora in the woods,
Spreading its leafless blooms in a damp nook,
To please the desert and the sluggish brook.
The purple petals, fallen in the pool,
Made the black water with their beauty gay;
Here might the redbird come his plumes to cool,
And court the flower that cheapens his array.
Rhodora! if the sages ask thee why
This charm is wasted on the earth and sky,
Tell them, dear, that if eyes were made for seeing,
Then Beauty is its own excuse for being:
Why thou wert there, O rival of the rose!
I never thought to ask, I never knew:
But, in my simple ignorance, suppose
The selfsame Power that brought me there brought you.

THE HUMBLEBEE

Burly, dozing humblebee,
Where thou art is clime for me.
Let them sail for Porto Rique,
Far-off heats through seas to seek;
I will follow thee alone,
Thou animated torrid zone!
Zigzag steerer, desert cheerer,
Let me chase thy waving lines;
Keep me nearer, me thy hearer,
Singing over shrubs and vines.

Insect lover of the sun.
Joy of thy dominion!
Sailor of the atmosphere;
Swimmer through the waves of air;
Voyager of light and noon;
Epicurean of June;
Wait, I prithee; till I come
Within earshot of thy hum—
All without is martyrdom.

When the south wind, in May days,
With a net of shining haze
Silvers the horizon wall,
And with softness touching all,
Tints the human countenance
With a color of romance,
And infusing subtle heats,
Turns the sod to violets,
Thou, in sunny solitudes,
Rover of the underwoods,
The green silence dost displace
With thy mellow, breezy bass.

Hot midsummer's petted crone,
Sweet to me thy drowsy tone
Tells of countless sunny hours,
Long days, and solid banks of flowers;
Of gulfs of sweetness without bound
In Indian wildernesses found;
Of Syrian peace, immortal leisure,
Firmest cheer, and birdlike pleasure.

Aught unsavory or unclean
Hath my insect never seen;
But violets and bilberry bells,
Maple sap and daffodils,
Grass with green flag half-mast high,
Succory to match the sky,
Columbine with horn of honey,
Scented fern, and agrimony,
Clover, catchfly, adder's tongue
And brier roses, dwelt among;
All beside was unknown waste,
All was picture as he passed.

Wiser far than human seer,
Yellow-breeched philosopher!
Seeing only what is fair,
Sipping only what is sweet,
Thou dost mock at fate and care,
Leave the chaff, and take the wheat.
When the fierce northwestern blast
Cools sea and land so far and fast,
Thou already slumberest deep;
Woe and want thou canst outsleep;
Want and woe, which torture us,
Thy sleep makes ridiculous.

EACH AND ALL

Little thinks, in the field, yon red-cloaked clown
Of thee from the hilltop looking down;
The heifer that lows in the upland farm,
Far-heard, lows not thine ear to charm;
The sexton, tolling his bell at noon,
Deems not that great Napoleon
Stops his horse, and lists with delight,
Whilst his files sweep round yon Alpine height;
Nor knowest thou what argument
Thy life to thy neighbor's creed has lent.
All are needed by each one;
Nothing is fair or good alone.
I thought the sparrow's note from heaven,
Singing at dawn on the alder bough;
I brought him home, in his nest, at even;
He sings the song, but it cheers not now,
For I did not bring home the river and sky;—
He sang to my ear,—they sang to my eye.
The delicate shells lay on the shore;
The bubbles of the latest wave
Fresh pearls to their enamel gave,
And the bellowing of the savage sea
Greeted their safe escape to me.
I wiped away the weeds and foam,
I fetched my sea-born treasures home;
But the poor, unsightly, noisome things
Had left their beauty on the shore
With the sun and the sand and the wild uproar.
The lover watched his graceful maid,
As 'mid the virgin train she strayed,

Nor knew her beauty's best attire
Was woven still by the snow-white choir.
At last she came to his hermitage,
Like the bird from the woodlands to the cage;—
The gay enchantment was undone,
A gentle wife, but fairy none.
Then I said, "I covet truth;
Beauty is unripe childhood's cheat;
I leave it behind with the games of youth."—
As I spoke, beneath my feet
The ground pine curled its pretty wreath,
Running over the club moss burs;
I inhaled the violet's breath;
Around me stood the oaks and firs;
Pine cones and acorns lay on the ground;
Over me soared the eternal sky,
Full of light and of diety;
Again I say, again I heard,
The rolling river, the morning bird;—
Beauty through my senses stole;
I yielded myself to the perfect whole.

THE PROBLEM

l like a church; I like a cowl;
I love a prophet of the soul;
And on my heart monastic aisles
Fall like sweet strains, or pensive smiles;
Yet not for all his faith can see
Would I that cowlèd churchman be.

Why should the vest on him allure,
Which I could not on me endure?

Not from a vain or shallow thought
His awful Jove young Phidias brought;
Never from lips of cunning fell
The thrilling Delphic oracle;
Out from the heart of nature rolled
The burdens of the Bible old;
The litanies of nations came,
Like the volcano's tongue of flame,
Up from the burning core below,—
The canticles of love and woe:
The hand that rounded Peter's dome

And groined the aisles of Christian Rome
Wrought in a sad sincerity;
Himself from God he could not free;
He builded better than he knew;—
The conscious stone to beauty grew.

Knowst thou what wove yon wood bird's nest
Of leaves, and feathers from her breast?
Or how the fish outbuilt her shell,
Painting with morn each annual cell?
Or how the sacred pine tree adds
To her old leaves new myriads?
Such and so grew these holy piles,
Whilst love and terror laid the tiles.
Earth proudly wears the Parthenon,
As the best gem upon her zone,
And Morning opes with haste her lids
To gaze upon the Pyramids;
O'er England's abbeys bends the sky,
As on its friends, with kindred eye;
For out of Thought's interior sphere
These wonders rose to upper air;
And Nature gladly gave them place,
Adopted them into her race,
And granted them an equal date
With Andes and with Ararat.

These temples grew as grows the grass;
Art might obey, but not surpass.
The passive Master lent his hand
To the vast soul that o'er him planned;
And the same power that reared the shrine
Bestrode the tribes that knelt within.
Ever the fiery Pentecost
Girds with one flame the countless host,
Trances the heart through chanting choirs,
And through the priest the mind inspires.
The word unto the prophet spoken
Was writ on tables yet unbroken;
The word by seers or sibyls told,
In groves of oak, or fanes of gold,
Still floats upon the morning wind,
Still whispers to the willing mind.
One accent of the Holy Ghost
The heedless world hath never lost.
I know what say the fathers wise,—

The Book itself before me lies,
Old *Chrysostom*, best Augustine,
And he who blent both in his line,
The younger *Golden Lips* or mines,
Taylor, the Shakespeare of divines.
His words are music in my ear.
I see his cowlèd portrait dear;
And yet, for all his faith could see,
I would not the good bishop be.

WOODNOTES

In unplowed Maine he sought the lumberers' gang
Where from a hundred lakes young rivers sprang;
He trode the unplanted forest floor, whereon
The all-seeing sun for ages hath not shone;
Where feeds the moose, and walks the surly bear,
And up the tall mast runs the woodpecker.
He saw beneath dim aisles, in odorous beds,
The slight Linnaea hang its twin-born heads,
And blessed the monument of the man of flowers,
Which breathes his sweet frame through the northern bowers.
He heard, when in the grove, at intervals,
With sudden roar the aged pine tree falls,—
One crash, the death hymn of the perfect tree,
Declares the close of its green century.
Low lies the plant to whose creation went
Sweet influence from every element;
Whose living towers the years conspired to build,
Whose giddy top the morning loved to gild.
Through these green tents, by eldest Nature dressed,
He roamed, content alike with man and beast.
Where darkness found him he lay glad at night;
There the red morning touched him with its light.
Three moons his great heart him a hermit made,
So long he roved at will the boundless shade.
The timid it concerns to ask their way,
And fear what foe in caves and swamps can stray,
To make no step until the event is known,
And ills to come as evils past bemoan.
Not so the wise; no coward watch he keeps
To spy what danger on his pathway creeps;
Go where he will, the wise man is at home,

His hearth the earth,—his hall the azure dome;
Where his clear spirit leads him, there's his road
By God's own light illumined and foreshadowed.

THE SNOWSTORM

Announced by all the trumpets of the sky,
Arrives the snow, and, driving o'er the fields,
Seems nowhere to alight: the whited air
Hides hills and woods, the river, and the heaven,
And veils the farmhouse at the garden's end.
The sled and traveler stopped, the courier's feet
Delayed, all friends shut out, the housemates sit
Around the radiant fireplace, enclosed
In a tumultuous privacy of storm.

Come see the north wind's masonry.
Out of an unseen quarry evermore
Furnished with tile, the fierce artificer
Curves his white bastions with projected roof
Round every windward stake, or tree, or door.
Speeding, the myriad-handed, his wild work
So fanciful, so savage, nought cares he
For number or proportion. Mockingly,
On coop or kennel he hangs Parian wreaths;
A swanlike form invests the hidden thorn;
Fills up the farmer's lane from wall to wall,
Mauger the farmer's sighs; and at the gate
A tapering turret overtops the work.
And when his hours are numbered, and the world
Is all his own, retiring, as he were not,
Leaves, when the sun appears, astonished Art
To mimic in slow structures, stone by stone,
Built in an age, the mad wind's night work.
The frolic architecture of the snow.

FABLE

The mountain and the squirrel
Had a quarrel,
And the former called the latter "Little Prig";
Bun replied,
"You are doubtless very big;
But all sorts of things and weather

Must be taken in together,
To make up a year
And a sphere.
And I think it no disgrace
To occupy my place.
If I'm not so large as you,
You are not so small as I,
And not half so spry.
I'll not deny you make
A very pretty squirrel track;
Talents differ; all is well and wisely put;
If I cannot carry forests on my back,
Neither can you crack a nut."

DAYS

Daughters of Time, the hypocritic Days,
Muffled and dumb like barefoot dervishes,
And marching single in an endless file,
Bring diadems and fagots in their hands.
To each they offer gifts after his will,
Bread, kingdoms, stars, and sky that holds them all.
I, in my pleached garden, watched the pomp,
Forgot my morning wishes, hastily
Took a few herbs and apples, and the Day
Turned and departed silent. I, too late,
Under her solemn fillet saw the scorn.

SAADI

Trees in groves,
Kine in droves,
In ocean sport the scaly herds,
Wedgelike cleave the air the birds,
To northern lakes fly wind-borne ducks,
Browse the mountain sheep in flocks,
Men consort in camp and town,
But the poet dwells alone.

God, who gave to him the lyre,
Of all mortals the desire,
For all breathing men's behoof,
Straitly charged him, "Sit aloof";
Annexed a warning, poets say,

To the bright premium,—
Ever, when twain together play,
Shall the harp be dumb.

Many may come,
But one shall sing;
Two touch the string,
The harp is dumb,
Though there come a million,
Wise Saadi dwells alone.

Yet Saadi loved the race of men,—
No churl, immured in cave or den;
In bower and hall
He wants them all,
Nor can dispense
With Persia for his audience;
They must give ear,
Grow red with joy and white with fear;
But he has no companion;
Come ten, or come a million,
Good Saadi dwells alone.

Be thou ware where Saadi dwells;
Wisdom of the gods is he,—
Entertain it reverently.
Gladly round that golden lamp
Sylvan deities encamp,
And simple maids and noble youth
Are welcome to the man of truth.
Most welcome they who need him most,
They feed the spring which they exhaust;
For greater need
Draws better deed:
But, critic, spare thy vanity,
Nor show thy pompous parts,
To vex with odious subtlety
The cheerer of men's hearts.

Sad-eyed Fakirs swiftly say
Endless dirges to decay,
Never in the blaze of light
Lose the shudder of midnight;
Pale at overflowing noon
Hear wolves barking at the moon;
In the bower of dalliance sweet

Hear the far Avenger's feet:
And shake before those awful Powers,
Who in their pride forgive not ours.
Thus the sad-eyed fakirs preach:
"Bard, when thee would Allah teach,
And lift thee to his holy mount,
He sends thee from his bitter fount
Wormwood,—saying, 'Go thy ways;
Drink not the Malaga of praise,
But do the deed thy fellows hate,
And compromise thy peaceful state;
Smite the white breasts which thee fed,
Stuff sharp thorns beneath the head
Of them thou shouldst have comforted;
For out of woe and out of crime
Draws the heart a lore sublime.' "
And yet it seemeth not to me
That the high gods love tragedy;
For Saadi sat in the sun,
And thanks was his contrition;
For haircloth and for bloody whips,
Had active hands and smiling lips;
And yet his runes he rightly read,
And to his folk his message sped.
Sunshine in his heart transferred
Lighted each transparent word,
And well could honoring Persia learn
What Saadi wished to say;
For Saadi's nightly stars did burn
Brighter than Jami's day.

Whispered the Muse in Saadi's cot:
"O gentle Saadi, listen not,
Tempted by thy praise of wit,
Or by thirst and appetite
For the talents not thine own,
To sons of contradiction.
Never, son of eastern morning,
Follow falsehood, follow scorning.
Denounce who will, who will deny,
And pile the hills to scale the sky;
Let theist, atheist, pantheist,
Define and wrangle how they list,
Fierce conserver, fierce destroyer,—
But thou, joy-giver and enjoyer,
Unknowing war, unknowing crime,

Gentle Saadi, mind thy rhyme;
Heed not what the brawlers say,
Heed thou only Saadi's lay.

"Let the great world bustle on
With war and trade, with camp and town;
A thousand men shall dig and eat;
At forge and furnace thousands sweat;
And thousands sail the purple sea,
And give or take the stroke of war,
Or crowd the market and bazaar;
Oft shall war end, and peace return,
And cities rise where cities burn,
Ere one man my hill shall climb,
Who can turn the golden rhyme.
Let them manage how they may,
Heed thou only Saadi's lay.
Seek the living among the dead.—
Man in man is imprisonèd;
Barefooted dervish is not poor,
If fate unlock his bosom's door,
So that what his eye hath seen
His tongue can paint as bright, as keen;
And what his tender heart hath felt
With equal fire thy heart shalt melt.
For, whom the Muses smile upon,
And touch with soft persuasion,
His words like a storm wind can bring
Terror and beauty on their wing;
In his every syllable
Lurketh Nature veritable;
And though he speak in midnight dark,—
In heaven no star, on earth no spark,—
Yet before the listener's eye
Swims the world in ecstasy,
The forest waves, the morning breaks,
The pastures sleep, ripple the lakes,
Leaves twinkle, flowers like persons be,
And life pulsates in rock or tree.
Saadi, so far thy words shall reach:
Suns rise and set in Saadi's speech!"

And thus to Saadi said the Muse:
"Eat thou the bread which men refuse;
Flee from the goods which from thee flee;
Seek nothing,—Fortune seeketh thee.

Nor mount, nor dive; all good things keep
The midway of the eternal deep.
Wish not to fill the isles with eyes
To fetch thee birds of paradise:
On thine orchard's edge belong
All the brags of plume and song;
Wise Ali's sun-bright sayings pass
For proverbs in the market place:
Through mountains bored by regal art,
Toil whistles as he drives his cart.
Nor scour the seas, nor sift mankind,
A poet or a friend to find:
Behold, he watches at the door!
Behold his shadow on the floor!
Open innumerable doors
The heaven where unveiled Allah pours
The flood of truth, the flood of good,
The seraph's and the cherub's food.
Those doors are men: the pariah hind
Admits thee to the perfect Mind.
Seek not beyond thy cottage wall
Redeemers that can yield thee all:
While thou sittest at thy door
On the desert's yellow floor,
Listening to the gray-haired crones,
Foolish gossips, ancient drones,
Saadi, see! they rise in stature
To the height of mighty Nature,
And the secret stands revealed
Fraudulent time in vain concealed,—
That blessed gods in servile masks
Plied for thee thy household tasks."

HAMATREYA

Bulkeley, Hunt, Willard, Hosmer, Meriam, Flint,
Possessed the land which rendered to their toil
Hay, corn, roots, hemp, flax, apples, wool and wood.
Each of these landlords walked amidst his farm,
Saying, "'Tis mine, my children's and my name's.
How sweet the west wind sounds in my own trees!
How graceful climb those shadows on my hill!
I fancy these pure waters and the flags
Know me, as does my dog: we sympathize;
And, I affirm, my actions smack of the soil."

Where are these men? Asleep beneath their grounds:
And strangers, fond as they, their furrows plow.
Earth laughs in flowers, to see her boastful boys
Earth-proud, proud of the earth which is not theirs;
Who steer the plow, but cannot steer their feet
Clear of the grave.
They added ridge to valley, brook to pond,
And sighed for all that bounded their domain;
'This suits me for a pasture; that's my park;
We must have clay, lime, gravel, granite ledge,
And misty lowland, where to go for peat.
The land is well,—lies fairly to the south.
'Tis good, when you have crossed the sea and back,
To find the sitfast acres where you left them."
Ah! the hot owner sees not Death, who adds
Him to his land, a lump of mold the more.
Hear what the Earth says:—

Earth Song

"Mine and yours;
  Mine, not yours.
  Earth endures;
  Stars abide—
  Shine down in the old sea;
  Old are the shores;
  But where are old men?
  I who have seen much,
  Such have I never seen.

"The lawyer's deed
  Ran sure,
  In tail,
  To them, and to their heirs
  Who shall succeed,
  Without fail,
  Forevermore.

"Here is the land,
  Shaggy with wood,

With its old valley,
  Mound and flood.
  But the heritors?—
  Fled like the flood's foam.
  The lawyer, and the laws,
  And the kingdom,
  Clean swept herefrom.

"They called me theirs,
  Who so controlled me;
  Yet every one
  Wished to stay, and is gone.
  How am I theirs,
  If they cannot hold me,
  But I hold them?"

When I heard the Earth song
I was no longer brave;
My avarice cooled
Like lust in the chill of the
    grave.

EXPERIENCE

The lords of life, the lords of life,—
I saw them pass
In their own guise,
Like and unlike,
Portly and grim,—
Use and surprise,
Surface and dream,
Succession swift, and spectral wrong,
Temperament without a tongue,
And the inventor of the game
Omnipresent without name;—
Some to see, some to be guessed,
They marched from east to west:
Little man, least of all,
Among the legs of his guardians tall,
Walked about with puzzled look.
Him by the hand dear Nature took,
Dearest Nature, strong and kind,
Whispered, "Darling, never mind!
Tomorrow they will wear another face,
The founder thou; these are thy race!"

COMPENSATION

Why should I keep holiday
    When other men have none?
Why but because, when these are gay,
    I sit and mourn alone?

And why, when mirth unseals all tongues,
    Should mine alone be dumb?
Ah! late I spoke to silent throngs,
    And now their hour is come.

FORBEARANCE

Hast thou named all the birds without a gun?
Loved the wood rose, and left it on its stalk?
At rich men's tables eaten bread and pulse?
Unarmed, faced danger with a heart of trust?
And loved so well a high behavior,
In man or maid, that thou from speech refrained,
Nobility more nobly to repay?
O, be my friend, and teach me to be thine!

THE PAST

The debt is paid,
The verdict said,
The Furies laid,
The plague is stayed,
All fortunes made;
Turn the key and bolt the door,
Sweet is death forevermore.
Nor haughty hope, nor swart chagrin,
Nor murdering hate, can enter in.
All is now secure and fast;
Not the gods can shake the past;
Flies-to the adamantine door
Bolted down forevermore.
None can re-enter there—
No thief so politic,
No Satan with a royal trick
Steal in by window, chink, or hole,
To bind or unbind, add what lacked,
Insert a leaf, or forge a name,
New-face or finish what is packed,
Alter or mend eternal fact.

ODE

Inscribed to W. H. Channing

Though loath to grieve
The evil time's sole patriot,
I cannot leave
My honeyed thought
For the priest's cant,
Or statesman's rant.

If I refuse
My study for their politic,
Which at the best is trick,
The angry Muse
Puts confusion in my brain.

But who is he that prates
Of the culture of mankind,
Of better arts and life?
Go, blindworm, go,
Behold the famous States
Harrying Mexico
With rifle and with knife!

Or who, with accent bolder
Dare praise the freedom-
    loving mountaineer?
I found by thee, O rushing
    Contoocook!
And in thy valleys,
    Agiochook!
The jackals of the Negro-
    holder.

The God who made New
    Hampshire
Taunted the lofty land
With little men;—
Small bat and wren
House in the oak:—
If earth-fire cleave
The upheaved land, and bury
    the folk,

The southern crocodile would
   grieve.
Virtue palters; Right is hence;
Freedom praised, but hid;
Funeral eloquence
Rattles the coffin lid.

What boots thy zeal,
O glowing friend,
That would indignant rend
The northland from the
   south?
Wherefore? to what good
   end?
Boston Bay and Bunker Hill
Would serve things still;—
Things are of the snake.

The horseman serves the
   horse,
The neatherd serves the
   neat,
The merchant serves the
   purse,
The eater serves his meat;
'Tis the day of the chattel,
Web to weave, and corn to
   grind;
Things are in the saddle,
And ride mankind.

There are two laws discrete,
Not reconciled,—
Law for man, and law for
   thing;
The last builds town and fleet,
But it runs wild,
And doth the man unking.

'Tis fit the forest fall,
The steep be graded,
The mountain tunneled,
The sand shaded,
The orchard planted,
The glebe tilled,
The prairie granted
The steamer built.

Let man serve law for man;
Live for friendship, live for
   love,
For truth's and harmony's
   behoof;
The state may follow how
   it can,
As Olympus follows Jove.

Yet do not I implore
The wrinkled shopman to my
   sounding woods,
Nor did the unwilling senator
Ask votes of thrushes in the
   solitudes.
Everyone to his chosen
   work—
Foolish hands may mix and
   mar;
Wise and sure the issues are.
Round they roll till dark is
   light,
Sex to sex, and even to
   odd;—
The overgod
Who marries Right to Might,
Who peoples, unpeoples,—
He who exterminates
Races by stronger races,
Black by white faces,—
Knows to bring honey
Out of the lion;
Grafts gentlest scion
On pirate and Turk.

The Cossack eats Poland,
Like stolen fruit;
Her last noble is ruined,
Her last poet mute;
Straight, into double band
The victors divide;
Half for freedom strike and
   stand;—
The astonished Muse finds
   thousands at her side.

GIVE ALL TO LOVE

Give all to love;
Obey thy heart;
Friends, kindred, days,
Estate, good fame,
Plans, credit, and the Muse,—
Nothing refuse.

'Tis a brave master;
Let it have scope:
Follow it utterly,
Hope beyond hope:
High and more high
It dives into noon,
With wing unspent,
Untold intent;
But it is god,
Knows its own path
And the outlets of the sky.

It was never for the mean;
It requireth courage stout.
Souls above doubt,
Valor unbending,
It will reward,—
They shall return
More than they were,
And ever ascending.

Leave all for love;
Yet, hear me, yet,

One word more thy heart
    behoved,
One pulse more of firm
    endeavor,—
Keep thee today,
Tomorrow, forever,
Free as an Arab
Of thy beloved.

Cling with life to the maid;
But when the surprise,
First vague shadow of
    surmise
Flits across her bosom young,
Of a joy apart from thee,
Free be she, fancy free;
Nor thou detain her vesture's
    hem,
Nor the palest rose she flung
From her summer diadem.

Though thou loved her as
    thyself,
As a self of purer clay,
Though her parting dims the
    day,
Stealing grace from all alive;
Heartily know,
When half gods go,
The gods arrive.

TERMINUS

It is time to be old,
To take in sail:—
The god of bounds,
Who sets to seas a shore,
Come to me in his fatal rounds,
And said: "No more!
No farther shoot
Thy broad ambitious branches, and thy root.
Fancy departs: no more invent;
Contract thy firmament

To compass of a tent.
There's not enough for this and that,
Make thy option which of two;
Economize the failing river,
Not the less revere the Giver,
Leave the many and hold the few.
Timely wise accept the terms,
Soften the fall with wary foot;
A little while
Still plan and smile,
And,—fault of novel germs,—
Mature the unfallen fruit.
Curse, if thou wilt, thy sires,
Bad husbands of their fires,
Who, when they gave thee breath,
Failed to bequeath
The needful sinew stark as once,
The baresark marrow to thy bones,
But left a legacy of ebbing veins,
Inconstant heat and nerveless reins,—
Amid the Muses, left thee deaf and dumb,
Amid the gladiators, halt and numb."

As the bird trims her to the gale,
I trim myself to the storm of time,
I man the rudder, reef the sail,
Obey the voice at eve obeyed at prime:
"Lowly faithful, banish fear,
Right onward drive unharmed;
The port, well worth the cruise, is near,
And every wave is charmed."

GOOD-BYE

Good-bye, proud world! I'm going home:
Thou art not my friend, and I'm not thine.
Long through thy weary crowds I roam;
A river ark on the ocean brine,
Long I've been tossed like the driven foam;
But now, proud world! I'm going home.

Good-bye to Flattery's fawning face;
To Grandeur with his wise grimace;
To upstart Wealth's averted eye;
To supple Office, low and high;

To crowded halls, to court and street;
To frozen hearts and hasting feet;
To those who go, and those who come;
Good-bye, proud world! I'm going home.

I am going to my own hearthstone,
Bosomed in yon green hills alone,—
A secret nook in a pleasant land,
Whose groves the frolic fairies planned;
Where arches green, the livelong day,
Echo the blackbird's roundelay,
And vulgar feet have never trod
A spot that is sacred to thought and God.

O, when I am safe in my sylvan home
I tread on the pride of Greece and Rome;
And when I am stretched beneath the pines,
Where the evening star so holy shines,
I laugh at the lore and the pride of man,
At the sophist schools, and the learned clan;
For what are they all, in their high conceit
When man in the bush with God may meet?

HENRY WADSWORTH LONGFELLOW
(1807–1882)

HYMN TO THE NIGHT

Ἀστασίη, τρίλλιστος

I heard the trailing garments of the Night
    Sweep through her marble halls!
I saw her sable skirts all fringed with light
    From the celestial walls!

I felt her presence, by its spell of might,
    Stoop o'er me from above;
The calm, majestic presence of the Night,
    As of the one I love.

I heard the sounds of sorrow and delight,
    The manifold, soft chimes,
That fill the haunted chambers of the Night,
    Like some old poet's rhymes.

From the cool cisterns of the midnight air
    My spirit drank repose;
The fountain of perpetual peace flows there,—
    From those deep cisterns flows.

O holy Night! from thee I learn to bear
    What man has borne before!
Thou layest thy finger on the lips of Care,
    And they complain no more.

Peace! Peace! Orestes-like I breathe this prayer!
    Descend with broad-winged flight,
The welcome, the thrice-prayed for, the most fair,
    The best-beloved Night!

THE DAY IS DONE

The day is done, and the darkness
   Falls from the wings of Night,
As a feather is wafted downward
   From an eagle in his flight.

I see the lights of the village
   Gleam through the rain and the mist,
And a feeling of sadness comes o'er me
   That my soul cannot resist:

A feeling of sadness and longing,
   That is not akin to pain,
And resembles sorrow only
   As the mist resembles the rain.

Come, read to me some poem,
   Some simple and heartfelt lay,
That shall soothe this restless feeling,
   And banish the thoughts of day.

Not from the grand old masters,
   Not from the bards sublime,
Whose distant footsteps echo
   Through the corridors of Time.

For, like strains of martial music,
   Their mighty thoughts suggest
Life's endless toil and endeavor;
   And tonight I long for rest.

Read from some humbler poet,
   Whose songs gushed from his heart,
As showers from the clouds of summer,
   Or tears from the eyelids start;

Who, through long days of labor,
   And nights devoid of ease,
Still heard in his soul the music
   Of wonderful melodies.

Such songs have power to quiet
   The restless pulse of care,
And come like the benediction
   That follows after prayer.

Then read from the treasured volume
  The poem of thy choice,
And lend to the rhyme of the poet
  The beauty of thy voice.

And the night shall be filled with music,
  And the cares, that infest the day,
Shall fold their tents, like the Arabs,
  And as silently steal away.

CURFEW

I

Solemnly, mournfully,
  Dealing its dole,
The curfew bell
  Is beginning to toll.

Cover the embers,
  And put out the light;
Toil comes with the morning,
  And rest with the night.

Dark grow the windows,
  And quenched is the fire;
Sound fades into silence,—
  All footsteps retire.

No voice in the chambers,
  No sound in the hall!
Sleep and oblivion
  Reign over all!

II

The book is completed,
  And closed, like the day;
And the hand that has written it
  Lays it away.

Dim grow its fancies;
  Forgotten they lie;
Like coals in the ashes,
  They darken and die.

Song sinks into silence,
  The story is told,
The windows are darkened,
  The hearthstone is cold.

Darker and darker
  The black shadows fall;
Sleep and oblivion
  Reign over all.

THE JEWISH CEMETERY AT NEWPORT

How strange it seems! These Hebrews in their graves,
  Close by the street of their fair seaport town,
Silent beside the never-silent waves,
  At rest in all this moving up and down!

The trees are white with dust, that o'er their sleep
  Wave their broad curtains in the south wind's breath,
While underneath these leafy tents they keep
  The long, mysterious Exodus of Death.

And these sepulchral stones, so old and brown,
  That pave with level flags their burial place,
Seem like the tablets of the Law, thrown down
  And broken by Moses at the mountain's base.

The very names recorded here are strange,
  Of foreign accent, and of different climes;
Alvares and Rivera interchange
  With Abraham and Jacob of old times.

"Blessed be God, for he created death!"
  The mourners said, "and death is rest and peace";
Then added, in the certainty of faith,
  "And giveth life that nevermore shall cease."

Closed are the portals of their synagogue,
  No Psalms of David now the silence break,
No Rabbi reads the ancient Decalogue
  In the grand dialect the prophets spake.

Gone are the living, but the dead remain,
  And not neglected; for a hand unseen,
Scattering its bounty, like a summer rain,
  Still keeps their graves and their remembrance green.

How came they here? What burst of Christian hate,
  What persecution, merciless and blind,
Drove o'er the sea—that desert desolate—
  These Ishmaels and Hagars of mankind?

They lived in narrow streets and lanes obscure,
  Ghetto and Judenstrass, in murk and mire;
Taught in the school of patience to endure
  The life of anguish and the death of fire.

All their lives long, with the unleavened bread
  And bitter herbs of exile and its fears,
The wasting famine of the heart they fed,
  And slaked its thirst with Marah of their tears.

Anathema maranatha! was the cry
  That rang from town to town, from street to street:
At every gate the accursed Mordecai
  Was mocked and jeered, and spurned by Christian feet.

Pride and humiliation hand in hand
  Walked with them through the world where'er they went;
Trampled and beaten were they as the sand,
  And yet unshaken as the continent.

For in the background figures vague and vast
  Of patriarchs and of prophets rose sublime,
And all the great traditions of the past
  They saw reflected in the coming time.

And thus forever with reverted look
  The mystic volume of the world they read,
Spelling it backward, like a Hebrew book,
  Till life became a legend of the dead.

But ah! what once has been shall be no more!
  The groaning earth in travail and in pain
Brings forth its races, but does not restore,
  And the dead nations never rise again.

MY LOST YOUTH

  Often I think of the beautiful town
    That is seated by the sea;
  Often in thought go up and down
    The pleasant streets of that dear old town,

And my youth comes back to me.
   And a verse of a Lapland song
Is haunting my memory still:
   "A boy's will is the wind's will,
And the thoughts of youth are long, long thoughts."

I can see the shadowy lines of its trees,
   And catch, in sudden gleams,
The sheen of the far-surrounding seas,
And islands that were the Hesperides
   Of all my boyish dreams.
      And the burden of that old song,
      It murmurs and whispers still:
      "A boy's will is the wind's will,
And the thoughts of youth are long, long thoughts."

I remember the black wharves and the slips,
   And the sea tides tossing free;
And Spanish sailors with bearded lips,
And the beauty and mystery of the ships,
   And the magic of the sea.
      And the voice of that wayward song
      Is singing and saying still:
      "A boy's will is the wind's will,
And the thoughts of youth are long, long thoughts."

I remember the bulwarks by the shore,
   And the fort upon the hill;
The sunrise gun, with its hollow roar,
The drumbeat repeated o'er and o'er,
   And the bugle wild and shrill.
      And the music of that old song
      Throbs in my memory still:
      "A boy's will is the wind's will,
And the thoughts of youth are long, long thoughts."

I remember the sea fight far away,
   How it thundered o'er the tide!
And the dead captains, as they lay
In their graves, o'erlooking the tranquil bay
   Where they in battle died.
      And the sound of that mournful song
      Goes through me with a thrill:
      "A boy's will is the wind's will,
And the thoughts of youth are long, long thoughts."

I can see the breezy dome of groves,
  The shadows of Deering's Woods;
And the friendships old and the early loves
Come back with a Sabbath sound, as of doves
    In quiet neighborhoods.
      And the verse of that sweet old song,
      It flutters and murmurs still:
      "A boy's will is the wind's will,
And the thoughts of youth are long, long thoughts."

I remember the gleams and glooms that dart
  Across the schoolboy's brain;
The song and the silence in the heart,
That in part are prophecies, and in part
    Are longings wild and vain.
      And the voice of that fitful song
      Sings on, and is never still:
      "A boy's will is the wind's will,
And the thoughts of youth are long, long thoughts."

There are things of which I may not speak;
  There are dreams that cannot die;
There are thoughts that make the strong heart weak,
And bring a pallor into the cheek,
    And a mist before the eye.
      And the words of that fatal song
      Come over me like a chill:
      "A boy's will is the wind's will,
And the thoughts of youth are long, long thoughts."

Strange to me now are the forms I meet
  When I visit the dear old town;
But the native air is pure and sweet,
And the trees that o'ershadow each well-known street,
    As they balance up and down,
      Are singing the beautiful song,
      Are sighing and whispering still:
      "A boy's will is the wind's will,
And the thoughts of youth are long, long thoughts."

And Deering's Woods are fresh and fair,
  And with joy that is almost pain
My heart goes back to wander there,
And among the dreams of the days that were,
    I find my lost youth again.
      And the strange and beautiful song,

The groves are repeating it still:
"A boy's will is the wind's will,
And the thoughts of youth are long, long thoughts."

THE BIRDS OF KILLINGWORTH

It was the season, when through all the land
   The merle and mavis build, and building sing
Those lovely lyrics, written by His hand,
   Whom Saxon Caedmon calls the Blitheheart King;
When on the boughs the purple buds expand,
   The banners of the vanguard of the spring,
And rivulets, rejoicing, rush and leap,
And wave their fluttering signals from the steep.

The robin and the bluebird, piping loud,
   Filled all the blossoming orchards with their glee;
The sparrows chirped as if they were still proud
   Their race in Holy Writ should mentioned be;
And hungry crows, assembled in a crowd,
   Clamored their piteous prayer incessantly,
Knowing who hears the ravens cry, and said:
"Give us, O Lord, this day, our daily bread! '

Across the sound the birds of passage sailed,
   Speaking some unknown language strange and sweet
Of tropic isle remote, and passing hailed
   The village with the cheers of all their fleet;
Or quarreling together, laughed and railed
   Like foreign sailors, landed in the street
Of seaport town, and with outlandish noise
Of oaths and gibberish frightening girls and boys.

Thus came the jocund spring in Killingworth,
   In fabulous days, some hundred years ago;
And thrifty farmers, as they tilled the earth,
   Heard with alarm the cawing of the crow,
That mingled with the universal mirth,
   Cassandra-like, prognosticating woe;
They shook their heads, and doomed with dreadful words
To swift destruction the whole race of birds.

And a town meeting was convened straightway
   To set a price upon the guilty heads
Of these marauders, who, in lieu of pay,

Levied blackmail upon the garden beds
And cornfields, and beheld without dismay
    The awful scarecrow, with his fluttering shreds;
The skeleton that waited at their feast,
Whereby their sinful pleasure was increased.

Then from his house, a temple painted white,
    With fluted columns, and a roof of red,
The squire came forth, august and splendid sight!
    Slowly descending, with majestic tread,
Three flights of steps, nor looking left nor right,
    Down the long street he walked, as one who said,
"A town that boasts inhabitants like me
Can have no lack of good society!"

The parson, too, appeared, a man austere,
    The instinct of whose nature was to kill;
The wrath of God he preached from year to year,
    And read, with fervor, Edwards on the will;
His favorite pastime was to slay the deer
    In summer on some Adirondac hill;
E'en now, while walking down the rural lane,
He lopped the wayside lilies with his cane.

From the Academy, whose belfry crowned
    The hill of science with its vane of brass
Came the preceptor, gazing idly round,
    Now at the clouds, and now at the green grass,
And all absorbed in reveries profound
    Of fair Almira in the upper class,
Who was, as in a sonnet he had said,
As pure as water, and as good as bread.

And next the deacon issued from his door,
    In his voluminous neckcloth, white as snow;
A suit of sable bombazine he wore;
    His form was ponderous, and his step was slow;
There never was so wise a man before;
    He seemed the incarnate "Well, I told you so!"
And to perpetuate his great renown
There was a street named after him in town.

These came together in the new town hall,
    With sundry farmers from the region round.
The Squire presided, dignified and tall,
    His air impressive and his reasoning sound;

Ill fared it with the birds, both great and small;
   Hardly a friend in all that crowd they found,
But enemies enough, who every one
Charged them with all the crimes beneath the sun.

When they had ended, from his place apart
   Rose the preceptor, to redress the wrong,
And, trembling like a steed before the start,
   Looked round bewildered on the expectant throng;
Then thought of fair Almira, and took heart
   To speak out what was in him, clear and strong,
Alike regardless of their smile or frown,
And quite determined not to be laughed down.

"Plato, anticipating the reviewers,
   From his Republic banished without pity
The poets; in this little town of yours,
   You put to death, by means of a committee,
The ballad singers, and the troubadours,
   The street musicians of the heavenly city,
The birds, who make sweet music for us all
In our dark hours, as David did for Saul.

"The thrush that carols at the dawn of day
   From the green steeples of the piny wood;
The oriole in the elm; the noisy jay,
   Jargoning like a foreigner at his food;
The bluebird balanced on some topmost spray,
   Flooding with melody the neighborhood;
Linnet and meadowlark, and all the throng
That dwell in nests, and have the gift of song.

"You slay them all! and wherefore? for the gain
   Of a scant handful more or less of wheat,
Or rye, or barley, or some other grain,
   Scratched up at random by industrious feet,
Searching for worm or weevil after rain!
   Or a few cherries, that are not so sweet
As are the songs these uninvited guests
Sing at their feast with comfortable breasts.

"Do you ne'er think what wondrous beings these?
   Do you ne'er think who made them, and who taught
The dialect they speak, where melodies
   Alone are the interpreters of thought?
Whose household words are songs in many keys,

Sweeter than instrument of man e'er caught!
Whose habitations in the treetops even
Are halfway houses on the road to heaven!

"Think, every morning when the sun peeps through
    The dim, leaf-latticed windows of the grove,
How jubilant the happy birds renew
    Their old, melodious madrigals of love!
And when you think of this, remember too
    'Tis always morning somewhere, and above
The awakening continents, from shore to shore,
Somewhere the birds are singing evermore.

"Think of your woods and orchards without birds!
    Of empty nests that cling to boughs and beams
As in an idiot's brain remembered words
    Hang empty 'mid the cobwebs of his dreams!
Will bleat of flocks or bellowing of herds
    Make up for the lost music, when your teams
Drag home the stingy harvest, and no more
The feathered gleaners follow to your door?

"What! would you rather see the incessant stir
    Of insects in the windrows of the hay,
And hear the locust and the grasshopper
    Their melancholy hurdy-gurdies play?
Is this more pleasant to you than the whir
    Of meadowlark, and her sweet roundelay,
Or twitter of little fieldfares, as you take
Your nooning in the shade of bush and brake?

"You call them thieves and pillagers; but know,
    They are the wingèd wardens of your farms,
Who from the cornfields drive the insidious foe,
    And from your harvests keep a hundred harms;
Even the blackest of them all, the crow,
    Renders good service as your man-at-arms,
Crushing the beetle in his coat of mail,
And crying havoc on the slug and snail.

"How can I teach your children gentleness,
    And mercy to the weak, and reverence
For life, which, in its weakness or excess,
    Is still a gleam of God's omnipotence,
Or death, which, seeming darkness, is no less
    The selfsame light, although averted hence,

When by your laws, your actions, and your speech,
You contradict the very things I teach?"

With this he closed; and through the audience went
   A murmur, like the rustle of dead leaves;
The farmers laughed and nodded, and some bent
   Their yellow heads together like their sheaves;
Men have no faith in fine-spun sentiment
   Who put their trust in bullocks and in beeves.
The birds were doomed; and, as the record shows,
A bounty offered for the heads of crows.

There was another audience out of reach,
   Who had no voice nor vote in making laws,
But in the papers read his little speech,
   And crowned his modest temples with applause;
They made him conscious, each one more than each,
   He still was victor, vanquished in their cause.
Sweetest of all the applause he won from thee,
O fair Almira at the Academy!

And so the dreadful massacre began;
   O'er fields and orchards, and o'er woodland crests,
The ceaseless fusillade of terror ran.
   Dead fell the birds, with bloodstains on their breasts;
Or wounded crept away from sight of man,
   While the young died of famine in their nests;
A slaughter to be told in groans, not words,
The very St. Bartholomew of birds!

The summer came, and all the birds were dead;
   The days were like hot coals; the very ground
Was burned to ashes; in the orchards fed
   Myriads of caterpillars, and around
The cultivated fields and garden beds
   Hosts of devouring insects crawled, and found
No foe to check their march, till they had made
The land a desert without leaf or shade.

Devoured by worms, like Herod, was the town,
   Because, like Herod, it had ruthlessly
Slaughtered the innocents. From the trees spun down
   The cankerworms upon the passers-by,
Upon each woman's bonnet, shawl, and gown,
   Who shook them off with just a little cry;
They were the terror of each favorite walk,
The endless theme of all the village talk.

The farmers grew impatient, but a few
  Confessed their error, and would not complain,
For after all, the best thing one can do
  When it is raining, is to let it rain.
Then they repealed the law, although they knew
  It would not call the dead to life again;
As schoolboys, finding their mistake too late,
Draw a wet sponge across the accusing slate.

That year in Killingworth the autumn came
  Without the light of his majestic look,
The wonder of the falling tongues of flame,
  The illumined pages of his Doomsday Book.
A few lost leaves blushed crimson with their shame,
  And dwarfed themselves despairing in the brook,
While the wild wind went moaning everywhere,
Lamenting the dead children of the air!

But the next spring a stranger sight was seen,
  A sight that never yet by bard was sung,
As great a wonder as it would have been
  If some dumb animal had found a tongue!
A wagon, overarched with evergreen,
  Upon whose boughs were wicker cages hung,
All full of singing birds, came down the street,
Filing the air with music wild and sweet.

From all the country round these birds were brought,
  By order of the town, with anxious quest,
And, loosened from their wicker prisons, sought
  In woods and fields the places they loved best,
Singing loud canticles, which many thought
  Were satires to the authorities addressed,
While others, listening in green lanes, averred
Such lovely music never had been heard!

But blither still and louder caroled they
  Upon the morrow, for they seemed to know
It was the fair Almira's wedding day,
  And everywhere, around, above, below,
When the preceptor bore his bride away,
  Their songs burst forth in joyous overflow,
And a new heaven bent over a new earth
Amid the sunny farms of Killingworth.

DIVINA COMMEDIA

I

Oft have I seen at some cathedral door
  A laborer, pausing in the dust and heat,
  Lay down his burden, and with reverent feet
  Enter, and cross himself, and on the floor
Kneel to repeat his paternoster o'er;
  Far off the noises of the world retreat;
  The loud vociferations of the street
Become an undistinguishable roar.
So, as I enter here from day to day,
  And leave my burden at this minster gate,
  Kneeling in prayer, and not ashamed to pray,
The tumult of the time disconsolate
  To inarticulate murmurs dies away,
  While the eternal ages watch and wait.

II

How strange the sculptures that adorn these towers!
  This crowd of statues, in whose folded sleeves
  Birds build their nests; while canopied with leaves
  Parvis and portal bloom like trellised bowers,
And the vast minster seems a cross of flowers!
  But fiends and dragons on the gargoyled eaves
  Watch the dead Christ between the living thieves,
  And, underneath, the traitor Judas lowers!
Ah! from what agonies of heart and brain,
  What exultations trampling on despair,
  What tenderness, what tears, what hate of wrong,
What passionate outcry of a soul in pain,
  Uprose this poem of the earth and air,
  This medieval miracle of song!

III

I enter, and I see thee in the gloom
  Of the long aisles, O poet saturnine!
  And strive to make my steps keep pace with thine.
  The air is filled with some unknown perfume;
The congregation of the dead make room
  For thee to pass; the votive tapers shine;
  Like rooks that haunt Ravenna's groves of pine
  The hovering echoes fly from tomb to tomb.

From the confessionals I hear arise
  Rehearsals of forgotten tragedies,
  And lamentations from the crypts below;
And then a voice celestial that begins
  With the pathetic words, "Although your sins
  As scarlet be," and ends with "as the snow."

IV

With snow-white veil and garments as of flame,
  She stands before thee, who so long ago
  Filled thy young heart with passion and the woe
From which thy song and all its splendors came;
And while with stern rebuke she speaks thy name,
  The ice about thy heart melts as the snow
  On mountain heights, and in swift overflow
Comes gushing from thy lips in sobs of shame.
Thou makest full confession; and a gleam,
  As of the dawn on some dark forest cast,
  Seems on thy lifted forehead to increase;
Lethe and Eunoë—the remembered dream
  And the forgotten sorrow—bring at last
  That perfect pardon which is perfect peace.

V

I lift mine eyes, and all the windows blaze
  With forms of saints and holy men who died,
  Here martyred and hereafter glorified;
And the great rose upon its leaves displays
Christ's triumph, and the angelic roundelays,
  With splendor upon splendor multiplied;
  And Beatrice again at Dante's side
No more rebukes, but smiles her words of praise.
And then the organ sounds, and unseen choirs
  Sing the old Latin hymns of peace and love
  And benedictions of the Holy Ghost;
And the melodious bells among the spires
  O'er all the housetops and through heaven above
  Proclaim the elevation of the Host!

VI

O star of morning and of liberty!
  O bringer of the light, whose splendor shines
  Above the darkness of the Apennines,

Forerunner of the day that is to be!
The voices of the city and the sea,
  The voices of the mountains and the pines,
  Repeat thy song, till the familiar lines
  Are footpaths for the thought of Italy!
Thy flame is blown abroad from all the heights,
  Through all the nations, and a sound is heard,
  As of a mighty wind, and men devout,
Strangers of Rome, and the new proselytes,
  In their own language hear thy wondrous word,
  And many are amazed and many doubt.

THE FIRE OF DRIFTWOOD
Devereux Farm, near Marblehead

We sat within the farmhouse old,
  Whose windows, looking o'er the bay,
Gave to the sea breeze damp and cold
  An easy entrance, night and day.

Not far away we saw the port,
  The strange, old-fashioned, silent town,
The lighthouse, the dismantled fort,
  The wooden houses, quaint and brown.

We sat and talked until the night,
  Descending, filled the little room;
Our faces faded from the sight,
  Our voices only broke the gloom.

We spake of many a vanished scene,
  Of what we once had thought and said,
Of what had been, and might have been,
  And who was changed, and who was dead;

And all that fills the hearts of friends,
  When first they feel, with secret pain,
Their lives henceforth have separate ends,
  And never can be one again;

The first slight swerving of the heart,
  That words are powerless to express,
And leave it still unsaid in part,
  Or say it in too great excess.

The very tones in which we spake
    Had something strange, I could but mark;
The leaves of memory seemed to make
    A mournful rustling in the dark.

Oft died the words upon our lips,
    As suddenly, from out the fire
Built of the wreck of stranded ships,
    The flames would leap and then expire.

And, as their splendor flashed and failed,
    We thought of wrecks upon the main,
Of ships dismasted, that were hailed
    And sent no answer back again.

The windows, rattling in their frames,
    The ocean, roaring up the beach,
The gusty blast, the bickering flames,
    All mingled vaguely in our speech;

Until they made themselves a part
    Of fancies floating through the brain,
The long-lost ventures of the heart,
    That send no answers back again.

O flames that glowed! O hearts that yearned!
    They were indeed too much akin,
The driftwood fire without that burned,
    The thoughts that burned and glowed within.

CHAUCER

An old man in a lodge within a park;
    The chamber walls depicted all around
    With portraitures of huntsman, hawk, and hound,
    And the hurt deer. He listeneth to the lark,
Whose song comes with the sunshine through the dark
    Of painted glass in leaden lattice bound;
    He listeneth and he laugheth at the sound,
    Then writeth in a book like any clerk.
He is the poet of the dawn, who wrote
    The Canterbury Tales, and his old age
    Made beautiful with song; and as I read
I hear the crowing cock, I hear the note
    Of lark and linnet, and from every page
    Rise odors of plowed field or flowery mead.

THE TIDE RISES, THE TIDE FALLS

The tide rises, the tide falls,
The twilight darkens, the curlew calls;
Along the sea sands damp and brown
The traveler hastens toward the town,
    And the tide rises, the tide falls.

Darkness settles on roofs and walls,
But the sea, the sea in the darkness calls;
The little waves, with their soft, white hands,
Efface the footprints in the sands,
    And the tide rises, the tide falls.

The morning breaks; the steeds in their stalls
Stamp and neigh, as the hostler calls;
The day returns, but nevermore
Returns the traveler to the shore,
    And the tide rises, the tide falls.

THE CROSS OF SNOW

In the long, sleepless watches of the night,
    A gentle face—the face of one long dead—
    Looks at me from the wall, where round its head
The night lamp casts a halo of pale light.
Here in this room she died; and soul more white
    Never through martyrdom of fire was led
    To its repose; nor can in books be read
The legend of a life more benedight.
There is a mountain in the distant West
    That, sun-defying, in its deep ravines
    Displays a cross of snow upon its side.
Such is the cross I wear upon my breast
    These eighteen years, through all the changing scenes
    And seasons, changeless since the day she died.

THE BELLS OF SAN BLAS

What say the bells of San Blas
To the ships that southward pass
    From the harbor of Mazatlán?
To them it is nothing more
Than the sound of surf on the shore,—
    Nothing more to master or man.

But to me, a dreamer of dreams,
To whom what is and what seems
    Are often one and the same,—
The bells of San Blas to me
Have a strange, wild melody,
    And are something more than a name.

For bells are the voice of the church;
They have tones that touch and search
    The hearts of young and old;
One sound to all, yet each
Lends a meaning to their speech,
    And the meaning is manifold.

They are a voice of the past,
Of an age that is fading fast,
    Of a power austere and grand;
When the flag of Spain unfurled
Its folds o'er this western world,
    And the priest was lord of the land.

The chapel that once looked down
On the little seaport town
    Has crumbled into the dust;
And on oaken beams below
The bells swing to and fro,
    And are green with mold and rust.

"Is, then, the old faith dead,"
They say, "and in its stead
    Is some new faith proclaimed,
That we are forced to remain
Naked to sun and rain
    Unsheltered and ashamed?

"Once in our tower aloof
We rang over wall and roof
    Our warnings and our complaints;
And round about us there
The white doves filled the air,
    Like the white souls of the saints.

"The saints! Ah, have they grown
Forgetful of their own?
    Are they asleep, or dead,
That open to the sky

Their ruined missions lie,
    No longer tenanted?

"Oh, bring us back once more
The vanished days of yore,
    When the world with faith was filled;
Bring back the fervid zeal,
The hearts of fire and steel,
    The hands that believe and build.

"Then from our tower again
We will send over land and main
    Our voices of command,
Like exiled kings who return
To their thrones, and the people learn
    That the priest is lord of the land!"

O bells of San Blas, in vain
Ye call back the past again!
    The past is deaf to your prayer;
Out of the shadows of night
The world rolls into light;
    It is daybreak everywhere.

THE ARROW AND THE SONG

I shot an arrow into the air,
It fell to earth, I knew not where;
For, so swiftly it flew, the sight
Could not follow it in its flight.

I breathed a song into the air,
It fell to earth, I knew not where;
For who has sight so keen and strong,
That it can follow the flight of song?

Long, long afterward, in an oak
I found the arrow, still unbroke;
And the song, from beginning to end,
I found again in the heart of a friend.

POSSIBILITIES

Where are the poets, unto whom belong
  The Olympian heights; whose singing shafts were sent
  Straight to the mark, and not from bows half bent,
  But with the utmost tension of the thong?
Where are the stately argosies of song,
  Whose rushing keels made music as they went
  Sailing in search of some new continent,
  With all sail set, and steady winds and strong?
Perhaps there lives some dreamy boy, untaught
  In schools, some graduate of the field or street,
  Who shall become a master of the art,
An admiral sailing the high seas of thought,
  Fearless and first, and steering with his fleet
  For lands not yet laid down in any chart.

THE ROPEWALK

In that building, long and low,
With its windows all a row,
  Like the portholes of a hulk,
Human spiders spin and spin,
Backward down their threads so thin
  Dropping, each a hempen bulk.

At the end, an open door;
Squares of sunshine on the floor
  Light the long and dusky lane;
And the whirring of a wheel,
Dull and drowsy, makes me feel
  All its spokes are in my brain.

As the spinners to the end
Downward go and reascend,
  Gleam the long threads in the sun;
While within this brain of mine
Cobwebs brighter and more fine
  By the busy wheel are spun.

Two fair maidens in a swing,
Like white doves upon the wing,
  First before my vision pass;
Laughing, as their gentle hands
Closely clasp the twisted strands,
  At their shadow on the grass.

Then a booth of mountebanks,
With its smell of tan and planks,
   And a girl poised high in air
On a cord, in spangled dress,
With a faded loveliness
   And a weary look of care.

Then a homestead among farms,
And a woman with bare arms
   Drawing water from a well;
As the bucket mounts apace,
With it mounts her own fair face,
   As at some magician's spell.

Then an old man in a tower,
Ringing loud the noontide hour,
   While the rope coils round and round
Like a serpent at his feet,
And again, in swift retreat,
   Nearly lifts him from the ground.

Then within a prison yard,
Faces fixed, and stern and hard,
   Laughter and indecent mirth;
Ah! it is the gallows tree!
Breath of Christian charity,
   Blow, and sweep it from the earth!

Then a schoolboy, with his kite
Gleaming in a sky of light,
   And an eager, upward look;
Steeds pursued through lane and field;
Fowlers with their snares concealed;
   And an angler by a brook.

Ships rejoicing in the breeze,
Wrecks that float o'er unknown seas,
   Anchors dragged through faithless sand;
Sea fog drifting overhead,
And, with lessening line and lead,
   Sailors feeling for the land.

All these scenes do I behold,
These, and many left untold,
   In that building long and low;
While the wheel goes round and round,
With a drowsy, dreamy sound,
   And the spinners backward go.

EVANGELINE

PROEM

This is the forest primeval. The murmuring pines and the
    hemlocks,
Bearded with moss, and in garments green, indistinct in the
    twilight,
Stand like Druids of eld, with voices sad and prophetic,
Stand like harpers hoar, with beards that rest on their bosoms.
Loud from its rocky caverns, the deep-voiced neighboring
    ocean
Speaks, and in accents disconsolate answers the wail of the
    forest.

This is the forest primeval; but where are the hearts that
    beneath it
Leaped like the roe, when he hears in the woodland the voice
    of the huntsman?
Where is the thatch-roofed village, the home of Acadian
    farmers,—
Men whose lives glided on like rivers that water the wood-
    lands,
Darkened by shadows of earth, but reflecting an image of
    heaven?
Waste are those pleasant farms, and the farmers forever
    departed!
Scattered like dust and leaves, when the mighty blasts of
    October
Seize them, and whirl them aloft, and sprinkle them far o'er
    the ocean.
Naught but tradition remains of the beautiful village of
    Grand-Pré.

Ye who believe in affection that hopes, and endures, and is
    patient,
Ye who believe in the beauty and strength of woman's
    devotion,
List to the mournful tradition, still sung by the pines of the
    forest;
List to a tale of love in Acadie, home of the happy.

from *Evangeline*

THE SONG OF HIAWATHA

INTRODUCTION

Should you ask me, whence these stories?
Whence these legends and traditions,
With the odors of the forest,
With the dew and damp of meadows,
With the curling smoke of wigwams,
With the rushing of great rivers,
With their frequent repetitions,
And their wild reverberations,
As of thunder in the mountains?

I should answer, I should tell you.
"From the forests and the prairies,
From the great lakes of the Northland,
From the land of the Ojibways,
From the land of the Dakotas,
From the mountains, moors, and fenlands
Where the heron, the Shuh-shuh-gah
Feeds among the reeds and rushes.
I repeat them as I heard them
From the lips of Nawadaha,
The musician, the sweet singer."

Should you ask where Nawadaha
Found these songs so wild and wayward,
Found these legends and traditions,
I should answer, I should tell you,
"In the bird's nests of the forest,
In the lodges of the beaver,
In the hoofprints of the bison,
In the eyrie of the eagle!

"All the wild fowl sang them to him,
In the moorlands and the fenlands,
In the melancholy marshes;
Chetowaik, the plover, sang them,
Mahug, the loon, the wild goose, Wawa,
The blue heron, the Shuh-shuh-gah,
And the grouse, the Mushkodasa!"

If still further you should ask me,
Saying, "Who was Nawadaha?
Tell us of this Nawadaha,"

I should answer your inquiries
Straightway in such words as follow.

"In the vale of Tawasentha,
In the green and silent valley,
By the pleasant watercourses,
Dwelt the singer Nawadaha.
Round about the Indian village
Spread the meadows and the cornfields,
And beyond them stood the forest,
Stood the groves of singing pine trees,
Green in summer, white in winter,
Ever sighing, ever singing.

"And the pleasant watercourses,
You could trace them through the valley,
By the rushing in the springtime,
By the alders in the summer,
By the white fog in the autumn,
By the black line in the winter;
And beside them dwelt the singer,
In the vale of Tawasentha,
In the green and silent valley.

"There he sang of Hiawatha,
Sang the Song of Hiawatha,
Sang his wondrous birth and being,
How he prayed and how he fasted,
How he lived, and toiled, and suffered,
That the tribes of men might prosper,
That he might advance his people!"

Ye who love the haunts of nature,
Love the sunshine of the meadow,
Love the shadow of the forest,
Love the wind among the branches,
And the rain shower and the snowstorm,
And the rushing of great rivers
Through their palisades of pine trees
And the thunder in the mountains,
Whose innumerable echoes
Flap like eagles in their eyries;—
Listen to these wild traditions,
To this Song of Hiawatha!

Ye who love a nation's legends,

Love the ballads of a people,
That like voices from afar off
Call to us to pause and listen,
Speak in tones so plain and childlike
Scarcely can the ear distinguish
Whether they are sung or spoken;—
Listen to this Indian legend,
To this Song of Hiawatha!

Ye whose hearts are fresh and simple,
Who have faith in God and Nature,
Who believe that in all ages
Every human heart is human,
That in even savage bosoms
There are longings, yearnings, strivings
For the good they comprehend not,
That the feeble hands and helpless,
Groping blindly in the darkness,
Touch God's right hand in that darkness
And are lifted up and strengthened;—
Listen to this simple story,
To this Song of Hiawatha!

Ye, who sometimes, in your rambles
Through the green lanes of the country,
Where the tangled barberry bushes
Hang their tufts of crimson berries
Over stone walls gray with mosses,
Pause by some neglected graveyard,
For a while to muse, and ponder
On a half-effaced inscription,
Written with little skill of songcraft,
Homely phrases, but each letter
Full of hope and yet of heartbreak,
Full of all the tender pathos
Of the Here and the Hereafter;—
Stay and read this rude inscription,
Read this Song of Hiawatha!

from *The Song of Hiawatha*

EDGAR ALLAN POE
(1809-1849)

DREAMS

Oh! that my young life were a lasting dream!
My spirit not awak'ning till the beam
Of an eternity should bring the morrow.
Yes! though that long dream were of hopeless sorrow,
'Twere better than the cold reality
Of waking life, to him whose heart must be,
And hath been still, upon the lovely earth,
A chaos of deep passion, from his birth.
But should it be—that dream eternally
Continuing—as dreams have been to me
In my young boyhood—should it thus be given,
'Twere folly still to hope for higher heaven.
For I have reveled, when the sun was bright
I' the summer sky, in dreams of living light
And loveliness,—have left my very heart
In climes of mine imagining, apart
From mine own home, with beings that have been
Of mine own thought—what more could I have seen?
'Twas once—and only once—and the wild hour
From my remembrance shall not pass—some pow'r
Or spell had bound me—'twas the chilly wind
Came o'er me in the night, and left behind
Its image on my spirit—or the moon
Shone on my slumbers in her lofty noon
Too coldly—or the stars—howe'er it was,
That dream was on that night wind—let it pass.
I *have been* happy, though but in a dream.
I have been happy—and I love the theme:
Dreams! in their vivid coloring of life,
As in that fleeting, shadowy, misty strife
Of semblance with reality which brings
To the delirious eye, more lovely things
Of paradise and love—and all our own!
Than young hope in his sunniest hour hath known.

A DREAM WITHIN A DREAM

Take this kiss upon the brow!
And, in parting from you now,
Thus much let me avow:
You are not wrong, who deem
That my days have been a dream;
Yet if hope has flown away
In a night, or in a day,
In a vision, or in none,
Is it therefore the less *gone?*
All that we see or seem
Is but a dream within a dream.

I stand amid the roar
Of a surf-tormented shore,
And I hold within my hand
Grains of the golden sand—
How few! yet how they creep
Through my fingers to the deep,
While I weep—while I weep!
O God! can I not grasp
Them with a tighter clasp?
O God! can I not save
One from the pitiless wave?
Is *all* that we see or seem
But a dream within a dream?

"THE HAPPIEST DAY, THE HAPPIEST HOUR"

The happiest day, the happiest hour
   My seared and blighted heart hath known,
The highest hope of pride and power,
   I feel hath flown.

Of power! said I? yes! such I ween;
   But they have vanished long, alas!
The visions of my youth have been—
   But let them pass.

And, pride, what have I now with thee?
   Another brow may ev'n inherit
The venom thou hast poured on me—
   Be still, my spirit!

The happiest day, the happiest hour
  Mine eyes shall see, have ever seen,
The brightest glance of pride and power,
  I feel—have been:

But were that hope of pride and power
  Now offered, with the pain
Ev'n *then* I felt—that brightest hour
  I would not live again:

For on its wing was dark alloy,
  And as it fluttered, fell
An essence—powerful to destroy
  A soul that knew it well.

SONNET—TO SCIENCE

Science! true daughter of old Time thou art!
  Who alterest all things with thy peering eyes.
Why preyest thou thus upon the poet's heart,
  Vulture, whose wings are dull realities?
How should he love thee? or how deem thee wise,
  Who wouldst not leave him in his wandering
To seek for treasure in the jeweled skies,
  Albeit he soared with an undaunted wing?
Hast thou not dragged Diana from her car,
  And driven the hamadryad from the wood
To seek a shelter in some happier star?
  Hast thou not torn the naiad from her flood,
The elfin from the green grass, and from me
The summer dream beneath the tamarind tree?

ROMANCE

Romance, who loves to nod and sing,
With drowsy head and folded wing,
Among the green leaves as they shake
Far down within some shadowy lake,
To me a painted paroquet
Hath been—a most familiar bird—
Taught me my alphabet to say,
To lisp my very earliest word,
While in the wild wood I did lie,
A child—with a most knowing eye.

Of late, eternal condor years
So shake the very heaven on high
With tumult as they thunder by,
I have no time for idle cares
Through gazing on the unquiet sky.
And when an hour with calmer wings
Its down upon my spirit flings—
That little time with lyre and rhyme
To while away—forbidden things!
My heart would feel to be a crime
Unless it trembled with the strings.

TO HELEN

Helen, thy beauty is to me
   Like those Nicéan barks of yore,
That gently, o'er a perfumed sea,
   The weary, way-worn wanderer bore
To his own native shore.

On desperate seas long wont to roam,
   Thy hyacinth hair, thy classic face,
Thy naiad airs have brought me home
   To the glory that was Greece
And the grandeur that was Rome.

Lo! in yon brilliant window niche
   How statuelike I see thee stand,
   The agate lamp within thy hand!
Ah, Psyche, from the regions which
   Are holy land!

ISRAFEL

*And the angel Israfel, whose heartstrings are a lute, and who
has the sweetest voice of all God's creatures.*—KORAN.

In heaven a spirit doth dwell
   "Whose heartstrings are a lute";
None sing so wildly well
As the angel Israfel,
And the giddy stars (so legends tell),
Ceasing their hymns, attend the spell
   Of his voice, all mute.

Tottering above
   In her highest noon,
   The enamored moon
Blushes with love,
   While, to listen, the red levin
   (With the rapid Pleiads, even,
   Which were seven),
   Pauses in heaven.

And they say (the starry choir
   And the other listening things)
That Israfeli's fire
Is owing to that lyre
   By which he sits and sings—
The trembling living wire
   Of those unusual strings.

But the skies that angel trod,
   Where deep thoughts are a duty,
Where Love's a grown-up god,
   Where the houri glances are
Imbued with all the beauty
   Which we worship in a star.

Therefore, thou art not wrong,
   Israfeli, who despisest
An unimpassioned song;
To thee the laurels belong,
   Best bard, because the wisest!
Merrily live, and long!

The ecstasies above
   With thy burning measures suit—
Thy grief, thy joy, thy hate, thy love,
   With the fervor of thy lute—
   Well may the stars be mute!

Yes, heaven is thine; but this
   Is a world of sweets and sours,
   Our flowers are merely—flowers,
And the shadow of thy perfect bliss
   Is the sunshine of ours.

If I could dwell
Where Israfel
   Hath dwelt, and he where I,

He might not sing so wildly well
   A mortal melody,
While a bolder note than this might swell
   From my lyre within the sky.

THE CITY IN THE SEA

Lo! Death has reared himself a throne
In a strange city lying alone
Far down within the dim West,
Where the good and the bad and the worst and the best
Have gone to their eternal rest.
There shrines and palaces and towers
(Time-eaten towers that tremble not!)
Resemble nothing that is ours.
Around, by lifting winds forgot,
Resignedly beneath the sky
The melancholy waters lie.

No rays from the holy heaven come down
On the long nighttime of that town;
But light from out the lurid sea
Streams up the turrets silently—
Gleams up the pinnacles far and free—
Up domes—up spires—up kingly halls—

Up fanes—up Babylon-like walls—
Up shadowy long-forgotten bowers
Of sculptured ivy and stone flowers—
Up many and many a marvelous shrine
Whose wreathèd friezes intertwine
The viol, the violet, and the vine.

Resignedly beneath the sky
The melancholy waters lie.
So blend the turrets and shadows there
That all seem pendulous in air,
While from a proud tower in the town
Death looks gigantically down.

There open fanes and gaping graves
Yawn level with the luminous waves;
But not the riches there that lie
In each idol's diamond eye—
Not the gaily jeweled dead

Tempt the waters from their bed;
For no ripples curl, alas!
Along that wilderness of glass—
No swellings tell that winds may be
Upon some far-off happier sea—
No heavings hint that winds have been
On seas less hideously serene.

But lo, a stir is in the air!
The wave—there is a movement there!
As if the towers had thrust aside,
In slightly sinking, the dull tide—
As if their tops had feebly given
A void within the filmy heaven.
The waves have now a redder glow—
The hours are breathing faint and low—
And when, amid no earthly moans,
Down, down that town shall settle hence,
Hell, rising from a thousand thrones,
Shall do it reverence.

THE SLEEPER

At midnight, in the month of June,
I stand beneath the mystic moon.
An opiate vapor, dewy, dim,
Exhales from out her golden rim,
And softly dripping, drop by drop,
Upon the quiet mountaintop,
Steals drowsily and musically
Into the universal valley.
The rosemary nods upon the grave;
The lily lolls upon the wave;
Wrapping the fog about its breast,
The ruin molders into rest;
Looking like Lethe, see! the lake
A conscious slumber seems to take,
And would not, for the world, awake.
All Beauty sleeps!—and lo! where lies
Irene, with her Destinies!

Oh, lady bright! can it be right—
This window open to the night?
The wanton airs, from the treetop,
Laughingly through the lattice drop—

The bodiless airs, a wizard rout,
Flit through thy chamber in and out,
And wave the curtain canopy
So fitfully—so fearfully—
Above the closed and fringèd lid
'Neath which thy slumb'ring soul lies hid,
That, o'er the floor and down the wall,
Like ghosts the shadows rise and fall!
Oh, lady dear, hast thou no fear?
Why and what art thou dreaming here?
Sure thou art come o'er far-off seas,
A wonder to these garden trees!
Strange is thy pallor! strange thy dress!
Strange, above all, thy length of tress,
And this all solemn silentness!

The lady sleeps! Oh, may her sleep,
Which is enduring, so be deep!
Heaven have her in its sacred keep!
This chamber changed for one more holy,
This bed for one more melancholy,
I pray to God that she may lie
Forever with unopened eye,
While the pale sheeted ghosts go by!

My love, she sleeps! Oh, may her sleep,
As it is lasting, so be deep!
Soft may the worms about her creep!
Far in the forest, dim and old,
For her may some tall vault unfold—
Some vault that oft hath flung its black
And wingèd panels fluttering back,
Triumphant, o'er the crested palls
Of her grand family funerals—
Some sepulcher, remote, alone,
Against whose portal she hath thrown,
In childhood, many an idle stone—
Some tomb from out whose sounding door
She ne'er shall force an echo more,
Thrilling to think, poor child of sin!
It was the dead who groaned within.

TO ONE IN PARADISE

Thou wast that all to me, love,
   For which my soul did pine—
A green isle in the sea, love,
   A fountain and a shrine,
All wreathed with fairy fruits and flowers,
   And all the flowers were mine.

Ah, dream too bright to last!
   Ah, starry hope! that didst arise
But to be overcast!
   A voice from out the future cries,
"On! on!"—but o'er the past
   (Dim gulf!) my spirit hovering lies
Mute, motionless, aghast!

For, alas! alas! with me
   The light of life is o'er!
No more—no more—no more—
   (Such language holds the solemn sea
To the sands upon the shore)
   Shall bloom the thunder-blasted tree,
Or the stricken eagle soar!

And all my days are trances,
   And all my nightly dreams
Are where thy gray eye glances,
   And where thy footstep gleams—
In what ethereal dances,
   By what eternal streams.

THE HAUNTED PALACE

In the greenest of our valleys
   By good angels tenanted,
Once a fair and stately palace—
   Radiant palace—reared its head.
In the monarch Thought's dominion,
   It stood there!
Never seraph spread a pinion
   Over fabric half so fair!

Banners yellow, glorious, golden,
   On its roof did float and flow

(This—all this—was in the olden
   Time long ago),
And every gentle air that dallied,
   In that sweet day,
Along the ramparts plumed and pallid,
   A wingèd odor went away.

Wanderers in that happy valley,
   Through two luminous windows, saw
Spirits moving musically,
   To a lute's well-tunèd law,
Round about a throne where, sitting,
   Porphyrogene!
In state his glory well befitting,
   The ruler of the realm was seen.

And all with pearl and ruby glowing
   Was the fair palace door,
Through which came flowing, flowing, flowing,
   And sparkling evermore,
A troop of Echoes, whose sweet duty
   Was but to sing,
In voices of surpassing beauty,
   The wit and wisdom of their king.

But evil things, in robes of sorrow,
   Assailed the monarch's high estate.
(Ah, let us mourn!—for never morrow
   Shall dawn upon him, desolate!)
And round about his home the glory
   That blushed and bloomed,
Is but a dim-remembered story
   Of the old time entombed.

And travelers, now, within that valley,
   Through the red-litten windows see
Vast forms that move fantastically
   To a discordant melody,
While, like a ghastly rapid river,
   Through the pale door
A hideous throng rush out forever,
   And laugh—but smile no more.

SONNET—SILENCE

There are some qualities—some incorporate things,
    That have a double life, which thus is made
A type of that twin entity which springs
    From matter and light, evinced in solid and shade.
There is a twofold Silence—sea and shore—
    Body and soul. One dwells in lonely places,
    Newly with grass o'ergrown; some solemn graces,
Some human memories and tearful lore,
Render him terrorless: his name's "No More."
He is the corporate Silence: dread him not!
    No power hath he of evil in himself;
But should some urgent fate (untimely lot!)
    Bring thee to meet his shadow (nameless elf,
That haunteth the lone regions where hath trod
No foot of man), commend thyself to God!

THE CONQUEROR WORM

    Lo! 'tis a gala night
        Within the lonesome latter years!
    An angel throng, bewinged, bedight
        In veils, and drowned in tears,
    Sit in a theater, to see
        A play of hopes and fears,
    While the orchestra breathes fitfully
        The music of the spheres.

    Mimes, in the form of God on high,
        Mutter and mumble low,
    And hither and thither fly—
        Mere puppets they, who come and go
    At bidding of vast formless things
        That shift the scenery to and fro,
    Flapping from out their condor wings
        Invisible woe!

    That motley drama—oh, be sure
        It shall not be forgot!
    With its phantom chased forevermore
        By a crowd that seize it not,
    Through a circle that ever returneth in
        To the selfsame spot,
    And much of madness, and more of sin,
        And horror the soul of the plot.

But see, amid the mimic rout,
  A crawling shape intrude!
A blood-red thing that writhes from out
  The scenic solitude!
It writhes!—it writhes!—with mortal pangs
  The mimes become its food,
And seraphs sob at vermin fangs
  In human gore imbued.

Out—out are the lights—out all!
  And, over each quivering form,
The curtain, a funeral pall,
  Comes down with the rush of a storm,
While the angels, all pallid and wan,
  Uprising, unveiling, affirm
That the play is the tragedy, "Man,"
  And its hero, the Conqueror Worm.

DREAMLAND

By a route obscure and lonely,
Haunted by ill angels only,
Where an eidolon, named Night,
On a black throne reigns upright,
I have reached these lands but newly
From an ultimate dim Thule—
From a wild weird clime that lieth, sublime,
      Out of space—out of time

Bottomless vales and boundless floods,
And chasms, and caves, and titan woods,
With forms that no man can discover
For the tears that drip all over;
Mountains toppling evermore
Into seas without a shore;
Seas that restlessly aspire,
Surging, unto skies of fire;
Lakes that endlessly outspread
Their lone waters, lone and dead,—
Their still waters, still and chilly
With the snows of the lolling lily.

By the lakes that thus outspread
Their lone waters, lone and dead,—
Their sad waters, sad and chilly

With the snows of the lolling lily,—
By the mountains—near the river
Murmuring lowly, murmuring ever,—
By the gray woods,—by the swamp
Where the toad and the newt encamp,—
By the dismal tarns and pools
   Where dwell the ghouls,—
By each spot the most unholy—
In each nook most melancholy,—
There the traveler meets, aghast,
Sheeted memories of the past—
Shrouded forms that start and sigh
As they pass the wanderer by—
White-robed forms of friends long given,
In agony, to the earth—and heaven.

For the heart whose woes are legion
'Tis a peaceful, soothing region—
For the spirit that walks in shadow
'Tis—oh, 'tis an Eldorado!
But the traveler, traveling through it,
May not—dare not openly view it;
Never its mysteries are exposed
To the weak human eye unclosed;
So wills its king, who hath forbid
The uplifting of the fringèd lid;
And thus the sad soul that here passes
Beholds it but through darkened glasses.

By a route obscure and lonely,
Haunted by ill angels only,
Where an eidolon, named Night,
On a black throne reigns upright,
I have wandered home but newly
From this ultimate dim Thule.

THE RAVEN

Once upon a midnight dreary, while I pondered, weak and
   weary,
Over many a quaint and curious volume of forgotten lore—
While I nodded, nearly napping, suddenly there came a tapping,
As of someone gently rapping, rapping at my chamber door.
" 'Tis some visitor," I muttered, "tapping at my chamber
   door—
     Only this and nothing more."

Ah, distinctly I remember it was in the bleak December;
And each separate dying ember wrought its ghost upon the
 floor.
Eagerly I wished the morrow;—vainly I had sought to borrow
From my books surcease of sorrow—sorrow for the lost
 Lenore—
For the rare and radiant maiden whom the angels name
 Lenore—
    Nameless *here* forevermore.

And the silken, sad, uncertain rusting of each purple curtain
Thrilled me—filled me with fantastic terrors never felt before;
So that now, to still the beating of my heart, I stood repeating,
" 'Tis some visitor entreating entrance at my chamber door—
Some late visitor entreating entrance at my chamber door;—
    This it is and nothing more."

Presently my soul grew stronger; hesitating then no longer,
"Sir," said I, "or madam, truly your forgiveness I implore;
But the fact is I was napping, and so gently you came rapping,
And so faintly you came tapping, tapping at my chamber door,
That I scarce was sure I heard you"—here I opened wide the
 door;—
    Darkness there and nothing more.

Deep into that darkness peering, long I stood there wondering,
 fearing,
Doubting, dreaming dreams no mortal ever dared to dream
 before;
But the silence was unbroken, and the stillness gave no token,
And the only word there spoken was the whispered word,
 "Lenore?"
This I whispered, and an echo murmured back the word,
 "Lenore!"
    Merely this and nothing more.

Back into the chamber turning, all my soul within me burning,
Soon again I heard a tapping somewhat louder than before.
"Surely," said I, "surely that is something at my window lattice;
Let me see, then, what thereat is, and this mystery explore—
Let my heart be still a moment and this mystery explore;—
    'Tis the wind and nothing more!"

Open here I flung the shutter, when, with many a flirt and
 flutter,
In there stepped a stately Raven of the saintly days of yore;

Not the least obeisance made he; not a minute stopped or
    stayed he;
But, with mien of lord or lady, perched above my chamber
    door—
Perched upon a bust of Pallas just above my chamber door—
      Perched, and sat, and nothing more.

Then this ebony bird beguiling my sad fancy into smiling,
By the grave and stern decorum of the countenance it wore,
"Though thy crest be shorn and shaven, thou," I said, "art sure
    no craven,
Ghastly grim and ancient Raven wandering from the nightly
    shore—
Tell me what thy lordly name is on the night's Plutonian
    shore!"
      Quoth the Raven, "Nevermore."

Much I marveled this ungainly fowl to hear discourse so
    plainly,
Though its answer little meaning—little relevancy bore;
For we cannot help agreeing that no living human being
Ever yet was blessed with seeing bird above his chamber
    door—
Bird or beast upon the sculptured bust above his chamber door,
      With such name as "Nevermore."

But the Raven, sitting lonely on the placid bust, spoke only
That one word, as if his soul in that one word he did outpour.
Nothing farther then he uttered—not a feather then he
    fluttered—
Till I scarcely more than muttered, "Other friends have flown
    before—
On the morrow *he* will leave me, as my hopes have flown
    before."
      Then the bird said, "Nevermore."

Startled at the stillness broken by reply so aptly spoken,
"Doubtless," said I, "what it utters is its only stock and store
Caught from some unhappy master whom unmerciful disaster
Followed fast and followed faster till his songs one burden
    bore—
Till the dirges of his hope that melancholy burden bore
      Of 'Never—nevermore'."

But the Raven still beguiling my sad fancy into smiling,
Straight I wheeled a cushioned seat in front of bird and bust
    and door;

Then, upon the velvet sinking, I betook myself to linking
Fancy unto fancy, thinking what this ominous bird of yore—
What this grim, ungainly, ghastly, gaunt, and ominous bird of
    yore
        Meant in croaking "Nevermore."

This I sat engaged in guessing, but no syllable expressing
To the fowl whose fiery eyes now burned into my bosom's core;
This and more I sat divining, with my head at ease reclining
On the cushion's velvet lining that the lamplight gloated o'er,
But whose velvet-violet lining with the lamplight gloating o'er,
    She shall press, ah, nevermore!

Then, methought, the air grew denser, perfumed from an
    unseen censer
Swung by seraphim whose footfalls tinkled on the tufted floor.
"Wretch," I cried, "thy God hath lent thee—by these angels
    he hath sent thee
Respite—respite and nepenthe from thy memories of Lenore;
Quaff, oh, quaff this kind nepenthe and forget this lost Lenore!"
        Quoth the Raven, "Nevermore."

"Prophet!" said I, "thing of evil!—prophet still, if bird or
    devil!—
Whether Tempter sent, or whether tempest tossed thee here
    ashore,
Desolate yet all undaunted, on this desert land enchanted—
On this home by horror haunted—tell me truly, I implore—
Is there—*is* there balm in Gilead?—tell me—tell me, I
    implore!"
        Quoth the Raven, "Nevermore."

"Prophet!" said I, "thing of evil—prophet still, if bird or devil!
By that heaven that bends above us—by that God we both
    adore—
Tell this soul with sorrow laden if, within the distant Aidenn,
It shall clasp a sainted maiden whom the angels name Lenore—
Clasp a rare and radiant maiden whom the angels name
    Lenore."
        Quoth the Raven, "Nevermore."

"Be that word our sign of parting, bird or fiend!" I shrieked,
    upstarting—
"Get thee back into the tempest and the night's Plutonian
    shore!
Leave no black plume as a token of that lie thy soul hath
    spoken!

Leave my loneliness unbroken!—quit the bust above my door!
Take thy beak from out my heart, and take they form from off
  my door!"
    Quoth the Raven, "Nevermore."

And the Raven, never flitting, still is sitting, *still* is sitting
On the pallid bust of Pallas just above my chamber door;
And his eyes have all the seeming of a demon's that is
  dreaming,
And the lamplight o'er him streaming throws his shadow on
  the floor;
And my soul from out that shadow that lies floating on the
  floor
    Shall be lifted—nevermore!

THE BELLS

I

Hear the sledges with the bells—
    Silver bells!
What a world of merriment their melody foretells!
  How they tinkle, tinkle, tinkle,
    In the icy air of night!
  While the stars that oversprinkle
  All the heavens, seem to twinkle
    With a crystalline delight;
  Keeping time, time, time,
  In a sort of runic rhyme,
To the tintinnabulation that so musically wells
  From the bells, bells, bells, bells,
      Bells, bells, bells—
From the jingling and the tinkling of the bells.

II

Hear the mellow wedding bells—
    Golden bells!
What a world of happiness their harmony foretells!
  Through the balmy air of night
  How they ring out their delight!—
    From the molten-golden notes,
      And all in tune,
    What a liquid ditty floats
  To the turtledove that listens, while she gloats

On the moon!
Oh, from out the sounding cells,
What a gush of euphony voluminously wells!
How it swells!
How it dwells
On the future!—how it tells
Of the rapture that impels
To the swinging and the ringing
Of the bells, bells, bells—
Of the bells, bells, bells, bells,
Bells, bells, bells—
To the rhyming and the chiming of the bells!

III

Hear the loud alarum bells—
Brazen bells!
What a tale of terror, now, their turbulency tells!
In the startled ear of night
How they scream out their affright!
Too much horrified to speak,
They can only shriek, shriek,
Out of tune,
In a clamorous appealing to the mercy of the fire,
In a mad expostulation with the deaf and frantic fire,
Leaping higher, higher, higher,
With a desperate desire,
And a resolute endeavor
Now—now to sit, or never,
By the side of the pale-faced moon.
Oh, the bells, bells, bells!
What a tale their terror tells
Of despair!
How they clang, and clash, and roar!
What a horror they outpour
On the bosom of the palpitating air!
Yet the ear, it fully knows
By the twanging
And the clanging,
How the danger ebbs and flows;
Yet the ear distinctly tells,
In the jangling
And wrangling,
How the danger sinks and swells,
By the sinking or the swelling in the anger of the bells—
Of the bells,—

Of the bells, bells, bells, bells,
  Bells, bells, bells—
In the clamor and the clangor of the bells!

IV

Hear the tolling of the bells—
    Iron bells!
What a world of solemn thought their monody compels!
    In the silence of the night,
    How we shiver with affright
At the melancholy menace of their tone!
  For every sound that floats
  From the rust within their throats
      Is a groan.
And the people—ah, the people—
They that dwell up in the steeple,
      All alone,
And who tolling, tolling, tolling,
  In that muffled monotone,
Feel a glory in so rolling
  On the human heart a stone—
They are neither man nor woman—
They are neither brute nor human—
    They are ghouls:—
  And their king it is who tolls:—
  And he rolls, rolls, rolls,
      Rolls
  A paean from the bells!
And his merry bosom swells
With the paean of the bells!
And he dances, and he yells;
Keeping time, time, time,
In a sort of runic rhyme,
  To the paean of the bells—
      Of the bells—
Keeping time, time, time,
In a sort of runic rhyme,
  To the throbbing of the bells—
    Of the bells, bells, bells—
  To the sobbing of the bells;
Keeping time, time, time,
  As he knells, knells, knells,
In a happy runic rhyme,
  To the rolling of the bells—
  Of the bells, bells, bells:—

To the tolling of the bells—
Of the bells, bells, bells, bells,
    Bells, bells, bells—
To the moaning and the groaning of the bells.

ULALUME—A BALLAD

The skies they were ashen and sober;
    The leaves they were crispèd and sere—
    The leaves they were withering and sere:
It was night, in the lonesome October
    Of my most immemorial year:
It was hard by the dim lake of Auber,
    In the misty mid-region of Weir—
It was down by the dank tarn of Auber,
    In the ghoul-haunted woodland of Weir.

Here once, through an alley titanic,
    Of cypress, I roamed with my soul—
    Of cypress with Psyche, my soul
These were days when my heart was volcanic
    As the scoriac rivers that roll—
    As the lavas that restlessly roll
Their sulphurous currents down Yaanek
    In the ultimate climes of the Pole—
That groan as they roll down Mount Yaanek
    In the realms of the boreal Pole.

Our talk had been serious and sober,
    But our thoughts they were palsied and sere—
    Our memories were treacherous and sere;
For we knew not the month was October,
    And we marked not the night of the year
    (Ah, night of all nights in the year!)—
We noted not the dim lake of Auber
    (Though once we had journeyed down here)—
We remembered not the dank tarn of Auber,
    Nor the ghoul-haunted woodland of Weir.

And now, as the night was senescent
    And star dials pointed to morn—
    As the star dials hinted of morn—
At the end of our path a liquescent
    And nebulous luster was born,
Out of which a miraculous crescent

      Arose with a duplicate horn—
Astarte's bediamonded crescent
      Distinct with its duplicate horn.

And I said: "She is warmer than Dian;
      She rolls through an ether of sighs—
      She revels in a region of sighs.
She has seen that the tears are not dry on
      These cheeks, where the worm never dies,
And has come past the stars of the Lion,
      To point us the path to the skies—
      To the Lethean peace of the skies—
Come up, in despite of the Lion,
      To shine on us with her bright eyes—
Come up through the lair of the Lion,
      With love in her luminous eyes."

But Psyche, uplifting her finger,
      Said: "Sadly this star I mistrust—
      Her pallor I strangely mistrust:
Ah, hasten!—ah, let us not linger.
      Ah, fly!—let us fly!—for we must."
In terror she spoke, letting sink her
      Wings till they trailed in the dust—
In agony sobbed, letting sink her
      Plumes till they trailed in the dust—
      Till they sorrowfully trailed in the dust.

I replied: "This is nothing but dreaming:
      Let us on by this tremulous light!
      Let us bathe in this crystalline light!
Its sibylic splendor is beaming
      With hope and in beauty tonight:—
      See!—it flickers up the sky through the night!
Ah, we safely may trust to its gleaming,
      And be sure it will lead us aright—
We surely may trust to a gleaming,
      That cannot but guide us aright,
      Since it flickers up to heaven through the night."

Thus I pacified Psyche and kissed her,
      And tempted her out of her gloom—
      And conquered her scruples and gloom;
And we passed to the end of the vista,
      But were stopped by the door of a tomb—
      By the door of a legended tomb;

And I said: "What is written, sweet sister,
   On the door of this legended tomb?"
   She replied: "Ulalume—Ulalume!—
'Tis the vault of thy lost Ulalume!"

Then my heart it grew ashen and sober
   As the leaves that were crispèd and sere—
   As the leaves that were withering and sere;
And I said: "It was surely October
   On *this* very night of last year
   That I journeyed—I journeyed down here!—
   That I brought a dread burden down here—
   On this night of all nights in the year,
   Ah, what demon hath tempted me here?
Well I know, now, this dim lake of Auber—
   This misty mid-region of Weir—
Well I know, now, this dank tarn of Auber,
   This ghoul-haunted woodland of Weir."

Said we, then—the two, then: "Ah, can it
   Have been that the woodlandish ghouls—
   The pitiful, the merciful ghouls—
To bar up our way and to ban it
   From the secret that lies in these wolds—
   From the thing that lies hidden in these wolds—
Have drawn up the specter of a planet
   From the limbo of lunary souls—
This sinful scintillant planet
   From the hell of the planetary souls?"

ELDORADO

Gaily bedight,
  A gallant knight,
In sunshine and in shadow,
  Had journeyed long,
  Singing a song,
In search of Eldorado.

But he grew old—
  This knight so bold—
And o'er his heart a shadow
  Fell as he found
  No spot of ground
That looked like Eldorado.

And, as his strength
  Failed him at length,
He met a pilgrim shadow—
  "Shadow," said he,
  "Where can it be—
This land of Eldorado?"

"Over the mountains
  Of the moon,
Down the valley of the shadow,
  Ride, boldly ride,"
  The shade replied,—
"If you seek for Eldorado!"

FOR ANNIE

Thank heaven! the crisis,
　The danger, is past,
And the lingering illness
　Is over at last—
And the fever called "living"
　Is conquered at last.

Sadly, I know
　I am shorn of my strength,
And no muscle I move
　As I lie at full length—
But no matter!—I feel
　I am better at length.

And I rest so composedly,
　Now, in my bed,
That any beholder
　Might fancy me dead—
Might start at beholding me,
　Thinking me dead.

The moaning and groaning,
　The sighing and sobbing,
Are quieted now, with
　That horrible throbbing
At heart:—ah, that horrible,
　Horrible throbbing!

The sickness—the nausea—
　The pitiless pain—
Have ceased, with the fever
　That maddened my brain—
With the fever called "living"
　That burned in my brain.

And oh! of all tortures
　That torture the worst
Has abated—the terrible
　Torture of thirst
For the naphthaline river
　Of passion accurst:—
I have drank of a water
　That quenches all thirst:—

Of a water that flows,
　With a lullaby sound,
From a spring but a very few
　Feet underground—
From a cavern not very far
　Down underground.

And ah! let it never
　Be foolishly said
That my room it is gloomy
　And narrow my bed;
For man never slept
　In a different bed—
And, to *sleep,* you must slumber
　In just such a bed.

My tantalized spirit
　Here blandly reposes,
Forgetting, or never
　Regretting, its roses—
Its old agitations
　Of myrtles and roses:

For now, while so quietly
　Lying, it fancies
A holier odor
　About it, of pansies—
A rosemary odor,
　Commingled with pansies
With rue and the beautiful
　Puritan pansies.

And so it lies happily,
　Bathing in many
A dream of the truth
　And the beauty of Annie—
Drowned in a bath
　Of the tresses of Annie.

She tenderly kissed me,
　She fondly caressed,
And then I fell gently

To sleep on her breast—
Deeply to sleep
   From the heaven of her
     breast.

When the light was extin-
   guished,
She covered me warm,
And she prayed to the angels
   To keep me from harm—
To the queen of the angels
   To shield me from harm.

And I lie so composedly,
   Now, in my bed
(Knowing her love),
   That you fancy me dead—

And I rest so contentedly,
   Now, in my bed
(With her love at my breast),
   That you fancy me dead—
That you shudder to look at
   me,
   Thinking me dead:—

But my heart it is brighter
   Than all of the many
Stars in the sky,
   For it sparkles with
     Annie—
It glows with the light
   Of the love of my Annie—
With the thought of the light
   Of the eyes of my Annie.

ANNABEL LEE

It was many and many a year ago,
     In a kingdom by the sea,
That a maiden there lived whom you may know
     By the name of Annabel Lee;—
And this maiden she lived with no other thought
     Than to love and be loved by me.

She was a child and *I* was a child,
     In this kingdom by the sea,
But we loved with a love that was more than love—
     I and my Annabel Lee—
With a love that the wingèd seraphs of heaven
     Coveted her and me.

And this was the reason that, long ago,
     In this kingdom by the sea,
A wind blew out of a cloud by night
     Chilling my Annabel Lee;
So that her highborn kinsmen came
     And bore her away from me,
To shut her up in a sepulcher
     In this kingdom by the sea.

The angels, not half so happy in heaven,
     Went envying her and me:—

Yes! that was the reason (as all men know,
  In this kingdom by the sea)
That the wind came out of the cloud, chilling
  And killing my Annabel Lee.

But our love it was stronger by far than the love
  Of those who were older than we—
  Of many far wiser than we—
And neither the angels in heaven above
  Nor the demons down under the sea,
Can ever dissever my soul from the soul
  Of the beautiful Annabel Lee:—

For the moon never beams without bringing me dreams
  Of the beautiful Annabel Lee;
And the stars never rise but I see the bright eyes
  Of the beautiful Annabel Lee;
And so, all the nighttide, I lie down by the side
Of my darling, my darling, my life and my bride,
  In her sepulcher there by the sea—
  In her tomb by the side of the sea.

THE LAKE: TO ———

In spring of youth it was my lot
To haunt of the wide world a spot
The which I could not love the less—
So lovely was the loneliness
Of a wild lake, with black rock bound,
And the tall pines that towered around.

But when the night had thrown her pall
Upon that spot, as upon all,
And the mystic wind went by
Murmuring in melody,
Then—ah, then—I would awake
To the terror of the lone lake.

Yet that terror was not fright,
But a tremulous delight—
A feeling not the jeweled mine
Could teach or bribe me to define—
Nor love—although the love were thine.

Death was in that poisonous wave,
And in its gulf a fitting grave
For him who thence could solace bring
To his lone imagining,
Whose solitary soul could make
An Eden of that dim lake.

ALONE

From childhood's hour I have not been
As others were—I have not seen
As others saw—I could not bring
My passions from a common spring—
From the same source I have not taken
My sorrow—I could not awaken
My heart to joy at the same tone—
And all I loved—*I* loved alone.
Then—in my childhood—in the dawn
Of a most stormy life—was drawn
From ev'ry depth of good and ill
The mystery which binds me still—
From the torrent, or the fountain—
From the red cliff of the mountain—
From the sun that round me rolled
In its autumn tint of gold—
From the lightning in the sky
As it passed me flying by—
From the thunder, and the storm—
And the cloud that took the form
(When the rest of heaven was blue)
Of a demon in my view.

WALT WHITMAN
(1819–1892)

SONG OF MYSELF

1

I celebrate myself, and sing myself,
And what I assume you shall assume,
For every atom belonging to me as good belongs to you.
I loaf and invite my soul,
I lean and loaf at my ease observing a spear of summer grass.
My tongue, every atom of my blood, formed from this soil,
    this air,
Born here of parents born here from parents the same, and
    their parents the same,
I, now thirty-seven years old in perfect health begin,
Hoping to cease not till death.
Creeds and schools in abeyance,
Retiring back awhile sufficed at what they are, but never
    forgotten,
I harbor for good or bad, I permit to speak at every hazard,
Nature without check with original energy.

2

Houses and rooms are full of perfumes, the shelves are
    crowded with perfumes,
I breathe the fragrance myself and know it and like it,
The distillation would intoxicate me also, but I shall not let it.

The atmosphere is not a perfume, it has no taste of the dis-
    tillation, it is odorless,
It is for my mouth forever, I am in love with it,
I will go to the bank by the wood and become undisguised
    and naked,
I am mad for it to be in contact with me.

The smoke of my own breath,
Echoes, ripples, buzzed whispers, love root, silk thread, crotch
    and vine,

My respiration and inspiration, the beating of my heart, the
        passing of blood and air through my lungs,
The sniff of green leaves and dry leaves, and of the shore and
        dark-colored sea rocks, and of hay in the
        barn,
The sound of the belched words of my voice loosed to the
        eddies of the wind,
A few light kisses, a few embraces, a reaching around of
        arms,
The play of shine and shade on the trees as the supple boughs
        wag,
The delight alone or in the rush of the streets, or along the
        fields and hillsides,
The feeling of health, the full-noon trill, the song of me rising
        from bed and meeting the sun.

Have you reckoned a thousand acres much? have you reckoned
        the earth much?
Have you practiced so long to learn to read?
Have you felt so proud to get at the meaning of poems?

Stop this day and night with me and you shall possess the
        origin of all poems,
You shall possess the good of the earth and sun (there are
        millions of suns left),
You shall no longer take things at second or third hand, nor
        look through the eyes of the dead, nor feed
        on the specters in books,
You shall not look through my eyes either, nor take things
        from me,
You shall listen to all sides and filter them from yourself.

3

I have heard what the talkers were talking, the talk of the
        beginning and the end,
But I do not talk of the beginning or the end.

There was never any more inception than there is now,
Nor any more youth or age than there is now,
And will never be any more perfection than there is now,
Nor any more heaven or hell than there is now.

Urge and urge and urge,
Always the procreant urge of the world.
Out of the dimness opposite equals advance, always substance
        and increase, always sex,

Always a knit of identity, always distinction, always a breed
of life.

To elaborate is no avail, learned and unlearned feel that it is so.

Sure as the most certain sure, plumb in the uprights, well
entretied, braced in the beams,
Stout as a horse, affectionate, haughty, electrical,
I and this mystery here we stand.

Clear and sweet is my soul, and clear and sweet is all that
is not my soul.

Lack one lacks both, and the unseen is proved by the seen,
Till that becomes unseen and receives proof in its turn.

Showing the best and dividing it from the worst age vexes age,
Knowing the perfect fitness and equanimity of things, while
they discuss I am silent, and go bathe and
admire myself.

Welcome is every organ and attribute of me, and of any man
hearty and clean,
Not an inch nor a particle of an inch is vile, and none shall be
less familiar than the rest.

I am satisfied—I see, dance, laugh, sing;
As the hugging and loving bedfellow sleeps at my side through
the night, and withdraws at the peep of the
day with stealthy tread,
Leaving me baskets covered with white towels swelling the
house with their plenty,
Shall I postpone my acceptation and realization and scream
at my eyes,
That they turn from gazing after and down the road,
And forthwith cipher and show me to a cent,
Exactly the value of one and exactly the value of two, and
which is ahead?

4

Trippers and askers surround me,
People I meet, the effect upon me of my early life or the ward
and city I live in, or the nation,
The latest dates, discoveries, inventions, societies, authors old
and new,

My dinner, dress, associates, looks, compliments, dues,
The real or fancied indifference of some man or woman I
love,
The sickness of one of my folks or of myself, or ill-doing
or loss or lack of money, or depressions or
exaltations,
Battles, the horrors of fratricidal war, the fever of doubtful
news, the fitful events;
These come to me days and nights and go from me again,
But they are not the Me myself.
Apart from the pulling and hauling stands what I am,
Stands amused, complacent, compassionating, idle, unitary,
Looks down, is erect, or bends an arm on an impalpable cer-
tain rest,
Looking with side-curved head curious what will come next,
Both in and out of the game and watching and wondering at it.
Backward I see in my own days where I sweated through fog
with linguists and contenders,
I have no mockings or arguments, I witness and wait.

5

I believe in you my soul, the other I am must not abase itself
to you,
And you must not be abased to the other.
Loaf with me on the grass, loose the stop from your throat,
Not words, not music or rhyme I want, not custom or lecture,
not even the best,
Only the lull I like, the hum of your valvèd voice.
I mind how once we lay such a transparent summer morning,
How you settled your head athwart my hips, and gently turned
over upon me,
And parted the shirt from my bosom bone, and plunged your
tongue to my bare-stripped heart,
And reached till you felt my beard, and reached till you held
my feet.
Swiftly arose and spread around me the peace and knowledge
that pass all the argument of the earth,
And I know that the hand of God is the promise of my own,
And I know that the spirit of God is the brother of my own,
And that all the men ever born are also my brothers, and the
women my sisters and lovers,
And that a kelson of the creation is love,
And limitless are leaves stiff or drooping in the fields,
And brown ants in the little wells beneath them,
And mossy scabs of the worm fence, heaped stones, elder,
mullein and pokeweed.

6

A child said *What is the grass?* fetching it to me with full
    hands,
How could I answer the child? I do not know what it is any
    more than he.
I guess it must be the flag of my disposition, out of hopeful
    green stuff woven.
Or I guess it is the handkerchief of the Lord,
A scented gift and remembrancer designedly dropped,
Bearing the owner's name someway in the corners, that we may
    see and remark, and say *Whose?*

Or I guess the grass is itself a child, the produced babe of the
    vegetation.

Or I guess it is a uniform hieroglyphic,
And it means, Sprouting alike in broad zones and narrow
    zones,
Growing among black folks as among white,
Canuck, Tuckahoe, Congressman, Cuff, I give them the same,
    I receive them the same.

And now it seems to me the beautiful uncut hair of graves.
Tenderly will I use you curling grass,
It may be you transpire from the breasts of young men,
It may be if I had known them I would have loved them,
It may be you are from old people, or from offspring taken
    soon out of their mothers' laps,
And here you are the mothers' laps.
This grass is very dark to be from the white heads of old
    mothers,
Darker than the colorless beards of old men,
Dark to come from under the faint red roof of mouths.
O I perceive after all so many uttering tongues,
And I perceive they do not come from the roofs of mouths for
    nothing.
I wish I could translate the hints about the dead young men
    and women,
And the hints about old men and mothers, and the offspring
    taken soon out of their laps.
What do you think has become of the young and old men?
And what do you think has become of the women and
    children?
They are alive and well somewhere,
The smallest sprout shows there is really no death,

And if ever there was it led forward life, and does not wait at
                    the end to arrest it,
And ceased the moment life appeared.
All goes onward and outward, nothing collapses,
And to die is different from what anyone supposed, and luckier.

7

Has anyone supposed it lucky to be born?
I hasten to inform him or her it is just as lucky to die, and I
                    know it.
I pass death with the dying and birth with the new-washed
                    babe, and am not contained between my hat
                    and boots,
And peruse manifold objects, no two alike and everyone good,
The earth good and the stars good, and their adjuncts all good.
I am not an earth nor an adjunct of an earth,
I am the mate and companion of people, all just as immortal
                    and fathomless as myself,
(They do not know how immortal, but I know.)
Every kind for itself and its own, for me mine male and female,
For me those that have been boys and that love women,
For me the man that is proud and feels how it stings to be
                    slighted,
For me the sweetheart and the old maid, for me mothers and
                    the mothers of mothers,
For me lips that have smiled, eyes that have shed tears,
For me children and the begetters of children.
Undrape! you are not guilty to me, nor stale nor discarded,
I see through the broadcloth and gingham whether or no,
And am around, tenacious, acquisitive, tireless, and cannot be
                    shaken away.

8

The little one sleeps in its cradle,
I lift the gauze and look a long time, and silently brush away
                    flies with my hand.
The youngster and the red-faced girl turn aside up the bushy
                    hill,
I peeringly view them from the top.
The suicide sprawls on the bloody floor of the bedroom,
I witness the corpse with its dabbled hair, I note where the
                    pistol has fallen.
The blab of the pave, tires of carts, sluff of boot soles, talk of
                    the promenaders,

The heavy omnibus, the driver with his interrogating thumb,
        the clank of the shod horses on the granite
        floor,
The snow sleighs, clinking, shouted jokes, pelts of snowballs,
The hurrahs for popular favorites, the fury of roused mobs,
The flap of the curtained litter, a sick man inside borne to the
        hospital,
The meeting of enemies, the sudden oath, the blows and fall,
The excited crowd, the policeman with his star quickly work-
        ing his passage to the center of the crowd,
The impassive stones that receive and return so many echoes,
What groans of overfed or half-starved who fall sunstruck or
        in fits,
What exclamations of women taken suddenly who hurry home
        and give birth to babes,
What living and buried speech is always vibrating here, what
        howls restrained by decorum,
Arrests of criminals, slights, adulterous offers made, accept-
        ances, rejections with convex lips,
I mind them or the show or resonance of them—I come and
        I depart.

9

The big doors of the country barn stand open and ready,
The dried grass of the harvest time loads the slow-drawn
        wagon,
The clear light plays on the brown gray and green intertinged,
The armfuls are packed to the sagging mow.
I am there, I help, I came stretched atop of the load,
I felt its soft jolts, one leg reclined on the other,
I jump from the crossbeams and seize the clover and timothy,
And roll head over heels and tangle my hair full of wisps.

10

Alone far in the wilds and mountains I hunt,
Wandering amazed at my own lightness and glee,
In the late afternoon choosing a safe spot to pass the night,
Kindling a fire and broiling the fresh-killed game,
Falling asleep on the gathered leaves with my dog and gun by
        my side.

The Yankee clipper is under her sky sails, she cuts the sparkle
        and scud,
My eyes settle the land, I bend at her prow or shout joyously
        from the deck.

The boatmen and clam-diggers arose early and stopped for me,
I tucked my trouser ends in my boots and went and had a good
    time;
You should have been with us that day round the chowder
    kettle.

I saw the marriage of the trapper in the open air in the far
    west, the bride was a red girl,
Her father and his friends sat near cross-legged and dumbly
    smoking, they had moccasins to their feet
    and large thick blankets hanging from their
    shoulders,
On a bank lounged the trapper, he was dressed mostly in skins,
    his luxuriant beard and curls protected his
    neck, he held his bride by the hand,
She had long eyelashes, her head was bare, her coarse straight
    locks descended upon her voluptuous limbs
    and reached to her feet.

The runaway slave came to my house and stopped outside,
I heard his motions crackling the twigs of the woodpile,
Through the swung half-door of the kitchen I saw him limpsy
    and weak,
And went where he sat on a log and led him in and assured
    him,
And brought water and filled a tub for his sweated body and
    bruised feet,
And gave him a room that entered from my own, and gave him
    some coarse clean clothes,
And remember perfectly well his revolving eyes and his awk-
    wardness,
And remember putting plasters on the galls of his neck and
    ankles;
He stayed with me a week before he was recuperated and
    passed north,
I had him sit next me at table, my firelock leaned in the corner.

11

Twenty-eight young men bathe by the shore,
Twenty-eight young men and all so friendly;
Twenty-eight years of womanly life and all so lonesome.
She owns the fine house by the rise of the bank,
She hides handsome and richly dressed aft the blinds of the
    window.
Which of the young men does she like the best?
Ah, the homeliest of them is beautiful to her.

Where are you off to, lady? for I see you,
You splash in the water there, yet stay stock still in your room.
Dancing and laughing along the beach came the twenty-ninth
          bather,
The rest did not see her, but she saw them and loved them.
The beards of the young men glistened with wet, it ran from
          their long hair,
Little streams passed all over their bodies.
An unseen hand also passed over their bodies,
It descended tremblingly from their temples and ribs.

The young men float on their backs, their white bellies bulge to
          the sun, they do not ask who seizes fast to
          them,
They do not know who puffs and declines with pendant and
          bending arch,
They do not think whom they souse with spray.

12

The butcher boy puts off his killing clothes, or sharpens his
          knife at the stall in the market,
I loiter enjoying his repartee and his shuffle and breakdown.
Blacksmiths with grimed and hairy chests environ the anvil,
Each has his main sledge, they are all out, there is a great heat
          in the fire.
From the cinder-strewed threshold I follow their movements,
The lithe sheer of their waists plays even with their massive
          arms,
Overhand the hammers swing, overhand so slow, overhand so
          sure,
They do not hasten, each man hits in his place.

13

The Negro holds firmly the reins of his four horses, the block
          swags underneath on its tied-over chain.
The Negro that drives the long dray of the stoneyard, steady
          and tall he stands poised on one leg on the
          stringpiece,
His blue shirt exposes his ample neck and breast and loosens
          over his hip band,
His glance is calm and commanding, he tosses the slouch of his
          hat away from his forehead,
The sun falls on his crispy hair and mustache, falls on the
          black of his polished and perfect limbs.

I behold the picturesque giant and love him, and I do not stop
                    there,
I go with the team also.

In me the caresser of life wherever moving, backward as well
                    as forward sluing,
To niches aside and junior bending, not a person or object
                    missing,
Absorbing all to myself and for this song.

Oxen that rattle the yoke and chain or halt in the leafy shade,
                    what is that you express in your eyes?
It seems to me more than all the print I have read in my life.

My tread scares the wood drake and wood duck on my distant
                    and day-long ramble,
They rise together, they slowly circle around.

I believe in those winged purposes,
And acknowledge red, yellow, white, playing within me.
And consider green and violet and the tufted crown inten-
                    tional,
And do not call the tortoise unworthy because she is not some-
                    thing else,
And the jay in the woods never studied the gamut, yet trills
                    pretty well to me,
And the look of the bay mare shames silliness out of me.

14

The wild gander leads his flock through the cool night,
Ya-honk he says, and sounds it down to me like an invitation,
The pert may suppose it meaningless, but I listening close,
Find its purpose and place up there toward the wintry sky.

The sharp-hoofed moose of the north, the cat on the house
                    sill, the chickadee, the prairie dog,
The litter of the grunting sow as they tug at her teats,
The brood of the turkey hen and she with her half-spread
                    wings,
I see in them and myself the same old law.

The press of my foot to the earth springs a hundred affections,
They scorn the best I can do to relate them.

I am enamored of growing outdoors,

Of men that live among cattle or taste of the ocean or woods,
Of the builders and steerers of ships and the wielders of axes
 and mauls, and the drivers of horses,
I can eat and sleep with them week in and week out.

What is commonest, cheapest, nearest, easiest, is Me,
Me going in for my chances, spending for vast returns,
Adorning myself to bestow myself on the first that will take me,
Not asking the sky to come down to my good will,
Scattering it freely forever.

15

The pure contralto sings in the organ loft,
The carpenter dresses his plank, the tongue of his foreplane
 whistles its wild ascending lisp,
The married and unmarried children ride home to their
 Thanksgiving dinner,
The pilot seizes the kingpin, he heaves down with a strong
 arm,
The mate stands braced in the whaleboat, lance and harpoon
 are ready,
The duck shooter walks by silent and cautious stretches,
The deacons are ordained with crossed hands at the altar,
The spinning girl retreats and advances to the hum of the big
 wheel,
The farmer stops by the bars as he walks on a First-day loaf
 and looks at the oats and rye,
The lunatic is carried at last to the asylum a confirmed case,
(He will never sleep any more as he did in the cot in his moth-
 er's bedroom);
The jour printer with gray head and gaunt jaws works at his
 case,
He turns his quid of tobacco while his eyes blur with the
 manuscript;
The malformed limbs are tied to the surgeon's table,
What is removed drops horribly in a pail;
The quadroon girl is sold at the auction stand, the drunkard
 nods by the barroom stove,
The machinist rolls up his sleeves, the policeman travels his
 beat, the gatekeeper marks who pass.
The young fellow drives the express wagon (I love him,
 though I do not know him);
The half-breed straps on his light boots to compete in the race,
The western turkey-shooting draws old and young, some lean
 on their rifles, some sit on logs,

Out from the crowd steps the marksman, takes his position,
        levels his piece;

The groups of newly come immigrants cover the wharf or
        levee,

As the wooly-pates hoe in the sugar field, the overseer views
        them from his saddle,

The bugle calls in the ballroom, the gentlemen run for their
        partners, the dancers bow to each other,

The youth lies awake in the cedar-roofed garret and harks to
        the musical rain,

The Wolverine sets traps on the creek that helps fill the Huron,

The squaw wrapped in her yellow-hemmed cloth is offering
        moccasins and bead bags for sale,

The connoisseur peers along the exhibition gallery with half-
        shut eyes bent sideways,

As the deck hands make fast the steamboat the plank is thrown
        for the shore-going passengers,

The young sister holds out the skein while the elder sister winds
        it off in a ball, and stops now and then for
        the knots,

The one-year wife is recovering and happy having a week ago
        borne her first child.

The clean-haired Yankee girl works with her sewing machine
        or in the factory or mill,

The paving man leans on his two-handed rammer, the re-
        porter's lead flies swiftly over the notebook,
        the sign painter is lettering with blue and
        gold,

The canal boy trots on the towpath, the bookkeeper counts at
        his desk, the shoemaker waxes his thread,

The conductor beats time for the band and all the performers
        follow him,

The child is baptized, the convert is making his first profes-
        sions,

The regatta is spread on the bay, the race is begun (how the
        white sails sparkle!);

The drover watching his drove sings out to them that would
        stray,

The peddler sweats with his pack on his back (the purchaser
        higgling about the odd cent);

The bride unrumples her white dress, the minute hand of the
        clock moves slowly,

The opium eater reclines with rigid head and just-opened lips,

The prostitute draggles her shawl, her bonnet bobs on her tipsy
        and pimpled neck,

The crowd laugh at her blackguard oaths, the men jeer and
    wink to each other,
(Miserable! I do not laugh at your oaths nor jeer you);
The President holding a Cabinet council is surrounded by the
    great Secretaries,
On the piazza walk three matrons stately and friendly with
    twined arms,
The crew of the fish smack pack repeated layers of halibut in
    the hold,
The Missourian crosses the plains toting his wares and his
    cattle,
As the fare collector goes through the train he gives notice by
    the jingling of loose change,
The floormen are laying the floor, the tinners are tinning the
    roof, the masons are calling for mortar,
In single file each shouldering his hod pass onward the labor-
    ers;
Seasons pursuing each other the indescribable crowd is gath-
    ered, it is the fourth of Seventh-month (what
    salutes of cannon   and small arms!);
Seasons pursuing each other the plower plows, the mower
    mows, and the winter grain falls in the
    ground;
Off on the lakes the pike fisher watches and waits by the hole
    in the frozen surface,
The stumps stand thick round the clearing, the squatter strikes
    deep with his ax,
Flatboatmen make fast towards dusk near the cottonwood or
    pecan trees,
Coon seekers go through the regions of the Red River or
    through those drained by the Tennessee, or
    through those of the Arkansas,
Torches shine in the dark that hangs on the Chattahoochee or
    Altamahaw,
Patriarchs sit at supper with sons and grandsons and great-
    grandsons around them,
In walls of adobe, in canvas tents, rest hunters and trappers
    after their day's sport,
The city sleeps and the country sleeps,
The living sleep for their time, the dead sleep for their time,
The old husband sleeps by his wife and the young husband
    sleeps by his wife;
And these tend inward to me, and I tend outward to them,
And such as it is to be of these more or less I am,
And of these one and all I weave the song of myself.

16

I am of old and young, of the foolish as much as the wise,
Regardless of others, ever regardful of others,
Maternal as well as paternal, a child as well as a man,
Stuffed with the stuff that is coarse and stuffed with the stuff
            that is fine,
One of the Nation of many nations, the smallest the same and
            the largest the same,
A Southerner soon as a Northerner, a planter nonchalant and
            hospitable down by the Oconee I live,
A Yankee bound my own way ready for trade, my joints the
            limberest joints on earth and the sternest
            joints on earth,
A Kentuckian walking the vale of the Elkhorn in my deerskin
            leggings, a Louisianian or Georgian,
A boatman over lakes or bays or along coasts, a Hoosier, a
            Badger, Buckeye;
At home on Canadian snowshoes or up in the bush, or with
            fishermen off Newfoundland,
At home in the fleet of iceboats, sailing with the rest and
            tacking,
At home on the hills of Vermont or in the woods of Maine,
            or the Texan ranch,
Comrade of Californians, comrade of Free Northwesterners,
            (loving their big proportions),
Comrade of raftsmen and coalmen, comrade of all who shake
            hands and welcome to drink and meat,
A learner with the simplest, a teacher of the thoughtfulest,
A novice beginning yet experient of myriads of seasons,
Of every hue and caste am I, of every rank and religion,
A farmer, mechanic, artist, gentleman, sailor, Quaker,
Prisoner, fancy man, rowdy, lawyer, physician, priest.

I resist anything better than my own diversity,
Breathe the air but leave plenty after me,
And am not stuck up, and am in my place.

(The moth and the fish eggs are in their place,
The bright suns I see and the dark suns I cannot see are in their
            place,
The palpable is in its place and the impalpable is in its place.)

17

These are really the thoughts of all men in all ages and lands,
            they are not original with me,

If they are not yours as much as mine they are nothing, or
        next to nothing,
If they are not the riddle and the untying of the riddle they
        are nothing,
If they are not just as close as they are distant they are nothing
This is the grass that grows wherever the land is and the
        water is,
This is the common air that bathes the globe.

18

With music strong I come, with my cornets and my drums,
I play not marches for accepted victors only, I play marches
        for conquered and slain persons.
Have you heard that it was good to gain the day?
I also say it is good to fall, battles are lost in the same spirit
        in which they are won.
I beat and pound for the dead,
I blow through my embouchures my loudest and gayest for
        them.
Vivas to those who have failed!
And to those whose war vessels sank in the sea!
And to those themselves who sank in the sea!
And to all generals that lost engagements, and all overcome
        heroes!
And the numberless unknown heroes equal to the greatest
        heroes known!

19

This is the meal equally set, this the meat for natural hunger,
It is for the wicked just the same as the righteous, I make
        appointments with all,
I will not have a single person slighted or left away,
The kept woman, sponger, thief, are hereby invited,
The heavy-lipped slave is invited, the venerealee is invited;
There shall be no difference between them and the rest.
This is the press of a bashful hand, this the float and odor of
        hair,
This the touch of my lips to yours, this the murmur of
        yearning,
This the far-off depth and height reflecting my own face,
This the thoughtful merge of myself, and the outlet again.
Do you guess I have some intricate purpose?
Well I have, for the Fourth-month showers have, and the mica
        on the side of a rock has.
Do you take it I would astonish?

Does the daylight astonish? does the early redstart twittering
                through the woods?
Do I astonish more than they?
This hour I tell things in confidence,
I might not tell everybody, but I will tell you.

20

Who goes there? hankering, gross, mystical, nude;
How is it I extract strength from the beef I eat?
What is a man anyhow? what am I? what are you?
All I mark as my own you shall offset it with your own,
Else it, were time lost listening to me.
I do not snivel that snivel the world over,
That months are vacuums and the ground but wallow and
                filth.
Whimpering and truckling fold with powders for invalids,
                conformity goes to the fourth-removed,
I wear my hat as I please indoors or out.
Why should I pray? why should I venerate and be ceremo-
                nious?
Having pried through the strata, analyzed to a hair, counseled
                with doctors and calculated close,
I find no sweeter fat than sticks to my own bones.
In all people I see myself, none more and not one a barley-
                corn less,
And the good or bad I say of myself I say of them.
I know I am solid and sound,
To me the converging objects of the universe perpetually
                flow,
All are written to me, and I must get what the writing means.
I know I am deathless,
I know this orbit of mine cannot be swept by a carpenter's
                compass,
I know I shall not pass like a child's carlacue cut with a
                burnt stick at night.
I know I am august,
I do not trouble my spirit to vindicate itself or be understood,
I see that the elementary laws never apologize,
(I reckon I behave no prouder than the level I plant my house
                by, after all.)
I exist as I am, that is enough,
If no other in the world be aware I sit content,
And if each and all be aware I sit content.
One world is aware and by far the largest to me, and that is
                myself,

And whether I come to my own today or in ten thousand or
    ten million years,
I can cheerfully take it now, or with equal cheerfulness I can
    wait.
My foothold is tenoned and mortised in granite,
I laugh at what you call dissolution,
And I know the amplitude of time.

21

I am the poet of the Body and I am the poet of the Soul,
The pleasures of heaven are with me and the pains of hell are
    with me,
The first I graft and increase upon myself, the latter I trans-
    late into a new tongue.
I am the poet of the woman the same as the man,
And I say it is as great to be a woman as to be a man,
And I say there is nothing greater than the mother of men.
I chant the chant of dilation or pride,
We have had ducking and deprecating about enough,
I show that size is only development.
Have you outstripped the rest? are you the President?
It is a trifle, they will more than arrive there every one, and
    still pass on.
I am he that walks with the tender and growing night,
I call to the earth and sea half-held by the night.
Press close bare-bosomed night—press close magnetic nour-
    ishing night!
Night of south winds—night of the large few stars!
Still nodding night—mad naked summer night.
Smile O voluptuous cool-breathed earth!
Earth of the slumbering and liquid trees!
Earth of departed sunset—earth of the mountains misty-
    topped!
Earth of the vitreous pour of the full moon just tinged with
    blue!
Earth of shine and dark mottling the tide of the river!
Earth of the limpid gray of clouds brighter and clearer for
    my sake!
Far-swooping elbowed earth—rich apple-blossomed earth!
Smile, for your lover comes.
Prodigal, you have given me love—therefore I to you give
    love!
O unspeakable passionate love.

22

You sea! I resign myself to you also—I guess what you mean,
I behold from the beach your crooked inviting fingers,
I believe you refuse to go back without feeling of me,
We must have a turn together, I undress, hurry me out of
    sight of the land,
Cushion me soft, rock me in billowy drowse,
Dash me with amorous wet, I can repay you.
Sea of stretched ground swells,
Sea breathing broad and convulsive breaths,
Sea of the brine of life and of unshoveled yet always-ready
    graves,
Howler and scooper of storms, capricious and dainty sea,
I am integral with you, I too am of one phase and of all
    phases.
Partaker of influx and efflux I, extoller of hate and conciliation,
Extoller of armies and those that sleep in each other's arms,
I am he attesting sympathy,
(Shall I make my list of things in the house and skip the house
    that supports them?)
I am not the poet of goodness only, I do not decline to be the
    poet of wickedness also.
What blurt is this about virtue and about vice?
Evil propels me and reform of evil propels me, I stand indif-
    ferent,
My gait is no faultfinder's or rejector's gait;
I moisten the roots of all that has grown.
Did you fear some scrofula out of the unflagging pregnancy?
Did you guess the celestial laws are yet to be worked over and
    rectified?
I find one side a balance and the antipodal side a balance,
Soft doctrine as steady help as stable doctrine,
Thoughts and deeds of the present our rouse and early start.
This minute that comes to me over the past decillions,
There is no better than it and now.
What behaved well in the past or behaves well today is not such
    a wonder,
The wonder is always and always how there can be a mean
    man or an infidel.

23

Endless unfolding of words of ages!
And mine a word of the modern, the word En Masse.
A word of the faith that never balks,

Here or henceforward it is all the same to me, I accept Time
absolutely.
It alone is without flaw, it alone rounds and completes all,
That mystic baffling wonder alone completes all.
I accept Reality and dare not question it,
Materialism first and last imbuing.
Hurrah for positive science! long live exact demonstration!
Fetch stonecrop mixed with cedar and branches of lilac,
This is the lexicographer, this the chemist, this made a gram-
mar of the old cartouches,
These mariners put the ship through dangerous unknown seas,
This is the geologist, this works with the scalpel. and this is
a mathematician.
Gentlemen, to you the first honors always!
Your facts are useful, and yet they are not my dwelling,
I but enter by them to an area of my dwelling.
Less the reminders of properties told my words,
And more the reminders they of life untold, and of freedom
and extrication,
And make short account of neuters and geldings, and favor
men and women fully equipped.
And beat the gong of revolt, and stop with fugitives and them
that plot and conspire.

24

Walt Whitman, a cosmos, of Manhattan the son,
Turbulent, fleshy, sensual, eating, drinking and breeding,
No sentimentalist, no stander above men and women or apart
from them,
No more modest than immodest.
Unscrew the locks from the doors!
Unscrew the doors themselves from their jambs!
Whoever degrades another degrades me,
And whatever is done or said returns at last to me.
Through me the afflatus surging and surging, through me the
current and index.
I speak the password primeval, I give the sign of democracy,
By God! I will accept nothing which all cannot have their
counterpart of on the same terms.
Through me many long dumb voices,
Voices of the interminable generations of prisoners and slaves.
Voices of the diseased and despairing and of thieves and
dwarfs,
Voices of cycles of preparation and accretion,
And of the threads that connect the stars, and of wombs and
of the father stuff,

And of the rights of them the others are down upon,
Of the deformed, trivial, flat, foolish, despised,
Fog in the air, beetles rolling balls of dung.
Through me forbidden voices,
Voices of sexes and lusts, voices veiled and I remove the veil,
Voices indecent by me clarified and transfigured.
I do not press my fingers across my mouth,
I keep as delicate around the bowels as around the head and
heart,
Copulation is no more rank to me than death is.
I believe in the flesh and the appetites,
Seeing, hearing, feeling, are miracles, and each part and tag
of me is a miracle.
Divine am I inside and out, and I make holy whatever I touch
or am touched from,
The scent of these armpits aroma finer than prayer,
This head more than churches, bibles, and all the creeds.
If I worship one thing more than another it shall be the spread
of my own body, or any part of it,
Translucent mold of me it shall be you!
Shaded ledges and rests it shall be you!
Firm masculine colter it shall be you!
Whatever goes to the tilth of me it shall be you!
You my rich blood! your milky stream pale strippings of my
life!
Breast that presses against other breasts it shall be you!
My brain it shall be your occult convolutions!
Root of washed sweet flag! timorous pond snipe! nest of guard-
ed duplicate eggs! it shall be you!
Mixed tussled hay of head, beard, brawn, it shall be you!
Trickling sap of maple, fiber of manly wheat, it shall be you!
Sun so generous it shall be you!
Vapors lighting and shading my face it shall be you!
You sweaty brooks and dews it shall be you!
Winds whose soft-tickling genitals rub against me it shall be
you!
Broad muscular fields, branches of live oak, loving lounger in
my winding paths, it shall be you!
Hands I have taken, face I have kissed, mortal I have ever
touched, it shall be you.
I dote on myself, there is that lot of me and all so luscious,
Each moment and whatever happens thrills me with joy,
I cannot tell how my ankles bend, nor whence the cause of
my faintest wish,
Nor the cause of the friendship I emit, nor the cause of the
friendship I take again.

That I walk up my stoop, I pause to consider if it really be,
A morning glory at my window satisfies me more than the
metaphysics of books.
To behold the daybreak!
The little light fades the immense and diaphanous shadows,
The air tastes good to my palate.
Hefts of the moving world at innocent gambols silently rising,
freshly exuding,
Scooting obliquely high and low.
Something I cannot see puts upward libidinous prongs,
Seas of bright juice suffuse heaven.
The earth by the sky stayed with, the daily close of their junc-
tion,
The heaved challenge from the east that moment over my
head,
The mocking taunt, See then whether you shall be master!

25

Dazzling and tremendous how quick the sunrise would kill
me,
If I could not now and always send sunrise out of me.
We also ascend dazzling and tremendous as the sun,
We found our own O my soul in the calm and cool of the
daybreak.
My voice goes after what my eyes cannot reach,
With the twirl of my tongue I encompass worlds and volumes
of worlds.
Speech is the twin of my vision, it is unequal to measure
itself,
It provokes me forever, it says sarcastically,
Walt you contain enough, why don't you let it out then?
Come now I will not be tantalized, you conceive too much of
articulation,
Do you not know O speech how the buds beneath you are
folded?
Waiting in gloom, protected by frost,
The dirt receding before my prophetical screams,
I underlying causes to balance them at last,
My knowledge my live parts, it keeping tally with the mean-
ing of all things,
Happiness (which whoever hears me let him or her set out
in search of this day).
My final merit I refuse you, I refuse putting from me what
I really am,
Encompass worlds, but never try to encompass me,

I crowd your sleekest and best by simply looking toward you.
Writing and talk do not prove me,
I carry the plenum of proof and everything else in my face,
With the hush of my lips I wholly confound the skeptic.

26

Now I will do nothing but listen,
To accrue what I hear into this song, to let sounds contribute
          toward it.
I hear bravuras of birds, bustle of growing wheat, gossip of
          flames, clack of sticks cooking my meals,
I hear the sound I love, the sound of the human voice,
I hear all sounds running together, combined, fused or fol-
          lowing,
Sounds of the city and sounds out of the city, sounds of the
          day and night,
Talkative young ones to those that like them, the loud laugh
          of work people at their meals,
The angry base of disjointed friendship, the faint tones of the
          sick,
The judge with hands tight to the desk, his pallid lips pro-
          nouncing a death sentence,
The heave'e'yo of stevedores unloading ships by the wharves,
          the refrain of the anchor lifters,
The ring of alarm bells, the cry of fire, the whirr of swift-
          streaking engines and hose carts with pre-
          monitory tinkles and colored lights,
The steam whistle, the solid roll of the train of approaching
          cars,
The slow march played at the head of the association march-
          ing two and two,
(They go to guard some corpse, the flag tops are draped with
          black muslin.)
I hear the violoncello ('tis the young man's heart s complaint),
I hear the keyed cornet, it glides quickly in through my ears,
It shakes mad-sweet pangs through my belly and breast.
I hear the chorus, it is a grand opera,
Ah this indeed is music—this suits me.
A tenor large and fresh as the creation fills me,
The orbic flex of his mouth is pouring and filling me full.
I hear the trained soprano (what work with hers is this?)
The orchestra whirls me wider than Uranus flies,
It wrenches such ardors from me I did not know I possessed
          them,
It sails me, I dab with bare feet, they are licked by the indo-
          lent waves,

I am cut by bitter and angry hail, I lose my breath,
Steeped amid honeyed morphine, my windpipe throttled in
    fakes of death,
At length let up again to feel the puzzle of puzzles,
And that we call Being.

27

To be in any form, what is that?
(Round and round we go, all of us, and ever come back
    thither),
If nothing lay more developed the quahog in its callous shell
    were enough.
Mine is no callous shell,
I have instant conductors all over me whether I pass or stop,
They seize every object and lead it harmlessly through me.
I merely stir, press, feel with my fingers, and am happy,
To touch my person to someone else's is about as much as
    I can stand.

28

Is this then a touch? quivering me to a new identity,
Flames and ether making a rush for my veins,
Treacherous tip of me reaching and crowding to help them,
My flesh and blood playing out lightning to strike what is
    hardly different from myself,
On all sides prurient provokers stiffening my limbs,
Straining the udder of my heart for its withheld drip,
Behaving licentious toward me, taking no denial,
Depriving me of my best as for a purpose,
Unbuttoning my clothes, holding me by the bare waist,
Deluding my confusion with the calm of the sunlight and
    pasture fields,
Immodestly sliding the fellow senses away,
They bribed to swap off with touch and go and graze at the
    edges of me,
No consideration, no regard for my draining strength or my
    anger,
Fetching the rest of the herd around to enjoy them awhile,
Then all uniting to stand on a headland and worry me.
The sentries desert every other part of me,
They have left me helpless to a red marauder,
They all come to the headland to witness and assist against me.

I am given up by traitors,

I talk wildly, I have lost my wits, I and nobody else am the
      greatest traitor,
I went myself first to the headland, my own hands carried
      me there.
You villain touch! what are you doing? my breath is tight
      in its throat,
Unclench your floodgates, you are too much for me.

29

Blind loving wrestling touch, sheathed hooded sharp-toothed
      touch!
Did it make you ache so, leaving me?
Parting tracked by arriving, perpetual payment of perpetual
      loan,
Rich showering rain, and recompense richer afterward.
Sprouts take and accumulate, stand by the curb prolific and
      vital,
Landscapes projected masculine, full-sized and golden.

30

All truths wait in all things,
They neither hasten their own delivery nor resist it,
They do not need the obstetric forceps of the surgeon,
The insignificant is as big to me as any,
(What is less or more than a touch?)
Logic and sermons never convince,
The damp of the night drives deeper into my soul.
(Only what proves itself to every man and woman is so,
Only what nobody denies is so.)
A minute and a drop of me settle my brain,
I believe the soggy clods shall become lovers and lamps,
And a compend of compends is the meat of a man or woman,
And a summit and flower there is the feeling they have for
      each other,
And they are to branch boundlessly out of that lesson until
      it becomes omnific,
And until one and all shall delight us, and we them.

31

I believe a leaf of grass is no less than the journeywork of
      the stars,
And the pismire is equally perfect, and a grain of sand, and
      the egg of the wren,

And the tree toad is a chef-d'oeuvre for the highest,
And the running blackberry would adorn the parlors of heaven,
And the narrowest hinge in my hand puts to scorn all ma-
 chinery,
And the cow crunching with depressed head surpasses any
 statue,
And a mouse is miracle enough to stagger sextillions of
 infidels.
I find I incorporate gneiss, coal, long-threaded moss, fruits,
 grains, esculent roots,
And am stuccoed with quadrupeds and birds all over,
And have distanced what is behind me for good reasons,
But call anything back again when I desire it.
In vain the speeding or shyness,
In vain the plutonic rocks send their old heat against my ap-
 proach,
In vain the mastodon retreats beneath its own powdered bones,
In vain objects stand leagues off and assume manifold shapes,
In vain the ocean settling in hollows and the great monsters
 lying low,
In vain the buzzard houses herself with the sky,
In vain the snake slides through the creepers and logs,
In vain the elk takes to the inner passes of the woods,
In vain the razor-billed auk sails far north to Labrador,
I follow quickly, I ascend to the nest in the fissure of the cliff.

32

I think I could turn and live with animals, they are so placid
 and self-contained,
I stand and look at them long and long.
They do not sweat and whine about their condition,
They do not lie awake in the dark and weep for their sins,
They do not make me sick discussing their duty to God,
Not one is dissatisfied, not one is demented with the mania
 of owning things,
Not one kneels to another, nor to his kind that lived thousands
 of years ago,
Not one is respectable or unhappy over the whole earth.
So they show their relations to me and I accept them,
They bring me tokens of myself, they evince them plainly in
 their possession.

I wonder where they get those tokens,
Did I pass that way huge times ago and negligently drop them?

Myself moving forward then and now and forever,
Gathering and showing more always and with velocity,
Infinite and omnigenous, and the like of these among them,
Not too exclusive toward the reachers of my remembrancers,
Picking out here one that I love, and now go with him on
        brotherly terms.
A gigantic beauty of a stallion, fresh and responsive to my
        caresses,
Head high in the forehead, wide between the ears,
Limbs glossy and supple, tail dusting the ground,
Eyes full of sparkling wickedness, ears finely cut, flexibly
        moving.
His nostrils dilate as my heels embrace him,
His well-built limbs tremble with pleasure as we race around
        and return.
I but use you a minute, then I resign you, stallion,
Why do I need your paces when I myself outgallop them?
Even as I stand or sit passing faster than you.

33

Space and Time! now I see it is true, what I guessed at,
What I guessed when I loafed on the grass,
What I guessed while I lay alone in my bed,
And again as I walked the beach under the paling stars of the
        morning.
My ties and ballasts leave me, my elbows rest in sea gaps,
I skirt sierras, my palms cover continents,
I am afoot with my vision.
By the city's quadrangular houses—in log huts, camping with
        lumbermen,
Along the ruts of the turnpike, along the dry gulch and rivulet
        bed,
Weeding my onion patch or hoeing rows of carrots and pars-
        nips, crossing savannas, trailing in forests,
Prospecting, gold digging, girdling the trees of a new pur-
        chase,
Scorched ankle-deep by the hot sand, hauling my boat down
        the shallow river,
Where the panther walks to and fro on a limb overhead,
        where the buck turns furiously at the hunter,
Where the rattlesnake suns his flabby length on a rock, where
        the otter is feeding on fish,
Where the alligator in his tough pimples sleeps by the bayou,
Where the black bear is searching for roots or honey, where
        the beaver pats the mud with his paddle-
        shaped tail;

Over the growing sugar, over the yellow-flowered cotton plant,
over the rice in its low moist field,

Over the sharp-peaked farmhouse, with its scalloped scum and
slender shoots from the gutters,

Over the western persimmon, over the long-leaved corn, over
the delicate blue-flower flax,

Over the white and brown buckwheat, a hummer and buzzer
there with the rest,

Over the dusky green of the rye as it ripples and shades in the
breeze;

Scaling mountains, pulling myself cautiously up, holding on
by low scragged limbs,

Walking the path worn in the grass and beat through the
leaves of the brush,

Where the quail is whistling betwixt the woods and the wheat
lot,

Where the bat flies in the Seventh-month eve, where the great
goldbug drops through the dark,

Where the brook puts out of the roots of the old tree and flows
to the meadow,

Where cattle stand and shake away flies with the tremulous
shuddering of their hides,

Where the cheesecloth hangs in the kitchen, where andirons
straddle the hearth slab, where cobwebs fall
in festoons from the rafters;

Where trip hammers crash, where the press is whirling its
cylinders,

Where the human heart beats with terrible throes under its
ribs,

Where the pear-shaped balloon is floating aloft (floating in it
myself and looking composedly down),

Where the life car is drawn on the slip noose, where the heat
hatches pale-green eggs in the dented sand,

Where the she-whale swims with her calf and never forsakes it,

Where the steamship trails hindways its long pennant of
smoke,

Where the fin of the shark cuts like a black chip out of the
water,

Where the half-burned brig is riding on unknown currents,

Where shells grow to her slimy deck, where the dead are cor-
rupting below;

Where the dense-starred flag is borne at the head of the regi-
ments,

Approaching Manhattan up by the long-stretching island,

Under Niagara, the cataract falling like a veil over my coun-
tenance,

Upon a doorstep, upon the horse block of hardwood outside,
Upon the race course, or enjoying picnics or jigs or a good
    game of baseball,
At he-festivals, with blackguard gibes, ironical license, bull
    dances, drinking, laughter,
At the cider mill tasting the sweets of the brown mash, sucking
    the juice through a straw,
At apple peelings wanting kisses for all the red fruit I find,
At musters, beach parties, friendly bees, huskings, house
    raisings;
Where the mockingbird sounds his delicious gurgles, cackles,
    screams, weeps,
Where the hayrick stands in the barnyard, where the dry
    stalks are scattered, where the brood cow
    waits in the hovel,
Where the bull advances to do his masculine work, where the
    stud to the mare, where the cock is treading
    the hen,
Where the heifers browse, where geese nip their food with
    short jerks,
Where sundown shadows lengthen over the limitless and lone-
    some prairie,
Where herds of buffalo make a crawling spread of the square
    miles far and near,
Where the hummingbird shimmers, where the neck of the
    long-lived swan is curving and winding,
Where the laughing gull scoots by the shore, where she laughs
    her near-human laugh,
Where beehives range on a gray bench in the garden half hid
    by the high weeds,
Where band-necked partridges roost in a ring on the ground
    with their heads out,
Where burial coaches enter the arched gates of a cemetery,
Where winter wolves bark amid wastes of snow and icicled
    trees,
Where the yellow-crowned heron comes to the edge of the
    marsh at night and feeds upon small crabs,
Where the splash of swimmers and divers cools the warm
    noon,
Where the katydid works her chromatic reed on the walnut
    tree over the well,
Through patches of citrons and cucumbers with silver-wired
    leaves,
Through the salt lick or orange glade, or under conical firs,
Through the gymnasium, through the curtained saloon,
    through the office or public hall;

Pleased with the native and pleased with the foreign, pleased
   with the new and old,
Pleased with the homely woman as well as the handsome,
Pleased with the Quakeress as she puts off her bonnet and
   talks melodiously,
Pleased with the tune of the choir of the whitewashed church,
Pleased with the earnest words of the sweating Methodist
   preacher, impressed seriously at the camp
   meeting;
Looking in at the shop windows of Broadway the whole fore-
   noon, flatting the flesh of my nose on the
   thick plate glass,
Wandering the same afternoon with my face turned up to
   the clouds, or down a lane or along the
   beach,
My right and left arms round the sides of two friends, and
   I in the middle;
Coming home with the silent and dark-cheeked bush boy,
   (behind me he rides at the drape of the day),
Far from the settlements studying the print of animals' feet,
   or the moccasin print,
By the cot in the hospital reaching lemonade to a feverish
   patient,
Nigh the coffined corpse when all is still, examining with a
   candle;
Voyaging to every port to dicker and adventure,
Hurrying with the modern crowd as eager and fickle as any,
Hot toward one I hate, ready in my madness to knife him,
Solitary at midnight in my back yard, my thoughts gone from
   me a long while,
Walking the old hills of Judea with the beautiful gentle God
   by my side,
Speeding through space, speeding through heaven and the
   stars,
Speeding amid the seven satellites and the broad ring, and
   the diameter of eighty thousand miles,
Speeding with tailed meteors, throwing fireballs like the rest,
Carrying the crescent child that carries its own full mother in
   its belly,
Storming, enjoying, planning, loving, cautioning,
Backing and filling, appearing and disappearing,
I tread day and night such roads.
I visit the orchards of spheres and look at the product,
And look at quintillions ripened and look at quintillions green.
I fly those flights of a fluid and swallowing soul,
My course runs below the soundings of plummets.

I help myself to material and immaterial,
No guard can shut me off, no law prevent me.
I anchor my ship for a little while only,
My messengers continually cruise away or bring their returns
    to me.
I go hunting polar furs and the seal, leaping chasms with a
    pike-pointed staff, clinging to topples of brit-
    tle and blue.
I ascend to the foretruck,
I take my place late at night in the crow's nest,
We sail the arctic sea, it is plenty light enough,
Through the clear atmosphere I stretch around on the wonder-
    ful beauty,
The enormous masses of ice pass me and I pass them, the
    scenery is plain in all directions,
The white-topped mountains show in the distance, I fling out
    my fancies toward them,
We are approaching some great battlefield in which we are
    soon to be engaged,
We pass the colossal outposts of the encampment, we pass
    with still feet and caution,
Or we are entering by the suburbs some vast and ruined city,
The blocks and fallen architecture more than all the living
    cities of the globe.
I am a free companion, I bivouac by invading watchfires,
I turn the bridegroom out of bed and stay with the bride
    myself,
I tighten her all night to my thighs and lips.
My voice is the wife's voice, the screech by the rail of the
    stairs,
They fetch my man's body up dripping and drowned.
I understand the large hearts of heroes,
The courage of present times and all times,
How the skipper saw the crowded and rudderless wreck of
    the steamship, and Death chasing it up and
    down the storm,
How he knuckled tight and gave not back an inch, and was
    faithful of days and faithful of nights,
And chalked in large letters on a board, *Be of good cheer,
we will not desert you;*
How he followed with them and tacked with them three days
    and would not give it up,
How he saved the drifting company at last,
How the lank loose-gowned women looked when boated from
    the side of their prepared graves,

How the silent old-faced infants and the lifted sick, and the
        sharp-lipped unshaven men;
All this I swallow, it tastes good, I like it well, it becomes
        mine,
I am the man, I suffered, I was there.

The disdain and calmness of martyrs,
The mother of old, condemned for a witch, burnt with dry
        wood, her children gazing on,
The hounded slave that flags in the race, leans by the fence,
        blowing, covered with sweat,
The twinges that sting like needles his legs and neck, the mur-
        derous buckshot and the bullets,
All these I feel or am.

I am the hounded slave, I wince at the bite of the dogs,
Hell and despair are upon me, crack and again crack the
        marksmen,
I clutch the rails of the fence, my gored ribs, thinned with
        the ooze of my skin,
I fall on the weeds and stones,
The riders spur their unwilling horses, haul close,
Taunt my dizzy ears and beat me violently over the head
        with whipstocks.

Agonies are one of my changes of garments.
I do not ask the wounded person how he feels, I myself be-
        come the wounded person,
My hurts turn livid upon me as I lean on a cane and observe.

I am the mashed fireman with breastbone broken,
Tumbling walls buried me in their debris,
Heat and smoke I inspired, I heard the yelling shouts of my
        comrades,
I heard the distant click of their picks and shovels,
They have cleared the beams away, they tenderly lift me forth.

I lie in the night air in my red shirt, the pervading hush is
        for my sake,
Painless after all I lie exhausted but not so unhappy,
White and beautiful are the faces around me, the heads are
        bared of their fire caps,
The kneeling crowd fades with the light of the torches.

Distant and dead resuscitate.
They show as the dial or move as the hands of me, I am the
        clock myself.

I am an old artillerist, I tell of my fort's bombardment,
I am there again.

Again the long roll of the drummers,
Again the attacking cannon, mortars,
Again to my listening ears the cannon responsive.

I take part, I see and hear the whole,
The cries, curses, roar, the plaudits for well-aimed shots,
The ambulanza slowly passing trailing its red drip,
Workmen searching after damages, making indispensable
            repairs,
The fall of grenades through the rent roof, the fan-shaped
            explosion,
The whizz of limbs, heads, stone, wood, iron, high in the air.

Again gurgles the mouth of my dying general, he furiously
            waves with his hand,
He gasps through the clot *Mind not me—mind—the entrench-
            ments.*

34

Now I tell what I know in Texas in my early youth,
(I tell not the fall of Alamo,
Not one escaped to tell the fall of Alamo,
The hundred and fifty are dumb yet at Alamo,)
'Tis the tale of the murder in cold blood of four hundred and
            twelve young men.

Retreating they had formed in a hollow square with their
            baggage for breastworks,
Nine hundred lives out of the surrounding enemy's, nine times
            their number, was the price they took in
            advance,
Their colonel was wounded and their ammunition gone,
They treated for an honorable capitulation, received writing
            and seal, gave up their arms and marched
            back prisoners of war.

They were the glory of the race of rangers,
Matchless with horse, rifle, song, supper, courtship,
Large, turbulent, generous, handsome, proud, and affectionate,
Bearded, sunburnt, dressed in the free costume of hunters,
Not a single one over thirty years of age.

The second First-day morning they were brought out in squads
            and massacred, it was beautiful early sum-
            mer,

The work commenced about five o'clock and was over by
eight.

None obeyed the command to kneel,
Some made a mad and helpless rush, some stood stark and
straight,
A few fell at once, shot in the temple or heart, the living and
dead lay together,
The maimed and mangled dug in the dirt, the newcomers saw
them there,
Some half-killed attempted to crawl away,
These were dispatched with bayonets or battered with the
blunts of muskets.
A youth not seventeen years old seized his assassin till two
more came to release him,
The three were all torn and covered with the boy's blood.

At eleven o'clock began the burning of the bodies;
That is the tale of the murder of the four hundred and twelve
young men.

35

Would you hear of an old-time sea fight?
Would you learn who won by the light of the moon and stars?
List to the yarn, as my grandmother's father the sailor told
it to me.

Our foe was no skulk in his ship I tell you (said he),
His was the surly English pluck, and there is no tougher or
truer, and never was, and never will be;
Along the lowered eve he came horribly raking us.

We closed with him, the yards entangled, the cannon touched,
My captain lashed fast with his own hands.

We had received some eighteen-pound shots under the water,
On our lower gun deck two large pieces had burst at the first
fire, killing all around and blowing up over-
head.

Fighting at sundown, fighting at dark,
Ten o'clock at night, the full moon well up, our leaks on the
gain, and five feet of water reported
The master-at-arms loosing the prisoners confined in the
afterhold to give them a chance for them-
selves.

The transit to and from the magazine is now stopped by the
sentinels,

They see so many strange faces they do not know whom to trust.

Our frigate takes fire,
The other asks if we demand quarter?
If our colors are struck and the fighting done?

Now I laugh content, for I hear the voice of my little captain,
We have not struck, he composedly cries, *we have just begun our part of the fighting.*

Only three guns are in use,
One is directed by the captain himself against the enemy's mainmast,
Two well served with grape and canister silence his musketry and clear his decks.

The tops alone second the fire of this little battery, especially the maintop,
They hold out bravely during the whole of the action.

Not a moment's cease,
The leaks gain fast on the pumps the fire eats toward the powder magazine.
One of the pumps has been shot away, it is generally thought we are sinking.
Serene stands the little captain,
He is not hurried, his voice is neither high nor low,
His eyes give more light to us than our battle lanterns.

Toward twelve there in the beams of the moon they surrender to us.

36

Stretched and still lies the midnight,
Two great hulls motionless on the breast of the darkness,
Our vessel riddled and slowly sinking, preparations to pass to the one we have conquered,
The captain on the quarterdeck coldly giving his orders through a countenance white as a sheet,
Nearby the corpse of the child that served in the cabin,
The dead face of an old salt with long white hair and carefully curled whiskers,
The flames spite of all that can be done flickering aloft and below,
The husky voices of the two or three officers yet fit for duty,
Formless stacks of bodies and bodies by themselves, dabs of flesh upon the masts and spars,

Cut of cordage, dangle of rigging, slight shock of the soothe
        of waves,
Black and impassive guns, litter of powder parcels, strong
        scent,
A few large stars overhead, silent and mournful shining,
Delicate sniffs of sea breeze, smells of sedgy grass and fields
        by the shore, death messages given in charge
        to survivors,
The hiss of the surgeon's knife, the gnawing teeth of his saw,
Wheeze, cluck, swash of falling blood, short wild scream, and
        long, dull, tapering groan,
These so, these irretrievable.

37

You laggards there on guard! look to your arms!
In at the conquered doors they crowd! I am possessed!
Embody all presences outlawed or suffering,
See myself in prison shaped like another man.
And feel the dull unintermitted pain,
For me the keepers of convicts shoulder their carbines and
        keep watch.
It is I let out in the morning and barred at night.

Not a mutineer walks handcuffed to jail but I am handcuffed
        to him and walk by his side,
(I am less the jolly one there, and more the silent one with
        sweat on my twitching lips,)

Not a youngster is taken for larceny but I go up too, and am
        tried and sentenced.

Not a cholera patient lies at the last gasp but I also lie at the
        last gasp,
My face is ash-colored, my sinews gnarl, away from me people
        retreat.

Askers embody themselves in me and I am embodied in
        them,
I project my hat, sit shamefaced, and beg.

38

Enough! enough! enough!
Somehow I have been stunned. Stand back!
Give me a little time beyond my cuffed head, slumbers,
        dreams, gaping,
I discover myself on the verge of a usual mistake.

That I could forget the mockers and insults!
That I could forget the trickling tears and the blows of the
    bludgeons and hammers!
That I could look with a separate look on my own crucifixion
    and bloody crowning!

I remember now,
I resume the overstaid fraction,
The grave of rock multiplies what has been confided to it,
    or to any graves,
Corpses rise, gashes heal, fastenings roll from me.

I troop forth replenished with supreme power, one of an
    average unending procession,
Inland and seacoast we go, and pass all boundary lines,
Our swift ordinances on their way over the whole earth,
The blossoms we wear in our hats the growth of thousands
    of years.

Élèves, I salute you! come forward!
Continue your annotations, continue your questionings.

39

The friendly and flowing savage, who is he?
Is he waiting for civilization, or past it and mastering it?

Is he some Southwesterner raised outdoors? is he Canadian?
Is he from the Mississippi country? Iowa, Oregon, California?
The mountains? prairie life, bush life? or sailor from the sea?
Wherever he goes men and women accept and desire him,
They desire he should like them, touch them, speak to them,
    stay with them.

Behavior lawless as snowflakes, words simple as grass, un-
    combed head, laughter, and naïveté,
Slow-stepping feet, common features, common modes and
    emanations,
They descend in new forms from the tips of his fingers,
They are wafted with the odor of his body or breath, they fly
    out of the glance of his eyes.

40

Flaunt of the sunshine I need not your bask—lie over!
You light surfaces only, I force surfaces and depths also.

Earth! you seem to look for something at my hands,
Say, old topknot, what do you want?

Man or woman, I might tell how I like you, but cannot,
And might tell what it is in me and what it is in you, but
cannot,
And might tell that pining I have, that pulse of my nights and
days.

Behold, I do not give lectures or a little charity,
When I give I give myself.

You there, impotent, loose in the knees,
Open your scarfed chops till I blow grit within you,
Spread your palms and lift the flaps of your pockets,
I am not to be denied, I compel, I have stores plenty and to
spare,
And anything I have I bestow.

I do not ask who you are, that is not important to me,
You can do nothing and be nothing but what I will infold you.

To cotton-field drudge or cleaner of privies I lean,
On his right cheek I put the family kiss,
And in my soul I swear I never will deny him.

On women fit for conception I start bigger and nimbler babes,
(This day I am jetting the stuff of far more arrogant republics.)

To anyone dying, thither I speed and twist the knob of the
door,
Turn the bedclothes toward the foot of the bed,
Let the physician and the priest go home.

I seize the descending man and raise him with resistless will,
O despairer, here is my neck,
By God, you shall not go down! hang your whole weight
upon me.

I dilate you with tremendous breath, I buoy you up,
Every room of the house do I fill with an armed force,
Lovers of me, bafflers of graves.

Sleep—I and they keep guard all night,
Not doubt, not disease shall dare to lay finger upon you,
I have embraced you, and henceforth possess you to myself,
And when you rise in the morning you will find what I tell
you is so.

41

I am he bringing help for the sick as they pant on their backs,

And for strong upright men I bring yet more needed help.

I heard what was said of the universe,
Heard it and heard it of several thousand years;
It is middling well as far as it goes—but is that all?

Magnifying and applying come I,
Outbidding at the start the old cautious hucksters,
Taking myself the exact dimensions of Jehovah,
Lithographing Cronos, Zeus his son, and Hercules his grand-
    son,
Buying drafts of Osiris, Isis Belus, Brahma, Buddha,
In my portfolio placing Manito loose, Allah on a leaf, the
    crucifix engraved,
With Odin and the hideous-faced Mexitli and every idol and
    image,
Taking them all for what they are worth and not a cent more,
Admitting they were alive and did the work of their days,
(They bore mites as for unfledged birds who have now to
    rise and fly and sing for themselves,)
Accepting the rough deific sketches to fill out better in myself,
    bestowing them freely on each man and
    woman I see,
Discovering as much or more in a framer framing a house,
Putting higher claims for him there with his rolled-up sleeves
    driving the mallet and chisel,
Not objecting to special revelations, considering a curl of
    smoke or a hair on the back of my hand just
    as curious as any revelation,
Lads ahold of fire engines and hook-and-ladder ropes no less
    to me than the gods of the antique wars,
Minding their voices peal through the crash of destruction,
Their brawny limbs passing safe over charred laths, their white
    foreheads whole and unhurt out of the
    flames;
By the mechanic's wife with her babe at her nipple interceding
    for every person born,
Three scythes at harvest whizzing in a row from three lusty
    angels with shirts bagged out at their waists,
The snag-toothed hostler with red hair redeeming sins past
    and to come,
Selling all he possesses, traveling on foot to fee lawyers for
    his brother and sit by him while he is tried
    for forgery;
What was strewn in the amplest strewing the square rod about
    me, and not filling the square rod then,

The bull and the bug never worshiped half enough,
Dung and dirt more admirable than was dreamed,
The supernatural of no account, myself waiting my time to be
one of the supremes,
The day getting ready for me when I shall do as much good
as the best, and be as prodigious;
But my life lumps! becoming already a creator,
Putting myself here and now to the ambushed womb of the
shadows.

42

A call in the midst of the crowd,
My own voice, orotund sweeping and final.

Come my children,
Come my boys and girls, my women, household and inti-
mates,
Now the performer launches his nerve, he has passed his
prelude on the reeds within.

Easily written loose-fingered chords—I feel the thrum of your
climax and close.

My head slues round on my neck,
Music rolls, but not from the organ,
Folks are around me, but they are no household of mine.

Ever the hard unsunk ground,
Ever the eaters and drinkers, ever the upward and downward
sun, ever the air and the ceaseless tides,
Ever myself and my neighbors, refreshing, wicked, real,
Ever the old inexplicable query, ever that thorned thumb, that
breath of itches and thirsts,
Ever the vexer's *hoot! hoot!* till we find where the sly one
hides and bring him forth,
Ever love, ever the sobbing liquid of life,
Ever the bandage under the chin, ever the trestles of death.

Here and there with dimes on the eyes walking,
To feed the greed of the belly the brains liberally spooning,
Tickets buying, taking, selling, but into the feast never once
going,
Many sweating, plowing, thrashing, and then the chaff for
payment receiving,
A few idly owning, and they the wheat continually claiming.

This is the city and I am one of the citizens,

Whatever interests the rest interests me, politics, wars, mar-
kets, newspapers, schools,
The mayor and councils, banks, tariffs, steamships, factories,
stocks, stores, real estate and personal estate.

The little plentiful manikins skipping around in collars and
tailed coats,
I am aware who they are (they are positively not worms or
fleas),
I acknowledge the duplicates of myself, the weakest and
shallowest is deathless with me,
What I do and say the same waits for them,
Every thought that flounders in me the same flounders in them.

I know perfectly well my own egotism,
Know my omnivorous lines and must not write any less,
And would fetch you whoever you are flush with myself.

Not words of routine this song of mine,
But abruptly to question, to leap beyond yet nearer bring;
This printed and bound book—but the printer and the print-
ing-office boy?
The well-taken photographs—but your wife or friend close
and solid in your arms?
The black ship mailed with iron, her mighty guns in her
turrets—but the pluck of the captain and
engineers?
In the houses the dishes and fare and furniture—but the host
and hostess, and the look out of their eyes?
The sky up there—yet here or next door, or across the way?
The saints and sages in history—but you yourself?
Sermons, creeds, theology—but the fathomless human brain,
And what is reason? and what is love? and what is life?

43

I do not despise you priests, all time, the world over,
My faith is the greatest of faiths and the least of faiths,
Enclosing worship ancient and modern and all between an-
cient and modern,
Believing I shall come again upon the earth after five thou-
sand years,
Waiting responses from oracles, honoring the gods, saluting
the sun,
Making a fetish of the first rock or stump, powwowing with
sticks in the circle of obis,
Helping the lama or Brahman as he trims the lamps of the
idols,

Dancing yet through the streets in a phallic procession, rapt
   and austere in the woods a gymnosophist,
Drinking mead from the skullcap, to shastras and Vedas ad-
   mirant, minding the Koran,
Walking the teokallis, spotted with gore from the stone and
   knife, beating the serpent-skin drum,
Accepting the Gospels, accepting him that was crucified,
   knowing assuredly that he is divine,
To the Mass kneeling or the puritan's prayer rising, or sitting
   patiently in a pew,
Ranting and frothing in my insane crisis, or waiting dead-
   like till my spirit arouses me,
Looking forth on pavement and land, or outside of pavement
   and land,
Belonging to the winders of the circuit of circuits.

One of that centripetal and centrifugal gang I turn and talk
   like a man leaving charges before a journey.

Downhearted doubters dull and excluded,
Frivolous, sullen, moping, angry, affected, disheartened,
   atheistical,
I know every one of you, I know the sea of torment, doubt,
   despair and unbelief.

How the flukes splash!
How they contort rapid as lightning, with spasms and spouts
   of blood!

Be at peace bloody flukes of doubters and sullen mopers,
I take my place among you as much as among any,
The past is the push of you, me, all, precisely the same,
And what is yet untried and afterward is for you, me, all pre-
   cisely the same.

I do not know what is untried and afterward,
But I know it will in its turn prove sufficient, and cannot fail.

Each who passes is considered, each who stops is considered,
   not a single one can it fail.

It cannot fail the young man who died and was buried,
Nor the young woman who died and was put by his side,
Nor the little child that peeped in at the door, and then drew
   back and was never seen again,
Nor the old man who has lived without purpose, and feels it
   with bitterness worse than gall,
Nor him in the poorhouse tubercled by rum and the bad
   disorder,

Nor the numberless slaughtered and wrecked, nor the brutish
    koboo called the ordure of humanity,
Nor the sacs merely floating with open mouths for food to
    slip in,
Nor anything in the earth, or down in the oldest graves of the
    earth,
Nor anything in the myriads of spheres, nor the myriads of
    myriads that inhabit them,
Nor the present, nor the least wisp that is known.

44

It is time to explain myself—let us stand up.
What is known I strip away,
I launch all men and women forward with me into the Un-
    known.
The clock indicates the moment—but what does eternity
    indicate?
We have thus far exhausted trillions of winters and summers,
There are trillions ahead, and trillions ahead of them.
Births have brought us richness and variety,
And other births will bring us richness and variety.
I do not call one greater and one smaller,
That which fills its period and place is equal to any.

Were mankind murderous or jealous upon you, my brother,
    my sister?
I am sorry for you, they are not murderous or jealous upon
    me,
All has been gentle with me, I keep no account with lamen-
    tation,
(What have I to do with lamentation?)

I am an acme of things accomplished, and I an encloser of
    things to be.
My feet strike an apex of the apices of the stairs,
On every step bunches of ages, and larger bunches between
    the steps,
All below duly traveled, and still I mount and mount.
Rise after rise bow the phantoms behind me,
Afar down I see the huge first Nothing, I know I was even
    there,
I waited unseen and always, and slept through the lethargic
    mist,
And took my time, and took no hurt from the fetid carbon.

Long I was hugged close—long and long.

Immense have been the preparations for me,
Faithful and friendly the arms that have helped me.

Cycles ferried my cradle, rowing and rowing like cheerful
      boatmen,
For room to me stars kept aside in their own rings,
They sent influences to look after what was to hold me.
Before I was born out of my mother generations guided me,
My embryo has never been torpid, nothing could overlay it.

For it the nebula cohered to an orb,
The long slow strata piled to rest it on,
Vast vegetables gave it sustenance,
Monstrous sauroids transported it in their mouths and de-
      posited it with care.
All forces have been steadily employed to complete and delight
      me,
Now on this spot I stand with my robust soul.

45

O span of youth! ever-pushed elasticity.
O manhood, balanced, florid and full.

My lovers suffocate me,
Crowding my lips, thick in the pores of my skin,
Jostling me through streets and public halls, coming naked to
      me at night,
Crying by day *Ahoy!* from the rocks of the river, swinging
      and chirping over my head,
Calling my name from flower beds, vines, tangled underbrush,
Lighting on every moment of my life,
Bussing my body with soft balsamic busses,
Noiselessly passing handfuls out of their hearts and giving
      them to be mine.

Old age superbly rising! O welcome, ineffable grace of dying
      days!

Every condition promulges not only itself, it promulges what
      grows after and out of itself,
And the dark hush promulges as much as any.

I open my scuttle at night and see the far-sprinkled systems,
And all I see multiplied as high as I can cipher edge but the
      rim of the farther systems.
Wider and wider they spread, expanding, always expanding,
Outward and outward and forever outward.

My sun has his sun and round him obediently wheels,
He joins with his partners a group of superior circuit,
And greater sets follow, making specks of the greatest inside
    them.

There is no stoppage and never can be stoppage,
If I, you, and the worlds, and all beneath or upon their sur-
    faces, were this moment reduced back to a
    pallid float, it would not avail in the long run,
We should surely bring up again where we now stand,
And surely go as much farther, and then farther and farther.

A few quadrillions of eras, a few octillions of cubic leagues,
    do not hazard the span or make it impatient,
They are but parts, anything is but a part.

See ever so far, there is limitless space outside of that,
Count ever so much, there is limitless time around that.
My rendezvous is appointed, it is certain,
The Lord will be there and wait till I come on perfect terms,
The great Camerado, the lover true for whom I pine will be
    there.

46

I know I have the best of time and space, and was never
    measured and never will be measured.
I tramp a perpetual journey (come listen all!),
My signs are a rainproof coat, good shoes, and a staff cut from
    the woods,
No friend of mine takes his ease in my chair,
I have no chair, no church, no philosophy,
I lead no man to a dinner table, library, exchange,
But each man and each woman of you I lead upon a knoll,
My left hand hooking you round the waist,
My right hand pointing to landscapes of continents and the
    public road.
Not I, not anyone else can travel that road for you,
You must travel it for yourself.
It is not far, it is within reach,
Perhaps you have been on it since you were born and did not
    know,
Perhaps it is everywhere on water and on land.
Shoulder your duds, dear son, and I will mine, and let us
    hasten forth,
Wonderful cities and free nations we shall fetch as we go.

If you tire, give me both burdens, and rest the chuff of your
        hand on my hip,
And in due time you shall repay the same service to me,
For after we start we never lie by again.
This day before dawn I ascended a hill and looked at the
        crowded heaven,
And I said to my spirit *When we become the enfolders of those*
        orbs, and the pleasure and knowledge of
        everything in them, shall we be filled and
        satisfied then?
And my spirit said *No, we but level that lift to pass and con-*
        tinue beyond.
You are also asking me questions and I hear you,
I answer that I cannot answer, you must find out for yourself.
Sit awhile, dear son,
Here are biscuits to eat and here is milk to drink,
But as soon as you sleep and renew yourself in sweet clothes,
        I kiss you with a good-by kiss and open the
        gate for your egress hence.
Long enough have you dreamed contemptible dreams,
Now I wash the gum from your eyes,
You must habit yourself to the dazzle of the light and of every
        moment of your life.
Long have you timidly waded holding a plank by the shore,
Now I will you to be a bold swimmer,
To jump off in the midst of the sea, rise again, nod to me,
        shout, and laughingly dash with your hair.

47

I am the teacher of athletes,
He that by me spreads a wider breast than my own proves
        the width of my own,
He most honors my style who learns under it to destroy the
        teacher.
The boy I love, the same becomes a man not through derived
        power, but in his own right,
Wicked rather than virtuous out of conformity or fear,
Fond of his sweetheart, relishing well his steak,
Unrequited love or a slight cutting him worse than sharp steel
        cuts,
First-rate to ride, to fight, to hit the bull's-eye, to sail a skiff,
        to sing a song or play on the banjo,
Preferring scars and the beard and faces pitted with smallpox
        over all latherers,
And those well-tanned to those that keep out of the sun.

I teach straying from me, yet who can stray from me?
I follow you whoever you are from the present hour,
My words itch at your ears till you understand them.
I do not say these things for a dollar or to fill up the time while
            I wait for a boat,
(It is you talking just as much as myself, I act as the tongue
            of you,
Tied in your mouth, in mine it begins to be loosened.)
I swear I will never again mention love or death inside a house,
And I swear I will never translate myself at all, only to him or
            her who privately stays with me in the open
            air.

If you would understand me go to the heights or water shore,
The nearest gnat is an explanation, and a drop or motion of
            waves a key,
The maul, the oar, the handsaw, second my words.
No shuttered room or school can commune with me,
But roughs and little children better than they.

The young mechanic is closest to me, he knows me well,
The woodman that takes his ax and jug with him shall take
            me with him all day,
The farm boy plowing in the field feels good at the sound of
            my voice,
In vessels that sail my words sail, I go with fishermen and
            seamen and love them.

The soldier camped or upon the march is mine,
On the night ere the pending battle many seek me, and I do
            not fail them,
On that solemn night (it may be their last) those that know
            me seek me.
My face rubs to the hunter's face when he lies down alone in
            his blanket,
The driver thinking of me does not mind the jolt of his wagon,
The young mother and old mother comprehend me,
The girl and the wife rest the needle a moment and forget
            where they are,
They and all would resume what I have told them.

48

I have said that the soul is not more than the body,
And I have said that the body is not more than the soul,
And nothing, not God, is greater to one than one's self is,
And whoever walks a furlong without sympathy walks to his
            own funeral dressed in his shroud,

And I or you pocketless of a dime may purchase the pick of
    the earth,
And to glance with an eye or show a bean in its pod confounds
    the learning of all times,
And there is no trade or employment but the young man fol-
    lowing it may become a hero,
And there is no object so soft but it makes a hub for the
    wheeled universe,
And I say to any man or woman, Let your soul stand cool and
    composed before a million universes.

And I say to mankind, Be not curious about God,
For I who am curious about each am not curious about God.
(No array of terms can say how much I am at peace about
    God and about death.)
I hear and behold God in every object, yet understand God
    not in the least,
Nor do I understand who there can be more wonderful than
    myself.
Why should I wish to see God better than this day?
I see something of God each hour of the twenty-four, and
    each moment then,
In the faces of men and women I see God, and in my own
    face in the glass,
I find letters from God dropped in the street, and every one is
    signed by God's name,
And I leave them where they are, for I know that wheresoe'er
    I go
Others will punctually come forever and ever.

49

And as to you Death, and you bitter hug of mortality, it is
    idle to try to alarm me.
To his work without flinching the accoucheur comes,
I see the elder hand pressing receiving supporting,
I recline by the sills of the exquisite flexible doors,
And mark the outlet, and mark the relief and escape.
And as to you Corpse I think you are good manure, but that
    does not offend me,
I smell the white roses sweet-scented and growing.
I reach to the leafy lips, I reach to the polished breasts of
    melons.

And as to you Life I reckon you are the leavings of many
    deaths,

(No doubt I have died myself ten thousand times before.)
I hear you whispering there O stars of heaven,
O suns—O grass of graves—O perpetual transfers and pro-
  motions,
If you do not say anything how can I say anything?
Of the turbid pool that lies in the autumn forest,
Of the moon that descends the steeps of the soughing twi-
  light,
Toss, sparkles of day and dusk—toss on the black stems that
  decay in the muck,
Toss to the moaning gibberish of the dry limbs.
I ascend from the moon, I ascend from the night,
I perceive that the ghastly glimmer is noonday sunbeams
  reflected,
And debouch to the steady and central from the offspring
  great or small.

50

There is that in me—I do not know what it is—but I know it
  is in me.
Wrenched and sweaty—calm and cool then my body becomes,
I sleep—I sleep long.
I do not know it—it is without name—it is a word unsaid,
It is not in any dictionary, utterance, symbol.
Something it swings on more than the earth I swing on,
To it the creation is the friend whose embracing awakes me.
Perhaps I might tell more. Outlines! I plead for my brothers
  and sisters.
Do you see O my brothers and sisters?
It is not chaos or death—it is form, union, plan—it is eternal
  life—it is Happiness.

51

The past and present wilt—I have filled them, emptied them,
And proceed to fill my next fold of the future.
Listener up there! what have you to confide to me?
Look in my face while I snuff the sidle of evening,
(Talk honestly, no one else hears you, and I stay only a
  minute longer.)
Do I contradict myself?
Very well then I contradict myself,
(I am large, I contain multitudes.)
I concentrate toward them that are nigh, I wait on the door
  slab.

Who has done his day's work? who will soonest be through
　　　　with his supper?
Who wishes to walk with me?
Will you speak before I am gone? will you prove already too
　　　　late?

52

The spotted hawk swoops by and accuses me, he complains
　　　　of my gab and my loitering.
I too am not a bit tamed, I too am untranslatable,
I sound my barbaric yawp over the roofs of the world.

The last scud of day holds back for me,
It flings my likeness after the rest and true as any on the
　　　　shadowed wilds,
It coaxes me to the vapor and the dusk.

I depart as air, I shake my white locks at the runaway sun,
I effuse my flesh in eddies, and drift it in lacy jags.

I bequeath myself to the dirt to grow from the grass I love
If you want me again look for me under your boot soles.

You will hardly know who I am or what I mean,
But I shall be good health to you nevertheless,
And filter and fiber your blood.

Failing to fetch me at first keep encouraged,
Missing me one place search another,
I stop somewhere waiting for you.

NATIVE MOMENTS

Native moments—when you come upon me—ah you are here
　　　　now,
Give me now libidinous joys only,
Give me the drench of my passions, give me lite coarse and
　　　　rank,
Today I go consort with Nature's darlings, tonight too,
I am for those who believe in loose delights, I share the mid-
　　　　night orgies of young men,
I dance with the dancers and drink with the drinkers,
The echoes ring with our indecent calls, I pick out some low
　　　　person for my dearest friend,

He shall be lawless, rude, illiterate, he shall be one condemned
  by others for deeds done,
I will play a part no longer, why should I exile myself from
  my companions?
O you shunned persons, I at least do not shun you,
I come forthwith in your midst, I will be your poet,
I will be more to you than to any of the rest.

EARTH, MY LIKENESS

Earth, my likeness,
Though you look so impassive, ample and spheric there,
I now suspect that is not all;
I now suspect there is something fierce in you eligible to burst
  forth,
For an athlete is enamored of me, and I of him,
But toward him there is something fierce and terrible in me
  eligible to burst forth,
I dare not tell it in words, not even in these songs.

OUT OF THE CRADLE ENDLESSLY ROCKING

Out of the cradle endlessly rocking,
Out of the mockingbird's throat, the musical shuttle,
Out of the Ninth-month midnight,
Over the sterile sands and the fields beyond, where the child
  leaving his bed wandered alone, bareheaded, barefoot,
Down from the showered halo,
Up from the mystic play of shadows twining and twisting as
  if they were alive,
Out from the patches of briers and blackberries,
From the memories of the bird that chanted to me,
From your memories sad brother, from the fitful risings and
  fallings I heard,
From under that yellow half-moon late-risen and swollen as
  if with tears,
From those beginning notes of yearning and love there in the
  mist,
From the thousand responses of my heart never to cease,
From the myriad thence-aroused words,
From the word stronger and more delicious than any,
From such as now they start the scene revisiting,
As a flock, twittering, rising, or overhead passing,
Borne hither, ere all eludes me, hurriedly,

A man, yet by these tears a little boy again,
Throwing myself on the sand, confronting the waves,
I, chanter of pains and joys, uniter of here and hereafter,
Taking all hints to use them, but swiftly leaping beyond them,
A reminiscence sing.

Once Paumanok,
When the lilac scent was in the air and Fifth-month grass was
      growing,
Up this seashore in some briers,
Two feathered guests from Alabama, two together,
And their nest, and four light-green eggs spotted with brown,
And every day the he-bird to and fro near at hand,
And every day the she-bird crouched on her nest, silent, with
      bright eyes,
And every day I, a curious boy, never too close, never disturb-
      ing them,
Cautiously peering, absorbing, translating.

Shine! shine! shine!
Pour down your warmth, great sun!
While we bask, we two together.
Two together!
Winds blow south, or winds blow north,
Day come white, or night come black,
Home, or rivers and mountains from home,
Singing all time, minding no time,
While we two keep together.

Till of a sudden,
Maybe killed, unknown to her mate,
One forenoon the she-bird crouched not on the nest,
Nor returned that afternoon, nor the next,
Nor ever appeared again.
And thenceforward all summer in the sound of the sea,
And at night under the full of the moon in calmer weather
Over the hoarse surging of the sea,
Or flitting from brier to brier by day,
I saw, I heard at intervals the remaining one, the he-bird,
The solitary guest from Alabama.

Blow! blow! blow!
Blow up sea winds along Paumanok's shore;
I wait and I wait till you blow my mate to me.

Yes, when the stars glistened,

All night long on the prong of a moss-scalloped stake,
Down almost amid the slapping waves,
Sat the lone singer wonderful causing tears.
He called on his mate,
He poured forth the meanings which I of all men know.
Yes my brother I know,
The rest might not, but I have treasured every note,
For more than once dimly down to the beach gliding,
Silent, avoiding the moonbeams, blending myself with the
          shadows,
Recalling now the obscure shapes, the echoes, the sounds and
          sights after their sorts,
The white arms out in the breakers tirelessly tossing,
I, with bare feet, a child, the wind wafting my hair,
Listened long and long.
Listened to keep, to sing, now translating the notes,
Following you my brother.

Soothe! soothe! soothe!
Close on its wave soothes the wave behind,
And again another behind embracing and lapping, every one
          close,
But my love soothes not me, not me.
Low hangs the moon, it rose late,
It is lagging—O I think it is heavy with love, with love.
O madly the sea pushes upon the land,
With love, with love.
O night! do I not see my love fluttering out among the
          breakers?
What is that little black thing I see there in the white?

Loud! loud! loud!
Loud I call to you, my love!
High and clear I shoot my voice over the waves,
Surely you must know who is here, is here,
You must know who I am, my love.
Low-hanging moon!
What is that dusky spot in your brown yellow?
O it is the shape, the shape of my mate!
O moon do not keep her from me any longer.
Land! land! O land!
Whichever way I turn, O I think you could give me my mate
          back again if you only would,
For I am almost sure I see her dimly whichever way I look.
O rising stars!

Perhaps the one I want so much will rise, will rise with some
of you.
O throat! O trembling throat!
Sound clearer through the atmosphere!
Pierce the woods, the earth,
Somewhere listening to catch you must be the one I want.

Shake out carols.
Solitary here, the night's carols!
Carols of lonesome love! death's carols!
Carols under that lagging, yellow, waning moon!
O under the moon where she droops almost down into the sea!
O reckless despairing carols.
But soft! sink low!
Soft! let me just murmur,
And do you wait a moment you husky-noised sea,
For somewhere I believe I heard my mate responding to me,
So faint, I must be still, be still to listen,
But not altogether still, for then she might not come imme-
diately to me.

Hither my love!
Here I am! here!
With this just-sustained note I announce myself to you,
This gentle call is for you my love, for you.
Do not be decoyed elsewhere,
That is the whistle of the wind, it is not my voice,
That is the fluttering, the fluttering of the spray,
Those are the shadows of leaves.

O darkness! O in vain!
O I am very sick and sorrowful.
O brown halo in the sky near the moon, drooping upon the sea!
O troubled reflection in the sea!
O throat! O throbbing heart!
And I singing uselessly, uselessly all the night.
O past! O happy life! O songs of joy!
In the air, in the woods, over fields,
Loved! loved! loved! loved! loved!
But my mate no more, no more with me!
We two together no more.

The aria sinking,
All else continuing, the stars shining,
The winds blowing, the notes of the bird continuous echoing,
With angry moans the fierce old mother incessantly moaning,

On the sands of Paumanok's shore gray and rustling,
The yellow half-moon enlarged, sagging down, drooping, the
    face of the sea almost touching,
The boy ecstatic, with his bare feet the waves, with his hair
    the atmosphere dallying,
The love in the heart long pent, now loose, now at last tumul-
    tuously bursting,
The aria's meaning, the ears, the soul, swiftly depositing,
The strange tears down the cheeks coursing,
The colloquy there, the trio, each uttering,
The undertone, the savage old mother incessantly crying,
To the boy's soul's questions sullenly timing, some drowned
    secret hissing,
To the outsetting bard.

Demon or bird! (said the boy's soul).
Is it indeed toward your mate you sing? or is it really to me?
For I, that was a child, my tongue's use sleeping, now I have
    heard you,
Now in a moment I know what I am for, I awake,
And already a thousand singers, a thousand songs, clearer,
    louder and more sorrowful than yours,
A thousand warbling echoes have started to life within me,
    never to die.

O you singer solitary, singing by yourself, projecting me,
O solitary me listening, never more shall I cease perpetuating
    you
Never more shall I escape, never more the reverberations,
Never more the cries of unsatisfied love be absent from me,
Never again leave me to be the peaceful child I was before
    what there in the night,
By the sea under the yellow and sagging moon,
The messenger there aroused, the fire, the sweet hell within,
The unknown want, the destiny of me.

O give me the clue! (it lurks in the night here somewhere),
O if I am to have so much, let me have more!
A word then (for I will conquer it),
The word final, superior to all,
Subtle, sent up—what is it?—I listen;
Are you whispering it, and have been all the time, you sea
    waves?
Is that it from your liquid rims and wet sands?
Whereto answering, the sea,
Delaying not, hurrying not,

Whispered me through the night, and very plainly before
    daybreak,
Lisped to me the low and delicious word death,
And again death, death, death, death,
Hissing melodious, neither like the bird nor like my aroused
    child's heart,
But edging near as privately for me rustling at my feet,
Creeping thence steadily up to my ears and laving me soft
    all over,
Death, death, death, death, death.

Which I do not forget,
But fuse the song of my dusky demon and brother,
That he sang to me in the moonlight on Paumanok's gray
    beach,
With the thousand responsive songs at random,
My own songs awaked from that hour,
And with them the key, the word up from the waves,
The word of the sweetest song and all songs,
That strong and delicious word which, creeping to my feet,
(Or like some old crone rocking the cradle, swathed in sweet
    garments, bending aside),
The sea whispered me.

I SIT AND LOOK OUT

I sit and look out upon all the sorrows of the world, and upon
    all oppression and shame,
I hear secret convulsive sobs from young men at anguish with
    themselves, remorseful after deeds done,
I see in low life the mother misused by her children, dying,
    neglected, gaunt, desperate,
I see the wife misused by her husband, I see the treacherous
    seducer of young women,
I mark the ranklings of jealousy and unrequited love attempted
    to be hid, I see these sights on the earth,
I see the workings of battle, pestilence, tyranny, I see martyrs
    and prisoners,
I observe a famine at sea, I observe the sailors casting lots who
    shall be killed to preserve the lives of the rest,
I observe the slights and degradations cast by arrogant persons
    upon laborers, the poor, and upon Negroes, and the
    like;
All these—all the meanness and agony without end I sitting
    look out upon,
See, hear, and am silent.

VIGIL STRANGE I KEPT ON THE FIELD ONE NIGHT

Vigil strange I kept on the field one night;
When you my son and my comrade dropped at my side that
day,
One look I but gave which your dear eyes returned with a
look I shall never forget,
One touch of your hand to mine O boy, reached up as you
lay on the ground,
Then onward I sped in the battle, the even-contested battle,
Till late in the night relieved to the place at last again I made
my way,
Found you in death so cold dear comrade, found your body
son of responding kisses (never again on
earth responding),
Bared your face in the starlight, curious the scene, cool blew
the moderate night wind,
Long there and then in vigil I stood, dimly around me the
battlefield spreading.
Vigil wondrous and vigil sweet there in the fragrant silent
night,
But not a tear fell, not even a long-drawn sigh, long, long I
gazed,
Then on the earth partially reclining sat by your side leaning
my chin in my hands,
Passing sweet hours, immortal and mystic hours with you
dearest comrade—not a tear, not a word,
Vigil of silence, love and death, vigil for you my son and my
soldier,
As onward silently stars aloft, eastward new ones upward stole,
Vigil final for you brave boy (I could not save you, swift was
your death
I faithfully loved you and cared for you living, I think we
shall surely meet again),
Till at latest lingering of the night, indeed just as the dawn
appeared,
My comrade I wrapped in his blanket, enveloped well his form,
Folded the blanket well, tucking it carefully over head and
carefully under feet,
And there and then and bathed by the rising sun, my son in
his grave, in his rude-dug grave I deposited,
Ending my vigil strange with that, vigil of night and battle-
field dim,
Vigil for boy of responding kisses (never again on earth re-
sponding),

Vigil for comrade swiftly slain, vigil I never forget, how as
        day brightened,
I rose from the chill ground and folded my soldier well in his
        blanket,
And buried him where he fell.

RECONCILIATION

Word over all, beautiful as the sky,
Beautiful that war and all its deeds of carnage must in time
        be utterly lost,
That the hands of the sisters Death and Night incessantly
        softly wash again, and ever again, this soiled
        world;
For my enemy is dead, a man divine as myself is dead,
I look where he lies white-faced and still in the coffin—I draw
        near,
Bend down and touch lightly with my lips the white face in
        the coffin.

WHEN LILACS LAST IN THE DOORYARD BLOOMED

1

When lilacs last in the dooryard bloomed,
And the great star early drooped in the western sky in the
        night,
I mourned, and yet shall mourn with ever-returning spring.

Ever-returning spring, trinity sure to me you bring,
Lilac blooming perennial and drooping star in the west,
And thought of him I love.

2

O powerful western fallen star!
O shades of night—O moody, tearful night!
O great star disappeared—O the black murk that hides the
        star!
O cruel hands that hold me powerless—O helpless soul of me!
O harsh surrounding cloud that will not free my soul.

3

In the dooryard fronting an old farmhouse near the white-
        washed palings,

Stands the lilac bush tall-growing with heart-shaped leaves of
    rich green,
With many a pointed blossom rising delicate, with the per-
    fume strong I love,
With every leaf a miracle—and from this bush in the dooryard,
With delicate-colored blossoms and heart-shaped leaves of
    rich green,
A sprig with its flower I break.

4

In the swamp in secluded recesses,
A shy and hidden bird is warbling a song.

Solitary the thrush,
The hermit withdrawn to himself, avoiding the settlements,
Sings by himself a song.

Song of the bleeding throat,
Death's outlet song of life (for well dear brother I know,
If thou wast not granted to sing thou wouldst surely die).

5

Over the breast of the spring, the land, amid cities,
Amid lanes and through old woods, where lately the violets
    peeped from the ground, spotting the gray
    debris,
Amid the grass in the fields each side of the lanes, passing the
    endless grass,
Passing the yellow-speared wheat, every grain from its shroud
    in the dark-brown fields uprisen,
Passing the apple-tree blows of white and pink in the orchards,
Carrying a corpse to where it shall rest in the grave,
Night and day journeys a coffin.

6

Coffin that passes through lanes and streets,
Through day and night with the great cloud darkening the
    land,
With the pomp of the inlooped flags with the cities draped in
    black,
With the show of the States themselves as of crape-veiled
    women standing,
With processions long and winding and the flambeaus of the
    night,
With the countless torches lit, with the silent sea of faces and
    the unbared heads,
With the waiting depot, the arriving coffin, and the somber
    faces,

With dirges through the night, with the thousand voices rising
strong and solemn,
With all the mournful voices of the dirges poured around the
coffin,
The dim-lit churches and the shuddering organs—where amid
these you journey,
With the tolling tolling bells' perpetual clang,
Here, coffin that slowly passes,
I give you my sprig of lilac.

7

(Nor for you, for one alone,
Blossoms and branches green to coffins all I bring,
For fresh as the morning, thus would I chant a song for you
O sane and sacred death.
All over bouquets of roses,
O death, I cover you over with roses and early lilies,
But mostly and now the lilac that blooms the first,
Copious I break, I break the sprigs from the bushes,
With loaded arms I come, pouring for you,
For you and the coffins all of you O death.)

8

O western orb sailing the heaven,
Now I know what you must have meant as a month since I
walked,
As I walked in silence the transparent shadowy night,
As I saw you had something to tell as you bent to me night
after night,
As you drooped from the sky low down as if to my side (while
the other stars all looked on),
As we wandered together the solemn night (for something I
know not what kept me from sleep),
As the night advanced, and I saw on the rim of the west how
full you were of woe,
As I stood on the rising ground in the breeze in the cool trans-
parent night,
As I watched where you passed and was lost in the netherward
black of the night,
As my soul in its trouble dissatisfied sank, as where you sad orb,
Concluded, dropped in the night, and was gone.

9

Sing on there in the swamp,
O singer bashful and tender, I hear your notes, I hear your call,

I hear, I come presently, I understand you,
But a moment I linger, for the lustrous star has detained me,
The star my departing comrade holds and detains me.

10

O how shall I warble myself for the dead one there I loved?
And how shall I deck my song for the large sweet soul that
      has gone?
And what shall my perfume be for the grave of him I love?
Sea winds blown from east and west,
Blown from the Eastern sea and blown from the Western sea,
      till there on the prairies meeting,
These and with these and the breath of my chant,
I'll perfume the grave of him I love.

11

O what shall I hang on ue chamber walls?
And what shall the pictures be that I hang on the walls,
To adorn the burial house of him I love?
Pictures of growing spring and farms and homes,
With the Fourth-month eve at sundown, and the gray smoke
      lucid and bright,
With floods of the yellow gold of the gorgeous, indolent, sink-
      ing sun, burning, expanding the air
With the fresh sweet herbage underfoot, and the pale green
      leaves of the trees prolific,
In the distance the flowing glaze, the breast of the river, with
      a wind dapple here and there,
With ranging hills on the banks, with many a line against the
      sky, and shadows,
And the city at hand with dwellings so dense, and stacks of
      chimneys,
And all the scenes of life and the workshops, and the workmen
      homeward returning.

12

Lo, body and soul—this land,
My own Manhattan with spires, and the sparkling and hurry-
      ing tides, and the ships,
The varied and ample land, the South and the North in the
      light, Ohio's shores and flashing Missouri,
And ever the far-spreading prairies covered with grass and
      corn.
Lo, the most excellent sun so calm and haughty,
The violet and purple morn with just-felt breezes,

The gentle soft-born measureless light,
The miracle spreading bathing all, the fulfilled noon,
The coming eve delicious, the welcome night and the stars,
Over my cities shining all, enveloping man and land.

13

Sing on, sing on you gray-brown bird,
Sing from the swamps, the recesses, pour your chant from the
　　　bushes,
Limitless out of the dusk, out of the cedars and pines.
Sing on dearest brother, warble your reedy song,
Loud human song, with voice of uttermost woe.
O liquid and free and tender!
O wild and loose to my soul—O wondrous singer!
You only I hear—yet the star holds me (but will soon depart),
Yet the lilac with mastering odor holds me.

14

Now while I sat in the day and looked forth,
In the close of the day with its light and the fields of spring,
　　　and the farmers preparing their crops,
In the large unconscious scenery of my land with its lakes
　　　and forests,
In the heavenly aerial beauty (after the perturbed winds and
　　　the storms),
Under the arching heavens of the afternoon swift passing, and
　　　the voices of children and women,
The many-moving sea tides, and I saw the ships how they
　　　sailed,
And the summer approaching with richness, and the fields all
　　　busy with labor,
And the infinite separate houses, how they all went on, each
　　　with its meals and minutia of daily usages,
And the streets how their throbbings throbbed, and the cities
　　　pent—lo, then and there,
Falling upon them all and among them all, enveloping me
　　　with the rest,
Appeared the cloud, appeared the long black trail,
And I knew death, its thought, and the sacred knowledge of
　　　death.

Then with the knowledge of death as walking one side of me,
And the thought of death close-walking the other side of me,
And I in the middle as with companions, and as holding the
　　　hands of companions,

I fled forth to the hiding receiving night that talks not,
Down to the shores of the water the path by the swamp in
        the dimness,
To the solemn shadowy cedars and ghostly pines so still.
And the singer so shy to the rest received me,
The gray-brown bird I know received us comrades three,
And he sang the carol of death, and a verse for him I love.
From deep secluded recesses
From the fragrant cedars and the ghostly pines so still,
Came the carol of the bird.
And the charm of the carol rapt me,
As I held as if by their hands my comrades in the night,
And the voice of my spirit tallied the song of the bird.

Come lovely and soothing death,
Undulate round the world, serenely arriving, arriving,
In the day, in the night, to all, to each,
Sooner or later delicate death.
Praised be the fathomless universe,
For life and joy, and for objects and knowledge curious,
And for love, sweet love—but praise! praise! praise!
For the sure-enwinding arms of cool-enfolding death.
Dark mother always gliding near with soft feet,
Have none chanted for thee a chant of fullest welcome?
Then I chant it for thee, I glorify thee above all,
I bring thee a song that when thou must indeed come, come
        unfalteringly.
Approach strong deliveress,
When it is so, when thou hast taken them I joyously sing the
        dead,
Lost in the loving floating ocean of thee,
Laved in the flood of thy bliss O death.
From me to thee glad serenades,
Dances for thee I propose saluting thee, adornments and
        feastings for thee,
And the sights of the open landscape and the high-spread sky
        are fitting,
And life and the fields, and the huge and thoughtful night.
The night in silence under many a star,
The ocean shore and the husky whispering wave whose voice
        I know,
And the soul turning to thee O vast and well-veiled death,
And the body gratefully nestling close to thee.
Over the treetops I float thee a song,
Over the rising and sinking waves, over the myriad fields and
        the prairies wide,

*Over the dense-packed cities all and the teeming wharves and
ways,*
I float this carol with joy, with joy to thee O death.

15

To the tally of my soul,
Loud and strong kept up the gray-brown bird,
With pure deliberate notes spreading filling the night.
Loud in the pines and cedars dim,
Clear in the freshness moist and the swamp perfume,
And I with my comrades there in the night.
While my sight that was bound in my eyes unclosed,
As to long panoramas of visions.
And I saw askant the armies,
I saw as in noiseless dreams hundreds of battle flags,
Borne through the smoke of the battles and pierced with
missiles I saw them,
And carried hither and yon through the smoke, and torn and
bloody,
And at last but a few shreds left on the staffs (and all in
silence),
And the staffs all splintered and broken.
I saw battle corpses, myriads of them,
And the white skeletons of young men, I saw them,
I saw the debris and debris of all the slain soldiers of the war,
But I saw they were not as was thought,
They themselves were fully at rest, they suffered not,
The living remained and suffered, the mother suffered,
And the wife and the child and the musing comrade suffered,
And the armies that remained suffered.

16

Passing the visions, passing the night,
Passing, unloosing the hold of my comrades' hands,
Passing the song of the hermit bird and the tallying song of
my soul,
Victorious song, death's outlet song, yet varying ever-altering
song,
As low and wailing, yet clear the notes, rising and falling,
flooding the night,
Sadly sinking and fainting, as warning and warning, and yet
again bursting with joy,
Covering the earth and filling the spread of the heaven,
As that powerful psalm in the night I heard from recesses,
Passing, I leave thee lilac with heart-shaped leaves,

I leave thee there in the dooryard, blooming, returning with
　　　　　spring.
I cease from my song for thee,
From my gaze on thee in the west, fronting the west, com-
　　　　　muning with thee,
O comrade lustrous with silver face in the night.

Yet each to keep and all, retrievements out of the night,
The song, the wondrous chant of the gray-brown bird,
And the tallying chant, the echo aroused in my soul,
With the lustrous and drooping star with the countenance
　　　　　full of woe,
With the holders holding my hand nearing the call of the bird,
Comrades mine and I in the midst, and their memory ever
　　　　　to keep, for the dead I loved so well,
For the sweetest, wisest soul of all my days and lands—and
　　　　　this for his dear sake,
Lilac and star and bird twined with the chant of my soul,
There in the fragrant pines and the cedars dusk and dim.

O CAPTAIN! MY CAPTAIN!

O Captain! my Captain! our fearful trip is done,
The ship has weathered every rack, the prize we sought is won,
The port is near, the bells I hear, the people all exulting,
While follow eyes the steady keel, the vessel grim and daring;
　　　　But O heart! heart! heart!
　　　　　O the bleeding drops of red,
　　　　　　Where on the deck my Captain lies,
　　　　　　Fallen cold and dead.

O Captain! my Captain! rise up and hear the bells;
Rise up—for you the flag is flung—for you the bugle trills,
For you bouquets and ribboned wreaths—for you the shores
　　　　　acrowding,
For you they call, the swaying mass, their eager faces turning;
　　　　Here Captain! dear father!
　　　　　The arm beneath your head!
　　　　　　It is some dream that on the deck,
　　　　　　You've fallen cold and dead.

My Captain does not answer, his lips are pale and still,
My father does not feel my arm, he has no pulse nor will,
The ship is anchored safe and sound, its voyage closed and
　　　　done,

From fearful trip the victor ship comes in with object won:
    Exult O shores, and ring O bells!
      But I with mournful tread,
        Walk the deck my Captain lies,
        Fallen cold and dead.

TO THINK OF TIME

1

To think of time—of all that retrospection,
To think of today, and the ages continued henceforward.
Have you guessed you yourself would not continue?
Have you dreaded these earth beetles?
Have you feared the future would be nothing to you?
Is today nothing? is the beginningless past nothing?
If the future is nothing they are just as surely nothing.
To think that the sun rose in the east—that men and women
        were flexible, real, alive—that everything was
        alive,
To think that you and I did not see, feel, think, nor bear our
        part,
To think that we are now here and bear our part.

2

Not a day passes, not a minute or second without an accouche-
        ment,
Not a day passes, not a minute or second without a corpse.
The dull nights go over and the dull days also,
The soreness of lying so much in bed goes over,
The physician after long putting off gives the silent and terrible
        look for an answer,
The children come hurried and weeping, and the brothers and
        sisters are sent for,
Medicines stand unused on the shelf (the camphor smell has
        long pervaded the rooms),
The faithful hand of the living does not desert the hand of the
        dying,
The twitching lips press lightly on the forehead of the dying,
The breath ceases and the pulse of the heart ceases,
The corpse stretches on the bed and the living look upon it,
It is palpable as the living are palpable.
The living look upon the corpse with their eyesight,
But without eyesight lingers a different living and looks curi-
        ously on the corpse.

3

To think the thought of death merged in the thought of mate-
rials,
To think of all these wonders of city and country, and others
taking great interest in them, and we taking
no interest in them.
To think how eager we are in building our houses,
To think others shall be just as eager, and we quite indifferent.
(I see one building the house that serves him a few years, or
seventy or eighty years at most,
I see one building the house that serves him longer than that.)
Slow-moving and black lines creep over the whole earth—they
never cease—they are the burial lines,
He that was President was buried, and he that is now President
shall surely be buried.

4

A reminiscence of the vulgar fate,
A frequent sample of the life and death of workmen,
Each after his kind.
Cold dash of waves at the ferry wharf, posh and ice in the
river, half-frozen mud in the streets,
A gray discouraged sky overhead, the short last daylight of
December,
A hearse and stages, the funeral of an old Broadway stage
driver, the cortege mostly drivers.
Steady the trot to the cemetery, duly rattles the death bell,
The gate is passed, the new-dug grave is halted at, the living
alight, the hearse uncloses,
The coffin is passed out, lowered and settled, the whip is laid
on the coffin, the earth is swiftly shoveled in,
The mound above is flatted with the spades—silence,
A minute—no one moves or speaks—it is done,
He is decently put away—is there anything more?
He was a good fellow, free-mouthed, quick-tempered, not bad
looking,
Ready with life or death for a friend, fond of women, gambled,
ate hearty, drank hearty,
Had known what it was to be flush, grew low-spirited toward
the last, sickened, was helped by a contribu-
tion,
Died, aged forty-one years—and that was his funeral.
Thumb extended, finger uplifted, apron, cape, gloves, strap,
wet-weather clothes, whip carefully chosen,

Boss, spotter, starter, hostler, somebody loafing on you, you
loafing on somebody, headway, man before
and man behind,
Good day's work, bad day's work, pet stock, mean stock, first
out, last out, turning in at night,
To think that these are so much and so nigh to other drivers,
and he there takes no interest in them.

5

The markets, the government, the workingman's wages, to
think what account they are through our
nights and days,
To think that other workingmen will make just as great account
of them, yet we make little or no account.
The vulgar and the refined, what you call sin and what you
call goodness, to think how wide a difference,
To think the difference will still continue to others, yet we lie
beyond the difference.
To think how much pleasure there is,
Do you enjoy yourself in the city? or engaged in business? or
planning a nomination and election? or with
your wife and family?
Or with your mother and sisters? or in womanly housework?
or the beautiful maternal cares?
These also flow onward to others, you and I flow onward,
But in due time you and I shall take less interest in them.
Your farm, profits, crops—to think how engrossed you are,
To think there will still be farms, profits, crops, yet for you of
what avail?

6

What will be will be well, for what is is well,
To take interest is well, and not to take interest shall be well.
The domestic joys, the daily housework or business, the build-
ing of houses, are not phantasms, they have
weight, form, location,
Farms, profits, crops, markets, wages, government, are none
of them phantasms,
The difference between sin and goodness is no delusion,
The earth is not an echo, man and his life and all the things
of his life are well-considered.
You are not thrown to the winds, you gather certainly and
safely around yourself,
Yourself, yourself! yourself, forever and ever!

7

It is not to diffuse you that you were born of your mother and
   father, it is to identify you,
It is not that you should be undecided, but that you should be
   decided,
Something long preparing and formless is arrived and formed
   in you,
You are henceforth secure, whatever comes or goes,
The threads that were spun are gathered, the weft crosses the
   warp, the pattern is systematic.
The preparations have every one been justified,
The orchestra have sufficiently tuned their instruments, the
   baton has given the signal.
The guest that was coming, he waited long, he is now housed,
He is one of those who are beautiful and happy, he is one of
   those that to look upon and be with is enough.
The law of the past cannot be eluded,
The law of the present and future cannot be eluded,
The law of the living cannot be eluded, it is eternal,
The law of promotion and transformation cannot be eluded,
The law of heroes and good-doers cannot be eluded,
The law of drunkards, informers, mean persons, not one iota
   thereof can be eluded.

8

Slow moving and black lines go ceaselessly over the earth,
Northerner goes carried and Southerner goes carried, and they
   on the Atlantic side and they on the Pacific,
And they between, and all through the Mississippi country, and
   all over the earth.
The great masters and cosmos are well as they go, the heroes
   and good-doers are well,
The known leaders and inventors and the rich owners and
   pious and distinguished may be well,
But there is more account than that, there is strict account
   of all.

The interminable hordes of the ignorant and wicked are not
   nothing,
The barbarians of Africa and Asia are not nothing,
The perpetual successions of shallow people are not nothing as
   they go.

Cf and in all these things,
I have dreamed that we are not to be changed so much, nor the
      law of us changed,
I have dreamed that heroes and good-doers shall be under the
      present and past law,
And that murderers, drunkards, liars, shall be under the pres-
      ent and past law,
For I have dreamed that the law they are under now is enough.
And I have dreamed that the purpose and essence of the known
      life, the transient,
Is to form and decide identity for the unknown life, the per-
      manent.
If all came but to ashes of dung,
If maggots and rats ended us, then Alarum! for we are be-
      trayed,
Then indeed suspicion of death.
Do you suspect death? if I were to suspect death I should die
      now,
Do you think I could walk pleasantly and well-suited toward
      annihilation?
Pleasantly and well-suited I walk,
Whither I walk I cannot define, but I know it is good,
The whole universe indicates that it is good,
The past and the present indicate that it is good.
How beautiful and perfect are the animals!
How perfect the earth, and the minutest thing upon it!
What is called good is perfect, and what is called bad is just
      as perfect,
The vegetables and minerals are all perfect, and the impon-
      derable fluids perfect;
Slowly and surely they have passed on to this, and slowly and
      surely they yet pass on.

9

I swear I think now that everything without exception has an
      eternal soul!
The trees have, rooted in the ground! the weeds of the sea
      have! the animals!
I swear I think there is nothing but immortality!
That the exquisite scheme is for it, and the nebulous float is for
      it, and the cohering is for it!
And all preparation is for it—and identity is for it—and life
      and materials are altogether for it!

JOY, SHIPMATE, JOY!

Joy, shipmate, joy!
(Pleased to my soul at death I cry.)
Our life is closed, our life begins,
The long, long anchorage we leave,
The ship is clear at last, she leaps!
She swiftly courses from the shore.
Joy, shipmate, joy!

GOOD-BYE MY FANCY!

Good-bye my Fancy!
Farewell dear mate, dear love!
I'm going away, I know not where.
Or to what fortune, or whether I may ever see you again,
So Good-bye my Fancy.

Now for my last—let me look back a moment;
The slower fainter ticking of the clock is in me,
Exit, nightfall, and soon the heart-thud stopping.
Long have we lived, joyed, caressed together;
Delightful!—now separation—Good-bye my Fancy.

Yet let me not be too hasty,
Long indeed have we lived, slept, filtered, become really
              blended into one;
Then if we die together (yes, we'll remain one),
If we go anywhere we'll go together to meet what happens,
Maybe we'll be better off and blither, and learn something,
Maybe it is yourself now really ushering me to the true songs,
              (who knows?),
Maybe it is you the mortal knob really undoing, turning—so
              now finally,
Good-bye—and hail! my Fancy.

EMILY DICKINSON
(1830–1886)

SUCCESS IS COUNTED SWEETEST

Success is counted sweetest
By those who ne'er succeed.
To comprehend a nectar
Requires sorest need.

Not one of all the purple host
Who took the flag today
Can tell the definition
So clear of victory

As he defeated, dying,
On whose forbidden ear
The distant strains of triumph
Burst agonized and clear.

ONE DIGNITY DELAYS FOR ALL

One dignity delays for all,
One mitered afternoon,
None can avoid this purple,
None evade this crown.

Coach it insures and footmen,
Chamber, and state, and throng,
Bells also in the village
As we ride grand along.

What dignified attendants,
What service when we pause,
How loyally at parting
Their hundred hats they raise!

How pomp surpassing ermine
When simple You and I
Present our meek escutcheon
And claim the rank to die!

NEW FEET WITHIN MY GARDEN GO

New feet within my garden go—
New fingers stir the sod.
A troubadour upon the elm
Betrays the solitude.

New children play upon the green—
New weary sleep below,
And still the pensive spring returns,
And still the punctual snow.

SURGEONS MUST BE VERY CAREFUL

Surgeons must be very careful
When they take the knife.
Underneath their fine incisions
Stirs the culprit, life.

FAITH IS A FINE INVENTION

Faith is a fine invention
When gentlemen can see,
But microscopes are prudent
In an emergency.

HOPE IS THE THING WITH FEATHERS

Hope is the thing with feathers
That perches in the soul
And sings the tune without the words
And never stops at all.

And sweetest in the gale is heard;
And sore must be the storm
That could abash the little bird
That kept so many warm.

I've heard it in the chillest land
And on the strangest sea,
Yet never in extremity
It asked a crumb of me.

I SHOULD NOT DARE TO LEAVE MY FRIEND

I should not dare to leave my friend,
Because—because if he should die
While I was gone, and I too late
Should reach the heart that wanted me,

If I should disappoint the eyes
That hunted—hunted so to see,
And could not bear to shut until
They noticed me—they noticed me,

If I should stab the patient faith
So sure I'd come—so sure I'd come,
It listening—listening went to sleep
Telling my tardy name,

My heart would wish it broke before,
Since breaking then—since breaking then
Were useless as next morning's sun
Where midnight frosts had lain.

I TASTE A LIQUOR NEVER BREWED

I taste a liquor never brewed
From tankards scooped in pearl.
Not all the Frankfort berries
Yield such an alcohol.

Inebriate of air am I
And debauchee of dew,
Reeling through endless summer days
From inns of molten blue.

When landlords turn the drunken bee
Out of the foxglove's door,
When butterflies renounce their drams,
I shall but drink the more,

Till seraphs swing their snowy hats
And saints to windows run
To see the little tippler
From manzanilla come!

THERE'S A CERTAIN SLANT OF LIGHT

There's a certain slant of light,
Winter afternoons,
That oppresses like the heft
Of cathedral tunes.

Heavenly hurt it gives us.
We can find no scar
But internal difference
Where the meanings are.

None may teach it anything
'Tis the seal despair,
An imperial affliction
Sent us of the air.

When it comes the landscape listens,
Shadows hold their breath.
When it goes 'tis like the distance
On the look of death.

I FELT A FUNERAL IN MY BRAIN

I felt a funeral in my brain,
And mourners to and fro
Kept treading, treading, till it seemed
That sense was breaking through.

And when they all were seated,
A service like a drum
Kept beating, beating, till I thought
My mind was going numb.

And then I heard them lift a box
And creak across my soul
With those same boots of lead again,
Then space began to toll,

As all the heavens were a bell,
And being but an ear,
And I and silence some strange race
Wrecked solitary here.

And then a plank in reason broke,
And I dropped down and down
And hit a world at every plunge,
And finished knowing then.

I'M NOBODY. WHO ARE YOU?

I'm nobody. Who are you?
Are you nobody too?
Then there's a pair of us.
Don't tell—they'd banish us, you know.

How dreary to be somebody,
How public—like a frog—
To tell your name the livelong June
To an admiring bog.

THE SOUL SELECTS HER OWN SOCIETY

The soul selects her own society,
Then shuts the door.
To her divine majority
Present no more.

Unmoved she notes the chariots pausing
At her low gate;
Unmoved, an emperor be kneeling
Upon her mat.

I've known her from an ample nation
Choose one,
Then close the valves of her attention
Like stone.

I SHOULD HAVE BEEN TOO GLAD, I SEE

I should have been too glad, I see,
Too lifted for the scant degree
Of life's penurious round;
My little circuit would have shamed
This new circumference, have blamed
The homelier time behind.

I should have been too saved, I see,
Too rescued; fear too dim to me
That I could spell the prayer
I knew so perfect yesterday,
That scalding one, "Sabachthani,"
Recited fluent here.

Earth would have been too much, I see,
And heaven not enough for me.
I should have had the joy
Without the fear to justify,
The palm without the Calvary.
So, Saviour, crucify.

Defeat whets victory, they say.
The reefs in old Gethsemane
Endear the shore beyond.
'Tis beggars banquets best define,
'Tis thirsting vitalizes wine.
Faith bleats to understand.

BEFORE I GOT MY EYE PUT OUT

Before I got my eye put out
I liked as well to see
As other creatures that have eyes
And know no other way;

But were it told to me today
That I might have the sky
For mine, I tell you that my heart
Would split for size of me—

The meadows mine,
The mountains mine,
All forests, stintless stars,
As much of noon as I could take
Between my finite eyes.

The motions of the dipping birds,
The lightning's jointed road,
For mine to look at when I liked—
The news would strike me dead.

So, safer, guess, with just my soul
Upon the windowpane,
Where other creatures put their eyes,
Incautious of the sun.

A BIRD CAME DOWN THE WALK

A bird came down the walk:
He did not know I saw;
He bit an angleworm in halves
And ate the fellow raw.

And then he drank a dew
From a convenient grass,
And then hopped sidewise to the wall
To let a beetle pass.

He glanced with rapid eyes
That hurried all around;
They looked like frightened beads, I thought;
He stirred his velvet head

Like one in danger; cautious,
I offered him a crumb,
And he unrolled his feathers
And rowed him softer home

Than oars divide the ocean,
Too silver for a seam,
Or butterflies, off banks of noon,
Leap, plashless, as they swim.

I DREADED THAT FIRST ROBIN SO

I dreaded that first robin so,
But he is mastered now;
I'm some accustomed to him grown—
He hurts a little, though.

I thought if I could only live
Till that first shout got by,
Not all pianos in the woods
Had power to mangle me.

I dared not meet the daffodils
For fear their yellow gown
Would pierce me with a fashion
So foreign to my own.

I wished the grass would hurry,
So when 'twas time to see,
He'd be too tall, the tallest one
Could stretch to look at me.

I could not bear the bees should come;
I wished they'd stay away
In those dim countries where they go.
What word had they for me?

They're here though; not a creature failed.
No blossom stayed away
In gentle deference to me,
The Queen of Calvary,

Each one salutes me as he goes,
And I my childish plumes
Lift, in 'bereaved acknowledgement
Of their unthinking drums.

NO RACK CAN TORTURE ME

No rack can torture me,
My soul at liberty;
Behind this mortal bone
There knits a bolder one

You cannot prick with saw
Nor pierce with scimitar.
Two bodies therefore be.
Bind one, the other fly.

The eagle of his nest
No easier divest
And gain the sky
Than mayest thou,

Except thyself may be
Thine enemy;
Captivity is consciousness,
So's liberty.

THERE'S BEEN A DEATH IN THE OPPOSITE HOUSE

There's been a death in the opposite house
As lately as today.
I know it by the numb look
Such houses have alway.

The neighbors rustle in and out;
The doctor drives away.
A window opens like a pod,
Abrupt, mechanically;

Somebody flings a mattress out.
The children hurry by;
They wonder if it died on that.
I used to, when a boy.

The minister goes stiffly in
As if the house were his
And he owned all the mourners now,
And little boys besides;

And then the milliner, and the man
Of the appalling trade
To take the measure of the house.
There'll be that dark parade

Of tassels and of coaches soon.
It's easy as a sign—
The intuition of the news
In just a country town.

WHAT SOFT CHERUBIC CREATURES

What soft cherubic creatures
These gentlewomen are.
One would as soon assault a plush
Or violate a star.

Such dimity convictions,
A horror so refined
Of freckled human nature,
Of deity ashamed—

It's such a common glory,
A fisherman's degree.
Redemption, brittle lady,
Be so ashamed of thee.

MUCH MADNESS IS DIVINEST SENSE

Much madness is divinest sense
To a discerning eye—
Much sense the starkest madness.
'Tis the majority
In this, as all, prevail.
Assent and you are sane;
Demur, you're straightway dangerous
And handled with a chain.

THE WIND TAPPED LIKE A TIRED MAN

The wind tapped like a tired man,
And like a host "Come in"
I boldly answered. Entered then
My residence within

A rapid footless guest,
To offer whom a chair
Were as impossible as hand
A sofa to the air.

No bone had he to bind him;
His speech was like the push
Of numerous hummingbirds at once
From a superior bush;

His countenance a billow;
His fingers as he passed
Let go a music as of tunes
Blown tremulous in glass.

He visited still flitting,
Then like a timid man
Again he tapped. 'Twas flurriedly,
And I became alone.

THIS IS MY LETTER TO THE WORLD

This is my letter to the world
That never wrote to me,
The simple news that nature told
With tender majesty.

Her message is committed
To hands I cannot see.
For love of her, sweet countrymen,
Judge tenderly of me.

I DIED FOR BEAUTY

I died for beauty, but was scarce
Adjusted in the tomb
When one who died for truth was lain
In an adjoining room.

He questioned softly why I failed,
"For beauty" I replied.
"And I for truth. Themself are one.
We brethren are" he said.

And so, as kinsmen met a night,
We talked between the rooms,
Until the moss had reached our lips
And covered up our names.

I HEARD A FLY BUZZ WHEN I DIED

I heard a fly buzz when I died.
The stillness in the room
Was like the stillness in the air
Between the heaves of storm.

The eyes around had wrung them dry,
And breaths were gathering firm
For that last onset when the king
Be witnessed in the room.

I willed my keepsakes, signed away
What portion of me be
Assignable; and then it was
There interposed a fly

With blue uncertain stumbling buzz
Between the light and me;
And then the windows failed; and then
I could not see to see.

IT WAS NOT DEATH, FOR I STOOD UP

It was not death, for I stood up,
And all the dead lie down.
It was not night, for all the bells
Put out their tongues for noon.

It was not frost, for on my flesh
I felt siroccos crawl;
Nor fire, for just my marble feet
Could keep a chancel cool—

And yet it tasted like them all.
The figures I have seen
Set orderly for burial
Reminded me of mine,

As if my life were shaven
And fitted to a frame
And could not breathe without a key;
And 'twas like midnight some

When everything that ticked has stopped
And space stares all around,
Or grisly frosts, first autumn morns,
Repeal the beating ground,

But most like chaos—stopless, cool,
Without a chance or spar,
Or even a report of land
To justify despair.

I STARTED EARLY, TOOK MY DOG

I started early, took my dog,
And visited the sea.
The mermaids in the basement
Came out to look at me

And frigates in the upper floor
Extended hempen hands,
Presuming me to be a mouse
Aground upon the sands,

But no man moved me till the tide
Went past my simple shoe
And past my apron and my belt
And past my bodice too,

And made as he would eat me up
As wholly as a dew
Upon a dandelion's sleeve;
And then I started too

And he, he followed close behind;
I felt his silver heel
Upon my ankle, then my shoes
Would overflow with pearl,

Until we met the solid town.
No one he seemed to know
And bowing with a mighty look
At me, the sea withdrew.

THE HEART ASKS PLEASURE FIRST

The heart asks pleasure first,
And then excuse from pain,
And then those little anodynes
That deaden suffering,

And then to go to sleep,
And then if it should be
The will of its inquisitor
The privilege to die.

I HAD BEEN HUNGRY ALL THE YEARS

I had been hungry all the years.
My noon had come to dine.
I trembling drew the table near
And touched the curious wine.

'Twas this on tables I had seen
When turning hungry home
I looked in windows for the wealth
I could not hope for mine.

I did not know the ample bread.
'Twas so unlike the crumb
The birds and I had often shared
In nature's dining room.

The plenty hurt me, 'twas so new.
Myself felt ill and odd,
As berry of a mountain bush
Transplanted to the road.

Nor was I hungry, so I found
That hunger was a way
Of persons outside windows
The entering takes away.

I LAUGHED A CRUMBLING LAUGH

I laughed a crumbling laugh
That I could fear a door
Who consternation compassed
And never winced before.

I fitted to the latch
My hand with trembling care,
Lest back the awful door should spring
And leave me in the floor;

Then moved my fingers off
As cautiously as glass,
And held my ears, and like a thief
Fled gasping from the house.

BECAUSE I COULD NOT STOP FOR DEATH

Because I could not stop for Death
He kindly stopped for me.
The carriage held but just ourselves
And immortality.

We slowly drove. He knew no haste,
And I had put away
My labor and my leisure too
For his civility.

We passed the school where children strove
At recess in the ring.
We passed the fields of gazing grain;
We passed the setting sun—

Or rather, he passed us.
The dews drew quivering and chill,
For only gossamer my gown,
My tippet only tulle.

We paused before a house that seemed
A swelling of the ground.
The roof was scarcely visible,
The cornice in the ground.

Since then 'tis centuries, and yet
Feels shorter than the day
I first surmised the horses' heads
Were toward eternity.

A NARROW FELLOW IN THE GRASS

A narrow fellow in the grass
Occasionally rides.
You may have met him—did you not?
His notice sudden is.

The grass divides as with a comb,
A spotted shaft is seen,
And then it closes at your feet
And opens further on.

He likes a boggy acre,
A floor too cool for corn;
Yet when a boy and barefoot,
I more than once at noon

Have passed, I thought, a whiplash
Unbraiding in the sun;
When, stooping to secure it,
It wrinkled and was gone.

Several of nature's people
I know, and they know me;
I feel for them a transport
Of cordiality,

But never met this fellow,
Attended or alone,
Without a tighter breathing
And zero at the bone.

THE SKY IS LOW, THE CLOUDS ARE MEAN

The sky is low, the clouds are mean.
A traveling flake of snow
Across a barn or through a rut
Debates if it will go.

A narrow wind complains all day
How someone treated him.
Nature, like us, is sometimes caught
Without her diadem.

I NEVER SAW A MOOR

I never saw a moor;
I never saw the sea,
Yet know I how the heather looks
And what a billow be.

I never spoke with God,
Nor visited in heaven.
Yet certain am I of the spot
As if the checks were given.

THE LAST NIGHT THAT SHE LIVED

The last night that she lived,
It was a common night
Except the dying—this to us
Made nature different.

We noticed smallest things,
Things overlooked before,
By this great light upon our minds
Italicized, as 'twere.

As we went out and in
Between her final room
And rooms where those to be alive
Tomorrow were, a blame

That others could exist
While she must finish quite,
A jealousy for her arose
So nearly infinite.

We waited while she passed;
It was a narrow time.
Too jostled were our souls to speak.
At length the notice came.

She mentioned, and forgot;
Then lightly as a reed
Bent to the water, struggled scarce,
Consented, and was dead.

And we, we placed the hair
And drew the head erect;
And then an awful leisure was,
Belief to regulate.

WHILE WE WERE FEARING IT, IT CAME

While we were fearing it, it came,
But came with less of fear
Because that fearing it so long
Had almost made it fair.

There is a fitting—a dismay;
A fitting—a despair.
'Tis harder knowing it is due
Than knowing it is here.

The trying on the utmost,
The morning it is new,
Is terribler than wearing it
A whole existence through.

THERE CAME A WIND LIKE A BUGLE

There came a wind like a bugle.
It quivered through the grass,
And a green chill upon the heat
So ominous did pass.
We barred the windows and the doors
As from an emerald ghost.
The doom's electric moccasin
That very instant passed.
On a strange mob of panting trees
And fences fled away
And rivers where the houses ran
Those looked that lived that day.
The bell within the steeple wild
The flying tidings told—
How much can come
And much can go,
And yet abide the world.

OF GOD WE ASK ONE FAVOR

Of God we ask one favor,
That we may be forgiven—
For what, he is presumed to know:
The crime from us is hidden.
Immured the whole of life
Within a magic prison,
We reprimand the happiness
That too competes with heaven.

MY LIFE CLOSED TWICE BEFORE ITS CLOSE

My life closed twice before its close.
It yet remains to see
If immortality unveil
A third event to me.

So huge, so hopeless to conceive
As these that twice befell.
Parting is all we know of heaven.
And all we need of hell.

THE DISTANCE THAT THE DEAD HAVE GONE

The distance that the dead have gone
Does not at first appear;
Their coming back seems possible
For many an ardent year.

And then that we have followed them
We more than half suspect,
So intimate have we become
With their dear retrospect.

THE SADDEST NOISE, THE SWEETEST NOISE

The saddest noise, the sweetest noise,
The maddest noise that grows,
The birds, they make it in the spring,
At night's delicious close

Between the March and April line,
That magical frontier
Beyond which summer hesitates,
Almost too heavenly near.

It makes us think of all the dead
That sauntered with us here,
By separation's sorcery
Made cruelly more dear.

It makes us think of what we had,
And what we now deplore.
We almost wish those siren throats
Would go, and sing no more.

An ear can break a human heart
As quickly as a spear;
We wish the ear had not a heart
So dangerously near.

EDWIN ARLINGTON ROBINSON
(1869–1935)

FLAMMONDE

The man Flammonde, from God knows where,
With firm address and foreign air,
With news of nations in his talk
And something royal in his walk,
With glint of iron in his eyes,
But never doubt, nor yet surprise,
Appeared, and stayed, and held his head
As one by kings accredited.

Erect, with his alert repose
About him, and about his clothes,
He pictured all tradition hears
Of what we owe to fifty years.
His cleansing heritage of taste
Paraded neither want nor waste;
And what he needed for his fee
To live, he borrowed graciously.

He never told us what he was,
Or what mischance, or other cause,
Had banished him from better days
To play the Prince of Castaways.
Meanwhile he played surpassing well
A part, for most, unplayable;
In fine, one pauses, half afraid
To say for certain that he played.

For that, one may as well forgo
Conviction as to yes or no;
Nor can I say just how intense
Would then have been the difference
To several, who, having striven
In vain to get what he was given,
Would see the stranger taken on
By friends not easy to be won.

Moreover, many a malcontent
He soothed and found munificent;
His courtesy beguiled and foiled
Suspicion that his years were soiled;
His mien distinguished any crowd,
His credit strengthened when he bowed;
And women, young and old, were fond
Of looking at the man Flammonde.

There was a woman in our town
On whom the fashion was to frown;
But while our talk renewed the tinge
Of a long-faded scarlet fringe,
The man Flammonde saw none of that,
And what he saw we wondered at—
That none of us, in her distress,
Could hide or find our littleness.

There was a boy that all agreed
Had shut within him the rare seed
Of learning. We could understand,
But none of us could lift a hand.
The man Flammonde appraised the youth,
And told a few of us the truth;
And thereby, for a little gold,
A flowered future was unrolled.

There were two citizens who fought
For years and years, and over nought;
They made life awkward for their friends,
And shortened their own dividends.
The man Flammonde said what was wrong
Should be made right; nor was it long
Before they were again in line,
And had each other in to dine.

And these I mention are but four
Of many out of many more.
So much for them. But what of him—
So firm in every look and limb?
What small satanic sort of kink
Was in his brain? What broken link
Withheld him from the destinies
That came so near to being his?

What was he, when we came to sift
His meaning, and to note the drift
Of incommunicable ways
That make us ponder while we praise?
Why was it that his charm revealed
Somehow the surface of a shield?
What was it that we never caught?
What was he, and what was he not?

How much it was of him we met
We cannot ever know; nor yet
Shall all he gave us quite atone
For what was his, and his alone;
Nor need we now, since he knew best,
Nourish an ethical unrest:
Rarely at once will nature give
The power to be Flammonde and live.

We cannot know how much we learn
From those who never will return,
Until a flash of unforeseen
Remembrance falls on what has been.
We've each a darkening hill to climb;
And this is why, from time to time
In Tilbury Town, we look beyond
Horizons for the man Flammonde.

LUKE HAVERGAL

Go to the western gate, Luke Havergal,
There where the vines cling crimson on the wall,
And in the twilight wait for what will come.
The leaves will whisper there of her, and some,
Like flying words, will strike you as they fall;
But go, and if you listen, she will call.
Go to the western gate, Luke Havergal—
Luke Havergal.

No, there is not a dawn in eastern skies
To rift the fiery night that's in your eyes;
But there, where western glooms are gathering,
The dark will end the dark, if anything:
God slays himself with every leaf that flies,
And hell is more than half of paradise.

No; there is not a dawn in eastern skies—
In eastern skies.

Out of a grave I come to tell you this,
Out of a grave I come to quench the kiss
That flames upon your forehead with a glow
That blinds you to the way that you must go.
Yes, there is yet one way to where she is,
Bitter, but one that faith may never miss.
Out of a grave I come to tell you this—
To tell you this.

There is the western gate, Luke Havergal,
There are the crimson leaves upon the wall.
Go, for the winds are tearing them away,—
Nor think to riddle the dead words they say,
Nor any more to feel them as they fall;
But go, and if you trust her she will call.
There is the western gate, Luke Havergal—
Luke Havergal.

CHARLES CARVILLE'S EYES

A melancholy face Charles Carville had,
But not so melancholy as it seemed,
When once you knew him, for his mouth redeemed
His insufficient eyes, forever sad:
In them there was no life-glimpse, good or bad,
Nor joy nor passion in them ever gleamed;
His mouth was all of him that ever beamed,
His eyes were sorry, but his mouth was glad.

He never was a fellow that said much,
And half of what he did say was not heard
By many of us: we were out of touch
With all his whims and all his theories
Till he was dead, so those blank eyes of his
Might speak them. Then we heard them, every word.

REUBEN BRIGHT

Because he was a butcher and thereby
Did earn an honest living (and did right),
I would not have you think that Reuben Bright

Was any more a brute than you or I;
For when they told him that his wife must die,
He stared at them, and shook with grief and fright,
And cried like a great baby half the night,
And made the women cry to see him cry.

And after she was dead, and he had paid
The singers and the sexton and the rest,
He packed a lot of things that she had made
Most mournfully away in an old chest

Of hers, and put some chopped-up cedar boughs
In with them, and tore down the slaughterhouse.

RICHARD CORY

Whenever Richard Cory went downtown,
  We people on the pavement looked at him:
He was a gentleman from sole to crown,
  Clean favored, and imperially slim.

And he was always quietly arrayed,
  And he was always human when he talked;
But still he fluttered pulses when he said,
  "Good morning," and he glittered when he walked.

And he was rich—yes, richer than a king,
  And admirably schooled in every grace:
In fine, we thought that he was everything
  To make us wish that we were in his place.

So on we worked, and waited for the light,
  And went without the meat, and cursed the bread;
And Richard Cory, one calm summer night,
  Went home and put a bullet through his head.

JOHN EVERELDOWN

"Where are you going tonight, tonight,—
  Where are you going, John Evereldown?
There's never the sign of a star in sight,
  Nor a lamp that's nearer than Tilbury Town.
Why do you stare as a dead man might?
Where are you pointing away from the light?

And where are you going tonight, tonight,—
    Where are you going, John Evereldown?"

"Right through the forest, where none can see,
    There's where I'm going, to Tilbury Town.
The men are asleep,—or awake, maybe,—
    But the women are calling John Evereldown.
Ever and ever they call for me,
And while they call can a man be free?
So right through the forest, where none can see,
    There's where I'm going, to Tilbury Town."

"But why are you going so late, so late,—
    Why are you going, John Evereldown?
Though the road be smooth and the way be straight,
    There are two long leagues to Tilbury Town.
Come in by the fire, old man, and wait!
Why do you chatter out there by the gate?
And why are you going so late, so late,—
    Why are you going, John Evereldown?"

"I follow the women wherever they call,—
    That's why I'm going to Tilbury Town.
God knows if I pray to be done with it all,
    But God is no friend to John Evereldown.
So the clouds may come and the rain may fall,
The shadows may creep and the dead men crawl,—
But I follow the women wherever they call,
    And that's why I'm going to Tilbury Town."

AARON STARK

Withal a meager man was Aaron Stark—
Cursed and unkempt, shrewd, shriveled, and morose.
A miser was he, with a miser's nose,
And eyes like little dollars in the dark.
His thin, pinched mouth was nothing but a mark;
And when he spoke there came like sullen blows
Through scattered fangs a few snarled words and close,
As if a cur were chary of its bark.

Glad for the murmur of his hard renown,
Year after year he shambled through the town—
A loveless exile moving with a staff;

And oftentimes there crept into his ears
A sound of alien pity, touched with tears—
And then (and only then) did Aaron laugh.

FLEMING HELPHENSTINE

At first I thought there was a superfine
Persuasion in his face; but the free glow
That filled it when he stopped, and cried, "Hello!"
Shone joyously, and so I let it shine.
He said his name was Fleming Helphenstine,
But be that as it may;— I only know
He talked of this and that and So-and-So,
And laughed and chaffed like any friend of mine.

But soon, with a queer, quick frown, he looked at me,
And I looked hard at him; and there we gazed
In a strained way that made us cringe and wince:
Then, with a wordless clogged apology
That sounded half confused and half amazed,
He dodged,—and I have never seen him since.

CLIFF KLINGENHAGEN

Cliff Klingenhagen had me in to dine
With him one day; and after soup and meat,
And all the other things there were to eat,
Cliff took two glasses and filled one with wine
And one with wormwood. Then, without a sign
For me to choose at all, he took the draught
Of bitterness himself, and lightly quaffed
It off, and said the other one was mine.
And when I asked him what the deuce he meant
By doing that, he only looked at me
And grinned, and said it was a way of his.
And though I know the fellow, I have spent
Long time awondering when I shall be
As happy as Cliff Klingenhagen is.

GEORGE CRABBE

Give him the darkest inch your shelf allows,
Hide him in lonely garrets, if you will,—
But his hard, human pulse is throbbing still
With the sure strength that fearless truth endows.

In spite of all fine science disavows,
Of his plain excellence and stubborn skill
There yet remains what fashion cannot kill,
Though years have thinned the laurel from his brows.

Whether or not we read him, we can feel
From time to time the vigor of his name
Against us like a finger for the shame
And emptiness of what our souls reveal
In books that are as altars where we kneel
To consecrate the flicker, not the flame.

CREDO

I cannot find my way: there is no star
In all the shrouded heavens anywhere;
And there is not a whisper in the air
Of any living voice but one so far
That I can hear it only as a bar
Of lost, imperial music, played when fair
And angel fingers wove, and unaware,
Dead leaves to garlands where no roses are.

No, there is not a glimmer, nor a call,
For one that welcomes, welcomes when he fears,
The black and awful chaos of the night;
For through it all—above, beyond it all—
I know the far-sent message of the years,
I feel the coming glory of the Light.

BEWICK FINZER

Time was when his half million drew
    The breath of six per cent;
But soon the worm of what-was-not
    Fed hard on his content;
And something crumbled in his brain
    When his half million went.

Time passed, and filled along with his
    The place of many more;

Time came, and hardly one of us
  Had credence to restore,
From what appeared one day, the man
  Whom we had known before.

The broken voice, the withered neck,
  The coat worn out with care,
The cleanliness of indigence,
  The brilliance of despair,
The fond imponderable dreams
  Of affluence,—all were there.

Poor Finzer, with his dreams and schemes,
  Fares hard now in the race,
With heart and eye that have a task
  When he looks in the face
Of one who might so easily
  Have been in Finzer's place.

He comes unfailing for the loan
  We give and then forget;
He comes, and probably for years
  Will he be coming yet,—
Familiar as an old mistake,
  And futile as regret.

MANY ARE CALLED

The Lord Apollo, who has never died,
Still holds alone his immemorial reign,
Supreme in an impregnable domain
That with his magic he has fortified;
And though melodious multitudes have tried
In ecstasy, in anguish, and in vain,
With invocation sacred and profane
To lure him, even the loudest are outside.

Only at unconjectured intervals,
By will of him on whom no man may gaze,
By word of him whose law no man has read,
A questing light may rift the sullen walls,
To cling where mostly its infrequent rays
Fall golden on the patience of the dead.

NEW ENGLAND

Here where the wind is lways north-northeast
And children learn to walk on frozen toes,
Wonder begets an envy of all those
Who boil elsewhere with such a lyric yeast
Of love that you will hear them at a feast
Where demons would appeal for some repose,
Still clamoring where the chalice overflows
And crying wildest who have drunk the least.

Passion is here a soilure of the wits,
We're told, and Love a cross for them to bear;
Joy shivers in the corner where she knits
And Conscience always has the rocking chair,
Cheerful as when she tortured into fits
The first cat that was ever killed by Care.

THE MILLER'S WIFE

The miller's wife had waited long,
  The tea was cold, the fire was dead;
And there might yet be nothing wrong
  In how he went and what he said:
"There are no millers any more,"
  Was all that she had heard him say;
And he had lingered at the door
  So long that it seemed yesterday.

Sick with a fear that had no form
  She knew that she was there at last;
And in the mill there was a warm
  And mealy fragrance of the past.
What else there was would only seem
  To say again what he had meant;
And what was hanging from a beam
  Would not have heeded where she went.

And if she thought it followed her,
  She may have reasoned in the dark
That one way of the few there were
  Would hide her and would leave no mark:
Black water, smooth above the weir
  Like starry velvet in the night,
Though ruffled once, would soon appear
  The same as ever to the sight.

AS IT LOOKED THEN

In a sick shade of spruce, moss-webbed, rock-fed,
Where, long unfollowed by sagacious man,
A scrub that once had been a pathway ran
Blindly from nowhere and to nowhere led,
One might as well have been among the dead
As halfway there alive; so I began
Like a malingering pioneer to plan
A vain return—with one last look ahead.

And it was then that like a spoken word
Where there was none to speak, insensibly
A flash of blue that might have been a bird
Grew soon to the calm wonder of the sea—
Calm as a quiet sky that looked to be
Arching a world where nothing had occurred.

ANOTHER DARK LADY

Think not, because I wonder where you fled,
That I would lift a pin to see you there;
You may, for me, be prowling anywhere,
So long as you show not your little head:
No dark and evil story of the dead
Would leave you less pernicious or less fair—
Not even Lilith, with her famous hair;
And Lilith was the devil, I have read.

I cannot hate you, for I loved you then.
The woods were golden then. There was a road
Through beeches; and I said their smooth feet showed
Like yours. Truth must have heard me from afar,
For I shall never have to learn again
That yours are cloven as no beech's are.

"IF THE LORD WOULD MAKE WINDOWS IN HEAVEN"

She who had eyes but had not wherewithal
To see that he was doomed to his own way,
Dishonored his illusions day by day,
And year by year was more angelical.
Flaunting an injured instinct for the small,
She stifled always more than she would say;

Nursing a fear too futile to betray,
She sewed, and waited for the roof to fall.

A seer at home, she saw that his high lights
That were not shining, and were not afire,
Were such as never would be seen from there;
A saint abroad, she saw him on the heights,
And feared for him—who, if he went much higher,
Might one day not be seen from anywhere.

RECALLED

Long after there were none of them alive
About the place—where there is now no place
But a walled hole where fruitless vines embrace
Their parent skeletons that yet survive
In evil thorns—none of us could arrive
At a more cogent answer to their ways
Than one old Isaac in his latter days
Had humor or compassion to contrive.

I mentioned them and Isaac shook his head:
"The Power that you call yours and I call mine
Extinguished in the last of them a line
That Satan could have disinherited.
When we are done with all but the Divine,
We die." And there was no more to be said.

HAUNTED HOUSE

Here was a place where none would ever come
For shelter, save as we did from the rain.
We saw no ghost, yet once outside again
Each wondered why the other should be dumb;
For we had fronted nothing worse than gloom
And ruin, and to our vision it was plain
Where thrift, outshivering fear, had let remain
Some chairs that were like skeletons of home.

There were no trackless footsteps on the floor
Above us, and there were no sounds elsewhere.
But there was more than sound; and there was more
Than just an ax that once was in the air
Between us and the chimney, long before
Our time. So townsmen said who found her there.

A MIGHTY RUNNER

(Nicarchus)

The day when Charmus ran with five
In Arcady, as I'm alive,
He came in seventh—"Five and one
Make seven, you say? It can't be done"—
Well, if you think it needs a note,
A friend in a fur overcoat
Ran with him, crying all the while,
"You'll beat him, Charmus, by a mile!"
And so he came in seventh.
Therefore, good Zoilus, you see
The thing is plain as plain can be;
And with four more for company,
He would have been eleventh.

THE STORY OF THE ASHES AND THE FLAME

No matter why, nor whence, nor when she came,
There was her place. No matter what men said,
No matter what she was; living or dead,
Faithful or not, he loved her all the same.
The story was as old as human shame,
But ever since that lonely night she fled,
With books to blind him, he had only read
The story of the ashes and the flame.

There she was always coming pretty soon
To fool him back, with penitent scared eyes
That had in them the laughter of the moon
For baffled lovers, and to make him think—
Before she gave him time enough to wink—
Her kisses were the keys to paradise.

HILLCREST

(To Mrs. Edward MacDowell)

No sound of any storm that shakes
Old island walls with older seas
Comes here where now September makes
An island in a sea of trees.

Between the sunlight and the shade
A man may learn till he forgets
The roaring of a world remade,
And all his ruins and regrets;

And if he still remembers here
Poor fights he may have won or lost,—
If he be ridden with the fear
Of what some other fight may cost,—

If, eager to confuse too soon
What he has known with what may be
He reads a planet out of tune
For cause of his jarred harmony,—

If here he venture to unroll
His index of adagios,
And he be given to console
Humanity with what he knows,—

He may by contemplation learn
A little more than what he knew,
And even see great oaks return
To acorns out of which they grew.

He may, if he but listen well,
Through twilight and the silence here
Be told what there are none may tell
To vanity's impatient ear;

And he may never dare again
Say what awaits him, or be sure
What sunlit labyrinth of pain
He may not enter and endure.

Who knows today from yesterday
May learn to count no thing too strange:
Love builds of what time takes away,
Till death itself is less than change.

Who sees enough in his duress
May go as far as dreams have gone;
Who sees a little may do less
Than many who are blind have done;

Who sees unchastened here the soul
Triumphant has no other sight
Than has a child who sees the whole
World radiant with his own delight.

Far journeys and hard wandering
Await him in whose crude surmise
Peace, like a mask, hides everything
That is and has been from his eyes;

And all his wisdom is unfound,
Or like a web that error weaves
On airy looms that have a sound
No louder now than falling leaves.

EROS TURANNOS

She fears him, and will always ask
    What fated her to choose him;
She meets in his engaging mask
    All reasons to refuse him;
But what she meets and what she fears
Are less than are the downward years,
Drawn slowly to the foamless weirs
    Of age, were she to lose him.

Between a blurred sagacity
    That once had power to sound him,
And love, that will not let him be
    The Judas that she found him,
Her pride assuages her almost,
As if it were alone the cost.
He sees that he will not be lost,
    And waits and looks around him.

A sense of ocean and old trees
    Envelops and allures him;
Tradition, touching all he sees,
    Beguiles and reassures him;
And all her doubts of what he says
Are dimmed with what she knows of days—
Till even prejudice delays
    And fades, and she secures him.

The falling leaf inaugurates
   The reign of her confusion;
The pounding wave reverberates
   The dirge of her illusion;
And home, where passion lived and died,
Becomes a place where she can hide.
While all the town and harborside
   Vibrate with her seclusion.

We tell you, tapping on our brows,
   The story as it should be,
As if the story of a house
   Were told, or ever could be;
We'll have no kindly veil between
Her visions and those we have seen,—
As if we guessed what hers have been,
   Or what they are or would be.

Meanwhile we do no harm; for they
   That with a god have striven,
Not hearing much of what we say,
   Take what the god has given;
Though like waves breaking it may be,
Or like a changed familiar tree,
Or like a stairway to the sea
   Where down the blind are driven.

MR. FLOOD'S PARTY

Old Eben Flood, climbing alone one night
Over the hill between the town below
And the forsaken upland hermitage
That held as much as he should ever know
On earth again of home, paused warily.
The road was his with not a native near;
And Eben, having leisure, said aloud,
For no man else in Tilbury Town to hear:

"Well, Mr. Flood, we have the harvest moon
Again, and we may not have many more;
The bird is on the wing, the poet says,
And you and I have said it here before.
Drink to the bird." He raised up to the light
The jug that he had gone so far to fill,
And answered huskily: "Well, Mr. Flood,
Since you propose it, I believe I will."

Alone, as if enduring to the end
A valiant armor of sacred hopes outworn,
He stood there in the middle of the road
Like Roland's ghost winding a silent horn.
Below him, in the town among the trees,
Where friends of other days had honored him,
A phantom salutation of the dead
Rang thinly till old Eben's eyes were dim.

Then, as a mother lays her sleeping child
Down tenderly, fearing it may awake,
He set the jug down slowly at his feet
With trembling care, knowing that most things break;
And only when assured that on firm earth
It stood, as the uncertain lives of men
Assuredly did not, he paced away,
And with his hand extended paused again:

"Well, Mr. Flood, we have not met like this
In a long time; and many a change has come
To both of us, I fear, since last it was
We had a drop together. Welcome home!"
Convivially returning with himself,
Again he raised the jug up to the light
And with an acquiescent quaver said:
"Well, Mr. Flood, if you insist, I might

"Only a very little, Mr. Flood—
For auld lang syne. No more, sir; that will do."
So, for the time, apparently it did,
And Eben evidently thought so too;
For soon amid the silver loneliness
Of night he lifted up his voice and sang,
Secure, with only two moons listening,
Until the whole harmonious landscape rang—

"For auld lang syne." The weary throat gave out,
The last word wavered; and the song being done,
He raised again the jug regretfully
And shook his head, and was again alone.
There was not much that was ahead of him,
And there was nothing in the town below—
Where strangers would have shut the many doors
That many friends had opened long ago.

CASSANDRA

I heard one who said: "Verily,
    What word have I for children here?
Your dollar is your only word,
    The wrath of it your only fear.

"You build it altars tall enough
    To make you see, but you are blind;
You cannot leave it long enough
    To look before you or behind.

"When reason beckons you to pause,
    You laugh and say that you know best;
But what it is you know, you keep
    As dark as ingots in a chest.

"You laugh and answer, 'We are young;
    Oh, leave us now, and let us grow':
Not asking how much more of this
    Will time endure or fate bestow.

"Because a few complacent years
    Have made your peril of your pride,
Think you that you are to go on
    Forever pampered and untried?

"What lost eclipse of history,
    What bivouac of the marching stars,
Has given the sign for you to see
    Millenniums and last great wars?

"What unrecorded overthrow
    Of all the world has ever known,
Or ever been, has made itself
    So plain to you, and you alone?

"Your dollar, dove, and eagle make
    A trinity that even you
Rate higher than you rate yourselves;
    It pays, it flatters, and it's new.

"And though your very flesh and blood
    Be what your eagle eats and drinks,
You'll praise him for the best of birds,
    Not knowing what the eagle thinks.

"The power is yours, but not the sight;
  You see not upon what you tread;
You have the ages for your guide,
  But not the wisdom to be led.

"Think you to tread forever down
  The merciless old verities?
And are you never to have eyes
  To see the world for what it is?

"Are you to pay for what you have
  With all you are?"—No other word
We caught, but with a laughing crowd
  Moved on. None heeded, and few heard.

STEPHEN CRANE
(1871–1900)

IN THE DESERT

In the desert
I saw a creature, naked, bestial,
Who, squatting upon the ground,
Held his heart in his hands,
And ate of it.
I said, "Is it good, friend?"
"It is bitter—bitter," he answered,
"But I like it
Because it is bitter,
And because it is my heart."

A GOD IN WRATH

A god in wrath
Was beating a man;
He cuffed him loudly
With thunderous blows
That rang and rolled over the earth.
All people came running.
The man screamed and struggled,
And bit madly at the feet of the god.
The people cried,
"Ah, what a wicked man!"
And—
"Ah, what a redoubtable god!"

I SAW A MAN PURSUING

I saw a man pursuing the horizon;
Round and round they sped.
I was disturbed at this;
I accosted the man.

"It is futile," I said,
"You can never—"

"You lie," he cried,
And ran on.

BEHOLD, THE GRAVE

Behold, the grave of a wicked man,
And near it, a stern spirit.

There came a drooping maid with violets,
But the spirit grasped her arm.
"No flowers for him," he said.
The maid wept:
"Ah, I loved him."
But the spirit, grim and frowning:
"No flowers for him."

Now, this is it—
If the spirit was just,
Why did the maid weep?

MANY WORKMEN

Many workmen
Built a huge ball of masonry
Upon a mountaintop.
Then they went to the valley below,
And turned to behold their work.
"It is grand," they said;
They loved the thing.

Of a sudden, it moved:
It came upon them swiftly;
It crushed them all to blood.
But some had opportunity to squeal.

A LEARNED MAN CAME TO ME ONCE

A learned man came to me once.
He said, "I know the way—come."
And I was overjoyed at this.
Together we hastened.

Soon, too soon, were we
Where my eyes were useless,
And I knew not the ways of my feet.
I clung to the hand of my friend;
But at last he cried, "I am lost."

THERE WAS SET BEFORE ME A MIGHTY HILL

There was set before me a mighty hill,
And long days I climbed
Through regions of snow.
When I had before me the summit view,
It seemed that my labor
Had been to see gardens
Lying at impossible distances.

A YOUTH IN APPAREL THAT GLITTERED

A youth in apparel that glittered
Went to walk in a grim forest.
There he met an assassin
Attired all in garb of old days;
He, scowling through the thickets,
And dagger poised quivering,
Rushed upon the youth.
"Sir," said this latter,
"I am enchanted, believe me,
To die, thus,
In this medieval fashion,
According to the best legends;
Ah, what joy!"
Then took he the wound, smiling,
And died, content.

THERE WAS ONE I MET

There was one I met upon the road
Who looked at me with kind eyes.
He said, "Show me of your wares."
And this I did,
Holding forth one.
He said, "It is a sin."
Then held I forth another;

He said, "It is a sin."
Then held I forth another;
He said, "It is a sin."
And so to the end;
Always he said, "It is a sin."
And, finally, I cried out,
"But I have none other."
Then did he look at me
With kinder eyes.
"Poor soul!" he said.

A MAN SAW A BALL OF GOLD

A man saw a ball of gold in the sky;
He climbed for it,
And eventually he achieved it—
It was clay.

Now this is the strange part:
When the man went to the earth
And looked again,
Lo, there was the ball of gold.
Now this is the strange part:
It was a ball of gold.
Ay, by the heavens, it was a ball of gold.

ON THE HORIZON

On the horizon, the peaks assembled;
And as I looked,
The march of the mountains began.
As they marched, they sang,
"Ay! we come! we come!"

I WALKED IN A DESERT

I walked in a desert.
And I cried,
"Ah, God, take me from this place!"
A voice said, "It is no desert."
I cried, "Well, but—
The sand, the heat, the vacant horizon."
A voice said, "It is no desert."

TRADITION, THOU ART FOR SUCKLING CHILDREN

Tradition, thou art for suckling children,
Thou art the enlivening milk for babes;
But no meat for men is in thee.
Then—
But, alas, we all are babes.

MANY RED DEVILS

Many red devils ran from my heart
And out upon the page.
They were so tiny
The pen could mash them.
And many struggled in the ink.
It was strange
To write in this red muck
Of things from my heart.

YOU SAY YOU ARE HOLY

You say you are holy,
And that
Because I have not seen you sin.
Ay, but there are those
Who see you sin, my friend.

"IT WAS WRONG TO DO THIS"

"It was wrong to do this," said the angel.
"You should live like a flower,
Holding malice like a puppy,
Waging war like a lambkin."

"Not so," quoth the man
Who had no fear of spirits;
"It is only wrong for angels
Who can live like the flowers,
Holding malice like the puppies,
Waging war like the lambkins."

A MAN FEARED

A man feared that he might find an assassin;
Another that he might find a victim.
One was more wise than the other.

THE SAGE LECTURED

The sage lectured brilliantly.
Before him, two images:
"Now this one is a devil,
And this one is me."
He turned away.
Then a cunning pupil
Changed the positions.
Turned the sage again:
"Now this one is a devil,
And this one is me."
The pupils sat, grinning,
And rejoiced in the game.
But the sage was a sage.

GOD LAY DEAD

God lay dead in heaven;
Angels sang the hymn of the end;
Purple winds went moaning,
Their wings drip-dripping
With blood
That fell upon the earth.
It, groaning thing,
Turned black and sank.
Then from the far caverns
Of dead sins
Came monsters, livid with desire.
They fought,
Wrangled over the world,
A morsel.
But of all sadness this was sad—
A woman's arms tried to shield
The head of a sleeping man
From the jaws of the final beast.

WAR IS KIND

Do not weep, maiden, for war is kind.
Because your lover threw wild hands toward the sky
And the affrighted steed ran on alone,
Do not weep.
War is kind.

> Hoarse, booming drums of the regiment,
> Little souls who thirst for fight,
> These men were born to drill and die.
> The unexplained glory flies above them,
> Great is the battle god, great, and his kingdom—
> A field where a thousand corpses lie.

Do not weep, babe, for war is kind.
Because your father tumbled in the yellow trenches,
Raged at his breast, gulped and died,
Do not weep.
War is kind.

> Swift blazing flag of the regiment,
> Eagle with crest of red and gold,
> These men were born to drill and die.
> Point for them the virtue of slaughter,
> Make plain to them the excellence of killing
> And a field where a thousand corpses lie.

Mother whose heart hung humble as a button
On the bright splendid shroud of your son,
Do not weep.
War is kind.

A LITTLE INK MORE OR LESS

A little ink more or less!
It surely can't matter?
Even the sky and the opulent sea,
The plains and the hills, aloof.
Hear the uproar of all these books.
But it is only a little ink more or less.

What?
You define me God with these trinkets?
Can my misery meal on an ordered walking

Of surpliced numskulls?
And a fanfare of lights?
Or even upon the measured pulpitings
Of the familiar false and true?
Is this God?
Where, then, is hell?
Show me some bastard mushroom
Sprung from a pollution of blood.
It is better.

Where is God?

FAST RODE THE KNIGHT

Fast rode the knight
With spurs, hot and reeking,
Ever waving an eager sword,
"To save my lady!"
Fast rode the knight,
And leaped from saddle to war.
Men of steel flickered and gleamed
Like riot of silver lights,
And the gold of the knight's good banner
Still waved on a castle wall.

A horse,
Blowing, staggering, bloody thing,
Forgotten at foot of castle wall.
A horse
Dead at foot of castle wall.

A NEWSPAPER

A newspaper is a collection of half injustices
Which, bawled by boys from mile to mile,
Spreads its curious opinion
To a million merciful and sneering men,
While families cuddle the joys of the fireside
When spurred by tale of dire lone agony.
A newspaper is a court
Where everyone is kindly and unfairly tried
By a squalor of honest men.
A newspaper is a market
Where wisdom sells its freedom

And melons are crowned by the crowd.
A newspaper is a game
Where his error scores the player victory
While another's skill wins death.
A newspaper is a symbol;
It is feckless life's chronicle,
A collection of loud tales
Concentrating eternal stupidities,
That in remote ages lived unhaltered,
Roaming through a fenceless world.

THE WAYFARER

The wayfarer
Perceiving the pathway to truth,
Was struck with astonishment.
It was thickly grown with weeds.
"Ha," he said,
"I see that none has passed here
In a long time."
Later he saw that each weed
Was a singular knife.
"Well," he mumbled at last,
"Doubtless there are other roads."

A SLANT OF SUN

A slant of sun on dull brown walls,
A forgotten sky of bashful blue.

Toward God a mighty hymn,
A song of collisions and cries,
Rumbling wheels, hoofbeats, bells,
Welcomes, farewells, love calls, final moans,
Voices of joy, idiocy, warning, despair,
The unknown appeals of brutes,
The chanting of flowers,
The screams of cut trees,
The senseless babble of hens and wise men—
A cluttered incoherency that says at the stars:
"O God, save us!"

THE IMPACT OF A DOLLAR

The impact of a dollar upon the heart
Smiles warm red light,
Sweeping from the hearth rosily upon the white table,
With the hanging cool velvet shadows
Moving softly upon the door.

The impact of a million dollars
Is a crash of flunkies,
And yawning emblems of Persia
Cheeked against oak, France and a saber,
The outcry of old beauty
Whored by pimping merchants
To submission before wine and chatter.
Silly rich peasants stamp the carpets of men,
Dead men who dreamed fragrance and light
Into their woof, their lives;
The rug of an honest bear
Under the feet of a cryptic slave
Who speaks always of baubles,
Forgetting state, multitude, work, and state,
Champing and mouthing of hats,
Making ratful squeak of hats,
Hats.

AY, WORKMAN

Ay, workman, make me a dream,
A dream for my love.
Cunningly weave sunlight,
Breezes, and flowers.
Let it be of the cloth of meadows.
And—good workman—
And let there be a man walking thereon.

THERE WAS A MAN WITH TONGUE OF WOOD

There was a man with tongue of wood
Who essayed to sing,
And in truth it was lamentable.
But there was one who heard
The clip-clapper of this tongue of wood
And knew what the man
Wished to sing,
And with that the singer was content.

I STOOD UPON A HIGH PLACE

I stood upon a high place,
And saw, below, many devils
Running, leaping,
And carousing in sin.
One looked up, grinning,
And said, "Comrade! Brother!"

ROBERT FROST
(b. 1874)

MENDING WALL

Something there is that doesn t love a wall,
That sends the frozen ground swell under it,
And spills the upper boulders in the sun;
And makes gaps even two can pass abreast.
The work of hunters is another thing:
I have come after them and made repair
Where they have left not one stone on a stone,
But they would have the rabbit out of hiding,
To please the yelping dogs. The gaps I mean,
No one has seen them made or heard them made,
But at spring mending time we find them there.
I let my neighbor know beyond the hill;
And on a day we meet to walk the line
And set the wall between us once again.
We keep the wall between us as we go.
To each the boulders that have fallen to each.
And some are loaves and some so nearly balls
We have to use a spell to make them balance:
"Stay where you are until our backs are turned!"
We wear our fingers rough with handling them.
Oh, just another kind of outdoor game,
One on a side. It comes to little more:
There where it is we do not need the wall:
He is all pine and I am apple orchard.
My apple trees will never get across
And eat the cones under his pines, I tell him.
He only says, "Good fences make good neighbors."
Spring is the mischief in me, and I wonder
If I could put a notion in his head:
"Why do they make good neighbors? Isn't it
Where there are cows? But here there are no cows.
Before I built a wall I'd ask to know
What I was walling in or walling out,
And to whom I was like to give offense.
Something there is that doesn't love a wall,

That wants it down." I could say "Elves" to him,
But it's not elves exactly, and I'd rather
He said it for himself. I see him there
Bringing a stone grasped firmly by the top
In each hand, like an old-stone savage armed.
He moves in darkness as it seems to me,
Not of woods only and the shade of trees.
He will not go behind his father's saying,
And he likes having thought of it so well
He says again, "Good fences make good neighbors."

6   *AFTER APPLE PICKING*

My long two-pointed ladder's sticking through a tree
Toward heaven still,
And there's a barrel that I didn't fill
Beside it, and there may be two or three
Apples I didn't pick upon some bough.
But I am done with apple picking now.
Essence of winter sleep is on the night,
The scent of apples: I am drowsing off.
I cannot rub the strangeness from my sight
10 I got from looking through a pane of glass
I skimmed this morning from the drinking trough
And held against the world of hoary grass.
It melted, and I let it fall and break.
But I was well
Upon my way to sleep before it fell,
And I could tell
What form my dreaming was about to take.
Magnified apples appear and disappear
Stem end and blossom end,
20 And every fleck of russet showing clear.
My instep arch not only keeps the ache,
It keeps the pressure of a ladder round.
I feel the ladder sway as the boughs bend.
And I keep hearing from the cellar bin
The rumbling sound
Of load on load of apples coming in.
For I have had too much
Of apple picking: I am overtired
Of the great harvest I myself desired.
30 There were ten thousand thousand fruit to touch,
Cherish in hand, lift down, and not let fall.
For all

That struck the earth,
No matter if not bruised or spiked with stubble,
35 Went surely to the cider-apple heap
As of no worth.
One can see what will trouble
This sleep of mine, whatever sleep it is.
Were he not gone,
40 The woodchuck could say whether it's like his
Long sleep, as I describe its coming on,
Or just some human sleep.

THE OVEN BIRD

There is a singer everyone has heard,
Loud, a midsummer and a midwood bird,
Who makes the solid tree trunks sound again.
He says that leaves are old and that for flowers
Midsummer is to spring as one to ten.
He says the early petal fall is past
When pear and cherry bloom went down in showers
On sunny days a moment overcast;
And comes that other fall we name the fall.
10 He says the highway dust is over all.
The bird would cease and be as other birds
But that he knows in singing not to sing.
The question that he frames in all but words
Is what to make of a diminished thing.

BIRCHES

When I see birches bend to left and right
Across the lines of straighter darker trees,
I like to think some boy's been swinging them.
But swinging doesn't bend them down to stay.
Ice storms do that. Often you must have seen them
Loaded with ice a sunny winter morning
After a rain. They click upon themselves
As the breeze rises, and turn many-colored
As the stir cracks and crazes their enamel.
Soon the sun's warmth makes them shed crystal shells
Shattering and avalanching on the snow crust—
Such heaps of broken glass to sweep away
You'd think the inner dome of heaven had fallen.
They are dragged to the withered bracken by the load,

And they seem not to break; though once they are bowed
So low for long, they never right themselves:
You may see their trunks arching in the woods
Years afterwards, trailing their leaves on the ground
Like girls on hands and knees that throw their hair
Before them over their heads to dry in the sun.
But I was going to say when Truth broke in
With all her matter-of-fact about the ice storm
I should prefer to have some boy bend them
As he went out and in to fetch the cows—
Some boy too far from town to learn baseball,
Whose only play was what he found himself,
Summer or winter, and could play alone.
One by one he subdued his father's trees
By riding them down over and over again
Until he took the stiffness out of them.
And not one but hung limp, not one was left
For him to conquer. He learned all there was
To learn about not launching out too soon
And so not carrying the tree away
Clear to the ground. He always kept his poise
To the top branches, climbing carefully
With the same pains you use to fill a cup
Up to the brim, and even above the brim.
Then he flung outward, feet first, with a swish,
Kicking his way down through the air to the ground.
So was I once myself a swinger of birches,
And so I dream of going back to be.
It's when I'm weary of considerations,
And life is too much like a pathless wood
Where your face burns and tickles with the cobwebs
Broken across it, and one eye is weeping
From a twig's having lashed across it open.
I'd like to get away from earth awhile
And then come back to it and begin over.
May no fate willfully misunderstand me
And half grant what I wish and snatch me away
Not to return. Earth's the right place for love:
I don't know where it's likely to go better.
I'd like to go by climbing a birch tree,
And climb black branches up a snow-white trunk
Toward heaven, till the tree could bear no more,
But dipped its top and set me down again.
That would be good both going and coming back.
One could do worse than be a swinger of birches.

THE SUBVERTED FLOWER

She drew back; he was calm:
"It is this that had the power."
And he lashed his open palm
With the tender-headed flower.
He smiled for her to smile,
But she was either blind
Or willfully unkind.
He eyed her for awhile
For a woman and a puzzle.
He flicked and flung the flower,
And another sort of smile
Caught up like fingertips
The corners of his lips
And cracked his ragged muzzle.
She was standing to the waist
In goldenrod and brake,
Her shining hair displaced.
He stretched her either arm
As if she made it ache
To clasp her—not to harm;
As if he could not spare
To touch her neck and hair.
"If this has come to us
And not to me alone—"
So she thought she heard him say;
Though with every word he spoke
His lips were sucked and blown
And the effort made him choke
Like a tiger at a bone.
She had to lean away.
She dared not stir a foot,
Lest movement should provoke
The demon of pursuit
That slumbers in a brute.
It was then her mother's call
From inside the garden wall
Made her steal a look of fear
To see if he could hear
And would pounce to end it all
Before her mother came.
She looked and saw the shame:
A hand hung like a paw,
An arm worked like a saw
As if to be persuasive,

An ingratiating laugh
That cut the snout in half,
An eye become evasive.
A girl could only see
That a flower had marred a man,
But what she could not see
Was that the flower might be
Other than base and fetid:
That the flower had done but part,
And what the flower began
Her own too meager heart
Had terribly completed.
She looked and saw the worst.
And the dog or what it was,
Obeying bestial laws,
A coward save at night,
Turned from the place and ran.
She heard him stumble first
And use his hands in flight.
She heard him bark outright.
And oh, for one so young
The bitter words she spit
Like some tenacious bit
That will not leave the tongue.
She plucked her lips for it,
And still the horror clung
Her mother wiped the foam
From her chin, picked up her comb
And drew her backward home.

THE GIFT OUTRIGHT

The land was ours before we were the land's.
She was our land more than a hundred years
Before we were her people. She was ours
In Massachusetts, in Virginia,
But we were England's, still colonials,
Possessing what we still were unpossessed by,
Possessed by what we now no more possessed.
Something we were withholding made us weak
Until we found out that it was ourselves
We were withholding from our land of living,
And forthwith found salvation in surrender.
Such as we were we gave ourselves outright

(The deed of gift was many deeds of war)
To the land vaguely realizing westward,
But still unstoried, artless, unenhanced,
Such as she was, such as she would become.

TO EARTHWARD

Love at the lips was touch
As sweet as I could bear;
And once that seemed too much;
I lived on air

That crossed me from sweet things,
The flow of—was it musk
From hidden grapevine springs
Downhill at dusk?

I had the swirl and ache
From sprays of honeysuckle
That when they're gathered shake
Dew on the knuckle.

I craved strong sweets, but those
Seemed strong when I was young;
The petal of the rose
It was that stung.

Now no joy but lacks salt
That is not dashed with pain
And weariness and fault;
I crave the stain

Of tears, the aftermark
Of almost too much love,
The sweet of bitter bark
And burning clove.

When stiff and sore and scarred
I take away my hand
From leaning on it hard
In grass and sand,

The hurt is not enough:
I long for weight and strength
To feel the earth as rough
To all my length.

TREE AT MY WINDOW

Tree at my window, window tree,
My sash is lowered when night comes on;
But let there never be curtain drawn
Between you and me.

Vague dream head lifted out of the ground,
And thing next most diffuse to cloud,
Not all your light tongues talking aloud
Could be profound.

But tree, I have seen you taken and tossed,
And if you have seen me when I slept,
You have seen me when I was taken and swept
And all but lost.

That day she put our heads together,
Fate had her imagination about her,
Your head so much concerned with outer,
Mine with inner, weather.

(2)

TWO TRAMPS IN MUD TIME

Out of the mud two strangers came
And caught me splitting wood in the yard,
And one of them put me off my aim
By hailing cheerily "Hit them hard!"
I knew pretty well why he dropped behind
And let the other go on a way.
I knew pretty well what he had in mind:
He wanted to take my job for pay.

Good blocks of beech it was I split,
As large around as the chopping block;
And every piece I squarely hit
Fell splinterless as a cloven rock.
The blows that a life of self-control
Spares to strike for the common good
That day, giving a loose to my soul,
I spent on the unimportant wood.

The sun was warm but the wind was chill.
You know how it is with an April day
When the sun is out and the wind is still,

You're one month on in the middle of May.
But if you so much as dare to speak,
A cloud comes over the sunlit arch,
A wind comes off a frozen peak,
And you're two months back in the middle of March.

A bluebird comes tenderly up to alight
And fronts the wind to unruffle a plume
His song so pitched as not to excite
A single flower as yet to bloom.
It is snowing a flake: and he half knew
Winter was only playing possum.
Except in color he isn't blue,
But he wouldn't advise a thing to blossom.

The water for which we may have to look
In summertime with a witching wand,
In every wheel rut's now a brook,
In every print of a hoof a pond.
Be glad of water, but don't forget
The lurking frost in the earth beneath
That will steal forth after the sun is set
And show on the water its crystal teeth.

The time when most I loved my task
These two must make me love it more
By coming with what they came to ask.
You'd think I never had felt before
The weight of an axhead poised aloft
The grip on earth of outspread feet.
The life of muscles rocking soft
And smooth and moist in vernal heat.

Out of the woods two hulking tramps
(From sleeping God knows where last night,
But not long since in the lumber camps.)
They thought all chopping was theirs of right.
Men of the woods and lumberjacks,
They judged me by their appropriate tool.
Except as a fellow handled an ax,
They had no way of knowing a fool.

Nothing on either side was said.
They knew they had but to stay their stay
And all their logic would fill my head:
As that I had no right to play

With what was another man's work for gain.
My right might be love but theirs was need.
And where the two exist in twain
Theirs was the better right—agreed.

But yield who will to their separation,
My object in living is to unite
My avocation and my vocation
As my two eyes make one in sight.
Only where love and need are one,
And the work is play for mortal stakes,
Is the deed ever really done
For heaven and the future's sakes.

THE WITCH OF COÖS

I stayed the night for shelter at a farm
Behind the mountain, with a mother and son,
Two old-believers. They did all the talking.

MOTHER. Folks think a witch who has familiar spirits
She could call up to pass a winter evening,
But won't, should be burned at the stake or something
Summoning spirits isn't "Button, button,
Who's got the button," I would have them know.

SON. Mother can make a common table rear
And kick with two legs like an army mule.

MOTHER. And when I've done it, what good have I done?
Rather than tip a table for you, let me
Tell you what Ralle the Sioux Control once told me.
He said the dead had souls, but when I asked him
How could that be—I thought the dead were souls,
He broke my trance. Don't that make you suspicious
That there's something the dead are keeping back?
Yes, there's something the dead are keeping back.

SON. You wouldn't want to tell him what we have
Up attic, mother?

MOTHER. Bones—a skeleton.

SON. But the headboard of mother's bed is pushed
Against the attic door: the door is nailed.

It's harmless. Mother hears it in the night
Halting perplexed behind the barrier
Of door and headboard. Where it wants to get
Is back into the cellar where it came from.

MOTHER. We'll never let them, will we, son! We'll never!

SON. It left the cellar forty years ago
And carried itself like a pile of dishes
Up one flight from the cellar to the kitchen,
Another from the kitchen to the bedroom,
Another from the bedroom to the attic,
Right past both father and mother, and neither stopped it.
Father had gone upstairs; mother was downstairs.
I was a baby: I don't know where I was.

MOTHER. The only fault my husband found with me—
I went to sleep before I went to bed,
Especially in winter when the bed
Might just as well be ice and the clothes snow.
The night the bones came up the cellar stairs
Toffile had gone to bed alone and left me,
But left an open door to cool the room off
So as to sort of turn me out of it.
I was just coming to myself enough
To wonder where the cold was coming from,
When I heard Toffile upstairs in the bedroom
And thought I heard him downstairs in the cellar.
The board we had laid down to walk dry shod on
When there was water in the cellar in spring
Struck the hard cellar bottom. And then someone
Began the stairs, two footsteps for each step,
The way a man with one leg and a crutch,
Or a little child, comes up. It wasn't Toffile:
It wasn't anyone who could be there.
The bulkhead double doors were double locked
And swollen tight and buried under snow.
The cellar windows were banked up with sawdust
And swollen tight and buried under snow.
It was the bones. I knew them—and good reason.
My first impulse was to get to the knob
And hold the door. But the bones didn't try
The door; they halted helpless on the landing;
Waiting for things to happen in their favor.
The faintest restless rustling ran all through them.
I never could have done the thing I did

If the wish hadn't been too strong in me
To see how they were mounted for this walk.
I had a vision of them put together
Not like a man, but like a chandelier.
So suddenly I flung the door wide on him.
A moment he stood balancing with emotion,
And all but lost himself. (A tongue of fire
Flashed out and licked along his upper teeth.
Smoke rolled inside the sockets of his eyes.)
Then he came at me with one hand outstretched,
The way he did in life once; but this time
I struck the hand off brittle on the floor,
And fell back from him on the floor myself.
The finger pieces slid in all directions.
(Where did I see one of those pieces lately?
Hand me my button box—it must be there.)
I sat up on the floor and shouted, "Toffile,
It's coming up to you." It had its choice
Of the door to the cellar or the hall.
It took the hall door for the novelty,
And set off briskly for so slow a thing,
Still going every which way in the joints, though,
So that it looked like lightning or a scribble,
From the slap I had just now given its hand.
I listened till it almost climbed the stairs
From the hall to the only finished bedroom,
Before I got up to do anything;
Then ran and shouted, "Shut the bedroom door,
Toffile, for my sake!" "Company?" he said,
"Don't make me get up; I'm too warm in bed."
So lying forward weakly on the handrail
I pushed myself upstairs, and in the light
(The kitchen had been dark) I had to own
I could see nothing. "Toffile, I don't see it.
It's with us in the room though. It's the bones."
"What bones?" "The cellar bones—out of the grave."
That made him throw his bare legs out of bed
And sit up by me and take hold of me.
I wanted to put out the light and see
If I could see it, or else mow the room,
With our arms at the level of our knees,
And bring the chalk pile down. "I'll tell you what—
It's looking for another door to try.
The uncommonly deep snow has made him think
Of his old song, 'The Wild Colonial Boy,'
He always used to sing along the tote road.

He's after an open door to get outdoors.
Let's trap him with an open door up attic."
Toffile agreed to that, and sure enough,
Almost the moment he was given an opening,
The steps began to climb the attic stairs.
I heard them. Toffile didn't seem to hear them.
"Quick!" I slammed to the door and held the knob,
"Toffile, get nails. I made him nail the door shut,
And push the headboard of the bed against it.
Then we asked was there anything
Up attic that we'd ever want again.
The attic was less to us than the cellar.
If the bones liked the attic, let them have it.
Let them stay in the attic. When they sometimes
Come down the stairs at night and stand perplexed
Behind the door and headboard of the bed,
Brushing their chalky skull with chalky fingers,
With sounds like the dry rattling of a shutter,
That's what I sit up in the dark to say—
To no one any more since Toffile died.
Let them stay in the attic since they went there.
I promised Toffile to be cruel to them
For helping them be cruel once to him.

SON. We think they had a grave down in the cellar.

MOTHER. We know they had a grave down in the cellar.

SON. We never could find out whose bones they were.

MOTHER. Yes, we could too, son. Tell the truth for once
They were a man's his father killed for me.
I mean a man he killed instead of me.
The least I could do was to help dig their grave.
We were about it one night in the cellar.
Son knows the story: but 'twas not for him
To tell the truth, suppose the time had come.
Son looks surprised to see me end a lie
We'd kept all these years between ourselves
So as to have it ready for outsiders.
But tonight I don't care enough to lie—
I don't remember why I ever cared.
Toffile, if he were here, I don't believe
Could tell you why he ever cared himself. . . .

She hadn't found the finger bone she wanted

Among the buttons poured out in her lap.
I verified the name next morning: Toffile.
The rural letter box said Toffile Lajway.

ONCE BY THE PACIFIC

The shattered water made a misty din.
Great waves looked over others coming in,
And thought of doing something to the shore
That water never did to land before.

The clouds were low and hairy in the skies,
Like locks blown forward in the gleam of eyes.
You could not tell, and yet it looked as if
The shore was lucky in being backed by cliff,

The cliff in being backed by continent;
It looked as if a night of dark intent
Was coming, and not only a night, an age.
Someone had better be prepared for rage.

There would be more than ocean water broken
Before God's last *Put out the Light* was spoken.

ACQUAINTED WITH THE NIGHT

I have been one acquainted with the night.
I have walked out in rain—and back in rain.
I have outwalked the further city light.

I have looked down the saddest city lane.
I have passed by the watchman on his beat
And dropped my eyes, unwilling to explain.

I have stood still and stopped the sound of feet
When far away an interrupted cry
Came over houses from another street,

But not to call me back or say good-bye;
And further still at an unearthly height,
One luminary clock against the sky

Proclaimed the time was neither wrong nor right.
I have been one acquainted with the night.

ON LOOKING UP BY CHANCE AT THE CONSTELLATIONS

You'll wait a long, long time for anything much
To happen in heaven beyond the floats of cloud
And the Northern Lights that run like tingling nerves.
The sun and moon get crossed, but they never touch,
Nor strike out fire from each other, nor crash out loud.
The planets seem to interfere in their curves,
But nothing ever happens, no harm is done.
We may as well go patiently on with our life.
And look elsewhere than to stars and moon and sun
For the shocks and changes we need to keep us sane.
It is true the longest drought will end in rain,
The longest peace in China will end in strife.
Still it wouldn't reward the watcher to stay awake
In hopes of seeing the calm of heaven break
On his particular time and personal sight.
That calm seems certainly safe to last tonight.

STOPPING BY WOODS ON A SNOWY EVENING

Whose woods these are I think I know.
His house is in the village though;
He will not see me stopping here
To watch his woods fill up with snow.

My little horse must think it queer
To stop without a farmhouse near
Between the woods and frozen lake
The darkest evening of the year.

He gives his harness bells a shake
To ask if there is some mistake.
The only other sound's the sweep
Of easy wind and downy flake.

The woods are lovely, dark and deep.
But I have promises to keep,
And miles to go before I sleep,
And miles to go before I sleep.

THE ROAD NOT TAKEN

Two roads diverged in a yellow wood,
And sorry I could not travel both
And be one traveler, long I stood
And looked down one as far as I could
To where it bent in the undergrowth;

Then took the other, as just as fair,
And having perhaps the better claim,
Because it was grassy and wanted wear;
Though as for that the passing there
Had worn them really about the same,

And both that morning equally lay
In leaves no step had trodden black.
Oh, I kept the first for another day!
Yet knowing how way leads on to way,
I doubted if I should ever come back.

I shall be telling this with a sigh
Somewhere ages and ages hence:
Two roads diverged in a wood, and I—
I took the one less traveled by,
And that has made all the difference.

NEITHER OUT FAR NOR IN DEEP

The people along the sand
All turn and look one way.
They turn their back on the land.
They look at the sea all day.

As long as it takes to pass
A ship keeps raising its hull;
The wetter ground like glass
Reflects a standing gull.

The land may vary more;
But wherever the truth may be—
The water comes ashore,
And the people look at the sea.

They cannot look out far.
They cannot look in deep.
But when was that ever a bar
To any watch they keep?

THE VANTAGE POINT

If tired of trees I seek again mankind,
    Well I know where to hie me—in the dawn,
    To a slope where the cattle keep the lawn.
There amid lolling juniper reclined,
Myself unseen, I see in white defined
    Far off the homes of men, and farther still,
    The graves of men on an opposing hill,
Living or dead, whichever are to mind.

And if by noon I have too much of these,
    I have but to turn on my arm, and lo,
    The sun-burned hillside sets my face aglow,
My breathing shakes the bluet like a breeze,
    I smell the earth, I smell the bruised plant,
    I look into the crater of the ant.

THE TUFT OF FLOWERS

I went to turn the grass once after one
Who mowed it in the dew before the sun.

The dew was gone that made his blade so keen
Before I came to view the leveled scene.

I looked for him behind an isle of trees;
I listened for his whetstone on the breeze.

But he had gone his way, the grass all mown,
And I must be, as he had been,—alone.

"As all must be," I said within my heart,
"Whether they work together or apart."

But as I said it, swift there passed me by
On noiseless wing a bewildered butterfly,

Seeking with memories grown dim o'ernight
Some resting flower of yesterday's delight.

And once I marked his flight go round and round,
As where some flower lay withering on the ground.

And then he flew as far as eye could see,
And then on tremulous wing came back to me.

I thought of questions that have no reply,
And would have turned to toss the grass to dry;

But he turned first, and led my eye to look
At a tall tuft of flowers beside a brook,

A leaping tongue of bloom the scythe had spared
Beside a reedy brook the scythe had bared.

I left my place to know them by their name,
Finding them butterfly weed when I came.

The mower in the dew had loved them thus,
By leaving them to flourish, not for us,

Nor yet to draw one thought of ours to him,
But from sheer morning gladness at the brim.

The butterfly and I had lit upon,
Nevertheless, a message from the dawn,

That made me hear the wakening birds around,
And hear his long scythe whispering to the ground,

And feel a spirit kindred to my own;
So that henceforth I worked no more alone;

But glad with him, I worked as with his aid,
And weary, sought at noon with him the shade;

And dreaming, as it were, held brotherly speech
With one whose thought I had not hoped to reach.

"Men work together," I told him from the heart,
"Whether they work together or apart."

DIRECTIVE

Back out of all this now too much for us,
Back in a time made simple by the loss
Of detail, burned, dissolved, and broken off
Like graveyard marble sculpture in the weather,
There is a house that is no more a house
Upon a farm that is no more a farm
And in a town that is no more a town.
The road there, if you'll let a guide direct you
Who only has at heart your etting lost,
May seem as if it should have been a quarry—
Great monolithic knees the former town
Long since gave up pretense of keeping covered.
And there's a story in a book about it:
Besides the wear of iron wagon wheels
The ledges show lines ruled southeast northwest,
The chisel work of an enormous Glacier
That braced his feet against the Arctic Pole.
You must not mind a certain coolness from him
Still said to haunt this side of Panther Mountain
Nor need you mind the serial ordeal
Of being watched from forty cellar holes
As if by eye pairs out of forty firkins.
As for the woods' excitement over you
That sends light rustle rushes to their leaves,
Charge that to upstart inexperience.
Where were they all not twenty years ago?
They think too much of having shaded out
A few old pecker-fretted apple trees.
Make yourself up a cheering song of how
Someone's road home from work this once was,
Who may be just ahead of you on foot
Or creaking with a buggy load of grain.
The height of the adventure is the height
Of country where two village cultures faded
Into each other. Both of them are lost.
And if you're lost enough to find yourself
By now, pull in your ladder road behind you
And put a sign up CLOSED to all but me.
Then make yourself at home. The only field
Now left's no bigger than a harness gall.
First there's the children's house of make believe,
Some shattered dishes underneath a pine,
The playthings in the playhouse of the children.
Weep for what little things could make them glad.

Then for the house that is no more a house,
But only a belilaced cellar hole,
Now slowly closing like a dent in dough.
This was no playhouse but a house in earnest.
Your destination and your destiny's
A brook that was the water of the house,
Cold as a spring as yet so near its source,
Too lofty and original to rage.
(We know the valley streams that when aroused
Will leave their tatters hung on barb and thorn.)
I have kept hidden in the instep arch
Of an old cedar at the waterside
A broken drinking goblet like the Grail
Under a spell so the wrong ones can't find it,
So can't get saved, as Saint Mark says they mustn't.
(I stole the goblet from the children's playhouse.)
Here are your waters and your watering place.
Drink and be whole again beyond confusion.

VACHEL LINDSAY
(1879–1931)

THE LEADEN-EYED

Let not young souls be smothered out before
They do quaint deeds and fully flaunt their pride.
It is the world's one crime its babes grow dull,
Its poor are oxlike, limp and leaden-eyed.
Not that they starve, but starve so dreamlessly;
Not that they sow, but that they seldom reap;
Not that they serve, but have no gods to serve;
Not that they die, but that they die like sheep.

THE UNPARDONABLE SIN

This is the sin against the Holy Ghost:—
To speak of bloody power as right divine,
And call on God to guard each vile chief's house,
And for such chiefs, turn men to wolves and swine:—

To go forth killing in White Mercy's name,
Making the trenches stink with spattered brains,
Tearing the nerves and arteries apart,
Sowing with flesh the unreaped golden plains.

In any church's name, to sack fair towns,
And turn each home into a screaming sty,
To make the little children fugitive,
And have their mothers for a quick death cry,—

This is the sin against the Holy Ghost:
This is the sin no purging can atone:—
To send forth rapine in the name of Christ:—
To set the face, and make the heart a stone.

SIMON LEGREE—A NEGRO SERMON

(To be read in your own variety of Negro dialect)

Legree's big house was white and green.
His cotton fields were the best to be seen.
He had strong horses and opulent cattle,
And bloodhounds bold, with chains that would rattle.
His garret was full of curious things:
Books of magic, bags of gold,
And rabbits' feet on long twine strings.
But he went down to the Devil.

Legree, he sported a brass-buttoned coat,
A snakeskin necktie, a blood-red shirt.
Legree he had a beard like a goat,
And a thick hairy neck, and eyes like dirt.
His puffed-out cheeks were fish-belly white,
He had great long teeth, and an appetite.
He ate raw meat, 'most every meal,
And rolled his eyes till the cat would squeal.
His fist was an enormous size
To mash poor niggers that told him lies:
He was surely a witchman in disguise.
But he went down to the Devil.

He wore hip boots, and would wade all day
To capture his slaves that had fled away.
But he went down to the Devil.

He beat poor Uncle Tom to death
Who prayed for Legree with his last breath.
Then Uncle Tom to Eva flew,
To the high sanctoriums bright and new;
And Simon Legree stared up beneath,
And cracked his heels, and ground his teeth:
And went down to the Devil.

He crossed the yard in the storm and gloom;
He went into his grand front room.
He said, "I liked him, and I don't care."
He kicked a hound, he gave a swear;
He tightened his belt, he took a lamp,
Went down cellar to the webs and damp.
There in the middle of the moldy floor
He heaved up a slab, he found a door—
And went down to the Devil.

His lamp blew out, but his eyes burned bright.
Simon Legree stepped down all night—
Down, down to the Devil.
Simon Legree he reached the place,
He saw one half of the human race,
He saw the Devil on a wide green throne,
Gnawing the meat from a big ham bone,
And he said to Mister Devil:
  "I see that you have much to eat—
  A red ham bone is surely sweet.
  I see that you have lion's feet;
  I see your frame is fat and fine,
  I see you drink your poison wine—
  Blood and burning turpentine."

And the Devil said to Simon Legree:
  "I like your style, so wicked and free.
  Come sit and share my throne with me,
  And let us bark and revel."
And there they sit and gnash their teeth,
And each one wears a hop-vine wreath.
They are matching pennies and shooting craps,
They are playing poker and taking naps.
And old Legree is fat and fine:
He heats the fire, he drinks the wine—
Blood and burning turpentine—
            Down, down with the Devil;
            Down, down with the Devil;
            Down, down with the Devil.

THE EAGLE THAT IS FORGOTTEN

*(John P. Altgeld. Born December 30, 1847; died
March 12, 1902)*

Sleep softly . . . eagle forgotten . . . under the stone.
Time has its way with you there, and the clay has its own.

"We have buried him now," thought your foes, and in secret
    rejoiced.
They made a brave show of their mourning, their hatred
    unvoiced.
They had snarled at you, barked at you, foamed at you day
    after day.
Now you were ended. They praised you, . . . and laid you away.

The others that mourned you in silence and terror and truth,
The widow bereft of her crust, and the boy without youth,
The mocked and the scorned and the wounded, the lame and
    the poor
That should have remembered forever, . . . remember no more.

Where are those lovers of yours, on what name do they call
The lost, that in armies wept over your funeral pall?
They call on the names of a hundred high-valiant ones,
A hundred white eagles have risen the sons of your sons,
The zeal in their wings is a zeal that your dreaming began
The valor that wore out your soul in the service of man.

Sleep softly, . . . eagle forgotten . . . under the stone.
Time has its way with you there and the clay has its own.
Sleep on, O bravehearted, O wise man, that kindled the
    flame—
To live in mankind is far more than to live in a name,
To live in mankind, far, far more . . . than to live in a name.

THE BRONCO THAT WOULD NOT BE BROKEN

A little colt—bronco, loaned to the farm
To be broken in time without fury or harm,
Yet black crows flew past you, shouting alarm,
Calling "Beware," with lugubrious singing . . .
The butterflies there in the bush were romancing,
The smell of the grass caught your soul in a trance,
So why be afearing the spurs and the traces,
O bronco that would not be broken of dancing?

You were born with the pride of the lords great and olden
Who danced, through the ages, in corridors golden.
In all the wide farm place the person most human.
You spoke out so plainly with squealing and capering,
With whinnying, snorting, contorting and prancing,
As you dodged your pursuers, looking askance,
With Greek-footed figures, and Parthenon paces,
O bronco that would not be broken of dancing.

The grasshoppers cheered. "Keep whirling," they said.
The insolent sparrows called from the shed
"If men will not laugh, make them wish they were dead."
But arch were your thoughts, all malice displacing,
Though the horse killers came, with snake whips advancing.

You bantered and cantered away your last chance.
And they scourged you, with hell in their speech and their
     faces,
O bronco that would not be broken of dancing.

"Nobody cares for you," rattled the crows,
As you dragged the whole reaper, next day, down the rows.
The three mules held back, yet you danced on your toes.
You pulled like a racer, and kept the mules chasing.
You tangled the harness with bright eyes side-glancing,
While the drunk driver bled you—a pole for a lance—
And the giant mules bit at you—keeping their places,
O bronco that would not be broken of dancing.

In that last afternoon your boyish heart broke.
The hot wind came down like a sledge-hammer stroke.
The bloodsucking flies to a rare feast awoke.
And they searched out your wounds, your death warrant
     tracing.
And the merciful men, their religion enhancing,
Stopped the red reaper, to give you a chance.
Then you died on the prairie, and scorned all disgraces,
O bronco that would not be broken of dancing.

THE GHOSTS OF THE BUFFALOES

Last night at black midnight I woke with a cry,
The windows were shaking, there was thunder on high,
The floor was atremble, the door was ajar,
White fires, crimson fires, shone from afar.
I rushed to the dooryard. The city was gone.
My home was a hut without orchard or lawn.
It was mud smear and logs near a whispering stream,
Nothing else built by man could I see in my dream. . . .

Then . . .
Ghost kings came headlong, row upon row,
Gods of the Indians, torches aglow.
They mounted the bear and the elk and the deer,
And eagles gigantic, agèd and sere,
They rode longhorn cattle, they cried "A-la-la."
They lifted the knife, the bow, and the spear,
They lifted ghost torches from dead fires below,
The midnight made grand with the cry "A-la-la."

The midnight made grand with a red-god charge,
A red-god show,
A red-god show,
"A-la-la, a-la-la, a-la-la, a-la-la."

With bodies like bronze, and terrible eyes
Came the rank and the file, with catamount cries,
Gibbering, yipping, with hollow-skull clacks,
Riding white broncos with skeleton backs,
Scalp hunters, beaded and spangled and bad,
Naked and lustful and foaming and mad,
Flashing primeval demoniac scorn,
Blood thirst and pomp amid darkness reborn,
Power and glory that sleep in the grass
While the winds and the snows and the great rains pass.
They crossed the gray river, thousands abreast,
They rode out in infinite lines to the west,
Tide upon tide of strange fury and foam,
Spirits and wraiths, the blue was their home,
The sky was their goal where the star flags are furled,
And on past those far golden splendors they whirled.
They burned to dim meteors, lost in the deep,
And I turned in dazed wonder, thinking of sleep.

And the wind crept by
Alone, unkempt, unsatisfied,
The wind cried and cried—
Muttered of massacres long past,
Buffaloes in shambles vast . . .
An owl said, "Hark, what is awing?"
I heard a cricket caroling,
I heard a cricket caroling,
I heard a cricket caroling.

Then . . .
Snuffing the lightning that crashed from on high
Rose royal old buffaloes, row upon row.
The lords of the prairie came galloping by.
And I cried in my heart "A-la-la, a-la-la.
A red-god show,
A red-god show,
A-la-la, a-la-la, a-la-la."
Buffaloes, buffaloes, thousands abreast,
A scourge and amazement, they swept to the west.
With black bobbing noses, with red rolling tongues,
Coughing forth steam from their leather-wrapped lungs,

Cows with their calves, bulls big and vain,
Goring the laggards, shaking the mane,
Stamping flint feet, flashing moon eyes,
Pompous and owlish, shaggy and wise.

Like sea cliffs and caves resounded their ranks
With shoulders like waves, and undulant flanks.
Tide upon tide of strange fury and foam,
Spirits and wraiths, the blue was their home,
The sky was their goal where the star flags are furled,
And on past those far golden splendors they whirled.
They burned to dim meteors, lost in the deep,
And I turned in dazed wonder, thinking of sleep.

I heard a cricket's cymbals play,
A scarecrow lightly flapped his rags,
And a pan that hung by his shoulder rang,
Rattled and thumped in a listless way,
And now the wind in the chimney sang,
The wind in the chimney,
The wind in the chimney,
The wind in the chimney,
Seemed to say:—   "Dream, boy, dream,
                     If you anywise can.
                   To dream is the work
                   Of beast or man.
Life is the west-going dream storm's breath,
Life is a dream, the sigh of the skies,
The breath of the stars, that nod on their pillows
With their golden hair mussed over their eyes."
The locust played on his musical wing,
Sang to his mate of love's delight.
I heard the whippoorwill's soft fret.
I heard a cricket caroling,
I heard a cricket caroling,
I heard a cricket say: "Good night, good night,
Good night, good night, . . . good night."

FACTORY WINDOWS ARE ALWAYS BROKEN

Factory windows are always broken.
Somebody's always throwing bricks,
Somebody's always heaving cinders,
Playing ugly Yahoo tricks.

Factory windows are always broken.
Other windows are let alone.
No one throws through the chapel window
The bitter, snarling derisive stone.

Factory windows are always broken.
Something or other is going wrong.
Something is rotten—I think, in Denmark.
End of the factory-window song.

THE PONTOON-BRIDGE MIRACLE

Prophets, preaching in new stars,
Have come in ships of sleep
And built a ghostly pontoon bridge that Michigan Avenue
Can keep.
Have built a causeway bright with sails
Where hares and tortoises may creep,
Where burbling bullfinches, laughing hyenas, whinnying
Shetlands
Climb the steep.

Oh the harp song of our sand dunes
Up this arching avenue,
Oh the voices in the prophet sails
Oh the lovers strolling slowly, two and two!

Though every Yankee patents some iron animals at last,
And does invent his own world's fair,
And world's fair tunes to cheer the air,
This is wild America, not orderly Timbuktu.
So Barnum's old procession holds proud Michigan Avenue,
Again moves by up the pontoon bridge
To the Prophet Avenue.
The thought goes again through the night so dark,
Going up to the North Star ark,
Ostriches two and two,
Kangaroos two and two, behemoths two and two,
Hippogriffs two and two, chimeras two and two.

Oh Radio, Oh Saxophone, Oh Slide Trombone, Oh Horns that
moan:—
The lion, the lion, goes roaring from his cage,
Ten thousand years before your jazz he roared a deeper rage.
And Jumbo, great Jumbo, goes swaying left and right,

Ten thousand years before your jazz his trumpet shook the
night.
But Jenny Lind outsings him still upon the heaven-born wind,
Stands up in Barnum's carriage on that bridge across the vast,
That pontoon span of comet boats arching above the past,
That silvery bridge of dawn across the cold.
In the rigging of their ships the prophets old
Sing with her their songs across the cold.

So, come let us forget our ivory towers, brothers,
Come let us be bold with our songs.

BRYAN, BRYAN, BRYAN, BRYAN

*The Campaign of Eighteen Ninety-Six, as Viewed at
The Time by a Sixteen-Year-Old, etc.*

I

In a nation of one hundred fine, mob-hearted, lynching,
 relenting, repenting millions,
There are plenty of sweeping, swinging, stinging, gorgeous
 things to shout about,
And knock your old blue devils out.

I brag and chant of Bryan, Bryan, Bryan,
Candidate for president who sketched a silver Zion,
The one American Poet who could sing outdoors,
He brought in tides of wonder, of unprecedented splendor
Wild roses from the plains, that made hearts tender,
All the funny circus silks
Of politics unfurled,
Bartlett pears of romance that were honey at the cores,
And torchlights down the street, to the end of the world.

There were truths eternal in the gab and tittle-tattle.
There were real heads broken in the fustian and the rattle.
There were real lines drawn:
Not the silver and the gold,
But Nebraska's cry went eastward against the dour and old,
The mean and cold.
It was eighteen ninety-six, and I was just sixteen
And Altgeld ruled in Springfield, Illinois.
When there came from the sunset Nebraska's shout of joy:
In a coat like a deacon, in a black Stetson hat

He scourged the elephant plutocrats
With barbed wire from the Platte.
The scales dropped from their mighty eyes.
They saw that summer's noon
A tribe of wonders coming
To a marching tune.

Oh, the longhorns from Texas,
The jayhawks from Kansas,
The plop-eyed bungaroo and giant giassicus,
The varmint, chipmunk, bugaboo,
The horned toad, prairie dog and ballyhoo,
From all the newborn states arow,
Bidding the eagles of the West fly on,
Bidding the eagles of the West fly on.
The fawn, prodactyl and thing-a-ma-jig,
The rakaboor, the hellangone,
The whangdoodle, batfowl and pig,
The coyote, wildcat and grizzly in a glow,
In a miracle of health and speed, the whole breed abreast,
They leaped the Mississippi, blue border of the West,
From the Gulf to Canada, two thousand miles long:—
Against the towns of Tubal Cain,
Ah,—sharp was their song.
Against the ways of Tubal Cain, too cunning for the young,
The longhorn calf, the buffalo and wampus gave tongue.

These creatures were defending things Mark Hanna never
        dreamed:
The moods of airy childhood that in desert dews gleamed,
The gossamers and whimsies,
The monkeyshines and didoes
Rank and strange
Of the canyons and the range,
The ultimate fantastics
Of the far western slope,
And of prairie-schooner children
Born beneath the stars.
Beneath falling snows,
Of the babies born at midnight
In the sod huts of lost hope,
With no physician there,
Except a Kansas prayer,
With the Indian raid ahowling through the air.
And all these in their helpless days
By the dour East oppressed,

Mean paternalism
Making their mistakes for them,
Crucifying half the West,
Till the whole Atlantic coast
Seemed a giant spider's nest.

And these children and their sons
At last rode through the cactus,
A cliff of mighty cowboys
On the lope,
With gun and rope.
And all the way to frightened Maine the old East heard them
    call,
And saw our Bryan by a mile lead the wall
Of men and whirling flowers and beasts,
The bard and the prophet of them all.
Prairie avenger, mountain lion,
Bryan, Bryan, Bryan, Bryan,
Gigantic troubadour, speaking like a siege gun,
Smashing Plymouth Rock with his boulders from the West,
And just a hundred miles behind, tornadoes piled across
    the sky,
Blotting out sun and moon,
A sign on high.

Headlong, dazed and blinking in the weird green light,
The scalawags made moan, afraid to fight.

II

When Bryan came to Springfield, and Altgeld gave him greet-
    ing,
Rochester was deserted, Divernon was deserted,
Mechanicsburg, Riverton, Chickenbristle, Cotton Hill,
Empty: for all Sangamon drove to the meeting—
In silver-decked racing cart,
Buggy, buckboard, carryall.
Carriage, phaeton, whatever would haul,
And silver-decked farm wagons gritted, banged and rolled,
With the new tale of Bryan by the iron tires told.
The State House loomed afar,
A speck, a hive, a football,
A captive balloon!
And the town was all one spreading wing of bunting, plumes,
    and sunshine,
Every rag and flag, and Bryan picture sold,

When the rigs in many a dusty line
Jammed our streets at noon,
And joined the wild parade against the power of gold.

We roamed, we boys from high school,
With mankind,
While Springfield gleamed, silk-lined.
Oh, Tom Dines, and Art Fitzgerald,
And the gangs that they could get!
I can hear them yelling yet.
Helping the incantation, defying aristocracy,
With every bridle gone,
Ridding the world of the low-down mean,
Bidding the eagles of the West fly on,
Bidding the eagles of the West fly on,
We were bully, wild and woolly,
Never yet curried below the knees.
We saw flowers in the air,
Fair as the Pleiades, bright as Orion,
Hopes of all mankind,
Made rare, resistless, thrice refined.
Oh, we bucks from every Springfield ward!
Colts of democracy—
Yet time winds out of Chaos from the star fields of the Lord.

The long parade rolled on. I stood by my best girl.
She was a cool young citizen, with wise and laughing eyes.
With my necktie by my ear, I was stepping on my dear,
But she kept like a pattern, without a shaken curl.

She wore in her hair a brave prairie rose.
Her gold chums cut her, for that was not the pose.
No Gibson Girl would wear it in that fresh way.
But we were fairy Democrats, and this was our day.

The earth rocked like the ocean, the sidewalk was a deck.
The houses for the moment were lost in the wide wreck.
And the bands played strange and stranger music as they
    trailed along.
Against the ways of Tubal Cain,
Ah, sharp was their song!
The demons in the bricks, the demons in the grass,
The demons in the bank vaults peered out to see us pass,
And the angels in the trees, the angels in the grass,
The angels in the flags peered out to see us pass.

And the sidewalk was our chariot, and the flowers bloomed
        higher,
And the street turned to silver and the grass turned to fire,
And then it was but grass, and the town was there again,
A place for women and men.

III

Then we stood where we could see every band,
And the speaker's stand.
And Bryan took the platform.
And he was introduced.
And he lifted his hand
And cast a new spell.
Progressive silence fell
In Springfield,
In Illinois,
Around the world.
Then we heard these glacial boulders across the prairie rolled:
"The people have a right to make their own mistakes. . . .
You shall not crucify mankind
Upon a cross of gold."

And everybody heard him—
In the streets and State House yard.
And everybody heard him
In Springfield, in Illinois,
Around and around and around the world,
That danced upon its axis
And like a darling bronco whirled.

IV

July, August, suspense.
Wall Street lost to sense.
August, September, October,
More suspense,
And the whole East down like a wind-smashed fence.

Then Hanna to the rescue,
Hanna of Ohio,
Rallying the roller tops,
Rallying the bucket shops.
Threatening drouth and death,
Promising manna,
Rallying the trusts against the bawling flannelmouth;

Invading misers' cellars,
Tin cans, socks,
Melting down the rocks,
Pouring out the long green to a million workers,
Spondulix by the mountain load, to stop each new tornado,
And beat the cheapskate, blatherskite,
Populistic, anarchistic,
Deacon—desperado.

V

Election night at midnight:
Boy Bryan's defeat.
Defeat of western silver.
Defeat of the wheat.
Victory of letter files
And plutocrats in miles
With dollar signs upon their coats,
Diamond watch chains on their vests
And spats on their feet.
Victory of custodians, Plymouth Rock,
And all that inbred landlord stock.
Victory of the neat.
Defeat of the aspen groves of Colorado valleys,
The bluebells of the Rockies,
And bluebonnets of old Texas, by the Pittsburgh alleys.
Defeat of alfalfa and the Mariposa lily.
Defeat of the Pacific and the long Mississippi.
Defeat of the young by the old and silly.
Defeat of tornadoes by the poison vats supreme.
Defeat of my boyhood, defeat of my dream.

VI

Where is McKinley, that respectable McKinley,
The man without an angle or a tangle,
Who soothed down the city man and soothed down the farmer,
The German, the Irish, the Southerner, the Northerner,
Who climbed every greasy pole, and slipped through every
  crack;
Who soothed down the gambling hall, the barroom, the church,
The devil vote, the angel vote, the neutral vote,
The desperately wicked, and their victims on the rack,
The gold vote, the silver vote, the brass vote, the lead vote,
Every vote? . . .

Where is McKinley, Mark Hanna's McKinley,
His slave, his echo, his suit of clothes?
Gone to join the shadows, with the pomps of that time,
And the flame of that summer's prairie rose.

Where is Cleveland whom the Democratic platform
Read from the party in a glorious hour,
Gone to join the shadows with pitchfork Tillman,
And sledge-hammer Altgeld who wrecked his power.

Where is Hanna, bulldog Hanna,
Low-browed Hanna, who said: "Stand pat"?
Gone to his place with old Pierpont Morgan.
Gone somewhere . . . with lean rat Platt.

Where is Roosevelt, the young dude cowboy,
Who hated Bryan, then aped his way?
Gone to join the shadows with mighty Cromwell
And tall King Saul, till the judgment day.

Where is Altgeld, brave as the truth,
Whose name the few still say with tears?
Gone to join the ironies with old John Brown,
Whose fame rings loud for a thousand years.

Where is that boy, that heaven-born Bryan,
That Homer Bryan, who sang from the West?
Gone to join the shadows with Altgeld the Eagle,
Where the kings and the slaves and the troubadours rest.

GENERAL WILLIAM BOOTH
ENTERS INTO HEAVEN

*(To be sung to the tune of "The Blood of the Lamb"
with indicated instrument.)*

(Bass drum beaten loudly)
Booth led boldly with his big bass drum—
(Are you washed in the blood of the Lamb?)
The saints smiled gravely and they said: "He's come."
(Are you washed in the blood of the Lamb?)
Walking lepers followed, rank on rank,
Lurching bravoes from the ditches dank,
Drabs from the alleyways and drug fiends pale—
Minds still passion-ridden, soul powers frail:—
Vermin-eaten saints with moldy breath,

Unwashed legions with the ways of death—
(Are you washed in the blood of the Lamb?)

(Banjos)
Every slum had sent its half a score
The round world over. (Booth had groaned for more.)
Every banner that the wide world flies
Bloomed with glory and transcendent dyes.
Big-voiced lasses made their banjos bang;
Tranced, fanatical they shrieked and sang:—
"Are you washed in the blood of the Lamb?"
Hallelujah! It was queer to see
Bull-necked convicts with that land make free.
Loons with trumpets blowed a blare, blare, blare
On, on upward thro' the golden air!
(Are you washed in the blood of the Lamb?)

(Bass drum slower and softer)
Booth died blind and still by faith he trod,
Eyes still dazzled by the ways of God.
Booth led boldly, and he looked the chief,
Eagle countenance in sharp relief,
Beard aflying, air of high command
Unabated in that holy land.

(Sweet flute music)
Jesus came from out the courthouse door,
Stretched his hands above the passing poor.
Booth saw not, but led his queer ones there
Round and round the mighty courthouse square.
Then, in an instant all that blear review
Marched on spotless, clad in raiment new.
The lame were straightened, withered limbs uncurled
And blind eyes opened on a new, sweet world.

(Bass drum louder)
Drabs and vixens in a flash made whole!
Gone was the weasel head, the snout, the jowl!
Sages and sibyls now, and athletes clean,
Rulers of empires, and of forests green!

*(Grand chorus of all instruments. Tambourine
to the foreground)*
The hosts were sandaled, and their wings were fire!
(Are you washed in the blood of the Lamb?)
But their noise played havoc with the angel choir.

(Are you washed in the blood of the Lamb?)
Oh, shout salvation! It was good to see
Kings and princes by the Lamb set free.
The banjos rattled and the tambourines
Jing-jing-jingled in the hands of queens.

(*Reverently sung, no instruments*)
And when Booth halted by the curb for prayer
He saw his Master thro' the flag-filled air.
Christ came gently with a robe and crown
For Booth the soldier, while the throng knelt down.
He saw King Jesus. They were face to face,
And he knelt aweeping in that holy place.
Are you washed in the blood of the Lamb?

THE CONGO

A Study of the Negro Race

(*Being a memorial to Ray Eldred, a Disciple missionary
of the Congo River*)

I. THEIR BASIC SAVAGERY

Fat black bucks in a wine-barrel room,
Barrel-house kings, with feet unstable,

A deep, rolling bass.

Sagged and reeled and pounded on the table,
Pounded on the table,
Beat an empty barrel with the handle of a
broom,
Hard as they were able,
Boom, boom, BOOM,
With a silk umbrella and the handle of a
broom,
Boomlay, boomlay, boomlay, BOOM.
THEN I had religion, THEN I had a vision.
I could not turn from their revel in derision.

More deliberate. Solemnly chanted.

THEN I SAW THE CONGO, CREEPING
THROUGH THE BLACK,
CUTTING THROUGH THE FOREST WITH A
GOLDEN TRACK.
Then along that riverbank
A thousand miles
Tattooed cannibals danced in files;
Then I heard the boom of the blood-lust song

A rapidly piling climax of speed and racket.

And a thigh bone beating on a tin-pan gong.
And "BLOOD" screamed the whistles and the
    fifes of the warriors,
"BLOOD" screamed the skull-faced, lean witch
    doctors,
"Whirl ye the deadly voodoo rattle,
Harry the uplands,
Steal all the cattle,
Rattle-rattle, rattle-rattle,
Bing.

With a philosophic pause.

Boomlay, boomlay, boomlay, BOOM,"
A roaring, epic, ragtime tune
From the mouth of the Congo
To the Mountains of the Moon.
Death is an elephant,
Torch-eyed and horrible,

Shrilly and with a heavily accented meter.

Foam-flanked and terrible,
BOOM, steal the pygmies,
BOOM, kill the Arabs,
BOOM, kill the white men,
Hoo, Hoo, Hoo.

Like the wind in the chimney.

Listen to the yell of Leopold's ghost
Burning in hell for his hand-maimed host.
Hear how the demons chuckle and yell
Cutting his hands off, down in hell.
Listen to the creepy proclamation,
Blown through the lairs of the forest nation,
Blown past the white ants' hill of clay,
Blown past the marsh where the butterflies
    play:—

All the "o" sounds very golden. Heavy accents very heavy. Light accents very light. Last line whispered.

"Be careful what you do,
Or Mumbo-Jumbo, god of the Congo,
And all of the other
Gods of the Congo,
Mumbo-Jumbo will hoo-doo you,
Mumbo-Jumbo will hoo-doo you,
Mumbo-Jumbo will hoo-doo you."

II. THEIR IRREPRESSIBLE HIGH SPIRITS

Rather shrill and high.

Wild crap shooters with a whoop and a call
Danced the juba in their gambling hall
And laughed fit to kill, and shook the town,
And guyed the policemen and laughed them down
With a boomlay, boomlay, boomlay, BOOM.

Read exactly as in first section.

THEN I SAW THE CONGO, CREEPING THROUGH THE
    BLACK

CUTTING THROUGH THE FOREST WITH A GOLDEN
                                    TRACK,

Lay emphasis   A Negro fairyland swung into view,
on the   A minstrel river
delicate
ideas.   Where dreams come true.
Keep as light- The ebony palace soared on high
footed as
possible.   Through the blossoming trees to the evening sky.
                 The inlaid porches and casements shone
                 With gold and ivory and elephant bone.
                 And the black crowd laughed till their sides were
                                    sore
                 At the baboon butler in the agate door,
                 And the well-known tunes of the parrot band
                 That trilled on the bushes of that magic land.
With   A troupe of skull-faced witchmen came
pomposity.   Through the agate doorway in suits of flame,
                 Yea, long-tailed coats with a gold-leaf crust
                 And hats that were covered with diamond dust.
                 And the crowd in the court gave a whoop and a
                                    call
                 And danced the juba from wall to wall.
With a great   But the witchmen suddenly stilled the throng
deliberation   With a stern cold glare, and a stern old song:—
and
ghostliness.   "Mumbo-Jumbo will hoo-doo you." . . .
With over-   Just then from the doorway, as fat as shotes,
whelming as-   Came the cakewalk princes in their long red coats,
surance,
good cheer,   Canes with a brilliant lacquer shine,
and pomp.   And tall silk hats that were red as wine.
                 And they pranced with their butterfly partners
                                    there,
With grow-   Coal-black maidens with pearls in their hair,
ing speed and Knee skirts trimmed with the jassamine sweet,
sharply
marked   And bells on their ankles and little black feet.
dance   And the couples railed at the chant and the
rhythm.   frown
                 Of the witchmen lean, and laughed them down.
                 (Oh, rare was the revel, and well worth while,
                 That made those glowering witchmen smile.)
                 The cakewalk royalty then began
                 To walk for a cake that was tall as a man
                 To the tune of "Boomlay, boomlay, BOOM,"
With a touch   While the witchmen laughed, with a sinister air,
of Negro dia- And sang with the scalawags prancing there:-
lect, and as
rapidly as   "Walk with care, walk with care,
possible   Or Mumbo-Jumbo, god of the Congo,
toward the
end.   And all of the other gods of the Congo,

Mumbo-Jumbo will hoo-doo you.
Beware, beware, walk with care,
Boomlay, boomlay, boomlay, boom.
Boomlay, boomlay, boomlay, boom.
Boomlay, boomlay, boomlay, boom.
Boomlay, boomlay, boomlay, BOOM."

Slow philo-
sophic calm. (Oh, rare was the revel, and well worth while
That made those glowering witchmen smile.)

III. THE HOPE OF THEIR RELIGION

Heavy bass. A good old Negro in the slums of the town
With a literal Preached at a sister for her velvet gown.
imitation of Howled at a brother for his low-down ways,
camp-meet- His prowling, guzzling, sneak-thief days.
ing racket, Beat on the Bible till he wore it out
and trance. Starting the jubilee revival shout.
And some had visions, as they stood on chairs,
And sang of Jacob, and the golden stairs,
And they all repented, a thousand strong
From their stupor and savagery and sin and wrong
And slammed with their hymnbooks till they shook
    the room
With "glory, glory, glory."
And "Boom, boom, BOOM."

THEN I SAW THE CONGO, CREEPING THROUGH THE
Exactly as in   BLACK,
the first CUTTING THROUGH THE JUNGLE WITH A GOLDEN
section.   TRACK.
Begin with And the gray sky opened like a new-rent veil
terror and And showed the apostles with their coats of mail.
power, end In bright white steel they were seated round
with joy. And their fire eyes watched where the Congo
    wound.
And the twelve apostles, from their thrones on high
Thrilled all the forest with their heavenly cry:—

Sung to the "Mumbo-Jumbo will die in the jungle;
tune of Never again will he hoo-doo you,
"Hark, ten Never again will he hoo-doo you."
thousand
harps and
voices."

With Then along that river, a thousand miles
growing The vine-snared trees fell down in files.
deliberation Pioneer angels cleared the way
and joy. For a Congo paradise, for babes at play,
For sacred capitals, for temples clean.
Gone were the skull-faced witchmen lean.

In a rather high key—as delicately as possible.

There, where the wild ghost gods had wailed
A million boats of the angels sailed
With oars of silver, and prows of blue
And silken pennants that the sun shone through.
'Twas a land transfigured, 'twas a new creation.
Oh, a singing wind swept the Negro nation

To the tune of "Hark, ten thousand harps and voices."

And on through the backwoods clearing flew:—
"Mumbo-Jumbo is dead in the jungle.
Never again will he hoo-doo you.
Never again will he hoo-doo you."

Redeemed were the forests, the beasts and the men,
And only the vulture dared again
By the far, lone mountains of the moon
To cry, in the silence, the Congo tune:—

Dying down into a penetrating, terrified whisper.

"Mumbo-Jumbo will hoo-doo you,
Mumbo-Jumbo will hoo-doo you.
Mumbo . . . Jumbo . . . will . . . hoo-doo . . . you."

ABRAHAM LINCOLN WALKS AT MIDNIGHT

(In Springfield, Illinois)

It is portentous, and a thing of state
That here at midnight, in our little town
A mourning figure walks, and will not rest,
Near the old courthouse pacing up and down,

Or by his homestead, or in shadowed yards
He lingers where his children used to play,
Or through the market, on the well-worn stones
He stalks until the dawn stars burn away.

A bronzed, lank man! His suit of ancient black,
A famous high top hat and plain worn shawl
Make him the quaint great figure that men love,
The prairie lawyer, master of us all.

He cannot sleep upon his hillside now.
He is among us—as in times before!
And we who toss and lie awake for long
Breathe deep, and start, to see him pass the door.

His head is bowed. He thinks on men and kings.
Yea, when the sick world cries, how can he sleep?

Too many peasants fight, they know not why,
Too many homesteads in black terror weep.

The sins of all the war lords burn his heart.
He sees the dreadnaughts scouring every main.
He carries on his shawl-wrapped shoulders now
The bitterness, the folly and the pain.

He cannot rest until a spirit-dawn
Shall come;—the shining hope of Europe free:
The league of sober folk, the Workers' Earth,
Bringing long peace to Cornland, Alp and Sea.

It breaks his heart that kings must murder still,
That all his hours of travail here for men
Seem yet in vain. And who will bring white peace
That he may sleep upon his hill again?

WALLACE STEVENS
(1879–1955)

PETER QUINCE AT THE CLAVIER

I

Just as my fingers on these keys
Make music, so the selfsame sounds
On my spirit make a music, too.

Music is feeling, then, not sound;
And thus it is that what I feel,
Here in this room, desiring you,

Thinking of your blue-shadowed silk,
Is music. It is like the strain
Waked in the elders by Susanna.

Of a green evening, clear and warm,
She bathed in her still garden, while
The red-eyed elders watching, felt

The basses of their beings throb
In witching chords, and their thin blood
Pulse pizzicati of Hosanna.

II

In the green water, clear and warm,
Susanna lay.
She searched
The touch of springs,
And found
Concealed imaginings.
She sighed,
For so much melody.

Upon the bank, she stood
In the cool
Of spent emotions.

She felt, among the leaves,
The dew
Of old devotions.

She walked upon the grass,
Still quavering.
The winds were like her maids,
On timid feet,
Fetching her woven scarves,
Yet wavering.

A breath upon her hand
Muted the night.
She turned—
A cymbal crashed,
And roaring horns.

III

Soon, with a noise like tambourines,
Came her attendant Byzantines.

They wondered why Susanna cried
Against the elders by her side;

And as they whispered, the refrain
Was like a willow swept by rain.

Anon, their lamps' uplifted flame
Revealed Susanna and her shame.

And then, the simpering Byzantines
Fled, with a noise like tambourines.

IV

Beauty is momentary in the mind—
The fitful tracing of a portal;
But in the flesh it is immortal.

The body dies; the body's beauty lives.
So evenings die, in their green going,
A wave, interminably flowing.
So gardens die, their meek breath scenting
The cowl of winter, done repenting.
So maidens die, to the auroral
Celebration of a maiden's choral.

Susanna's music touched the bawdy strings
Of those white elders; but, escaping,
Left only Death's ironic scraping.
Now, in its immortality, it plays
On the clear viol of her memory,
And makes a constant sacrament of praise.

SUNDAY MORNING

I

Complacencies of the peignoir, and late
Coffee and oranges in a sunny chair,
And the green freedom of a cockatoo
Upon a rug mingle to dissipate
The holy hush of ancient sacrifice.
She dreams a little, and she feels the dark
Encroachment of that old catastrophe,
As a calm darkens among water lights.
The pungent oranges and bright, green wings
Seem things in some procession of the dead,
Winding across wide water, without sound.
The day is like wide water, without sound,
Stilled for the passing of her dreaming feet
Over the seas, to silent Palestine,
Dominion of the blood and sepulcher.

II

Why should she give her bounty to the dead?
What is divinity if it can come
Only in silent shadows and in dreams?
Shall she not find in comforts of the sun,
In pungent fruit and bright, green wings, or else
In any balm or beauty of the earth,
Things to be cherished like the thought of heaven?
Divinity must live within herself:
Passions of rain, or moods in falling snow;
Grievings in loneliness, or unsubdued
Elations when the forest blooms; gusty
Emotions on wet roads on autumn nights;
All pleasures and all pains, remembering
The bough of summer and the winter branch.
These are the measures destined for her soul.

III

Jove in the clouds had his inhuman birth.
No mother suckled him, no sweet land gave
Large-mannered motions to his mythy mind.
He moved among us, as a muttering king,
Magnificent, would move among his hinds,
Until our blood, commingling, virginal,
With heaven, brought such requital to desire
The very hinds discerned it, in a star.
Shall our blood fail? Or shall it come to be
The blood of paradise? And shall the earth
Seem all of paradise that we shall know?
The sky will be much friendlier then than now,
A part of labor and a part of pain,
And next in glory to enduring love,
Not this dividing and indifferent blue.

IV

She says, "I am content when wakened birds,
Before they fly, test the reality
Of misty fields, by their sweet questionings;
But when the birds are gone, and their warm fields
Return no more, where, then, is paradise?"
There is not any haunt of prophecy,
Nor any old chimera of the grave,
Neither the golden underground, nor isle
Melodious, where spirits gat them home,
Nor visionary south, nor cloudy palm
Remote on heaven's hill, that has endured
As April's green endures; or will endure
Like her remembrance of awakened birds,
Or her desire for June and evening, tipped
By the consummation of the swallow's wings.

V

She says, "But in contentment I still feel
The need of some imperishable bliss."
Death is the mother of beauty; hence from her,
Alone, shall come fulfillment to our dreams
And our desires. Although she strews the leaves
Of sure obliteration on our paths,
The path sick sorrow took, the many paths
Where triumph rang its brassy phrase, or love
Whispered a little out of tenderness,

She makes the willow shiver in the sun
For maidens who were wont to sit and gaze
Upon the grass, relinquished to their feet.
She causes boys to pile new plums and pears
On disregarded plate. The maidens taste
And stray impassioned in the littering leaves.

VI

Is there no change of death in paradise?
Does ripe fruit never fall? Or do the boughs
Hang always heavy in that perfect sky,
Unchanging, yet so like our perishing earth,
With rivers like our own that seek for seas
They never find, the same receding shores
That never touch with inarticulate pang?
Why set the pear upon those riverbanks
Or spice the shores with odors of the plum?
Alas, that they should wear our colors there,
The silken weavings of our afternoons,
And pick the strings of our insipid lutes!
Death is the mother of beauty, mystical,
Within whose burning bosom we devise
Our earthly mothers waiting, sleeplessly.

VII

Supple and turbulent, a ring of men
Shall chant in orgy on a summer morn
Their boisterous devotion to the sun,
Not as a god, but as a god might be,
Naked among them, like a savage source.
Their chant shall be a chant of paradise,
Out of their blood, returning to the sky;
And in their chant shall enter, voice by voice,
The windy lake wherein their lord delights,
The trees, like seraphim, and echoing hills,
That choir among themselves long afterward.
They shall know well the heavenly fellowship
Of men that perish and of summer morn.
And whence they came and whither they shall go
The dew upon their feet shall manifest.

VIII

She hears, upon that water without sound,
A voice that cries, "The tomb in Palestine

Is not the porch of spirits lingering.
It is the grave of Jesus, where he lay."
We live in an old chaos of the sun,
Or old dependency of day and night,
Or island solitude, unsponsored, free,
Of that wide water, inescapable.
Deer walk upon our mountains, and the quail
Whistle about us their spontaneous cries;
Sweet berries ripen in the wilderness;
And, in the isolation of the sky,
At evening, casual flocks of pigeons make
Ambiguous undulations as they sink,
Downward to darkness, on extended wings.

LE MONOCLE DE MON ONCLE

"Mother of heaven, regina of the clouds,
O scepter of the sun, crown of the moon,
There is not nothing, no, no, never nothing,
Like the clashed edges of two words that kill."
And so I mocked her in magnificent measure.
Or was it that I mocked myself alone?
I wish that I might be a thinking stone.
The sea of spuming thought foists up again
The radiant bubble that she was. And then
A deep uppouring from some saltier well
Within me, bursts its watery syllable.

II

A red bird flies across the golden floor.
It is a red bird that seeks out his choir
Among the choirs of wind and wet and wing.
A torrent will fall from him when he finds.
Shall I uncrumple this much-crumpled thing?
I am a man of fortune greetings heirs;
For it has come that thus I greet the spring.
These choirs of welcome choir for me farewell.
No spring can follow past meridian.
Yet you persist with anecdotal bliss
To make believe a starry *connaissance*.

III

Is it for nothing, then, that old Chinese
Sat tittivating by their mountain pools

Or in the Yangtse studied out their beards?
I shall not play the flat historic scale.
You know how Utamaro's beauties sought
The end of love in their all-speaking braids.
You know the mountainous coiffures of Bath.
Alas! Have all the barbers lived in vain
That not one curl in nature has survived?
Why, without pity on these studious ghosts.
Do you come dripping in your hair from sleep?

IV

This luscious and impeccable fruit of life
Falls, it appears, of its own weight to earth.
When you were Eve, its acrid juice was sweet,
Untasted, in its heavenly, orchard air.
An apple serves as well as any skull
To be the book in which to read a round,
And is an excellent, in that it is composed
Of what, like skulls, comes rotting back to ground.
But it excels in this, that as the fruit
Of love, it is a book too mad to read
Before one merely reads to pass the time.

V

In the high west there burns a furious star.
It is for fiery boys that star was set
And for sweet-smelling virgins close to them.
The measure of the intensity of love
Is measure, also, of the verve of earth.
For me, the firefly's quick, electric stroke
Ticks tediously the time of one more year.
And you? Remember how the crickets came
Out of their mother grass, like little kin,
In the pale nights, when your first imagery
Found inklings of your bond to all that dust.

VI

If men at forty will be painting lakes
The ephemeral blues must merge for them in one,
The basic slate, the universal hue.
There is a substance in us that prevails.
But in our amours amorists discern
Such fluctuations that their scrivening
Is breathless to attend each quirky turn.

When amorists grow bald, then amours shrink
Into the compass and curriculum
Of introspective exiles, lecturing.
It is a theme for Hyacinth alone.

VII

The mules that angels ride come slowly down
The blazing passes, from beyond the sun.
Descensions of their tinkling bells arrive.
These muleteers are dainty of their way.
Meantime, centurions guffaw and beat
Their shrilling tankards on the table boards.
This parable, in sense, amounts to this:
The honey of heaven may or may not come,
But that of earth both comes and goes at once.
Suppose these couriers brought amid their train
A damsel heightened by eternal bloom.

VIII

Like a dull scholar, I behold, in love,
An ancient aspect touching a new mind.
It comes, it blooms, it bears its fruit and dies.
This trivial trope reveals a way of truth.
Our bloom is gone. We are the fruit thereof.
Two golden gourds distended on our vines,
Into the autumn weather, splashed with frost,
Distorted by hale fatness, turned grotesque.
We hang like warty squashes, streaked and rayed,
The laughing sky will see the two of us
Washed into rinds by rotting winter rains.

IX

In verses wild with motion, full of din,
Loudened by cries, by clashes, quick and sure
As the deadly thought of men accomplishing
Their curious fates in war, come, celebrate
The faith of forty, ward of Cupido.
Most venerable heart, the lustiest conceit
Is not too lusty for your broadening.
I quiz all sounds, all thoughts, all everything
For the music and manner of the paladins
To make oblation fit. Where shall I find
Bravura adequate to this great hymn?

X

The fops of fancy in their poems leave
Memorabilia of the mystic spouts,
Spontaneously watering their gritty soils.
I am a yeoman, as such fellows go.
I know no magic trees, no balmy boughs,
No silver-ruddy, go d-vermilion fruits.
But, after all, I know a tree that bears
A semb.ance to the thing I have in mind.
It stands gigantic, with a certain tip
To which all birds come sometime in their time.
But when they go that tip still tips the tree.

XI

If sex were all, then every trembling hand
Could make us squeak, ike do ls, the wished-for words.
But note the unconscionable treachery oi ate,
That makes us weep iaugh grunt and groan, and shout
Doleful heroics, pinching gestures iorth
From madness or de ght, without regard
To that first, foremost law. Anguishing hour!
Last night, we sat beside a pool of pink,
Clippered with lilies scudding the bright chromes,
Keen to the point of starlight, while a frog
Boomed from his very belly odious chords.

XII

A blue pigeon it is, that circles the blue sky.
On sidelong wing, around and round and round.
A white pigeon it is, that flutters to the ground,
Grown tired of flight. Like a dark rabbi, I
Observed, when young, the nature of mankind,
In lordly study. Every day, I found
Man proved a gobbet in my mincing world.
Like a rose rabbi, later, I pursued,
And still pursue, the origin and course
Of love, but until now I never knew
That fluttering things have so distinct a shade.

FLYER'S FALL

This man escaped the dirty fates,
Knowing that he did nobly, as he died.

Darkness, nothingness of human afterdeath,
Receive and keep him in the deepnesses of space—

Profundum, physical thunder, dimension in which
We believe without belief, beyond belief.

MEN MADE OUT OF WORDS

What should we be without the sexual myth,
The human reverie or poem of death?

Castratos of moon-mash—Life consists
Of propositions about life. The human

Reverie is a solitude in which
We compose these propositions, torn by dreams,

By the terrible incantations of defeats
And by the fear that defeats and dreams are one.

The whole race is a poet that writes down
The eccentric propositions of its fate.

THE GLASS OF WATER

That the glass would melt in heat,
That the water would freeze in cold,
Shows that this object is merely a state,
One of many, between two poles. So,
In the metaphysical, there are these poles.

Here in the center stands the glass. Light
Is the lion that comes down to drink. There
And in that state, the glass is a pool.
Ruddy are his eyes and ruddy are his claws
When light comes down to wet his frothy jaws

And in the water winding weeds move round.
And there and in another state—the refractions,

The *metaphysica*, the plastic parts of poems
Crash in the mind— But, fat Jocundus, worrying
About what stands here in the center, not the glass,

But in the center of our lives, this time, this day,
It is a state, this spring among the politicians
Playing cards. In a village of the indigenes,
One would have still to discover. Among the dogs and dung,
One would continue to contend with one's ideas.

ANECDOTE OF THE JAR

I placed a jar in Tennessee,
And round it was, upon a hill.
It made the slovenly wilderness
Surround that hill.

The wilderness rose up to it,
And sprawled around, no longer wild.
The jar was round upon the ground
And tall and of a port in air.

It took dominion everywhere.
The jar was gray and bare.
It did not give of bird or bush,
Like nothing else in Tennessee.

THE EMPEROR OF ICE CREAM

Call the roller of big cigars,
The muscular one, and bid him whip
In kitchen cups concupiscent curds.
Let the wenches dawdle in such dress
As they are used to wear, and let the boys
Bring flowers in last month's newspapers.
Let be be finale of seem.
The only emperor is the emperor of ice cream.

Take from the dresser of deal,
Lacking the three glass knobs, that sheet
On which she embroidered fantails once
And spread it so as to cover her face.
If her horny feet protrude, they come
To show how cold she is, and dumb.
Let the lamp affix its beam.
The only emperor is the emperor of ice cream.

DRY LOAF

It is equal to living in a tragic land
To live in a tragic time.
Regard now the sloping, mountainous rocks
And the river that batters its way over stones,
Regard the hovels of those that live in this land.

That was what I painted behind the loaf,
The rocks not even touched by snow,
The pines along the river and the dry men blown
Brown as the bread, thinking of birds
Flying from burning countries and brown sand shores,

Birds that came like dirty water in waves
Flowing above the rocks, flowing over the sky,
As if the sky was a current that bore them along,
Spreading them as waves spread flat on the shore,
One after another washing the mountains bare.

It was the battering of drums I heard
It was hunger, it was the hungry that cried
And the waves, the waves were soldiers moving,
Marching and marching in a tragic time
Below me, on the asphalt, under the trees.

It was soldiers went marching over the rocks
And still the birds came, came in watery flocks,
Because it was spring and the birds had to come.
No doubt that soldiers had to be marching
And that drums had to be rolling, rolling rolling.

TO THE ONE OF FICTIVE MUSIC

Sister and mother and diviner love,
And of the sisterhood of the living dead
Most near, most clear, and of the clearest bloom,
And of the fragrant mothers the most dear
And queen, and of diviner love the day
And flame and summer and sweet fire, no thread
Of cloudy silver sprinkles in your gown
Its venom of renown, and on your head
No crown is simpler than the simple hair.

Now, of the music summoned by the birth
That separates us from the wind and sea,
Yet leaves us in them, until earth becomes,
By being so much of the things we are,
Gross effigy and simulacrum, none
Gives motion to perfection more serene
Than yours, out of our imperfections wrought,
Most rare, or ever of more kindred air
In the laborious weaving that you wear.

For so retentive of themselves are men
That music is intensest which proclaims
The near, the clear, and vaunts the clearest bloom,
And of all vigils musing the obscure,
That apprehends the most which sees and names,
As in your name, an image that is sure,
Among the arrant spices of the sun,
O bough and bush and scented vine, in whom
We give ourselves our likest issuance.

Yet not too like, yet not so like to be
Too near, too clear, saving a little to endow
Our feigning with the strange unlike, whence springs
The difference that heavenly pity brings.
For this, musician, in your girdle fixed
Bear other perfumes. On your pale head wear
A band entwining, set with fatal stones.
Unreal, give back to us what once you gave:
The imagination that we spurned and crave.

BANTAMS IN PINE WOODS

Chieftain Iffucan of Azcan in caftan
Of tan with henna hackles, halt!

Damned universal cock, as if the sun
Was blackamoor to bear your blazing tail.

Fat! Fat! Fat! Fat! I am the personal.
Your world is you. I am my world.

You ten-foot poet among inchlings. Fat!
Begone! An inchling bristles in these pines,

Bristles, and points their Appalachian tángs,
And fears not portly Azcan nor his hoos.

THE IDEA OF ORDER AT KEY WEST

She sang beyond the genius of the sea.
The water never formed to mind or voice,
Like a body wholly body, fluttering
Its empty sleeves; and yet its mimic motion
Made constant cry, caused constantly a cry,
That was not ours although we understood,
Inhuman, of the veritable ocean.

The sea was not a mask. No more was she.
The song and water were not medleyed sound
Even if what she sang was what she heard,
Since what she sang was uttered word by word.
It may be that in all her phrases stirred
The grinding water and the gasping wind;
But it was she and not the sea we heard.

For she was the maker of the song she sang.
The ever-hooded, tragic-gestured sea
Was merely a place by which she walked to sing.
Whose spirit is this? we said, because we knew
It was the spirit that we sought and knew
That we should ask this often as she sang.

If it was only the dark voice of the sea
That rose, or even colored by many waves;
If it was only the outer voice of sky
And cloud, of the sunken coral water-walled,
However clear, it would have been deep air,
The heaving speech of air, a summer sound
Repeated in a summer without end
And sound alone. But it was more than that,
More even than her voice, and ours, among
The meaningless plungings of water and the wind,
Theatrical distances, bronze shadows heaped
On high horizons, mountainous atmospheres
Of sky and sea.

       It was her voice that made
The sky acutest at its vanishing.
She measured to the hour its solitude.
She was the single artificer of the world
In which she sang. And when she sang, the sea,
Whatever self it had, became the self
That was her song, for she was the maker. Then we,
As we beheld her striding there alone,

Knew that there never was a world for her
Except the one she sang and, singing, made.

Ramon Fernandez, tell me, if you know,
Why, when the singing ended and we turned
Toward the town, tell why the glassy lights,
The lights in the fishing boats at anchor there,
As the night descended, tilting in the air,
Mastered the night and portioned out the sea,
Fixing emblazoned zones and fiery poles,
Arranging, deepening, enchanting night.

Oh! Blessed rage for order, pale Ramon,
The maker's rage to order words of the sea,
Words of the fragrant portals, dimly starred,
And of ourselves and of our origins,
In ghostlier demarcations, keener sounds.

A POSTCARD FROM THE VOLCANO

Children picking up our bones
Will never know that these were once
As quick as foxes on the hill;

And that in autumn, when the grapes
Made sharp air sharper by their smell
These had a being, breathing frost;

And least will guess that with our bones
We left much more, left what still is
The look of things, left what we felt

At what we saw. The spring clouds blow
Above the shuttered mansion house,
Beyond our gate and the windy sky

Cries out a literate despair.
We knew for long the mansion's look
And what we said of it became

A part of what it is. . . . Children,
Still weaving budded aureoles,
Will speak our speech and never know,

Will say of the mansion that it seems
As if he that lived there left behind
A spirit storming in blank walls,

A dirty house in a gutted world,
A tatter of shadows peaked to white,
Smeared with the gold of the opulent sun.

CUISINE BOURGEOISE

These days of disinheritance, we feast
On human heads. True, birds rebuild
Old nests and there is blue in the woods.
The church bells clap one night in the week.
But that's all done. It is what used to be,
As they used to lie in the grass, in the heat,
Men on green beds and women half of sun.
The words are written, though not yet said.

It is like the season when, after summer,
It is summer and it is not, it is autumn
And it is not, it is day and it is not,
As if last night's lamps continued to burn,
As if yesterday's people continued to watch
The sky, half porcelain, preferring that
To shaking out heavy bodies in the glares
Of this present, this science, this unrecognized,

This outpost, this douce, this dumb, this dead, in which
We feast on human heads, brought in on leaves,
Crowned with the first, cold buds. On these we live,
No longer on the ancient cake of seed,
The almond and deep fruit. This bitter meat
Sustains us. . . . Who, then, are they, seated here?
Is the table a mirror in which they sit and look?
Are they men eating reflections of themselves?

POETRY IS A DESTRUCTIVE FORCE

That's what misery is,
Nothing to have at heart.
It is to have or nothing.

It is a thing to have,
A lion, an ox in his breast,
To feel it breathing there.

Corazon, stout dog,
Young ox, bowlegged bear,
He tastes its blood, not spit.

He is like a man
In the body of a violent beast.
Its muscles are his own. . . .

The lion sleeps in the sun.
Its nose is on its paws.
It can kill a man.

THE POEMS OF OUR CLIMATE

I

Clear water in a brilliant bowl,
Pink and white carnations. The light
In the room more like a snowy air,
Reflecting snow. A newly fallen snow
At the end of winter when afternoons return.
Pink and white carnations—one desires
So much more than that. The day itself
Is simplified: a bowl of white,
Cold, a cold porcelain, low and round,
With nothing more than the carnations there.

II

Say even that this complete simplicity
Stripped one of all one's torments, concealed
The evilly compounded, vital I
And made it fresh in a world of white,
A world of clear water, brilliant-edged,
Still one would want more, one would need more,
More than a world of white and snowy scents.

III

There would still remain the never-resting mind,
So that one would want to escape, come back

To what had been so long composed.
The imperfect is our paradise.
Note that, in this bitterness, delight,
Since the imperfect is so hot in us,
Lies in flawed words and stubborn sounds.

MARTIAL CADENZA

I

Only this evening I saw again low in the sky
The evening star, at the beginning of winter, the star
That in spring will crown every western horizon,
Again . . . as if it came back, as if life came back,
Not in a later son, a different daughter, another place,
But as if evening found us young, still young,
Still walking in a present of our own.

II

It was like sudden time in a world without time,
This world, this place, the street in which I was,
Without time: as that which is not has no time,
Is not, or is of what there was, is full
Of the silence before the armies, armies without
Either trumpets or drums, the commanders mute, the arms
On the ground, fixed fast in a profound defeat.

III

What had this star to do with the world it lit,
With the blank skies over England, over France
And above the German camps? It looked apart.
Yet it is this that shall maintain— Itself
Is time, apart from any past, apart
From any future, the ever-living and being,
The ever-breathing and moving, the constant fire,

IV

The present close, the present realized,
Not the symbol but that for which the symbol stands,
The vivid thing in the air that never changes,
Though the air change. Only this evening I saw it again,
At the beginning of winter, and I walked and talked
Again, and lived and was again, and oreathed again
And moved again and flashed again, time flashed again.

THE DWARF

Now it is September and the web is woven.
The web is woven and you have to wear it.

The winter is made and you have to bear it,
The winter web, the winter woven, wind and wind,

For all the thoughts of summer that go with it
In the mind, pupa of straw, moppet of rags.

It is the mind that is woven, the mind that was jerked
And tufted in straggling thunder and shattered sun.

It is all that you are, the final dwarf of you,
That is woven and woven and waiting to be worn,

Neither as mask nor as garment but as a being,
Torn from insipid summer, for the mirror of cold,

Sitting beside your lamp, there citron to nibble
And coffee dribble. . . . Frost is in the stubble.

NO POSSUM, NO SOP, NO TATERS

He is not here, the old sun,
As absent as if we were asleep.

The field is frozen. The leaves are dry.
Bad is final in this light.

In this bleak air the broken stalks
Have arms without hands. They have trunks

Without legs or, for that, without heads.
They have heads in which a captive cry

Is merely the moving of a tongue.
Snow sparkles like eyesight falling to earth,

Like seeing fallen brightly away.
The leaves hop, scraping on the ground.

It is deep January. The sky is hard.
The stalks are firmly rooted in ice.

It is in this solitude, a syllable,
Out of these gawky flitterings,

Intones its single emptiness,
The savagest hollow of winter sound.

It is here, in this bad, that we reach
The last purity of the knowledge of good.

The crow looks rusty as he rises up.
Bright is the malice in his eye. . . .

One joins him there for company,
But at a distance, in another tree.

ESTHÉTIQUE DU MAL

I

He was at Naples writing letters home
And, between his letters, reading paragraphs
On the sublime. Vesuvius had groaned
For a month. It was pleasant to be sitting there,
While the sultriest fulgurations, flickering,
Cast corners in the glass. He could describe
The terror of the sound because the sound
Was ancient. He tried to remember the phrases: pain
Audible at noon, pain torturing itself,
Pain killing pain on the very point of pain.
The volcano trembled in another ether,
As the body trembles at the end of life.

It was almost time for lunch. Pain is human.
There were roses in the cool café. His book
Made sure of the most correct catastrophe.
Except for us, Vesuvius might consume
In solid fire the utmost earth and know
No pain (ignoring the cocks that crow us up
To die). This is a part of the sublime
From which we shrink. And yet, except for us,
The total past felt nothing when destroyed.

II

At a town in which acacias grew, he lay
On his balcony at night. Warblings became

Too dark, too far, too much the accents of
Afflicted sleep, too much the syllables
That would form themselves, in time, and communicate
The intelligence of his despair, express
What meditation never quite achieved.
The moon rose up as if it had escaped
His meditation. It evaded his mind.
It was part of a supremacy always
Above him. The moon was always free from him,
As night was free from him. The shadow touched
Or merely seemed to touch him as he spoke
A kind of elegy he found in space:

It is pain that is indifferent to the sky
In spite of the yellow of the acacias, the scent
Of them in the air still hanging heavily
In the hoary-hanging night. It does not regard
This freedom, this supremacy, and in
Its own hallucination never sees
How that which rejects it saves it in the end.

III

His firm stanzas hang like hives in hell
Or what hell was, since now both heaven and hell
Are one, and here, O terra infidel.

The fault lies with an overhuman god,
Who by sympathy has made himself a man
And is not to be distinguished, when we cry

Because we suffer, our oldest parent, peer
Of the populace of the heart, the reddest lord,
Who has gone before us in experience.

If only he would not pity us so much,
Weaken our fate, relieve us of woe both great
And small, a constant fellow of destiny,

A too, too human god, self-pity's kin
And uncourageous genesis. . . . It seems
As if the health of the world might be enough.

It seems as if the honey of common summer
Might be enough, as if the golden combs
Were a part of a sustenance itself enough,

As if hell, so modified, had disappeared,
As if pain, no longer satanic mimicry,
Could be borne, as we were sure to find our way.

IV

Livre de Toutes Sortes de Fleurs d'après Nature.
All sorts of flowers. That's the sentimentalist.
When B. sat down at the piano and made
A transparence in which we heard music, made music,
I₁ which we heard transparent sounds, did he play
All sorts of notes? Or did he play only one
In an ecstasy o.. its associates,
Variations in the tones o.. a single sound,
The last, or sounds so single they seemed one?

And then that Spaniard of the rose, itself
Hot-hooded anu dark-blooded, rescued the rose
From nature, each time he saw it, making it,
As he saw it, exist in his own especial eye.
Can we conceive of him as rescuing less,
As muffing the mistress for her several maids,
As foregoing the nakedest passion for barefoot
Philandering? . . . The genius of misfortune
Is not a sentimentalist. He is
That evil, that evil in the sel., from which
In desperate hallow, rugged gesture, fault
Falls out on everything: the genius of
The mind, which is our being, wrong and wrong,
The genius of the body, which is our world,
Spent in the false engagements of the mind.

V

Softly let all true sympathizers come,
Without the inventions of sorrow or the sob
Beyond invention. Within what we permit,
Within the actual, the warm, the near,
So great a unity, that it is bliss,
Ties us to those we love. For this familiar,
This brother even in the father's eye,
This brother half-spoken in the mother's throat
And these regalia, these things disclosed,
These nebulous brilliancies in the smallest look
Of the being's deepest darling, we forgo
Lament, willingly forfeit the ai-ai
Of parades in the obscurer selvages.

Be near me, come closer, touch my hand, phrases
Compounded of dear relation, spoken twice,
Once by the lips, once by the services
Of central sense, these minutiae mean more
Than clouds, benevolences, distant heads.
These are within what we permit, in-bar
Exquisite in poverty against the suns
Of ex-bar, in-bar retaining attributes
With which we vested, once, the golden forms
And the damasked memory of the golden forms
And ex-bar's flowers and fire of the festivals
Of the damasked memory of the golden forms,
Before we were wholly human and knew ourselves.

VI

The sun, in clownish yellow, but not a clown,
Brings the day to perfection and then fails. He dwells
In a consummate prime, yet still desires
A further consummation. For the lunar month
He makes the tenderest research, intent
On a transmutation which, when seen, appears
To be askew. And space is filled with his
Rejected years. A big bird pecks at him
For food. The big bird's bony appetite
Is as insatiable as the sun's. The bird
Rose from an imperfection of its own
To feed on the yellow bloom of the yellow fruit
Dropped down from turquoise leaves. In the landscape of
The sun, its grossest appetite becomes less gross,
Yet, when corrected, has its curious lapses,
Its glitters, its divinations of serene
Indulgence out of all celestial sight.

The sun is the country wherever he is. The bird
In the brightest landscape downwardly revolves
Disdaining each astringent ripening,
Evading the point of redness, not content
To repose in an hour or season or long era
Of the country colors crowding against it, since
The yellow grassman's mind is still immense,
Still promises perfection cast away.

VII

How red the rose that is the soldier's wound,
The wounds of many soldiers, the wounds of all
The soldiers that have fallen, red in blood,
The soldier of time grown deathless in great size.

A mountain in which no ease is ever found,
Unless indifference to deeper death
In ease, stands in the dark, a shadows' hill,
And there the soldier of time has deathless rest.

Concentric circles of shadows, motionless
Of their own part, yet moving on the wind,
Form mystical convolutions in the sleep
Of time's red soldier deathless on his bed.

The shadows of his fellows ring him round
In the high night, the summer breathes for them
Its fragance, a heavy somnolence, and for him,
For the soldier of time, it breathes a summer sleep,

In which his wound is good because life was.
No part of him was ever part of death.
A woman smoothes her forehead with her hand
And the soldier of time lies calm beneath that stroke.

VIII

The death of Satan was a tragedy
For the imagination. A capital
Negation destroyed him in his tenement
And, with him, many blue phenomena.
It was not the end he had foreseen. He knew
That his revenge created filial
Revenges. And negation was eccentric.
It had nothing of the Julian thundercloud:
The assassin flash and rumble. . . . He was denied.
Phantoms, what have you left? What underground?
What place in which to be is not enough
To be? You go, poor phantoms, without place
Like silver in the sheathing of the sight,
As the eye closes. . . . How cold the vacancy
When the phantoms are gone and the shaken realist
First sees reality. The mortal no
Has its emptiness and tragic expirations.
The tragedy, however, may have begun,

Again, in the imagination's new beginning,
In the yes of the realist spoken because he must
Say yes, spoken because under every no
Lay a passion for yes that had never been broken.

IX

Panic in the face of the moon—round effendi
Or the phosphored sleep in which he walks abroad
Or the majolica dish heaped up with phosphored fruit
That he sends ahead, out of the goodness of his heart,
To anyone that comes—panic, because
The moon is no longer these nor anything
And nothing is left but comic ugliness
Or a lustered nothingness. Effendi, he
That has lost the folly of the moon becomes
The prince of the proverbs of pure poverty.
To lose sensibility, to see what one sees,
As if sight had not its own miraculous thrift,
To hear only what one hears, one meaning alone,
As if the paradise of meaning ceased
To be paradise, it is this to be destitute.
This is the sky divested of its fountains.
Here in the west indifferent crickets chant
Through our indifferent crises. Yet we require
Another chant, an incantation, as in
Another and later genesis, music
That buffets the shapes of its possible halcyon
Against the haggardie. . . . A loud, large water
Bubbles up in the night and drowns the crickets' sound.
It is a declaration, a primitive ecstasy,
Truth's favors sonorously exhibited.

X

He had studied the nostalgias. In these
He sought the most grossly maternal, the creature
Who most fecundly assuaged him, the softest
Woman with a vague moustache and not the mauve
Maman. His anima liked its animal
And liked it unsubjugated, so that home
Was a return to birth, a being born
Again in the savagest severity,
Desiring fiercely, the child of a mother fierce
In his body, fiercer in his mind, merciless
To accomplish the truth in his intelligence.

It is true there were other mothers, singular
In form, lovers of heaven and earth, she-wolves
And forest tigresses and women mixed
With the sea. These were fantastic. There were homes
Like things submerged with their englutted sounds,
That were never wholly still. The softest woman,
Because she is as she was, reality,
The gross, the fecund, proved him against the touch
Of impersonal pain. Reality explained.
It was the last nostalgia: that he
Should understand. That he might suffer or that
He might die was the innocence of living, if life
Itself was innocent. To say that it was
Disentangled him from sleek ensolacings.

XI

Life is a bitter aspic. We are not
At the center of a diamond. At dawn,
The paratroopers fall and as they fall
They mow the lawn. A vessel sinks in waves
Of people, as big bell-billows from its bell
Bell-bellow in the village steeple. Violets,
Great tufts, spring up from buried houses
Of poor, dishonest people, for whom the steeple,
Long since, rang out farewell, farewell, farewell.

Natives of poverty, children of malheur,
The gaiety of language is our seigneur.

A man of bitter appetite despises
A well-made scene in which paratroopers
Select adieux; and he despises this:
A ship that rools on a confected ocean,
The weather pink, the wind in motion; and tnis:
A steeple that tiptops the classic sun's
Arrangements; and the violets' exhumo.
The tongue caresses these exacerbations.
They press it as epicure, distinguishing
Themselves from its essential savor,
Like hunger that feeds on its own hungriness.

XII

He disposes the world in categories, thus:
The peopled and the unpeopled. In both, he is

Alone. But in the peopled world, there is,
Besides the people, his knowledge of them. In
The unpeopled, there is his knowledge of himself.
Which is more desperate in the moments when
The will demands that what he thinks be true?

Is it himself in them that he knows or they
In him? If it is himself in them, they have
No secret from him. If it is they in him,
He has no secret from them. This knowledge
Of them and of himself destroys both worlds,
Except when he escapes from it. To be
Alone is not to know them or himself.

This creates a third world without knowledge,
In which no one peers, in which the will makes no
Demands. It accepts whatever is as true,
Including pain, which, otherwise, is false.
In the third world, then, there is no pain. Yes, but
What lover has one in such rocks, what woman,
However known, at the center of the heart?

XIII

It may be that one life is a punishment
For another, as the son's life for the father's.
But that concerns the secondary characters.
It is a fragmentary tragedy
Within the universal whole. The son
And the father alike and equally are spent,
Each one, by the necessity of being
Himself, the unalterable necessity
Of being this unalterable animal.
This force of nature in action is the major
Tragedy. This is destiny unperplexed,
The happiest enemy. And it may be
That in his Mediterranean cloister a man,
Reclining, eased of desire, establishes
The visible, a zone of blue and orange
Versicolorings, establishes a time
To watch the fire-feinting sea and calls it good,
The ultimate good, sure of a reality
Of the longest meditation, the maximum,
The assassin's scene. Evil in evil is
Comparative. The assassin discloses himself,
The force that destroys us is disclosed, within

This maximum, an adventure to be endured
With the politest helplessness. Ay-mi!
One feels its action moving in the blood.

XIV

Victor Serge said, "I followed his argument
With the blank uneasiness which one might feel
In the presence of a logical lunatic."
He said it of Konstantinov. Revolution
Is the affair of logical lunatics.
The politics of emotion must appear
To be an intellectual structure. The cause
Creates a logic not to be distinguished
From lunacy. . . . One wants to be able to walk
By the lake at Geneva and consider logic:
To think of the logicians in their graves
And of the worlds of logic in their great tombs.
Lakes are more reasonable than oceans. Hence,
A promenade amid the grandeurs of the mind,
By a lake, with clouds like lights among great tombs,
Gives one a blank uneasiness, as if
One might meet Konstantinov, who would interrupt
With his lunacy. He would not be aware of the lake.
He would be the lunatic of one idea
In a world of ideas, who would have all the people
Live, work, suffer and die in that idea
In a world of ideas. He would not be aware of the clouds,
Lighting the martyrs of logic with white fire.
His extreme of logic would be illogical.

XV

The greatest poverty is not to live
In a physical world, to feel that one's desire
Is too difficult to tell from despair. Perhaps,
After death, the nonphysical people, in paradise,
Itself nonphysical, may, by chance, observe
The green corn gleaming and experience
The minor of what we feel. The adventurer
In humanity has not conceived of a race
Completely physical in a physical world.
The green corn gleams and the metaphysicals
Lie sprawling in majors of the August heat,
The rotund emotions, paradise unknown.
This is the thesis scrivened in delight,
The reverberating psalm, the right chorale.

One might have thought of sight, but who could think
Of what it sees, for all the ill it sees?
Speech found the ear, for all the evil sound,
But the dark italics it could not propound.
And out of what one sees and hears and out
Of what one feels, who could have thought to make
So many selves, so many sensuous worlds,
As if the air, the midday air, was swarming
With the metaphysical changes that occur,
Merely in living as and where we live.

THE GOOD MAN HAS NO SHAPE

Through centuries he lived in poverty.
God only was his only elegance.

Then generation by generation he grew
Stronger and freer, a little better off.

He lived each life because, if it was bad,
He said a good life would be possible.

At last the good life came, good sleep, bright fruit,
And Lazarus betrayed him to the rest,

Who killed him, sticking feathers in his flesh
To mock him. They placed with him in his grave

Sour wine to warm him, an empty book to read;
And over it they set a jagged sign,

Epitaphium to his death, which read,
The Good Man Has No Shape, as if they knew.

CREDENCES OF SUMMER

I

Now in midsummer come and all fools slaughtered
And spring's infuriations over and a long way
To the first autumnal inhalations, young broods
Are in the grass, the roses are heavy with a weight
Of fragrance and the mind lays by its trouble.

Now the mind lays by its trouble and considers.
The fidgets of remembrance come to this.
This is the last day of a certain year
Beyond which there is nothing left of time.
It comes to this and the imagination's life.

There is nothing more inscribed nor thought nor felt
And this must comfort the heart's core against
Its false disasters—these fathers standing round,
These mothers touching, speaking, being near,
These lovers waiting in the soft dry grass.

II

Postpone the anatomy of summer, as
The physical pine, the metaphysical pine.
Let's see the very thing and nothing else.
Let's see it with the hottest fire of sight.
Burn everything not part of it to ash.

Trace the gold sun about the whitened sky
Without evasion by a single metaphor.
Look at it in its essential barrenness
And say this, this is the center that I seek.
Fix it in an eternal foliage

And fill the foliage with arrested peace,
Joy of such permanence, right ignorance
Of change still possible. Exile desire
For what is not. This is the barrenness
Of the fertile thing that can attain no more.

III

It is the natural tower of all the world,
The point of survey, green's green apogee,
But a tower more precious than the view beyond,
A point of survey squatting like a throne,
Axis of everything, green's apogee

And happiest folkland, mostly marriage hymns.
It is the mountain on which the tower stands,
It is the final mountain. Here the sun,
Sleepless, inhales his proper air, and rests.
This is the refuge that the end creates.

It is the old man standing on the tower,
Who reads no book. His ruddy ancientness
Absorbs the ruddy summer and is appeased,
By an understanding that fulfills his age,
By a feeling capable of nothing more.

IV

One of the limits of reality
Presents itself in Oley when the hay,
Baked through long days, is piled in mows. It is
A land too ripe for enigmas, too serene.
There the distant fails the clairvoyant eye

And the secondary senses of the ear
Swarm, not with secondary sounds, but choirs,
Not evocations but last choirs, last sounds
With nothing else compounded, carried full,
Pure rhetoric of a language without words.

Things stop in that direction and since they stop
The direction stops and we accept what is
As good. The utmost must be good and is
And is our fortune and honey hived in the trees
And mingling of colors at a festival.

V

One day enriches a year. One woman makes
The rest look down. One man becomes a race,
Lofty like him, like him perpetual.
Or do the other days enrich the one?
And is the queen humble as she seems to be,

The charitable majesty of her whole kin?
The bristling soldier, weather-foxed, who looms
In the sunshine is a filial form and one
Of the land's children, easily born, its flesh,
Not fustian. The more than casual blue

Contains the year and other years and hymns
And people, without souvenir. The day
Enriches the year, not as embellishment.
Stripped of remembrance, it displays its strength—
The youth, the vital son, the heroic power.

VI

The rock cannot be broken. It is the truth.
It rises from land and sea and covers them.
It is a mountain halfway green and then,
The other immeasurable half, such rock
As placid air becomes. But it is not

A hermit's truth nor symbol in hermitage.
It is the visible rock, the audible,
The brilliant mercy of a sure repose,
On this present ground, the vividest repose,
Things certain sustaining us in certainty.

It is the rock of summer, the extreme,
A mountain luminous halfway in bloom
And then halfway in the extremest light
Of sapphires flashing from the central sky,
As if twelve princes sat before a king.

VII

Far in the woods they sang their unreal songs,
Secure. It was difficult to sing in face
Of the object. The singers had to avert themselves
Or else avert the object. Deep in the woods
They sang of summer in the common fields.

They sang desiring an object that was near,
In face of which desire no longer moved,
Nor made of itself that which it could not find. . . .
Three times the concentered self takes hold, three times
The thrice-concentered self, having possessed

The object, grips it in savage scrutiny,
Once to make captive, once to subjugate
Or yield to subjugation, once to proclaim
The meaning of the capture, this hard prize,
Fully made, fully apparent, fully found.

VIII

The trumpet of morning blows in the clouds and through
The sky. It is the visible announced,
It is the more than visible, the more
Than sharp, illustrious scene. The trumpet cries
This is the successor of the invisible.

This is its substitute in stratagems
Of the spirit. This, in sight and memory,
Must take its place, as what is possible
Replaces what is not. The resounding cry
Is like ten thousand tumblers tumbling down

To share the day. The trumpet supposes that
A mind exists, aware of division, aware
Of its cry as clarion, its diction's way
As that of a personage in a multitude:
Man's mind grown venerable in the unreal.

IX

Fly low, cock bright, and stop on a bean pole. Let
Your brown breast redden, while you wait for warmth.
With one eye watch the willow, motionless.
The gardener's cat is dead, the gardener gone
And last year's garden grows salacious weeds.

A complex of emotions falls apart,
In an abandoned spot. Soft, civil bird,
The decay that you regard: of the arranged
And of the spirit of the arranged, *douceurs,*
Tristesses, the fund of life and death, suave bush

And polished beast, this complex falls apart.
And on your bean pole, it may be, you detect
Another complex of other emotions, not
So soft, so civil, and you make a sound,
Which is not part of the listener's own sense.

X

The personae of summer play the characters
Of an inhuman author, who meditates
With the gold bugs, in blue meadows, late at night.
He does not hear his characters talk. He sees
Them mottled, in the moodiest costumes,

Of blue and yellow, sky and sun, belted
And knotted, sashed and seamed, half pales of red,
Half pales of green, appropriate habit for
The huge decorum, the manner of the time,
Part of the mottled mood of summer's whole,

In which the characters speak because they want
To speak, the fat, the roseate characters,
Free, for a moment, from malice and sudden cry,
Complete in a completed scene, speaking
Their parts as in a youthful happiness.

TWO THINGS OF OPPOSITE NATURES SEEM TO DEPEND

Two things of opposite natures seem to depend
On one another, as a man depends
On a woman, day on night, the imagined

On the real. This is the origin of change.
Winter and spring, cold copulars, embrace
And forth the particulars of rapture come.

Music falls on the silence like a sense,
A passion that we feel, not understand.
Morning and afternoon are clasped together

And north and south are an intrinsic couple
And sun and rain a plural, like two lovers
That walk away as one in the greenest body.

In solitude the trumpets of solitude
Are not of another solitude resounding;
A little string speaks for a crowd of voices.

The partaker partakes of that which changes him.
The child that touches takes character from the thing,
The body, it touches. The captain and his men

Are one and the sailor and the sea are one.
Follow after, O my companion, my fellow, my self,
Sister and solace, brother and delight.

from *"It Must Change," IV, Notes toward a Supreme Fiction*

TO AN OLD PHILOSOPHER IN ROME

On the threshold of heaven, the figures in the street
Become the figures of heaven, the majestic movement
Of men growing small in the distances of space,
Singing, with smaller and still smaller sound,
Unintelligible absolution and an end—

The threshold, Rome, and that more merciful Rome
Beyond, the two alike in the make of the mind.
It is as if in a human dignity
Two parallels become one, a perspective, of whicn
Men are part both in the inch and in the mile.

How easily the blown banners change to wings. . . .
Things dark on the horizons of perception,
Become accompaniments of fortune, but
Of the fortune of the spirit, beyond the eye,
Not of its sphere, and yet not far beyond,

The human end in the spirit's greatest reach,
The extreme of the known in the presence of the extreme
Of the unknown. The newsboys' muttering
Becomes another murmuring; the smell
Of medicine, a fragrantness not to be spoiled. . . .

The bed, the books, the chair, the moving nuns,
The candle as it evades the sight, these are
The sources of happiness in the shape of Rome,
A shape within the ancient circles of shapes,
And these beneath the shadow of a shape

In a confusion on bed and books, a portent
On the chair, a moving transparence on the nuns,
A light on the candle tearing against the wick
To join a hovering excellence, to escape
From fire and be part only of that of which

Fire is the symbol: the celestial possible.
Speak to your pillow as if it was yourself.
Be orator but with an accurate tongue
And without eloquence, O half-asleep,
Of the pity that is the memorial of this room,

So that we feel, in this illumined large,
The veritable small, so that each of us
Beholds himself in you, and hears his voice
In yours, master and commiserable man,
Intent on your particles of nether-do,

Your dozing in the depths of wakefulness,
In the warmth of your bed, at the edge of your chair, alive
Yet living in two worlds, impenitent

As to one, and, as to one, most penitent,
Impatient for the grandeur that you need

In so much misery; and yet finding it
Only in misery, the afflatus of ruin,
Profound poetry of the poor and of the dead,
As in the last drop of the deepest blood,
As it falls from the heart and lies there to be seen,

Even as the blood of an empire, it might be,
For a citizen of heaven though still of Rome.
It is poverty's speech that seeks us out the most.
It is older than the oldest speech of Rome.
This is the tragic accent of the scene.

And you—it is you that speak it, without speech,
The loftiest syllables among loftiest things,
The one invulnerable man among
Crude captains, the naked majesty, if you like,
Of bird-nest arches and of rain-stained vaults.

The sounds drift in. The buildings are remembered.
The life of the city never lets go, nor do you
Ever want it to. It is part of the life in your room.
Its domes are the architecture of your bed.
The bells keep on repeating solemn names

In choruses and choirs of choruses,
Unwilling that mercy should be a mystery
Of silence, that any solitude of sense
Should give you more than their peculiar chords
And reverberations clinging to whisper still.

It is a kind of total grandeur at the end,
With every visible thing enlarged and yet
No more than a bed, a chair and moving nuns,
The immensest theatre, the pillared porch,
The book and candle in your ambered room,

Total grandeur of a total edifice,
Chosen by an inquisitor of structures
For himself. He stops upon this threshold,
As if the design of all his words takes form
And frame from thinking and is realized.

NOT IDEAS ABOUT THE THING
BUT THE THING ITSELF

At the earliest ending of winter,
In March, a scrawny cry from outside
Seemed like a sound in his mind.

He knew that he heard it,
A bird's cry, at daylight or before,
In the early March wind.

The sun was rising at six,
No longer a battered panache above snow. . . .
It would have been outside.

It was not from the vast ventriloquism
Of sleep's faded papier-mâché. . . .
The sun was coming from outside.

That scrawny cry—it was
A chorister whose C preceded the choir.
It was part of the colossal sun,

Surrounded by its choral rings,
Still far away. It was like
A new knowledge of reality.

CRUDE FOYER

Thought is false happiness: the idea
That merely by thinking one can,
Or may, penetrate, not may,
But can, that one is sure to be able—

That there lies at the end of thought
A foyer of the spirit in a landscape
Of the mind, in which we sit
And wear humanity's bleak crown;

In which we read the critique of paradise
And say it is the work
Of a comedian, this critique;
In which we sit and breathe

An innocence of an absolute,
False happiness, since we know that we use
Only the eye as faculty, that the mind
Is the eye, and that this landscape of the mind

Is a landscape only of the eye; and that
We are ignorant men incapable
Of the least, minor, vital metaphor, content,
At last, there, when it turns out to be here.

WILLIAM CARLOS WILLIAMS
(b. 1883)

THE YACHTS

contend in a sea which the land partly encloses
shielding them from the too heavy blows
of an ungoverned ocean which when it chooses

tortures the biggest hulls, the best man knows
to pit against its beatings, and sinks them pitilessly.
Mothlike in mists, scintillant in the minute

brilliance of cloudless days, with broad bellying sails
they glide to the wind tossing green water
from their sharp prows while over them the crew crawls

ant-like, solicitously grooming them, releasing,
making fast as they turn, lean far over and having
caught the wind again, side by side, head for the mark.

In a well guarded arena of open water surrounded by
lesser and greater craft which, sycophant, lumbering
and flittering follow them, they appear youthful, rare

as the light of a happy eye, live with the grace
of all that in the mind is fleckless, free and
naturally to be desired. Now the sea which holds them

is moody, lapping their glossy sides, as if feeling
for some slightest flaw but fails completely.
Today no race. Then the wind comes again. The yachts

move, jockeying for a start, the signal is set and they
are off. Now the waves strike at them but they are too
well made, they slip through, though they take in canvas.

Arms with hands grasping seek to clutch at the prows.
Bodies thrown recklessly in the way are cut aside.
It is a sea of faces about them in agony, in despair

until the horror of the race dawns staggering the mind,
the whole sea become an entanglement of watery bodies
lost to the world bearing what they cannot hold. Broken,

beaten, desolate, reaching from the dead to be taken up
they cry out, failing, failing! their cries rising
in waves still as the skillful yachts pass over.

TO A POOR OLD WOMAN

munching a plum on
the street a paper bag
of them in her hand

They taste good to her
They taste good
to her. They taste
good to her

You can see it by
the way she gives herself
to the one half
sucked out in her hand

Comforted
a solace of ripe plums
seeming to fill the air
They taste good to her

THE SEA ELEPHANT

Trundled from
the strangeness of the sea—
a kind of
heaven—

the gigantic
sea elephant! O wallow
of flesh where
are

Ladies and Gentlemen!
the greatest
sea monster ever exhibited
alive

there fish enough for
that
appetite stupidity
cannot lessen?

Sick
of April's smallness
the little
leaves—

Flesh has lief of you
enormous sea—
Speak!
Blouaugh! (feed

me) my
flesh is riven—
fish after fish into his maw
unswallowing

to let them glide down
gulching back
half spittle half
brine

the
troubled eyes—torn
from the sea.
(In

a practical voice) They
ought
to put it back where
it came from.

Gape.
Strange head—
told by old sailors—
rising

bearded
to the surface—and
the only
sense out of them

is that woman's
Yes
it's wonderful but they
ought to

put it
back into the sea where
it came from.
Blouaugh!

Swing—ride
walk
on wires—toss balls
stoop and

contort yourselves—
But I
am love. I am
from the sea—

Blouaugh!
there is no crime save
the too-heavy
body

the sea
held playfully—comes
to the surface
the water

boiling
about the head the cows
scattering
fish dripping from

the bounty
of . . . and Spring
they say
Spring is icummen in—

LEAR

When the world takes over for us
and the storm in the trees
replaces our brittle consciences
(like ships, female to all seas)

when the few last yellow leaves
stand out like flags on tossed ships
at anchor—our minds are rested

Yesterday we sweated and dreamed
or sweated in our dreams walking
at a loss through the bulk of figures
that appeared solid, men or women,
but as we approached down the paved
corridor melted—Was it I?—like
smoke from bonfires blowing away

Today the storm, inescapable, has
taken the scene and we return
our hearts to it, however made, made
wives by it and though we secure
ourselves for a dry skin from the drench
of its passionate approaches we
yield and are made quiet by its fury

Pitiful Lear, not even you could
out-shout the storm—to make a fool
cry! Wife to its power might you not
better have yielded earlier? as on ships
facing the seas were carried once
the figures of women at repose to
signify the strength of the waves' lash.

THESE

are the desolate, dark weeks
when nature in its barrenness
equals the stupidity of man.

The year plunges into night
and the heart plunges
lower than night

to an empty, windswept place
without sun, stars or moon
but a peculiar light as of thought

that spins a dark fire—
whirling upon itself until,
in the cold, it kindles

to make a man aware of nothing
that he knows, not loneliness
itself—Not a ghost but

would be embraced—emptiness
despair—(They
whine and whistle) among

the flashes and booms of war;
houses of whose rooms
the cold is greater than can be thought,

the people gone that we loved,
the beds lying empty, the couches
damp, the chairs unused—

Hide it away somewhere
out of the mind, let it get roots
and grow, unrelated to jealous

ears and eyes—for itself.
In this mine they come to dig—all.
Is this the counterfoil to sweetest

music? The source of poetry that
seeing the clock stopped, says,
The clock has stopped

that ticked yesterday so well?
and hears the sound of lakewater
splashing—that is now stone.

BURNING THE CHRISTMAS GREENS

Their time past, pulled down
cracked and flung to the fire
—go up in a roar

All recognition lost, burnt clean
clean in the flame, the green

dispersed, a living red,
flame red, red as blood wakes
on the ash—

and ebbs to a steady burning
the rekindled bed become
a landscape of flame

At the winter's midnight
we went to the trees, the coarse
holly, the balsam and
the hemlock for their green

At the thick of the dark
the moment of the cold's
deepest plunge we brought branches
cut from the green trees

to fill our need, and over
doorways, about paper Christmas
bells covered with tinfoil
and fastened by red ribbons

we stuck the green prongs,
in the windows hung
woven wreaths and above pictures
the living green. On the

mantle we built a green forest
and among those hemlock
sprays put a herd of small
white deer as if they

were walking there. All this!
and it seemed gentle and good
to us. Their time past,
relief! The room bare. We

stuffed the dead grate
with them upon the half burnt out
log's smoldering eye, opening
red and closing under them

and we stood there looking down.
Green is a solace

a promise of peace, a fort
against the cold (though we

did not say so) a challenge
above the snow's
hard shell. Green (we might
have said) that, where

small birds hide and dodge
and lift their plaintive
rallying cries, blocks for them
and knocks down

the unseeing bullets of
the storm. Green spruce boughs
pulled down by a weight of
snow—Transformed!

Violence leaped and appeared.
Recreant! roared to life
as the flame rose through and
our eyes recoiled from it.

In the jagged flames green
to red, instant and alive. Green!
those sure abutments . . . Gone!
lost to mind

and quick in the contracting
tunnel of the grate
appeared a world! Black
mountains, black and red—as

yet uncolored—and ash white,
an infant landscape of shimmering
ash and flame and we, in
that instant, lost,

breathless to be witnesses,
as if we stood
ourselves refreshed among
the shining fauna of that fire.

THE DANCE

In Breughel's great picture, The Kermess,
the dancers go round, they go round and
around, the squeal and the blare and the
tweedle of bagpipes, a bugle and fiddles
tipping their bellies (round as the thick-
sided glasses whose wash they impound)
their hips and their bellies off balance
to turn them. Kicking and rolling about
the Fair Grounds, swinging their butts, those
shanks must be sound to bear up under such
rollicking measures, prance as they dance
in Breughel's great picture, The Kermess.

ON GAY WALLPAPER

The green-blue ground
is ruled with silver lines
to say the sun is shining

And on this moral sea
of grass or dreams lie flowers
or baskets of desires

Heaven knows what they are
between cerulean shapes
laid regularly round

Mat roses and tridentate
leaves of gold
threes, threes and threes

Three roses and three stems
the basket floating
standing in the horns of blue

Repeating to the ceiling
to the windows
where the day

Blows in
the scalloped curtains to
the sound of rain

THE PURE PRODUCTS OF AMERICA

The pure products of America
go crazy—
mountain folk from Kentucky

or the ribbed north end of
Jersey
with its isolate lakes and

valleys, its deaf-mutes, thieves
old names
and promiscuity between

devil-may-care men who have taken
to railroading
out of sheer lust of adventure—

and young slatterns, bathed
in filth
from Monday to Saturday

to be tricked out that night
with gauds
from imaginations which have no

peasant traditions to give them
character
but flutter and flaunt

sheer rags—succumbing without
emotion
save numbed terror

under some hedge of choke-cherry
or viburnum—
which they cannot express—

Unless it be that marriage
perhaps
with a dash of Indian blood

will throw up a girl so desolate
so hemmed round
with disease or murder

that she'll be rescued by an
 agent—
reared by the state and

sent out at fifteen to work in
some hard-pressed
house in the suburbs—

some doctor's family, some Elsie—
voluptuous water
expressing with broken

brain the truth about us—
her great
ungainly hips and flopping breasts

addressed to cheap
jewelry
and rich young men with fine eyes

as if the earth under our feet
were
an excrement of some sky

and we degraded prisoners
destined
to hunger until we eat filth

while the imagination strains
after deer
going by fields of goldenrod in

the stifling heat of September
Somehow
it seems to destroy us

It is only in isolate flecks that
something
is given off

No one
to witness
and adjust, no one to drive the car

BY THE ROAD TO THE CONTAGIOUS HOSPITAL

By the road to the contagious hospital
under the surge of the blue
mottled clouds driven from the
northeast—a cold wind. Beyond, the
waste of broad, muddy fields
brown with dried weeds, standing and fallen

patches of standing water
the scattering of tall trees

All along the road the reddish
purplish, forked, upstanding, twiggy
stuff of bushes and small trees
with dead, brown leaves under them
leafless vines—

Lifeless in appearance, sluggish
dazed spring approaches—

They enter the new world naked,
cold, uncertain of all
save that they enter. All about them
the cold, familiar wind—

Now the grass, tomorrow
the stiff curl of wildcarrot leaf

One by one objects are defined—
It quickens: clarity, outline of leaf

But now the stark dignity of
entrance—Still, the profound change
has come upon them: rooted they
grip down and begin to awaken

QUEEN-ANN'S-LACE

Her body is not so white as
anemone petals nor so smooth—nor
so remote a thing. It is a field
of the wild carrot taking
the field by force; the grass
does not raise above it.
Here is no question of whiteness,
white as can be, with a purple mole
at the center of each flower.
Each flower is a hand's span
of her whiteness. Wherever
his hand has lain there is
a tiny purple blemish. Each part
is a blossom under his touch
to which the fibers of her being
stem one by one, each to its end.
until the whole field is a
white desire, empty, a single stem,
a cluster, flower by flower,
a pious wish to whiteness gone over—
or nothing.

TRACT

I will teach you my townspeople
how to perform a funeral—
for you have it over a troop
of artists—
unless one should scour the world—
you have the ground sense necessary.

See! the hearse leads.
I begin with a design for a hearse.
For Christ's sake not black—

nor white either—and not polished!
Let it be weathered—like a farm wagon—
with gilt wheels (this could be
applied fresh at small expense)
or no wheels at all:
a rough dray to drag over the ground.

Knock the glass out!
My God—glass, my townspeople!
For what purpose? Is it for the dead
to look out or for us to see
how well he is housed or to see
the flowers or the lack of them—
or what?
To keep the rain and snow from him?
He will have a heavier rain soon:
pebbles and dirt and what not.
Let there be no glass—
and no upholstery phew!
and no little brass rollers
and small easy wheels on the bottom—
my townspeople what are you thinking of?

A rough plain hearse then
with gilt wheels and no top at all.
On this the coffin lies
by its own weight.

                        No wreaths please—
especially no hothouse flowers.
Some common memento is better,
something he prized and is known by:
his old clothes—a few books perhaps—
God knows what! You realize
how we are about these things
my townspeople—
something will be found—anything
even flowers if he had come to that.
So much for the hearse.

For heaven's sake though see to the driver!
Take off the silk hat! In fact
that's no place at all for him—
up there unceremoniously
dragging our friend out to his own dignity!
Bring him down—bring him down!

Low and inconspicuous! I'd not have him ride
on the wagon at all—damn him—
the undertaker's understrapper!
Let him hold the reins
and walk at the side
and inconspicuously too!

Then briefly as to yourselves:
Walk behind—as they do in France,
seventh class, or if you ride
Hell take curtains! Go with some show
of inconvenience; sit openly—
to the weather as to grief.
Or do you think you can shut grief in?
What—from us? We who have perhaps
nothing to lose? Share with us
share with us—it will be money
in your pockets.
              Go now
I think you are ready.

SIX POEMS FROM PATERSON

I

Paterson lies in the valley under the Passaic Falls
its spent waters forming the outline of his back. He
lies on his right side, head near the thunder
of the waters filling his dreams! Eternally asleep,
his dreams walk about the city where he persists
incognito. Butterflies settle on his stone ear.
Immortal he neither moves nor rouses and is seldom
seen, though he breathes and the subtleties of his machinations
drawing their substance from the noise of the pouring river
animate a thousand automatons. Who because they
neither know their sources nor the sills of their
disappointments walk outside their bodies aimlessly
      for the most part,
locked and forgot in their desires—unroused.

   —Say it, no ideas but in things—
nothing but the blank faces of the houses
and cylindrical trees
bent, forked by preconception and accident—

split, furrowed, creased, mottled, stained—
secret—into the body of the light!

From above, higher than the spires, higher
even than the office towers, from oozy fields
abandoned to gray beds of dead grass,
black sumac, withered weed-stalks,
mud and thickets cluttered with dead leaves—
the river comes pouring in above the city
and crashes from the edge of the gorge
in a recoil of spray and rainbow mists—

    (What common language to unravel?
  . . combed into straight lines
  from that rafter of a rock's
  lip.)

A man like a city and a woman like a flower
—who are in love. Two women. Three women.
Innumerable women, each like a flower.

                    But

only one man—like a city.

II

        I remember
a *Geographic* picture, the 9 women
of some African chief semi-naked
astraddle a log, an official log to
be presumed, heads left:

            Foremost
froze the young and latest,
erect, a proud queen, conscious of her power,
mud-caked, her monumental hair
slanted above the brows—violently frowning.

Behind her, packed tight up
in a descending scale of freshness
stiffened the others
            and then . .
the last, the first wife,
present! supporting all the rest growing
up from her—whose careworn eyes

serious, menacing—but unabashed; breasts
sagging from hard use . .

Whereas the uppointed breasts
of that other, tense, charged with
pressures unrelieved .
and the rekindling they bespoke
was evident.

Not that the lightnings
do not stab at the mystery of a man
from both ends—and the middle, no matter
how much a chief he may be, rather the more
because of it, to destroy him at home

. . Womanlike, a vague smile,
unattached, floating like a pigeon
after a long flight to his cote.

III

Two halfgrown girls hailing hallowed Easter,
(an inversion of all out-of-doors) weaving
about themselves, from under
the heavy air, whorls of thick translucencies
poured down, cleaving them away,
shut from the light; bare-
headed, their clear hair dangling—

Two—
      disparate among the pouring
waters of their hair in which nothing is
molten—

two, bound by an instinct to be the same:
ribbons, cut from a piece,
cerise pink, binding their hair: one—
a willow twig pulled from a low
leafless bush in full bud in her hand,
(or eels or a moon!)
holds it, the gathered spray,
upright in the air, the pouring air,
strokes the soft fur—

                Ain't they beautiful!

IV

                    The sun
winding the yellow bindweed about a
bush; worms and gnats, life under a stone.
The pitiful snake with its mosaic skin
and frantic tongue. The horse, the bull
the whole din of fracturing thought
as it falls tinnily to nothing upon the streets
and the absurd dignity of a locomotive
hauling freight—

                    Pithy philosophies of
daily exits and entrances, with books
propping up one end of the shaky table—
The vague accuracies of events dancing two
and two with language which they
forever surpass—and dawns
tangled in darkness—

    The giant in whose apertures we
    cohabit, unaware of what air supports
    us—the vague, the particular
    no less vague

                    his thoughts, the stream
    and we, we two, isolated in the stream,
    we also: three alike—

                            we sit and talk
    I wish to be with you abed, we two
    as if the bed were the bed of a stream
    —I have much to say to you

                    We sit and talk,
    quietly, with long lapses of silence
    and I am aware of the stream
    that has no language, coursing
    beneath the quiet heaven of
    your eyes

                    which has no speech; to
    go to bed with you, to pass beyond
    the moment of meeting, while the
    currents float still in mid-air, to
    fall—
    With you from the brink, before
    the crash—

                    to seize the moment.

We sit and talk, sensing a little
the rushing impact of the giants'
violent torrent rolling over us, a
few moments.

v

                          What
irritation of offensively red brick is this,
red as poor-man's flesh? Anachronistic?
                          The mystery
of streets and back rooms—
wiping the nose on sleeves, come here
to dream

Tenement windows, sharp edged, in which
no face is seen—though curtainless, into
which no more than birds and insects look or
the moon stares, concerning which they dare
look back, by times.

It is the complement exact of vulgar streets,
a mathematic calm, controlled, the architecture
mete, sinks there, lifts here
the same blank and staring eyes.

                          An incredible
clumsiness of address,
senseless rapes—caught on hands and knees
scrubbing a greasy corridor; the blood
boiling as though in a vat, where they soak—

Plaster saints, glass jewels
and those apt paper flowers, bafflingly
complex—have here
their forthright beauty, beside:

Things, things unmentionable,
the sink with the waste farina in it and
lumps of rancid meat, milk-bottle tops: have
here a tranquillity and loveliness
Have here (in his thoughts)
a complement tranquil and chaste.

        He shifts his change:

VI

    Thought clambers up,
snail like, upon the wet rocks
hidden from sun and sight—
        hedged in by the pouring torrent—
and has its birth and death there
in that moist chamber, shut from
the world—and unknown to the world,
cloaks itself in mystery—

                And the myth
that holds up the rock,
that holds up the water thrives there—
in that cavern, that profound cleft,
                a flickering green
inspiring terror, watching . .

And standing, shrouded there, in that din,
Earth, the chatterer, father of all
speech . . . .

EZRA POUND
(b. 1885)

NA AUDIART

Que be-m vols mal

NOTE: *Anyone who has read anything of the troubadours knows well the tale of Bertran of Born and My Lady Maent of Montaignac, and knows also the song he made when she would none of him, the song wherein he, seeking to find or make her equal, begs of each pre-eminent lady of Langue d'Oc some trait or some fair semblance: thus of Cembelins her "esgart amoros" to wit, her love-lit glance, of Aelis her speech free-running, of the Vicomtess of Chalais her throat and her two hands, at Roacoart of Anhes her hair golden as Iseult's; and even in this fashion of Lady Audiart "although she would that ill come unto him" he sought and praised the lineaments of the torse. And all this to make "Una dompna soiseubuda" a borrowed lady or as the Italians translated it "Una donna ideale."*

Though thou well dost wish me ill
          Audiart, Audiart,
Where thy bodice laces start
As ivy fingers clutching through
Its crevices,
          Audiart, Audiart,
Stately, tall and lovely tender
Who shall render
          Audiart, Audiart,
Praises meet unto thy fashion?
Here a word kiss!
          Pass I on
Unto Lady "Miels-de-Ben,"
Having praised thy girdle's scope
How the stays ply back from it;
I breathe no hope
That thou shouldst . . .
          Nay no whit
Bespeak thyself for anything.
Just a word in thy praise, girl,
Just for the swirl
Thy satins make upon the stair,
'Cause never a flaw was there

Where thy torse and limbs are met
Though thou hate me, read it set
In rose and gold.[1]
Or when the minstrel, tale half told,
Shall burst to lilting at the praise
                    "Audiart, Audiart" . . .
Bertrans, master of his lays,
Bertrans of Aultaforte thy praise
Sets forth, and though thou hate me well,
Yea though thou wish me ill,
                    Audiart, Audiart.
Thy loveliness is here writ till,
                    Audiart,
Oh, till thou come again.[2]
And being bent and wrinkled, in a form
That hath no perfect limning, when the warm
Youth dew is cold
Upon thy hands, and thy old soul
Scorning a new, wry'd casement,
Churlish at seemed misplacement,
Finds the earth as bitter
As now seems it sweet,
Being so young and fair
As then only in dreams,
Being then young and wry'd,
Broken of ancient pride,
Thou shalt then soften,
Knowing, I know not how,
Thou wert once she
                    Audiart, Audiart
For whose fairness one forgave
                    Audiart,
Audiart
        Que be-m vols mal.

BALLAD OF THE GOODLY FERE

Simon Zelotes speaking after the Crucifixion. Fere = Mate,
Companion.

Ha' we lost the goodliest fere o' all
For the priests and the gallows tree?
Aye lover he was of brawny men,
O' ships and the open sea.

[1] I.e., in illumed manuscript.
[2] Reincarnate.

When they came wi' a host to take Our Man
His smile was good to see,
"First let these go!" quo' our Goodly Fere,
"Or I'll see ye damned," says he.

Aye he sent us out through the crossed high spears
And the scorn of his laugh rang free,
"Why took ye not me when I walked about
Alone in the town?" says he.

Oh we drank his "Hale" in the good red wine
When we last made company,
No capon priest was the Goodly Fere
But a man o' men was he.

I ha' seen him drive a hundred men
Wi' a bundle o' cords swung free,
That they took the high and holy house
For their pawn and treasury.

They'll no' get him a' in a book I think
Though they write it cunningly;
No mouse of the scrolls was the Goodly Fere
But aye loved the open sea.

If they think they ha' snared our Goodly Fere
They are fools to the last degree.
"I'll go to the feast," quo' our Goodly Fere,
"Though I go to the gallows tree."

"Ye ha' seen me heal the lame and blind,
And wake the dead," says he,
"Ye shall see one thing to master all:
'Tis how a brave man dies on the tree."

A son of God was the Goodly Fere
That bade us his brothers be.
I ha' seen him cow a thousand men.
I have seen him upon the tree.

He cried no cry when they drave the nails
And the blood gushed hot and free,
The hounds of the crimson sky gave tongue
But never a cry cried he.

I ha' seen him cow a thousand men
On the hills o' Galilee,
They whined as he walked out caïm between,
Wi' his eyes like the grey o' the sea,

Like the sea that brooks no voyaging
With the winds unleashed and free,
Like the sea that he cowed at Genseret
Wi' twey words spoke' suddently.

A master of men was the Goodly Fere,
A mate of the wind and sea,
If they think they ha' slain our Goodly Fere
They are fools eternally.

I ha' seen him eat o' the honey-comb
Sin' they nailed him to the tree.

PORTRAIT D'UNE FEMME

Your mind and you are our Sargasso Sea,
London has swept about you this score years
And bright ships left you this or that in fee:
Ideas, old gossip, oddments of all things,
Strange spars of knowledge and dimmed wares of price.
Great minds have sought you—lacking someone else.
You have been second always. Tragical?
No. You preferred it to the usual thing:
One dull man, dulling and uxorious,
One average mind—with one thought less, each year.
Oh, you are patient. I have seen you sit
Hours, where something might have floated up.
And now you pay one. Yes, you richly pay.
You are a person of some interest, one comes to you
And takes strange gain away:
Trophies fished up; some curious suggestion;
Fact that leads nowhere; and a tale or two,
Pregnant with mandrakes, or with something else
That might prove useful and yet never proves,
That never fits a corner or shows use,
Or finds its hour upon the loom of days:
The tarnished, gaudy, wonderful old work;
Idols and ambergris and rare inlays,
These are your riches, your great store; and yet
For all this sea-hoard of deciduous things,

Strange woods half sodden, and new brighter stuff:
In the slow float of different light and deep,
No! there is nothing! In the whole and all,
Nothing that's quite your own.
     Yet this is you.

A VIRGINAL

No, no! Go from me. I have left her lately.
I will not spoil my sheath with lesser brightness,
For my surrounding air hath a new lightness;
Slight are her arms, yet they have bound me straitly
And left me cloaked as with a gauze of aether;
As with sweet leaves; as with subtle clearness.
Oh, I have picked up magic in her nearness
To sheathe me half in half the things that sheathe her.
No, no! Go from me. I have still the flavour,
Soft as spring wind that's come from birchen bowers.
Green come the shoots, aye April in the branches,
As winter's wound with her sleight hand she staunches,
Hath of the trees a likeness of the savour:
As white their bark, so white this lady's hours.

THE RETURN

See, they return; ah, see the tentative
Movements, and the slow feet,
The trouble in the pace and the uncertain
Wavering!

See, they return, one, and by one,
With fear, as half awakened;
As if the snow should hesitate
And murmur in the wind,
     and half turn back;
These were the "Wing'd-with-Awe,"
     Inviolable,

Gods of the wingèd shoe!
With them the silver hounds,
     sniffing the trace of air!

Haie! Haie!
  These were the swift to harry;

These the keen-scented;
These were the souls of blood.

Slow on the leash,
                    pallid the leash-men!

TENZONE

Will people accept them?
          (i.e. these songs).
As a timorous wench from a centaur
          (or a centurion),
Already they flee, howling in terror.

Will they be touched with the verisimilitudes?
          Their virgin stupidity is untemptable.
I beg you, my friendly critics,
Do not set about to procure me an audience.

I mate with my free kind upon the crags;
          the hidden recesses
Have heard the echo of my heels,
          in the cool light,
          in the darkness.

SALUTATION

O generation of the thoroughly smug
          and thoroughly uncomfortable,
I have seen fishermen picnicking in the sun,
I have seen them with untidy families,
I have seen their smiles full of teeth
          and heard ungainly laughter.
And I am happier than you are,
And they were happier than I am;
And the fish swim in the lake
          and do not even own clothing.

A PACT

I make a pact with you, Walt Whitman—
I have detested you long enough.
I come to you as a grown child
Who has had a pig-headed father;

I am old enough now to make friends.
It was you that broke the new wood,
Now is a time for carving.
We have one sap and one root—
Let there be commerce between us.

THE REST

O helpless few in my country,
O remnant enslaved!

Artists broken against her,
A-stray, lost in the villages,
Mistrusted, spoken-against,

Lovers of beauty, starved,
Thwarted with systems,
Helpless against the control;

You who can not wear yourselves out
By persisting to successes,
You who can only speak,
Who can not steel yourselves into reiteration;

You of the finer sense,
Broken against false knowledge,
You who can know at first hand,
Hated, shut in, mistrusted:

Take thought:
I have weathered the storm,
I have beaten out my exile.

THE TEMPERAMENTS

Nine adulteries, 12 liaisons, 64 fornications and something
    approaching a rape
Rest nightly upon the soul of our delicate friend Florialis,
And yet the man is so quiet and reserved in demeanor
That he passes for both bloodless and sexless.
Bastidides, on the contrary, who both talks and writes of noth-
    ing save copulation,
Has become the father of twins.

But he accomplished this feat at some cost;
He had to be four times cuckold.

IN A STATION OF THE METRO

The apparition of these faces in the crowd;
Petals on a wet, black bough.

THE RIVER-MERCHANT'S WIFE: A LETTER

While my hair was still cut straight across my forehead
Played I about the front gate, pulling flowers.
You came by on bamboo stilts, playing horse,
You walked about my seat, playing with blue plums.
And we went on living in the village of Chokan:
Two small people, without dislike or suspicion.

At fourteen I married My Lord you.
I never laughed, being bashful.
Lowering my head, I looked at the wall.
Called to, a thousand times, I never looked back.

At fifteen I stopped scowling,
I desired my dust to be mingled with yours
Forever and forever and forever.
Why should I climb the look out?

At sixteen you departed,
You went into far Ku-to-yen, by the river of swirling eddies,
And you have been gone five months.
The monkeys make sorrowful noise overhead.

You dragged your feet when you went out.
By the gate now, the moss is grown, the different mosses,
Too deep to clear them away!
The leaves fall early this autumn, in wind.
The paired butterflies are already yellow with August
Over the grass in the West garden;
They hurt me. I grow older.
If you are coming down through the narrows of the river
     Kiang,
Please let me know beforehand,
And I will come out to meet you
                As far as Cho-fu-Sa.

                                    By Rihaku

HUGH SELWYN MAUBERLEY

E. P. Ode Pour L Election de Son Sepulchre

For three years, out of key with his time,
He strove to resuscitate the dead·art
Of poetry; to maintain "the sublime"
In the old sense. Wrong from the start—

No, hardly, but seeing he had been born
In a half-savage country, out of date;
Bent resolutely on wringing lilies from the acorn;
Capaneus; trout for factitious bait;

Ἴδμεν γάρ τοι πάνθ', ὅσ' ἐνὶ Τροίῃ
Caught in the unstopped ear;
Giving the rocks small lee-way
The chopped seas held him, therefore, that year.

His true Penelope was Flaubert,
He fished by obstinate isles;
Observed the elegance of Circe's hair
Rather than the mottoes on sun-dials.

Unaffected by "the march of events,"
He passed from men's memory in *l'an trentuniesme
De son eage;* the case presents
No adjunct to the Muses' diadem.

II

The age demanded an image
Of its accelerated grimace,
Something for the modern stage,
Not, at any rate, an Attic grace;

Not, not certainly, the obscure reveries
Of the inward gaze;
Better mendacities
Than the classics in paraphrase!

The "age demanded" chiefly a mould in plaster,
Made with no loss of time,
A prose kinema, not, not assuredly, alabaster
Or the "sculpture" of rhyme.

III

The tea-rose tea-gown, etc.
Supplants the mousseline of Cos,
The Pianola "replaces"
Sappho's barbitos.

Christ follows Dionysus,
Phallic and ambrosial
Made way for macerations;
Caliban casts out Ariel.

All things are a flowing,
Sage Heracleitus says;
But a tawdry cheapness
Shall outlast our days.

Even the Christian beauty
Defects—after Samothrace;
We see τὸ καλὸν
Decreed in the market place.

Faun's flesh is not to us,
Nor the saint's vision.
We have the press for wafer;
Franchise for circumcision.

All men, in law, are equals.
Free of Pisistratus,
We choose a knave or an eunuch
To rule over us.

O bright Apollo,
τίν' ἄνδρα, τίν' ἥρωα, τίνα θεὸν,
What god, man, or hero
Shall I place a tin wreath upon!

IV

These fought in any case,
and some believing,
          pro domo, in any case . . .

Some quick to arm,
some for adventure,
some from fear of weakness,
some from fear of censure,

some for love of slaughter, in imagination,
learning later . . .
some in fear, learning love of slaughter;
Died some, pro patria,
                    non "dulce" non "et decor" . . .
walked eye-deep in hell
believing in old men's lies, then unbelieving
came home, home to a lie,
home to many deceits,
home to old lies and new infamy;
usury age-old and age-thick
and liars in public places.

Daring as never before, wastage as never before.
Young blood and high blood,
fair cheeks, and fine bodies;

fortitude as never before

frankness as never before,
disillusions as never told in the old days,
hysterias, trench confessions,
laughter out of dead bellies.

V

There died a myriad,
And of the best, among them,
For an old bitch gone in the teeth,
For a botched civilization,

Charm, smiling at the good mouth,
Quick eyes gone under earth's lid,

For two gross of broken statues,
For a few thousand battered books.

Yeux Glauques

Gladstone was still respected,
When John Ruskin produced
"King's Treasuries"; Swinburne
And Rossetti still abused.

Fetid Buchanan lifted up his voice
When that faun's head of hers
Became a pastime for
Painters and adulterers.

The Burne-Jones cartons
Have preserved her eyes;
Still, at the Tate, they teach
Cophetua to rhapsodize;

Thin like brook-water,
With a vacant gaze.
The English Rubáiyát was still-born
In those days.

The thin, clear gaze, the same
Still darts out faunlike from the half-ruin'd face,
Questing and passive. . . .
"Ah, poor Jenny's case" . . .

Bewildered that a world
Shows no surprise
At her last maquero's
Adulteries.

"Siena Mi Fe'; Disfecemi Maremma"

Among the pickled fetuses and bottled bones,
Engaged in perfecting the catalogue,
I found the last scion of the
Senatorial families of Strasbourg, Monsieur Verog.

For two hours he talked of Gallifet;
Of Dowson; of the Rhymers' Club;
Told me how Johnson (Lionel) died
By falling from a high stool in a pub . . .

But showed no trace of alcohol
At the autopsy, privately performed—
Tissue preserved—the pure mind
Arose toward Newman as the whiskey warmed.

Dowson found harlots cheaper than hotels;
Headlam for uplift; Image impartially imbued
With raptures for Bacchus, Terpsichore and the Church.
So spoke the author of "The Dorian Mood,"

M. Verog, out of step with the decade,
Detached from his contemporaries,
Neglected by the young,
Because of these reveries.

Brennbaum

The skylike limpid eyes,
The circular infant's face,
The stiffness from spats to collar
Never relaxing into grace;

The heavy memories of Horeb, Sinai and the forty years,
Showed only when the daylight fell
Level across the face
Of Brennbaum "The Impeccable."

Mr. Nixon

In the cream gilded cabin of his steam yacht
Mr. Nixon advised me kindly, to advance with fewer
Dangers of delay. "Consider
        "Carefully the reviewer.

"I was as poor as you are;
"When I began I got, of course,
"Advance on royalties, fifty at first," said Mr. Nixon,
"Follow me, and take a column,
"Even if you have to work free.

"Butter reviewers. From fifty to three hundred
"I rose in eighteen months;
"The hardest nut I had to crack
"Was Dr. Dundas.

"I never mentioned a man but with the view
"Of selling my own works.
"The tip's a good one, as for literature
"It gives no man a sinecure.

"And no one knows, at sight, a masterpiece.
"And give up verse, my boy,
"There's nothing in it."

*   *   *   *

Likewise a friend of Bloughram's once advised me:
Don't kick against the pricks,
Accept opinion. The "Nineties" tried your game
And died, there's nothing in it.

X

Beneath the sagging roof
The stylist has taken shelter,
Unpaid, uncelebrated,
At last from the world's welter

Nature receives him;
With a placid and uneducated mistress
He exercises his talents
And the soil meets his distress.

The haven from sophistications and contentions
Leaks through its thatch;
He offers succulent cooking;
The door has a creaking latch.

XI

"Conservatrix of Milésian"
Habits of mind and feeling,
Possibly. But in Ealing
With the most bank-clerkly of Englishmen?

No, "Milésian" is an exaggeration.
No instinct has survived in her
Older than those her grandmother
Told her would fit her station.

XII

"Daphne with her thighs in bark
"Stretches toward me her leafy hands,"—
Subjectively. In the stuffed-satin drawing-room
I await The Lady Valentine's commands,

Knowing my coat has never been
Of precisely the fashion
To stimulate, in her,
A durable passion;

Doubtful, somewhat, of the value
Of well-gowned approbation
Of literary effort,
But never of The Lady Valentine's vocation:

Poetry, her border of ideas,
The edge, uncertain, but a means of blending
With other strata
Where the lower and higher have ending;

A hook to catch the Lady Jane's attention,
A modulation toward the theatre,
Also, in the case of revolution,
A possible friend and comforter.

* * * *

Conduct, on the other hand, the soul
"Which the highest cultures have nourished"
To Fleet St. where
Dr. Johnson flourished;

Beside this thoroughfare
The sale of half-hose has
Long since superseded the cultivation
Of Pierian roses.

Envoi (1919)

Go, dumb-born book,
Tell her that sang me once that song of Lawes:
Hadst thou but song
As thou hast subjects known,
Then were there cause in thee that should condone
Even my faults that heavy upon me lie,
And build her glories their longevity.

Tell her that sheds
Such treasure in the air,
Recking naught else but that her graces give
Life to the moment,
I would bid them live
As roses might, in magic amber laid,
Red overwrought with orange and all made
One substance and one colour
Braving time.

Tell her that goes
With song upon her lips
But sings not out the song, nor knows
The maker of it, some other mouth,
May be as fair as hers,
Might, in new ages, gain her worshippers,
When our two dusts with Waller's shall be laid,
Siftings on siftings in oblivion,
Till change hath broken down
All things save Beauty alone.

Mauberley (1920)

"VACUOS EXERCET AERA MORSUS."

Turned from the "eau-forte
Par Jaquemart"
To the strait head
Of Messalina:

"His true Penelope
Was Flaubert,"
And his tool
The engraver's.

Firmness,
Not the full smile,
His art, but an art
In profile;

Colourless
Pier Francesca,
Pisanello lacking the skill
To forge Achaia.

II

"QU'EST CE QU'ILS SAVENT DE L'AMOUR, ET QU'EST CE QU'ILS
PEUVENT COMPRENDRE?

S'ILS NE COMPRENNENT PAS LA POÉSIE, S'ILS NE SENTENT
PAS LA MUSIQUE, QU'EST CE QU'ILS PEUVENT COMPRENDRE DE
CETTE PASSION EN COMPARAISON AVEC L QUELLE LA ROSE EST
GROSSIÈRE ET LE PARFUM DES VIOLETTES UN TONNERRE?"
CAID ALI

For three years, diabolus in the scale,
He drank ambrosia,
All passes, ANANGKE prevails,
Came end, at last, to that Arcadia.

He had moved amid her phantasmagoria,
Amid her galaxies,
NUKTIS'AGALMA

    *   *   *   *

Drifted . . . drifted precipitate,
Asking time to be rid of . . .
Of his bewilderment; to designate
His new found orchid. . . .

To be certain . . . certain . . .
(Amid aerial flowers) . . . time for arrangements—
Drifted on
To the final estrangement;

Unable in the supervening blankness
To sift TO AGATHON from the chaff
Until he found his sieve . . .
Ultimately, his seismograph:

—Given that is his "fundamental passion,"
This urge to convey the relation
Of eye-lid and cheek-bone
By verbal manifestations;

To present the series
Of curious heads in medallion—

He had passed, inconscient, full gaze,
The wide-banded irides
And botticellian sprays implied
In their diastasis;

Which anesthesis, noted a year late,
And weighed, revealed his great affect,
(Orchid), mandate
Of Eros, a retrospect.

    *   *   *   *

Mouths biting empty air,
The still stone dogs,

Caught in metamorphosis, were
Left him as epilogues.

"The Age Demanded"

Vide Poem II, Page (342)

For this agility chance found
Him of all men, unfit
As the red-beaked steeds of
The Cytherean for a chain bit.

The glow of porcelain
Brought no reforming sense
To his perception
Of the social inconsequence.

Thus, if her colour
Came against his gaze,
Tempered as if
It were through a perfect glaze

He made no immediate application
Of this to relation of the state
To the individual, the month was more temperate
Because this beauty had been.

       The coral isle, the lion-coloured sand
       Burst in upon the porcelain revery:
       Impetuous troubling
       Of his imagery.

Mildness, amid the neo-Nietzschean clatter,
His sense of graduations,
Quite out of place amid
Resistance to current exacerbations,

Invitation, mere invitation to perceptivity
Gradually led him to the isolation
Which these presents place
Under a more tolerant, perhaps, examination.

By constant elimination
The manifest universe
Yielded an armour
Against utter consternation,

A Minoan undulation,
Seen, we admit, amid ambrosial circumstances
Strengthened him against
The discouraging doctrine of chances.

And his desire for survival,
Faint in the most strenuous moods,
Became an Olympian *apathein*
In the presence of selected perceptions.

A pale gold, in the aforesaid pattern,
The unexpected palms
Destroying, certainly, the artist's urge,
Left him delighted with the imaginary
Audition of the phantasmal sea-surge,

Incapable of the least utterance or composition,
Emendation, conservation of the "better tradition,"
Refinement of medium, elimination of superfluities,
August attraction or concentration.

Nothing, in brief, but maudlin confession,
Irresponse to human aggression,
Amid the precipitation, down-float
Of insubstantial manna,
Lifting the faint susurrus
Of his subjective hosanna.
Ultimate affronts to
Human redundancies;

Non-esteem of self-styled "his betters"
Leading, as he well knew,
To his final
Exclusion from the world of letters.

IV

Scattered Moluccas
Not knowing, day to day,
The first day's end, in the next noon;
The placid water
Unbroken by the Simoon;

Thick foliage
Placid beneath warm suns,
Tawn fore-shores
Washed in the cobalt o. oblivions;

Or through dawn-mist
The grey and rose
Of the juridical
Flamingoes;

A consciousness disjunct,
Being but this overblotted
Series
Of intermittences;

Coracle of Pacific voyages,
The unforecasted beach;
Then on an oar
Read this:

"I was
"And I no more exist;
"Here drifted
"An hedonist."

Medallion

Luini in porcelain!
The grand piano
Utters a profane
Protest with her clear soprano.

The sleek head emerges
From the gold-yellow frock
As Anadyomene in the opening
Pages of Reinach.

Honey-red, closing the face-oval,
A basket-work of braids which seem as if they were
Spun in King Minos' hall
From metal, or intractable amber;

The face-oval beneath the glaze,
Bright in its suave bounding-line, as,
Beneath half-watt rays,
The eyes turn topaz.

from *HOMAGE TO SEXTUS PROPERTIUS*

III

Midnight, and a letter comes to me from
      our mistress:
    Telling me to come to Tibur:
                        At once!!
"Bright tips reach up from twin towers,
"Anienan spring water falls into flat-spread pools."

What *is* to be done about it?
        Shall I entrust myself to entangled shadows,
Where bold hands may do violence to my person?

Yet if I postpone my obedience
               because of this respectable terror,
I shall be prey to lamentations worse than a noctural assailant.
And I shall be in the wrong,
             and it will last a twelve-month,
For her hands have no kindness me-ward,
Nor is there anyone to whom lovers are not sacred
    at midnight
    And in the Via Sciro.
If any man would be a lover
         he may walk on the Scythian coast,
No barbarism would go to the extent of doing him harm,
The moon will carry his candle,
       the stars will point out the stumbles,
Cupid will carry lighted torches before him
            and keep mad dogs off his ankles.
Thus all roads are perfectly safe
               and at any hour;
Who so indecorous as to shed the pure gore of a suitor?!
    Cypris is his cicerone.

What if undertakers follow my track,
              such a death is worth dying.
She would bring frankincense and wreaths to my tomb,
    She would sit like an ornament on my pyre.

God's aid, let not my bones lie in a public location
With crowds too assiduous in their crossing of it;
For thus are tombs of lovers most desecrated.

May a woody and sequestered place cover me with its foliage

Or may I inter beneath the hummock
                of some as yet uncatalogued sand;
At any rate I shall not have my epitaph in a high road.

IV

Difference of Opinion with Lygdamus

Tell me the truths which you hear of our constant young lady,
           Lygdamus,
And may the bought yoke of a mistress lie with
              equitable weight on your shoulders;
For I am swelled up with inane pleasurabilities
              and deceived by your reference
To things which you think I would like to believe.

No messenger should come wholly empty
            and a slave should fear plausibilities;
Much conversation is as good as having a home.
    Out with it, tell it to me, all of it, from the beginning,
I guzzle with outstretched ears.
Thus? She wept into uncombed hair,
                  And you saw it.
Vast waters flowed from her eyes?
                You, you Lygdamus
Saw her stretched on her bed,—
           it was no glimpse in a mirror;
No gawds on her snowy hands, no orfevrerie,
Sad garment draped on her slender arms.
Her escritoires lay shut by the bed-feet.
Sadness hung over the house, and the desolated female attendants
Were desolated because she had told them her dreams.

She was veiled in the midst of that place,
Damp woolly handkerchiefs were stuffed into her
           undryable eyes,
And a querulous noise responded to our solicitous reprobations.
For which things you will get a reward from me, Lygdamus?
To say many things is equal to having a home.
And the other woman "has not enticed me
              by her pretty manners,
"She has caught me with herbaceous poison,
           she twiddles the spiked wheel of a rhombus,
"She stews puffed frogs, snake s bones, the moulted feathers of
           screech owls,

"She binds me with ravvles of shrouds.
        "Black spiders spin in her bed!
"Let her lovers snore at her in the morning!
        "May the gout cramp up her feet!
"Does he like me to sleep here alone,
        Lygdamus?
"Will he say nasty things at my funeral?"

And you expect me to believe this
        after twelve months of discomfort?

VI

When, when, and whenever death closes our eyelids,
Moving naked over Acheron
Upon the one raft, victor and conquered together,
Marius and Jugurtha together,
        one tangle of shadows.

Caesar plots against India,
Tigris and Euphrates shall, from now on, flow at his bidding,
Tibet shall be full of Roman policemen,
The Parthians shall get used to our statuary
        and acquire a Roman religion;
One raft on the veiled flood of Acheron,
        Marius and Jugurtha together.

Nor at my funeral either will there be any long trail;
        bearing ancestral lares and images;
No trumpets filled with my emptiness,
Nor shall it be on an Atalic bed;
        The perfumed cloths will be absent.
A small plebeian procession.
        Enough, enough and in plenty
There will be three books at my obsequies
Which I take, my not unworthy gift, to Persephone.

You will follow the bare scarified breast
Nor will you be weary of calling my name, nor too weary
        To place the last kiss on my lips
When the Syrian onyx is broken.

        "He who is now vacant dust
        "Was once the slave of one passion:"
Give that much inscription
        "Death why tardily come?"

You, sometimes, will lament a lost friend,
      For it is a custom:
This care for past men,

Since Adonis was gored in Idalia, and the Cytherean
Ran crying with out-spread hair
      In vain, you call back the shade,
In vain, Cynthia. Vain call to unanswering shadow,
      Small talk comes from small bones.

VII

Me happy, night, night full of brightness;
Oh couch made happy by my long delectations;
How many words talked out with abundant candles;
Struggles when the lights were taken away;
Now with bared breasts she wrestled against me,
      Tunic spread in delay;
And she then opening my eyelids fallen in sleep,
Her lips upon them; and it was her mouth saying:
    Sluggard!

In how many varied embraces, our changing arms,
Her kisses, how many, lingering on my lips.
"Turn not Venus into a blinded motion,
      Eyes are the guides of love,
Paris took Helen naked coming from the bed of Menelaus,
Endymion's naked body, bright bait for Diana,"
    —such at least is the story.

While our fates twine together, sate we our eyes with love;
For long night comes upon you
        and a day when no day returns.
Let the gods lay chains upon us
      so that no day shall unbind them.

Fool who would set a term to love's madness,
For the sun shall drive with black horses,
      earth shall bring wheat from barley,
The flood shall move toward the fountain
      Ere love know moderations,
      The fish shall swim in dry streams.
No, now while it may be, let not the fruit of life cease.

    Dry wreaths drop their petals,
        their stalks are woven in baskets,

To-day we take the great breath of lovers,
    to-morrow fate shuts us in.

Though you give all your kisses
     you give but few.

Nor can I shift my pains to other,
   Hers will I be dead,
If she confer such nights upon me,
     long is my life, long in years,
If she give me many,
   God am I for the time.

IX

I

The twisted rhombs ceased their clamour of accompaniment;
The scorched laurel lay in the fire-dust;
The moon still declined to descend out of heaven,

But the black ominous owl hoot was audible.

And one raft bears our fates
     on the veiled lake toward Avernus
Sails spread on Cerulean waters, I would shed tears
   for two;
I shall live, if she continue in life,
    If she dies, I shall go with her.
Great Zeus, save the woman,
    or she will sit before your feet in a veil,
    and tell out the long list of her troubles.

II

Persephone and Dis, Dis, have mercy upon her,
There are enough women in hell,
     quite enough beautiful women,
Iope, and Tyro, and Pasiphaë and the formal girls of Achaia,
And out of Troad, and from Campania,
Death has his tooth in the lot,
    Avernus lusts for the lot of them,
Beauty is not eternal, no man has perennial fortune,
Slow foot, or swift foot, death delays but for a season.

III

My light, light of my eyes,
                    you are escaped from great peril,
Go back to Great Dian's dances bearing suitable gifts,
Pay up your vow of night watches
                              to Dian, goddess of virgins,
And unto me also pay debt:
The ten nights of your company you have
                              promised me.

CANTO I

And then went down to the ship,
Set keel to breakers, forth on the godly sea, and
We set up mast and sail on that swart ship,
Bore sheep aboard her, and our bodies also
Heavy with weeping, and winds from sternward
Bore us out onward with bellying canvas,
Circe's this craft, the trim-coifed goddess.
Then sat we amidships, wind jamming the tiller,
Thus with stretched sail, we went over sea till day's end.
Sun to his slumber, shadows o'er all the ocean,
Came we then to the bounds of deepest water,
To the Kimmerian lands, and peopled cities
Covered with close-webbed mist, unpierced ever
With glitter of sun-rays
Nor with stars stretched, nor looking back from heaven
Swartest night stretched over wretched men there.
The ocean flowing backward, came we then to the place
Aforesaid by Circe.
Here did they rites, Perimedes and Eurylochus,
And drawing sword from my hip
I dug the ell-square pitkin;
Poured we libations unto each the dead,
First mead and then sweet wine, water mixed with white flour.
Then prayed I many a prayer to the sickly death's-heads;
As set in Ithaca, sterile bulls of the best
For sacrifice, heaping the pyre with goods,
A sheep to Tiresias only, black and a bell-sheep.
Dark blood flowed in the fosse,
Souls out of Erebus, cadaverous dead, of brides
Of youths and of the old who had borne much;
Souls stained with recent tears, girls tender,
Men many, mauled with bronze lance heads,
Battle spoil, bearing yet dreory arms,

These many crowded about me; with shouting,
Pallor upon me, cried to my men for more beasts;
Slaughtered the herds, sheep slain of bronze;
Poured ointment, cried to the gods,
To Pluto the strong, and praised Proserpine;
Unsheathed the narrow sword,
I sat to keep off the impetuous impotent dead,
Till I should hear Tiresias.
But first Elpenor came, our friend Elpenor,
Unburied, cast on the wide earth,
Limbs that we left in the house of Circe,
Unwept, unwrapped in sepulchre, since toils urged other.
Pitiful spirit. And I cried in hurried speech:
"Elpenor, how art thou come to this dark coast?
"Cam'st thou afoot, outstripping seamen?"
                And he in heavy speech:
"Ill fate and abundant wine. I slept in Circe's ingle.
"Going down the long ladder unguarded,
"I fell against the buttress,
"Shattered the nape-nerve, the soul sought Avernus.
"But thou, O King, I bid remember me, unwept, unburied,
"Heap up mine arms, be tomb by sea-bord, and inscribed:
"A man of no fortune, and with a name to come.
"And set my oar up, that I swung mid fellows."

And Anticlea came, whom I beat off, and then Tiresias Theban,
Holding his golden wand, knew me, and spoke first:
"A second time? why? man of ill star,
"Facing the sunless dead and this joyless region?
"Stand from the fosse, leave me my bloody bever
"For soothsay."
                And I stepped back,
And he strong with the blood, said then: "Odysseus
"Shalt return through spiteful Neptune, over dark seas,
"Lose all companions." Then Anticlea came.
Lie quiet Divus. I mean, that is Andreas Divus,
In officina Wecheli, 1538, out of Homer.
And he sailed, by Sirens and thence outward and away
And unto Circe.
            Venerandam,
In the Cretan's phrase, with the golden crown, Aphrodite,
Cypri munimenta sortita est, mirthful, oricalchi, with golden
Girdle and breast bands, thou with dark eyelids
Bearing the golden bough of Argicida. So that:

CANTO II

Hang it all, Robert Browning,
there can be but the one "Sordello.'
But Sordello, and my Sordello?
Lo Sordels si fo di Mantovana.
So-shu churned in the sea.
Seal sports in the spray-whited circles of cliff-wash,
Sleek head, daughter of Lir,
           eyes of Picasso
Under black fur-hood, lithe daughter of Ocean;
And the wave runs in the beach-groove.
"Eleanor, ἐλέναυς and ἐλέπτολις!"
                And poor old Homer blind, blind, as a bat,
Ear, ear for the sea-surge, murmur of old men s voices:
"Let her go back to the ships,
"Back among Grecian faces, lest evil come on our own,
"Evil and further evil, and a curse cursed on our children,
"Moves, yes she moves like a goddess
"And has the face of a god
           and the voice of Schoeney's daughters,
"And doom goes with her in walking,
"Let her go back to the ships,
           back among Grecian voices."
And by the beach-run, Tyro,
           Twisted arms of the sea-god,
Lithe sinews of water, gripping her, cross-hold,
And the blue-gray glass of the wave tents them,
Glare azure of water, cold-welter, close cover.
Quiet sun-tawny sand-stretch,
The gulls broad out their wings,
           nipping between the splay feathers;
Snipe come for their bath,
           bend out their wing-joints,
Spread wet wings to the sun-film,
And by Scios,
           to left of the Naxos passage,
Naviform rock overgrown,
           algae cling to its edge,
There is a wine-red glow in the shallows,
           a tin flash in the sun-dazzle.

The ship landed in Scios,
           men wanting spring-water,
And by the rock-pool a young boy loggy with vine-must,

      "To Naxos? Yes, we'll take you to Naxos,
Cum' along lad." "Not that way!"
"Aye, that way is Naxos."
            And I said: "It's a straight ship."
And an ex-convict out of Italy
         knocked me into the fore-stays,
(He was wanted for manslaughter in Tuscany)
         And the whole twenty against me,
Mad for a little slave money.
         And they took her out of Scios
And off her course . . .
         And the boy came to, again, with the racket,
And looked out over the bows,
         and to eastward, and to the Naxos passage.
God-sleight then, god-sleight:
         Ship stock fast in sea-swirl,
Ivy upon the oars, King Pentheus,
         grapes with no seed but sea-foam,
Ivy in scupper-hole.
Aye, I, Acoetes, stood there,
         and the god stood by me,
Water cutting under the keel,
Sea-break from stern forrards,
         wake running off from the bow,
And where was gunwale, there now was vine-trunk,
And tenthril where cordage had been,
         grape-leaves on the rowlocks,
Heavy vine on the oarshafts,
And, out of nothing, a breathing,
         hot breath on my ankles,
Beasts like shadows in glass,
         a furred tail upon nothingness.
Lynx-purr, and heathery smell of beasts,
         where tar smell had been,
Sniff and pad-foot of beasts,
         eye-glitter out of black air.
The sky overshot, dry, with no tempest,
Sniff and pad-foot of beasts,
         fur brushing my knee-skin,
Rustle of airy sheaths,
         dry forms in the *æther*.
And the ship like a keel in ship-yard,
         slung like an ox in smith's sling,
Ribs stuck fast in the ways,
         grape-cluster over pin-rack,
         void air taking pelt.

Lifeless air become sinewed,
           e eisure of panthers,
Leopards sniffing the grape shoots by scupper-hole,
Crouched pa thers by fore-hatch,
And the sea blue-deep about us,
          green-ruddy in shadows,
And Lyæus: "From now, Acoetes, my altars,
Fearing no bondage,
          fearing no cat of the wood,
Safe with my lynxes,
          feeding grapes to my leopards,
Olibanum is my incense,
          the vines grow in my homage."

The back-swell now smooth in the rudder-chains,
Black snout of a porpoise
          where Lycabs had been,
Fish-scales on the oarsmen.
          And I worship.
I have seen what I have seen.
          When they brought the boy I said:
"He has a god in him,
          though I do not know which god."
And they kicked me into the fore-stays.
I have seen what I have seen:
          Medon's face like the face of a dory,
Arms shrunk into fins. And you, Pentheus,
Had as well listen to Tiresias, and to Cadmus,
          or your luck will go out of you.
Fish-scales over groin muscles,
          lynx-purr amid sea . . .
And of a later year,
          pale in the wine-red algae,
If you will lean over the rock,
          the coral face under wave-tinge,
Rose-paleness under water-shift,
          Ileuthyeria, fair Dafne of sea-bords,
The swimmer's arms turned to branches,
Who will say in what year,
          fleeing what band of tritons,
The smooth brows, seen, and half seen,
          now ivory stillness.

And So-shu churned in the sea, So-shu also,
          using the long moon for a churn-stick . . .

Lithe turning of water,
        sinews of Poseidon,
Black azure and hyaline,
        glass wave over Tyro,
Close cover, unstillness,
        bright welter of wave-cords,
Then quiet water,
        quiet in the buff sands,
Sea-fowl stretching wing-joints,
        splashing in rock-hollows and sand-hollows
In the wave-runs by the half-dune;
Glass-glint of wave in the tide-rips against sunlight,
        pallor of Hesperus,
Grey peak of the wave,
        wave, colour of grape's pulp,

Olive grey in the near,
        far, smoke grey of the rock-slide,
Salmon-pink wings of the fish-hawk
        cast grey shadows in water,
The tower like a one-eyed great goose
        cranes up out of the olive-grove,

And we have heard the fauns chiding Proteus
        in the smell of hay under the olive-trees,
And the frogs singing against the fauns
        in the half-light.
And . . .

CANTO III

I sat on the Dogana's steps
For the gondolas cost too much, that year,
And there were not "those girls," there was one face,
And the Buccéntoro twenty yards off, howling "Stretti,"
The lit cross-beams, that year, in the Morosini,
And peacocks in Koré's house, or there may have been.
        Gods float in the azure air,
Bright gods and Tuscan, back before dew was shed.
Light: and the first light, before ever dew was fallen.
Panisks, and from the oak, dryas,
And from the apple, maelid,
Through all the wood, and the leaves are full of voices,
A-whisper, and the clouds bowe over the lake,
And there are gods upon them,

And in the water, the almond-white swimmers,
The silvery water glazes the upturned nipple,
        As Poggio has remarked.
Green veins in the turquoise,
Or, the gray steps lead up under the cedars.

My Cid rode up to Burgos,
Up to the studded gate between two towers,
Beat with his lance butt, and the child came out,
Una niña de nueve años,
To the little gallery over the gate, between the towers,
Reading the writ, voce tinnula:
That no man speak to, feed, help Ruy Diaz,
On pain to have his heart out, set on a pike spike
And both his eyes torn out, and all his goods sequestered,
"And here, Myo Cid, are the seals,
The big seal and the writing."
And he came down from Bivar, Myo Cid,
With no hawks left there on their perches,
And no clothes there in the presses,
And left his trunk with Raquel and Vidas,
That big box of sand, with the pawn-brokers,
To get pay for his menie;
Breaking his way to Valencia.
Ignez da Castro murdered, and a wall
Here stripped, here made to stand.
Drear waste, the pigment flakes from the stone,
Or plaster flakes, Mantegna painted the wall.
Silk tatters, "Nec Spe Nec Metu."

CANTO XVII

So that the vines burst from my fingers
And the bees weighted with pollen
Move heavily in the vine-shoots:
        chirr—chirr—chir-rikk—a purring sound,
And the birds sleepily in the branches.
        ZAGREUS! IO ZAGREUS!
With the first pale-clear of the heaven
And the cities in their hills,
And the goddess of the fair knees
Moving there, with the oak-wood behind her,
The green slope, with white hounds
        leaping about her;

And thence down to the creek's mouth, until evening,
Flat water before me,
            and the trees growing in water,
Marble trunks out of stillness,
On past the palazzi,
                        in the stillness,
The light now, not of the sun.
                        Chrysophrase,
And the water green clear, and blue clear;
On, to the great cliffs of amber.
                                    Between them,
Cave of Nerea,
        she like a great shell curved,
And the boat drawn without sound,
Without odour of ship-work,
Nor bird-cry, nor any noise of wave moving,
Nor splash of porpoise, nor any noise of wave moving,
Within her cave, Nerea,
                        she like a great shell curved
In the suavity of the rock,
                        cliff green-gray in the far,
In the near, the gate-cliffs of amber,
And the wave
                    green clear, and blue clear,
And the cave salt-white, and glare-purple,
            cool, porphyry smooth,
            the rock sea-worn.
No gull-cry, no sound of porpoise,
Sand as of malachite, and no cold there,
            the light not of the sun.

Zagreus, feeding his panthers,
            the turf clear as on hills under light.
And under the almond-trees, gods,
            with them, *choros nympharum*. Gods,
Hermes and Athene,
            As shaft of compass,
Between them, trembled—
To the left is the place of fauns,
            sylva nympharum;
The low wood, moor-scrub,
            the doe, the young spotted deer,
            leap up through the broom-plants,
                        as dry leaf amid yellow.
And by one cut of the hills,
            the great alley of Memnons.

Beyond, sea, crests seen over dune
Night sea churning shingle,
To the left, the alley of cypress.
                              A boat came,
One man holding her sail,
Guiding her with oar caught over gunwale, saying:
          "There, in the forest of marble,
          "the stone trees—out of water—
          "the arbours of stone—
          "marble leaf, over leaf,
          "silver, steel over steel,
          "silver beaks rising and crossing,
          "prow set against prow,
          "stone, ply over ply,
          "the gilt beams flare of an evening"
Borso, Carmagnola, the men of craft, *i vitrei,*
Thither, at one time, time after time,
And the waters richer than glass,
Bronze gold, the blaze over the silver,
Dye-pots in the torch-light,
The flash of wave under prows,
And the silver beaks rising and crossing,
          Stone trees, white and rose-white in the darkness,
Cypress there by the towers,
          Drift under hulls in the night.

          "In the gloom the gold
Gathers the light about it." . . .

Now supine in burrow, half over-arched bramble,
One eye for the sea, through that peek-hole,
Gray light, with Athene.
Zothar and her elephants, the gold loin-cloth,
The sistrum, shaken, shaken,
          the cohort of her dancers.
And Aletha, by bend of the shore,
          with her eyes seaward,
          and in her hands sea-wrack
Salt-bright with the foam.
Koré through the bright meadow,
          with green-gray dust in the grass:
"For this hour, brother of Circe."
Arm laid over my shoulder,
Saw the sun for three days, the sun fulvid,
As a lion lift over sand-plain;
                              and that day,

And for three days, and none after,
Splendour, as the splendour of Hermes,
And shipped thence
              to the stone place,
Pale white, over water,
                  known water,
And the white forest of marble, bent bough over bough,
The pleached arbour of stone,
Thither Borso, when they shot the barbed arrow at him,
And Carmagnola, between the two columns,
Sigismundo, after that wreck in Dalmatia.
      Sunset like the grasshopper flying.

CANTO XLV

With *Usura*
With usura hath no man a house of good stone
each block cut smooth and well fitting
that design might cover their face,
with usura
hath no man a pointed paradise on his church wall
harpes et luthes
or where virgin receiveth message
and halo projects from incision,
with usura
seeth no man Gonzaga his heirs and his concubines
no picture is made to endure nor to live with
but it is made to sell and sell quickly
with usura, sin against nature,
is thy bread ever more of stale rags
is thy bread dry as paper,
with no mountain wheat, no strong flour
with usura the line grows thick
with usura is no clear demarcation
and no man can find site for his dwelling.
Stone cutter is kept from his stone
weaver is kept from his loom
WITH USURA
wool comes not to market
sheep bringeth no gain with usura
Usura is a murrain, usura
blunteth the needle in the maid's hand
and stoppeth the spinner's cunning. Pietro Lombardo
came not by usura
Duccio came not by usura

nor Pier della Francesca; Zuan Bellin' not by usura
nor was "La Calunnia" painted.
Came not by usura Angelico; came not Ambrogio Praedis,
Came no church of cut stone signed: *Adamo me fecit.*
Not by usura St Trophime
Not by usura Saint Hilaire,
Usura rusteth the chisel
It rusteth the craft and the crafstman
It gnaweth the thread in the loom
None learneth to weave gold in her pattern;
Azure hath a canker by usura; cramoisi is unbroidered
Emerald findeth no Memling
Usura slayeth the child in the womb
It stayeth the young man's courting
It hath brought palsey to bed, lyeth
between the young bride and her bridgegroom
                    CONTRA NATURAM
They have brought whores for Eleusis
Corpses are set to banquet
at behest of usura.

from *CANTO LXXXI*

Yet
Ere the season died a-cold
Borne upon a zephyr's shoulder
I rose through the aureate sky
            Lawes and Jenkyns guard thy rest
            Dolmetsch ever be thy guest,
Has he tempered the viol's wood
To enforce both the grave and the acute?
Has he curved us the bowl of the lute?
            Lawes and Jenkyns guard thy rest
            Dolmetsch ever be thy guest
Hast 'ou fashioned so airy a mood
     To draw up leaf from the root?
Hast 'ou found a cloud so light
     As seemed neither mist nor shade?

                Then resolve me, tell me aright
                If Waller sang or Dowland played.

        Your eyen two wol sleye me sodenly
        I may the beauté of hem nat susteyne

And for 180 years almost nothing.

Ed ascoltando al leggier mormorio
    there came new subtlety of eyes into my tent,
whether of spirit or hypostasis,
    but what the blindfold hides
or at carneval

                nor any pair showed anger
    Saw but the eyes and stance between the eyes,
colour, diastasis,
    careless or unaware it had not the
  whole tent's room
nor was place for the full image,
interpass, penetrate
    casting but shade beyond the other lights
        sky's clear
        night's sea
        green of the mountain pool
        shone from the unmasked eyes in half-mask's space.
What thou lovest well remains,
                the rest is dross
What thou lov'st well shall not be reft from thee
What thou lov'st well is thy true heritage
Whose world, or mine or theirs
             or is it of none?
First came the seen, then thus the palpable
    Elysium, though it were in the halls of hell,
What thou lovest well is thy true heritage

The ant's a centaur in his dragon world.
Pull down thy vanity, it is not man
Made courage, or made order, or made grace,
    Pull down thy vanity, I say pull down.
Learn of the green world what can be thy place
In scaled invention or true artistry,
Pull down thy vanity,
           Paquin pull down!
The green casque has outdone your elegance.

"Master thyself, then others shall thee beare"
    Pull down thy vanity
Thou art a beaten dog beneath the hail,
A swollen magpie in a fitful sun,
Half black half white
Nor knowst'ou wing from tail

Pull down thy vanity
                    How mean thy hates
Fostered in falsity,
                    Pull down thy vanity,
Rathe to destroy, niggard in charity,
Pull down thy vanity,
                    I say pull down.

But to have done instead of not doing
                    this is not vanity
To have, with decency, knocked
That a Blunt should open
                    To have gathered from the air a live tradition
or from a fine old eye the unconquered flame
This is not vanity.
                    Here error is all in the not done,
all in the diffidence that faltered.

MARIANNE MOORE
(b. 1887)

NO SWAN SO FINE

"No water so still as the
   dead fountains of Versailles." No swan,
with swart blind look askance
and gondoliering legs, so fine
   as the chintz china one with fawn-
brown eyes and toothed gold
collar on to show whose bird it was.

Lodged in the Louis Fifteenth
   candelabrum-tree of cockscomb-
tinted buttons, dahlias,
sea-urchins, and everlastings,
   it perches on the branching foam
of polished sculptured
flowers—at ease and tall. The king is dead.

THE FISH

wade
through black jade.
   Of the crow-blue mussel-shells, one keeps
   adjusting the ash-heaps;
      opening and shutting itself like

an
injured fan.
   The barnacles which encrust the side
   of the wave, cannot hide
      there for the submerged shafts of the

sun,
split like spun
   glass, move themselves with spotlight swiftness
   into the crevices—
      in and out, illuminating

the
turquoise sea
   of bodies. The water drives a wedge
   of iron through the iron edge
      of the cliff; whereupon the stars,

pink
rice-grains, ink-
   bespattered jelly-fish, crabs like green
   lilies, and submarine
      toadstools, slide each on the other.

All
external
   marks of abuse are present on this
   defiant edifice—
      all the physical features of

ac-
cident—lack
   of cornice, dynamite grooves, burns, and
   hatchet strokes, these things stand
      out on it; the chasm-side is

dead.
Repeated
   evidence has proved that it can live
   on what can not revive
      its youth. The sea grows old in it.

IN THIS AGE OF HARD TRYING, NONCHALANCE IS GOOD AND

"really, it is not the
   business of the gods to bake clay pots." They did not
      do it in this instance. A few
         revolved upon the axes of their worth
  as if excessive popularity might be a pot;

they did not venture the
   profession of humility. The polished wedge
      that might have split the firmament
         was dumb. At last it threw itself away
and falling down, conferred on some poor fool, a privilege.

"Taller by the length of
    a conversation of five hundred years than all
        the others," there was one, whose tales
            of what could never have been actual—
were better than the haggish, uncompanionable drawl

of certitude; his by-
    play was more terrible in its effectiveness
        than the fiercest frontal attack.
            The staff, the bag, the feigned inconsequence
of manner, best bespeak that weapon, self-protectiveness.

CRITICS AND CONNOISSEURS

There is a great amount of poetry in unconscious
    fastidiousness. Certain Ming
        products, imperial floor-coverings of coach-
wheel yellow, are well enough in their way but I have seen
                something
        that I like better—a
            mere childish attempt to make an imperfectly ballasted
                animal stand up,
            similar determination to make a pup
                eat his meat from the plate.

I remember a swan under the willows in Oxford,
    with flamingo-coloured, maple-
        leaflike feet. It reconnoitered like a battle-
ship. Disbelief and conscious fastidiousness were the staple
    ingredients in its
        disinclination to move. Finally its hardihood was
            not proof against its
        proclivity to more fully appraise such bits
            of food as the stream

bore counter to it; it made away with what I gave it
    to eat. I have seen this swan and
        I have seen you; I have seen ambition without
    understanding in a variety of forms. Happening to stand
            by an ant-hill, I have
        seen a fastidious ant carrying a stick north, south,
            east, west, till it turned on
        itself, struck out from the flower-bed into the lawn,
            and returned to the point

from which it had started. Then abandoning the stick as
   useless and overtaxing its
        jaws with a particle of whitewash—pill-like but
heavy, it again went through the same course of procedure.
             What is
        there in being able
             to say that one has dominated the stream in an
                 attitude of self-defence;
        in proving that one has had the experience
             of carrying a stick?

THE MONKEYS

winked too much and were afraid of snakes. The zebras
        supreme in
their abnormality; the elephants with the fog-coloured skin
   and strictly practical appendages
        were there, the small cats; and the parakeet—
             trivial and humdrum on examination, destroying
        bark and portions of the food it could not eat.

I recall their magnificence, now not more magnificent
than it is dim. It is difficult to recall the ornament,
   speech, and precise manner of what one might
        call the minor acquaintances twenty
             years back; but I shall not forget him—that Gilgamesh
                 among
        the hairy carnivora—that cat with the

Wedge-shaped, slate-grey marks on its forelegs and the
        resolute tail,
astringently remarking, "They have imposed on us with their
        pale
   half-fledged protestations, trembling about
        in inarticulate frenzy, saying
             it is not for us to understand art; finding it
        all so difficult, examining the thing

as if it were inconceivably arcanic, as symmet-
rically frigid as if it had been carved out of chrysoprase
   or marble—strict with tension, malignant
        in its power over us and deeper
             than the sea when it proffers flattery in exchange for
                 hemp,
        rye, flax, horses, platinum, timber, and fur."

IN THE DAYS OF PRISMATIC COLOUR

not in the days of Adam and Eve, but when Adam
    was alone; when there was no smoke and colour was
fine, not with the refinement
    of early civilization art, but because
of its originality; with nothing to modify it but the

mist that went up, obliqueness was a varia-
    tion of the perpendicular, plain to see and
to account for: it is no
    longer that; nor did the blue-red-yellow band
of incandescence that was colour keep its stripe: it also is one of

those things into which much that is peculiar can be
    read; complexity is not a crime, but carry
it to the point of murki-
    ness and nothing is plain. Complexity,
moreover, that has been committed to darkness, instead of
        granting it-

self to be the pestilence that it is, moves all a-
    bout as if to bewilder us with the dismal
fallacy that insistance
    is the measure of achievement and that all
truth must be dark. Principally throat, sophistication is as it al-

ways has been—at the antipodes from the init-
    ial great truths. "Part of it was crawling, part of it
was about to crawl, the rest
    was torpid in its lair." In the short-legged, fit-
ful advance, the gurgling and all the minutiae—we have
        the classic

multitude of feet. To what purpose! Truth is no Apollo
    Belvedere, no formal thing. The wave may go over it if
        it likes.
Know that it will be there when it says,
    "I shall be there when the wave has gone by."

ENGLAND

with its baby rivers and little towns, each with its abbey or its
        cathedral,
with voices—one voice perhaps, echoing through the transept
        —the

criterion of suitability and convenience; and Italy with its equal
shores—contriving an epicureanism from which the grossness
    has been

extracted: and Greece with its goat and its gourds, the nest
    of modified illusions:
and France, the "chrysalis of the nocturnal butterfly," in
whose products mystery of construction diverts one from
    what was originally one's
object—substance at the core: and the East with its snails,
    its emotional

shorthand and jade cockroaches, its rock crystal and its im-
    perturbability,
all of museum quality: and America where there
is the little old ramshackle victoria in the south, where cigars
    are smoked on the
street in the north; where there are no proof-readers, no
    silk-worms, no digressions;

the wild man's land; grassless, linksless, languageless country
    in which letters are written
not in Spanish, not in Greek, not in Latin, not in shorthand,
but in plain American which cats and dogs can read! The
    letter *a* in psalm and calm when
pronounced with the sound of *a* in candle, is very notice-
    able, but

why should continents of misapprehension have to be ac-
    counted for by the
fact? Does it follow that because there are poisonous toad-
    stools
which resemble mushrooms, both are dangerous? In the case
    of mettlesomeness which may be
mistaken for appetite, of heat which may appear to be haste,
    no con-

clusions may be drawn. To have misapprehended the matter
    is to have confessed
that one has not looked far enough. The sublimated wisdom
of China, Egyptian discernment, the cataclysmic torrent of
    emotion compressed
in the verbs of the Hebrew language, the books of the man
    who is able

to say, "I envy nobody but him, and him only, who catches
    more fish than
I do,"—the flower and fruit of all that noted superi-
ority—should one not have stumbled upon it in America, must
    one imagine
that it is not there? It has never been confined to one locality.

A GRAVE

Man looking into the sea,
taking the view from those who have a. much right to it as
    you have to it yourself,
it is human nature to stand in the middle of a thing,
but you cannot stand in the middle of this;
the sea has nothing to give but a well-excavated grave.
The firs stand in a procession, each with an emerald turkey-
    foot at the top,
reserved as their contours, saying nothing;
repression, however, is not the most obvious characteristic
    of the sea;
the sea is a collector, quick to return a rapacious look.
There are others besides you who have worn that look—
whose expression is no longer a protest; the fish no longer
    investigate them
for their bones have not lasted:
men lower nets, unconscious of the fact that they are dese-
    crating a grave,
and row quickly away—the blades of the oars
moving together like the feet of water-spiders as if there
    were no such thing as death.
The wrinkles progress among themselves in a phalanx—
    beautiful under networks of foam,
and fade breathlessly while the sea rustles in and out of the
    seaweed;
the birds swim through the air at top speed, emitting cat-
    calls as heretofore—
the tortoise-shell scourges about the feet of the cliffs, in motion
    beneath them;
and the ocean, under the pulsation of lighthouses and noise
    of bell-buoys.
advances as usual, looking as if it were not that ocean in
    which dropped things are bound to sink—
in which if they turn and twist, it is neither with volition nor
    consciousness.

THE LABOURS OF HERCULES

To popularize the mule, its neat exterior
expressing the principle of accommodation reduced to a
    minimum:
to persuade one of austere taste, proud in the possession of
    home and a musician—
that the piano is a free field for etching; that his "charming
    tadpole notes"
belong to the past when one had time to play them:
to persuade those self-wrought Midases of brains
whose fourteen-carat ignorance aspires to rise in value
till the sky is the limit,
that excessive conduct augurs disappointment,
that one must not borrow a long white beard and tie it on
and threaten with the scythe of time the casually curious:
to teach the bard with too elastic a selectiveness
that one detects creative power by its capacity to conquer
    one's detachment,
that while it may have more elasticity than logic,
it knows where it is going;
it flies along in a straight line like electricity,
depopulating areas that boast of their remoteness,
to prove to the high priests of caste
that snobbishness is a stupidity,
the best side out, of age-old toadyism,
kissing the feet of the man above,
kicking the face of the man below;
to teach the patron-saints-to-atheists, the Coliseum
meet-me-alone-by-moonlight maudlin troubadour
that kickups for catstrings are not life
nor yet appropriate to death—that we are sick of the earth,
sick of the pig-sty, wild geese and wild men;
to convince snake-charming controversialists
that it is one thing to change one's mind,
another to eradicate it—that one keeps on knowing
"that the Negro is not brutal,
that the Jew is not greedy,
that the Oriental is not immoral,
that the German is not a Hun."

TO A STEAM ROLLER

The illustration
is nothing to you without the application.
    You lack half wit. You crush all the particles down
        into close conformity, and then walk back and forth
          on them.

Sparkling chips of rock
are crushed down to the level of the parent block.
    Were not "impersonal judgment in aesthetic
        matters, a metaphysical impossibility," you

might fairly achieve
it. As for butterflies, I can hardly conceive
    of one's attending upon you, but to question
        the congruence of the complement is vain, if it exists.

TO A SNAIL

If "compression is the first grace of style,"
you have it. Contractility is a virtue
as modesty is a virtue.
It is not the acquisition of any one thing
that is able to adorn,
or the incidental quality that occurs
as a concomitant of something well said,
that we value in style,
but the principle that is hid:
in the absence of feet, "a method of conclusions";
"a knowledge of principles,"
in the curious phenomenon of your occipital horn.

TO THE PEACOCK OF FRANCE

In "taking charge of your possessions when you saw them"
        you became a golden jay.
Scaramouche said you charmed his charm away,
    But not his colour? Yes, his colour when you liked.
Of chiselled setting and black-opalescent dye,
      You were the jewelry of sense;
        Of sense, not licence; you but trod the pace
        Of liberty in market-place
          And court. Molière,

The huggermugger repertory of your first adven-
ture, is your own affair.

"Anchorites do not dwell in theatres," and peacocks do not
flourish in a cell.
Why make distinctions? The results were well
When you were on the boards; nor were your triumphs
bought
At horrifying sacrifice of stringency.
You hated sham; you ranted up
And down through the conventions of excess;
Nor did the King love you the less
Nor did the world,
In whose chief interest and for whose spontaneous
delight, your broad tail was unfurled.

THE PAST IS THE PRESENT

If external action is effete
and rhyme is outmoded,
I shall revert to you,
Habakkuk, as on a recent occasion I was goaded
into doing by XY, who was speaking of unrhymed
verse.
This man said—I think that I repeat
his identical words:
"Hebrew poetry is
prose with a sort of heightened consciousness." Ecstasy
affords the occasion and expediency determines the
form.

WHAT ARE YEARS?

What is our innocence,
what is our guilt? All are
naked, none is safe. And whence
is courage: the unanswered question,
the resolute doubt,—
dumbly calling, deafly listening—that
in misfortune, even death,
encourages others
and in its defeat, stirs

the soul to be strong? He
sees deep and is glad, who

   accedes to mortality
   and in his imprisonment rises
   upon himself as
   the sea in a chasm, struggling to be
   free and unable to be,
     in its surrendering
     finds its continuing.

   So he who strongly feels,
   behaves. The very bird,
    grown taller as he sings, steels
   his form straight up. Though he is captive,
   his mighty singing
   says, satisfaction is a lowly
   thing, how pure a thing is joy.
     This is mortality.
     this is eternity.

SPENSER'S IRELAND

has not altered;—
 a place as kind as it is green,
 the greenest place I've never seen.
Every name is a tune.
Denunciations do not affect
  the culprit; nor blows, but it
is torture to him to not be spoken to.
They're natural,—
   the coat, like Venus'
mantle lined with stars,
buttoned close at the neck,—the sleeves new from disuse.

If in Ireland
 they play the harp backward at need,
 and gather at midday the seed
of the fern, eluding
their "giants all covered with iron," might
  there be fern seed for unlearn-
ing obduracy and for reinstating
the enchantment?
   Hindered characters
seldom have mothers
in Irish stories, but they all have grandmothers.

It was Irish;
  a match not a marriage was made
  when my great great grandmother'd said
with native genius for
disunion, "although your suitor be
    perfection, one objection
is enough; he is not
Irish." Outwitting
    the fairies, befriending the furies,
whoever again
and again says, "I'll never give in," never sees

that you're not free
  until you've been made captive by
  supreme belief,—credulity
you say? When large dainty
fingers tremblingly divide the wings
    of the fly for mid-July
with a needle and wrap it with peacock-tail,
or tie wool and
    buzzard's wing, their pride,
like the enchanter's
is in care, not madness. Concurring hands divide

flax for damask
  that when bleached by Irish weather
  has the silvered chamois-leather
water-tightness of a
skin. Twisted torcs and gold new-moon-shaped
    lunulae aren't jewelry
like the purple-coral fuchsia-tree's. Eire—
the guillemot
    so neat and the hen
of the heath and the
linnet spinet-sweet—bespeak relentlessness? Then

they are to me
  like enchanted Earl Gerald who
  changed himself into a stag, to
a great green-eyed cat of
the mountain. Discommodity makes
    them invisible; they've dis-
appeared. The Irish say your trouble is their
trouble and your
    joy their joy? I wish
I could believe it;
I am troubled, I'm dissatisfied, I'm Irish.

NEVERTHELESS

you've seen a strawberry
    that's had a struggle; yet
    was, where the fragments met,

a hedgehog or a star-
    fish for the multitude
    of seeds. What better food

than apple-seeds—the fruit
    within the fruit—locked in
    like counter-curved twin

hazel-nuts? Frost that kills
    the little rubber-plant-
    leaves of *kok-saghyz*-stalks, can't

harm the roots; they still grow
    in frozen ground. Once where
    there was a prickly-pear-

leaf clinging to barbed wire,
    a root shot down to grow
    in earth two feet below;

as carrots form mandrakes
    or a ram's-horn root some-
    times. Victory won't come

to me unless I go
    to it; a grape-tendril
    ties a knot in knots till

knotted thirty times,—so
    the bound twig that's under-
    gone and over-gone, can't stir.

The weak overcomes its
    menace, the strong over-
    comes itself. What is there

like fortitude! What sap
    went through that little thread
    to make the cherry red!

THE MIND IS AN ENCHANTING THING

is an enchanted thing
    like the glaze on a
katydid-wing
        subdivided by sun
        till the nettings are legion.
Like Gieseking playing Scarlatti;

like the apteryx-awl
    as a beak, or the
kiwi's rain-shawl
        of haired feathers, the mind
        feeling its way as though blind,
walks along with its eyes on the ground.

It has memory's ear
    that can hear without
having to hear.
        Like the gyroscope's fall,
        truly unequivocal
because trued by regnant certainty,

it is a power of
    strong enchantment. It
is like the dove-
        neck animated by
        sun; it is memory's eye;
it's conscientious inconsistency.

It tears off the veil; tears
    the temptation, the
mist the heart wears,
        from its eyes,—if the heart
        has a face; it takes apart
dejection. It's fire in the dove-neck's

iridescence; in the
    inconsistencies
of Scarlatti.
        Unconfusion submits
        its confusion to proof; it's
not a Herod's oath that cannot change.

IN DISTRUST OF MERITS

Strengthened to live, strengthened to die for
    medals and positioned victories?
They're fighting, fighting, fighting the blind
    man who thinks he sees,—
who cannot see that the enslaver is
enslaved; the hater, harmed. O shining O
        firm star, O tumultuous
            ocean lashed till small things go
      as they will, the mountainous
         wave makes us who look, know

depth. Lost at sea before they fought! O
    star of David, star of Bethlehem,
O black imperial lion
    of the Lord—emblem
of a risen world—be joined at last, be
joined. There is hate's crown beneath which all is
        death; there's love's without which none
         is king; the blessed deeds bless
      the halo. As contagion
        of sickness makes sickness,

contagion of trust can make trust. They're
    fighting in deserts and caves, one by
one, in battalions and squadrons;
    they're fighting that I
may yet recover from the disease, My
Self; some have it lightly; some will die. "Man
        wolf to man" and we devour
         ourselves. The enemy could not
      have made a greater breach in our
        defences. One pilot-

ing a blind man can escape him, but
    Job disheartened by false comfort knew
that nothing can be so defeating
    as a blind man who
can see. O alive who are dead, who are
proud not to see, O small dust of the earth
        that walks so arrogantly,
          trust begets power and faith is
      an affectionate thing. We
        vow, we make this promise

to the fighting—it's a promise—"We'll
    never hate black, white, red, yellow, Jew,
Gentile, Untouchable." We are
    not competent to
make our vows. With set jaw they are fighting,
fighting, fighting,—some we love whom we know,
       some we love but know not—that
          hearts may feel and not be numb.
      It cures me; or am I what
        I can't believe in? Some

in snow, some on crags, some in quicksands,
    little by little, much by much, they
are fighting fighting fighting that where
    there was death there may
be life. "When a man is prey to anger,
he is moved by outside things; when he holds
       his ground in patience patience
          patience, that is action or
      beauty," the soldier's defence
        and hardest armour for

the fight. The world's an orphans' home. Shall
    we never have peace without sorrow?
without pleas of the dying for
    help that won't come? O
quiet form upon the dust, I cannot
look and yet I must. If these great patient
       dyings—all these agonies
         and woundbearings and bloodshed—
      can teach us how to live, these
        dyings were not wasted.

Hate-hardened heart, O heart of iron,
    iron is iron till it is rust.
There never was a war that was
    not inward; I must
fight till I have conquered in myself what
causes war, but I would not believe it.
      I inwardly did nothing.
        O Iscariotlike crime!
      Beauty is everlasting
        and dust is for a time.

JOHN CROWE RANSOM
(b. 1888)

WINTER REMEMBERED

Two evils, monstrous either one apart,
Possessed me, and were long and loath at going:
A cry of Absence, Absence, in the heart,
And in the wood the furious winter blowing.

Think not, when fire was bright upon my bricks,
And past the tight boards hardly a wind could enter,
I glowed like them, the simple burning sticks,
Far from my cause, my proper heat and center.

Better to walk forth in the frozen air
And wash my wound in the snows; that would be healing;
Because my heart would throb less painful there,
Being caked with cold, and past the smart of feeling.

And where I walked, the murderous winter blast
Would have this body bowed, these eyeballs streaming,
And though I think this heart's blood froze not fast
It ran too small to spare one drop for dreaming.

Dear love, these fingers that had known your touch,
And tied our separate forces first together,
Were ten poor idiot fingers not worth much,
Ten frozen parsnips hanging in the weather.

NECROLOGICAL

The friar had said his paternosters duly
And scourged his limbs, and afterwards would have slept;
But with much riddling his head became unruly,
He arose, from the quiet monastery he crept.

Dawn lightened the place where the battle had been won.
The people were dead—it is easy he thought to die—
These dead remained, but the living all were gone,
Gone with the wailing trumps of victory.

The dead men wore no raiment against the air,
Bartholomew's men had spoiled them where they fell;
In defeat the heroes' bodies werc whitely bare,
The field was white like meads of asphodel.

Not all were white; some gory and fabulous
Whom the sword had pierced and then the gray wolf eaten;
But the brother reasoned that heroes' flesh was thus.
Flesh fails, and the postured bones lie weather-beaten.

The lords of chivalry lay prone and shattered.
The gentle and the bodyguard of yeomen;
Bartholomew's stroke went home—but little it mattered,
Bartholomew went to be stricken of other foemen.

Beneath the blue ogive of the firmament
Was a dead warrior, clutching whose mighty knees
Was a leman, who with her flame had warmed his tent,
For him enduring all men's pleasantries.

Close by the sable stream that purged the plain
Lay the white stallion and his rider thrown,
The great beast had spilled there his little brain,
And the little groin of the knight was spilled by a stone.

The youth possessed him then of a crooked blade
Deep in the belly of a lugubrious wight;
He fingered it well, and it was cunningly made;
But strange apparatus was it for a Carmelite.

Then he sat upon a hill and bowed his head
As under a riddle, and in a deep surmise
So still that he likened himself unto those dead
Whom the kites of Heaven solicited with sweet cries.

BELLS FOR JOHN WHITESIDE'S DAUGHTER

There was such speed in her little body,
And such lightness in her footfall,
It is no wonder her brown study
Astonishes us all.

Her wars were bruited in our high window.
We looked among orchard trees and beyond
Where she took arms against her shadow,
Or harried unto the pond

The lazy geese, like a snow cloud
Dripping their snow on the green grass,
Tricking and stopping, sleepy and proud,
Who cried in goose, Alas,

For the tireless heart within the little
Lady with rod that made them rise
From their noon apple-dreams and scuttle
Goose-fashion under the skies!

But now go the bells, and we are ready,
In one house we are sternly stopped
To say we are vexed at her brown study,
Lying so primly propped.

DEAD BOY

The little cousin is dead, by foul subtraction,
A green bough from Virginia's aged tree,
And none of the county kin like the transaction,
Nor some of the world of outer dark, like me.

A boy not beautiful, nor good, nor clever,
A black cloud full of storms too hot for keeping,
A sword beneath his mother's heart—yet never
Woman bewept her babe as this is weeping.

A pig with a pasty face, so I had said,
Squealing for cookies, kinned by poor pretense
With a noble house. But the little man quite dead,
I see the forebears' antique lineaments.

The elder men have strode by the box of death
To the wide flag porch, and muttering low send round
The bruit of the day. O friendly waste of breath!
Their hearts are hurt with a deep dynastic wound.

He was pale and little, the foolish neighbors say;
The first fruits, saith the Preacher, the Lord hath taken;
But this was the old tree's late branch wrenched away,
Grieving the sapless limbs, the shorn and shaken.

GOOD SHIPS

Fleet ships encountering n the high seas
Who speak, and the unto the vast diverge,
These hailed each other, poised on the loud surge
Of one of Mrs. Grundy's Tuesday teas,
Nor trimmed one sail to baffle the driving breeze.
A macaroon absorbed all her emotion;
His hue was ashy but an effect of ocean;
They exchanged the nautical technicalities.

It was only a nothing or so, and thus they parted.
Away they sailed, most certainly bound for port,
So seaworthy one felt they could not sink;
Still there was a tremor shook them, I should think,
Beautiful timbers fit for storm and sport
And unto miserly merchant hulks converted.

EMILY HARDCASTLE, SPINSTER

We shall come tomorrow morning, who were not to have her
    love,
We shall bring no face of envy but a gift of praise and lilies
To the stately ceremonial we are not the heroes of.

Let the sisters now attend her, who are red-eyed, who are
    wroth;
They were younger, she was finer, for they wearied of the
    waiting
And they married them to merchants, being unbelievers both.

I was dapper when I dangled in my pepper-and-salt;
We were only local beauties, and we beautifully trusted
If the proud one had to tarry we would have her by default.

But right across her threshold has her Grizzled Baron come;
Let them wrap her as a princess, who'd go softly down a
    stairway
And seal her to the stranger for his castle in the gloom.

HERE LIES A LADY

Here lies a lady of beauty and high degree.
Of chills and fever she died, of fever and chills,
The delight of her husband, her aunt, an infant of three,
And of medicos marveling sweetly on her ills.

For either she burned, and her confident eyes would blaze,
And her fingers fly in a manner to puzzle their heads—
What was she making? Why, nothing; she sat in a maze
Of old scraps of laces, snipped into curious shreds—

Or this would pass, and the light of her fire decline
Till she lay discouraged and cold, like a thin stalk white and
　　blown,
And would not open her eyes, to kisses, to wine;
The sixth of these states was her last; the cold settled down.

Sweet ladies, long may ye bloom, and toughly I hope ye may
　　thole,
But was she not lucky? In flowers and lace and mourning,
In love and great honor we bade God rest her soul
After six little spaces of chill, and six of burning.

CONRAD IN TWILIGHT

Conrad, Conrad, aren't you old
To sit so late in your moldy garden?
And I think Conrad knows it well,
Nursing his knees, too rheumy and cold
To warm the wraith of a Forest of Arden.

Neuralgia in the back of his neck,
His lungs filling with such miasma,
His feet dipping in leafage and muck:
Conrad! you've forgotten asthma.

Conrad's house has thick red walls,
The log on Conrad's hearth is blazing,
Slippers and pipe and tea are served,
Butter and toast are meant for pleasing!
Still Conrad's back is not uncurved
And here's an autumn on him, teasing.

Autumn days in our section
Are the most used-up thing on earth
(Or in the waters under the earth)
Having no more color nor predilection
Than cornstalks too wet for the fire,
A ribbon rotting on the byre,
A man's face as weathered as straw
By the summer's flare and winter's flaw.

ARMAGEDDON

Antichrist, playing his lissome flute and merry
As was his wont, debouched upon the plain;
Then came a swirl of dust, and Christ drew rein,
Brooding upon his frugal breviary.

Now which shall die, the roundel, rose, and hall,
Or else the tonsured beadsman's monkery?
For Christ and Antichrist are cap-a-pie,
The prospect charms the soul of the lean jackal.

But Antichrist got down from the Barbary beast
And doffed his plume in courteous prostration;
Christ left his jennet's back in deprecation
And raised him, his own hand about the waist.

Then next they fingered chivalry's quaint page,
Of precedence discoursing by the letter.
The oratory of Antichrist was better,
He invested Christ with the elder lineage.

He set Christ on his own Mahomet's back
Where Christ sat fortressed up like Diomede;
The cynical hairy jennet was his steed,
Obtuse, and most indifferent to attack.

The lordings measured lances and stood still,
And each was loath to let the other's blood;
Orginally they were one brotherhood;
There stood the white pavilion on the hill.

To the pavilion went then the hierarchs,
If they might truce their honorable dispute;
Firm was the Christian's chin and he was mute,
And Antichrist ejected scant remarks.

Antichrist tendered a spray of rosemary
To serve his brother for a buttonhole;
Then Christ about his adversary's poll
Wrapped a dry palm that grew on Calvary.

Christ wore a dusty cassock, and the knight
Did him the honors of his tiring hall,
Whence Christ did not come forth too finical,
But his egregious beauty richly dight.

With feasting they concluded every day,
And when the other shaped his phrases thicker
Christ, introducing water in the liquor,
Made wine of more ethereal bouquet.

At wassail Antichrist would pitch the strain
For unison of all the retinue;
Christ beat the time, and hummed a stave or two,
But did not say the words, which were profane.

Perruquiers were privily presented,
Till, knowing his need extreme and his heart pure,
Christ let them dress him his thick chevelure,
And soon his beard was glozed and sweetly scented.

And so the Wolf said Brother to the Lamb,
The True Heir keeping with the poor Impostor,
The rubric and the holy paternoster
Were jangled strangely with the dithyramb.

It could not be. There was a patriarch,
A godly liege of old malignant brood,
Who could not fathom the new brotherhood
Between the children of the light and dark.

He sought the ear of Christ on these strange things,
But in the white pavilion when he stood,
And saw them favored and dressed like twins at food,
Profound and mad became his misgivings.

The voices, and their burdens, he must hear,
But equal between the pleasant Princes flew
Theology, the arts, the old customs and the new;
Hoarsely he ran and hissed in the wrong ear.

He was discomfited, but Christ much more.
Christ sheds unmannerly his devil's pelf,
Takes ashes from the hearth and smears himself,
Calls for his smock and jennet as before.

His trump recalls his own to right opinions,
With scourage they mortify their carnal selves,
With stone they whet the axheads on the helves
And seek the Prince Beelzebub and minions.

Christ and his myrmidons, Christ at the head,
Chanted of death and glory and no complaisance;
Antichrist and the armies of malfeasance
Made songs of innocence and no bloodshed.

The immortal Adversary shook his head:
If now they fought too long, then he would famish;
And if much blood was shed, why, he was squeamish:
"These Armageddons weary me much," he said.

JUDITH OF BETHULIA

Beautiful as the flying legend of some leopard
She had not yet chosen her great captain or prince
Depositary to her flesh, and our defense;
And a wandering beauty is a blade out of its scabbard.
You know how dangerous, gentlemen of threescore?
May you know it yet ten more.

Nor by process of veiling she grew the less fabulous.
Gray or blue veils, we were desperate to study
The invincible emanations of her white body,
And the winds at her ordered raiment were ominous.
Might she walk in the market, sit in the council of soldiers?
Only of the extreme elders.

But a rare chance was the girl's then, when the Invader
Trumpeted from the south, and rumbled from the north,
Beleaguered the city from four quarters of the earth,
Our soldiery too craven and sick to aid her—
Where were the arms could countervail this horde?
Her beauty was the sword.

She sat with the elders, and proved on their blear visage
How bright was the weapon unrusted in her keeping,
While he lay surfeiting on their harvest heaping,
Wasting the husbandry of their rarest vintage—
And dreaming of the broad-breasted dames for concubine?
These floated on his wine.

He was lapped with bay leaves, and grass and fumiter weed,
And from under the wine-film encountered his mortal vision,
For even within his tent she accomplished his derision;
She loosed one veil and another, standing unafraid;

And he perished. Nor brushed her with even so much as a
    daisy?
She found his destruction easy.

The heathen are all perished. The victory was furnished,
We smote them hiding in our vineyards, barns, annexes,
And now their white bones clutter the holes of foxes,
And the chieftain's head, with grinning sockets, and var-
    nished—
Is it hung on the sky with a hideous epitaphy?
No, the woman keeps the trophy.

May God send unto our virtuous lady her prince.
It is stated she went reluctant to that orgy,
Yet a madness fevers our young men, and not the clergy
Nor the elders have turned them unto modesty since.
Inflamed by the thought of her naked beauty with desire?
Yes, and chilled with fear and despair.

BLUE GIRLS

Twirling your blue skirts, traveling the sward
Under the towers of your seminary,
Go listen to your teachers old and contrary
Without believing a word.

Tie the white fillets then about your hair
And think no more of what will come to pass
Than bluebirds that go walking on the grass
And chattering on the air.

Practice your beauty, blue girls, before it fail;
And I will cry with my loud lips and publish
Beauty which all our power shall never establish,
It is so frail.

For I could tell you a story which is true;
I know a lady with a terrible tongue,
Blear eyes fallen from blue,
All her perfections tarnished—yet it is not long
Since she was lovelier than any of you.

OLD MAN PLAYING WITH CHILDREN

A discreet householder exclaims on the grandsire
In war paint and feathers, with fierce grandsons and axes
Dancing round a backyard fire of boxes:
"Watch grandfather, he'll set the house on fire."

But I will unriddle for you the thought of his mind,
An old one you cannot open with conversation.
What animates the thin legs in risky motion?
Mixes the snow on the head with snow on the wind?

"Grandson, grandsire. We are equally boy and boy.
Do not offer your reclining chair and slippers
With tedious old women talking in wrappers.
This life is not good but in danger and in joy.

"It is you the elder to these and younger to me
Who are penned as slaves by properties and causes
And never walk from your insupportable houses
And shamefully, when boys shout, go in and flee.

"May God forgive me, I know your middling ways,
Having taken care and performed ignominies unreckoned
Between the first brief childhood and the brief second,
But I will be more honorable in these days."

CAPTAIN CARPENTER

Captain Carpenter rose up in his prime
Put on his pistols and went riding out
But had got well-nigh nowhere at that time
Till he fell in with ladies in a rout.

It was a pretty lady and all her train
That played with him so sweetly but before
An hour she'd taken a sword with all her main
And twined him of his nose for evermore.

Captain Carpenter mounted up one day
And rode straightway into a stranger rogue
That looked unchristian but be that as may
The Captain did not wait upon prologue.

But drew upon him out of his great heart
The other swung against him with a club

And cracked his two legs at the shinny part
And let him roll and stick like any tub.

Captain Carpenter rode many a time
From male and female took he sundry harms
He met the wife of Satan crying "I'm
The she-wolf bids you shall bear no more arms."

Their strokes and counters whistled in the wind
I wish he had delivered half his blows
But where she should have made off like a hind
The bitch bit off his arms at the elbows.

And Captain Carpenter parted with his ears
To a black devil that used him in this wise
O Jesus ere his threescore and ten years
Another had plucked out his sweet blue eyes.

Captain Carpenter got up on his roan
And sallied from the gate in hell's despite
I heard him asking in the grimmest tone
If any enemy yet there was to fight?

"To any adversary it is fame
If he risk to be wounded by my tongue
Or burnt in two beneath my red heart's flame
Such are the perils he is cast among.

"But if he can he has a pretty choice
From an anatomy with little to lose
Whether he cut my tongue and take my voice
Or whether it be my round red heart he choose."

It was the neatest knave that ever was seen
Stepping in perfume from his lady's bower
Who at this word put in his merry mien
And fell on Captain Carpenter like a tower.

I would not knock old fellows in the dust
But there lay Captain Carpenter on his back
His weapons were the old heart in his bust
And a blade shook between rotten teeth alack.

The rogue in scarlet and gray soon knew his mind
He wished to get his trophy and depart
With gentle apology and touch refined
He pierced him and produced the Captain's heart.

God's mercy rest on Captain Carpenter now
I thought him sirs an honest gentleman
Citizen husband soldier and scholar enow
Let jangling kites eat of him if they can.

But God's deep curses follow after those
That shore him of his goodly nose and ears
His legs and strong arms at the two elbows
And eyes that had not watered seventy years.

The curse of hell upon the sleek upstart
That got the Captain finally on his back
And took the red red vitals of his heart
And made the kites to whet their beaks clack clack.

OLD MANSION

As an intruder I trudged with careful innocence
To mask in decency a meddlesome stare,
Passing the old house often on its eminence,
Exhaling my foreign weed on its weighted air.

Here age seemed newly imaged for the historian
After his monstrous châteaux on the Loire,
A beauty not for depicting by old vulgarian
Reiterations which gentle readers abhor.

Each time of seeing I absorbed some other feature
Of a house whose annals in no wise could be brief
Nor ignoble; for it expired as sweetly as Nature,
With her tinge of oxidation on autumn leaf.

It was a Southern manor. One need hardly imagine
Towers, white monoliths, or even ivied walls;
But sufficient state if its peacock *was* a pigeon;
Where no courts kept, but grave rites and funerals.

Indeed, not distant, possibly not external
To the property, were tombstones, where the catafalque
Had carried their dead; and projected a note too charnel
But for the honeysuckle on its intricate stalk.

Stability was the character of its rectangle
Whose line was seen in part and guessed in part
Through trees. Decay was the tone of old brick and shingle.
Green blinds dragging frightened the watchful heart

To assert, "Your mansion, long and richly inhabited,
Its exits and entrances suiting the children of men,
Will not forever be thus, O man, exhibited,
And one had best hurry to enter it if one can."

And at last, with my happier angel's own temerity,
Did I clang their brazen knocker against the door,
To beg their dole of a look, in simple charity,
Or crumbs of legend dropping from their great store.

But it came to nothing—and may so gross denial
Which has been deplored with a beating of the breast
Never shorten the tired historian, loyal
To acknowledge defeat and discover a new quest—

The old mistress was ill, and sent my dismissal
By one even more wrappered and lean and dark
Than that wrapped concierge and imperturbable vassal
Who bids you begone from her master's Gothic park.

Emphatically, the old house crumbled; the ruins
Would litter, as already the leaves, this petted sward;
And no annalist went in to the lords or the peons;
The antiquary would finger the bits of shard.

But on retreating I saw myself in the token,
How loving from my foreign weed the feather curled
On the languid air; and I went with courage shaken
To dip, alas, into some unseemlier world.

PIAZZA PIECE

—I am a gentleman in a dust coat trying
To make you hear. Your ears are soft and small
And listen to an old man not at all,
They want the young men's whispering and sighing.
But see the roses on your trellis dying
And hear the spectral singing of the moon;
For I must have my lovely lady soon,
I am a gentleman in a dust coat trying.

—I am a lady young in beauty waiting
Until my truelove comes, and then we kiss.
But what gray man among the vines is this
Whose words are dry and faint as in a dream?
Back from my trellis, sir, before I scream!
I am a lady young in beauty waiting.

VISION BY SWEETWATER

Go and ask Robin to bring the girls over
To Sweetwater, said my aunt; and that was why
It was like a dream of ladies sweeping by
The willows, clouds, deep meadowgrass, and the river.

Robin's sisters and my aunt's lily daughter
Laughed and talked, and tinkled light as wrens
If there were a little colony all hens
To go walking by the steep turn of Sweetwater.

Let them alone, dear aunt, just for one minute
Till I go fishing in the dark of my mind:
Where have I seen before, against the wind,
These bright virgins, robed and bare of bonnet,

Flowing with music of their strange quick tongue
And adventuring with delicate paces by the stream,—
Myself a child, old suddenly at the scream
From one of the white throats which it hid among?

HER EYES

To a woman that I knew
Were eyes of an extravagant hue:
Viz., china blue.

Those I wear upon my head
Are sometimes green and sometimes red,
I said.

My mother's eyes are wet and blear,
My little sister's are not clear,
Poor silly dear.

It must be given to but few,
A pair of eyes so utter blue
And new;

Where does she keep them from this glare
Of the monstrous sun and the wind's flare
Without any wear;

And were they never in the night
Poisoned by artificial light
Much too bright;

And had the splendid beast no heart
That boiled with tears and baked with smart
The ocular part?

I'll have no business with those eyes,
They are not kind, they are not wise,
They are two great lies.

A woman shooting such blue flame
I apprehend will get some blame
On her good name.

PARTING, WITHOUT A SEQUEL

She has finished and sealed the letter
At last, which he so richly has deserved,
With characters venomous and hatefully curved,
And nothing could be better.

But even as she gave it
Saying to the blue-capped functioner of doom,
"Into his hands," she hoped the leering groom
Might somewhere lose and leave it.

Then all the blood
Forsook the face. She was too pale for tears,
Observing the ruin of her younger years.
She went and stood

Under her father's vaunting oak
Who kept his peace in wind and sun, and glistened
Stoical in the rain; to whom she listened
If he spoke.

And now the agitation of the rain
Rasped his sere leaves, and he talked low and gentle
Reproaching the wan daughter by the lintel;
Ceasing and beginning again.

Away went the messenger's bicycle,
His serpent's track went up the hill forever,
And all the time she stood there hot as fever
And cold as any icicle.

JANET WAKING

Beautifully Janet slept
Till it was deeply morning. She woke then
And thought about her dainty-feathered hen,
To see how it had kept.

One kiss she gave her mother.
Only a small one gave she to her daddy
Who would have kissed each curl of his shining baby;
No kiss at all for her brother.

"Old Chucky, old Chucky!" she cried,
Running across the world upon the grass
To Chucky's house, and listening. But alas,
Her Chucky had died.

It was a transmogrifying bee
Came droning down on Chucky's old bald head
And sat and put the poison. It scarcely bled,
But how exceedingly

And purply did the knot
Swell with the venom and communicate
Its rigor! Now the poor comb stood up straight
But Chucky did not.

So there was Janet
Kneeling on the wet grass, crying her brown hen
(Translated far beyond the daughters of men)
To rise and walk upon it.

And weeping fast as she had breath
Janet implored us, "Wake her from her sleep!"
And would not be instructed in how deep
Was the forgetful kingdom of death.

TWO IN AUGUST

Two that could not have lived their single lives
As can some husbands and wives
Did something strange: they tensed their vocal cords
And attacked each other with silences and words
Like catapulted stones and arrowed knives.

Dawn was not yet; night is for loving or sleeping,
Sweet dreams or safekeeping;
Yet he of the wide brows that were used to laurel
And she, the famed for gentleness, must quarrel.
Furious both of them, and scared, and weeping.

How sleepers groan, twitch, wake to such a mood
Is not well understood,
Nor why two entities grown almost one
Should rend and murder trying to get undone,
With individual tigers in their blood.

She in terror fled from the marriage chamber
Circuiting the dark rooms like a string of amber
Round and round and back,
And would not light one lamp against the black,
And heard the clock that clanged: Remember,
    Remember.

And he must tread barefooted the dim lawn,
Soon he was up and gone;
High in the trees the night-mastered birds were crying
With fear upon their tongues, no singing nor flying
Which are their lovely attitudes by dawn.

Whether those bird cries were of heaven or hell
There is no way to tell;
In the long ditch of darkness the man walked
Under the hackberry trees where the birds talked
With words too sad and strange to syllable.

OUR TWO WORTHIES

All the here and all the there
Ring with the praises of the pair:
Jesus the Paraclete
And Saint Paul the Exegete.

Jesus proclaimed the truth.
Paul's missionary tooth
Shredded it fine, and made a paste,
No particle going to waste,
Kneaded it and caked it
And buttered it and baked it
(And indeed all but digested

While Jesus went to death and rested)
Into a marketable compound
Ready to lay on any wound,
Meet to prescribe to our distress
And feed unto our emptiness.

And this is how the Pure Idea
Became our perfect panacea,
Both external and internal
And supernal and infernal.

When the great captains die,
There is some faithful standing by
To whom the chieftain hands his sword.
Proud Paul received—a Word.

This was the man who, given his cause,
Gave constitution and bylaws,
Distinguished pedagogue
Who invaded the synagogue
And in a little while
Was proselyting the Gentile.

But what would there have been for Paul
If the Source had finished all?
He blessed the mighty Paraclete
For needing him, to miss defeat,
He couldn't have done anything
But for his Captain spiriting.

He knew that he was competent
For any sort of punishment,
With his irresistible urge
To bare his back unto the scourge,
Teasing his own neck
In prodigious shipwreck;
Hunger and rats and gaol
With mere detail.

Paul was every inch of him
Valiant as the Seraphim,
And all he went among
Confessed his marvelous tongue,
And Satan fearing the man's spell
Embittered smote the gates of Hell.

So he finished his fight
And he too went from sight.

Then let no cantankerous schism
Corrupt this our catechism
But one and all let us repeat:
Who then is Jesus?
He is our Paraclete.
And Paul, out of Tarsus?
He is our Exegete.

MAN WITHOUT SENSE OF DIRECTION

Tell this to ladies: how a hero man
Assail a thick and scandalous giant
Who casts true shadow in the sun,
And die, but play no truant.

This is more horrible: that the darling egg
Of the chosen people hatch a creature
Of noblest mind and powerful leg
Who cannot fathom nor perform his nature.

The larks' tongues are never stilled
Where the pale spread straw of sunlight lies.
Then what invidious gods have willed
Him to be seized so otherwise?

Birds of the field and beasts of the stable
Are swollen with rapture and make uncouth
Demonstration of joy, which is a babble
Offending the ear of the fervorless youth.

Love—is it the cause? the proud shamed spirit?
Love has slain some whom it possessed,
But his was requited beyond his merit
And won him in bridal the loveliest.

Yet scarcely he issues from the warm chamber,
Flushed with her passion, when cold as dead
Once more he walks where waves past number
Of sorrow buffet his curse-hung head.

Whether by street, or in field full of honey,
Attended by clouds of the creatures of air

Or shouldering the city's companioning many,
His doom is on him; and how can he care

For the shapes that would fiddle upon his senses,
Wings and faces and mists that move,
Words, sunlight, the blue air which rinses
The pure pale head which he must love?

And he writhes like an antique man of bronze
That is beaten by furies visible,
Yet he is punished not knowing his sins
And for his innocence walks in hell.

He flails his arms, he moves his lips:
"Rage have I none, cause, time, nor country—
Yet I have traveled land and ships
And knelt my seasons in the chantry."

So he stands muttering; and rushes
Back to the tender thing in his charge
With clamoring tongue and taste of ashes
And a small passion to feign large.

But let his cold lips be her omen,
She shall not kiss that harried one
To peace, as men are served by women
Who comfort them in darkness and in sun.

SURVEY OF LITERATURE

In all the good Greek of Plato
I lack my roast beef and potato.

A better man was Aristotle,
Pulling steady on the bottle.

I dip my hat to Chaucer,
Swilling soup from his saucer,

And to Master Shakespeare
Who wrote big on small beer.

The abstemious Wordsworth
Subsisted on a curd's-worth,

But a slick one was Tennyson,
Putting gravy on his venison.

What these men had to eat and drink
Is what we say and what we think.

The influence of Milton
Came wry out of Stilton.

Sing a song for Percy Shelley,
Drowned in pale lemon jelly,

And for precious John Keats,
Dripping blood of pickled beets.

Then there was poor Willie Blake,
He foundered on sweet cake.

God have mercy on the sinner
Who must write with no dinner,

No gravy and no grub,
No pewter and no pub,

No belly and no bowels,
Only consonants and vowels.

THE EQUILIBRISTS

Full of her long white arms and milky skin
He had a thousand times remembered sin.
Alone in the press of people traveled he,
Minding her jacinth, and myrrh, and ivory.

Mouth he remembered: the quaint orifice
From which came heat that flamed upon the kiss,
Till cold words came down spiral from the head.
Gray doves from the officious tower ill sped.

Body: it was a white field ready for love.
On her body's field, with the gaunt tower above,
The lilies grew, beseeching him to take,
If he would pluck and wear them, bruise and break.

Eyes talking: Never mind the cruel words,
Embrace my flowers, but not embrace the swords.
But what they said, the doves came straightway flying
And unsaid: Honor. Honor, they came crying.

Importunate her doves. Too pure, too wise,
Clambering on his shoulder, saying, Arise,
Leave me now, and never let us meet,
Eternal distance now command thy feet.

Predicament indeed, which thus discovers
Honor among thieves, Honor between lovers.
O such a little word is Honor, they feel!
But the gray word is between them cold as steel.

At length I saw these lovers fully were come
Into their torture of equilibrium;
Dreadfully had forsworn each other, and yet
They were bound each to each, and they did not forget.

And rigid as two painful stars, and twirled
About the clustered night their prison world,
They burned with fierce love always to come near,
But honor beat them back and kept them clear.

Ah, the strict lovers, they are ruined now!
I cried in anger. But with puddled brow
Devising for those gibbeted and brave
Came I descanting: Man, what would you have?

For spin your period out, and draw your breath,
A kinder saeculum begins with Death.
Would you ascend to Heaven and bodiless dwell?
Or take your bodies honorless to Hell?

In Heaven you have heard no marriage is,
No white flesh tinder to your lecheries,
Your male and female tissue sweetly shaped
Sublimed away, and furious blood escaped.

Great lovers lie in Hell, the stubborn ones
Infatuate of the flesh upon the bones;
Stuprate, they rend each other when they kiss,
The pieces kiss again, no end to this.

But still I watched them spinning, orbited nice.
Their flames were not more radiant than their ice.
I dug in the quiet earth and wrought the tomb
And made these lines to memorize their doom:—

Epitaph
Equilibrists lie here; stranger, tread light;
Close, but untouching in each other's sight;
Moldered the lips and ashy the tall skull.
Let them lie perilous and beautiful.

PAINTED HEAD

By dark severance the apparition head
Smiles from the air a capital on no
Column or a Platonic perhaps head
On a canvas sky depending from nothing;

Stirs up an old illusion of grandeur
By tickling the instinct of heads to be
Absolute and to try decapitation
And to play truant from the body bush;

But too happy and beautiful for those sorts
Of head (home-keeping heads are happiest)
Discovers maybe thirty unwidowed years
Of not dishonoring the faithful stem;

Is nameless and has authored for the evil
Historian head-hunters neither book
Nor state and is therefore distinct from tart
Heads with crowns and guilty gallery heads;

So that the extravagant device of art
Unhousing by abstraction this once head
Was capital irony by a loving hand
That knew the no treason of a head like this;

Makes repentance in an unlovely head
For having vinegarly traduced the flesh
Till, the hurt flesh recusing, the hard egg
Is shrunken to its own deathlike surface;

And an image thus. The body bears the head
(So hardly one they terribly are two)

Feeds and obeys and unto please what end?
Not to the glory of tyrant head but to

The increase of body. Beauty is of body.
The flesh contouring shallowly on a head
Is a rock garden needing body's love
And best bodiness to colorify

The big blue birds sitting and seashell flats
And caves, and on the iron acropolis
To spread the hyacinthine hair and rear
The olive garden for the nightingales.

ADDRESS TO THE SCHOLARS OF NEW ENGLAND

(Harvard Phi Beta Kappa Poem, June 23, 1939)

When Sarah Pierrepont let her spirit rage
Her love and scorn refused the bauble earth
(Which took bloom even here, under the Bear)
And groped for the Essence sitting in himself,
Subtle, I think, for a girl's unseasoned rage.

The late and sudden extravagance of soul
By which they all were swollen exalted her
At seventeen years to Edwards' canopy,
A match pleasing to any Heaven, had not
The twelve mortal labors harassed her soul.

Thrifty and too proud were the sea-borne fathers
Who fetched the Pure Idea in a bound box
And fastened him in a steeple, to have his court
Shabby with an unkingly establishment
And Sabbath levees for the minion fathers.

The majesty of Heaven has a great house,
And even if the Indian kingdom or the fox
Ran barking mad in a wide forest place,
They had his threshold, and you had the dream
Of property in him by a steepled house.

If once the entail shall come on raffish sons,
Knife-wit scholar and merchant sharp in thumb,
With positive steel they'll pry into the steeple,
And blinking through the cracked ribs at the void
A judgment laughter rakes the cynic sons.

But like prevailing wind New England's honor
Carried, and teased small Southern boys in school,
Whose heads the temperate birds fleeing your winter
Construed for, but the stiff heroes abashed
With their frozen fingers and unearthly honor.

Scared by the holy megrims of those Pilgrims,
I thought the unhumbled and outcast and cold
Were the rich Heirs traveling incognito,
Bred too fine for the country's sweet produce
And but affecting that dog's life of pilgrims.

There used to be debate of soul and body,
The soul storming incontinent with shrew's tongue
Against what natural brilliance body had loved,
Even the green phases though deciduous
Of earth's zodiac homage to the body.

Plato, before Plotinus gentled him,
Spoke the soul's part, and though its vice is known
We're in his shadow still, and it appears
Your founders most of all the nations held
By his scandal-mongering, and established him.

Perfect was the witch foundering in water,
The blasphemer that spraddled in the stocks,
The woman branded with her sin, the whales
Of ocean taken with a psalmer's sword,
The British tea infusing the bay's water,

But they reared heads into the always clouds
And stooped to the event of war or bread,
The secular perforces and short speech
Being labors surlily done with the left hand,
The chief strength giddying with transcendent clouds.

The tangent Heavens mocked the fathers' strength,
And how the young sons know it, and study now
To take fresh conquest of the conquered earth,
But they're too strong for that, you've seen them whip
The laggard will to deeds of lunatic strength.

To incline the powerful living unto peace
With Heaven is easier now, with Earth is hard,
Yet a rare metaphysic makes them one,
A gentle Majesty, whose myrtle and rain
Enforce the fathers' gravestones unto peace.

I saw the youngling bachelors of Harvard
Lit like torches, and scrambling to disperse
Like aimless firebrands pitiful to slake,
And if there's passion enough for half their flame,
Your wisdom has done this, sages of Harvard.

EDNA ST. VINCENT MILLAY
(1892–1950)

RENASCENCE

All I could see from where I stood
Was three long mountains and a wood;
I turned and looked another way,
And saw three islands in a bay.
So with my eyes I traced the line
Of the horizon, thin and fine,
Straight around till I was come
Back to where I'd started from;
And all I saw from where I stood
Was three long mountains and a wood.
Over these things I could not see;
These were the things that bounded me;
And I could touch them with my hand,
Almost, I thought, from where I stand.
And all at once things seemed so small
My breath came short, and scarce at all.
But, sure, the sky is big, I said;
Miles and miles above my head;
So here upon my back I'll lie
And look my fill into the sky.
And so I looked, and, after all,
The sky was not so very tall.
The sky, I said, must somewhere stop,
And—sure enough!—I see the top!
The sky, I thought, is not so grand;
I 'most could touch it with my hand!
And, reaching up my hand to try,
I screamed to feel it touch the sky.

I screamed, and—lo!—Infinity
Came down and settled over me;
Forced back my scream into my chest,
Bent back my arm upon my breast,
And, pressing of the Undefined
The definition on my mind,
Held up before my eyes a glass

Through which my shrinking sight did pass
Until it seemed I must behold
Immensity made manifold;
Whispered to me a word whose sound
Deafened the air for worlds around,
And brought unmuffled to my ears
The gossiping of friendly spheres,
The creaking of the tented sky,
The ticking of Eternity.

I saw and heard, and knew at last
The How and Why of all things, past,
And present, and forevermore.
The universe, cleft to the core,
Lay open to my probing sense
That, sickening, I would fain pluck thence
But could not,—nay! But needs must suck
At the great wound, and could not pluck
My lips away till I had drawn
All venom out.—Ah, fearful pawn!
For my omniscience I paid toll
In infinite remorse of soul.
All sin was of my sinning, all
Atoning mine, and mine the gall
Of all regret. Mine was the weight
Of every brooded wrong, the hate
That stood behind each envious thrust,
Mine every greed, mine every lust.
And all the while for every grief,
Each suffering, I craved relief
With individual desire,—
Craved all in vain! And felt fierce fire
About a thousand people crawl;
Perished with each,—then mourned for all!
A man was starving in Capri;
He moved his eyes and looked at me;
I felt his gaze, I heard his moan,
And knew his hunger as my own.
I saw at sea a great fog bank
Between two ships that struck and sank;
A thousand screams the heavens smote;
And every scream tore through my throat;
No hurt I did not feel, no death
That was not mine; mine each last breath
That, crying, met an answering cry
From the compassion that was I.

All suffering mine, and mine its rod;
Mine, pity like the pity of God.

Ah, awful weight! Infinity
Pressed down upon the finite me!
My anguished spirit, like a bird,
Beating against my lips I heard;
Yet lay the weight so close about
There was no room for it without.
And so beneath the weight lay I
And suffered death, but could not die.

Long had I lain thus, craving death,
When quietly the earth beneath
Gave way, and inch by inch, so great
At last had grown the crushing weight,
Into the earth I sank till I
Full six feet underground did lie,
And sank no more,—there is no weight
Can follow here, however great.
From off my breast I felt it roll,
And as it went my tortured soul
Burst forth and fled in such a gust
That all about me swirled the dust.

Deep in the earth I rested now;
Cool is its hand upon the brow
And soft its breast beneath the head
Of one who is so gladly dead.
And all at once, and over all,
The pitying rain began to fall.
I lay and heard each pattering hoof
Upon my lowly, thatchèd roof.
And seemed to love the sound far more
Than ever I had done before.
For rain it hath a friendly sound
To one who's six feet underground;
And scarce the friendly voice or face:
A grave is such a quiet place.

The rain, I said, is kind to come
And speak to me in my new home.
I would I were alive again
To kiss the fingers of the rain,
To drink into my eyes the shine
Of every slanting silver line,

To catch the freshened, fragrant breeze
From drenched and dripping apple trees.
For soon the shower will be done,
And then the broad face of the sun
Will laugh above the rain-soaked earth
Until the world with answering mirth
Shakes joyously, and each round drop
Rolls, twinkling, from its grass-blade top.
How can I bear it; buried here,
While overhead the sky grows clear
And blue again after the storm?
O, multicolored, multiform,
Belovèd beauty over me,
That I shall never, never see
Again! Spring silver, autumn gold,
That I shall never more behold!
Sleeping your myriad magics through,
Close-sepulchered away from you!
O God, I cried, give me new birth,
And put me back upon the earth!
Upset each cloud's gigantic gourd
And let the heavy rain, downpoured
In one big torrent, set me free,
Washing my grave away from me!

I ceased; and through the breathless hush
That answered me, the far-off rush
Of herald wings came whispering
Like music down the vibrant string
Of my ascending prayer, and—crash!
Before the wild wind's whistling lash
The startled storm clouds reared on high
And plunged in terror down the sky,
And the big rain in one black wave
Fell from the sky and struck my grave.

I know not how such things can be,
I only know there came to me
A fragrance such as never clings
To aught save happy living things;
A sound as of some joyous elf
Singing sweet songs to please himself,
And, through and over everything,
A sense of glad awakening.
The grass, a tiptoe at my ear,
Whispering to me I could hear;

I felt the rain's cool fingertips
Brushed tenderly across my lips,
Laid gently on my sealèd sight,
And all at once the heavy night
Fell from my eyes and I could see,—
A drenched and dripping apple tree,
A last long line of silver rain,
A sky grown clear and blue again.
And as I looked a quickening gust
Of wind blew up to me and thrust
Into my face a miracle
Of orchard breath, and with the smell,—
I know not how such things can be!—
I breathed my soul back into me.

Ah! Up then from the ground sprang I
And hailed the earth with such a cry
As is not heard save from a man
Who has been dead and lives again.
About the trees my arms I wound;
Like one gone mad I hugged the ground;
I raised my quivering arms on high;
I laughed and laughed into the sky,
Till at my throat a strangling sob
Caught fiercely, and a great heartthrob
Sent instant tears into my eyes;
O God, I cried, no dark disguise
Can e'er hereafter hide from me
Thy radiant identity!
Thou canst not move across the grass
But my quick eyes will see Thee pass,
Nor speak, however silently,
But my hushed voice will answer Thee.
I know the path that tells Thy way
Through the cool eve of every day;
God, I can push the grass apart
And lay my finger on Thy heart!

The world stands out on either side
No wider than the heart is wide;
Above the world is stretched the sky,—
No higher than the soul is high.
The heart can push the sea and land
Farther away on either hand;
The soul can split the sky in two,
And let the face of God shine through.

But east and west will pinch the heart
That cannot keep them pushed apart;
And he whose soul is flat—the sky
Will cave in on him by and by.

DIRGE WITHOUT MUSIC

I am not resigned to the shutting away of loving hearts in the
hard ground.
So it is, and so it will be, for so it has been, time out of mind:
Into the darkness they go, the wise and the lovely.
Crowned with lilies and with laurel they go; but I am not
resigned.

Lovers and thinkers, into the earth with you.
Be one with the dull, the indiscriminate dust.
A fragment of what you felt, of what you knew,
A formula, a phrase remains—but the best is lost.

The answers quick and keen, the honest look, the laughter,
the love,—
They are gone. They are gone to feed the roses. Elegant and
curled
Is the blossom. Fragrant is the blossom. I know. But I do
not approve.
More precious was the light in your eyes than all the roses
in the world.

Down, down, down into the darkness of the grave
Gently they go, the beautiful, the tender, the kind;
Quietly they go, the intelligent, the witty, the brave.
I know. But I do not approve. And I am not resigned.

SPRING

To what purpose, April, do you return again?
Beauty is not enough.
You can no longer quiet me with the redness
Of little leaves opening stickily.
I know what I know.
The sun is hot on my neck as I observe
The spikes of the crocus.
The smell of the earth is good.
It is apparent that there is no death.

But what does that signify?
Not only underground are the brains of men
Eaten by maggots.
Life in itself
Is nothing,
An empty cup, a flight of uncarpeted stairs.
It is not enough that yearly, down this hill,
April
Comes like an idiot, babbling and strewing flowers.

THE BALLAD OF THE HARP-WEAVER

"Son," said my mother,
　When I was knee-high,
"You've need of clothes to
　　cover you,
　And not a rag have I.

"There's nothing in the house
　To make a boy breeches,
Nor shears to cut a cloth with,
　Nor thread to take stitches.

"There's nothing in the house
　But a loaf-end of rye,
And a harp with a woman's
　　head
　Nobody will buy,"
　And she began to cry.

That was in the early fall.
　When came the late fall,
"Son," she said, "the sight of
　　you
　Makes your mother's blood
　　crawl,—

"Little skinny shoulder blades
　Sticking through your
　　clothes!
And where you'll get a jacket
　　from
　God above knows.

"It's lucky for me, lad,
　Your daddy's in the
　　ground,
And can't see the way I let
　His son go around!"
　And she made a queer
　　sound.

That was in the late fall.
　When the winter came,
I'd not a pair of breeches
　Nor a shirt to my name

I couldn't go to school,
　Or out of doors to play.
And all the other little boys
　Passed our way.

"Son," said my mother,
　"Come, climb into my lap,
And I'll chafe your little
　　bones
　While you take a nap."

And, oh, but we were silly
　For half an hour or more,
Me with my long legs
　Dragging on the floor,

A-rock-rock-rocking
　To a Mother Goose rhyme!
Oh, but we were happy
　For half an hour's time!

But there was I, a great boy,
  And what would folks say
To hear my mother singing
    me
  To sleep all day,
  In such a daft way?

Men say the winter
  Was bad that year;
Fuel was scarce,
  And food was dear.

A wind with a wolf's head
  Howled about our door,
And we burned up the chairs
  And sat upon the floor.

All that was left us
  Was a chair we couldn't
    break,
And the harp with a woman's
    head
  Nobody would take,
  For song or pity's sake.

The night before Christmas
  I cried with the cold,
I cried myself to sleep
  Like a two-year-old.

And in the deep night
  I felt my mother rise,
And stare down upon me
  With love in her eyes.

I saw my mother sitting
  On the one good chair,
A light falling on her
  From I couldn't tell where,

Looking nineteen,
  And not a day older,
And the harp with a woman's
    head
  Leaned against her
    shoulder.

Her thin fingers, moving
  In the thin, tall strings,
Were weav-weav-weaving
  Wonderful things.

Many bright threads,
  From where I couldn't see,
Were running through the
    harp strings
  Rapidly,

And gold threads whistling
  Through my mother's
    hand.
I saw the web grow,
  And the pattern expand.

She wove a child's jacket,
  And when it was done
She laid it on the floor
  And wove another one.

She wove a red cloak
  So regal to see,
"She's made it for a king's
    son,"
  I said, "and not for me."
  But I knew it was for me.

She wove a pair of breeches
  Quicker than that!
She wove a pair of boots
  And a little cocked hat.

She wove a pair of mittens,
  She wove a little blouse,
She wove all night
  In the still, cold house.

She sang as she worked,
  And the harp strings spoke;
Her voice never faltered,
  And the thread never
    broke.
And when I awoke,—

There sat my mother
  With the harp against her
    shoulder,
Looking nineteen,
  And not a day older,

A smile about her lips,
  And a light about her head,

And her hands in the harp
    strings
  Frozen dead.

And piled up beside her
  And toppling to the skies,
Were the clothes of a king's
    son,
  Just my size.

MORITURUS

If I could have
Two things in one:
The peace of the grave,
And the light of the sun;

My hands across
My thin breastbone,
But aware of the moss
Invading the stone,

Aware of the flight
Of the golden flicker
With his wing to the light;
To hear him nicker

And drum with his bill
On the rotted window;
Snug and still
On a gray pillow

Deep in the clay
Where digging is hard,
One of the way—
The blue shard

Of a broken platter—
If I might be
Insensate matter
With sensate me

Sitting within,
Harking and prying,
I might begin
To dicker with dying.

For the body at best
Is a bundle of aches,
Longing for rest:
It cries when it wakes

"Alas, 'tis light!"
At set of sun
"Alas, 'tis night,
And nothing done!"

Death, however,
Is a spongy wall,
Is a sticky river,
Is nothing at all.

Summon the weeper,
Wail and sing;
Call him Reaper,
Angel, King;

Call him Evil
Drunk to the lees,
Monster, Devil—
He is less than these.

Call him Thief,
The Maggot in the Cheese,
The Canker in the Leaf—
He is less than these.

Dusk without sound,
Where the spirit by pain
Uncoiled, is wound
To spring again;

The mind enmeshed
Laid straight in repose,
And the body refreshed
By feeding the rose—

These are but visions;
These would be
The grave's derisions,
Could the grave see.

Here is the wish
Of one that died
Like a beached fish
On the ebb of the tide:

That he might wait
Till the tide came back,
To see if a crate,
Or a bottle, or a black

Boot, or an oar,
Or an orange peel
Be washed ashore. . . .
About his heel

The sand slips;
The last he hears
From the world's lips
Is the sand in his ears.

What thing is little?—
The aphis hid
In a house of spittle?
The hinge of the lid

Of the spider's eye
At the spider's birth?
"Greater am I
By the earth's girth

"Than Mighty Death!"
All creatures cry
That can summon breath—
And speak no lie.

For he is nothing;
He is less
Than Echo answering
"Nothingness!"—

Less than the heat
Of the furthest star
To the ripening wheat;
Less by far,

When all the lipping
Is said and sung,
Than the sweat dripping
From a dog's tongue.

This being so,
And I being such,
I would liever go
On a cripple's crutch,

Lopped and felled;
Liever be dependent
On a chair propelled
By a surly attendant

With a foul breath,
And be spooned my food,
Than go with Death
Where nothing good,

Not even the thrust
Of the summer gnat,
Consoles the dust
For being that.

Needy, lonely,
Stitched by pain,
Left with only
The drip of the rain

Out of all I had:
The books of the wise,
Badly read
By other eyes,

Lewdly bawled
At my closing ear;
Hated, called
A lingerer here—

Withstanding Death
Till Life be gone,
I shall treasure my breath,
I shall linger on.

I shall bolt my door
With a bolt and a cable;

I shall block my door
With a bureau and a table;

With all my might
My door shall be barred.
I shall put up a fight,
I shall take it hard.

With his hand on my mouth
He shall drag me forth,
Shrieking to the south
And clutching at the north.

RECUERDO

We were very tired, we were very merry—
We had gone back and forth all night on the ferry.
It was bare and bright, and smelled like a stable—
But we looked into a fire, we leaned across a table,
We lay on a hilltop underneath the moon;
And the whistles kept blowing, and the dawn came soon.

We were very tired, we were very merry—
We had gone back and forth all night on the ferry;
And you ate an apple, and I ate a pear,
From a dozen of each we had bought somewhere;
And the sky went wan, and the wind came cold,
And the sun rose dripping, a bucketful of gold.

We were very tired, we were very merry,
We had gone back and forth all night on the ferry.
We hailed, "Good morrow, mother!" to a shawl-covered head,
And bought a morning paper, which neither of us read;
And she wept, "God bless you!" for the apples and pears,
And we gave her all our money but our subway fares.

THE CAMEO

Forever over now, forever, forever gone
That day. Clear and diminished like a scene
Carven in cameo, the lighthouse, and the cove between
The sandy cliffs, and the boat drawn up on the beach;
And the long skirt of a lady innocent and young,

Her hand resting on her bosom, her head hung;
And the figure of a man in earnest speech.

Clear and diminished like a scene cut in cameo
The lighthouse, and the boat on the beach, and the two shapes
Of the woman and the man; lost like the lost day
Are the words that passed, and the pain,—discarded, cut away
From the stone, as from the memory the heat of the tears
    escapes.

O troubled forms, O early love unfortunate and hard,
Time has estranged you into a jewel cold and pure;
From the action of the waves and from the action of sorrow
    forever secure,
White against a ruddy cliff you stand, chalcedony on sard.

LAMENT

Listen, children:
Your father is dead.
From his old coats
I'll make you little jackets;
I'll make you little trousers
From his old pants.
There'll be in his pockets
Things he used to put there,
Keys and pennies
Covered with tobacco;
Dan shall have the pennies
To save in his bank;
Anne shall have the keys
To make a pretty noise with
Life must go on,
And the dead be forgotten;
Life must go on,
Though good men die;
Anne, eat your breakfast;
Dan, take your medicine:
Life must go on;
I forget just why.

ELEGY BEFORE DEATH

There will be rose and rhododendron
 When you are dead and underground;
Still will be heard from white syringas
 Heavy with bees, a sunny sound;

Still will the tamaracks be raining
 After the rain has ceased, and still
Will there be robins in the stubble,
 Gray sheep upon the warm green hill.

Spring will not ail nor autumn falter;
 Nothing will know that you are gone,—
Saving alone some sullen plowland
 None but yourself sets foot upon;

Saving the mayweed and the pigweed
 Nothing will know that you are dead,—
These, and perhaps a useless wagon
 Standing beside some tumbled shed.

Oh, there will pass with your great passing
 Little of beauty not your own,—
Only the light from common water,
 Only the grace from simple stone!

THE RETURN

Earth does not understand her child,
 Who from the loud gregarious town
Returns, depleted and defiled,
 To the still woods, to fling him down.

Earth cannot count the sons she bore:
 The wounded lynx, the wounded man
Come trailing blood unto her door;
 She shelters both as best she can.

But she is early up and out,
 To trim the year or strip its bones;
She has no time to stand about
 Talking of him in undertones

Who has no aim but to forget,
  Be left in peace, be lying thus
For days, for years, for centuries yet,
  Unshaven and anonymous;

Who, marked for failure, dulled by grief,
  Has traded in his wife and friend
For this warm ledge, this alder leaf:
  Comfort that does not comprehend.

CONSCIENTIOUS OBJECTOR

I shall die, but that is all that I shall do for Death.

I hear him leading his horse out of the stall; I hear the clatter
    on the barn floor.
He is in haste; he has business in Cuba, business in the Bal-
    kans, many calls to make this morning.
But I will not hold the bridle while he cinches the girth.
And he may mount by himself: I will not give him a leg up.

Though he flick my shoulders with his whip, I will not tell him
    which way the fox ran.
With his hoof on my breast, I will not tell him where the black
    boy hides in the swamp.
I shall die, but that is all that I shall do for Death; I am not
    on his payroll.

I will not tell him the whereabouts of my friends nor of my
    enemies either.
Though he promise me much, I will not map him the route to
    any man's door.
Am I a spy in the land of the living, that I should deliver men
    to Death?
Brother, the password and the plans of our city are safe with
    me; never through me
Shall you be overcome.

OH, THINK NOT I AM FAITHLESS TO A VOW!

Oh, think not I am faithful to a vow!
Faithless am I save to love's self alone.
Were you not lovely I would leave you now:
After the feet of beauty fly my own.

Were you not still my hunger's rarest food,
And water ever to my wildest thirst,
I would desert you—think not but I would!—
And seek another as I sought you first.

But you are mobile as the veering air,
And all your charms more changeful than the tide,
Wherefore to be inconstant is no care:
I have but to continue at your side.
So wanton, light and false, my love, are you.
I am most faithless when I most am true.

I SHALL FORGET YOU PRESENTLY, MY DEAR

I shall forget you presently, my dear,
So make the most of this, your little day,
Your little month, your little half a year,
Ere I forget, or die, or move away,
And we are done forever; by and by
I shall forget you, as I said, but now,
If you entreat me with your loveliest lie
I will protest you with my favorite vow.

I would indeed that love were longer-lived,
And oaths were not so brittle as they are,
But so it is, and nature has contrived
To struggle on without a break thus far,—
Whether or not we find what we are seeking
Is idle, biologically speaking.

NOT WITH LIBATIONS, BUT WITH SHOUTS AND LAUGHTER

Not with libations, but with shouts and laughter
We drenched the altars of Love's sacred grove,
Shaking to earth green fruits, impatient after
The launching of the colored moths of Love.
Love's proper myrtle and his mother's zone
We bound about our irreligious brows,
And fettered him with garlands of our own,
And spread a banquet in his frugal house.

Not yet the god has spoken; but I fear
Though we should break our bodies in his flame,

And pour our blood upon his altar, here
Henceforward is a grove without a name,
A pasture to the shaggy goats of Pan,
Whence flee forever a woman and a man.

AND YOU AS WELL MUST DIE, BELOVED DUST

And you as well must die, belovèd dust,
And all your beauty stand you in no stead;
This flawless, vital hand, this perfect head,
This body of flame and steel, before the gust
Of Death, or under his autumnal frost,
Shall be as any leaf, be no less dead
Than the first leaf that fell,—this wonder fled,
Altered, estranged, disintegrated, lost.

Nor shall my love avail you in your hour.
In spite of all my love, you will arise
Upon that day and wander down the air
Obscurely as the unattended flower,
It mattering not how beautiful you were,
Or how belovèd above all else that dies.

PITY ME NOT BECAUSE THE LIGHT OF DAY

Pity me not because the light of day
At close of day no longer walks the sky;
Pity me not for beauties passed away
From field and thicket as the year goes by;
Pity me not the waning of the moon,
Nor that the ebbing tide goes out to sea,
Nor that a man's desire is hushed so soon,
And you no longer look with love on me.

This have I known always: Love is no more
Than the wide blossom which the wind assails,
Than the great tide that treads the shifting shore,
Strewing fresh wreckage gathered in the gales:
Pity me that the heart is slow to learn
What the swift mind beholds at every turn.

I SHALL GO BACK AGAIN TO THE BLEAK SHORE

I shall go back again to the bleak shore
And build a little shanty on the sand,
In such a way that the extremest band
Of brittle seaweed will escape my door
But by a yard or two; and nevermore
Shall I return to take you by the hand;
I shall be gone to what I understand,
And happier than I ever was before.

The love that stood a moment in your eyes,
The words that lay a moment on your tongue,
Are one with all that in a moment dies,
A little undersaid and oversung.
But I shall find the sullen rocks and skies
Unchanged from what they were when I was young.

*WHAT LIPS MY LIPS HAVE KISSED,
AND WHERE, AND WHY*

What lips my lips have kissed, and where, and why,
I have forgotten, and what arms have lain
Under my head till morning; but the rain
Is full of ghosts tonight, that tap and sigh
Upon the glass and listen for reply,
And in my heart there stirs a quiet pain
For unremembered lads that not again
Will turn to me at midnight with a cry.
Thus in the winter stands the lonely tree,
Nor knows what birds have vanished one by one,
Yet knows its boughs more silent than before:
I cannot say what loves have come and gone,
I only know that summer sang in me
A little while, that in me sings no more.

EUCLID ALONE HAS LOOKED ON BEAUTY BARE

Euclid alone has looked on Beauty bare.
Let all who prate of Beauty hold their peace,
And lay them prone upon the earth and cease
To ponder on themselves, the while they stare
At nothing, intricately drawn nowhere
In shapes of shifting lineage; let geese
Gabble and hiss, but heroes seek release
From dusty bondage into luminous air.

O blinding hour, O holy, terrible day,
When first the shaft into his vision shone
Of light anatomized! Euclid alone
Has looked on Beauty bare. Fortunate they
Who, though once only and then but far away,
Have heard her massive sandal set on stone.

TO JESUS ON HIS BIRTHDAY

For this your mother sweated in the cold,
For this you bled upon the bitter tree:
A yard of tinsel ribbon bought and sold;
A paper wreath; a day at home for me.
The merry bells ring out, the people kneel;
Up goes the man of God before the crowd;
With voice of honey and with eyes of steel
He drones your humble gospel to the proud.
Nobody listens. Less than the wind that blows
Are all your words to us you died to save.
O Prince of Peace! O Sharon's dewy Rose!
How mute you lie within your vaulted grave.
The stone the angel rolled away with tears
Is back upon your mouth these thousand years.

ON HEARING A SYMPHONY OF BEETHOVEN

Sweet sounds, oh, beautiful music, do not cease!
Reject me not into the world again.
With you alone is excellence and peace,
Mankind made plausible, his purpose plain.
Enchanted in your air benign and shrewd,
With limbs asprawl and empty faces pale,
The spiteful and the stingy and the rude
Sleep like the scullions in the fairy tale.
This moment is the best the world can give:
The tranquil blossom on the tortured stem.
Reject me not, sweet sounds! oh, let me live,
Till Doom espy my towers and scatter them,
A city spellbound under the aging sun,
Music my rampart, and my only one.

LOVE IS NOT ALL: IT IS NOT MEAT NOR DRINK

Love is not all: it is not meat nor drink
Nor slumber nor a roof against the rain;
Nor yet a floating spar to men that sink
And rise and sink and rise and sink again;
Love cannot fill the thickened lung with breath,
Nor clean the blood, nor set the fractured bone;
Yet many a man is making friends with death
Even as I speak, for lack of love alone.
It well may be that in a difficult hour,
Pinned down by pain and moaning for release,
Or nagged by want past resolution's power,
I might be driven to sell your love for peace,
Or trade the memory of this night for food.
It well may be. I do not think I would.

ARCHIBALD MacLEISH
(b. 1892)

THE SILENT SLAIN

We too, we too, descending once again
The hills of our own land, we too have heard
Far off—Ah, que ce cor a longue haleine
The horn of Roland in the passages of Spain,
The first, the second blast, the failing third,
And with the third turned back and climbed once more
The steep road southward, and heard faint the sound
Of swords, of horses, the disastrous war,
And crossed the dark defile at last, and found
At Roncevaux upon the darkening plain
The dead against the dead and on the silent ground
The silent slain—

ELEVEN

And summer mornings, the mute child, rebellious,
Stupid, hating the words, the meanings, hating
The Think now, Think, the Oh but Think! would leave
On tiptoe the three chairs on the veranda
And crossing tree by tree the empty lawn
Push back the shed door and upon the sill
Stand pressing out the sunlight from his eyes
And enter and with outstretched fingers feel
The grindstone and behind it the bare wall
And turn and in the corner on the cool
Hard earth sit listening. And one by one,
Out of the dazzled shadow in the room,
The shapes would gather, the brown plowshare, spades,
Mattocks, the polished helves of picks, a scythe
Hung from the rafters, shovels, slender tines
Glinting across the curve of sickles—shapes
Older than men were, the wise tools, the iron
Friendly with earth. And sit there, quiet, breathing
The harsh dry smell of withered bulbs, the faint

Odor of dung, the silence. And outside
Beyond the half-shut door the blind leaves
And the corn moving. And at noon would come,
Up from the garden, his hard crooked hands
Gentle with earth, his knees still earth-stained, smelling
Of sun, of summer, the old gardener, like
A priest, like an interpreter, and bend
Over his baskets.
                    And they would not speak:
They would say nothing. And the child would sit there
Happy as though he had no name, as though
He had been no one: like a leaf, a stem,
Like a root growing—

ARS POETICA

A poem should be palpable and mute
As a globed fruit,

Dumb
As old medallions to the thumb,

Silent as the sleeve-worn stone
Of casement ledges where the moss has grown—

A poem should be wordless
As the flight of birds.

A poem should be motionless in time
As the moon climbs,

Leaving, as the moon releases
Twig by twig the night-entangled trees,

Leaving, as the moon behind the winter leaves,
Memory by memory the mind—

A poem should be motionless in time
As the moon climbs.

A poem should be equal to:
Not true.

For all the history of grief
An empty doorway and a maple leaf.

For love
The leaning grasses and two lights above the sea—

A poem should not mean
But be.

YOU, ANDREW MARVELL

And here face down beneath the sun
And here upon earth's noonward height
To feel the always coming on
The always rising of the night

To feel creep up the curving east
The earthy chill of dusk and slow
Upon those under lands the vast
And ever climbing shadow grow

And strange at Ecbatan the trees
Take leaf by leaf the evening strange
The flooding dark about their knees
The mountains over Persia change

And now at Kermanshah the gate
Dark empty and the withered grass
And through the twilight now the late
Few travelers in the westward pass

And Baghdad darken and the bridge
Across the silent river gone
And through Arabia the edge
Of evening widen and steal on

And deepen on Palmyra's street
The wheel rut in the ruined stone
And Lebanon fade out and Crete
High through the clouds and overblown

And over Sicily the air
Still flashing with the landward gulls
And loom and slowly disappear
The sails above the shadowy hulls

And Spain go under and the shore
Of Africa the gilded sand
And evening vanish and no more
The low pale light across that land

Nor now the long light on the sea

And here face downward in the sun
To feel how swift how secretly
The shadow of the night comes on . . .

THE END OF THE WORLD

Quite unexpectedly as Vasserot
The armless ambidextrian was lighting
A match between his great and second toe
And Ralph the lion was engaged in biting
The neck of Madame Sossman while the drum
Pointed, and Teeny was about to cough
In waltz time swinging Jocko by the thumb—
Quite unexpectedly the top blew off:

And there, there overhead, there, there, hung over
Those thousands of white faces, those dazed eyes,.
There in the starless dark the poise, the hover,
There with vast wings across the canceled skies,
There in the sudden blackness the black pall
Of nothing, nothing, nothing—nothing at all.

MEMORIAL RAIN

For Kenneth MacLeish, 1894-1918

Ambassador Puser the ambassador
Reminds himself in French, felicitous tongue,
What these (young men no longer) lie here for
In rows that once, and somewhere else, were young . . .

All night in Brussels the wind had tugged at my door:
I had heard the wind at my door and the trees strung
Taut, and to me who had never been before
In that country it was a strange wind, blowing
Steadily, stiffening the walls, the floor,
The roof of my room. I had not slept for knowing
He too, dead, was a stranger in that land
And felt beneath the earth in the wind's flowing
A tightening of roots and would not understand,
Remembering lake winds in Illinois,
That strange wind. I had felt his bones in the sand
Listening.

. . . Reflects that these enjoy
Their country's gratitude, that deep repose,
That peace no pain can break, no hurt destroy,
That rest, that sleep . . .

At Ghent the wind rose.
There was a smell of rain and a heavy drag
Of wind in the hedges but not as the wind blows
Over fresh water when the waves lag
Foaming and the willows huddle and it will rain:
I felt him waiting.

. . . Indicates the flag
Which (may he say) enisles in Flanders plain
This little field these happy, happy dead
Have made America . . .

In the ripe grain
The wind coiled glistening, darted, fled,
Dragging its heavy body: at Waereghem
The wind coiled in the grass above his head:
Waiting—listening . . .

. . . Dedicates to them
This earth their bones have hallowed, this last gift
A grateful country . . .

Under the dry grass stem
The words are blurred, are thickened, the words sift
Confused by the rasp of the wind, by the thin grating
Of ants under the grass, the minute shift
And tumble of dusty sand separating
From dusty sand. The roots of the grass strain,
Tighten, the earth is rigid, waits—he is waiting—

And suddenly, and all at once, the rain!

The living scatter, they run into houses, the wind
Is trampled under the rain, shakes free, is again
Trampled. The rain gathers, running in thinned
Spurts of water that ravel in the dry sand,
Seeping in the sand under the grass roots, seeping
Between cracked boards to the bones of a clenched hand:
The earth relaxes, loosens; he is sleeping,
He rests, he is quiet, he sleeps in a strange land.

"NOT MARBLE NOR THE GILDED MONUMENTS"

For Adele

The praisers of women in their proud and beautiful poems,
Naming the grave mouth and the hair and the eyes,
Boasted those they loved should be forever remembered:
These were lies.

The words sound but the face in the Istrian sun is forgotten.
The poet speaks but to her dead ears no more.
The sleek throat is gone—and the breast that was troubled to
    listen:
Shadow from door.

Therefore I will not praise your knees nor your fine walking
Telling you men shall remember your name as long
As lips move or breath is spent or the iron of English
Rings from a tongue.

I shall say you were young, and your arms straight, and your
    mouth scarlet:
I shall say you will die and none will remember you:
Your arms change, and none remember the swish of your
    garments,
Nor the click of your shoe.

Not with my hand's strength, not with difficult labor
Springing the obstinate words to the bones of your breast
And the stubborn line to your young stride and the breath to
    your breathing
And the beat to your haste
Shall I prevail on the hearts of unborn men to remember.

(What is a dead girl but a shadowy ghost
Or a dead man's voice but a distant and vain affirmation
Like dream words most)

Therefore I will not speak of the undying glory of women.
I will say you were young and straight and your skin fair
And you stood in the door and the sun was a shadow of leaves
    on your shoulders
And a leaf on your hair—

I will not speak of the famous beauty of dead women:
I will say the shape of a leaf lay once on your hair.
Till the world ends and the eyes are out and the mouths broken
Look! It is there!

PONY ROCK

For the memory of H.T.C.

One who has loved the hills and died, a man
Intimate with them—how their profiles fade
Large out of evening or through veils of rain
Vanish and reappear or how the sad
Long look of moonlight troubles their blind stones—
One who has loved them does not utterly,
Letting his fingers loosen and the green
Ebb from his eyeballs, close his eyes and go:

But other men, long after he is dead,
Seeing those hills will catch their breath and stare
As one who reading in a book some word
That calls joy back but can recall not where—
Only the crazy sweetness in the head—
Will stare at the black print till the page is blurred.

POLE STAR FOR THIS YEAR

Where the wheel of light is turned:
Where the axle of the night is
Turned: is motionless: where holds
And has held ancient sureness always:

Where of faring men the eyes
At oar bench at the rising bow
Have seen—torn shrouds between—the Wain
And that star's changelessness: not changing:

There upon that intent star:
Trust of wandering men: of truth
The most reminding witness: we
Fix our eyes also: waylost: the wanderers:

We too turn now to that star:
We too in whose trustless hearts
All truth alters and the lights
Of earth are out now turn to that star:

Liberty of man and mind
That once was mind's necessity
And made the West blaze up has burned
To bloody embers and the lamp's out:

Hope that was a noble flame
Has fanned to violence and feeds
On cities and the flesh of men
And chokes where unclean smoke defiles it:

Even the small spark of pride
That taught the tyrant once is dark
Where gunfire rules the starving street
And justice cheats the dead of honor:

Liberty and pride and hope
And every guide mark of the mind
That led our blindness once has vanished.
This star will not. Love's star will not.

Love that has beheld the face
A man has with a man's eyes in it
Bloody from the slugger's blows
Or heard the cold child cry for hunger—

Love that listens where the good:
The virtuous: the men of faith:
Proclaim the paradise on earth
And murder starve and burn to make it—

Love that cannot either sleep
Or keep rich music in the ear
Or lose itself for the wild beat
The anger in the blood makes raging—

Love that hardens into hate—
Love like hatred and as bright—
Love is that one waking light
That leads now when all others darken.

POEM IN PROSE

This poem is for my wife.
I have made it plainly and honestly:
The mark is on it
Like the burl on the knife.

I have not made it for praise.
She has no more need for praise
Than summer has
Or the bright days.

In all that becomes a woman
Her words and her ways are beautiful:
Love's lovely duty,
The well-swept room.

Wherever she is there is sun
And time and a sweet air:
Peace is there,
Work done.

There are always curtains and flowers
And candles and baked bread
And a cloth spread
And a clean house.

Her voice when she sings is a voice
At dawn by a freshening sea
Where the wave leaps in the
Wind and rejoices.

Wherever she is it is now.
It is here where the apples are:
Here in the stars,
In the quick hour.

The greatest and richest good,
My own life to live in,
This she has given me—

If giver could.

WHAT ANY LOVER LEARNS

Water is heavy silver over stone.
Water is heavy silver over stone's
Refusal. It does not fall. It fills. It flows
Every crevice, every fault of the stone,

Every hollow. River does not run.
River presses its heavy silver self
Down into stone and stone refuses.

                    What runs,
Swirling and leaping into sun, is stone's
Refusal of the river, not the river.

THE STEAMBOAT WHISTLE

Woman riding the two mares of her thighs
In July cotton and the Sunday morning
Moseying up the gutter, nudging the cats,
The house fronts rosy with the feints of heat,
And the Fall River boat going by, its scarlet bunting
Strung across the ending of the street,

When suddenly the crinkled sky was torn
To paper pigeons tumbling from the air
And She we know but have not ever seen
Rose from the river where the streets all end,
Her birds about her, and the silver nervous
Mares of morning, balky in the surf.

STARVED LOVERS

Chrysanthemums last too long for these ravenous ladies.
The flowers they prefer are brief, unfold
At evening filling the cool room then fade,
Budded at pleasure and at pleasure old.

Chrysanthemums stand too still for these starved ladies.
Staring like Vincent's sunlight, bright and still,
They burn until these feasters are afraid
Hunger may leave them and their lives be filled.

The ravenous ladies in the still-starved lives
Strip off the ever-burning leaves with silver knives.

WHAT THE SERPENT SAID TO ADAM

Which is you, old two-in-one?
Which is which, old one of two?
When the doubling is undone
Which one is you?

Is it you that so delights
By that woman in her bed?
Or you the glimmering sky afrights,
Vast overhead?

Are you body, are you ghost?
Were you got or had no father?
Is this you—the guest?—the host?
Who then's the other?

That woman says, old one-of-two,
In body was the soul begun:
Now two are one and one is you:—
Which one? Which one?

VICISSITUDES OF THE CREATOR

Fish has laid her succulent eggs
Safe in Sargasso weed
So wound and bound that crabbed legs
Nor clattering claws can find and feed.

Thus fish commits unto the sea
Her infinite future and the Trade
Blows westward toward eternity
The universe her love has made.

But when, upon this leeward beach,
The measureless sea journey ends
And ball breaks open, from the breach
A deft, gold, glossy crab extends

In ringside ritual of self-applause
The small ironic silence of his claws.

MY NAKED AUNT

Who puts off shift
Has love's concealment left.

Who puts off skin
Has pain to wind her in.

Who puts off flesh
Wears soul's enormous wish.

Who puts off bone
Has all of death for gown.

None go naked who have drawn this breath
Till love's put off and pain and wish and death.

THE GENIUS

Waked by the pale pink
Intimation to the eastward,
Cock, the prey of every beast,
Takes breath upon the hen-house rafter,
Leans above the fiery brink
And shrieks in brazen obscene burst
On burst of uncontrollable derisive laughter:
Cock has seen the sun! He first! He first!

REASONS FOR MUSIC

For Wallace Stevens

Why do we labor at the poem
Age after Age—even an age like
This one, when the living rock
No longer lives and the cut stone perishes?—

Hölderlin's question. Why be poet
Now when the meanings do not mean?—
When the stone shape is shaped stone?—
Dürftiger Zeit?—time without inwardness?

Why lie upon our beds at night
Holding a mouthful of words, exhausted
Most by the absence of the adversary?

Why be poet? Why be man!

Far out in the uttermost Andes
Mortised enormous stones are piled.
What is man? Who founds a poem
In the rubble of wild world—wilderness.

The acropolis of eternity that crumbles
Time and again is mine—my task.

The heart's necessity compels me:
Man I am: poet must be.

The labor of order has no rest:
To impose on the confused, fortuitous
Flowing away of the world, Form—
Still, cool, clean, obdurate,

Lasting forever, or at least
Lasting: a precarious monument
Promising immortality, for the wing
Moves and in the moving balances.

Why do we labor at the poem?
Out of the turbulence of the sea,
Flower by brittle flower, rises
The coral reef that calms the water.

Generations of the dying
Fix the sea's dissolving salts
In stone, still trees, their branches immovable,
Meaning
        the movement of the sea.

E. E. CUMMINGS
(b. 1894)

SPRING IS LIKE A PERHAPS HAND

Spring is like a perhaps hand
(which comes carefully
out of Nowhere)arranging
a window,into which people look(while
people stare
arranging and changing placing
carefully there a strange
thing and a known thing here)and

changing everything carefully

spring is like a perhaps
Hand in a window
(carefully to
and fro moving New and
Old things,while
people stare carefully
moving a perhaps
fraction of flower here placing
an inch of air there)and

without breaking anything.

DARLING!BECAUSE MY BLOOD CAN SING

darling!because my blood can sing
and dance(and does with each your least
your any most very amazing now
or here)let pitiless fear play host
to every isn't that's under the spring
—but if a look should april me,
down isn't's own isn't go ghostly they

doubting can turn men's see to stare
their faith to how their joy to why

their stride and breathing to limp and prove
—but if a look should april me,
some thousand million hundred more
 bright worlds than merely by doubting have
darkly themselves unmade makes love

armies(than hate itself and no
meanness unsmaller)armies can
immensely meet for centuries
and(except nothing)nothing's won
—but if a look should april me
for a half a when,whatever is less
alive than never begins to yes

but if a look should april me
(though such as perfect hope can feel
only despair completely strikes
forests of mind,mountains of soul)
quite at the hugest which of his who
death is killed dead. Hills jump with brooks:
trees tumble out of twigs and sticks;

WHEN SERPENTS BARGAIN FOR THE RIGHT TO SQUIRM

when serpents bargain for the right to squirm
and the sun strikes to gain a living wage—
when thorns regard their roses with alarm
and rainbows are insured against old age

when every thrush may sing no new moon in
if all screech-owls have not okayed his voice
—and any wave signs on the dotted line
or else an ocean is compelled to close

when the oak begs permission of the birch
to make an acorn—valleys accuse their
mountains of having altitude—and march
denounces april as a saboteur

then we'll believe in that incredible
unanimal mankind(and not until)

HANK YOU GOD FOR MOST THIS AMAZING

i thank You God for most this amazing
day:for the leaping greenly spirits of trees
and a blue true dream of sky;and for everything
which is natural which is infinite which is yes

(i who have died am alive again today,
and this is the sun's birthday;this is the birth
day of life and of love and wings:and of the gay
great happening illimitably earth)

how should tasting touching hearing seeing
breathing any—lifted from the no
of all nothing—human merely being
doubt unimaginable You?

(now the ears of my ears awake and
now the eyes of my eyes are opened)

ALL IGNORANCE TOBOGGANS INTO KNOW

all ignorance toboggans into know
and trudges up to ignorance again:
but winter's not forever,even snow
melts;and if spring should spoil the game,what then?

all history's a winter sport or three:
but were it five,i'd still insist that all
history is too small for even me;
for me and you,exceedingly too small.

Swoop(shrill collective myth)into thy grave
merely to toil the scale to shrillerness
per every madge and mabel dick and dave
—tomorrow is our permanent address

and there they'll scarcely find us(if they do,
we'll move away still further:into now

MAGGIE AND MILLY AND MOLLY AND M~

maggie and milly and molly and may
went down to the beach(to play one day)

and maggie discovered a shell that sang
so sweetly she couldn't remember her troubles,and

milly befriended a stranded star
whose rays five languid fingers were;

and molly was chased by a horrible thing
which raced sideways while blowing bubbles:and

may came home with a smooth round stone
as small as a world and as large as alone.

For whatever we lose(like a you or a me)
it's always ourselves we find in the sea

SO SHY SHY SHY(AND WITH A

So shy shy shy(and with a
look the very boldest man
can scarcely dare to meet no matter

how he'll try to try)

So wrong(wrong wrong)and with a
smile at which the rightest man
remembers there is such a thing

as spring and wonders why

So gay gay gay and with a
wisdom not the wisest man
will partly understand(although

the wisest man am i)

So young young young and with a
something makes the oldest man
(whoever he may be)the only

man who'll never die

IN TIME OF DAFFODILS(WHO KNOW

in time of daffodils(who know
the goal of living is to grow)
forgetting why,remember how

in time of lilacs who proclaim
the aim of waking is to dream,
remember so(forgetting seem)

in time of roses(who amaze
our now and here with paradise)
forgetting if,remember yes

in time of all sweet things beyond
whatever mind may comprehend.
remember seek(forgetting find)

and in a mystery to be
(when time from time shall set us free)
forgetting me,remember me

IF THERE ARE ANY HEAVENS MY MOTHER WILL (ALL BY HERSELF)HAVE

if there are any heavens my mother will(all by herself)have
one. It will not be a pansy heaven nor
a fragile heaven of lilies-of-the-valley but
it will be a heaven of blackred roses

my father will be(deep like a rose
tall like a rose)

standing near my

(swaying over her
silent)
with eyes which are really petals and see

nothing with the face of a poet really which
is a flower and not a face with
hands
which whisper
This is my beloved my

                    (suddenly in sunlight)

he will bow,

& the whole garden will bow)

MOUSE)WON

mouse)Won
derfully is
anyone else entirely who doesn't
move(Moved more suddenly than)whose

tiniest smile?may Be
bigger than the fear of all
hearts never which have
(Per

haps)loved(or than
everyone that will Ever love)we
've
hidden him in A leaf

and,
Opening
beautiful earth
put(only)a Leaf among dark

ness.sunlight's
thenlike?now
Disappears
some

thing(silent:
madeofimagination
;the incredible soft)ness
(his ears(eyes

THAT MELANCHOLY

that melancholy

fellow'll play
his handorgan
until you say

"i want a fortune"

.At which(smiling)he stops:
& pick
ing up a magical stick
t,a,p,s

this dingy cage:then with a ghost

's rainfaint windthin
voice-which-is
no-voice sobcries

"paw?lee"

—whereupon out(SlO
wLy)steps(to
mount the wand)a by no
means almost

white morethanPerson;who

(riding through space
to diminutive this
opened drawer)tweak

S with his brutebeak

one fatal faded(pinkish or
yellowish maybe)piece
of pitiful paper—
but now, as Mr bowing Cockatoo

proffers the meaning of the stars

14th st dis(because my tears
are full of eyes)appears.   Because
only the truest things always

are true because they can't be true

THANKSGIVING

(1956)

a monstering horror swallows
this unworld me by you
as the god of our fathers' fathers bows
to a which that walks like a who

but the voice-with-a-smile of democracy
announces night & day
"all poor little peoples that want to be free
just trust in the u s a"

suddenly uprose hungary
and she gave a terrible cry
"no slave's unlife shall murder me
for i will freely die"

she cried so high thermopylae
heard her and marathon
and all prehuman history
and finally The UN

"be quiet little hungary
and do as you are bid
a good kind bear is angary
we fear for the quo pro quid"

uncle sam shrugs his pretty
pink shoulders you know how
and he twitches a liberal titty
and lisps "i'm busy right now"

so rah-rah-rah democracy
let's all be as thankful as hell
and bury the statue of liberty
(because it begins to smell)

WHATEVER'S MERELY WILFUL

whatever's merely wilful,
and not miraculous
(be never it so skilful)
must wither fail and cease
—but better than to grow
beauty knows no

their goal(in calm and fury:
through joy and anguish)who've
made her,outglory glory
the little while they live—
unless by your thinking
forever's long

let beauty touch a blunder
(called life)we die to breathe,
itself becomes her wonder
—and wonderful is death;
but more,the older he's
the younger she's

STAND WITH YOUR LOVER ON THE ENDING EARTH

stand with your lover on the ending earth—

and while a(huge which by which huger than
huge)whoing sea leaps to greenly hurl snow

suppose we could not love,dear;imagine

ourselves like living neither nor dead these
(or many thousand hearts which don't and dream
or many million minds which sleep and move)
blind sands,at pitiless the mercy of

time time time time time

—how fortunate are you and i,whose home
is timelessness:we who have wandered down
from fragrant mountains of eternal now

to frolic in such mysteries as birth
and death a day(or maybe even less)

I AM A LITTLE CHURCH(NO GREAT CATHEDRAL)

i am a little church(no great cathedral)
far from the splendor and squalor of hurrying cities
—i do not worry if briefer days grow briefest,
i am not sorry when sun and rain make april

my life is the life of the reaper and the sower;
my prayers are prayers of earth's own clumsily striving
(finding and losing and laughing and crying)children
whose any sadness or joy is my grief or my gladness

around me surges a miracle of unceasing
birth and glory and death and resurrection:
over my sleeping self float flaming symbols
of hope,and i wake to a perfect patience of mountains

i am a little church(far from the frantic
world with its rapture and anguish)at peace with nature
—i do not worry if longer nights grow longest;
i am not sorry when silence becomes singing

winter by spring,i lift my diminutive spire to
merciful Him Whose only now is forever:
standing erect in the deathless truth of His presence
(welcoming humbly His light and proudly His darkness) •

I CARRY YOUR HEART WITH ME(I CARRY IT IN

i carry your heart with me(i carry it in
my heart)i am never without it(anywhere
i go you go,my dear;and whatever is done
by only me is your doing, my darling)
                         i fear
no fate(for you are my fate,my sweet)i want
no world(for beautiful you are my world,my true)
and it's you are whatever a moon has always meant
and whatever a sun will always sing is you

here is the deepest secret nobody knows
(here is the root of the root and the bud of the bud
and the sky of the sky of a tree called life;which grows
higher than soul can hope or mind can hide)
and this is the wonder that's keeping the stars apart

i carry your heart(i carry it in my heart)

IF UP'S THE WORD;AND A WORLD GROWS GREENER

if up's the word;and a world grows greener
minute by second and most by more—
if death is the loser and life is the winner
(and beggars are rich but misers are poor)
—let's touch the sky:
                    with a to and a fro
(and a here there where)and away we go

in even the laziest creature among us
a wisdom no knowledge can kill is astir—
now dull eyes are keen and now keen eyes are keener
(for young is the year,for young is the year)
—let's touch the sky:
                    with a great(and a gay
and a steep)deep rush through amazing day

it's brains without hearts have set saint against sinner;
put gain over gladness and joy under care—
let's do as an earth which can never do wrong does
(minute by second and most by more)
—let's touch the sky:
                    with a strange(and a true)
and a climbing fall into far near blue

if beggars are rich(and a robin will sing his
robin a song)but misers are poor—
let's love until noone could quite be(and young is
the year,dear)as living as i'm and as you're
—let's touch the sky:
                    with a you and a me
and an every(who's any who's some)one who's we

WHAT IF A MUCH OF A WHICH OF A WIND

what if a much of a which of a wind
gives the truth to summer's lie;
bloodies with dizzying leaves the sun
and yanks immortal stars awry?
Blow king to beggar and queen to seem
(blow friend to fiend:blow space to time)
—when skies are hanged and oceans drowned,
the single secret will still be man

what if a keen of a lean wind flays
screaming hills with sleet and snow:
strangles valleys by ropes of thing
and stifles forests in white ago?
Blow hope to terror;blow seeing to blind
(blow pity to envy and soul to mind)
—whose hearts are mountains,roots are trees,
it's they shall cry hello to the spring

what if a dawn of a doom of a dream
bites this universe in two,
peels forever out of his grave
and sprinkles nowhere with me and you?
Blow soon to never and never to twice
(blow life to isn't:blow death to was)
—all nothing's only our hugest home;
the most who die,the more we live

NO MAN,IF MEN ARE GODS;BUT IF GODS MUST

no man,if men are gods;but if gods must
be men,the sometimes only man is this
(most common,for each anguish is his grief;
and,for his joy is more than joy,most rare)

a fiend,if fiends speak truth;if angels burn

by their own generous completely light,
an angel;or(as various worlds he'll spurn
rather than fail immeasurable fate)
coward,clown,traitor,idiot,dreamer,beast—

such was a poet and shall be and is

—who'll solve the depths of horror to defend
a sunbeam's architecture with his life:
and carve immortal jungles of despair
to hold a mountain's heartbeat in his hand

I SING OF OLAF GLAD AND BIG

i sing of Olaf glad and big
whose warmest heart recoiled at war:
a conscientious object-or

his wellbelovèd colonel(trig
westpointer most succinctly bred)
took erring Olaf soon in hand;
but—though an host of overjoyed
noncoms(first knocking on the head
him)do through icy waters roll
that helplessness which others stroke
with brushes recently employed
anent this muddy toiletbowl,
while kindred intellects evoke
allegiance per blunt instruments—
Olaf(being to all intents
a corpse and wanting any rag
upon what God unto him gave)
responds,without getting annoyed
"I will not kiss your f.ing flag"

straightway the silver bird looked grave
(departing hurriedly to shave)

but—though all kinds of officers
(a yearning nation's blueeyed pride)
their passive prey did kick and curse
until for wear their clarion
voices and boots were much the worse,
and egged the firstclassprivates on
his rectum wickedly to tease
by means of skilfully applied
bayonets roasted hot with heat—
Olaf(upon what were once knees)
does almost ceaselessly repeat
"there is some s. I will not eat"

our president,being of which
assertions duly notified
threw the yellowsonofabitch
into a dungeon,where he died

Christ(of His mercy infinite)
i pray to see;and Olaf,too

preponderatingly because
unless statistics lie he was
more brave than me:more blond than you.

A MAN WHO HAD FALLEN AMONG THIEVES

a man who had fallen among thieves
lay by the roadside on his back
dressed in fifteenthrate ideas
wearing a round jeer for a hat

fate per a somewhat more than less
emancipated evening
had in return for consciousness
endowed him with a changeless grin

whereon a dozen staunch and leal
citizens did graze at pause
then fired by hypercivic zeal
sought newer pastures or because

swaddled with a frozen brook
of pinkest vomit out of eyes
which noticed nobody he looked
as if he did not care to rise

one hand did nothing on the vest
its wideflung friend clenched weakly dirt
while the mute trouserfly confessed
a button solemnly inert.

Brushing from whom the stiffened puke
i put him all into my arms
and staggered banged with terror through
a million billion trillion stars

"NEXT TO OF COURSE GOD AMERICA I

"next to of course god america i
love you land of the pilgrims' and so forth oh
say can you see by the dawn's early my
country 'tis of centuries come and go
and are no more what of it we should worry
in every language even deafanddumb
thy sons acclaim your glorious name by gorry
by jingo by gee by gosh by gum
why talk of beauty what could be more beau-

tiful than these heroic happy dead
who rushed like lions to the roaring slaughter
they did not stop to think they died instead
then shall the voice of liberty be mute?"

He spoke. And drank rapidly a glass of water

ANYONE LIVED IN A PRETTY HOW TOWN

anyone lived in a pretty how town
(with up so floating many bells down)
spring summer autumn winter
he sang his didn't he danced his did.

Women and men(both little and small)
cared for anyone not at all
they sowed their isn't they reaped their same
sun moon stars rain

children guessed(but only a few
and down they forgot as up they grew
autumn winter spring summer)
that noone loved him more by more

when by now and tree by leaf
she laughed his joy she cried his grief
bird by snow and stir by still
anyone's any was all to her

someones married their everyones
laughed their cryings and did their dance
(sleep wake hope and then)they
said their nevers they slept their dream

stars rain sun moon
(and only the snow can begin to explain
how children are apt to forget to remember
with up so floating many bells down)

one day anyone died i guess
(and noone stooped to kiss his face)
busy folk buried them side by side
little by little and was by was

all by all and deep by deep
and more by more they dream their sleep
noone and anyone earth by april
wish by spirit and if by yes.

Women and men(both dong and ding)
summer autumn winter spring
reaped their sowing and went their came
sun moon stars rain

PITY THIS BUSY MONSTER,MANUNKIND,

pity this busy monster,manunkind,

not. Progress is a comfortable disease:
your victim(death and life safely beyond)

plays with the bigness of his littleness
—electrons deify one razorblade
into a mountainrange;lenses extend

unwish through curving wherewhen till unwish
returns on its unself.
                  A world of made
is not a world of born—pity poor flesh

and trees,poor stars and stones,but never this
fine specimen of hypermagical

ultraomnipotence. We doctors know

a hopeless case if—listen:there's a hell
of a good universe next door;let's go

MY FATHER MOVED THROUGH DOOMS OF LOVE

my father moved through dooms of love
through sames of am through haves of give,
singing each morning out of each night
my father moved through depths of height

this motionless forgetful where
turned at his glance to shining here;
that if(so timid air is firm)
under his eyes would stir and squirm

newly as from unburied which
floats the first who,his april touch
drove sleeping selves to swarm their fates
woke dreamers to their ghostly roots

and should some why completely weep
my father's fingers brought her sleep:
vainly no smallest voice might cry
for he could feel the mountains grow.

Lifting the valleys of the sea
my father moved through griefs of joy;
praising a forehead called the moon
singing desire into begin

joy was his song and joy so pure
a heart of star by him could steer
and pure so now and now so yes
the wrists of twilight would rejoice

keen as midsummer's keen beyond
conceiving mind of sun will stand,
so strictly(over utmost him
so hugely)stood my father's dream

his flesh was flesh his blood was blood:
no hungry man but wished him food;
no cripple wouldn't creep one mile
uphill to only see him smile.

Scorning the pomp of must and shall
my father moved through dooms of feel;
his anger was as right as rain
his pity was as green as grain

septembering arms of year extend
less humbly wealth to foe and friend
than he to foolish and to wise
offered immeasurable is

proudly and(by octobering flame
beckoned)as earth will downward climb,
so naked for immortal work
his shoulders marched against the dark

his sorrow was as true as bread:
no liar looked him in the head;
if every friend became his foe
he'd laugh and build a world with snow.

My father moved through theys of we,
singing each new leaf out of each tree
(and every child was sure that spring
danced when she heard my father sing)

then let men kill which cannot share,
let blood and flesh be mud and mire,
scheming imagine,passion willed,
freedom a drug that's bought and sold

giving to steal and cruel kind,
a heart to fear,to doubt a mind,
to differ a disease of same,
conform the pinnacle of am

though dull were all we taste as bright,
bitter all utterly things sweet,
maggoty minus and dumb death
all we inherit,all bequeath

and nothing quite so least as truth
—i say though hate were why men breathe—
because my father lived his soul
love is the whole and more than all

HART CRANE
(1899–1932)

THE BRIDGE

*From going to and fro in the earth,
and from walking up and down in it.*
THE BOOK OF JOB

Proem: To Brooklyn Bridge

How many dawns, chill from his rippling rest
The seagull's wings shall dip and pivot him,
Shedding white rings of tumult, building high
Over the chained bay waters Liberty—

Then, with inviolate curve, forsake our eyes
As apparitional as sails that cross
Some page of figures to be filed away;
—Till elevators drop us from our day. . . .

I think of cinemas, panoramic sleights
With multitudes bent toward some flashing scene
Never disclosed, but hastened to again,
Foretold to other eyes on the same screen;

And Thee, across the harbor, silver-paced
As though the sun took step of thee, yet left
Some motion ever unspent in thy stride,—
Implicitly thy freedom staying thee!

Out of some subway scuttle, cell or loft
A bedlamite speeds to thy parapets,
Tilting there momently, shrill shirt ballooning,
A jest falls from the speechless caravan.

Down Wall, from girder into street noon leaks,
A rip-tooth of the sky's acetylene;
All afternoon the cloud-flown derricks turn. . . .
Thy cables breathe the North Atlantic still.

And obscure as that heaven of the Jews,
Thy guerdon. . . . Accolade thou dost bestow
Of anonymity time cannot raise:
Vibrant reprieve and pardon thou dost show.

O harp and altar, of the fury fused,
(How could mere toil align thy choiring strings!)
Terrific threshold of the prophet's pledge,
Prayer of pariah, and the lover's cry,—

Again the traffic lights that skim thy swift
Unfractioned idiom, immaculate sigh of stars,
Beading thy path—condense eternity:
And we have seen night lifted in thine arms.

Under thy shadow by the piers I waited;
Only in darkness is thy shadow clear.
The City's fiery parcels all undone,
Already snow submerges an iron year. . . .

O Sleepless as the river under thee,
Vaulting the sea, the prairies' dreaming sod,
Unto us lowliest sometimes sweep, descend
And of the curveship lend a myth to God.

I. Ave Maria

Venient annis, saecula seris,
Quibus Oceanus vincula rerum
Laxet et ingens pateat tellus
Tiphysque novos detegat orbes
Nec sit terris ultima Thule.
SENECA

[*Columbus, alone, gazing toward Spain, invokes the presence of two faithful partisans of his quest. . . .*]

Be with me, Luis de San Angel, now—
Witness before the tides can wrest away
The word I bring, O you who reined my suit
Into the Queen's great heart that doubtful day;
For I have seen now what no perjured breath
Of clown nor sage can riddle or gainsay;—
To you, too, Juan Perez, whose counsel fear
And greed adjourned,—I bring you back Cathay!

Here waves climb into dusk on gleaming mail;
Invisible valves of the sea,—locks, tendons
Crested and creeping, troughing corridors
That fall back yawning to another plunge.
Slowly the sun's red caravel drops light
Once more behind us. . . . It is morning there—
O where our Indian emperies lie revealed,
Yet lost, all, let this keel one instant yield!

I thought of Genoa; and this truth, now proved,
That made me exile in her streets, stood me
More absolute than ever—biding the moon
Til dawn should clear that dim frontier, first seen
—The Chan's great continent. . . . Then faith, not fear
Nigh surged me witless. . . . Hearing the surf near—
I, wonder-breathing, kept the watch,—saw
The first palm chevron the first lighted hill

And lowered. And they came out to us crying,
"The Great White Birds!" (O Madre Maria, still
One ship of these thou grantest safe returning;
Assure us through thy mantle's ageless blue!)
And record of more, floating in a casque,
Was tumbled from us under bare poles scudding;
And later hurricanes may claim more pawn. . . .
For here between two worlds, another, harsh,

This third, of water, tests the word; lo, here
Bewilderment and mutiny heap whelming
Laughter, and shadow cuts sleep from the heart
Almost as though the Moor's flung scimitar
Found more than flesh to fathom in its fall.
Yet under tempest lash and surfeitings
Some inmost sob, half heard, dissuades the abyss,
Merges the wind in measure to the waves,

Series on series, infinite,—till eyes
Starved wide on blackened tides, accrete—enclose
This turning rondure whole, this crescent ring
Sun-cusped and zoned with modulated fire
Like pearls that whisper through the Doge's hands
—Yet no delirium of jewels! O Fernando,
Take of that eastern shore, this western sea,
Yet yield thy God's, thy Virgin's charity!

—Rush down the plenitude, and you shall see
Isaiah counting famine on this lee!

*

An herb, a stray branch among salty teeth,
The jellied weeds that drag the shore,—perhaps
Tomorrow's moon will grant us Saltes Bar—
Palos again,—a land cleared of long war.
Some Angelus environs the cordage tree;
Dark waters onward shake the dark prow free.

*

O Thou who sleepest on Thyself, apart
Like ocean athwart lanes of death and birth,
And all the eddying breath between dost search
Cruelly with love thy parable of man.—
Inquisitor! incognizable Word
Of Eden and the enchained Sepulcher,
Into thy steep savannas, burning blue,
Utter to loneliness the sail is true.

Who grindest oar, and arguing the mast
Subscribed holocaust of ships, O Thou
Within whose primal scan consummately
The glistening seignories of Ganges swim;
Who sendest greeting by the corposant,
And Teneriffe's garnet—flamed it in a cloud,
Urging through night our passage to the Chan;—
Te Deum laudamus, for thy teeming span!

Of all that amplitude that time explores,
A needle in the sight, suspended north,—
Yielding by inference and discard, faith
And true appointment from the hidden shoal:
This disposition that thy night relates
From Moon to Saturn in one sapphire wheel:
The orbic wake of thy once whirling feet,
Elohim, still I hear thy sounding heel!

White toil of heaven's cordons, mustering
In holy rings all sails charged to the far
Hushed gleaming fields and pendent seething wheat
Of knowledge,—round thy brows unhooded now
—The kindled Crown! acceded of the poles
And biased by full sails, meridians reel

Thy purpose—still one shore beyond desire!
The sea's green crying towers asway, Beyond

And kingdoms
              naked in the
                          trembling heart—
  Te Deum laudamus
                  O Thou Hand of Fire

II. *Powhatan's Daughter*

> "—*Pocahuntus, a well-featured but wanton yong girle . . . of the age of eleven or twelve years, get the boyes forth with her into the market place, and make them wheele, falling on their hands, turning their heels upwards, whom she would followe, and wheele so herself, naked as she was, all the fort over.*"

THE HARBOR DAWN

[*400 years and more . . . or is it from the soundless shore of sleep that time*]

Insistently through sleep—a tide of voices—
They meet you listening midway in your dream,
The long, tired sounds, fog-insulated noises:
Gongs in white surplices, beshrouded wails,
Far strum of foghorns . . . signals dispersed in veils.

And then a truck will lumber past the wharves
As winch engines begin throbbing on some deck;
Or a drunken stevedore's howl and thud below
Comes echoing alley-upward through dim snow.

And if they take your sleep away sometimes
They give it back again. Soft sleeves of sound
Attend the darkling harbor, the pillowed bay;
Somewhere out there in blankness steam

Spills into steam, and wanders, washed away
—Flurried by keen fifings, eddied
Among distant chiming buoys—adrift. The sky,
Cool feathery fold, suspends, distills
This wavering slumber. . . . Slowly—
Immemorially the window, the half-covered chair,
Ask nothing but this sheath of pallid air.

[*recalls you to your love, there in a waking dream to merge your seed*]

And you beside me, blessèd now while sirens
Sing to us, stealthily weave us into day—
Serenely now, before day claims our eyes
Your cool arms murmurously about me lay.

While myriad snowy hands are clustering at the panes—

> *your hands within my hands are deeds;*
> *my tongue upon your throat—singing*
> *arms close; eyes wide, undoubtful*
> > *dark*
> > > *drink the dawn—*
> *a forest shudders in your hair!*

[*—with whom?*]

The window goes blond slowly. Frostily clears.
From Cyclopean towers across Manhattan waters
—Two—three bright window-eyes aglitter, disk
The sun, released—aloft with cold gulls hither.

[*Who is the woman with us in the dawn? . . . whose is the flesh*
our feet have moved upon?]

The fog leans one last moment on the sill.
Under the mistletoe of dreams, a star—
As though to join us at some distant hill—
Turns in the waking west and goes to sleep.

VAN WINKLE

[*Streets spread past store and factory—sped by sunlight and her*
smile. . . .]

Macadam, gun-gray as the tunny's belt,
Leaps from Far Rockaway to Golden Gate:
Listen! the miles a hurdy-gurdy grinds—
Down gold arpeggios mile on mile unwinds.

Times earlier, when you hurried off to school
—It is the same hour though a later day—
You walked with Pizarro in a copybook,
And Cortez rode up, reining tautly in—
Firmly as coffee grips the taste,—and away!

There was Priscilla's cheek close in the wind,
And Captain Smith, all beard and certainty,
And Rip Van Winkle bowing by the way,—
"Is this Sleepy Hollow, friend—?" And he—

[*Like Memory, she is time's truant, shall take you by the hand. . . .*]

And Rip forgot the office hours,
                    and he forgot the pay;
        Van Winkle sweeps a tenement
                    way down on Avenue A,—

The grind-organ says. . . . Remember, remember
The cinder pile at the end of the back yard
Where we stoned the family of young
Garter snakes under. . . . And the monoplanes
We launched—with paper wings and twisted
Rubber bands. . . . Recall—recall
                                        the rapid tongues
That flittered from under the ash heap day
After day whenever your stick discovered
Some sunning inch of unsuspecting fiber—
It flashed back at your thrust, as clean as fire.

And Rip was slowly made aware
        that he, Van Winkle, was not here
    nor there. He woke and swore he'd seen Broadway
            a Catskill daisy chain in May—

So memory, that strikes a rhyme out of a box
Or splits a random smell of flowers through glass—
Is it the whip stripped from the lilac tree
One day in spring my father took to me,
Or is it the Sabbatical, unconscious smile
My mother almost brought me once from church
And once only, as I recall—?

It flickered through the snow screen, blindly
It forsook her at the doorway, it was gone
Before I had left the window. It
Did not return with the kiss in the hall.

Macadam, gun-gray as the tunny's belt,
Leaps from Far Rockaway to Golden Gate. . . .
Keep hold of that nickel for car change, Rip,—
Have you got your *Times*—?
And hurry along, Van Winkle—it's getting late!

THE RIVER

[*. . . and past the din and slogans of the year*—]

Stick your patent name on a signboard
brother—all over—going west—young man
Tintex—Japalac—Certain-teed Overalls ads
and lands sakes! under the new playbill ripped
in the guaranteed corner—see Bert Williams what?
Minstrels when you steal a chicken just
save me the wing for if it isn't
Erie it ain't for miles around a
Mazda—and the telegraphic night coming on Thomas

a Ediford—and whistling down the tracks
a headlight rushing with the sound—can you
imagine—while an EXPRESS makes time like
SCIENCE—COMMERCE and the HOLYGHOST
RADIO ROARS IN EVERY HOME WE HAVE THE NORTHPOLE
WALLSTREET AND VIRGINBIRTH WITHOUT STONES OR
WIRES OR EVEN RUNning brooks connecting ears
and no more sermons windows flashing roar
Breathtaking—as you like it . . . eh?

                So the 20th Century—so
whizzed the Limited—roared by and left
three men, still hungry on the tracks, ploddingly
watching the tail lights wizen and converge, slip-
ping gimleted and neatly out of sight.

                *

[*to those whose addresses are never near*]

The last bear, shot drinking in the Dakotas
Loped under wires that span the mountain stream.
Keen instruments, strung to a vast precision
Bind town to town and dream to ticking dream.
But some men take their liquor slow—and count
—Though they'll confess no rosary nor clue—
The river's minute by the far brook's year.
Under a world of whistles, wires and steam
Caboose-like they go ruminating through
Ohio, Indiana—blind baggage—
To Cheyenne tagging. . . . Maybe Kalamazoo.

Time's rendings, time's blendings they construe
As final reckonings of fire and snow;
Strange bird-wit, like the elemental gist
Of unwalled winds they offer, singing low
"My Old Kentucky Home" and "Casey Jones,"
"Some Sunny Day." I heard a road gang chanting so.
And afterwards, who had a colt's eyes—one said,
"Jesus! Oh I remember watermelon days!" And sped
High in a cloud of merriment, recalled
"And when my Aunt Sally Simpson smiled," he drawled—
"It was almost Louisiana, long ago."
"There's no place like Booneville though, Buddy,"
One said, excising a last bur from his vest,
"—For early trouting." Then peering in the can,
"—But I kept on the tracks." Possessed, resigned,
He trod the fire down pensively and grinned,
Spreading dry shingles of a beard. . . .

                                                        Behind
My father's cannery works I used to see
Rail squatters ranged in nomad raillery,
The ancient men—wifeless or runaway
Hobo-trekkers that forever search
An empire wilderness of freight and rails.
Each seemed a child, like me, on a loose perch,
Holding to childhood like some termless play.
John, Jake, or Charley, hopping the slow freight
—Memphis to Tallahassee—riding the rods,
Blind fists of nothing, humpty-dumpty clods.

[but who have touched her, knowing her without name]

Yet they touch something like a key perhaps.
From pole to pole across the hills, the states
—They know a body under the wide rain;
Youngsters with eyes like fjords, old reprobates
With race-track jargon,—dotting immensity
They lurk across her, knowing her yonder breast
Snow silvered, sumac stained or smoky blue—
Is past the valley-sleepers, south or west.
—As I have trod the rumorous midnights, too,
And past the circuit of the lamp's thin flame
(O Nights that brought me to her body bare!)
Have dreamed beyond the print that bound her name.
Trains sounding the long blizzards out—I heard

Wail into distances I knew were hers.
Papooses crying on the wind's long mane
Screamed redskin dynasties that fled the brain,
—Dead echoes! But I knew her body there,
Time like a serpent down her shoulder, dark,
And space, an eaglet's wing, laid on her hair.

[*nor the myths of her fathers. . . .*]

Under the Ozarks, domed by Iron Mountain,
The old gods of the rain lie wrapped in pools
Where eyeless fish curvet a sunken fountain
And redescend with corn from querulous crows.
Such pilferings make up their timeless eatage,
Propitiate them for their timber torn
By iron, iron—always the iron dealt cleavage!
They doze now, below ax and powder horn.

And Pullman breakfasters glide glistening steel
From tunnel into field—iron strides the dew—
Straddles the hill, a dance of wheel on wheel.
You have a half hour's wait at Siskiyou,
Or stay the night and take the next train through.
Southward, near Cairo passing, you can see
The Ohio merging,—borne down Tennessee;
And if it's summer and the sun's in dusk
Maybe the breeze will lift the River's musk
—As though the waters breathed that you might know
"Memphis Johnny," "Steamboat Bill," "Missouri Joe."
Oh, lean from the window, if the train slows down,
As though you touched hands with some ancient clown,
—A little while gaze absently below
And hum "Deep River" with them while they go.

Yes, turn again and sniff once more—look see,
O Sheriff, Brakeman and Authority—
Hitch up your pants and crunch another quid,
For you, too, feed the River timelessly.
And few evade full measure of their fate;
Always they smile out eerily what they seem.
I could believe he joked at heaven's gate—
Dan Midland—jolted from the cold brake beam.

Down, down—born pioneers in time's despite,
Grimed tributaries to an ancient flow—
They win no frontier by their wayward plight,
But drift in stillness, as from Jordan's brow.

You will not hear it as the sea; even stone
Is not more hushed by gravity. . . . But slow,
As loath to take more tribute—sliding prone
Like one whose eyes were buried long ago

The River, spreading, flows—and spends your dream.
What are you, lost within this tideless spell?
You are your father's father, and the stream—
A liquid theme that floating niggers swell.

Damp tonnage and alluvial march of days—
Nights turbid, vascular with silted shale
And roots surrendered down of moraine clays:
The Mississippi drinks the farthest dale.

O quarrying passion, undertowed sunlight!
The basalt surface drags a jungle grace
Ochreous and lynx-barred in lengthening might;
Patience! and you shall reach the biding place!

Over De Soto's bones the freighted floors
Throb past the City storied of three thrones.
Down two more turns the Mississippi pours
(Anon tall ironsides up from salt lagoons)

And flows within itself, heaps itself free.
All fades but one thin skyline 'round. . . . Ahead
No embrace opens but the stinging sea;
The River lifts itself from its long bed,

Poised wholly on its dream, a mustard glow
Tortured with history, its one will—flow!
—The Passion spreads in wide tongues, choked and slow,
Meeting the Gulf, hosannas silently below.

THE DANCE

*[Then you shall see her truly—your blood remembering its first inva-
sion of her secrecy, its first encounters with her kin, her chieftain
lover . . . his shade that haunts the lakes and hills]*

The swift red flesh, a winter king—
Who squired the glacier woman down the sky?
She ran the neighing canyons all the spring;
She spouted arms; she rose with maize—to die.

And in the autumn drouth, whose burnished hands
With mineral wariness found out the stone
Where prayers, forgotten, streamed the mesa sands?
He holds the twilight's dim, perpetual throne.

Mythical brows we saw retiring—loath,
Disturbed and destined, into denser green.
Greeting they sped us, on the arrow's oath:
Now lie incorrigibly what years between. . . .

There was a bed of leaves, and broken play;
There was a veil upon you, Pocahontas, bride—
O Princess whose brown lap was virgin May;
And bridal flanks and eyes hid tawny pride.

I left the village for dogwood. By the canoe
Tugging below the mill race, I could see
Your hair's keen crescent running, and the blue
First moth of evening take wing stealthily.

What laughing chains the water wove and threw!
I learned to catch the trout's moon whisper; I
Drifted how many hours I never knew,
But, watching, saw that fleet young crescent die,—

And one star, swinging, take its place, alone,
Cupped in the larches of the mountain pass—
Until, immortally, it bled into the dawn.
I left my sleek boat nibbling margin grass. . . .

I took the portage climb, then chose
A further valley shed; I could not stop.
Feet nozzled wat'ry webs of upper flows;
One white veil gusted from the very top.

O Appalachian Spring! I gained the ledge;
Steep, inaccessible smile that eastward bends
And northward reaches in that violet wedge
Of Adirondacks!—wisped of azure wands,

Over how many bluffs, tarns, streams I sped!
—And knew myself within some boding shade:—
Gray tepees tufting the blue knolls ahead,
Smoke swirling through the yellow chestnut glade. . . .

A distant cloud, a thunder bud—it grew,
That blanket of the skies: the padded foot
Within,—I heard it; till its rhythm drew,
—Siphoned the black pool from the heart's hot root!

A cyclone threshes in the turbine crest,
Swooping in eagle feathers down your back;
Know, Maquokeeta, greeting; know death's best;
—Fall, sachem, strictly as the tamarack!

A birch kneels. All her whistling fingers fly.
The oak grove circles in a crash of leaves;
The long moan of a dance is in the sky.
Dance, Maquokeeta: Pocahontas grieves. . . .

And every tendon scurries toward the twangs
Of lightning deltaed down your saber hair.
Now snaps the flint in every tooth; red fangs
And splay tongues thinly busy the blue air. . . .

Dance, Maquokeeta! snake that lives before,
That casts his pelt, and lives beyond! Sprout, horn!
Spark, tooth! Medicine man, relent, restore—
Lie to us,—dance us back the tribal morn!

Spears and assemblies: black drums thrusting on—
O yelling battlements,—I, too, was liege
To rainbows currying each pulsant bone:
Surpassed the circumstance, danced out the siege!

And buzzard-circleted, screamed from the stake;
I could not pick the arrows from my side.
Wrapped in that fire, I saw more escorts wake—
Flickering, sprint up the hill groins like a tide.

I heard the hush of lava wrestling your arms,
And stag teeth foam about the raven throat;
Flame cataracts of heaven in seething swarms
Fed down your anklets to the sunset's moat.

O, like the lizard in the furious noon,
That drops his legs and colors in the sun,
—And laughs, pure serpent, Time itself, and moon
Of her own fate, I saw thy change begun!

And saw thee dive to kiss that destiny
Like one white meteor, sacrosanct and blent
At last with all that's consummate and free
There, where the first and last gods keep thy tent.

*

Thewed of the levin, thunder-shod and lean,
Lo, through what infinite seasons dost thou gaze—
Across what bivouacs of thin angered slain,
And see'st thy bride immortal in the maize!

Totem and fire gall, slumbering pyramid—
Though other calendars now stack the sky,
Thy freedom is her largesse, Prince, and hid
On paths thou knewest best to claim her by.

High unto Labrador the sun strikes free
Her speechless dream of snow, and stirred again,
She is the torrent and the singing tree;
And she is virgin to the last of men. . . .

West, west and south! winds over Cumberland
And winds across the llano grass resume
Her hair's warm sibilance. Her breasts are fanned
O stream by slope and vineyard—into bloom!

And when the caribou slant down for salt
Do arrows thirst and leap? Do antlers shine
Alert, star-triggered in the listening vault
Of dusk?—And are her perfect brows to thine?

We danced, O Brave, we danced beyond their farms
In cobalt desert closures made our vows. . . .
Now is the strong prayer folded in thine arms,
The serpent with the eagle in the boughs.

INDIANA

[. . . *and read her in a mother's farewell gaze.*]

The morning glory, climbing the morning long
   Over the lintel on its wiry vine,
Closes before the dusk, furls in its song
       As I close mine. . . .

And bison thunder rends my dreams no more
   As once my womb was torn, my boy, when you
Yielded your first cry at the prairie's door. . . .
       Your father knew

Then, though we'd buried him behind us, far
   Back on the gold trail—then his lost bones stirred. . . .
But you who drop the scythe to grasp the oar
       Knew not, nor heard.

How we too, Prodigal, once rode off, too—
   Waved Seminary Hill a gay good-bye. . . .
We found God lavish there in Colorado
       But passing sly.

The pebbles sang, the firecat slunk away
   And glistening through the sluggard freshets came
In golden syllables loosed from the clay
       His gleaming name.

A dream called Eldorado was his town,
   It rose up shambling in the nuggets' wake,
It had no charter but a promised crown
       Of claims to stake.

But we,—too late, too early, howsoever—
   Won nothing out of fifty-nine—those years—
But gilded promise, yielded to us never,
       And barren tears. . . .

The long trail back! I huddled in the shade
   Of wagon-tenting looked out once and saw
Bent westward, passing on a stumbling jade
       A homeless squaw—

Perhaps a half-breed. On her slender back
   She cradled a babe's body, riding without rein.
Her eyes, strange for an Indian's, were not black
       But sharp with pain

And like twin stars. They seemed to shun the gaze
   Of all our silent men—the long team line—
Until she saw me—when their violet haze
       Lit with love shine. . . .

I held you up—I suddenly the bolder,
   Knew that mere words could not have brought us nearer.
She nodded—and that smile across her shoulder
       Will still endear her

As long as Jim, your father's memory, is warm.
   Yes, Larry, now you're going to sea, remember
You were the first—before Ned and this farm,—
       First-born, remember—

And since then—all that's left to me of Jim
   Whose folks, like mine, came out of Arrowhead.
And you're the only one with eyes like him—
       Kentucky bred!

I'm standing still, I'm old, I'm half of stone!
   Oh, hold me in those eyes' engaging blue;
There's where the stubborn years gleam and atone,—
       Where gold is true!

Down the dim turnpike to the river's edge—
   Perhaps I'll hear the mare's hoofs to the ford. . . .
Write me from Rio . . . and you'll keep your pledge;
       I know your word!

Come back to Indiana—not too late!
   (Or will you be a ranger to the end?)
Good-bye . . . Good-bye . . . oh, I shall always wait
   You, Larry, traveler—
                stranger,
                    son,
                       —my friend—

III.   Cutty Sark

> *O, the navies old and oaken,*
> *O, the Temeraire no more!*
>   MELVILLE

I met a man in South Street, tall—
a nervous shark tooth swung on his chain.
His eyes pressed through green grass
—green glasses, or bar lights made them
so—
     shine—
          GREEN—
                eyes—
stepped out—forgot to look at you
or left you several blocks away—

in the nickel-in-the-slot piano jogged
"Stamboul Nights"—weaving somebody's nickel—
        sang—

    O Stamboul Rose—dreams weave the rose!

       Murmurs of Leviathan he spoke,
       and rum was Plato in our heads. . . .

"It's S.S. *Ala*—Antwerp—now remember kid
to put me out at three she sails on time.
I'm not much good at time any more keep
weak-eyed watches sometimes snooze—" his bony hands
got to beating time. . . . "A whaler once—
I ought to keep time and get over it—I'm a
Democrat—I know what time it is—No
I don't want to know what time it is—that
damned white Arctic killed my time. . . ."

    O Stamboul Rose—drums weave—

"I ran a donkey engine down there on the Canal
in Panama—got tired of that—
then Yucatán selling kitchenware—beads—
have you seen Popocatepetl—birdless mouth
with ashes sifting down—?
                  and then the coast again. . . ."

Rose of Stamboul O coral Queen—
teased remnants of the skeletons of cities—
and galleries, galleries of watergutted lava
snarling stone—green—drums—drown—

Sing!
"—that spiracle!" he shot a finger out the door. . . .
"O life's a geyser—beautiful—my lungs—
No—I can't live on land—!"

I saw the frontiers gleaming of his mind;
or are there frontiers—running sands sometimes
running sands—somewhere—sands running. . . .
Or they may start some white machine that sings.
Then you may laugh and dance the axletree—
steel—silver—kick the traces—and know—

> *ATLANTIS ROSE drums wreathe the rose,*
> *the star floats burning in a gulf of tears*
> *and sleep another thousand—*

                                   interminably
long since somebody's nickel—stopped—
playing—

A wind worried those wicker-neat lapels, the
swinging summer entrances to cooler hells. . . .
Outside a wharf truck nearly ran him down
—he lunged up Bowery way while the dawn
was putting the Statue of Liberty out—that
torch of hers you know—

I started walking home across the Bridge. . . .

*

Blithe Yankee vanities, turreted sprites, winged
                             British repartees, skill-
ful savage sea-girls
that bloomed in the spring—Heave, weave
those bright designs the trade winds drive. . . .

> *Sweet opium and tea, Yo-ho!*
> *Pennies for porpoises that bank the keel!*
> *Fins whip the breeze around Japan!*

Bright skysails ticketing the Line, wink round the Horn
to Frisco, Melbourne. . . .
                              Pennants, parabolas—
clipper dreams indelible and ranging,
baronial white on lucky blue!

    Perennial-*Cutty*-trophied-*Sark!*

Thermopylae, Black Prince, Flying Cloud through Sunda
—scarfed of foam, their bellies veered green esplanades,
locked in wind-humors, ran their eastings down;

    at Java Head freshened the nip
    (sweet opium and tea!)
    and turned and left us on the lee. . . .

Buntlines tusseling (91 days, 20 hours and anchored!)
                              Rainbow, Leander
(last trip a tragedy) where can you be
Nimbus? and you rivals two—

    a long tack keeping—

                        Taeping?
                        Ariel?

IV. Cape Hatteras

The seas all crossed,
weathered the capes, the voyage done . . .
           WALT WHITMAN

Imponderable the dinosaur
               sinks slow,
                    the mammoth saurian
                      ghoul, the eastern

                            Cape. . . .
While rises in the west the coastwise range,
                   slowly the hushed land—
Combustion at the astral core—the dorsal change
Of energy—convulsive shift of sand. . . .
But we, who round the capes, the promontories
Where strange tongues vary messages of surf
Below gray citadels, repeating to the stars
The ancient names—return home to our own
Hearths, there to eat an apple and recall
The songs that gypsies dealt us at Marseille
Or how the priests walked—slowly through Bombay—
Or to read you, Walt,—knowing us in thrall

To that deep wonderment, our native clay
Whose depth of red, eternal flesh of Pocahontas—
Those continental folded eons, surcharged
With sweetness below derricks, chimneys, tunnels—
Is veined by all that time has really pledged us. . . .
And from above, thin squeaks of radio static,
The captured fume of space foams in our ears—
What whisperings of far watches on the main
Relapsing into silence, while time clears
Our lenses, lifts a focus, resurrects
A periscope to glimpse what joys or pain
Our eyes can share or answer—then deflects
Us, shunting to a labyrinth submersed
Where each sees only his dim past reversed. . . .

But that star-glistered salver of infinity,
The circle, blind crucible of endless space,
Is sluiced by motion,—subjugated never.
Adam and Adam's answer in the forest
Left Hesperus mirrored in the lucid pool,
Now the eagle dominates our days, is jurist
Of the ambiguous cloud. We know the strident rule
Of wings imperious. . . . Space, instantaneous,
Flickers a moment, consumes us in its smile:
A flash over the horizon—shifting gears—
And we have laughter, or more sudden tears.
Dream cancels dream in this new realm of fact
From which we wake into the dream of act;
Seeing himself an atom in a shroud—
Man hears himself an engine in a cloud!

"—Recorders ages hence"—ah, syllables of faith!
Walt, tell me, Walt Whitman, if infinity
Be still the same as when you walked the beach
Near Paumanok—your lone patrol—and heard the wraith
Through surf, its bird note there a long time falling. . . .
For you, the panoramas and this breed of towers,
Of you—the theme that's statured in the cliff.
O Saunterer on free ways still ahead!
Not this our empire yet, but labyrinth
Wherein your eyes, like the Great Navigator's without ship,
Gleam from the great stones of each prison crypt
Of canyoned traffic. . . . Confronting the Exchange,
Surviving in a world of stocks,—they also range
Across the hills where second timber strays
Back over Connecticut farms, abandoned pastures,—
Sea eyes and tidal, undenying, bright with myth!

The nasal whine of power whips a new universe. . . .
Where spouting pillars spoor the evening sky,
Under the looming stacks of the gigantic powerhouse
Stars prick the eyes with sharp ammoniac proverbs,
New verities, new inklings in the velvet hummed
Of dynamos, where hearing's leash is strummed. . . .
Power's script,—wound, bobbin-bound, refined—
Is stropped to the slap of belts on booming spools, spurred
Into the bulging bouillon, harnessed jelly of the stars.
Towards what? The forked crash of split thunder parts
Our hearing momentwise; but fast in whirling armatures,
As bright as frogs' eyes, giggling in the girth
Of steely gizzards—axle-bound, confined
In coiled precision, bunched in mutual glee
The bearings glint,—O murmurless and shined
In oil-rinsed circles of blind ecstasy!

Stars scribble on our eyes the frosty sagas,
The gleaming cantos of unvanquished space. . . .
O sinewy silver biplane, nudging the wind's withers!
There, from Kill Devils Hill at Kitty Hawk
Two brothers in their twinship left the dune;
Warping the gale, the Wright windwrestlers veered
Capeward, then blading the wind's flank, banked and spun
What ciphers risen from prophetic script,
What marathons new-set between the stars!
The soul, by naphtha fledged into new reaches,
Already knows the closer clasp of Mars,—
New latitudes, unknotting, soon give place
To what fierce schedules, rife of doom apace!

Behold the dragon's covey—amphibian, ubiquitous
To hedge the seaboard, wrap the headland, ride
The blue's cloud-templed districts unto ether. . . .
While Iliads glimmer through eyes raised in pride
Hell's belt springs wider into heaven's plumed side.
O bright circumferences, heights employed to fly
War's fiery kennel masked in downy offings,—
This tournament of space, the threshed and chiseled height,
Is baited by marauding circles, bludgeon flail
Of rancorous grenades whose screaming petals carve us
Wounds that we wrap with theorems sharp as hail!

Wheeled swiftly, wings emerge from larval-silver hangars.
Taut motors surge, space-gnawing, into flight;
Through sparkling visibility, outspread, unsleeping,

Wings clip the last peripheries of light. . . .
Tellurian wind-sleuths on dawn patrol,
Each plane a hurtling javelin of winged ordnance,
Bristle the heights above a screeching gale to hover;
Surely no eye that Sunward Escadrille can cover!
There, meaningful, fledged as the Pleiades
With razor sheen they zoom each rapid helix!
Up-chartered choristers of their own speeding
They, cavalcade on escapade, shear Cumulus—
Lay siege and hurdle Cirrus down the skies!
While Cetus-like, O thou Dirigible, enormous Lounger
Of pendulous auroral beaches,—satellited wide
By convoy planes, moonferrets that rejoin thee
On fleeing balconies as thou dost glide,
—Hast splintered space!

                        Low, shadowed of the Cape,
Regard the moving turrets! From gray decks
See scouting griffons rise through gaseous crepe
Hung low . . . until a conch of thunder answers
Cloud-belfries, banging, while searchlights, like fencers,
Slit the sky's pancreas of foaming anthracite
Toward thee, O Corsair of the typhoon,—pilot, hear!
Thine eyes bicarbonated white by speed, O Skygak, see
How from thy path above the levin's lance
Thou sowest doom thou hast nor time nor chance
To reckon—as thy stilly eyes partake
What alcohol of space . . . ! Remember, Falcon Ace,
Thou hast there in thy wrist a Sanskrit charge
To conjugate infinity's dim marge—
Anew . . . !

                        But first, here at this height receive
The benediction of the shell's deep, sure reprieve!
Lead-perforated fuselage, escutcheoned wings
Lift agonized quittance, tilting from the invisible brink
Now eagle-bright, now
                        quarry-hid, twist-
                                        -ing, sink with
Enormous reprecussive list-
                        -ings down
Giddily spiraled
                        gauntlets, upturned, unlooping
In guerrilla sleights, trapped in combustion gyr-
Ing, dance the curdled depth
                        down whizzing

Zodiacs, dashed
                    (now nearing fast the Cape!)
                                        down gravitation's
                                          vortex into crashed
. . . dispersion . . . into mashed and shapeless debris. . . .
By Hatteras bunched the beached heap of high bravery!

*

The stars have grooved our eyes with old persuasions
Of love and hatred, birth,—surcease of nations. . . .
But who has held the heights more sure than thou,
O Walt!— Ascensions of thee hover in me now
As thou at junctions elegiac, there, of speed
With vast eternity, dost wield the rebound seed!
The competent loam, the probable grass,—travail
Of tides awash the pedestal of Everest, fail
Not less than thou in pure impulse inbred
To answer deepest soundings! O, upward from the dead
Thou bringest tally, and a pact, new bound,
Of living brotherhood!

                    Thou, there beyond—
Glacial sierras and the flight of ravens,
Hermetically past condor zones, through zenith havens
Past where the albatross has offered up
His last wing-pulse, and downcast as a cup
That's drained, is shivered back to earth—thy wand
Has beat a song, O Walt,—there and beyond!
And this, thine other hand, upon my heart
Is plummet ushered of those tears that start
What memories of vigils, bloody, by that Cape,—
Ghoul-mound of man's perversity at balk
And fraternal massacre! Thou, pallid there as chalk,
Hast kept of wounds, O Mourner, all that sum
That then from Appomattox stretched to Somme!

Cowslip and shad-blow, flaked like tethered foam
Around bared teeth of stallions, bloomed that spring
When first I read thy lines, rife as the loam
Of prairies, yet like breakers cliffward leaping!
O, early following thee, I searched the hill
Blue-writ and odor-firm with violets, till
With June the mountain laurel broke through green
And filled the forest with what clustrous sheen!
Potomac lilies,—then the Pontiac rose,
And Klondike edelweiss of occult snows!

White banks of moonlight came descending valleys—
How speechful on oak-vizored palisades,
As vibrantly I following down sequoia alleys
Heard thunder's eloquence through green arcades
Set trumpets breathing in each clump and grass tuft—till
Gold autumn, captured, crowned the trembling hill!

Panis Angelicus! Eyes tranquil with the blaze
Of love's own diametric gaze, of love's amaze!
Not greatest, thou,—not first, nor last,—but near
And onward yielding past my utmost year.
Familiar, thou, as mendicants in public places;
Evasive—too—as dayspring's spreading arc to trace is:—
Our Meistersinger, thou set breath in steel;
And it was thou who on the boldest heel
Stood up and flung the span on even wing
Of that great Bridge, our Myth, whereof I sing!

Years of the Modern! Propulsions toward what capes?
But thou, *Panis Angelicus,* hast thou not seen
And passed that Barrier that none escapes—
But knows it leastwise as death strife?—O, something green,
Beyond all sesames of science was thy choice
Wherewith to bind us throbbing with one voice,
New integers of Roman, Viking, Celt—
Thou, Vedic Caesar, to the greensward knelt!

And now, as launched in abysmal cupolas of space,
Toward endless terminals, Easters of speeding light—
Vast engines outward veering with seraphic grace
On clarion cylinders pass out of sight
To course that span of consciousness thou'st named
The Open Road—thy vision is reclaimed!
What heritage thou'st signaled to our hands!

And see! the rainbow's arch—how shimmeringly stands
Above the Cape's ghoul-mound, O joyous seer!
Recorders ages hence, yes, they shall hear
In their own veins uncanceled thy sure tread
And read thee by the aureole 'round thy head
Of pasture-shine, *Panis Angelicus!*

                              Yes, Walt,
Afoot again, and onward without halt,—
Not soon, nor suddenly,—No, never to let go
    My hand
          in yours,
                    Walt Whitman—
                         so—

V. Three Songs

The one Sestos, the other Abydos hight.
                                    MARLOWE

SOUTHERN CROSS

I wanted you, nameless Woman of the South,
No wraith, but utterly—as still more alone
The Southern Cross takes night
And lifts her girdles from her, one by one—
High, cool,
                wide from the slowly smoldering fire
Of lower heavens,—
                    vaporous scars!
Eve! Magdalene!
                or Mary, you?

Whatever call—falls vainly on the wave.
O simian Venus, homeless Eve,
Unwedded, stumbling gardenless to grieve
Windswept guitars on lonely decks forever;
Finally to answer all within one grave!

And this long wake of phosphor,
                            iridescent
Furrow of all our travel—trailed derision!
Eyes crumble at its kiss. Its long-drawn spell
Incites a yell. Slid on that backward vision
The mind is churned to spittle, whispering hell.

I wanted you. . . . The embers of the Cross
Climbed by aslant and huddling aromatically.
It is blood to remember; it is fire
To stammer back. . . . It is
God—your namelessness. And the wash—

All night the water combed you with black
Insolence. You crept out simmering, accomplished.
Water rattled that stinging coil, your
Rehearsed hair—docile, alas, from many arms.
Yes, Eve—wraith of my unloved seed!

The Cross, a phantom, buckled—dropped below the dawn.
Light drowned the lithic trillions of your spawn.

NATIONAL WINTER GARDEN

Outspoken buttocks in pink beads
Invite the necessary cloudy clinch
Of bandy eyes. . . . No extra mufflings here:
The world's one flagrant, sweating cinch.

And while legs waken salads in the brain
You pick your blonde out neatly through the smoke.
Always you wait for someone else though, always—
(Then rush the nearest exit through the smoke.)

Always and last, before the final ring
When all the fireworks blare, begins
A tom-tom scrimmage with a somewhere violin,
Some cheapest echo of them all—begins.

And shall we call her whiter than the snow?
Sprayed first with ruby, then with emerald sheen—
Least tearful and least glad (who knows her smile?)
A caught slide shows her sandstone gray between.

Her eyes exist in swivelings of her teats,
Pearls whip her hips, a drench of whirling strands.
Her silly snake rings begin to mount, surmount
Each other—turquoise fakes on tinseled hands.

We wait that writhing pool, her pearls collapsed
—All but her belly buried in the floor;
And the lewd trounce of a final muted beat!
We flee her spasm through a fleshless door. . . .

Yet, to the empty trapeze of your flesh,
O Magdalene, each comes back to die alone.
Then you, the burlesque of our lust—and faith,
Lug us back lifeward—bone by infant bone.

VIRGINIA

O rain at seven,
Pay check at eleven—
Keep smiling the boss away,
Mary (what are you going to do?)
Gone seven—gone eleven,
And I'm still waiting you—

O blue-eyed Mary with the claret scarf,
Saturday Mary, mine!

It's high carillon
From the popcorn bells!
Pigeons by the million—
And spring in Prince Street
Where green figs gleam
By oyster shells!

O Mary, leaning from the high wheat tower,
Let down your golden hair!

High in the noon of May
On cornices of daffodils
The slender violets stray.
Crap-shooting gangs in Bleecker reign,
Peonies with pony manes—
Forget-me-nots at windowpanes:

Out of the way-up nickel-dime tower shine,
Cathedral Mary,

shine!—

VI. Quaker Hill

*I see only the ideal. But no
ideals have ever been fully suc-
cessful on this earth.*
ISADORA DUNCAN

*The gentian weaves her fringes,
The maple's loom is red.*
EMILY DICKINSON

Perspective never withers from their eyes;
They keep that docile edict of the spring
That blends March with August Antarctic skies:
These are but cows that see no other thing
Than grass and snow, and their own inner being
Through the rich halo that they do not trouble
Even to cast upon the seasons fleeting
Though they should thin and die on last year's stubble.

And they are awkward, ponderous and uncoy . . .
While we who press the cider mill, regarding them—

We, who with pledges taste the bright annoy
Of friendship's acid wine, retarding phlegm,
Shifting reprisals (till who shall tell us when
The jest is too sharp to be kindly?) boast
Much of our store of faith in other men
Who would, ourselves, stalk down the merriest ghost.

Above them old Mizzentop, palatial white
Hostelry—floor by floor to cinquefoil dormer
Portholes the ceilings stack their stoic height.
Long tiers of windows staring out toward former
Faces—loose panes crown the hill and gleam
At sunset with a silent, cobwebbed patience. . . .
See them, like eyes that still uphold some dream
Through mapled vistas, canceled reservations!

High from the central cupola, they say
One's glance could cross the borders of three states;
But I have seen death's stare in slow survey
From four horizons that no one relates. . . .
Weekenders avid of their turf-won scores,
Here three hours from the semaphores, the czars
Of golf, by twos and threes in plaid plus fours
Alight with sticks abristle and cigars.

This was the Promised Land, and still it is
To the persuasive suburban land agent
In bootleg roadhouses where the gin fizz
Bubbles in time to Hollywood's new love-nest pageant.
Fresh from the radio in the old Meeting House
(Now the New Avalon Hotel) volcanoes roar
A welcome to high-steppers that no mouse
Who saw the Friends there ever heard before.

What cunning neighbors history has in fine!
The wood louse mortgages the ancient deal
Table that Powitzky buys for only nine-
Ty-five at Adams' auction,—eats the seal,
The spinster polish of antiquity. . . .
Who holds the lease on time and on disgrace?
What eats the pattern with ubiquity?
Where are my kinsmen and the patriarch race?

The resigned factions of the dead preside.
Dead rangers bled their comfort on the snow;
But I must ask slain Iroquois to guide

Me farther than scalped Yankees knew to go:
Shoulder the curse of sundered parentage,
Wait for the postman driving from Birch Hill
With birthright by blackmail, the arrant page
That unfolds a new destiny to fill. . . .

So, must we from the hawk's far-stemming view,
Must we descend as worm's eye to construe
Our love of all we touch, and take it to the Gate
As humbly as a guest who knows himself too late,
His news already told? Yes, while the heart is wrung,
Arise—yes, take this sheaf of dust upon your tongue!
In one last angelus lift throbbing throat—
Listen transmuting silence with that stilly note

Of pain that Emily, that Isadora knew!
While high from dim elm chancels hung with dew,
That triple-noted clause of moonlight—
Yes, whippoorwill, unhusks the heart of fright,
Breaks us and saves, yes, breaks the heart, yet yields
That patience that is armor and that shields
Love from despair—when love foresees the end—
Leaf after autumnal leaf
                    break off,
                                descend—
                                            descend—

VII. The Tunnel

To Find the Western path
Right thro' the Gates of Wrath.
                    BLAKE

Performances, assortments, résumés—
Up Times Square to Columbus Circle lights
Channel the congresses, nightly sessions,
Refractions of the thousand theaters, faces—
Mysterious kitchens. . . . You shall search them all.
Someday by heart you'll learn each famous sight
And watch the curtain lift in hell's despite;
You'll find the garden in the third act dead,
Finger your knees—and wish yourself in bed
With tabloid crime sheets perched in easy sight.

Then let you reach your hat

and go.
As usual, let you—also
walking down—exclaim
to twelve upward leaving
a subscription praise
for what time slays.

Or can't you quite make up your mind to ride;
A walk is better underneath the L a brisk
Ten blocks or so before? But you find yourself
Preparing penguin flexions of the arms,—
As usual you will meet the scuttle yawn:
The subway yawns the quickest promise home.

Be minimum, then, to swim the hiving swarms
Out of the Square, the Circle burning bright—
Avoid the glass doors gyring at your right,
Where boxed alone a second, eyes take fright
—Quite unprepared rush naked back to light:
And down beside the turnstile press the coin
Into the slot. The gongs already rattle.

And so
of cities you bespeak
subways, rivered under streets
and rivers. . . . In the car
the overtone of motion
underground, the monotone
of motion is the sound
of other faces, also underground—

"Let's have a pencil Jimmy—living now
at Floral park
Flatbush—on the Fourth of July—
like a pigeon's muddy dream—potatoes
to dig in the field—travlin the town—too—
night after night—the Culver line—the
girls all shaping up—it used to be—"

Our tongues recant like beaten weather vanes.
This answer lives like verdigris, like hair
Beyond extinction, surcease of the bone;
And repetition freezes—"What

"what do you want? getting weak on the links?
fandaddle daddy don't ask for change—IS THIS
FOURTEENTH? it's half past six she said—if

you don't like my gate why did you
swing on it, why *didja*
swing on it
anyhow—"

And somehow anyhow swing—

The phonographs of hades in the brain
Are tunnels that rewind themselves, and love
A burnt match skating in a urinal—
Somewhere above Fourteenth TAKE THE EXPRESS
To brush some new presentiment of pain—

"But I want service in this office SERVICE
I said—after
the show she cried a little afterwards but—"

Whose head is swinging from the swollen strap?
Whose body smokes along the bitten rails,
Bursts from a smoldering bundle far behind
In back forks of the chasms of the brain,—
Puffs from a riven stump far out behind
In interborough fissures of the mind . . . ?

And why do I often meet your visage here,
Your eyes like agate lanterns—on and on
Below the toothpaste and the dandruff ads?
—And did their riding eyes right through your side,
And did their eyes like unwashed platters ride?
And Death, aloft,—gigantically down
Probing through you—toward me, O evermore!
And when they dragged your retching flesh,
Your trembling hands that night through Baltimore—
That last night on the ballot rounds, did you
Shaking, did you deny the ticket, Poe?

For Gravesend Manor change at Chambers Street.
The platform hurries along to a dead stop.

The intent escalator lifts a serenade
Stilly
Of shoes, umbrellas, each eye attending its shoe, then
Bolting outright somewhere above where streets
Burst suddenly in rain. . . . The gongs recur:
Elbows and levers, guard and hissing door.
Thunder is galvothermic here below. . . . The car

Wheels off. The train rounds, bending to a scream,
Taking the final level for the dive

Under the river—
And somewhat emptier than before,
Demented, for a hitching second, humps; then
Lets go. . . . Toward corners of the floor
Newspapers wing, revolve and wing.
Blank windows gargle signals through the roar.

And does the Daemon take you home, also,
Wop washerwoman, with the bandaged hair?
After the corridors are swept, the cuspidors—
The gaunt sky-barracks cleanly now, and bare,
O Genoese, do you bring mother eyes and hands
Back home to children and to golden hair?

Daemon, demurring and eventful yawn!
Whose hideous laughter is a bellows mirth
—Or the muffled slaughter of a day in birth—
O cruelly to inoculate the brinking dawn
With antennae toward worlds that glow and sink;—
To spoon us out more liquid than the dim
Locution of the eldest star, and pack
The conscience naveled in the plunging wind,
Umbilical to call—and straightway die!

O caught like pennies beneath soot and steam,
Kiss of our agony thou gatherest;
Condensed, thou takest all—shrill ganglia
Impassioned with some song we fail to keep.
And yet, like Lazarus, to feel the slope,
The sod and billow breaking,—lifting ground,
—A sound of waters bending astride the sky
Unceasing with some Word that will not die . . . !

*

A tugboat, wheezing wreaths of steam,
Lunged past, with one galvanic blare stove up the River.
I counted the echoes assembling, one after one,
Searching, thumbing the midnight on the piers.
Lights, coasting, left the oily tympanum of waters;
The blackness somewhere gouged glass on a sky.
And this thy harbor, O my City, I have driven under,
Tossed from the coil of ticking towers. . . . Tomorrow,
And to be. . . . Here by the River that is East—

Here at the waters' edge the hands drop memory;
Shadowless in that abyss they unaccounting lie.
How far away the star has pooled the sea—
Or shall the hands be drawn away, to die?

Kiss of our agony Thou gatherest,
             O Hand of Fire
                        gatherest—

VIII. Alantis

*Music is then the knowledge of that which
relates to love in harmony and system.*
                                PLATO

Through the bound cable strands, the arching path
Upward, veering with light, the flight of strings,—
Taut miles of shuttling moonlight syncopate
The whispered rush, telepathy of wires.
Up the index of night, granite and steel—
Transparent meshes—fleckless the gleaming staves—
Sibylline voices flicker, waveringly stream
As though a god were issue of the strings. . . .

And through that cordage, threading with its call
One arc synoptic of all tides below—
Their labyrinthine mouths of history
Pouring reply as though all ships at sea
Complighted in one vibrant breath made cry,—
"Make thy love sure—to weave whose song we ply!"
From black embankments, moveless soundings hailed,
So seven oceans answer from their dream.

And on, obliquely up bright carrier bars
New octaves trestle the twin monoliths
Beyond whose frosted capes the moon bequeaths
Two worlds of sleep (O arching strands of song!)—
Onward and up the crystal-flooded aisle
White tempest nets file upward, upward ring
With silver terraces the humming spars,
The loft of vision, palladium helm of stars.

Sheerly the eyes, like sea gulls stung with rime—
Slit and propelled by glistening fins of light—
Pick biting way up towering looms that press
Sidelong with flight of blade on tendon blade

—Tomorrows into yesteryear—and link
What cipher script of time no traveler reads
But who, through smoking pyres of love and death,
Searches the timeless laugh of mythic spears.

Like hails, farewells—up planet-sequined heights
Some trillion whispering hammers glimmer Tyre:
Serenely, sharply up the long anvil cry
Of inchling eons silence rivets Troy.
And you, aloft there—Jason! hesting Shout!
Still wrapping harness to the swarming air!
Silvery the rushing wake, surpassing call,
Beams yelling Aeolus! splintered in the straits!

From gulfs unfolding, terrible of drums,
Tall Vision-of-the-Voyage, tensely spare—
Bridge, lifting night to cycloramic crest
Of deepest day—O Choir, translating time
Into what multitudinous Verb the suns
And synergy of waters ever fuse, recast
In myriad syllables,—Psalm of Cathay!
O Love, thy white, pervasive Paradigm . . . !

We left the haven hanging in the night—
Sheened harbor lanterns backward fled the keel.
Pacific here at time's end, bearing corn,—
Eyes stammer through the pangs of dust and steel.
And still the circular, indubitable frieze
Of heaven's meditation, yoking wave
To kneeling wave, one song devoutly binds—
The vernal strophe chimes from deathless strings!

O Thou steeled Cognizance whose leap commits
The agile precincts of the lark's return;
Within whose lariat sweep encinctured sing
In single chrysalis the many twain,—
Of stars Thou art the stitch and stallion glow
And like an organ, Thou, with sound of doom—
Sight, sound and flesh Thou leadest from time's realm
As love strikes clear direction for the helm.

Swift peal of secular light, intrinsic Myth
Whose fell unshadow is death's utter wound,—
O River-throated—iridescently upborne
Through the bright drench and fabric of our veins;
With white escarpments swinging into light,

Sustained in tears the cities are endowed
And justified conclamant with ripe fields
Revolving through their harvests in sweet torment.

Forever Deity's glittering Pledge, O Thou
Whose canticle fresh chemistry assigns
To rapt inception and beatitude,—
Always through blinding cables, to our joy,
Of thy white seizure springs the prophecy:
Always through spiring cordage, pyramids
Of silver sequel, Deity's young name
Kinetic of white choiring wings . . . ascends.

Migrations that must needs void memory,
Inventions that cobblestone the heart,—
Unspeakabe Thou Bridge to Thee, O Love.
Thy pardon for this history, whitest Flower,
O Answerer of all,—Anemone,—
Now while thy petals spend the suns about us, hold—
(O Thou whose radiance doth inherit me)
Atlantis,—hold thy floating singer late!

So to thine Everpresence, beyond time,
Like spears ensanguined of one tolling star
That bleeds infinity—the orphic strings,
Sidereal phalanxes, leap and converge:
—One Song, one Bridge of Fire! Is it Cathay,
Now pity steeps the grass and rainbows ring
The serpent with the eagle in the leaves . . . ?
Whispers antiphonal in azure swing.

BLACK TAMBOURINE

The interests of a black man in a cellar
Mark tardy judgment on the world's closed door.
Gnats toss in the shadow of a bottle,
And a roach spans a crevice in the floor.

Aesop, driven to pondering, found
Heaven with the tortoise and the hare;
Fox brush and sow ear top his grave
And mingling incantations on the air.

The black man, forlorn in the cellar,
Wanders in some mid-kingdom, dark, that lies,
Between his tambourine, stuck on the wall,
And, in Africa, a carcass quick with flies.

EMBLEMS OF CONDUCT

By a peninsula the wanderer sat and sketched
The uneven valley graves. While the apostle gave
Alms to the meek the volcano burst
With sulphur and aureate rocks . . .
For joy rides in stupendous coverings
Luring the living into spiritual gates.

Orators follow the universe
And radio the complete laws to the people.
The apostle conveys thought through discipline.
Bowls and cups fill historians with adorations,—
Dull lips commemorating spiritual gates.

The wanderer later chose this spot of rest
Where marble clouds support the sea
And where was finally borne a chosen hero.
By that time summer and smoke were past.
Dolphins still played, arching the horizons,
But only to build memories of spiritual gates.

PRAISE FOR AN URN

In Memoriam: Ernest Nelson

It was a kind and northern face
That mingled in such exile guise
The everlasting eyes of Pierrot
And, of Gargantua, the laughter.

His thoughts, delivered to me
From the white coverlet and pillows,
I see now, were inheritances—
Delicate riders of the storm.

The slant moon on the slanting hill
Once moved us toward presentiments
Of what the dead keep, living still,
And such assessments of the soul

As, perched in the crematory lobby,
The insistent clock commented on,
Touching as well upon our praise
Of glories proper to the time.

Still, having in mind gold hair,
I cannot see that broken brow
And miss the dry sound of bees
Stretching across a lucid space.

Scatter these well-meant idioms
Into the smoky spring that fills
The suburbs, where they will be lost.
They are no trophies of the sun.

GARDEN ABSTRACT

The apple on its bough is her desire,—
Shining suspension, mimic of the sun.
The bough has caught her breath up, and her voice,
Dumbly articulate in the slant and rise
Of branch on branch above her, blurs her eyes.
She is prisoner of the tree and its green fingers.

And so she comes to dream herself the tree,
The wind possessing her, weaving her young veins,
Holding her to the sky and its quick blue,
Drowning the fever of her hands in sunlight.
She has no memory, nor fear, nor hope
Beyond the grass and shadows at her feet.

STARK MAJOR

The lover's death, how regular
With lifting spring and starker
Vestiges of the sun that somehow
Filter in to us before we waken.

Not yet is there that heat and sober
Vivisection of more clamant air
That hands joined in the dark will answer
After the daily circuits of its glare.

It is the time of sundering . . .
Beneath the green silk counterpane
Her mound of undelivered life
Lies cool upon her—not yet pain.

And she will wake before you pass,
Scarcely aloud, beyond her door,
And every third step down the stair
Until you reach the muffled floor—

Will laugh and call your name; while you
Still answering her faint good-byes,
Will find the street, only to look
At doors and stone with broken eyes.

Walk now, and note the lover's death.
Henceforth her memory is more
Than yours, in cries, in ecstasies
You cannot ever reach to share.

VOYAGES

I

Above the fresh ruffles of the surf
Bright striped urchins flay each other with sand.
They have contrived a conquest for shell shucks,
And their fingers crumble fragments of baked weed
Gaily digging and scattering.

And in answer to their treble interjections
The sun beats lightning on the waves,
The waves fold thunder on the sand;
And could they hear me I would tell them:

O brilliant kids, frisk with your dog,
Fondle your shells and sticks, bleached
By time and the elements; but there is a line
You must not cross nor ever trust beyond it
Spry cordage of your bodies to caresses
Too lichen-faithful from too wide a breast.
The bottom of the sea is cruel.

II

And yet this great wink of eternity,
Of rimless floods, unfettered leewardings,
Samite sheeted and processioned where
Her undinal vast belly moonward bends,
Laughing the wrapt inflections of our love;

Take this Sea, whose diapason knells
On scrolls of silver snowy sentences,
The sceptered terror of whose sessions rends
As her demeanors motion well or ill,
All but the pieties of lovers' hands.

And onward, as bells off San Salvador
Salute the crocus lusters of the stars,
In these poinsettia meadows of her tides,—
Adagios of islands, O my Prodigal,
Complete the dark confessions her veins spell.

Mark how her turning shoulders wind the hours,
And hasten while her penniless rich palms
Pass superscription of bent foam and wave,—
Hasten, while they are true,—sleep, death, desire,
Close round one instant in one floating flower.

Bind us in time, O Seasons clear, and awe.
O minstrel galleons of Carib fire,
Bequeath us to no earthly shore until
Is answered in the vortex of our grave
The seal's wide spindrift gaze toward paradise.

III

Infinite consanguinity it bears—
This tendered theme of you that light
Retrieves from sea plains where the sky
Resigns a breast that every wave enthrones;
While ribboned water lanes I wind
Are laved and scattered with no stroke
Wide from your side, whereto this hour
The sea lifts, also, reliquary hands.

And so, admitted through black swollen gates
That must arrest all distance otherwise,—
Past whirling pillars and lithe pediments,
Light wrestling there incessantly with light,
Star kissing star through wave on wave unto
Your body rocking!
                        and where death, if shed,
Presumes no carnage, but this single change,—
Upon the steep floor flung from dawn to dawn
The silken skilled transmemberment of song;

Permit me voyage, love, into your hands. . . .

IV

Whose counted smile of hours and days, suppose
I know as spectrum of the sea and pledge
Vastly now parting gulf on gulf of wings
Whose circles bridge, I know (from palms to the severe
Chilled albatross's white immutability)
No stream of greater love advancing now
Than, singing, this mortality alone
Through clay aflow immortally to you.

All fragrance irrefragably, and claim
Madly meeting logically in this hour
And region that is ours to wreathe again,
Portending eyes and lips and making told
The chancel port and portion of our June—

Shall they not stem and close in our own steps
Bright staves of flowers and quills today as I
Must first be lost in fatal tides to tell?
In signature of the incarnate word
The harbor shoulders to resign in mingling
Mutual blood, transpiring as foreknown
And widening noon within your breast for gathering
All bright insinuations that my years have caught
For islands where must lead inviolably
Blue latitudes and levels of your eyes,—

In this expectant, still exclaim receive
The secret oar and petals of all love.

V

Meticulous, past midnight in clear rime,
Infrangible and lonely, smooth as though cast
Together in one merciless white blade—
The bay estuaries fleck the hard sky limits.

—As if too brittle or too clear to touch!
The cables of our sleep so swiftly filed,
Already hang, shred ends from remembered stars.
One frozen trackless smile. . . . What words
Can strangle this deaf moonlight? For we

Are overtaken. Now no cry, no sword
Can fasten or deflect this tidal wedge,

Slow tyranny of moonlight, moonlight loved
And changed. . . . "There's

Nothing like this in the world," you say,
Knowing I cannot touch your hand and look
Too, into that godless cleft of sky
Where nothing turns but dead sands flashing.

"—And never to quite understand!" No,
In all the argosy of your bright hair I dreamed
Nothing so flagless as this piracy.
                                    But now
Draw in your head, alone and too tall here.
Your eyes already in the slant of drifting foam;
Your breath sealed by the ghosts I do not know:
Draw in your head and sleep the long way home.

VI

Where icy and bright dungeons lift
Of swimmers their lost morning eyes,
And ocean rivers, churning, shift
Green borders under stranger skies,

Steadily as a shell secretes
Its beating leagues of monotone,
Or as many waters trough the sun's
Red kelson past the cape's wet stone;

O rivers mingling toward the sky
And harbor of the phoenix's breast—
My eyes pressed black against the prow,
—Thy derelict and blinded guest

Waiting, afire, what name, unspoke,
I cannot claim: let thy waves rear
More savage than the death of kings,
Some splintered garland for the seer.

Beyond siroccos harvesting
The solstice thunders, crept away,
Like a cliff swinging or a sail
Flung into April's inmost day—

Creation's blithe and petaled word
To the lounged goddess when she rose

Conceding dialogue with eyes
That smile unsearchable repose—

Still fervid covenant, Belle Isle,
—Unfolded floating dais before
Which rainbows twine continual hair—
Belle Isle, white echo of the oar!

The imaged Word, it is, that holds
Hushed willows anchored in its glow.
It is the unbetrayable reply
Whose accent no farewell can know.

THE BROKEN TOWER

The bell rope that gathers God at dawn
Dispatches me as though I dropped down the knell
Of a spent day—to wander the cathedral lawn
From pit to crucifix, feet chill on steps from hell.

Have you not heard, have you not seen that corps
Of shadows in the tower, whose shoulders sway
Antiphonal carillons launched before
The stars are caught and hived in the sun's ray?

The bells, I say, the bells break down their tower;
And swing I know not where. Their tongues engrave
Membrane through marrow, my long-scattered score
Of broken intervals. . . . And I, their sexton slave!

Oval encyclicals in canyons heaping
The impasse high with choir. Banked voices slain!
Pagodas, campaniles with reveilles outleaping—
O terraced echoes prostrate on the plain! . . .

And so it was I entered the broken world
To trace the visionary company of love, its voice
An instant in the wind (I know not whither hurled)
But not for long to hold each desperate choice.

My word I poured. But was it cognate, scored
Of that tribunal monarch of the air
Whose thigh embronzes earth, strikes crystal Word
In wounds pledged once to hope—cleft to despair?

The steep encroachments of my blood left me
No answer (could blood hold such a lofty tower

As flings the question true?)—or is it she
Whose sweet mortality stirs latent power?—

And through whose pulse I hear, counting the strokes
My veins recall and add, revived and sure
The angelus of wars my chest evokes:
What I hold healed, original now, and pure . . .

And builds, within, a tower that is not stone
(Not stone can jacket heaven)—but slip
Of pebbles—visible wings of silence sown
In azure circles, widening as they dip

The matrix of the heart, lift down the eye
That shrines the quiet lake and swells a tower. . . .
The commodious, tall decorum of that sky
Unseals her earth, and lifts love in its shower.

REPOSE OF RIVERS

The willows carried a slow sound,
A saraband the wind mowed on the mead.
I could never remember
That seething, steady leveling of the marshes
Till age had brought me to the sea.

Flags, weeds. And remembrance of steep alcoves
Where cypresses shared the noon's
Tyranny; they drew me into hades almost.
And mammoth turtles climbing sulphur dreams
Yielded, while sun-silt rippled them
Asunder. . . .

How much I would have bartered! the black gorge
And all the singular nestings in the hills
Where beavers learn stitch and tooth.
The pond I entered once and quickly fled—
I remember now its singing willow rim.

And finally, in that memory all things nurse;
After the city that I finally passed
With scalding unguents spread and smoking darts
The monsoon cut across the delta
At gulf gates. . . . There, beyond the dykes

I heard wind flaking sapphire, like this summer,
And willows could not hold more steady sound.

W. H. AUDEN
(b. 1907)

MUSÉE DES BEAUX ARTS

About suffering they were never wrong,
The Old Masters: how well they understood
Its human position; how it takes place
While someone else is eating or opening a window or just
    walking dully along;
How, when the aged are reverently, passionately waiting
For the miraculous birth, there always must be
Children who did not specially want it to happen, skating
On a pond at the edge of the wood:
They never forgot
That even the dreadful martyrdom must run its course
Anyhow in a corner, some untidy spot
Where the dogs go on with their doggy life and the torturer's
    horse
Scratches its innocent behind on a tree.

In Brueghel's *Icarus*, for instance: how everything turns away
Quite leisurely from the disaster; the ploughman may
Have heard the splash, the forsaken cry,
But for him it was not an important failure; the sun shone
As it had to on the white legs disappearing into the green
Water: and the expensive delicate ship that must have seen
Something amazing, a boy falling out of the sky,
Had somewhere to get to and sailed calmly on.

THE UNKNOWN CITIZEN

(To JS/07/M/378 This Marble Monument Is Erected
by the State)

He was found by the Bureau of Statistics to be
One against whom there was no official complaint,
And all the reports on his conduct agree
That, in the modern sense of an old-fashioned word, he was a
    saint,
For in everything he did he served the Greater Community.

Except for the War till the day he retired
He worked in a factory and never got fired
But satisfied his employers, Fudge Motors Inc.
Yet he wasn't a scab or odd in his views,
For his Union reports that he paid his dues,
(Our report on his Union shows it was sound)
And our Social Psychology workers found
That he was popular with his mates and liked a drink.
The Press are convinced that he bought a paper every day
And that his reactions to advertisements were normal in every
    way.
Policies taken out in his name prove that he was fully insured,
And his Health-card shows he was once in hospital but left it
    cured.
Both Producers Research and High-Grade Living declare
He was fully sensible to the advantages of the Installment Plan
And had everything necessary to the Modern Man,
A phonograph, a radio, a car and a frigidaire.
Our researchers into Public Opinion are content
That he held the proper opinions for the time of year;
When there was peace, he was for peace; when there was war,
    he went.
He was married and added five children to the population,
Which our Eugenist says was the right number for a parent of
    his generation.
And our teachers report that he never interfered with their
    education.

Was he free? Was he happy? The question is absurd:
Had anything been wrong, we should certainly have heard.

PETITION

Sir, no man's enemy, forgiving all
But will its negative inversion, be prodigal:
Send to us power and light, a sovereign touch
Curing the intolerable neural itch,
The exhaustion of weaning, the liar's quinsy,
And the distortions of ingrown virginity.
Prohibit sharply the rehearsed response
And gradually correct the coward's stance;
Cover in time with beams those in retreat
That, spotted, they turn though the reverse were great;
Publish each healer that in city lives
Or country houses at the end of drives;
Harrow the house of the dead; look shining at
New styles of architecture, a change of heart.

THE COMPOSER

All the others translate: the painter sketches
A visible world to love or reject;
Rummaging into his living, the poet fetches
The images out that hurt and connect,
From Life to Art by painstaking adaption
Relying on us to cover the rift;
Only your notes are pure contraption,
Only your song is an absolute gift.

Pour out your presence, O delight, cascading
The falls of the knee and the weirs of the spine,
Our climate of silence and doubt invading;
You, alone, alone, O imaginary song,
Are unable to say an existence is wrong,
And pour out your forgiveness like a wine.

IN MEMORY OF W. B. YEATS

(d. Jan. 1939)

I

He disappeared in the dead of winter:
The brooks were frozen, the air-ports almost deserted,
And snow disfigured the public statues;
The mercury sank in the mouth of the dying day.
O all the instruments agree
The day of his death was a dark cold day.

Far from his illness
The wolves ran on through the evergreen forests,
The peasant river was untempted by the fashionable quays;
By mourning tongues
The death of the poet was kept from his poems.

But for him it was his last afternoon as himself,
An afternoon of nurses and rumours;
The provinces of his body revolted,
The squares of his mind were empty,
Silence invaded the suburbs,
The current of his feeling failed: he became his admirers.

Now he is scattered among a hundred cities
And wholly given over to unfamiliar affections;
To find his happiness in another kind of wood
And be punished under a foreign code of conscience.
The words of a dead man
Are modified in the guts of the living.

But in the importance and noise of to-morrow
When the brokers are roaring like beasts on the floor of the
   Bourse,
And the poor have the sufferings to which they are fairly ac-
   customed,
And each in the cell of himself is almost convinced of his free-
   dom;
A few thousand will think of this day
As one thinks of a day when one did something slightly un-
   usual.

O all the instruments agree
The day of his death was a dark cold day.

II

You were silly like us: your gift survived it all;
The parish of rich women, physical decay,
Yourself; mad Ireland hurt you into poetry.
Now Ireland has her madness and her weather still,
For poetry makes nothing happen: it survives
In the valley of its saying where executives
Would never want to tamper; it flows south
From ranches of isolation and the busy griefs,
Raw towns that we believe and die in; it survives,
A way of happening, a mouth.

III

Earth, receive an honoured guest;
William Yeats is laid to rest:
Let the Irish vessel lie
Emptied of its poetry.

Time that is intolerant
Of the brave and innocent,
And indifferent in a week
To a beautiful physique,

Worships language and forgives
Everyone by whom it lives;
Pardons cowardice, conceit,
Lays its honours at their feet.

Time that with this strange excuse
Pardoned Kipling and his views,
And will pardon Paul Claudel,
Pardons him for writing well.

In the nightmare of the dark
All the dogs of Europe bark,
And the living nations wait,
Each sequestered in its hate;

Intellectual disgrace
Stares from every human face,
And the seas of pity lie
Locked and frozen in each eye.

Follow, poet, follow right
To the bottom of the night,
With your unconstraining Voice
Still persuade us to rejoice;

With the farming of a verse
Make a vineyard of the curse,
Sing of human unsuccess
In a rapture of distress;

In the deserts of the heart
Let the healing fountain start,
In the prison of his days
Teach the free man how to praise.

HERMAN MELVILLE

Towards the end he sailed into an extraordinary mildness,
And anchored in his home and reached his wife
And rode within the harbour of her hand,
And went across each morning to an office
As though his occupation were another island.

Goodness existed: that was the new knowledge.
His terror had to blow itself quite out
To let him see it; but it was the gale had blown him
Past the Cape Horn of sensible success
Which cries: "This rock is Eden. Shipwreck here."

But deafened him with thunder and confused with lightning:
—The maniac hero hunting like a jewel
The rare ambiguous monster that had maimed his sex,
Hatred for hatred ending in a scream,
The unexplained survivor breaking off the nightmare—
All that was intricate and false; the truth was simple.

Evil is unspectacular and always human,
And shares our bed and eats at our own table,
And we are introduced to Goodness every day,
Even in drawing-rooms among a crowd of faults;
He has a name like Billy and is almost perfect
But wears a stammer like a decoration:
And every time they meet the same thing has to happen;
It is the Evil that is helpless like a lover
And has to pick a quarrel and succeeds,
And both are openly destroyed before our eyes.

For now he was awake and knew
No one is ever spared except in dreams;
But there was something else the nightmare had distorted—
Even the punishment was human and a form of love:
The howling storm had been his father's presence
And all the time he had been carried on his father's breast.

Who now had set him gently down and left him.
He stood upon the narrow balcony and listened:
And all the stars above him sang as in his childhood
"All, all is vanity," but it was not the same;
For now the words descended like the calm of mountains—
—Nathaniel had been shy because his love was selfish—
But now he cried in exultation and surrender
"The Godhead is broken like bread. We are the pieces."

And sat down at his desk and wrote a story.

SOMETHING IS BOUND TO HAPPEN

Doom is dark and deeper than any sea-dingle:
Upon what man it fall
In spring, day-wishing flowers appearing,
Avalanche sliding, white snow from rock-face,
That he should leave his house;
No cloud-soft hands can hold him, restraint by women,
But ever that man goes
By place-keepers, by forest trees,
A stranger to strangers over undried sea,
Houses for fishes, suffocating water;
Or lonely on fell as chat,
By pot-holed becks
A bird stone-haunting, an unquiet bird.

There head falls forward, fatigued at evening,
And dreams of home:
Waving from window, spread of welcome,
Kissing of wife under single sheet;
But waking sees
Bird-flocks nameless to him, through doorway voices
Of new men making another love.

Save him from hostile capture
From sudden tiger's spring at corner:
Protect his house,
His anxious house where days are counted
From thunderbolt protect,
From gradual ruin spreading like a stain:
Converting number from vague to certain
Bring joy, bring day of his returning,
Lucky with day approaching, with leaning dawn.

THE DIASPORA

How he survived them they could never understand:
Had they not beggared him themselves to prove
They could not live without their dogmas or their land?
No worlds they drove him from were ever big enough:

How *could* it be the earth the Unconfined
Meant when It bade them set no limits to their love?
And he fulfilled the role for which he was designed:

On heat with fear, he drew their terrors to him,
And was a godsend to the lowest of mankind.
Till there was no place left where they could still pursue him
Except that exile which he called his Race.

But, envying him even that, they plunged right through him
Into a land of mirrors without time or space,
And all they had to strike now was the human face.

THE NOVELIST

Encased in talent like a uniform,
The rank of every poet is well known;
They can amaze us like a thunderstorm,
Or die so young, or live for years alone.

They can dash forward like hussars: but he
Must struggle out of his boyish gift and learn
How to be plain and awkward, how to be
One after whom none think it worth to turn.

For, to achieve his lightest wish, he must
Become the whole of boredom, subject to
Vulgar complaints like love, among the Just

Be just, among the Filthy filthy too,
And in his own weak person, if he can,
Must suffer dully all the wrongs of Man.

THE CLIMBERS

Fleeing the short-haired mad executives,
The sad and useless faces round my home,
Upon the mountains of my fear I climb;
Above, the breakneck scorching rock, the caves,
No col, no water; with excuse concocted,
Soon on a lower alp I fall and pant,
Cooling my face there in the faults that flaunt
The life which they have stolen and perfected.

Climbing with you was easy as a vow:
We reached the top not hungry in the least,
But it was eyes we looked at, not the view,
Saw nothing but ourselves, left-handed, lost;
Returned to shore, the rich interior still
Unknown. Love gave the power, but took the will.

ANOTHER TIME

For us like any other fugitive,
Like the numberless flowers that cannot number
And all the beasts that need not remember,
It is today in which we live.

So many try to say Not Now,
So many have forgotten how
To say I Am, and would be
Lost, if they could, in history.

Bowing, for instance, with such old-world grace
To a proper flag in a proper place,
Muttering like ancients as they stump upstairs
Of Mine and His or Ours and Theirs.

Just as if time were what they used to will
When it was gifted with possession still,
Just as if they were wrong
In no more wishing to belong.

No wonder then so many die of grief,
So many are so lonely as they die;
No one has yet believed or liked a lie,
Another time has other lives to live.

WHO'S WHO

A shilling life will give you all the facts:
How Father beat him, how he ran away,
What were the struggles of his youth, what acts
Made him the greatest figure of his day:

Of how he fought, fished, hunted, worked all night,
Though giddy, climbed new mountains; named a sea:
Some of the last researchers even write
Love made him weep his pints like you and me.

With all his honours on, he sighed for one
Who, say astonished critics, lived at home;
Did little jobs about the house with skill

And nothing else; could whistle; would sit still
Or potter round the garden; answered some
Of his long marvellous letters but kept none.

MACAO

A weed from Catholic Europe, it took root
Between the yellow mountains and the sea,
And bore these gay stone houses like a fruit,
And grew on China imperceptibly.
Rococo images of Saint and Saviour
Promise her gamblers fortunes when they die;
Churches beside the brothels testify
That faith can pardon natural behaviour.

This city of indulgence need not fear
The major sins by which the heart is killed,
And governments and men are torn to pieces:
Religious clocks will strike; the childish vices
Will safeguard the low virtues of the child;
And nothing serious can happen here.

O WHAT IS THAT SOUND

O what is that sound which so thrills the ear
  Down in the valley drumming, drumming?
Only the scarlet soldiers, dear,
  The soldiers coming.

O what is that light I see flashing so clear
  Over the distance brightly, brightly?
Only the sun on their weapons, dear,
  As they step lightly.

O what are they doing with all that gear,
  What are they doing this morning, this morning?
Only their usual manoeuvres, dear,
  Or perhaps a warning.

O why have they left the road down there,
  Why are they suddenly wheeling, wheeling?
Perhaps a change in their orders, dear.
  Why are you kneeling?

O haven't they stopped for the doctor's care,
  Haven't they reined their horses, their horses?
Why, they are none of them wounded, dear,
  None of these forces.

O is it the parson they want, with white hair,
  Is it the parson, is it, is it?
No, they are passing his gateway, dear,
  Without a visit.

O it must be the farmer who lives so near.
  It must be the farmer so cunning, so cunning?
They have passed the farmyard already, dear,
  And now they are running.

O where are you going? Stay with me here!
  Were the vows you swore deceiving, deceiving?
No, I promised to love you, dear,
  But I must be leaving.

O it's broken the lock and splintered the door,
  O it's the gate where they're turning, turning;
Their boots are heavy on the floor
  And their eyes are burning.

O WHERE ARE YOU GOING

"O where are you going?" said reader to rider,
"That valley is fatal when furnaces burn,
Yonder's the midden whose odors will madden,
That gap is the grave where the tall return."

"O do you imagine," said fearer to farer,
"That dusk will delay on your path to the pass,
Your diligent looking discover the lacking
Your footsteps feel from granite to grass?"

"O what was that bird," said horror to hearer,
"Did you see that shape in the twisted trees?
Behind you swiftly the figure comes softly,
The spot on your skin is a shocking disease."

"Out of this house"—said rider to reader,
"Yours never will"—said farer to fearer,
"They're looking for you"—said hearer to horror,
As he left them there, as he left them there.

MUNDUS ET INFANS

Kicking his mother until she let go of his soul
Has given him a healthy appetite: clearly, her role
   In the New Order must be
To supply and deliver his raw materials free;
   Should there be any shortage,
She will be held responsible; she also promises
To show him all such attentions as befit his age.
   Having dictated peace,

With one fist clenched behind his head, heel drawn up to thigh,
The cocky little ogre dozes off, ready,
   Though, to take on the rest
Of the world at the drop of a hat or the mildest
   Nudge of the impossible,
Resolved, cost what it may, to seize supreme power and
Sworn to resist tyranny to the death with all
   Forces at his command.

A pantheist not a solipsist, he co-operates
With a universe of large and noisy feeling-states
   Without troubling to place
Them anywhere special, for, to his eyes, Funnyface
   Or Elephant as yet
Mean nothing. His distinction between Me and Us
Is a matter of taste; his seasons are Dry and Wet;
   He think as his mouth does.

Still his loud iniquity is still what only the
Greatest of saints become—someone who does not lie:
   He because he cannot
Stop the vivid present to think, they by having got
   Past reflection into
A passionate obedience in time. We have our Boy-
Meets-Girl era of mirrors and muddle to work through,
   Without rest, without joy.

Therefore we love him because his judgments are so
Frankly subjective that his abuse carries no
   Personal sting. We should
Never dare offer our helplessness as a good
   Bargain; without at least
Promising to overcome a misfortune we blame
History or Banks or the Weather for: but this beast
   Dares to exist without shame.

Let him praise our Creator with the top of his voice,
Then, and the motions of his bowels; let us rejoice
   That he lets us hope, for
He may never become a fashionable or
   important personage:
However bad he may be, he has not yet gone mad;
Whoever we are now, we were no worse at his age;
   So of course we ought to be glad

When he bawls the house down. Has he not a perfect right
To remind us at every moment how we quite
   Rightly expect each other
To go upstairs or for a walk if we must cry over
   Spilt milk, such as our wish
That, since, apparently, we shall never be above
Either or both, we had never learned to distinguish
   Between hunger and love?

THE CHIMERAS

   Absence of heart—as in public buildings,
   Absence of mind—as in public speeches,
   Absence of words—as in goods intended for the public,

   Are telltale signs that a chimera has just dined
   On someone else; of him, poor foolish fellow,
   Not a scrap is left, not even his name.

   Indescribable—being neither this nor that,
   Uncountable—being any number,
   Unreal—being anything but what they are,

   And ugly customers for someone to encounter,
   It is our fault entirely if we do;
   They cannot touch us; it is we who will touch them.

   Curious from wantonness—to see what they are like,
   Cruel from fear—to put a stop to them,
   Incredulous from conceit—to prove they cannot be,

   We prod or kick or measure and are lost:
   The stronger we are the sooner all is over;
   It is our strength with which they gobble us up.

If someone, being chaste, brave, humble,
Get by them safely, he is still in danger,
With pity remembering what once they were,

Of turning back to help them. Don't.
What they were once was what they would not be;
Not liking what they are not is what now they are.

No one can help them; walk on, keep on walking,
And do not let your goodness self-deceive you:
It is good that they are but not that they are thus.

WORDS

A sentence uttered makes a world appear
Where all things happen as it says they do;
We doubt the speaker, not the tongue we hear:
Words have no word for words that are not true.

Syntactically, though, it must be clear;
One cannot change the subject halfway through,
Nor alter tenses to appease the ear:
Arcadian tales are hard-luck stories too.

But should we want to gossip all the time
Were fact not fiction for us at its best,
Or find a charm in syllables that rhyme,

Were not our fate by verbal chance expressed,
As rustics in a ring-dance pantomime
The Knight at some lone crossroads of his quest?

EPITAPH ON A TYRANT

Perfection, of a kind, was what he was after
And the poetry he invented was easy to understand;
He knew human folly like the back of his hand,
And was greatly interested in armies and fleets;
When he laughed, respectable senators burst with laughter,
And when he cried the little children died in the streets.

NARRATOR

Well, so that is that. Now we must dismantle the tree,
Putting the decorations back into their cardboard boxes—
Some have got broken—and carrying them up to the attic.
The holly and the mistletoe must be taken down and burnt,
And the children got ready for school. There are enough
Leftovers to do, warmed up, for the rest of the week—
Not that we have much appetitie, having drunk such a lot,
Stayed up so late, attempted—quite unsuccessfully—
To love all of our relatives, and in general
Grossly overestimated our powers. Once again
As in previous years we have seen the actual Vision and failed
To do more than entertain it as an agreeable
Possibility, once again we have sent Him away,
Begging though to remain His disobedient servant,
The promising child who cannot keep His word for long.
The Christmas Feast is already a fading memory,
And already the mind begins to be vaguely aware
Of an unpleasant whiff of apprehension at the thought
Of Lent and Good Friday which cannot, after all, now
Be very far off. But, for the time being, here we all are,
Back in the moderate Aristotelian city
Of darning and the Eight-Fifteen, where Euclid's geometry
And Newton's mechanics would account for our experience,
And the kitchen table exists because I scrub it.
It seems to have shrunk during the holidays. The streets
Are much narrower than we remembered; we had forgotten
The office was as depressing as this. To those who have seen
The Child, however dimly, however incredulously,
The Time Being is, in a sense, the most trying time of all.
For the innocent children who whispered so excitedly
Outside the locked door where they knew the presents to be
Grew up when it opened. Now, recollecting that moment
We can repress the joy, but the guilt remains conscious;
Remembering the stable where for once in our lives
Everything became a You and nothing was an It.
And craving the sensation but ignoring the cause,
We look round for something, no matter what, to inhibit
Our self-reflection, and the obvious thing for that purpose
Would be some great suffering. So, once we have met the Son,
We are tempted ever after to pray to the Father;
"Lead us into temptation and evil for our sake."
They will come, all right, don't worry; probably in a form
That we do not expect, and certainly with a force
More dreadful than we can imagine. In the meantime

There are bills to be paid, machines to keep in repair,
Irregular verbs to learn, the Time Being to redeem
From insignificance. The happy morning is over,
The night of agony still to come; the time is noon:
When the Spirit must practise his scales of rejoicing
Without even a hostile audience, and the Soul endure
A silence that is neither for nor against her faith
That God's Will will be done, that, in spite of her prayers,
God will cheat no one, not even the world of its triumph.

NOTES ON THE POETS

EDWARD TAYLOR (c. 1645–1729) was born in England and in his youth went to Massachusetts Bay, where he became a minister in the village of Westfield. Although his poetic career ran from 1680 to 1725, none of his poems was published until the discovery of his manuscripts in the Yale University library led to the issuance of his *Poetical Works* (1939), edited by T. H. Johnson.

RALPH WALDO EMERSON (1803–1882) was born in Boston, one of five sons of a Unitarian minister, who died in 1811. Despite their poverty, his mother's tenacity succeeded in getting Ralph as well as three other sons through college. He was graduated from Harvard at eighteen, taught for almost four years, then entered divinity school. He succeeded to his father's Boston parish in 1829, but resigned three years later because of a religious scruple concerning the administering of the Sacrament. The loss of his profession, the death of his wife and a brother, and his own poor health drove him abroad, where he toured Italy and visited Coleridge, Wordsworth, and Carlyle in England. In 1833 he returned home. He remarried, settled in Concord, Massachusetts, and embarked on a new career as a lecturer, poet, and essayist, becoming the most eminent and respected American intellectual of his day. His two speeches at Harvard, "The American Scholar" (1837) and "The Divinity School Address" (1838) were taken as heretical utterances, but have since become classical statements on American individualism. As a lifelong advocate of new ideas, he entertained and sought out both crackpots and men of genius, and defended the Brook Farm experiment, abolitionism, Henry Thoreau, John Brown, and Walt Whitman. Though famous as a public speaker, Emerson was a shy man who found the solitude of Concord and his own study more productive than the adulation he received as a traveling sage. Illness incapacitated him after the Civil War and kept him from sustaining his work in the last decade of his life. The best of Emerson's thought is revealed in the ten volumes of his *Journals* (1909–1914). His works include *Essays: First Series* (1841), *Essays: Second Series* (1844), two volumes of poems (1847 and 1867), and *Selected Poems* (1876).

HENRY WADSWORTH LONGFELLOW (1807–1882), born in Portland, Maine, was Hawthorne's classmate at Bowdoin College, where he was later professor of modern languages. He was also professor of modern languages and literature at Harvard College for eighteen years until 1854, and made his permanent home in Cambridge. Frequent travel abroad and a lifelong interest in European literature resulted in his many poetic translations from Spanish, Swedish, Danish, German, Italian, Portuguese, and French, as well as Latin and Anglo-Saxon. Generations of school children have been exposed to his "Evangeline," "The Song of Hiawatha," "Paul Revere's Ride," "The Wreck of the Hesperus," and "The Courtship of Miles Standish." Few American poets were more prolific than Longfellow, who wrote continually until a few days before his death. Undoubtedly a professional poet with wide cultural interests, his curiosity about verse forms made him experiment with meters and styles as omnivorously as Tennyson. At best he is a poet of graceful nostalgias, elegiac occasions, conscientious scruples, and lighthearted intelligence.

EDGAR ALLAN POE (1809–1849), who, like François Villon, helped to make "drunkard" synonymous with "poet" in the popular mind, was born in Boston to actor parents, orphaned at two, and adopted by the Virginians, Mr. and Mrs. John Allan. He was sent to school in England

and then spent a year at the University of Virginia, from which he was removed by his foster father because of excessive drinking and gambling. He had a four-year hitch of military service (1827-31), including some months at West Point, before he was disinherited by Mr. Allan. By that time he had published three books of poems: *Tamerlane and Other Poems* (1827), *Al Aaraaf, Tamerlane, and Minor Poems* (1829), and *Poems* (1831). To earn a living Poe began writing fiction and literary criticism. Like Whitman, however, he had little to do with the reigning literati of his time in Boston and New York. (Subsequently Whitman was the only notable poet to attend Poe's reburial in Baltimore in 1875.) He gave up drinking on marrying his thirteen-year-old cousin, Virginia Clemm, in 1836, but later relapsed when she become hopelessly ill; when she died (1847), Poe suffered a brain lesion. For over a decade he had a spotty career as an editor, successfully regenerating moribund magazines in Richmond, Philadelphia, and New York. The last two years of his life were blurred over by a haze of attachments to matrons and minor poetesses. Like Longfellow's, Poe's American reputation was routinely sustained by the public schools and literary clubs, although he was avidly taken up by the French symbolists, and subsequently, like Whitman, celebrated in Latin America. Like Whitman again, his personal life interested his critics more than his work—an interest climaxed in the two thick volumes by Marie Bonaparte, who undertook his psychoanalysis by means of his poems and stories.

WALT WHITMAN (1819-1892), of Dutch and English ancestry, was born in West Hills, Long Island, had very little formal schooling, and began to work in a print shop at the age of twelve. This led to a desultory career in newspaper work that was mediocre and poorly paid for twenty-five years. Besides editing and reporting, he was variously engaged in bookselling, carpentering, free-lance writing, volunteer nursing, and clerking. He found his real vocation when, after a psychological conversion in 1855, he published the first edition of *Leaves of Grass*. Emerson hailed the book privately, but then withdrew his endorsement after Whitman had made wide use of it and gotten himself a scandalous reputation among genteel readers. During the next thirty-seven years Whitman supervised eight editions of his book, which grew four and a half times its original length by 1892. Partial paralysis, poverty, and neglect reduced him to peddling his book on the streets. But his life and legend began to take hold. He addressed a Dartmouth College commencement, gave a round of annual lectures on Abraham Lincoln, visited the West and Canada, was the subject of a biography by R. M. Bucke (1883), and was even acclaimed for a time by British poets and critics. After he died in Camden, New Jersey, his idolators' effusions for thirty years did more to distort his reputation than earlier neglect and misunderstanding had accomplished during his lifetime. The present esteem in which his poetry is held was initiated by D. H. Lawrence's *Studies in Classic American Literature* in 1923.

EMILY DICKINSON (1830-1886) lived all her life in Amherst, Massachusetts, leaving only briefly to visit Philadelphia and Washington in 1854 and to consult a Boston eye doctor in 1864 and 1865. Her father was a well-known lawyer and a United States Congressman. She studied at Amherst Academy and South Hadley Female Seminary, (later Mt. Holyoke College). By the age of thirty-five she was a recluse in a world circumscribed by her father's house and garden and the few friends who visited her there. She died of Bright's disease at fifty-five. Speculation as to the mysterious subject of her love poems has at various times fixed on three men: Benjamin F. Newton, her father's law clerk; the Rev. Charles Wadsworth, whom she met briefly in Philadelphia when she was twenty-four, but did not see again till she was fifty; and a family friend, Judge Otis Lord. Only two of her now famous poems were published during her lifetime. The more than 1,500 poems she had secreted away on scraps of paper in boxes and drawers were from time to time brought out in scattered and defective editions, beginning with *Poems* (1890). It was not until 1955 that the definitive three-volume edition of her work was published, edited by T. H. Johnson.

EDWIN ARLINGTON ROBINSON (1869-1935) was born in Head Tide, Maine, and grew up in nearby Gardiner, the "Tilbury Town" of his best-known poems. Though he studied for two years at Harvard, he was as much a self-taught poet as Poe, Whitman, and Dickinson. He began writing verse at eleven and produced translations from Sophocles and Virgil in his early teens. While working as a subway checker in the New York subways, he published his third book of poems, *Captain Craig* (1902). The book came to the attention of President Theodore Roosevelt, who got him a clerkship in the New York Custom House, a job he held until 1910. Thereafter, until his death twenty-five years later, Robinson devoted himself exclusively to his writing, spending his summers at the MacDowell Colony in Peterborough, New Hampshire, and writing the long narrative poems—among them *Merlin, Lancelot, Tristram, Avon's Harvest, Roman Batholow, Dionysus in Doubt, and Cavender's House*—which made him a best-selling poet in the nineteen-twenties and three times the winner of the Pulitzer Prize. The complete edition of his *Collected Poems* was published in 1937.

STEPHEN CRANE (1871-1900), the fourteenth child of parents who were both writers, was born in Newark, New Jersey. Descended from a line of soldiers and clergymen (his father, Rev. Jonathan T. Crane, was an overworked Methodist minister), Crane seems to have gotten from them an obsessive subject, war, something of his stoical compassion, and, particularly in his poetry, a Biblical style. His short, phenomenal literary career, which began in 1891 when he quit Syracuse University as a freshman, yielded the major fictions, *The Red Badge of Courage* (1895), *The Open Boat* (1898), and *The Blue Hotel* (1899), as well as two volumes of poetry, *The Black Riders, and Other Lines* (1895) and *War Is Kind* (1899). His novel, *Maggie: A Girl of the Streets*, reputed to have been written in two days in 1891, first appeared under his own name in the 1896 edition; it is often credited with starting the naturalistic tradition in American fiction. He worked as a reporter in New York and later as a foreign correspondent following the wars. During his brief residence in England, he was befriended by Henry James, Conrad, H. G. Wells, and F. M. Ford, who commonly regarded him as a new master of fiction. Somewhat like James Joyce, a writer of similarly "ruthless literary courage," Crane's eminence as a fiction writer tended to obscure his surprising power as a poet, which is only now beginning to be estimated and understood.

ROBERT FROST (1874—) was born in San Francisco and grew up in Lawrence, Massachusetts. He attended Dartmouth College briefly, went back to Lawrence to work in a mill, and was married at twenty. He tried college again, but after two years at Harvard, left to go to work—this time as a shoemaker, schoolteacher, newspaper editor, and farmer. In 1912 he took his family to England where, aided by Rupert Brooke, Wilfrid Gibson, Lascelles Abercrombie, and Edward Thomas, his poetry was published and gained the recognition it had until then been denied in America. Three years later, the author of *A Boy's Will* (1913) and

North of Boston (1914) returned to find himself famous at home. There-
after, between periods of college teaching, summers at the Bread Loaf
School in Middlebury, Vermont, and public readings for which he became
widely known throughout the country, Frost wrote *Mountain Interval*
(1916), *New Hampshire* (1923), *West-Running Brook* (1928), *A Further
Range* (1936), *The Witness Tree* (1942), *A Masque of Reason* (1945),
Steeple Bush (1947) and *A Masque of Mercy* (1947). The latest edition
of his *Complete Poems* appeared in 1949, by which time he had won the
Pulitzer Prize four times. He is the most widely read of contemporary
poets today.

VACHEL LINDSAY (1879–1931) was born in Springfield, Illinois, and
lived for many years in the shadow of the governor's mansion, where the
subject of one of his best-known poems, John Altgeld, ended his tragic
career. From 1897 to 1905 Lindsay attended Hiram College, the Chicago
Art Institute, and the New York School of Art. A man of great personal
energy and a sense of mission, he set himself up as a poetic evangelist and
for many years made extensive walking tours through American towns
and villages, where he recited his poems both to make his way and to
preach the "gospel of beauty." His collections include *General William
Booth Enters Into Heaven and Other Poems* (1913), *The Congo and
Other Poems* (1914), and *The Chinese Nightingale and Other Poems*
(1917). His *Collected Poems* appeared in 1923, at the height of his career.
He died suddenly in 1931.

WALLACE STEVENS (1879–1955), a native of Reading, Pennsylvania,
was educated at Harvard and the New York Law School, and was ad-
mitted to the bar in 1904. From 1916 until his death he was associated
with the Hartford Accident and Indemnity Company (Connecticut),
where he became a vice president in 1934. These and other nonliterary
associations, as well as the fact that his first book was not published until
1923, gave him for many years, while his reputation slowly rose, the
notoriety of an isolato. His principal volumes are *Harmonium* (1923),
Ideas of Order (1935), *Parts of a World* (1942), *Auroras of Autumn*
(1950), *Collected Poems* (1954), and *The Necessary Angel* (1951),
a book of essays.

WILLIAM CARLOS WILLIAMS (1883–   ), born in Rutherford,
New Jersey, became a pediatrician and practiced medicine in his native
city until his recent retirement. His early association with Ezra Pound
(while both were students at the University of Pennsylvania) led to a
fierce and uneven friendship between the poet who made his peace with
America as a local doctor and the poet who went abroad and was forcibly
returned to America, charged with treason. Recognition of Williams's
poetic accomplishment came late, but since 1946 has grown steadily, partly
as a result of the publication of his long poem *Paterson*, the first four
books of which were issued between 1946 and 1951, and the fifth book in
1958. He has published many books of verse, fiction, criticism, auto-
biography, letters, and drama. Besides *Paterson*, his chief volumes of
poetry include *Collected Later Poems* (1950), *Collected Earlier Poems*
(1951), *The Desert Music and Other Poems* (1954), and *Journey to
Love* (1955).

EZRA POUND (1885–   ) was born in Hailey, Idaho, attended the
University of Pennsylvania and Hamilton College (Ph.B., 1905). He took
an M.A. at Pennsylvania in 1906, had a short, ill-fated spell as a college
instructor, then in 1907 departed from the United States. Dedicating
himself completely to literature, in London, Paris, and Rapallo, Italy, he
became the chief innovator, assisted by T. S. Eliot, of the modern

movement. In 1945 he was returned to the United States to be tried for treason as a result of his broadcasts in Italy during the Second World War, but did not stand trial because he was declared to be of unsound mind and was committed the following year to a mental hospital in Washington. Released in 1958, partly as a result of the intercession of Robert Frost, he now resides again in Italy, where he is completing the *Cantos*, a poem he has been writing for over forty years.

MARIANNE MOORE (1887–   ), born in St. Louis and brought up by her grandfather, a Presbyterian pastor, was educated at Bryn Mawr (B.A., 1909), and became in turn a teacher of commercial subjects, a library assistant, and an editor of *The Dial*. A volume, *Poems*, was published in 1921 without her knowledge by two members of the Imagist group (H. D. and Bryher) with whom she had been associated for several years. *Observations* (1924) was the first volume she supervised herself. Highly praised by T. S. Eliot and her fellow poets, her fastidious work, never very great in volume, had to wait until the past decade or so for the wider acclaim and honors she has come to enjoy. Her *Collected Poems* (1951) was followed by versions of *The Fables of La Fontaine* (1954) and by *O to Be a Dragon* (1959).

JOHN CROWE RANSOM (1888–   ), known for his literary criticism as well as his poetry, was born in Pulaski, Tennessee, and educated at Vanderbilt University (B.A., 1909) and at Christ College, Oxford, where he went as a Rhodes Scholar. He taught English at Vanderbilt from 1914 to 1937. He was an artillery lieutenant with the A.E.F. in France, then returned to the United States to continue his lifelong career as a teacher, critic, and editor, the last at Kenyon College, where he started the *Kenyon Review* in 1938. He has only recently (1959) retired from these jobs. Earlier (1922–1925) he was the influential founder of the *Fugitive* and the guiding spirit of the Fugitive Group, which included Allen Tate and Robert Penn Warren. Though his output has been small, it is one of the most distinguished in modern poetry. It includes *Poems about God* (1919), *Chills and Fever* (1924), *Two Gentlemen in Bonds* (1927), *Selected Poems* (1945). His best-known works of criticism are *The World's Body* (1938) and *The New Criticism* (1941).

EDNA ST. VINCENT MILLAY (1892–1950), probably the most widely read woman poet in America, was born in Rockland, Maine. By the time she was graduated from Vassar she had already published her first major work, *Renascence* (1912). She was an early member of the Provincetown Players in Greenwich Village, for which she wrote three verse plays as well as the libretto for Deems Taylor's opera *The King's Henchman* (1927). Her love poetry of the nineteen-twenties increasingly gave way to a poetry dealing with themes of social injustice—*Conversation at Midnight* (1937) and *Murder of Lidice* (1942)—though she is perhaps more justly famous as the author of *The Harp-Weaver and Other Poems* (1923), *The Buck in the Snow* (1928), *Fatal Interview* (1931) and her *Collected Sonnets* (1941). *Mine the Harvest* (1954), her last volume, appeared posthumously.

ARCHIBALD MACLEISH (1892–   ), born in Glencoe, Illinois, attended Hotchkiss School, then went to Yale (B.A., 1915) and Harvard Law School (LL.B., 1919). He transferred from an ambulance group to a field artillery unit in France during the First World War. After a few years in a Boston law office, he took his wife and children abroad, lived in France (1923–1928) and wrote poetry. During the nineteen-thirties he was the most influential of American poets who had espoused the social and political ideals of extreme liberalism against the encroachments of world fascism. In 1939 he was appointed Librarian of Congress, and during the Second World War was a trusted member of the President's inner cabinet. He also served as head of the Office of Facts and Figures, was assistant director of the Office of War Information, and then Assistant Secretary of State. After the war, he was chairman of the first American delegation at UNESCO in Paris. In 1949 he became Boylston Professor of Rhetoric and Oratory at Harvard. His chief books are *The Hamlet of A. MacLeish* (1928), *Conquistador* (1932), *Panic* (1935), *Public Speech* (1936), *The Fall of the City* (1937), and *Collected Poems 1917–1952* (1952).

E. E. CUMMINGS (1894–   ), a native of Cambridge, Massachusetts, and the son of a Harvard professor who was also a Congregationalist minister, was educated at Harvard (B.A., 1915; M.A., 1916). He drove an ambulance in France during the First World War, and for awhile was stationed in a U. S. Army camp. His brief experiences as a prisoner in a French jail provided the material for his novel, *The Enormous Room* (1922). After two years in New York Cummings went to Paris, where he wrote poetry and studied art. From 1924 to 1930 he lived in New York before returning to Paris again for several years. He is also a painter and has had several one-man shows. In 1952 he was Charles Eliot Norton Professor at Harvard. His *Poems 1923–1954* (1954) includes all his books of verse to that date. He is also known for his play *Him* (1927), his travel book on Russia, *Eimi* (1933), a ballet scenario, *Tom* (1935), and *Santa Claus: A Morality* (1946). The autobiographical *i; six nonlectures* was published late in 1953, and since 1954 he has published several new volumes of verse.

HART CRANE (1899–1932), born in Garrettsville, Ohio, spent his early years in Dayton and Cleveland. His parents' divorce and an early experience on the Isle of Pines in the Caribbean turned him toward poetry. With little formal education, he went to New York to write during the First World War. In Cleveland later, he held numerous jobs—in a bookshop, a munitions factory, and a shipyard; he was also a reporter for *The Plain Dealer*, then returned to live in New York more or less permanently except for a year abroad in Paris. He tried managing a tearoom and also, quite briefly, wrote advertising copy. A personal grant from the banker, Otto Kahn, enabled him to concentrate on the writing of *The Bridge* (1930). After a discouraging interval in Mexico, where he had gone to write on a Guggenheim fellowship (1931–1932), he committed suicide by jumping overboard on his return voyage to New York. His other books are *White Buildings* (1926) and the posthumous *Collected Poems* (1933).

W. H. AUDEN (1907–   ), the son of a doctor, was born in York, England, and educated at Gresham's School and Christ College. A short period as schoolmaster after leaving college was followed by his association with a young group of poets in London, who were in open revolt against middle-class society. He drove an ambulance for the Loyalists during the Civil War in Spain, then came to live in the United States in 1939, where he has since become an American citizen. His most influential books of verse are *Poems* (1930), *For the Time Being* (1944), *Collected Poetry* (1945), *The Age of Anxiety* (1947), *Nones* (1951) and *The Shield of Achilles* (1955). These works reflect Auden's shifting interest from the leftist liberal he was before the war to the High Church adherent he has since become. He is also the author of several verse plays and libretti, some of these in collaboration with others, and of *The Enchaféd Flood* (1950), a book of criticism.

INDEX

TITLES OF POEMS ARE SET IN ITALICS, AND FIRST LINES IN ROMAN TYPE. WHEN A
TITLE AND A FIRST LINE ARE THE SAME ONLY THE FIRST LINE APPEARS.

ABOUT THE EDITORS

OSCAR WILLIAMS is the author of four books of poetry, of which the most recent is *Selected Poems*, published by Charles Scribner's Sons. Dylan Thomas has written: "Oscar Williams is without a doubt a very real and important American poet. . . . His powerful imagery and unique personal idiom will add a permanent page to American poetry." Mr. Williams has edited many anthologies, of which there are more than one million copies in print. Among his important collections are Scribner's *The Little Treasury* series, New American Library's *The Golden Treasury* and *The Silver Treasury of Light Verse*, published in Mentor editions, and *The Mentor Book of Major British Poets*. Robert Lowell has written in the *Sewanee Review*: "Oscar Williams is probably the best anthologist in America." In 1958, Mr. Williams delivered an official reading of his poems at the Library of Congress. He died October 10, 1964, at the age of 64. At the time of his death he was the editor for a series of recordings by poets issued by Gryphon Records as well as being actively engaged in lecture tours and public readings of his poems and the works of other poets.

EDWIN HONIG is a poet (*The Moral Circus* and the *Gazabos*), a critic (*García Lorca* and *Dark Conceit: The Making of Allegory*), a translator (*Calderón: Four Plays* and *The Interludes of Cervantes*). He has published stories and essays in the quarterlies, has been twice awarded a Guggenheim fellowship, and is Professor of English at Brown University.

She look **sparkled b** **r** **Matilda a** **A tiny s**

She picked up the knife again and started on the other side of the duck and he stepped forward, took the knife from her, carved the rest of the bird with a practiced hand and laid the knife down on the table.

"Is there no one to help you?"

"They're having their supper. I'll stay down here until you've all gone home." She selected a slice of duck and popped it into her mouth.

It was Roseanne who spoke. "Look—" she sounded worried "—we must go back. They'll wonder where we are."

He looked as cross as two sticks, she thought lovingly. "I shall take a tray up to my room. Good night, Mr. Scott-Thurlow, or is it goodbye?"

THE BEST *of*

BETTY NEELS

The Most Marvellous Summer

Recycling programs
for this product may
not exist in your area.

ISBN-13: 978-0-373-24955-8

THE MOST MARVELLOUS SUMMER

Copyright © 1991 by Betty Neels

All rights reserved. Except for use in any review, the reproduction or
utilization of this work in whole or in part in any form by any electronic,
mechanical or other means, now known or hereafter invented, including
xerography, photocopying and recording, or in any information storage
or retrieval system, is forbidden without the written permission of the
publisher, Harlequin Enterprises Limited, 225 Duncan Mill Road,
Don Mills, Ontario, Canada M3B 3K9.

This is a work of fiction. Names, characters, places and incidents are
either the product of the author's imagination or are used fictitiously,
and any resemblance to actual persons, living or dead, business
establishments, events or locales is entirely coincidental.

This edition published by arrangement with Harlequin Books S.A.

For questions and comments about the quality of this book
please contact us at CustomerService@Harlequin.com.

® and TM are trademarks of Harlequin Enterprises Limited or its
corporate affiliates. Trademarks indicated with ® are registered in the
United States Patent and Trademark Office, the Canadian Trade Marks
Office and in other countries.

www.Harlequin.com

Printed in U.S.A.

CHAPTER ONE

MATILDA HAD FALLEN in love. She had had no intention of doing so, but there it was. She first saw the stranger during the reading of the first lesson by Sir Benjamin Fox, whose pompous voice, pronouncing biblical names with precise correctness, always set her thoughts wandering. She glanced along the pew at her two brothers, home for the half-term holidays, her two sisters and her mother and then allowed her gaze to wander to the manor pew at the side of the chancel, where Lady Fox sat with various members of her family. They all looked alike, she thought, with their fine beaky noses and thin mouths. She turned her head very slightly and looked across the main aisle and saw the stranger sitting by Dr Bramley. He appeared a very large man with broad shoulders, fair hair which she suspected had a sprinkling of grey, and a splendid profile. A pity that he didn't look round… Sir Benjamin rolled the last unpronounceable name off his tongue and she fixed her eyes on him once more— green eyes, shadowed by sweeping black lashes, in a lovely face crowned by a wealth of copper hair.

Her father announced the hymn and the congregation rose to sing it cheerfully, galloping ahead of the organ when it had the chance, and then sitting once more for the second lesson. The headmaster of the village infants' school read it in a clear unhurried voice and this time she listened, until something compelled her to glance across the aisle again. The stranger was looking at her and he was every bit as handsome as she had expected him to be; unsmiling—it wouldn't have done in church if he had smiled anyway—and somehow compelling. She went faintly pink and looked away from him quickly, feeling all at once as though she were in some kind of blissful heaven, knowing with certainty that she had fallen in love. It was a delightful sensation, and she pondered over it during her father's sermon, taking care not to look across the aisle again; the village was a small one and rather isolated, so that everyone was inclined to mind everyone else's business and turn a molehill into a mountain, preferably a romantic one, and that if a girl so much as glanced twice at the same man. She was aware that the village was disappointed that she hadn't married. She had had three proposals and although she had hesitated over them she had declined them kindly and watched her erstwhile suitors marry without regret. Twenty-six was getting on a bit, as Mrs Chump at the general stores so often reminded her, but she had waited. Now here he was, the man she wished to marry, dropped as it were from heaven into her path. He could of course be married, engaged or a confirmed bachelor—she would have to find out, but, as she was great friends with Dr Bramley, it would be easy to ask him.

The last hymn sung, the congregation filed out, stopping to chat as it went, and since the rector's family were well liked their progress was slow; they arrived at the church door just in time for her to see the stranger, still with the doctor, talking to Sir Benjamin, and even as Matilda looked Lady Fox tapped him on an arm and pushed Roseanne, her eldest daughter, forwards. Matilda watched him being swept away down the tree-lined avenue which led to the manor-house from the churchyard.

She watched him go, already planning to ask who he was when she got to the manor-house in the morning. Esme, her younger sister, fourteen and as sharp as a needle, tugged her arm. 'Hey, Tilly—come on,' and then, 'I bet you've fallen for him—I have. A bit old for me I suppose, but he'd do nicely for you.'

'Rubbish, love. What nonsense you do talk.'

'You went all pink when he looked at you—I expect it was your hair—it kind of glows, you know, even under a hat!'

They started to walk along the narrow path which led to the rectory garden and Esme said, 'Hilary's seen him too, but of course she's engaged...'

'Let's forget him,' said Matilda cheerfully. 'We'll probably never see him again.' She uttered the remark with the heartfelt wish that it might not be true. However could she marry anyone else now that she had seen him and knew that she had fallen in love at last? She would have to stay an old maid, if there was such a thing these days, helping with the parish and wearing dreary hats and worthy undateable clothes.

She sighed heavily at the very idea and Esme said, 'I bet you'll meet again—I dare say he's your fate.'

'Oh, what romantic nonsense,' said Matilda again and hurried to the kitchen to help her mother dish up the Sunday lunch.

Her mother had her head in the Aga oven, and was prodding the joint with a fork. 'Put the apples on for the sauce, will you, dear? I wonder who that giant was in church? Did you see him?' She didn't wait for an answer. 'He seemed to know the Foxes. I must keep my ears open in the village tomorrow.'

She emerged and closed the oven door, an older version of her lovely daughter although the hair was streaked with grey. 'That was a frightful hat Lady Fox was wearing—I wonder where she buys them?'

'Probably makes them herself.' Matilda was peeling apples and biting at the cores.

She was up early the next morning and while her mother cooked the breakfast she sorted the wash, got the machine going, made sure that Esme was up and had everything she needed before catching the bus to Sherborne where she was having extra coaching for her O Levels, and then roused the two boys. Hilary, her other sister, was going to stay with her fiancé and was already up, doing the last of her packing. They all sat down to breakfast presently, a meal taken with the minimum of conversation since everyone there had his or her plans for the day. Esme was the first to go, then the boys on a fishing expedition, the rector to visit a parishioner in hospital at Salisbury and then Hilary, leaving Mrs ffinch and Matilda to clear the table and leave the dishes for Mrs Coffin, who came three times a week to help in the house.

'Don't be late,' warned Mrs ffinch as Matilda got Nelson the cat's breakfast. She sighed as she said it—it irked her that her beautiful daughter should have to go to work each day. Not that it wasn't a suitable job for the daughter of the rector—social secretary to Lady Fox— even though it was badly paid and covered a multitude of odd jobs which no social secretary cognisant with her normal duties would have countenanced. But, as

Matilda pointed out, it paid for her clothes, and the fees for Esme's coaching, and helped towards the upkeep of the rectory, a large, rambling house with out-of-date plumbing always going wrong, draughty rooms and a boiler which swallowed coke by the ton. All the same, it was comfortable in a shabby way and the family was a happy one.

It was only a few minutes' walk to the manor-house; Matilda nipped smartly through the light rain and went in through the side-door—not that she wasn't expected to use the front entrance, but the polished floor of the wide hall showed every mark from damp feet and she was aware that Mrs Fletcher from the village, who obliged each day at the manor-house, would have just finished polishing it. She went along the passage to the kitchen, wished Cook and the kitchen maid good morning and made her way through the baize door into the front of the house. Lady Fox was coming down the staircase, holding a handful of letters.

'Good morning, Matilda.' She glanced at the long case clock in the hall, but since Matilda was exactly on time and she had no cause to find fault she went on, 'Such a number of letters this morning; really, my days are so busy...'

Lady Fox gave Matilda a faintly disapproving look; there was nothing wrong with her appearance—the striped shirt, navy pleated skirt and sensible shoes were, to say the least, not worthy of a second glance—but dowdy clothes couldn't dim the brightness of Matilda's hair or the sparkling green of her eyes, and those allied to a delightful nose, a curving mouth and a complexion as smooth and fresh as a child's. Lady Fox frowned slightly, remembering Roseanne's regrettable spots

and unfortunate nose. 'I have guests for lunch,' she
observed. 'I had better see Cook at once while you
deal with these.' She handed the letters to Matilda and
hurried away kitchenwards.

Matilda, sorting out butcher's and grocer's bills
from invitations to dinner and requests from charities,
reflected that Lady Fox wasn't in a very good mood and,
since there was no sign of that lady, she put the letters
on the desk in Lady Fox's sitting-room and went along
to the chilly little room where she arranged the flowers.
The gardener had brought in early tulips and daffodils
and some rather overpowering greenery and she was
trying to decide what to do with them when Lady Fox's
voice, high and penetrating, reached her. 'You might do
a small centre-piece for the table, Matilda—go into the
garden and see what you can find.'

Matilda, well brought up as she had been, allowed
herself the comfort of a childish grimace; if it hadn't
been for the useful money needed at the rectory, she
would have liked to flounce out of the manor-house
and never go back.

The garden was soothing, if chilly, and she took
a basket with her and picked primulas and grape-
hyacinths, late Christmas roses, lily of the valley and
a handful of brightly coloured polyanthus and bore the
lot back through the garden door and into the hall, intent
on fetching a particular bowl which would look just
right on the dining-room table.

Lady Fox was in the hall, talking animatedly to
the stranger. She paused to look at Matilda and her
companion looked too; Matilda, her fiery head a little
untidy, her pretty face glowing from the fresh air,
clutching her basket of flowers, was worth looking at.

'There you are,' observed Lady Fox with distinctly false *bonhomie*, 'but shouldn't you be arranging the flowers?' She turned to the man beside her. 'My companion-secretary, you know—I couldn't manage without help and Roseanne has her painting—quite talented.'

He gave her a grave, enquiring look and she went on hurriedly, 'This is Matilda ffinch, the rector's eldest daughter—Matilda, this is Mr Scott-Thurlow.'

Matilda transferred the basket to her other arm and held out a hand, to have it engulfed by his large firm grasp. Now that she could look at him face to face, she was even more certain that this was the man she had been waiting for. She beamed at him, full of delight, and he smiled a little in return. A firm mouth, perhaps a rather stern one, and his eyes were blue, heavy-lidded and cool; he would be at least thirty-five, perhaps nearer forty.

His polite 'How do you do?' was uttered in a deep quiet voice and her smile widened. Her 'hello' sounded like that of a little girl who had just been offered something she had longed for.

Lady Fox spoke in the voice she kept for recalcitrant children on those occasions when she had been asked to give away the Sunday school prizes.

'If you would see to the flowers, Matilda—and since I shan't need you for a few hours you may go home for your lunch.'

'Back after lunch?' asked Matilda.

'Half-past two.' Mr Scott-Thurlow would be gone by then; Roseanne on her own could be quite charming, reflected her fond parent, and there would be no competition...

'Very well, Lady Fox.' Matilda turned an emerald gaze upon Mr Scott-Thurlow. Her goodbye was cheerful; having found him she didn't for one moment expect fate to lose him again for her. She would have liked to have stayed for lunch—usually she did—but one lunch more or less would make no difference to the future.

She nipped smartly to the back of the house, arranged the flowers and then took herself off home. She passed Roseanne as she left the house, and since she was a kind-hearted girl she was sorry to see that she was wearing an expensive two-piece in the wrong shade of green—it showed up the spots.

Roseanne stopped when she saw her. 'I hate this outfit,' she declared, quite fiercely for her. 'Mother says it's elegant but I feel a fool in it.' She cast an envious eye upon Matilda's person. 'You always look right—why?'

'I don't know. You'd look nice in the greeny blue...'

'There's that man coming to lunch,' went on Roseanne unhappily. 'Mother says I must exert myself...'

She hurried indoors and Matilda went back to the rectory to give her mother and father a hand, prepare the lunch and then sit down and eat it.

'You aren't usually home at this time,' remarked her father, ladling shepherd's pie into exact portions.

'Got the sack?' asked Guy, and Thomas added, 'Shouldn't be surprised with that hair.'

'Visitors for lunch,' explained Matilda, ignoring her brothers. 'I'm to go back at half-past two.'

'You usually stay there even when there are visitors,' mused her mother.

Matilda turned limpid eyes upon her parent. 'Probably

I'd have made the numbers wrong, Mother.' She handed out the plates. 'Is it Esme's evening for dancing class? Do you want me to collect her?'

'Well, that would be nice, dear; the bus takes so long to get here.'

Matilda went back to the manor-house after lunch and found Lady Fox and Roseanne arguing about the green outfit. They both looked cross and Lady Fox said at once, 'This silly girl has been invited to stay in London and she doesn't want to go...'

Matilda had collected the second post as she went in, and she sat down and began to sort it. 'Why not?' she asked, pleasantly. 'I should think it would be the greatest fun.'

'I don't know anyone,' mumbled Roseanne.

'Well, you don't expect to until you're there,' said Matilda reasonably, 'but think of the theatres—you know, *The Phantom of the Opera* and *Aspects of Love* and *Cats* and there'll be exhibitions at the Tate and the National Gallery. You might meet some artists.'

Roseanne brightened. 'Well, yes—I suppose that I might; perhaps it wouldn't be so bad.'

Matilda went home again after tea, taken off a tray while she added up the household accounts for Lady Fox. It was a fine evening and the drive to Sherborne would be pleasant. Abner Magna was only a few miles from that town, but the roads were narrow and winding and the evening bus which Esme sometimes took stopped whenever someone wanted to board it or get off, making the journey twice as long. Matilda got a thick knitted jacket, poked at her hair and went to tell her mother that she was about to leave. There was no one in the kitchen but there were voices in her father's study. She opened the door, stuck her head round it and cried, 'I'm off to fetch Esme, we shouldn't be—' She came to a halt; Mr Scott-Thurlow was standing beside her father, surveying the rather untidy garden.

He said at once, 'Good evening, Miss ffinch,' and her father said mildly, 'John Bramley asked Mr Scott-Thurlow to bring a book over which he had promised to lend me. You have met?'

'Very briefly,' observed his guest. 'I mustn't keep you, sir. Do I understand Miss ffinch to say that she is driving into Sherborne? I'm on the point of going there myself and shall be glad to offer her a lift.'

A delightful prospect, which she had to refuse with regret. 'I'm going to fetch my sister—she's at dancing class, and we've no way of getting back here—the last bus would have gone…'

'I shall be coming back; I have to take something to the hospital for Dr Bramley, a matter of five minutes. We could collect your sister and I can stop at the hospital on our way back.'

'Oh, well, yes—thank you very much. Do you want to go now?'

'Certainly.' He said all the right things to the rector and then stopped in the hall for a moment to bid Mrs ffinch goodbye before ushering Matilda outside.

He opened the door of the car standing there and she skipped inside. 'What a treat,' she declared happily, 'a Rolls-Royce—wait till Esme sees it.' She added the information that such a vehicle was seldom seen in Abner Magna. 'Of course Sir Benjamin has a Daimler, but it's a bit worthy if you know what I mean.'

He made some non-committal answer, but since she felt strangely at ease with him she enlivened their short journey with odds and ends of information, all of them good-natured, about the village and its inhabitants. 'I dare say you live in London?' she wanted to know.

Mr Scott-Thurlow was sitting back, not driving fast; he said idly, 'Yes, I do. Your village is delightful.'

'Well, I like it, but I was born here. Have you known Dr Bramley long?'

'Er—he and my father knew each other in their youth...'

'Oh, well, I didn't think you were all that old,' said Matilda kindly. 'Dr Bramley is always saying that he'll retire so he must be getting on a bit.'

Her companion allowed himself a faint smile. 'I am thirty-eight,' he told her. 'And how old are you, Miss ffinch?'

'Me? Oh, twenty-six.'

'And heart-whole?'

A difficult question to answer. 'Well, I was... Are you married?'

They were in Sherborne now and he asked, 'Which way?' before saying, 'No, but I'm engaged.'

Matilda knew exactly how a balloon must feel when it was pricked. She said in a rigid voice, 'I expect you're looking forward to getting married. Here we are.'

He stopped the car and turned to look at her. 'Do you know, Miss ffinch, I cannot remember when I was cross-examined so thoroughly?'

She stared at him, stricken. 'I'm sorry, I didn't mean to pry—I just wanted—I was interested...'

He smiled then and her heart turned over. 'I rather enjoyed it. Is that your sister waving to us from the other side of the road?'

A snub, a gentle one, but still a snub. Matilda went a

delightful pink and frowned ferociously, remembering
the string of questions she had flung at him; he probably
thought her a dull country woman with nothing better
to do than poke her nose into other people's affairs.
Her daydream had been shattered by a few well-chosen
words on his part and life would never be the same
again. The quicker he went away and she never set eyes
on him again the better. She said in a sober voice, 'Yes,
that's Esme.'

It was a good thing that Esme elected to sit beside
him and chatter non-stop so that Matilda had no need to
say much; she thanked him rather primly as he stopped
at the rectory gates but it was Esme who urged him to
go in with them. An invitation he declined pleasantly
enough.

He had gone the next day, or so it seemed from a
remark her father made the following evening, and it
was then that she realised that she had no idea what
he did or who he really was. He had the calm self-
assured manner of a solicitor and she had heard him
discussing a point of law with the rector during his
brief visit. Solicitors, she had always supposed, earned
themselves a good living, good enough to run a Rolls—
she allowed her thoughts to wander—he might have
to get a cheaper car when he married though; his wife
would want clothes and the children would need to be
educated. She made a resolution then and there not to
think about him any more. That she had fallen in love
with a man who was on the point of getting married
to some other girl was a trick of unkind fate, and there
was nothing to do about it.

A week went by, the boys went back to school and
so did Esme, and Hilary was home again. Matilda's

days were full: Lady Fox each day, choir practice on Thursday evening, Sunday school, driving her father to one or two of the more distant farms; the pattern of her future, reflected Matilda, indulging in a rare attack of self-pity, and then forgetting to be sorry for herself when she went for a Sunday afternoon stroll through the woods above the village. It really was a delightful day; the sky was blue, the trees were turning green even as she looked at them and there were lambs racing around the fields, and when she sat on a tree stump to get her breath a squirrel came and sat within a yard or two of her. There were compensations, she told herself stoutly.

She was surprised to find Lady Fox waiting for her in the hall when she went there on the Monday morning. She wondered uneasily if she had done something really dire, like sending a letter in the wrong envelope, but from the smile on Lady Fox's face she thought that unlikely.

'There you are, Matilda,' said Lady Fox unnecessarily. 'Come into the sitting-room, will you? I should like a word with you.'

She nodded to a chair and Matilda sat down, wondering what to expect.

'Roseanne,' began Lady Fox, 'has consented to pay a visit to London—her godmother, you know, the Honourable Mrs Venables. I am delighted; she is bound to meet people.' Lady Fox really meant young men free to marry. 'There is simply no one of her age and class here.'

Matilda said nothing, although that was difficult; the ffinches had been in and around Dorset for centuries and were as good, if not better than the Foxes, and what was more her mother was distantly related to a peer of the realm—so distant, it must be said, that her family name was a mere dot on the outskirts of the lordly family tree—all the same, it was there.

'Such a pity,' went on Lady Fox in what she considered to be a confidential voice, 'that Mr Scott-Thurlow is engaged to be married, although of course he would have been rather old for Roseanne—a pity that I wasn't told.'

'You were telling me about Roseanne's visit,' prompted Matilda while she thought about Mr Scott-Thurlow.

'I am coming to that. She will go only on the condition that you go with her. The visit is for a month and you would go as her companion. Her godmother has no objection, and I shall of course pay you your usual salary. In a week's time.'

'I'll talk it over with my mother and father,' said Matilda in a quiet voice which her nearest and dearest would have recognised as the first sign of rage coming to the boil. 'I shall want to consider it myself.'

Lady Fox looked astounded. 'But my dear girl, it is such a splendid opportunity for you to see something of the sophisticated world—you might even meet some suitable young man. If you are worried about clothes I'm sure—'

'No, I'm not worried about clothes, Lady Fox. I'm not sure that I want to go to London. I really must have a day or two to think about it.'

Lady Fox's formidable frontage swelled alarmingly. 'Well, really, I don't know what to say. It is most important that Roseanne should go—she is so—so countrified and gauche. Vera and Mary are so much younger and already quite self-possessed.'

Matilda, who disliked the two teenagers, agreed politely; Roseanne was dull and had no backbone worth mentioning, but at least she wasn't rude.

Lady Fox rose. 'Well, since you seem to want time to think over this splendid offer, perhaps you will let me know as soon as you have decided? Now, will you see to the post and wash the Sèvres? I have to go in to Sherborne. I shall be back for lunch—Sir Benjamin is out so there will be just myself, Roseanne and yourself. Tell Cook, will you?'

She hurried away, looking cross, and Matilda wandered off to the kitchen where she discussed lunch with Cook and had a cup of tea before going through the post.

She was in the china pantry washing the precious Sèvres china when Roseanne wandered in.

'Matilda, you will come with me, won't you? I won't go unless you do. Mother keeps on and on, if I don't go I won't stay here either, I'll run away.'

Matilda eyed her carefully. Roseanne meant it. The worm had turned, and, let loose on an uncaring world, Roseanne wouldn't stand a chance...

'I'll have to discuss it with Mother and Father but I don't think they would mind, just for a few weeks.'

'You'll come? Oh, Matilda, I'll never be able to thank you enough—I'll do anything...'

'No need,' said Matilda prosaically, 'I dare say it will be quite fun.'

Her parents raised no objection; she told Lady Fox the next day that she was willing to go with Roseanne and listened to that lady's monologue about the benefits of London to a girl like Roseanne. 'Of course *you* may not get invited to the dinner parties and dances her godmother will arrange, but I dare say you will be glad of that.'

'Why?' asked Matilda with interest.

Lady Fox went an unbecoming red. 'Oh, I have no intention of being rude, Matilda—what I mean is that you will need time to yourself occasionally and there will be no need to attend all the parties Roseanne is bound to go to. I rely upon you to see that she buys only suitable clothes, and please discourage any friendships she may strike up if the—er—young man isn't suitable. She is very young...'

Twenty-two wasn't all that young, thought Matilda, and it was high time Roseanne found her own feet and stood on them.

At home, she inspected her wardrobe and decided that there was no need to buy anything new. She had two evening dresses, both off the peg and by no means new, but nevertheless pretty. She had a good suit, blouses and sweaters enough, a skirt or two and a rather nice jersey dress bought in the January sales. She climbed the narrow stairs to the attic, found a rather battered case, hauled it downstairs and packed it without enthusiasm. London in the spring would come a poor second to Abner Magna.

Each day she was taken aside and lectured by Lady Fox about the London visit; she must do this and not that, young men were to be scrutinised and Roseanne wasn't to go gallivanting off...

Matilda forbore from pointing out that the girl was the last person on earth to gallivant, and anyway with those spots and that unfortunate nose she wasn't likely to get the chance. Let the poor girl have her fling! However timid, she was a nice girl and perhaps with her mother out of the way she might even improve enormously.

She made suitable replies to Lady Fox's remarks and that lady, looking at her, wished for the hundredth time that it could have been someone else but Matilda ffinch who was going with Roseanne; the girl was too pretty—more than that, that hair and those wide eyes weren't to be ignored. She would have to drop a word in Roseanne's godmother's ear to make sure that Matilda attended as few dances and parties as possible; no one— no man—would look at the dear girl while Matilda was there, although give the girl her due she wasn't a young woman to push herself forward; she knew her place, Lady Fox reflected, happily unaware of the superiority of the ffinches over the Foxes.

They were to travel up to London in the Foxes' Daimler driven by Gregg the chauffeur and gardener. Matilda got up early, made a tour of the rather untidy garden, ate a good breakfast and presented herself at the manor at nine o'clock sharp.

Roseanne, wearing expensive mud-brown tweeds, quite unsuitable for the time of year, looked as though she would change her mind about going at any moment; Matilda bustled her briskly into the car with the promise that they would telephone as soon as they arrived and they drove away.

It was a pleasant morning, chilly still but the sun shone and Matilda, chatting bracingly about the pleasures in store, wanted very much to get out of the car and walk or get on to her old bike and potter off for the day. She listened sympathetically to Roseanne's uncertain hopes for the next few weeks, bolstered her up with the delights of London in store for her and whenever she had a moment thought about Mr Scott-Thurlow.

The Honourable Mrs Venables lived in Kensington, in a massive red brick flat, furnished with splendour and a regrettable tendency to overdo crimson velvet, gilding wherever possible and dark, heavy furniture. She received them graciously and somewhat absent-mindedly, since she was holding a lengthy telephone conversation when they arrived. They sat while she concluded this and were then handed over to a dour-looking woman who led them down a long corridor to two rooms at its end, overlooking a narrow garden and more red brick walls.

'There's the bathroom,' they were told. 'You share it. My name's Bertha.'

'I'm not going to like it,' declared Roseanne when they were alone in her room. Her lip quivered. 'I want to go home.'

'We've only just got here,' Matilda pointed out. 'At least let's give it a try. It's all a bit strange—you'll feel better after lunch.'

She was right; Mrs Venables had a great deal to say over the meal, laying out for Roseanne's approbations the various entertainments she had arranged for her. 'We shall have a quiet evening here today,' she said, 'but tomorrow we might go shopping and there's an excellent film we might see in the evening. I shall leave you two girls to amuse yourselves during the day—there is plenty to see and do. I have arranged a dinner party or two and there are several invitations for you.' It all sounded rather fun so that when Roseanne telephoned her mother after lunch she said nothing about wanting to return home.

They spent the next day or two finding their feet. The mornings were taken up with shopping; Roseanne had plenty of money and urged by Matilda bought the clothes she had always wanted and never had the smallest chance to since her mother had always accompanied her. It was a surprise what a difference they made to her appearance, especially when Matilda, given *carte blanche* at the cosmetic counters, found a cream to disguise the spots and chose lipstick, blusher and eye-shadow and applied them to her companion's face. 'Don't you want to buy anything?' asked Roseanne. 'Clothes?'

Matilda assured her, quite untruthfully, that she didn't.

It was their third day there and they had been shopping again. It was Matilda who stopped outside an art gallery with a discreet notice, 'Exhibition Within', and suggested that they might take a look.

The gallery was a series of rooms, very elegant and half filled with viewers, and the first person Matilda saw there was Mr Scott-Thurlow.

CHAPTER TWO

MR SCOTT-THURLOW WASN'T alone: there was a tall, willowy girl beside him, a fashion-plate, so slim that she might have been cut out of cardboard. She was exquisitely made up and her hair was a teased-out halo, lacquered into immobility. She was beautiful but there was no animation in her face; indeed, she looked bored, far more interested in arranging the pleats of her long skirt than viewing the large painting before which they stood.

Matilda, after the first shock of delight, wanted perversely nothing so much as to get as far away from Mr Scott-Thurlow as possible, but Roseanne had seen him too. She darted up to him and caught his sleeve.

'Fancy seeing you here, Mr Scott-Thurlow—' for once she had forgotten her shyness '—and Matilda's with me...'

He took her hand and shook it gently and his voice was kind. 'How delightful to see you again, Roseanne. Are you staying in town?' He turned to his companion. 'Rhoda, this is Roseanne Fox; we met in Dorset a few weeks ago.' He smiled at Roseanne. 'My fiancée, Rhoda Symes.'

He looked past her to where Matilda was waiting and his smile faded, indeed he looked angry but so fleetingly that watching him she decided that she had imagined it. There was nothing else to do but to join

Roseanne, greet him politely and be introduced in her turn to the girl with him.

Rhoda Symes was everything that she wasn't, reflected Matilda sadly, thinking of her own pleasant plumpness and kind of knowing that in the eyes of this girl she was just plain fat, size fourteen, wearing all the wrong make-up and with the wrong-coloured hair... All the same she gave the girl a friendly smile—if she was going to make Mr Scott-Thurlow a happy man, then she, Matilda, would make the best of it; she loved him too much to think otherwise.

The girl was lovely. Matilda supposed that in all fairness if she were a man she would undoubtedly fall for all that elegant beauty.

They stood and talked for a few minutes until Matilda observed that they still had almost the whole of the exhibition to see and since Roseanne was interested hadn't they better get started?

She bade Mr Scott-Thurlow a colourless goodbye and smiled without guile at Rhoda Symes, trying not to see the very large diamond on her left hand—a hand which that lady flourished rather too prominently.

'I say,' said Roseanne excitedly, 'isn't she absolutely lovely? I wonder if we'll get asked to the wedding?' She added, not meaning to be rude, 'Not you, of course.'

Matilda, contemplating a large oil-painting which she thought privately looked as though the artist had upset his paint pots over the canvas, agreed cheerfully to this remark; wild horses wouldn't drag her to Mr Scott-Thurlow's wedding—he was, as far as she was concerned, a closed book. Or so she told herself.

Roseanne's godmother gave a dinner party on the following evening; just a few friends, the Honourable

Mrs Venables had said, most of them unattached men of suitable age with a complement of safely married ladies; Roseanne must have her chance and a dinner party was a very good way of getting to know people. Matilda was to attend too although her hostess would have been happier not to have had the competition; she consoled herself with the thought that men didn't care for such bright red hair.

Matilda did her best to look inconspicuous; she did her hair in a severe french pleat, wore an unassuming gown—grey crêpe and several years out of date— and stayed in the background as much as possible. Nevertheless she attracted the attention of the company, and since she was a nice, unassuming girl the ladies of the party liked her as well as the men. She did her best to see that Roseanne was a success and her godmother had to admit that Matilda hadn't made any attempt to draw attention to herself. All the same, an excuse would have to be found for Roseanne to go without her to the dinner dance later that week, and Matilda, being told on the morning of that day that she looked poorly and perhaps it would be wise if she didn't go out that evening, agreed for Roseanne's sake that she had a very bad headache and an early night would do her the world of good.

Of course, during the days she was expected to accompany Roseanne wherever she had a fancy to go, leaving her godmother to pursue her own busy social life, and it was a day or so after the dinner dance that they found themselves in the National Gallery. It was while they were admiring some splendid examples of the Netherlandish school that the young man standing close by spoke to them, or rather to Roseanne.

'Forgive me,' he began, 'I overheard you discussing this picture—you know something about it, do you not? Are you interested in oil-paintings of that period?'

When Roseanne nodded, her beaky nose quivering with the unexpectedness of it all, he asked, 'You paint yourself?' Then when she nodded again, 'Then let me explain...'

Which he did at some length, taking her from one painting to the next with Matilda, intrigued, keeping discreetly in the background. He seemed all right; he had a nice open face, not good-looking, but his gaze was direct, and he had introduced himself and shaken hands. 'Bernard Stevens,' he told them, working as a picture restorer for a famous art gallery and painting when he had the time. Roseanne had to be prised away from him after half an hour or so but only after she had promised to meet him there on the following morning, ostensibly to discuss more paintings but Matilda, studying her face, thought that was only partly the reason.

'You won't tell Aunt Maud?' begged Roseanne.

'Roseanne, you're twenty-two, old enough to decide whom you want to know. Of course I shan't breathe a word.'

All the same she played discreet gooseberry the next morning, and again on the following afternoon, only now it was the Tate Gallery. She had been reassured to hear him mention the names of several people whom Roseanne's godmother had talked of from time to time and he appeared well dressed and had good manners; she was no snob, but just supposing the gentle little flirtation turned into something more serious—she would have to answer to Lady Fox.

They were to go to the theatre on the next evening,

quite a small party and Matilda found herself paired
off with an elderly man, a widower who told her at
great length about his late wife's ill health, and during
the interval, when she had hoped to escape him for
a short while, he led her firmly to the bar where he
fetched her a tonic and lemon without asking her what
she would like. 'I don't approve of pretty young ladies
drinking alcohol,' he told her and, because she had a
kind heart, she accepted it nicely and sipped at it. She
really needed something strong. Vodka? She had never
tasted it. Brandy and soda? She looked around her—
everyone there appeared to be drinking gin and tonic
or champagne.

She took another sip and while appearing attentive
to her companion's remarks—still about his wife too—
glanced around her. There were some lovely dresses,
and the grey crêpe was drowned in a sea of silks and
satins. There was a vivid scarlet gown worn by someone
with her back to Matilda and standing beside it, looking
over the silk shoulder, was Mr Scott-Thurlow, watching
her.

She went pale with the strength of her feelings at the
sight of him and then blushed. It seemed impossible
for her to look away but she managed it and she hadn't
smiled because he had looked unsmilingly at her.

She tossed off the tonic and lent a sympathetic ear to
her companion's description of his late wife's asthma,
murmuring in all the right places and not really hearing
a word.

She went to bed later, feeling unhappy, longing for
a scarlet gown in which she might dazzle Mr Scott-
Thurlow and at the same time wanting to go home then
and there. She even wept a little and then her common

sense came to the rescue; scarlet would look hideous with her hair and no way could she go home and leave Roseanne just as the girl was beginning to find her feet—perhaps she would find romance too.

And it seemed likely; two days later, attending a preview of an up-and-coming portrait painter and this time with their hostess, Matilda was intrigued and delighted to see Bernard Stevens. He was with a friend of Mrs Venables and naturally enough was introduced, and presently he bore Roseanne off to make a tour of the rooms while Matilda stood between the two older ladies and listened with interest while Mrs Venables asked endless questions about Mr Stevens. The answers seemed to satisfy her and Matilda reflected that their month in London would make one of them happy, at least. That night after they had gone to bed Roseanne came along to her room, brimming over with excitement. She should get excited more often, thought Matilda, sitting up in bed, lending a sympathetic ear; it added a sparkle to Roseanne's plain face; even the unfortunate nose seemed less prominent and her mouth had taken on a softer curve.

Bernard, Roseanne told her, now that he had made the acquaintance of her godmother, was going to find a way to meet her parents; her godmother was one of the few people her mother listened to, and Mrs Venables liked him. 'Isn't it wonderful?' breathed Roseanne. 'Our meeting like that? He thinks I'm pretty, only my clothes are wrong—you always said that too, didn't you? He's going to meet me one day and go with me to choose an outfit. I wish we were staying here forever.'

'Well, if you want a super wedding you'll have to go home to get ready for it, and the sooner you do that the sooner you can get married. Big weddings take an awful lot of organising.'

Which started Roseanne off again until she gave a final yawn and said goodnight, but on her way to the door she stopped. 'I'm ever so glad it's happened to me—I wish it could happen to you too.'

'Nothing,' declared Matilda in a falsely cheerful voice, 'ever happens to me.'

She was wrong; fate had a testy ear tuned in to that kind of remark.

THEY HAD BEEN for a morning walk and now they were hurrying home as rain, threatening to be heavy, began to fall. There was a short cut to the house through narrow streets lined with small, rather shabby shops and used a great deal by drivers avoiding the main roads. They were turning into it when they saw half a dozen people standing on the edge of the pavement looking down at something.

'I'm going to see what it is,' said Matilda and despite Roseanne's peevish reluctance went to look. A small dog was lying in the gutter, wet, pitifully thin, and also obviously injured.

No one was doing anything; Matilda bent down and put out a gentle hand. 'Leave it alone, miss,' said a large untidy man roughly. '"E'll bite yer—'it by a car, 'e'll be dead in no time.'

Matilda flashed a glance at him and got on to her knees, the better to look at the little beast. It cowered and showed its teeth and then put out a tongue and licked her hand.

'How long has it been here?' she demanded.

'"Arf an hour…'

'Then not one of you has done anything to help it?' She turned to look at them. 'Why, you're nothing but a bunch of heartless brutes.'

"'Ere, that won't do, lady—it's only a stray, 'arf starved too.'

No one had noticed the car which drew up on the other side of the street; Mr Scott-Thurlow was beside her, bending his great height, lifting her to her feet before anyone had spoken again.

'Oh, dear, oh, dear,' he said softly, 'Miss ffinch helping lame dogs...'

'Don't you start,' she warned him fiercely. 'This poor creature's been here for half an hour and no one has lifted a finger.'

Mr Scott-Thurlow wasted no time. 'Get me a piece of cardboard,' he ordered the man nearest him, 'flat, mind you, and please be quick about it.'

The people around suddenly became helpful; suggestions filled the air, even offers of help, unspecified. The cardboard was brought back and everyone stood aside watching; they weren't unkind deliberately, only indifferent—if the big gent liked to get bitten by a dog that was going to die anyway, that was his look-out and they might as well be there to see it.

He wasn't bitten; he slid the cardboard under the dog, lifted it with the animal trembling on it and carried it across the street to his car, closely followed by Matilda and Roseanne. Matilda turned back halfway across to address the untidy man.

'Now you know what to do next time an animal gets hurt,' she told him, and added kindly, 'I dare say you didn't think, did you? Standing and looking at something that needs to be done is such a waste of time.'

She smiled at him and he smiled back, mostly because he hadn't seen green eyes like hers before.

Roseanne was already in the car, sitting in the back. 'Get inside beside me,' ordered Mr Scott-Thurlow, 'and I'll lay the cardboard on your lap.'

'A vet?' asked Matilda. The little dog looked in a bad way.

'Yes.'

He had nothing more to say until he turned into a side-street and got out. 'Stay there, I'll be back,' he told her and opened a side-door in a long brick wall. He came back almost at once with a burly, bearded man who nodded at Matilda and cast an eye over the dog.

'Let's have him in,' he suggested, and lifted the cardboard neatly off her knees. 'Coming too?'

Matilda got out of the car, but Roseanne shook her head. 'I'd rather stay here…'

Mr Scott-Thurlow held the door open and they went in one after the other down a long passage with the surgery at its end. 'You wait here,' the vet told her. 'I'll do an X-ray first—you can give a hand, James.'

Matilda sat in the waiting-room on a rather hard chair, cherishing the knowledge that his name was James. It suited him, though she doubted if anyone had ever called him Jimmy or even Jim. Time passed unheeded since her thoughts were entirely taken up with James Scott-Thurlow; when he joined her she looked at him mistily, shaken out of her daydreams.

'The little dog?'

'A fractured pelvis, cracked ribs, starved and very, very dirty. He'll live.'

'May he stay here? What will happen to him? Will it take long? If no one wants him I'm sure Father will let me have him…'

'He'll stay here until he's fit and he'll be well looked after. I should suppose he'll be fit, more or less, in a month or six weeks.' Mr Scott-Thurlow paused and then went on in a resigned voice, 'I have a Labrador who will be delighted to have a companion.'

He was rewarded by an emerald blaze of gratitude. 'Oh, how good of you; I'm not sure what kind of a dog he is but I'm certain that when he's well again you'll be proud of him.'

Mr Scott-Thurlow doubted this but forbore to mention it. 'Were you on your way back to Kensington? I'll run you there; Mrs Venables may be getting anxious.'

'Oh, I don't suppose so,' said Matilda airily. 'We may do as we please during the day, you know, unless there is some suitable young man coming to lunch. Do you know Mrs Venables?'

They had reached the door but he made no move to open it. 'I have a slight acquaintance. Rhoda knows her quite well, I believe.'

'Oh, then I expect you will be at the dinner party next week—a kind of farewell before we go back to Abner Magna.'

He had categorically refused to accompany Rhoda when she had told him of the invitation. Now, on second thoughts, he decided that he would go with her after all.

He opened the door. 'Then we shall meet again,' he said as they reached the car. Before he drove off he reached for the phone and said into it, 'I shall be half an hour late—warn everyone, will you?'

He drove off without a word, leaving Matilda

guessing. Was he a barrister, defending some important client, she wondered, or someone in the banking world, making decisions about another person's money? It would be a clerk at the other end, middle-aged, rather shabby probably with a large family of growing children and a mortgage. Her imagination ran riot until he stopped outside the Kensington house, bade them a polite goodbye and drove off.

'He doesn't talk much, does he?' Roseanne wanted to know. 'I think I'm a bit—well—scared of him.'

Matilda looked at her in astonishment. 'Scared? Of him? Whatever for? I dare say he was wrapped up in some business transaction; of course he didn't want to talk. Anyway you'll change your mind next week—he's coming to your godmother's dinner party, so we shall see him then.'

She saw him before then.

The days had passed rapidly, too fast for Roseanne, not fast enough for Matilda; she wanted to go home—London, she felt, wasn't for her. True, while she was there there was always the chance that she would see Mr Scott-Thurlow, but what was the use of that when he was going to marry Rhoda? A girl who was undoubtedly beautiful, clever and wore all the right clothes regardless of expense. She and Roseanne had gone shopping, gone to more exhibitions than she could count, seen the latest films and plays and accompanied Mrs Venables on several occasions when that lady, an enthusiastic member of several committees, introduced them to their various other members, mostly middle-aged and not in the least interested in the two girls. Roseanne found them a waste of time when she might have spent it in the company of her Bernard.

There were only a few days left now and preparations for the dinner party that night were well ahead. They were finishing their breakfast, which they took alone since Mrs Venables had hers in bed, when the dining-room door was thrust open and the kitchen maid—who should have known better, as Roseanne was quick to point out—rushed up to the table.

'It's Cook—cut herself something awful and the others down at the market getting the food for tonight. Whatever shall I do?'

'My dear good girl,' began Roseanne, looking alarmingly like her mother, but she was not allowed to finish.

'I'll come and look, shall I?' suggested Matilda calmly. 'If it's very bad we can get her to the hospital, but perhaps it looks worse than it is.'

Cook was sitting at the table, her hand wrapped in a teatowel. She was a nasty green colour and moaning faintly. Matilda opened the towel gently, making soothing noises the while. There was a lot of blood, but if it was a deep cut she could tie the hand up tightly and get a taxi to the nearest hospital. Since both of her companions were on the edge of hysteria she told them bracingly to close their eyes and turned back the last of the towel. She would have liked to have closed her eyes too; Cook's first and second fingers had been neatly severed just above the second joints. Matilda gulped and hoped her breakfast would stay down.

'Milly—it is Milly?—please go and ring for a taxi. Be quick and say that it's very urgent. Then come back here.'

'Is it a bad cut?' asked Roseanne from the door. 'Should I tell Aunt Maud?'

'Presently. I'll go with Cook to the nearest hospital and perhaps you'll tell her then.' She glanced at the girl. 'Would you get a shawl or something to put round Cook?'

'There's blood everywhere,' said Roseanne, and handed over a cape hanging behind the door, carefully looking the other way.

Matilda hung on to her patience. 'Thanks. Now find a table napkin or a scarf and look sharp about it…'

'No one speaks to me like that,' declared Roseanne.

'Don't be silly! I dare say you'll find a cloth of some sort in that cupboard.'

Roseanne opened drawers in an aggrieved manner and came back with a small teacloth. It was fine linen and beautifully embroidered and Matilda fashioned it into some kind of a sling, draped the cloak round Cook's shaking shoulders and propelled her gently out of the kitchen across the hall and out to the waiting taxi. They left a trail of red spots across the floor and Matilda heard Milly's gasp of horror.

'The nearest hospital,' urged Matilda, supporting a half-fainting and sturdily built Cook, 'as quick as you can.'

The cabby drove well, taking short cuts, cutting corners, beating the lights by a hair's breadth. At the Casualty entrance they got out and he got out too and between them they got poor Cook in to Casualty.

There was a young man standing talking to a nurse near the door. Matilda paused by him. 'Would you please pay the cabby? I'll let you have the money as soon as I can leave Cook.'

He looked astonished, paid the man while Matilda

offered hasty thanks, then took his place on the other side of Cook.

'She's cut off her fingers—two of them—they're there, inside the towel. Could someone get a doctor?'

'That's me. Casualty officer on duty. Let's have her in here.'

The place was half full, patients on chairs waiting to be seen, nurses going to and fro, several people on trolleys and a fierce-looking sister coming towards them.

'Well, what's this?' she wanted to know and with a surprising gentleness turned back the towel. She lifted Cook's arm and pressed the bell beside the couch and, when a nurse came, gave her quick instructions and then glanced at the young man.

'Shall I get her ready for Theatre? Nurse is taking a message—the quicker the better.'

Matilda was holding the other hand and Cook was clinging to it as though she would never let it go. Her skirt and blouse were ruined and her hair was coming down but she didn't give them a thought. She felt sick.

The shock of seeing Mr Scott-Thurlow in a long white coat over an excellently tailored grey suit dispelled the sickness. He was coming towards them with calm speed and fetched up beside the couch. He gave her a cool nod and she said in a wondering voice, 'Oh, I've been wondering just what you did...' and blushed scarlet as he gave a faint smile as he bent over Cook. The casualty officer was doing things—a tourniquet?—some kind of pressure so that the bleeding wasn't so bad any more and Sister was handing swabs and instruments to Mr Scott-Thurlow. Matilda, feeling sick again, looked at the curtains around the couch.

She heard him say, 'Right, we'll have her up right away, please, before I start my list. Warn Theatre, will you?' He bent over Cook. 'Don't worry too much, my dear, I'm going to stitch your fingers on again and you can stay here for a few days while they heal. Nurse is going to give you a little injection now to help the pain.' He patted her shoulder. 'You're very brave.'

He spoke to Matilda then. 'What did she have for breakfast?' he wanted to know.

'I don't know, but she would have had it quite early—about seven o'clock. She was slicing bacon with one of those machines...'

Matilda felt cold and looked green; the thought of the bacon had been too much. 'I'm going to be...'

Mr Scott-Thurlow handed her a bowl with the manner of someone offering her a hanky she might have dropped or a glass of water she had asked for. He was just in time.

There was someone beside her, a young nurse being sympathetic and helpful, and when Matilda lifted a shamed face everyone had gone.

'Don't worry,' said the nurse, 'there's somewhere where you can wait and I'll get someone to bring you a cup of tea. Mr Scott-Thurlow is going to operate at once so you'll know what's happening quite soon. Do you want to phone anybody?'

'Yes, please, only I haven't any money.'

She was led away to a rather bare room lined with benches with a kind of canteen at one end and two telephones on the wall. The nurse gave her twenty pence, patted her on the shoulder in a motherly fashion and hurried away.

She phoned Mrs Venables. 'How could she?' cried

that lady in an outraged voice. 'When we have the dinner party this evening and absolutely no chance of getting a cook at such short notice. What am I to do? She must have been careless—'

'She's cut off two fingers,' said Matilda. 'I'll stay here until I know what is happening to her. She's been very brave.'

She didn't wait for Mrs Venables's reply.

She sat for an hour, revived by a cup of hot strong tea, thinking about Cook and Mr Scott-Thurlow. She shouldn't have blurted out her silly remark in Casualty—she went hot again just thinking about it—and then to have been sick… She wriggled with humiliation. He had been kind to Cook; she hoped that he would be able to sew the fingers back on—surgeons were clever and she supposed that he was very experienced.

The kind little nurse who had lent her the twenty pence came into the waiting-room and she got up to meet her.

'She's going to be all right,' said the nurse. 'Mr Scott-Thurlow did a good job, and her fingers will be as good as new—well, almost. He's a wizard with bones. Sister said will you arrange for Mrs Chubb's clothes—nighties and washing things and so on—to be brought in? She's to stay a few days.'

Matilda nodded. 'Yes, of course. Which ward is she in?'

'Women's Orthopaedic, second floor. You'll be able to see her.'

'I'll go and get everything now and come back as soon as I can. Thank you, you've all been awfully kind.'

She was back within the hour, Cook's necessities in a case, with a couple of paperbacks she had stopped to buy and a bunch of flowers, Mrs Venables's unfeeling, complaining voice still ringing in her ears.

'The woman will be of no use to me,' she had said impatiently. 'Now I shall have to get another cook.'

Matilda had turned a thoughtful green gaze on to her hostess. 'Has she worked for you for long?' she asked.

'Oh, years,' said Mrs Venables. 'I must say it is *most* inconvenient—'

'I dare say Cook finds it inconvenient too, and very painful.'

She had received a very cold look for that; a good thing they were going home in a few more days.

Cook was in a small ward, sitting up in bed, looking pale. Matilda put everything away in her locker, fetched a vase for the flowers and offered the paperbacks— light romantic reading which she hoped would take Cook's mind off her problems. She parried the awkward questions she was asked, skimming smoothly over the future, and invented one or two suitable messages from Mrs Venables. 'I'll pop in some time tomorrow,' she finished, 'just to see if there's anything you would like.'

'That's kind of you, miss. We all said in the kitchen what a kind young lady you were, and so very understanding.'

Matilda said goodbye and found her way out of the hospital, trying not to wish that she might meet Mr Scott-Thurlow. But of course she didn't.

She got back to the house to find Mrs Venables raging up and down the drawing-room floor while Roseanne sat in a corner looking obstinate. She had intended to spend the morning with Bernard and she had had to put him off. Her mouth was set in a thin line and she looked very like her mother.

Mrs Venables, pacing back to the door, saw Matilda. 'I've telephoned every agency I can think of,' she declared. 'There is not a decent cook to be had at a moment's notice. I am distraught.' She wrung her hands in a dramatic fashion and glared at Matilda.

'You will be relieved to know that Mrs Chubb's operation was successful and that she is comfortably in bed.' Matilda glared back. 'I can cook—I'll see to dinner this evening.'

Mrs Venables's glare turned to a melting sweetness. 'Matilda! Oh, can you really cook? I mean cordon bleu? My dear girl, however can I thank you—what a relief, you have no idea how worried I've been.' She reeled off the menu: consommé royale, poached salmon, roast duck with orange garnish and brandy, straw potatoes and a selection of vegetables, some sort of a salad—she had left that to Cook—and then peach condé and coffee mousse. 'Can you manage that?' She patted Matilda's arm. 'So good of you to do this for me.'

'I'm doing it for Cook,' said Matilda.

She didn't wait for Mrs Venables's outraged gasp but took herself off to the kitchen, where she explained matters to the domestic staff and sat down at the kitchen table to get organised. She had plenty of willing help, and, satisfied with the arrangements, she went away to tidy herself for lunch, an uncomfortable meal with Mrs Venables suppressing her ill temper in case Matilda should back out at the last minute, and Roseanne still sulking.

Matilda spent most of the afternoon preparing for the evening. She enjoyed cooking and she was an instinctive cook, quite ordinary food turning into delectable dishes under her capable hands. She had her tea in the kitchen,

which rather upset the butler and the kitchen maid and
certainly upset Bertha, who had disapproved of the
whole thing to start with. 'Ladies,' she had sniffed,
'don't belong in the kitchen,' a remark to which Matilda
didn't bother to reply.

Everything went well; as the first guests arrived and
the butler went to admit them, Matilda gave the ducks a
satisfied prod, tasted the consommé and began to make
a salad. There was half an hour before dinner would be
served and she enjoyed making a salad.

The Honourable Mrs Venables greeted her guests
with an almost feverish eagerness. She had planned the
evening carefully and if anything went wrong she would
never recover from it. She cast an anxious eye over
the laughing and talking people around her. Bernard
had come and she sighed with relief, for Roseanne had
stopped sulking at the sight of him and even looked a
bit pretty. There were two more to come, Rhoda Symes
and Mr Scott-Thurlow, and they entered the room at that
moment. A handsome couple, she conceded; Rhoda
looked magnificent, but then she always did. Mr Scott-
Thurlow looked much as he usually did, rather grave;
always courteous and lovely manners, though. She went
forward to welcome them.

Mr Scott-Thurlow had seen Roseanne as soon as he
entered the room but there was no sign of the bright
head of hair he had expected to see. He listened politely
to one of the guests trying to prise free advice from
him while he glanced round the room. Matilda wasn't
there. He caught Rhoda's eye and she smiled at him.
She was looking particularly beautiful, exquisitely
made up, her hair a blonde halo, her cerise dress the
very latest fashion. She would make him a very suitable

wife; she was a clever woman as well as attractive, completely at ease against a social background, cool and undemonstrative. The uneasy thought that her charming appearance hid a cold nature crossed his mind and he found himself wondering why he had asked her to marry him. He knew the answer to that: she made no demands upon him and appeared quite content with the lack of romance between them. He had been an only child and had lost his parents in a plane crash when he had been a small boy. He had gone to live with his grandparents, who had loved him dearly but had not known what to say to him, so he had learned to hide his loneliness and unhappiness and had grown up into a rather quiet man who seldom allowed his feelings to show, channelling his energy and interest into his work. It was his old nanny, Mrs Twigg, who kept house for him, who had begged him to find himself a wife and he had acknowledged the good sense of that; his friends were all married by now and despite his absorption in his work he was sometimes lonely.

He and the man to whom he was talking were joined by several more people and the conversation became general until they were summoned to dinner, where he sat between two young married women who flirted gently with him.

It was someone at the other end of the table who remarked loudly upon the delicious duck. 'You must have a splendid cook,' he remarked, laughing.

'I've had her for years,' declared Mrs Venables. 'She's a treasure,' and Mr Scott-Thurlow, happening to glance at Roseanne across the table, saw the look of surprised rage on her face and wondered why.

It was some time afterwards when they were all back

in the drawing-room that he made his way to her side. 'Nice to see you, Roseanne, and you look charming. Is Miss ffinch ill?'

Roseanne said softly, 'No, of course not—she never is. She's in the kitchen. She cooked the dinner.' She smiled suddenly. 'We'll go and see her if you like.' Before he could answer she said loudly, 'It's rather warm—shall we go on to the balcony for a minute?'

There was a small staircase at one end of the balcony and she led the way down it and round the house and in through a side-door.

The short passage was rather dark and smelled vaguely damp. Roseanne opened the door at its end, revealing the kitchen.

Matilda was standing at the kitchen table, carving slices off a roast duck. She wasn't doing it very well and there was a large pan of rather mangled bones and bits beside her. She looked up and saw them as they went in. She was flushed and untidy and swathed in one of Mrs Chubb's aprons, many sizes too large for her, and despite that she still contrived to look beautiful. When she saw them she smiled and said, 'Oh, hello...'

'What the devil do you think you're doing?' asked Mr Scott-Thurlow with a good deal of force.

She chose to misunderstand him. 'Well, I never could carve—the bones will make splendid soup and there's still plenty of meat...'

His tone was measured. 'That is not what I meant, and you know it. Why are you working in the kitchen when you should be in the drawing-room? That abominable woman...' He stopped, mindful of good manners. 'Do you mean to say that she asked you to cook dinner?'

'No. I said that I would—to help Mrs Chubb; you know she was in such a state. They tell me that you did a splendid job on her fingers. Are you a consultant or something?'

'Yes. Let us keep to the point, Matilda.'

She looked meek, but her eyes sparkled because he had called her Matilda and not Miss ffinch. A tiny step forwards perhaps?

She picked up the knife again and started on the other side of the duck and he stepped forwards, took the knife from her, carved the rest of the bird with a practised hand and laid the knife down on the table.

'Is there no one to help you?'

'They're having their supper. I'll stay down here until you've all gone home.' She selected a slice of duck and popped it into her mouth.

It was Roseanne who spoke. 'Look,' she sounded worried, 'we must go back—they'll wonder where we are.'

'Very well. Have you had your dinner, Matilda?'

He looked as cross as two sticks, she thought lovingly. 'I shall take a tray up to my room. Goodnight, Mr Scott-Thurlow, or is it goodbye?'

CHAPTER THREE

MATILDA, PACKING THE remainder of her things ready to leave in the morning, reflected sadly that it really had been goodbye and not goodnight. From upstairs at the landing window she had watched the dinner guests go home and it seemed to her that Mr Scott-Thurlow was quite devoted in his attention towards his fiancée as they left the house. Rhoda had really looked quite stunning.

She was glad to be going home; Mrs Venables had thanked her for her services rather coldly, remarking at the same time that she had no idea how she was going to manage with the temporary cook whom she had engaged. Matilda, who had been to see Mrs Chubb again, had observed rather tartly that she would appreciate Mrs Chubb's services all the more when she returned, 'Because, of course, she will be coming back here, will she not? After all these years?'

A remark which received no answer save a non-committal murmur which could have meant anything or nothing.

Gregg fetched them soon after breakfast and the two girls bade their hostess goodbye. She embraced Roseanne warmly and begged her to visit her again very soon, but when she shook Matilda's hand she observed rather distantly that she supposed that the daughter of a rector had much to occupy her and that they were unlikely to meet again.

Matilda, who had no wish to improve her acquaintance with the Honourable Mrs Venables, assured her that the likelihood of her visiting London in the foreseeable future was indeed remote.

Gregg obligingly stopped at the rectory and deposited Matilda and her case in the porch while Roseanne hung out of the car, calling to her to come up to the manor as soon as she could. 'Mother will want to know about Bernard...'

Matilda nodded and smiled, thanked Gregg and opened the door of her home to hear her mother's voice from somewhere upstairs and a moment later her father's deeper tones from his study before both parents converged in the hall to hug her warmly.

'We've missed you,' said her mother. 'It's lovely to have you back...'

'You're glad to be home?' enquired her father.

'Oh, Father, yes.' Her eyes shone with tears. 'I missed you all too.'

They went into the kitchen and presently sat down round the kitchen table to drink coffee.

'You enjoyed yourself, dear?' asked her mother. 'When you wrote and telephoned there was always a party or a dinner or something.' She added causally, 'Did you meet anyone you liked?'

Matilda cut herself a slice of the cake her mother had taken out of the oven and bit into it. She wiped the crumbs away from her mouth before she answered. 'Yes, but he's going to be married to a very beautiful woman.' She went on steadily, 'I met quite a few people

I liked too but not many young ones. They went to the dances and Roseanne mostly went with her godmother.'

Her mother nodded and smiled a little; she could imagine the Honourable Mrs Venables's disquiet when she had first set eyes on Matilda—Roseanne wouldn't stand much chance...And this man? She wondered who he was and where Matilda had met him and whether he had been aware that her darling daughter had lost her heart to him. She longed to know; instead she asked, 'And Roseanne, did she have a good time too?'

'Oh, yes—we met a young man, Bernard Stevens— at one of the picture galleries, and he fell for her. Luckily he knows friends of Mrs Venables so I can't see that Lady Fox could possibly object—Roseanne wants to marry him and she can be as stubborn as a mule. He'll be down for a weekend soon, I expect, and you'll meet him or at least see him in church.'

'What a relief for Lady Fox,' observed Mrs ffinch. 'There are three daughters and those unfortunate noses... Did you enjoy the big dinner party before you left? Did the grey crêpe do?'

Matilda took another slice of cake. 'Well, I didn't go...' She paused, smiling a little, remembering Mr Scott-Thurlow's visit to the kitchen. 'The cook cut herself,' she began and recounted the happenings of that eventful day, leaving out Mr Scott-Thurlow of course.

Her mother was indignant. 'Well, really—it was one thing letting you do the cooking but she could at least have told her guests and thanked you.'

Mrs ffinch looked quite fierce and the rector said, 'Now, now, my dear, Matilda had the thanks that mattered—the poor woman with the cut hand will remember her with gratitude, while Mrs Venables is to be pitied for her lack of charity.'

His wife cast him a resigned look; sometimes she wished that he would get really annoyed about something or someone, but he never did. She smiled suddenly at him. 'You're quite right, of course—you always are.'

Matilda went to the manor the following morning to resume her usual duties there. Roseanne met her at the door and said eagerly, 'You will tell Mother what a splendid man Bernard is, won't you? She's sure to ask you. If you could persuade her to invite him for a weekend…'

'I'll do my best,' said Matilda doubtfully. Lady Fox wasn't the kind of person one could persuade easily.

As it happened her task was made easy; Lady Fox had already had a good report of Bernard from Mrs Venables. All the same she cross-questioned Matilda about him at length. 'I should like to meet this young man,' she concluded.

Matilda was catching up on the household accounts. 'I expect you have already thought of a way to do that,' she suggested. 'A weekend here would give you the opportunity to get to know him.'

'That is true, and I had of course already decided to do so. I cannot have one of my girls throwing herself away on some unsuitable young man.'

Matilda murmured. She was of the private opinion that Roseanne intended to marry the young man whether her mother approved or not.

Lady Fox got up from her desk. 'Yes, I shall certainly do so,' she said in a voice which suggested that Matilda had begged her not to.

'How very wise of you, Lady Fox,' said Matilda, looking as meek as red hair and green eyes allowed her.

Life settled back into the quiet routine which had been interrupted by their visit to London. Matilda, soothed by the comparative leisurely progress of her days, was able to think about James Scott-Thurlow in a sensible way. She was in love with him and always would be, there was no gainsaying that, but she had known her case was hopeless when she had set eyes on Rhoda. It was now just a question of forgetting him, she told herself firmly. Unfortunately she soon discovered that this was impossible.

They had been back for ten days when Bernard Stevens was invited for the weekend. Roseanne was almost sick with excitement and despair as she examined her face. 'Look at the spots,' she said pettishly. 'What am I to do?'

'I'll come early tomorrow and do your face—some of that cream you bought in London. I know your mother doesn't like you to use make-up but if I'm careful I don't think she'll notice.'

So that, when Bernard arrived, Roseanne presented a passable face to him, skilfully made up and made almost pretty because she was in love. Anyway, he wouldn't have noticed because he loved the girl…

Matilda made herself scarce once she had greeted him; there were the flowers to do for the dinner table that evening and then she would go home for the weekend. Not, though, before Bernard and Roseanne came looking for her.

'I've a message for you—do you remember Mr Scott-Thurlow? He asked me to say that the little dog is doing well—oh, and the cook—Mrs Chubb?—is staying with her sister and then going to a new job where there will be plenty of help.'

Matilda bent over her flowers. 'Oh, what splendid news—thank you for telling me.'

'You're awfully red,' observed Roseanne. 'It is rather hot in here.'

'I've almost finished. Are you going to show Bernard the garden?' Then she added, unable to help herself, 'I didn't know that you knew Mr Scott-Thurlow.'

'Well, I don't—just an acquaintance really. Nice chap, but I don't like that girl he's going to marry.'

Matilda stopped herself just in time from agreeing with him.

There was a splendid congregation in church that Sunday—the village knew all about Bernard Stevens by now and everyone was agog to take a look at him; he sat in the manor-house pew with Lady Fox in one of her terrible hats on one side of him and Roseanne on the other with her sisters and Sir Benjamin. He looked quite at ease and happy; presumably Lady Fox had given him her blessing, which meant that Sir Benjamin, who did what he was told, had given his too.

Going out of the church, Matilda bumped into Mrs Chump. '''Er ladyship will be pleased,' she breathed, lowering her voice since they were still in the porch. '''E looks a likely young man. Not a patch on that there friend of Dr Bramley's—now there was a gent for you, Miss Matilda. Happen 'e'll come visiting again some time.'

'Unlikely, I should think, Mrs Chump. What a lovely day it is…'

BERNARD LEFT ON Monday morning and Matilda was met by an ecstatic Roseanne with the news that they were to become engaged. 'Isn't it marvellous?' she wanted to know. 'I'm going up to town tomorrow to meet him and choose the ring.' She danced away, calling as she went, 'I've been so afraid I'd get left like you and be an old maid!'

What a good start to a Monday morning, thought Matilda gloomily as she went along to Lady Fox's sitting-room and started on the post. That lady joined her almost at once and spent the next hour expressing her satisfaction at her daughter's engagement. 'Quite a good family,' she conceded of Bernard, 'related to the Crofts of Norfolk, and he has good prospects.' She glanced up from the bill she was frowning over. 'Why does the butcher send this account for the second time?'

'It wasn't paid, you said that he could wait for his money.'

Lady Fox went an unbecoming red. 'You must have misunderstood me, Matilda—see that it is paid at once.' She added, 'What a pity you can't find yourself a husband.'

Only by reminding herself that no ffinch would lower herself to answer such a vulgar remark from the inferior Fox family did Matilda manage to remain silent. It was becoming obvious to her that she would have to give up her job at the manor-house; the money was useful but there was a limit to what a girl could stand. She wasn't trained for anything but she was a good cook and she liked children; there must be something...

Roseanne came back the next day with a diamond ring on her finger; it wasn't as large or as brilliant as that of Mr Scott-Thurlow's fiancée, but it was worth the unstinted admiration Matilda gave it.

That evening, sitting round the supper table with

her mother and father and Esme, Matilda told them that she wanted to give up her job. It was a relief that no one asked why.

Her mother answered at once, 'Yes, dear, I think that will be a good thing. Lady Fox leans on you far too heavily,' and her father nodded his head in agreement, and as for Esme she gave a crow of delight.

'They'll never get anyone to do the chores like you do, Tilly, and they'll have to pay the earth too. What are you going to do?'

'Well, I don't know, I'll have to think about it.' Matilda looked anxiously at her father, who observed placidly,

'I should miss you helping around the parish, my dear, but Esme can take your place and Hilary will be back home in a week or so and will be here until the wedding. We must put our heads together...'

So Matilda went to the manor-house with a speech carefully prepared and all the answers likely to be needed as arguments as to why she wanted to leave. She was going in through the side-door when she heard the sound of breaking glass, bumps and screams.

She ran along the passage and into the hall and saw Roseanne lying in an untidy heap at the foot of the staircase, an excellent example of the Tudor period, wide, its treads worn smooth with age. It was obvious that the girl had missed her footing and hurtled down its length, scattering the contents of a tray of china and glass as she went.

Matilda bent over her and, as she did so, Roseanne opened her eyes and started to scream. Lady Fox, who had come hurrying to see what was the matter, started to scream too and Sir Benjamin, taking his time, joined her, only he didn't scream but swore. Various members of the staff had arrived by now and the noise was considerable.

'Phone Dr Bramley,' said Matilda briskly. 'Lady Fox, please stop screaming so that we can hear where Roseanne hurts.'

That was going to be difficult, for Roseanne was making a great deal of noise. 'My leg!' she shouted. 'My arm! I can't bear it, I'm dying.'

'No, you're not,' said Matilda firmly. 'Try and be quiet and tell me exactly where the pain is.'

Roseanne glared at her. 'My leg, I told you—above my knee, of course, can't you see for yourself? And my arm, it's my wrist…I'm in agony.'

Sir Benjamin, who had gone to telephone, came back and Matilda sent him for a cushion which she tucked carefully under Roseanne's head.

'You can't leave my poor girl like that!' bellowed Lady Fox. 'I'll get Gregg in to lift her.'

'Lady Fox, if there are broken bones they'll be even more broken if we move her.'

'Nonsense, I'm her mother and I know what's best for her.' She glared at Matilda. 'You have no idea…'

Matilda had prudently taken up a position by Roseanne which would fend off any efforts Lady Fox intended to make. It wasn't much use saying anything—poor Roseanne was screaming her head off, Sir Benjamin stood there looking useless and the housemaid together with the cleaning lady seemed rooted to the spot. If only Mr Scott-Thurlow were here, thought Matilda.

Dr Bramley came instead, nodded to everyone and got down on his knees beside Roseanne.

'No one moved her?' he asked, running gentle hands over arm and leg.

'I told them to fetch Gregg and have her carried to her room,' said Lady Fox loudly, 'but of course Matilda disobeyed me and left my poor girl lying there.'

'A very good thing too—more damage done by people moving injured people than you'd believe.' He was opening his bag and getting out a syringe. 'First we will stop the pain then she must go to hospital.'

'Certainly not, Dr Bramley. Roseanne is a sensitive girl; to be in a ward with other sick patients would do her a great deal of harm.'

He drew up an injection and gave it into a shrinking Roseanne. 'She must be X-rayed as soon as possible and the bones set by an expert.'

Sir Benjamin and Matilda spoke together. 'There's King's Hall...'

'Send her there. Matilda, go and phone for an ambulance, will you? Then pack whatever Roseanne will need for a short period there.'

Roseanne opened her eyes again. The injection was already doing its good work but she was rather vague. 'I won't go unless Matilda comes with me—and stays there.' And when no one said anything, 'You heard what I said—I won't go, I won't.'

'My darling child,' declared Lady Fox dramatically, 'of course she shall go with you. Matilda, pack her things and then pack some things for yourself—it's the least you can do.'

Matilda's eyes and hair seemed to glow with rage.

She caught the doctor's eye and he winked and nodded his head, knowing exactly how she felt. 'Please, Matilda, until Roseanne has quietened down.'

'I'll go because you asked me to,' said Matilda and marched off to phone for an ambulance.

By the time the ambulance had arrived she had packed a bag for Roseanne and gone home, packed one for herself, given a brief account of what had occurred to her mother and presented herself, outwardly calm and inwardly fuming still, at the manor-house again.

She would have liked to have flung her resignation at Lady Fox's head there and then, but Roseanne needed someone with her until her arm and leg had been put to rights. It should have been her mother, thought Matilda, casting that lady an accusing look.

Lady Fox interpreted it correctly for she said defensively, 'This has been a tremendous shock to me; my sensitive nature cannot face up to it.' She embraced a drowsy Roseanne gingerly. 'Dearest child, you will soon be better. Matilda will let me know what is to be done.'

Dr Bramley, supervising the patient's disposal in the ambulance, heard that. 'I shall phone you as soon as it's been decided what has to be done, Lady Fox, then you can make your own arrangements concerning Roseanne.'

Matilda got into the car beside him as the ambulance pulled away. 'Someone should let Bernard know,' she pointed out tartly as Dr Bramley started the car.

King's Hall was twenty minutes' drive away, a private hospital set in pleasant surroundings and with a high reputation. Roseanne was conveyed into it and taken straight to the X-ray department with no delay while Matilda sat patiently in the comfortably furnished waiting-room. Someone brought her coffee after a time and told her kindly that once the specialist had seen

Roseanne someone would be along to make whatever arrangements were necessary.

Matilda drank her coffee, ate all the biscuits and speculated about lunch, and not only lunch; Lady Fox had told her to stay with Roseanne but perhaps the hospital wouldn't approve of that—perhaps she ought to phone…

There was a small stir in the hall and a moment later the half-open door of the waiting-room was thrust open. Mr Scott-Thurlow, looking calm, grave and unhurried came in.

'Ah, Matilda, I felt in my bones…' He didn't go on. 'Be good enough not to go away—I'll see you presently…'

She sat staring at him, awash with delight. She should have known—Lady Fox would have demanded the very best treatment for her daughter and he was undoubtedly the very best. Suddenly the annoyance she had felt at being sent with Roseanne melted away; fate had very kindly thrust her in his path once more, which was delightful—probably he felt no delight at all though. A pity she couldn't have thought of something to say instead of gasping at him like a stranded fish.

She heard one o'clock strike somewhere and a moment later a smartly dressed domestic came in carrying a tray which she set on a small table. She smiled at Matilda. 'Your lunch, Miss,' and hard on her heels came a dignified lady in a grey dress and a fetching muslin cap.

'They're in Theatre now,' she explained, 'and it may be some time. Please make yourself comfortable in the meantime.' She smiled and went away and Matilda, a girl with a healthy appetite, lifted the lids covering the dishes on the tray. Soup in a pitkin, piping hot, fish and creamed potatoes, broccoli and carrots and a baked custard.

She sat herself down and ate the lot and the domestic came back with a tray of coffee just as she had finished. She went back to her easy chair then and since there was nothing else much to do she closed her eyes and dozed off.

Mr Scott-Thurlow, coming silently into the room, paused by the door. She made a delightful picture, her glorious fiery hair against the soft green of the chair in which she was sprawling. He stood for a few moments looking down at her and then bent and touched her shoulder gently.

She woke at once and smiled widely and sat up. 'Is everything all right?'

He sat down opposite her. 'Yes. Roseanne's arm is in plaster, a simple fracture which should knit quickly. Her leg is rather more complicated: a double fracture above the knee—rather unusual; it will have to be in extension for some weeks. She has come round from the anaesthetic but is asleep now. I've spoken to her mother—I gather that you are to stay here with her until such time as she feels she can cope without you.' He smiled faintly. 'An arrangement which I hope doesn't inconvenience you at all?'

'Well, as a matter of fact, it does. I was going to tell Lady Fox this morning that I wanted to leave, but before I could do that Roseanne fell down the stairs.'

'But you will stay here as long as you think it necessary?'

'I suppose so. Perhaps Lady Fox could come and

stay here. I'm not necessary here; there must be plenty of nurses.'

'There are.' He looked up as Dr Bramley came into the room and sat down.

'Hello, Matilda. They're bringing tea and presently you'll be taken to see Roseanne and then shown your room. James, what had Lady Fox got to say?'

'I had to refuse her—er—request to remain here. I have patients to see this evening and a list in the morning. I'll be down again in a couple of days and we'll take another X-ray but I foresee no complications.'

Tea was brought in then and Matilda was invited to pour out.

'I've had a talk with Matron,' said Mr Scott-Thurlow, 'and explained the position with regard to you, Matilda; I'm sure that you will find her and the nurses most kind and helpful. I have also asked her to allow Bernard Stevens to visit at any time—he seems to have a great deal of influence with Roseanne.'

'Thank you. How long do you suppose I must stay here?'

He raised his eyebrows. 'That is something I am unable to tell you. It depends on Lady Fox, does it not?'

'Well, yes, of course it does. But she will listen to you because you're an—eminent surgeon.'

'I'll do my best.' He spoke gravely but she had the feeling that he was laughing silently. 'I saw Mrs Chubb this morning. She is doing excellently—she sent her love. So did that little rascal of a dog...'

'He's still at the vet?'

'For another week. Can you suggest a name for him before I introduce him to my household?'

'He was in Theobald Avenue. Could you call him that?'

This time he allowed his amusement to show. 'I don't see why not.' He glanced at his watch. 'I must go. I'll take another look at Roseanne first.'

He went away with Dr Bramley, leaving Matilda to sit and dream. They didn't come back; presently she heard voices in the hall and then the sound of cars being driven away and when a nurse came to fetch her she asked if she might telephone. 'I told Lady Fox I would let her know if Roseanne was feeling more herself. Mr Scott-Thurlow has already talked to her, hasn't he? And I'm sure Dr Bramley will go and see her. And I'd like to ring my mother, if I may. I had to leave rather suddenly...'

Roseanne was awake now and fairly free from pain. She was also irritable and tearful. 'Now I'll never get married,' she wailed, 'with a broken arm and leg.'

'I can't think why not,' said Matilda hearteningly. 'In a matter of weeks you'll be as good as new and you weren't planning to marry for a month or two, were you?'

'No. Why doesn't he come? He should be here, comforting me...'

'Well, he'd have to be told first, wouldn't he? He might be out of town; you know he travels around to various museums. He's got to get here too, you know.'

'Do I look awful?'

Matilda examined the rather cross face on the pillows. 'No, if you could smile just a little you'd look pretty. It's not so bad, you know—this is a nice cheerful place and the nurses are awfully kind, and you had Mr

Scott-Thurlow to put you to rights and he's one of the best, so I've been told.'

'Who told you that?'

'Someone at the hospital where I took poor Mrs Chubb when she chopped off her fingers.'

'Oh, her...Mr Scott-Thurlow is stern, isn't he?'

'I don't know him well enough to say,' observed Matilda, rather at a loss as to what to say and relieved when a nurse came in with a basket of red roses.

'Just look at this,' she begged them. 'Here's the card.'

'Open it, Matilda,' ordered Roseanne, and added 'please' at the look of surprise she got. It was from Bernard, of course—she read the card Matilda handed to her, cried a little and then, to everyone's relief, smiled. 'He's coming to see me; he's going to stay with Mother and Father until I feel better. Now I don't mind any more—not much, anyway.'

Matilda stayed with her until supper was brought, a very small light meal because of the anaesthetic, but she ate most of it and, when a nurse came to make her ready for the night, Matilda was free to be shown her own room, next to the patient's. There was TV in one corner of it and she sat eating the supper which was brought to her, watching a film while she did so.

Lady Fox had been vague when Matilda phoned her. She would come to see Roseanne in the morning, she had said, and then they could discuss what was best to be done. 'Roseanne needs all the support she can get,' she had observed. 'Fortunately you are there with her.'

Matilda had frowned fiercely at the phone. She had said with asperity, 'I should be glad if you or one of her sisters will take over from me as quickly as possible—that is if she needs someone. I need to go back home,

Lady Fox; you must realise that I have to help my father in the village.'

Lady Fox had snorted angrily. 'Surely you realise that Roseanne is more urgent than anything else.'

'Yes, I'm sure that she is, but if you feel it's so urgent that someone is here with her, should you not come yourself?'

She had put down the phone before Lady Fox had caught her outraged breath. Tomorrow, she thought as she got ready for bed, she would be sent her notice and a good thing too. It would make it awfully awkward for her father, of course, and she was sorry about that, but she was sure that Dr Bramley would back her up. She got into her comfortable bed and put out the light and a second later someone tapped on the door. A nurse came in. 'I'm so sorry, Miss ffinch, but Miss Fox is being rather difficult. Perhaps if you came...'

Matilda, muttering under her breath, went.

Morning came and with it Lady Fox, in a nasty temper too, made worse since she had had to wait until the matron was free to see her. By the time she got to Roseanne's room she was rigid with annoyance because the matron had suggested that Roseanne would do much better if she had several days quiet, without visitors.

'I am her mother,' Lady Fox had said grandly.

'In that case,' Matron had replied smoothly, 'you will wish to co-operate in every way, will you not?'

Matilda was reading one of the more gossipy newspapers to Roseanne when her mother came into the room. Her eye lighted upon it at once.

'Gutter Press!' she cried. 'How dare you read that rubbish to Roseanne?'

'It's not my cup of tea either,' agreed Matilda

cheerfully, 'but it takes her mind off herself. I mean *The Times* or the *Telegraph* don't print titbits, do they?'

Lady Fox gobbled, bent to embrace her daughter, who burst into tears for no reason at all, and then sat down heavily by the bed.

The visit wasn't a success—mother and daughter were too much alike for that. Matilda, who had prudently skipped away, could hear their raised voices and presently the quiet, severe voice of the sister on duty, and later Lady Fox was ushered into her room.

'And what was all that rubbish on the phone last night?' demanded that lady. 'I must say I was amazed at your rudeness, Matilda.'

'Do please sit down,' said Matilda, 'and I wasn't rude, Lady Fox, only stating facts. Now that I have the opportunity I should like to give up my job with you. I really only stayed because of Roseanne, you know, but she will be getting married soon. Let me see, it's Thursday…I'll stay with you until Saturday week if you would like that; that gives you time to find someone to take my place.'

Her companion looked thunderstruck. 'But what am I to do? I shall never find someone who will come each day…'

Not from the village you won't, reflected Matilda naughtily—the salary Lady Fox paid was a pittance compared to other jobs. Matilda, who had been unnaturally meek for far too long, felt a surge of delight at the idea of being free from her petty chores at the manor-house. She would be free to choose what she wanted to do. Mr Scott-Thurlow's handsome features imprinted themselves behind her eyelids; what she wanted to do was marry him…

She was aware that Lady Fox was speaking rather loudly in a cross voice, to stop abruptly as the door opened once more and Dr Bramley and Dr Scott-Thurlow were ushered in.

'Interrupting a little chat?' asked Dr Bramley and winked at Matilda. 'Mr Scott-Thurlow has come to see Roseanne and then perhaps something can be arranged...'

Mr Scott-Thurlow wished Lady Fox good morning and then turned his attention to Matilda. 'Roseanne is more herself today?' he wished to know.

'Oh, yes. Rather a ragged night, though, but Bernard telephoned early this morning. He is coming down this afternoon.'

'In that case I suggest that we examine the patient.' The men went away and Matilda and Lady Fox sat without speaking until they returned.

'Quite satisfactory,' declared Mr Scott-Thurlow. 'I leave Roseanne in Dr Bramley's capable hands. I shall, of course, visit from time to time. It will be necessary to take further X-rays to monitor progress. Physiotherapy will be started as soon as possible.'

He stood just inside the door and Matilda thought how distinguished and handsome he was and so sure of himself... She heaved a sigh which he noticed with amusement. That there had been some kind of disagreement was obvious—the air was thick with it. Matilda had probably spoken her mind...

He went on gravely, 'I am of the opinion that Roseanne will make better progress if she is without constant companionship. Visitors by all means, and certainly Mr Stevens should be allowed to call at any time. The nursing staff here are excellent; she will not lack for sympathetic treatment.' He went to the door. 'You must forgive me if I leave now—I have a busy day ahead of me. This is an unfortunate accident for your daughter, Lady Fox, but I can assure you that within a very short time she will be fully restored to normal health and strength.'

He bade her goodbye and turned to Matilda. 'Thank you for your help,' he said and smiled and took her hand, and was interrupted by Lady Fox.

'Your bill, Mr Scott-Thurlow...'

The eyes smiling down at Matilda became icy. 'You will receive my account from my secretary in due course, Lady Fox.'

Matilda, who had done her best on several occasions to be sympathetic to Lady Fox, and failed, felt sorry for her; Mr Scott-Thurlow's voice had been courteous and straight from the North Pole, implying delicately that there had been a breach of good taste on her part.

When he had gone and Dr Bramley had gone to speak to the sister looking after Roseanne, Lady Fox spoke. 'Well, you had better get yourself back home,' she said crossly. 'It seems you're not needed here. I shall have to come over every day, I suppose. I shall forget all this nonsense about your leaving, Matilda, and expect you tomorrow morning as usual.'

'Certainly, Lady Fox, I did say that I would stay until Saturday week, but it was no nonsense. I shall leave then.'

CHAPTER FOUR

DR BRAMLEY GAVE Matilda a lift back home after a stormy ten minutes with Roseanne, whose threatened hysterics at the idea of being left on her own were curtailed by Matilda's timely reminder that Bernard when he arrived to visit her would expect to see a bravely smiling girl, looking her best and wearing the lacy bedjacket her mother had had the forethought to bring with her.

On the way back Dr Bramley asked cautiously, 'Have you and Lady Fox fallen out, Tilly? I detected a distinct coolness in the air...'

She explained. 'Anyway, it's time I found something else to do—Hilary will be home for some months and Esme's awfully good helping Father. I'd quite like to get a job not too far away from home, so that I could pop in regularly. I've no idea what. I don't suppose there are many people who want someone just to see to the post and the flowers and so on.'

'I'm given to understand that you are a splendid cook among other things. I don't doubt that something will turn up. Go and see Roseanne from time to time, won't you? She needs someone to stiffen her spine; she never could stand up to her mother. This chap she intends to marry seems nice enough.'

'Oh, he is—she's a different girl when he's with her.'

'It amazes me how love can alter a person.'

Matilda said yes, doesn't it and wondered if it had altered Rhoda Symes. She thought it unlikely. Perhaps that was because she didn't love James Scott-Thurlow, or even that he didn't love her. Wishful thinking.

She enquired after her companion's bees, a passionate hobby of his, and they were still discussing them when he stopped outside the rectory and, when invited to go in with her, followed her inside for a delayed cup of coffee.

The next ten days were a bit difficult; Matilda went to the manor-house each morning, obeying Lady Fox's beck and call without outward rancour although her feelings inside didn't bear scrutiny. Her successor had to be found—no easy task, for no one who knew Lady Fox and the miserable salary she paid was prepared to work for her.

Lady Fox was reduced to asking Matilda what to do.

'Well,' said Matilda thoughtfully, 'if you were to offer a bigger salary and advertise in the Salisbury or Yeovil papers...and there's room enough to offer a bed-sitting-room, free, of course.'

'Well, really,' observed Lady Fox indignantly and did so. There was one applicant, a middle-aged lady, rather stolid, who obviously would stand no nonsense, expected a good deal of free time and a month's holiday and showed not the least timidity towards Lady Fox. On the other hand, she had splendid references, a pleasant voice and manner and her typing, after Matilda's home-taught efforts, was excellent. She was engaged and Matilda sighed with relief for she had known all along that, if no one had been forthcoming to take her place, she would have felt compelled to stay until someone turned up.

She had gone to see Roseanne several times, driving herself in her father's elderly car, and found her much improved. Bernard had gone again but had promised to return each weekend and, since he had the good sense to take a pile of magazines with him, Roseanne was quite happy sitting up in bed, looking at soft furnishings, tables and chairs and the like, planning their home when they married.

Dr Bramley had been quite right, thought Matilda on her way home after a particularly cheerful visit; love worked wonders. Which thought, naturally enough, led her to Mr Scott-Thurlow.

She wished that she could see him again, but although he had been back to the hospital to see Roseanne she had never been there at the same time. Perhaps it was just as well. A job, she told herself firmly, something else to think about, new people to meet and occupy her mind.

She left Lady Fox's employ ostensibly on good terms with that lady. Her father saw a good deal of Sir Benjamin and it would never do to have ill feeling between the manor-house and the rectory. On Sunday, Miss Twisk, who had taken her place, was to be seen sitting where Roseanne usually sat in the family pew and Lady Fox, on her way out after the service, bowed graciously towards the rectory pew—on the surface at least bygones were to be bygones.

It was delightful to be free of her various little tasks at the manor-house; over the weeks she helped her mother make rhubarb jam, poked around very happily in the large untidy garden, painted one of the numerous sheds which were dotted haphazardly around and then, since the weather was warm and sunny, she embarked

on the drawing-room curtains, well worn and faded.
Mrs Chump had rummaged around her stock and found
a dye in a pleasant shade of old rose and Matilda set to.
It was a messy business but she was pleased with the
result as she hung them up to dry. Still in a serviceable
pinny, she went back into the house and sat down in the
kitchen to drink her coffee with her mother and Mrs
Coffin. The old fashioned bell, first in the row ranged
beside the dresser, disturbed their casual gossip.

'Front door, drat it,' said Mrs Coffin. 'It'll be Postie,
and why 'e 'as to make such a din…' She got up. 'The
dear knows what 'e'll be up to next.'

She went away and Matilda kicked off her sandals
and lolled back in her old basket chair. She said, 'Today
I shall go to Sherborne and look for a job.'

Mrs ffinch put down her coffee-mug. 'Darling, but
what will you do?'

'I've no idea—something will turn up…' She smiled
at her mother and turned round to see what Mrs Coffin
had been given by the postman.

Not a parcel and not the postman either. Mr Scott-
Thurlow came through the door behind Mrs Coffin,
bending his handsome head so as not to knock himself
out on its lintel.

Matilda, to her great annoyance, blushed at the sight
of him; her mother beamed a welcome and got to her
feet. 'Good morning, Mr Scott-Thurlow—you're just
in time for coffee. Do sit down. Have you been over at
the manor-house?'

She patted the Windsor armchair beside her and
Matilda, glad of something to do, got up to get the
coffee-pot from the Aga.

'You must forgive me for calling at such a time, Mrs

ffinch. Yes, I called at the manor on my way back from seeing Roseanne. She is doing well now.'

He took the mug Matilda offered him and Mrs Coffin said, 'Well, I'll get on with the bedrooms, me loves,' and took herself off.

Before she left the kitchen Matilda, strangely reluctant to be with Mr Scott-Thurlow, asked, 'Do you want any help with the beds?' and had actually got out of her chair again, intent on escape, when he said quietly,

'Please don't go, Matilda; it was you I came to talk to.'

'Me?' She sat down again. 'Whatever for?'

He smiled a little, and Mrs ffinch said briskly, 'Oh, well, I must get on—such a large house, you know, always something to do...'

'Please stay, Mrs ffinch. I have a suggestion to make to Matilda. I understand that she no longer goes to the manor and I wondered if she would be interested in a temporary job—not far away—between Sherborne and Montacute. An old gentleman whose wife is in hospital for a few weeks. There is a housekeeper and plenty of help in the house but he needs companionship, someone to read to him, play cards, potter in the garden with him, listen while he talks... You would of course need to live there but there is no reason why you shouldn't come home at the weekends. There is no hard work involved but it may be dull and perhaps at times demanding. The salary...' The sum he mentioned made Matilda's eyes open wide.

'Too much,' she said roundly.

'Indeed not,' he told her seriously, 'taking into account the fact that you will have very little time to yourself save at the weekend.' He didn't smile. 'I hope that you will consider it very seriously, Matilda.'

She loved him very much, but at the same time she was aware that she was just a little in awe of him; he looked and spoke exactly how an eminent surgeon should—courteous and impersonal and remote. She had no idea what he was thinking behind that calm face. She frowned. 'When do you want to know?'

'Now.'

She looked at her mother and found that lady smiling. 'You were only saying, Tilly dear, that you were going to look for a little job in Sherborne today.' Her parent gave her a guileless look.

'How would I get there? Is there a bus? And how do I get home for the weekend?'

'You would be driven there. You drive, do you not? I believe that there is a car you might use at weekends.'

'When would this gentleman want me to go?' She looked down at her pinny. 'I've been dyeing curtains...'

Mr Scott-Thurlow, who knew nothing of dyeing curtains, let this pass.

'Tomorrow afternoon?' he suggested gently. 'Try it for a week—if you aren't happy then the matter can be arranged.' He got up. 'I must get back to town—may I pick you up about three o'clock tomorrow?'

Matilda heard herself say yes as her mother went out of the room with him. It was only as she heard the front door squeak when it was opened that she realised that she didn't know the name of her new employer. She ran through the house, swept past her mother about to shut the door and raced down the garden path to where Mr Scott-Thurlow was getting into his car. He was in it by the time she reached it and she poked her head through the window, her bright hair all over the place, her lovely face inches from his.

'His name?' she demanded urgently. 'What's his name, this old gentleman?'

He allowed himself the pleasure of studying her face before he answered. 'Scott-Thurlow—Mr Charles Scott-Thurlow. My grandfather.'

A man of reserve, not given to impulse, he kissed the face, so temptingly close, raised a hand in grave salute and drove himself away.

Matilda stood staring after the car, a prey to mixed feelings: delight, surprise—and why had he kissed her? He was engaged, wasn't he? To a beautiful woman, and what would she say if she knew? Or perhaps in her particular social circle the odd kiss didn't count for anything. But it hadn't been an odd kiss...

Mr Scott-Thurlow was having mixed feelings too. After years of knowing exactly what he wanted, and that included a suitable marriage to someone who would make no demands upon his dedicated life, run his house well and take care of the social side of his life, he was experiencing an overpowering wish to see Matilda again and as often as possible. She would wreak havoc in his orderly life, she was impulsive, quick-tempered, given to speaking her mind upon occasion and, from what he had seen of her, uncaring about her appearance.

He shot past a busload of people who waved but he didn't notice. He must uproot the girl before she became important to him... He regretted now that he had offered to drive her to his grandfather's house, reflecting with his usual honesty that he had thought the whole thing up in the first place because he had wanted to see more of her. It was true that his grandfather was in need of company but he could have called upon any number of suitable middle-aged ladies to fulfil that office. He could of course take a few days off; a change of scene would help. Perhaps Rhoda would go with him. He viewed the idea with no enthusiasm.

He had a list that afternoon; he thrust Matilda out of his mind and concentrated upon pinning and plating a shattered leg, a laminectomy for the removal of a spinal tumour and a meniscectomy to relieve a torn cartilage. These done to his satisfaction, he drank the tea Theatre Sister had ready for him, bade her a courteous good day and repaired to the consultant's room where he found an urgent message from his secretary asking him to telephone her.

There had been a mine disaster in Spitsbergen and he was asked to go there to advise upon several cases which might require his particular skill. He accepted at once and spent the rest of the day making arrangements for his registrar to take over from him, booking a flight for the next day and then telephoning the rectory. Mrs ffinch answered.

'You want to fetch Matilda in the morning? Of course that's all right—she's out at the moment but she's quite ready to leave. I'll tell her—ten o'clock? She'll be waiting.'

Mr Scott-Thurlow put the phone down with a sigh; circumstances, unhappy for some, had dealt with his problem very nicely. He whistled the dogs, and with Theobald under one arm—for he was still something of an invalid—he walked to Regent's Park, which he strode from end to end and then back again, much to the dogs' delight. Despite the exercise he had little appetite for the excellent dinner Twigg, his man, served to him.

A circumstance which made that faithful servant observe to his wife, 'It's not like him, Mavis, not like him at all. Something's up and it's nothing to do with going to Spitsbergen; he's always off here, there and everywhere and never turns a hair.'

'That Miss Symes?' suggested Mrs Twigg, who didn't like her.

He shook his bald head. 'Can't be—he was on the phone to her, saying he couldn't go to some concert or other with her, quite affable too.'

MATILDA WAS QUITE ready when he arrived at the rectory the next morning. She had dressed carefully in a wide flowery skirt and a plain cotton blouse with a matching cardigan, and she had taken great pains with her hair and face. Mr Scott-Thurlow took one look at her and then wished her a coolly detached good morning. She supposed that he had had a busy time of it since she had seen him last, and at the thought blushed. She hadn't expected him to refuse the coffee her mother had ready. Pressure of work, he explained pleasantly, and ushered her out to the car without loss of time.

There was no need to go into Sherborne; country roads skirting round the north of the town took them to Mackrell Cantelo, a small village between the A303 and Yeovil and as remote as Abner Magna. Throughout the short journey Mr Scott-Thurlow had had little to say. Matilda had essayed a few remarks, to be met with pleasantly non-committal replies. She had been looking forward to the trip, longing for it, in fact, but now she felt uneasy; her companion having withdrawn behind a bland face and manner. They were almost there when she hit on the answer. He was letting her see that his interest in her was purely superficial; a chance acquaintance who most providentially could fill a needed job. The kiss had been sheer relief on his part—well, he need have no fears that she had imagined otherwise. She lapsed into a dignified silence, studying the scenery as though she had never seen it before and smouldering inwardly.

They swept through Mackrell Cantelo, turned in between stone pillars and drew up before a nice old house, eighteenth century, with stone mullioned windows and a red tiled roof and set in grounds planted with rhododendrons, ornamental trees and shrubs of all kinds and boasting a small lake to one side of the house. Mr Scott-Thurlow stopped before the front door, got out to help Matilda and crossed the gravel sweep with her beside him. He didn't ring the ancient bell-pull beside the door but opened it and without delay walked in. The lobby opened into a large square hall, very pleasant and light with a polished wood floor partly covered by Persian rugs, its walls, panelled in some light wood, hung with paintings and across which hurried a spruce middle-aged man, neatly dressed.

'Ah, Slocombe, how are you?' Mr Scott-Thurlow turned to Matilda. 'Slocombe runs the house for my grandparents and is a tower of strength. You will find him the greatest help. Slocombe, this is Miss ffinch— you already know that she will keep my grandfather company until my grandmother returns home.'

Slocombe bowed his head gravely at Matilda, who stepped forwards and offered a hand. 'I'm sure I shall be glad of your advice,' she told him and Mr Scott-Thurlow watched the older man succumb to her friendly smile and green eyes.

'Your grandfather is waiting for you, Mr James,' said Slocombe and led the way across the hall, into a large room with windows back and front.

The old gentleman who got up as they went in must have been as big a man as his grandson when he was younger and even now, in his eighties, he was upright and remarkably handsome with a fine head of white hair and the blue eyes his grandson had inherited. Matilda, as usual, allowed her imagination to go to work; in fifty years' time James would look exactly like that, it would be their golden wedding anniversary and they would be surrounded by children and grandchildren... She was suddenly aware that both gentlemen were looking at her, wearing the same half-smile, their eyebrows tilted at exactly the same angle.

'Matilda, this is my grandfather. I'm sure you will be able to help him pass the time until my grandmother comes home again.'

Matilda shook hands with the old gentleman—she liked him at once, but of course she would; he was James's grandfather and therefore to be cherished. 'I do hope so,' she said and smiled widely.

'You'll stay for lunch, James?'

'Regretfully, no. I must be on my way—I've a plane to catch.'

Matilda had an instant and vivid picture of him boarding Concorde with Rhoda, off to some exotic island.

'Ah, yes, of course, the mine disaster in Spitsbergen. Several in your line, no doubt.'

'I fear so.' He shook his grandfather's hand. 'I'll see you when I get back.'

'Taking Rhoda with you?' asked his grandfather.

His grandson looked astounded. 'Rhoda to Spitsbergen? I doubt if she knows where it is.'

'A very beautiful woman,' observed his grandparent. 'I wish I could come with you.'

'So do I.' The two men smiled at each other and Mr Scott-Thurlow turned to Matilda, standing so quietly beside them. 'Take care of him, Matilda,' he said pleasantly and had gone before she had even nodded her head.

'Now, my dear, shall we have a drink just to get to know each other? Slocombe will have taken your things upstairs and Mrs Slocombe will take you to your room presently. A pity James couldn't stay, but of course it's quite a longish flight to Spitsbergen.'

'You said a mine disaster—is that the one I read about in the paper this morning?'

'Yes, they're well equipped there for accidents and so on, there's an excellent hospital at Ny Alesund, but when there's a disaster of any sort then they need extra help. James has been before of course. A good chap— told me when he was quite a small chap that he would be as good a surgeon as his father, and he is. Bones, of course—it runs in the family.'

Matilda sipped her sherry. 'Your wife...' she began tentatively.

'Having a prosthesis—hip joint, you know. A colleague of James's did it last week. Normally she would come home but she's an independent woman, doesn't want to be an invalid in her own home, so she will stay at the nursing home until she is fit—three weeks or so, so she tells me.' He added, 'I do miss her.'

'I'm sure you do, but how nice to look forward to having her home again in a week or two with a new hip.'

'Yes, yes. She's a keen gardener, you know, able to name every flower she's ever grown.' He sighed, 'Never got over James's father dying like that. His mother too—a nice little thing she was, and quite devoted.'

He closed his eyes and was all at once asleep and she sat there quietly, her thoughts with Mr Scott-Thurlow driving himself to the airport, going hundreds of miles at a few hours' notice because he was needed. His grandfather had called him a 'good chap', which from that rather austere gentleman was probably high praise—she thought of him in warmer terms; he was everything she had ever hoped for in a husband, only there was no chance of his being that...

'Do you play chess, Matilda?'

Mr Scott-Thurlow senior had opened his very blue eyes and was watching her.

'Me? Chess? Well, in a manner of speaking—I'm really bad at it, so my father says.'

'Splendid. I shall beat you each evening after dinner. Now tell me all about your family.'

Which she did until Slocombe came quietly into the room to remind them that lunch would be in half an hour and would Miss ffinch like to go to her room first?

Matilda was led up the curved staircase by Mrs Slocombe, stout and friendly. Her room was at the side of the house, overlooking the gardens, and was rather charmingly furnished with white-painted bed and dressing-table, an easy chair or two, a pretty little lamp table and carpeted in a soft blue, echoed in the curtains and bedspread. There were flowers and books too and a small bathroom leading from it.

'Anything you want, my love, just you ask,' said Mrs Slocombe in her soft West Country voice. 'There's

Alice the housemaid lives in; she'll bring you tea in the morning. Mr Scott-Thurlow eats his breakfast early—eight o'clock sharp. Miss Symes, when she's visited here, has hers in her bed—don't like to rise before ten o'clock or thereabouts.'

'If it's all right I'd like to come down for breakfast—I'm used to getting up early. That is if Mr Scott-Thurlow won't mind.'

"'E don't hold with lying in bed of a morning, miss. You come down and welcome.'

She trotted off, leaving Matilda to explore her room, hang out of the window and finally sit down at the dressing-table to tidy her person.

They both enjoyed lunch; they discussed a variety of subjects, arguing happily and at length until they parted company for the afternoon, he to take a nap in the library, she to explore the house at his invitation.

'Tea at four o'clock,' he told her. 'I enjoy my tea, and if you have nothing better to do you can go through the post for me and deal with anything that needs looking into. And we might have that game of chess...'

It was that evening, after he had beaten her soundly and declared that he would go to bed that he observed, 'James will be in Norway by now.'

'How will he get to Spitsbergen from there?'

'Well, he will have flown to Oslo and then taken a plane to Tromso, that's in the north, and from there he'll get a light aircraft to Spitsbergen. Or perhaps a helicopter.'

'It will be late when he gets there.'

'Or early morning. I dare say there is other stuff being flown out—tools and so on.'

'He'll be tired,' said Matilda.

The old man agreed quietly, his eyes suddenly alert, but all he said was, 'Well, I'm for bed. Do I see you at breakfast?'

'If you would like that, yes.'

'My wife has never been one to languish in bed until all hours. Until she needed to go to hospital we breakfasted together every morning. We will visit her tomorrow. I go each day in the morning. James tells me that you drive. Slocombe will be delighted, for it has upset his morning's routine having to take me there and wait to bring me back.'

'Is the hospital far away?'

He mentioned a private hospital on the road to Bath. 'Half an hour or so, and it's a good road.'

Matilda slept soundly, ate a good breakfast in the old gentleman's company and then, a little nervously, got behind the wheel of the Daimler Slocombe had brought to the door, but she soon forgot to be nervous—the car ran like a dream and the roads were quiet. At the hospital Mr Scott-Thurlow broke the silence. 'Very nice, my dear. My dear wife does not drive, but of course all young women should do so nowadays—shopping, children to school. You will find it useful when you marry.'

Matilda said bleakly, 'I don't expect to marry...'

'But you will.' He smiled at her and looked exactly like his grandson, so that her heart lurched.

Mrs Scott-Thurlow was sitting in a pleasant room full of flowers. Her husband kissed her tenderly, told her that she looked beautiful and introduced Matilda.

'Ah, yes,' said Mrs Scott-Thurlow, 'James was quite right.' She smiled brilliantly. 'He told me that you were beautiful too. My grandson, you know.' She nodded her head so that the silvery hair danced around her pretty elderly face. 'He seldom notices women. It's time he took his nose out of that hospital and looked around him...'

'I fancy he has done so,' observed her husband and Matilda, turning the knife in the wound, said brightly, 'His fiancée is very beautiful; I met her once.'

'Ah, yes—you were in London, were you not? Did you enjoy your stay there?'

'Well, it was most interesting,' began Matilda carefully, 'but I'd rather live in the country.'

A nurse brought a tray of coffee and presently Matilda sauntered out, having said that she would like to look at the garden if no one minded, leaving the two old people together.

They were a delightful pair and they were fond of their grandson, but she suspected that they shared a life which they had made their own. For a small boy who had just lost his parents that had been a barrier, and he had sensed it and never overcome it although he must have come to terms with it now that he was a man with a well-established life of his own. 'But no roots,' said Matilda, talking to herself, and since there was no one else to talk to she added, 'He needs a home and a wife and a clutch of children to warm him and that Rhoda will never do that. He'll get more and more remote because she won't expect him to be anything else, and the children, if they have any, will see him for a few minutes each day and he won't know how to talk to them, just as his grandparents didn't know how to talk to him.' She plucked a weed with a good deal of unnecessary force. 'Something must be done.'

The choice wasn't great; even if she had been an

unscrupulous girl it would have been difficult to divert Mr Scott-Thurlow's affections from Rhoda, who was beautiful, amusing and shared his background. Matilda, aware that she was very pretty was none the less not conceited about it—besides, he had demonstrated clearly enough that he had absolutely no interest in her. Here she paused to mull over the kiss he had given her. It had been done on the spur of the moment; probably he had been thankful that she had agreed to stay with his grandfather… She dismissed the occurrence, although she would have like to linger over it, and returned to the vexed question of Rhoda. Perhaps if she got to know her? Persuaded her that James needed to be loved and teased a little and even annoyed a bit from time to time, made aware of the fact that there was a good life outside his working world? In ten years' time, thought Matilda unhappily, he would be so wrapped up in his world of surgery that he might just as well not have married.

She started to wander back, deep in thought. Why on earth had he decided to marry the girl? Rhoda liked a social life and, granted, she would be a splendid hostess and no doubt run his house admirably—would she like waiting up if he got called out in the evening, or getting his slippers when he got home or making sure that he had enough to eat? It would be easier if she knew more about his personal life—and Rhoda's too. 'I am an interfering busybody,' said Matilda softly to herself, 'and I want him for me not her, but I can't have him so I'd better try and help.'

A depressing thought struck her; perhaps he liked Rhoda like that, cool and undemonstrative and slightly bored—at least she had appeared so to Matilda, but who knew what she was like when she was alone with

James? It was a sobering thought; perhaps she would do well to hold her tongue and forget him, but she would have to wait until Mrs Scott-Thurlow was back home again and she could go home herself and wipe him clean out of her mind.

Mr Scott-Thurlow was ready to leave. Mrs Scott-Thurlow gave her a kind smile. 'I feel so much easier in my mind now that you are at home, my dear. The Slocombes are old servants and friends but it is company my husband needs. Do let me know the moment you hear from James.'

He telephoned that evening. Matilda happened to be by the phone in the sitting-room when it rang and Mr Scott-Thurlow, unable to get out of his chair with any kind of speed, asked her to answer it.

She said, 'Yes?' in a wispy voice, sure that it was James. It was; his voice, very clear from all those miles away, sent her heart racing.

'Matilda? I should like to speak to my grandfather...'

That was that as far as she was concerned. She went out of the room once the old gentleman was settled by the phone and went upstairs to her room and hung out of the window, looking at the late spring evening. He could at least have said how are you, or even hello. She went downstairs again and out of a side-door into the garden and stayed there until Slocombe opened the french window in the drawing-room and reminded her that the drinks had been poured.

Mr Scott-Thurlow was chatty. 'What a blessing the telephone can be,' he observed happily, 'although I suppose it must be complicated between here and Spitsbergen. A clear line though. James is busy, but he expected to be. He won't be back for a week—there were some bad injuries and the hospital is full. He will be ringing again in a few days' time. I let my wife know, of course—he sent a number of messages.'

None for me, thought Matilda peevishly. Out loud she said, 'I expect it's difficult telephoning all that way. I expect Miss Symes is anxious, but I dare say there's a way in which she can phone him.' To make it sound more casual she added, 'There's a time difference, isn't there?'

'Yes. I don't imagine Rhoda will telephone him; I believe that she leads a very busy life.' His voice was dry.

'I should think she would—she is so beautiful, and attractive too.' She spoke sincerely; she didn't like Rhoda but that was no reason to be spiteful about her, especially to this nice old man who would shortly be her grandfather-in-law.

The days passed pleasantly; chess, strolls in the garden, listening to Mr Scott-Thurlow talking about every subject under the sun. Matilda found that there wasn't a dull moment. They went each day to see Mrs Scott-Thurlow, although Matilda only stayed in the room for a few minutes, tactfully absenting herself for an hour or so. She got to know the grounds of the hospital rather well and she would stroll up and down thinking about James.

She would have liked to know so much more about him but his grandfather rarely spoke of his private life and she couldn't ask. He didn't talk about Rhoda either but Matilda was after all a stranger, filling a gap until his wife returned home. That wouldn't be too long, she was told, as it was now only a question of finding a suitable nurse to stay with her for a week or so until she felt quite able to be independent.

Matilda went home at the weekend, glad to see everyone again and tell them about her job.

'Sounds cushy to me,' said Esme. 'How long will you be there?'

'Not long, another week or two at the most.'

'It will be nice to have you at home again, Tilly,' said her mother.

'Yes, Mother, but I shall find another job as soon as possible. I can ask for a reference...'

She was welcomed back warmly. 'I missed you, Matilda,' said Mr Scott-Thurlow. 'The house seemed very quiet. We seldom have visitors, you know.'

One came the very next day—Rhoda Symes!

CHAPTER FIVE

RHODA DROVE UP in a Porsche just as they were getting ready to visit Mrs Scott-Thurlow. It was a bright red car and she wore a scarlet suede jacket over a black dress, not suitable for the country but very eye-catching. She got out of the car slowly and came towards them as they stood poised to get into the Daimler.

'Hello,' she called, 'I've been at Brooke House for the weekend and it seemed a good idea to come and see you on my way back to town.' She kissed Mr Scott-Thurlow's cheek. 'I've had a marvellous time—a pity James couldn't have been with me.' She looked at Matilda then. 'Haven't I seen you before? Of course, at that boring picture gallery with Roseanne Fox, and aren't you the girl who cooked the dinner? James told me about it—what a joke.' She turned back to the old gentleman. 'And where is Mrs Scott-Thurlow? Is she—' she nodded towards Matilda '—the new cook?'

Matilda admired Mr Scott-Thurlow's nice manners. 'My wife has had an operation; Matilda is most kindly staying here to keep me company until she is back home. Did you not know?'

'Oh, I believe James did say something about it—but I've got the most awful memory, especially about anything unpleasant.'

'Have you heard from him?'

'I told him not to bother to phone or write, he'll only be away for a week or so. Why he has to go to these awful God-forsaken places…! He can take his pick of all the private patients he wants in town.' She looked at the car. 'Are you going somewhere? Am I keeping you?'

'We're going to see my wife. Perhaps you would like to come along too?'

'Love to. Is she in that nice place outside Bath? A friend of mine went there to have something or other done; wildly expensive too.' She gave Mr Scott-Thurlow a charming smile. 'You tootle along, I'll follow.'

Matilda drove silently, afraid that if she spoke she might say something she would regret afterwards. She was on fire with rage and a strong wish to tear Rhoda's hair out by the roots and then take a pair of sharp scissors to that red jacket. She kept these reprehensible thoughts to herself with difficulty and was relieved when they arrived at the hospital. Mr Scott-Thurlow hadn't spoken either, only as they got out of the car he gave her an understanding smile.

The visit wasn't a success. Rhoda was charming but Matilda saw Mrs Scott-Thurlow bristle with anger when she was referred to as a poor old thing. Old she might be, but poor she certainly was not, and it was doubtful if anyone had ever dared to call her that before. She couldn't be faulted in her manner towards Rhoda; she listened to Rhoda's high and very clear voice, recounting the fun she had had over the weekend, and her plans for future entertainment. 'When James gets back I'll see that he gets out and about,' she declared. 'There are several good parties and it's months since we went to the theatre together.'

Matilda, after a decent interval, said that she would

take her usual stroll in the grounds and, mindful of the old people's wish to be alone for a time, invited Rhoda to go with her.

'Whatever for? Gardens bore me unless they're spectacular—besides, whatever should we talk about?' She gave a little rippling laugh. 'Cooking?'

Matilda kept her pretty face smiling although her eyes darted green fire. 'About half an hour?' she asked, and, receiving a nod from Mr Scott-Thurlow, wandered off. Trying to walk off her temper she reflected that if Rhoda was staying for lunch she herself would have a bad headache. 'What can he see in the girl?' she asked the hospital cat, sitting in a sunny corner. 'But perhaps she never talks like that when he's with her.'

They drove back presently and Rhoda, after the briefest of goodbyes and declining coffee or lunch, shot away in the Porsche.

Mr Scott-Thurlow led the way into the house as the car disappeared into the lane and there was no mistaking his air of relief although he said nothing, merely asking her to see if Slocombe would bring them some coffee. 'I know it's almost time for lunch, but a cup would be nice. Have one with me, Matilda.'

So she sat with him, drinking first coffee and then a glass of sherry and then going in to lunch, all the while chatting about nothing in particular and never a word about Rhoda, sensing that he was upset.

The days went by, pleasantly enough. Mrs Scott-Thurlow was to return home in a week's time, accompanied by a nurse, a placid little woman who didn't fuss. She was already at the hospital and her patient liked her. She joined Matilda on her morning strolls in the grounds and they got on well together.

'I shall go home as soon as you get back with Mrs Scott-Thurlow,' said Matilda. 'I came just to keep Mr Scott-Thurlow company. I've enjoyed every minute of it too; they have been so kind and really I've had nothing to do.'

'Well, there will be precious little work for me,' Nurse Watkins said. 'A couple of weeks, perhaps less, and I'll be off again.'

'Oh, don't you work at the hospital all the time?'

'No. I work for an agency but I take Mr Scott-Thurlow's—that's the grandson's—patients. I wouldn't want to work for anyone else; he's marvellous. I've been with him for years now. He's in Spitsbergen, operating on the bone injuries from that mine disaster, but, just fancy, he found time to telephone the agency asking for me to come and look after his granny. He's a wonderful man. Have you met him?'

'Well, yes, but I don't know him well...'

'He's engaged, you know. To a hoity-toity piece—well, I shouldn't have said that, I dare say she's all right, just not my sort. I don't think she's his sort either, but that's neither here nor there.'

It was the following morning that Mrs Scott-Thurlow, after greeting her husband, told him to take Nurse Watkins for a walk round the grounds. 'I want to talk to Matilda—all we ever say to each other is good morning and goodbye and she will be leaving us soon.'

As the door closed behind the other two she said, 'Come and sit down here beside me, my dear. I have to thank you for being such good company for Charles; it has been the greatest help to him during this tiresome time. I told my grandson that when he telephoned me yesterday. It was a splendid idea to ask you in the first place. He tells me that you were actually going to a job when he asked that you should come to us, and reminded me to allow you to leave just as soon as I am home again, so you must make your plans. Slocombe will drive you to your home.' She leaned over and patted Matilda's hands, lying idly in her lap. 'We shall miss you and I hope that you will visit us from time to time. And now that is settled tell me something of your family and your life.'

'There's not much to tell,' observed Matilda, and embarked on a description of life at Abner Magna while she seethed silently. James Scott-Thurlow didn't deserve to be loved—he was a nasty cold-blooded creature who, as soon as he had got what he wanted from someone, ignored them; got rid of them just as he was getting rid of her. He deserved Rhoda—in fact the girl was too good for him!

She was finishing a light-hearted account of bingo in the village hall when the others came back, and she said goodbye to Mrs Scott-Thurlow and tactfully went out to the car with Nurse Watkins.

'A very nice girl,' declared the old lady to her husband when they were alone, 'and such a charming voice and manner. I wonder what is worrying her…?'

'Worrying her? What should be? She seems content enough.'

'Yes, dear, I am sure that she's as happy as possible with you. All the same I must find out.' She added casually, 'I suppose she has met James?'

'Of course—he fixed her up with us, didn't he? Besides, I remember her saying that she had met him at some exhibition or other. Anyway, he drove her down, didn't he? So of course they've met even if that was for the first time. You can't count that exhibition—I dare say they were introduced and didn't speak. Why do you ask?'

'No reason, my dear,' said his wife airily. She bade him goodbye and, when she was alone, sat in deep thought, frowning a little.

The day came when they were to fetch Mrs Scott-Thurlow back home. The Slocombes had polished and cleaned and, with Matilda helping out, put flowers in every room, and a festive lunch had been arranged. She got into the car and drove it for the last time to the hospital. She was packed and ready to leave that very afternoon; Slocombe was to drive her home, and although she didn't want to go in the least she could see that it would be much easier for Nurse Watkins if she wasn't there. 'Too many cooks spoil the broth,' said Matilda, which wasn't quite what she meant but near enough.

They were met in the hall by the matron, looking apologetic.

'There is a slight hitch,' she began. 'Nurse Watkins had severe toothache during the night and she is even now at the dentist. I phoned just a few minutes ago and he tells me that he has taken the tooth out but recommends that she should have a day's quiet before resuming her work. Shall we keep Mrs Scott-Thurlow until tomorrow, when I'm sure that Nurse Watkins will be well enough to accompany her home, or would you be able to manage for a day?'

Mr Scott-Thurlow didn't hesitate. 'Miss ffinch here will look after my wife until Nurse Watkins can join us—we cannot disappoint her after our plans have been made.'

Matilda opened her mouth and then shut it again—
there was no point in making an awkward situation
more awkward—and when he turned to her and said,
'You don't mind, do you, Matilda?' she shook her head
meekly and murmured that of course it didn't matter
at all.

So they drove back again with Mrs Scott-Thurlow
sitting in the back with her husband, so delighted to be
going home again that she was on the verge of tears.

Everyone in the house came to welcome her home.
She was led tenderly into the sitting-room, sat in a
suitable chair, offered coffee and fussed over while the
old gentleman watched with a delighted smile.

There were enough people there, Matilda decided, so
she got the luggage from the boot and carried it upstairs
and unpacked it and put everything away in what she
hoped were the proper cupboards and drawers, and then
went down to the kitchen to tell Mrs Slocombe what she
had done and offer to give a hand with lunch. Mrs Scott-
Thurlow was quite comfortable, talking quietly with her
happy husband—they would have a lot to say to each
other before they sat down to the splendid meal which
Mrs Slocombe had prepared, and after that, Matilda
reflected, she would suggest a little nap until teatime.

Mrs Slocombe was standing at the table beating eggs.
'There you are, miss. Madam would like to go to her
room to tidy herself and won't take no for an answer...'

Matilda and the old lady went very slowly up the
staircase, watched by her anxious husband from the
hall. 'You see,' said Mrs Scott-Thurlow triumphantly
when they reached the gallery above, 'I knew I could
do it.'

All the same, Matilda persuaded her to sit down for

ten minutes while she combed the pretty white hair and powdered the haughty little nose. Mrs Scott-Thurlow was impatient. 'We will go back now and sit for a few minutes, and we will have a glass of sherry, my dear.'

So they trundled downstairs, which wasn't as easy as going up had been; all the same, they reached the drawing-room safely and Matilda sat her down in the chair again.

'I would like a shawl,' said Mrs Scott-Thurlow, 'just for my shoulders. Matilda, will you go to my room and get one? There should be several in the commode drawer, and when you come back we will all have that drink.'

Matilda closed the double doors behind her and started across the hall. She had taken herself half a dozen steps when the house door was flung open and James Scott-Thurlow strode in. He saw her at once and she gave him a delighted smile and started towards him.

'What in the name of the almighty are you doing here?' he demanded, his voice as cold as the Arctic regions he had just left. 'I arranged for a nurse...'

Not even a hello, thought Matilda crossly, and however did she allow herself to fall in love with such a rude, bad-tempered man?

'Arrangements go wrong sometimes,' she told him waspishly. '"There's many a slip," you know. Nurse Watkins had to have a tooth out, and I'm to stay until she gets here tomorrow. Too bad, isn't it? But I'll go the very moment she has put a foot inside the door.'

She turned her back on him and went up the staircase. She was in the gallery before she heard the drawing-room doors open and shut.

She took as long as possible finding the shawl; she

had no wish to go back to the drawing-room, but on the other hand if she didn't show herself he would think that she was feeling awkward about their meeting in the hall.

'Bother him,' she told her reflection in Mrs Scott-Thurlow's dressing-table mirror. 'I don't care if I never see him again.' Upon which heartening lie she took herself downstairs once more.

He was sitting between his grandparents but he got up when she went in. 'Ah, Matilda, come and sit down and have a glass of sherry.' He pulled a small armchair forwards for her and went to the drinks tray. 'It is most kind of you to stay until Nurse Watkins gets here. Have you had time to phone your mother?'

No one could have been more polite or easy-mannered. She accepted the sherry, muttered that yes, thank you, she had already phoned home, and lapsed into silence. Presently Slocombe came to tell them that lunch was ready and she went into the dining-room with the old gentleman behind his wife and grandson.

'Splendid to see James back, my dear. His grand-mother is delighted. We must get him to tell us some-thing of his work on Spitsbergen; I'm sure it will be most interesting. So delightful that he will be staying the night.'

Matilda agreed with him, her feelings mixed.

The conversation at table was general; the old gentleman asked about the weather in Spitsbergen, the local amenities and the scenery, but he asked no questions as to his grandson's work, nor did James mention it. Matilda, speaking when spoken to on such topics as the habitat of the wildlife there, the plants to be found and similar sidelights on life in the Arctic Circle, found it strange that no one was agog with questions about James's own life and work there. Now, if she had been at home, she reflected, just returned from some place or other, everyone would have wanted to know everything concerning her, never mind the flora and fauna. The three people at the table with her were all so polite and detached; she had no doubt that they were fond of each other but they seemed unable to show it. She wondered if they had been so detached when he was a small boy, thrust into their lives at a moment's notice, and if that was why he was so reserved. She made up her mind there and then to find out.

It would be difficult. She remembered James Scott-Thurlow's somewhat acid remarks when she had asked him rather a lot of questions in his car. He had called it a cross-examination; he wouldn't take kindly to any prying on her part.

She coaxed a rather tired old lady upstairs to have a nap when they had finished lunch and then went to her room and sat in a chair by the window. It was a splendid day and she would have liked to have gone into the garden, but she wanted to avoid Mr Scott-Thurlow: besides if he and his grandfather wanted to talk she would be a nuisance. She poked her head out into the summer sunshine and was accosted from below.

'Come on down, Matilda,' said old Mr Scott-Thurlow. 'James is going to tell me something of his stay in Spitsbergen.'

'Later perhaps?' She thought wildly for an excuse. 'Mrs Scott-Thurlow is a little unsettled; I thought I might read to her for a while.'

'A good idea. Please come down when you can.'

She withdrew her head and sat down again and since

she had said that she was going to read aloud she had better go and suggest it. The old lady was sound asleep.

For the rest of that day Matilda contrived to keep in the background, and since Mrs Scott-Thurlow had had strict instructions to go to bed in good time she was able to accompany her to her room to help her to bed. This took some time so that, beyond polite regrets, neither gentleman appeared put out when she bade them goodnight and went to bed herself. It was a lovely evening—just right for a stroll in the gardens. With James Scott-Thurlow, of course; such a pity that she was forced to go to bed instead. If she had been Rhoda... Matilda had a very hot bath and, as pink as a lobster, got into her bed and lay listening to the drone of the men's voices coming faintly from the open windows of the drawing-room below. Old Mr Scott-Thurlow's rather slow voice, and his grandson's, deep and deliberate. She closed her eyes and slept.

It was pouring with rain when she woke in the morning, dressed and went down to the dining-room. It was barely eight o'clock and she hoped that she would be able to eat her breakfast, or at least most of it, before anyone else came down. She was doomed to disappointment—Mr Scott-Thurlow the younger was already there, reading *The Times* newspaper and consuming bacon, mushrooms and eggs. He got up when she went in, gave her a polite good morning and begged her to help herself. She noticed that she folded the paper and put it on the table beside him with a faint air of annoyance, so that she said in a voice she strove to keep amiable, 'Don't stop reading for me; I don't mind in the least.'

She poured coffee, filled a plate with bacon and egg

and began to eat. There was a slight edge to her voice as she went on, 'So unfortunate that I should still be here, isn't it? I'm going immediately after I've seen to Mrs Scott-Thurlow.'

It was disconcerting when he didn't answer, and, quite reckless because she wouldn't be seeing him again, she added sharply, 'Well, has the cat got your tongue?'

He leaned back in his chair and looked her over. 'What an abominable girl you are, Matilda; I'm not surprised your hair is so fiery for you have a temper to match it.' He poured himself some more coffee. 'And why should you suppose that I should object to finding you still here?'

'The look on your face when you saw me,' she said, not beating about the bush. She glanced across at him and all her ill humour evaporated at the sight of his weary face. 'Heavens, you're worn out; was it very busy at Spitsbergen?'

His eyebrows rose. 'Why the volte-face? But yes, I was kept busy.'

'Then you should take a holiday,' said Matilda, 'and have some fun. Miss Symes was here, you know, and she said there were several parties she would take you to when you got back.'

'And is that your idea of fun?'

'Parties? No, well, I'm different, aren't I?'

She didn't hear his, 'Indeed you are.'

'I mean, I don't fit in awfully well—with your kind of people. I like dining out and dancing and going to the theatre, but there's no conversation at parties, is there? Or, if there is, I can never hear it.' She gave him an almost motherly smile. 'But I expect you will enjoy yourself.'

'I am touched by your solicitude, Matilda, but you have no need to concern yourself with my way of life.' He spoke gently in a cold voice so that she went very pink and blurted out,

'I'm interfering—'

Old Mr Scott-Thurlow coming into the room at that moment saved her from uttering whatever she had intended; she wished him good morning, murmured that she would go and see how his wife was and took herself off.

Beyond giving his grandson a good look, the old gentleman said nothing and it was James who spoke. 'The matron phoned soon after seven o'clock to say that Nurse Watkins should be here by half-past nine.'

'Good. I'll tell Slocombe to drive Matilda back.'

'No need, sir. I must call in on my way and see how my patient is getting on. She was taken to King's Hall. Matilda lives only a few miles further on—I'll drop her off.'

'Splendid. Have you told her?'

'No. Did grandmother have a good night?'

By mutual consent, they began to discuss his grandmother's health.

Nurse Watkins arrived soon after nine o'clock, by which time Matilda had got Mrs Scott-Thurlow out of her bed and into a comfortable chair while she got a bath ready and put everything in order so that she might dress. She was wondering just what she should do next when the nurse joined them and the following ten minutes were taken up with apologies, regrets and goodbyes. Mrs Scott-Thurlow put up her face for a kiss and pressed a small box into Matilda's hand. 'You have been so good, my dear, and we shall both miss you. You must come and see us again soon—and that isn't an empty remark, I really mean it. Now run along and I hope this job you're going to will be a pleasant one.'

Matilda kissed the elderly cheek, shook Nurse Watkins's hand and fetched her jacket and case from her bedroom. She still had to say goodbye to old Mr Scott-Thurlow and, although it broke her heart not to see James just once more, she was determined to avoid him.

He was in the hall with his grandfather and stood quietly by while she bade that gentleman goodbye. It was impossible to avoid him now; she gave a brief nod in his direction. 'Goodbye.'

'I'm driving you back.'

'Oh, but there's no need, thank you. Slocombe is taking me.'

He shook his head. 'No, I am—'

She didn't give up easily. 'But I saw him only a short time ago and he never said—'

'I told him not to. Come along; I have no time to waste.'

She was aware that his grandfather was standing there looking amused and at the same time thoughtful. She said with dignity, 'Very well,' gave the old gentleman a delightful smile, handed James her case with a scowl and a flash of her green eyes and marched out of the door. The Slocombes had come to wave goodbye so she changed the scowl to another smile, got into the car while her case was put in the boot and then waved until the group by the door was out of sight.

They drove for several miles without speaking until he asked, 'Still sulking, Matilda?'

'I don't sulk. I have no reason to do so.'

'Good. In that case let me talk sensibly...' He ignored her cross mutter. 'You will find your fee waiting for you at your home. What do you intend to do next?' He added, 'And don't tell me to mind my own business.'

'I had no intention of saying any such thing,' said Matilda, who had been on the point of uttering those very words. 'I have no idea what I shall do next; certainly I shall stay at home for a short time. I cannot think why you should want to know.'

'Nor can I.'

The conversation seemed to have come to an end, such as it was. But presently he said, 'Theobald should be quite recovered; he is a splendid companion for my Labrador, who mothers him relentlessly. He loves it.'

'It was kind of you to take him in,' she said stiffly.

'You have no dog of your own?'

'No. Our dog died last year. I would love to have another one, but if I get a job away from home it's hardly fair on the rest of the family.'

'And you intend to leave home?'

Now who was cross-questioning? 'I haven't decided.'

Mr Scott-Thurlow allowed a small sound to escape his lips—it could have been a chuckle or a grunt—and he said smoothly, 'I'm sure that you will find something worthwhile to do. But why not get married?' He gave her a quick sideways glance. 'I'm surprised that no man has snapped you up.'

She said fierily, 'And I am not a bargain—what a horrid thing to say.'

'Not a bargain—a prize. Once you have been tamed a little and have lost your prickles and your impulsiveness—but that, of course, is the fault of your hair—'

'If you weren't driving this car, I would box your ears—you're more than horrid, you're deliberately baiting me. I hope I never see you again.' She was being childish but she didn't care.

He went on talking just as though she hadn't spoken. 'And yet you were splendid when Mrs Chubb severed her fingers; I don't know of anyone else who would have dealt with the situation with such good sense, nor can I think of any woman I know who would have retired to the kitchen and cooked a meal to cordon bleu standard. And Theobald—you made it your business to help him and you didn't stop to think, did you? The men could have turned nasty; you had no idea what to do with him, had you? Yet you rushed to his aid—and you have been kindness itself to my grandmother and Roseanne. I am forced to the conclusion that it is I who rub you up the wrong way.'

'This is a pointless conversation, Mr Scott-Thurlow.'

She peeped at him; his profile looked grim. He had looked so tired… Her ill humour evaporated, she said, 'I'm sorry if I annoy you—you must be tired. Mother will have coffee ready; perhaps you would like a cup before you go to King's Hall?'

His stern mouth relaxed. 'Why, thank you, Matilda.'

Her mother flung the door open as the car stopped. 'There you are—how nice to see you, Mr Scott-Thurlow; come on in, both of you. There's coffee ready and I made a lardy cake.' She embraced Matilda and shook hands with Mr Scott-Thurlow. 'Dr Bramley told us that you had gone to Spitsbergen to help those poor men in that frightful accident.'

She led the way to the kitchen. 'Sit down, won't you? You don't mind having your coffee here? The sitting-room's being cleaned.'

Mr Scott-Thurlow sat down facing Matilda, made polite small talk with the rector and then said that he must go.

'I expect that you will take a little holiday,' said Mrs ffinch chattily. 'You must need a rest and a change. I dare say it's rather different at Spitsbergen.'

He agreed pleasantly. 'But I hear from Matilda that my fiancée has several parties lined up for me.' He bade her goodbye, shook the rector's hand and paused by Matilda's chair. 'I'll give Theobald your love,' he told her. 'Goodbye, Matilda.'

The rector went with him to his car and Mrs ffinch poured more coffee. 'Such a nice man,' she commented. 'He looked tired—he should go somewhere quiet for a few days but I dare say he won't get the chance; Lady Fox was telling me that his fiancée has been to visit Roseanne at the hospital and told her that she had planned dinner parties and theatres and I don't know what else; she said that he needed to be taken out of himself, whatever that means. I don't think she should be his wife—he needs someone more suitable.'

Matilda said slowly. 'But she is suitable, Mother: she comes from a similar background, she's lovely to look at and dresses marvellously and she'll be a perfect hostess…'

'I should have thought that what he needed was a perfect wife and mother of his children.' She saw the look on Matilda's face and went on quickly, 'Now do tell me about this nice old couple you've been staying with, and is Mrs Scott-Thurlow quite well again?'

Matilda listened to the gentle purr of the Rolls going down the drive—she would never see him again; she didn't want to believe it but it was true. She began to tell her mother about her stay. She looked unhappy but her mother pretended not to notice that. Her dear Tilly would tell her why in time, although she could guess very well who it was that had taken the happy look from her eyes. She frowned a little; Mr Scott-Thurlow had paid scant attention to Matilda—in fact he had behaved with the scrupulous civility of someone being polite at all costs towards a person they disliked. She had been very stiff too. They must have quarrelled. Somehow the thought cheered Mrs ffinch; at least they weren't indifferent to each other. He was of course engaged to marry that other girl but she dismissed that with a maternal single-mindedness. Tilly would make him a good wife. When Matilda had finished her disjointed tale, Mrs ffinch said brightly, 'There's a letter for you, Tilly. It's in the hall.'

It contained a cheque and a short businesslike note stating what it was for; it was signed 'J. Scott-Thurlow'. Or, at least, that was what she supposed it was; it was almost unreadable.

'Isn't it funny,' she observed to her mother, 'that someone who can put bones together again is unable to write legibly?'

'Yes, dear, but we can't excel in everything. I'm told that Roseanne is doing very well. I didn't realise that he was so well-known until Lady Fox waylaid me the other day—she has a new hat, dear, tweed and floppy, quite terrible—where was I? Oh, yes—well, she kept on and on about his brilliance and then told me what his fees were for the operation on Roseanne. Not that

I wanted to know; she is sometimes vulgar, you know. I must tell you something else, though; Dr Bramley told me that Mr Scott-Thurlow refuses his fees when he is asked to give his aid at some disaster. The trip to Spitsbergen must have left him very out of pocket.' She added thoughtfully, 'It's a pity that Lady Fox doesn't know that.'

She glanced at the tell-tale face Matilda turned to her and went on cheerfully, 'It's lovely to have you home again, Tilly. They missed you in Sunday school, though I must say Esme does very well, your Father did say.'

'It's grand to be back, Mother.' Matilda studied the cheque; it was quite a nice sum of money. 'I'll pop into Sherborne tomorrow and pay this in, and at the same time I'll poke around and see if there are any jobs going.'

She had friends there but none of them knew of any likely job; she had no qualifications, but they were full of suggestions as they sat over coffee at the café opposite the abbey. None of them very practical, though; Matilda parted from them presently and went off to do some shopping for her mother. That done, she wandered into the bookshop in Cheap Street and thumbed through the magazines. The *Lady* had pages of adverts, too many to skim through in the shop. She bought a copy and took herself off to the restaurant in Denners where she sat down with a pot of tea and a plate of sandwiches and began to search the pages.

There were dozens of jobs, mostly for trained nannies and married couples, and she had nearly given up when her eye lighted on a lengthy advertisement under the heading 'Educational'. A young lady was needed for the rest of the school term—barely a month now—

and the week subsequent to that, to take the place of a junior matron to work under the school matron, and to be in charge of the youngest girls—all boarders. No teaching would be required, but a sense of discipline and common sense were essential. The salary, from Matilda's point of view, was adequate, and to crown everything the school was situated in a small town north of Sherborne, a few miles on the other side of the A303, a mere matter of fifteen miles or so from her home.

Never one to beat about the bush, she gobbled her sandwich, drained the teapot and went off to find the nearest phone box.

The voice at the other end of the line sounded severe but faintly desperate. There had been several applicants but none of them had been satisfactory—the voice gave Matilda the strong impression that she wasn't expected to be satisfactory either, but she persevered. Having a rector for a father, once she disclosed this fact, was the turning-point in her favour. She was bidden to attend an interview on the following morning.

The occasion warranted recognition of some kind; she had paid her cheque into her bank account, put aside a good deal of it to give to her mother for Esme's fees, and went on an impulsive shopping spree. She didn't dare spend too much, though—probably the owner of the voice wouldn't think her good matron material—all the same she bought chocolates for Esme, tobacco for her father's pipe, a bottle of perfume for her mother and a charming little teapot from the china shop in Cheap Street for Hilary—it would do very nicely for her to use when she was married. The boys could have money— she would send it to them at school.

She bore her gifts home, told her family what she had

done, handed over the presents and went to select an outfit for the interview. Something sober, she decided, suitable for a junior matron. Eyeing her rather basic wardrobe she found herself thinking about Mr Scott-Thurlow—probably at one of the parties Rhoda had lined up for him. A pity she couldn't tell him that she had found something worthwhile, and in record time. Being Matilda, of course, she never doubted that she would get the job.

CHAPTER SIX

MATILDA, SOBERLY CLAD in a jacket and skirt, borrowed her father's car and drove herself to her appointment. It was for eleven o'clock and she allowed plenty of time. She knew where the school was; it was fairly well known, taking mostly boarders, children whose parents were overseas and, unlike most schools, it was for girls only.

She got there too soon and parked the car some distance from the wide gateway, thinking up suitable answers to the likely questions she might expect, but this palled after a time and she allowed herself to think of Mr Scott-Thurlow. What would he be doing? she wondered. Sitting in some handsome consulting-room, she supposed, behind an imposing desk, listening courteously to some wealthy patient complaining about his bones. On the other hand, he might be doing one of those ward rounds which always looked so impressive in films. He might even be spending the day with Rhoda...

Mr Scott-Thurlow was bending his large person over his patient on the operating table, meticulously piecing together bits of a bone in a boy's leg, wiring them together and fitting them into a whole with all the care of a jigsaw puzzle enthusiast. Unlike Matilda, he wasn't allowing his thoughts to wander...

Matilda glanced at her watch and started the car,

turned in through the gates and stopped neatly in front
of the front entrance of the school. It had at one time
been the country estate of a member of the eighteenth-
century nobility, a point stressed in the prospectus,
and any necessary additions and alterations which
had been done had been prudently carried out at the
back of it and its imposing Georgian front had been
left in its original state. Matilda got out, rang the bell
and waited composedly to be admitted. The maid who
came to the door was rather wooden-faced and dressed
in a print frock, white apron and cap. A nice touch,
thought Matilda, suitable for a school which had a high
reputation for the educating of girls. She gave her name,
was shown to a small room at the side of the hall, and sat
down, still composed. She wasn't kept waiting long; the
maid returned and led her across the hall, knocked on
a door and opened it for her. The room was light, high-
ceilinged and well furnished rather severely, a fitting
background for the stern lady sitting behind the desk.

She didn't get up but said, 'Good morning, Miss
ffinch. Please sit down.'

Matilda got to her feet fifteen minutes later—she
had got the job. Her quiet answers seemed to satisfy
her questioner; her references, from Dr Bramley and
her godfather, who was a bishop, were impeccable. She
was asked to start in two days' time and to remain until
one week after the end of term. 'You must understand,'
said Miss Tremble, 'that this is a temporary post only.
You will have one day a week free, that is from directly
after breakfast until ten o'clock. It will be one of your
duties to get up at night should you be needed. There
is a head matron, who will direct you in your work,
and another assistant matron who looks after the older

girls. Be good enough to come with me so that you may see the school.'

The classrooms were on the ground floor, hives of activity into which she wasn't taken. 'You will have nothing to do with the teaching of the girls, of course,' said Miss Tremble in a quelling voice and led the way up the handsome staircase. The dormitories were airy and comfortable, with four or six beds in each of them. 'The small girls sleep in these four rooms and your room is at the end of the corridor.'

She was shown a small, nicely furnished room with a bathroom leading from it. 'You share this with the assistant matron,' she was told, and, 'There is a small kitchenette where you make tea and coffee if you wish. Your free time will vary from day to day and you will be responsible for accompanying any child who needs to go to the dentist or doctor's surgery.'

She was led downstairs again, bidden goodbye in a voice only slightly less severe than earlier, had her hand shaken with the brisk reminder that she would be expected by ten o'clock on the second day from then, and was ushered out by the wooden-faced maid.

Matilda drove herself home, occasionally breaking into song and uttering little yelps of delight between mental calculations as to how much exactly she would earn. She would have to wait a month, of course, for her cheque and there would be only the extra week after that; all the same, it would be a useful sum. She drove the car round to the garage and went in through the kitchen door.

'Did they give you coffee?' her mother asked, shucking broad beans at the table. 'And did you get the job, Tilly?'

Matilda chucked her jacket over a chair. 'No to the coffee, and yes to the job.' She went to the Aga and fetched the coffee-pot and a mug. 'I start the day after tomorrow...'

'Sit down, darling, and tell me all about it—no, wait a minute, I'll get your father, he's in the study, and Hilary's somewhere...'

They gathered round while she told them and then sat back listening to their pleased remarks. How different from the polite talk when James had visited his grandparents; she felt sorry for him never to have had the simple pleasure of sitting in a loving family circle, knowing that everyone there was as pleased as you were, hanging on every word and then all talking at once. She mustn't think about him though. She was doing what she had said she would do, making a bid for independence. The job was temporary, but it was a first step in the right direction, and the money was three times what Lady Fox had paid her.

Hilary drove her to the school. 'Very impressive,' she observed as they arrived. 'Do you want me to wait?'

'No, love.' Matilda got her case off the back seat and stuck her head through the window. 'Thanks for bringing me. I'll phone as soon as I know when I can have a day off. Someone will have to fetch me and bring me back.'

'Oh, Max is down for the weekend to discuss the wedding—he'll come for you if you're free.'

The same maid opened the door and this time she said, 'Good morning, miss,' and when Matilda asked her name told her it was Winnie. 'And I'm to take you straight to Miss Tremble, miss.'

Matilda put her case down and, following her across

the hall, went in to Miss Tremble's room. This time Miss Tremble smiled as she entered. 'I hope that you are prepared to start work at once, Miss ffinch? Winnie will take you to your room and my senior matron, Mrs Down, will tell you exactly what your daily routine will be.'

Mrs Down was comfortably middle-aged and pleased to see Matilda. 'We've been run off our feet, me and Joan—that is, Miss Willis. We're making beds, as you can see, but now that you're here I shall be free to see to the sick-bay, check the laundry and inspect the dormitories. You'll need an overall. Come with me and I'll see if I can find one to fit you.'

Matilda was a girl of noble proportions and it was only after a good deal of searching through various linen cupboards that a garment was found that fitted more or less. 'There are two, thank heaven,' breathed Mrs Down. 'They belonged to a rather stout matron we had for a time. Not that you are stout, my dear. On the contrary, you have a lovely figure—such a small waist too.'

Matilda enveloped herself in the garment, belted it firmly and was led away to inspect the dormitories, where the assistant matron was making beds on her own. She looked cross and Mrs Down said, 'Supposing you give Miss Willis a hand first? Then we'll have a cup of coffee and explain the routine to you.'

When she had gone, Miss Willis said, 'Call me Joan—what's your name?'

'Matilda, and do call me that. Do the little girls call us by our Christian names?'

'Lord, no, Miss Tremble would never allow it. This isn't a free-and-easy place—the children have to behave and there's no familiarity allowed. They're happy enough though.'

The beds made, they went downstairs to a small sitting-room next to the kitchen. 'This is our room,' said Mrs Down. 'Not that we get much time to sit in it. We're supposed to have three hours off each day but it doesn't always work out that way—we take what we can get. You get a day off, of course, but Miss Tremble won't let any of us sleep out.'

'Yes, she told me that, but I don't live very far away—Abner Magna. Someone will fetch me after breakfast and bring me back in the evening.'

'That's nice. Now, Matilda, I'll explain your work…'

A busy day, thought Matilda, listening carefully, especially mornings and evenings, when a score of small girls would have to be readied for their day and bathed and bedded each night.

'Quite often at weekends parents come down and take them out for tea—that's allowed. We don't get our days off at weekends, by the way.'

Mrs Down bustled away and Matilda was led off to be shown the dining-room, the cloakrooms, the changing-rooms and the room where the children could play in their free time. Despite its imposing appearance and Miss Tremble's rather severe demeanour, the place seemed comfortable and homely and the girls she glimpsed looked happy as they hurried from one class to another.

After that first day she enjoyed her work. She had some twenty small girls in her care but over and above them there were a number of chores she was expected to do so that her days were filled. The food was good and her room, though small, was comfortable. She liked the little girls and they loved her; she tucked them into their beds each night, listened to their small worries, admired pictures of Mummy and Daddy, plaited hair, inspected fingernails and cuddled the tearful victims of bruises and grazed knees. At the end of a week she was given her day off and went home, fetched by Hilary. The day went too quickly—there was such a lot to talk about—and when she had exhausted her descriptions of her work at the school there was plenty of village gossip to be discussed.

'One shouldn't listen to gossip,' observed her mother, 'but one does hear things, you know… They say that Lady Fox has given the new secretary a week's notice, but I don't believe it; she looked very firmly entrenched in church last Sunday. Roseanne is still in hospital, of course. Her arm plaster is to come off next week. Lady Fox is fussing because Mr Scott-Thurlow hasn't sent in his account. I did point out that he wasn't likely to do that until Roseanne is on her feet again and he can discharge her. After all, he's not the butcher or the baker, is he?'

Matilda had gone a little pink at his name but all she said was, 'I wonder when Roseanne and Bernard are going to marry?'

'September, I believe. Dr Bramley told me that Mr Scott-Thurlow is working too hard. That fiancé of his tries to get him to go out in the evenings and spend the weekends with her friends in the country but he almost always refuses.' Mrs ffinch sighed. 'She seems so very unsuitable for him…'

'Well, he doesn't have to marry her,' said Matilda, and just for a moment her eyes shone at the thought. 'But I expect he will,' she added soberly.

Her father drove her back that evening and before she got into her bed she trod softly through the dormitories, making sure that the children were sleeping. Only one little girl was awake. One of the youngest there, Lucy Phelps, almost seven years old, whose parents were somewhere in South America where it wasn't wise to take children. Her father was head of a medical team sent out to get a new hospital started and her mother had gone with him; they wouldn't be home again for months and Lucy was homesick.

Matilda sat down on her bed, put her on her lap and cuddled her and let her cry quietly. 'Three months will go very quickly, darling. Where are you going for your holidays?'

'To my godfather—he's nice but he's not Daddy or Mummy.'

Matilda offered a handkerchief to mop at a small red nose. 'Of course he's not, but aren't you lucky to have him? When you come back after the holidays your mummy and daddy will be coming home in just a few weeks.'

She popped the moppet back into her bed and tucked her up and bent to kiss the wet cheek.

'I like you,' said Lucy, 'I like your name too. Do they call you Tilly at home? Have you got a mummy and daddy?'

'Indeed I have; brothers and sisters too.'

'Mummy promised me that I can have a baby brother or sister when they come home. I shan't have to be a boarder then.'

'Now, that is something nice to look forward to, love. Do go to sleep now.'

The days slipped away, filled with monotonous jobs

which seldom varied, but the little girls were fun, she got on well with Mrs Down and Joan and seldom saw Miss Tremble, and between them they mostly contrived to get an hour or so to themselves each day. On her next free day she had got Hilary to drive her to King's Hall on their way home and went to see how Roseanne was getting on. Her arm was out of plaster now and she was sitting up in bed, her leg still in extension. She was pleased to see Matilda and began at once to talk about herself and Bernard. 'You see my arm is quite all right now, but I've got to stay like this for weeks until my leg's all right. Mr Scott-Thurlow says it will be perfectly sound by September so we shall get married then.' She paused to eye Matilda. 'Mother said you'd got a job at a school. Do you like it?'

'Yes, I do…'

'Are there any men there?'

'Two gardeners and an odd-job man.'

'Don't you want to get married?'

'Not to a gardener or an odd-job man. I must fly; they're expecting me at home.'

The last few days of term came and Matilda was busy packing trunks, finding lost garments, writing labels and washing small heads of hair. Mrs Down was going with the children who had a train journey. The school bus would take them to Yeovil and it was her task to get the little girls into the right trains before boarding the London train herself. Joan was to leave next, to go home to her mother in the Midlands, leaving Matilda to see that the remaining children were collected by parents before beginning on the hefty job of stripping beds, getting the dormitories ready for the maids to clean, tidying the playroom, checking that nothing had been left in drawers or cupboards and then putting out clean bed linen by each bed ready for the beds to be made up before the new term started.

'A pity you won't be here,' commented Mrs Down, 'for you've fitted in very well, Matilda, and you're a good worker, but Joyce will be back—Miss Tremble told me this morning.'

The children were excited, getting them ready for their various journeys took all her time, and it was a relief to see the busload drive off. Joan, with the two little girls she was escorting to Manchester on her way home, left next and that left a bare dozen children, waiting more or less patiently for their parents to fetch them. Most of them were older girls with whom Matilda had had little to do and they went off in ones and twos until she was left with four of the smallest, Lucy among them.

They sat on a wall in the sunshine, hardly moving because they wanted to look their best, and Matilda, sensing their impatience, started a game of 'I spy with my little eye' to keep them occupied.

A car came up the drive and one of the children rushed to meet it; that left Lucy and two sisters. Their father came next, made polite conversation for a few minutes, scooped them up and bore them off. That left Lucy.

'He's not coming...'

'Of course he is, love. Perhaps he's got to drive miles and miles to get here.' As she spoke they both heard the car and stood up expectantly.

'It's here—it's Uncle James!' screamed Lucy as the Rolls came to a quiet stop and Mr Scott-Thurlow got out. He caught the little girl in his arms and hugged her but his eyes were upon Matilda, standing there in her outsize overall, her hair, as usual, rather untidy.

They stared at each other for a long moment until Matilda said inadequately, 'Hello.'

'You do pop up in the most unexpected places,' he said, 'just when I think…' He stopped because someone else had got out of the car—Rhoda, dressed as for a garden party and quite breathtakingly lovely.

She put a gloved hand on Lucy's head. 'Don't blame your uncle because he's late—it was naughty me; I couldn't find the right clothes to wear.' She glanced across to where Matilda was standing. 'The cook—how we do keep meeting, don't we? Is this your latest job?'

Matilda took no notice. She said, 'You're Lucy's godfather…?'

He had an arm round the little girl's shoulders. 'Indeed I am. And you, Matilda, what are you?'

'A school matron—you see, I found a job.'

'Permanent?'

She was so delighted to see him that she didn't stop to think. 'No, I finish at the end of the week…'

'So you will be out of work again,' drawled Rhoda in a sugary voice.

Matilda hadn't heard her. Somehow she and Mr Scott-Thurlow were in a world of their own—not for long, she knew that; he would make some chillingly polite remark and go away again.

She wasn't sure if she could bear that, but she would have to.

'Do you know Uncle James?' piped Lucy. 'You could come and stay with us, Miss ffinch.'

Matilda saw the look on Rhoda's face; she didn't dare look at James. 'Lucy, dear, I have to be here for another week and then I'm going home, but it's very kind of you to think of it.'

Lucy wasn't to be side-tracked. 'Will you be here next term? I won't come back unless you are.'

'Listen, love, your mummy and daddy will be home again in just a few weeks after you come back here and I expect you won't need to be a boarder then.'

'You're not coming back?'

'No. I came for a week or two while Miss Tring was ill. She's better now.'

'But I'll see you again.'

The conversation had gone on long enough. Matilda gave her a hug and kissed a round pink cheek. 'Won't it be fun if we do?' she admonished.

Mr Scott-Thurlow had remained silent; now he took Lucy's hand and started towards the car. His 'goodbye, Matilda' sounded very final.

Rhoda lingered. 'All this fuss over a child—and what are you hoping to get out of it, buttering her up like that? It's nauseating.'

She had lowered her voice, but it had a piercing quality which made it possible for Lucy to hear her. James heard her too.

Matilda put her clenched hands behind her back for fear she might slap Rhoda and turned her back. She stayed like that until she heard the car's engine. She turned round then and waved and called goodbye to Lucy sitting beside her godfather.

The big house was very quiet now that everyone had gone. Miss Tremble was still there but she would be going on holiday herself on the following day and several of the domestic staff had already gone, leaving the housekeeper, one maid and the gardeners to mind the place. Matilda took herself upstairs and started the beds, glad to have something to do, trying to dismiss from her thoughts Mr Scott-Thurlow's indifference. Yet when he had got out of his car and seen her she could have sworn that he had been pleased to see her. 'Oh, well, no good moping,' muttered Matilda, bundling up sheets as though her life depended on it.

Contrary to her expectations the week went quickly; there was a lot to do but there was the odd hour when she was free to roam the gardens or even, greatly daring, sit down at the piano in the assembly hall and thump out a few tunes. The housekeeper was kind, making sure that she ate the good food she got ready and not complaining when Matilda took her cup of tea and slice of cake out into the garden, to sit under a tree.

She hadn't been paid and she was a little worried about that, but on the day before she was due to go the postman left a letter for her. Miss Tremble had written her a kind note, promising a reference if she wanted one and enclosing her cheque. Matilda sat and admired it for quite a time, thinking of all the things for which it could be used.

Hilary came for her on the last morning and she bade goodbye to the remaining staff, quite sorry to go, but once in the car, exchanging news, her regret was soon forgotten.

'Roseanne knows you're coming home today; could you bear to see her for a few minutes on our way home?'

'Yes, all right. How is she?'

'Waiting impatiently until she's on her feet again. She's having physio so it shouldn't be too long now.' She added, 'She wants you to be one of the bridesmaids.'

'Me? Oh, no—anyway, I doubt if Lady Fox will allow her to invite me to the wedding.'

At the hospital Matilda got out of the car. 'Are you coming in?'

Hilary shook her head. 'I'll give you ten minutes.'

Roseanne was in good spirits and greeted her with delight. 'Only another few weeks,' she began at once, 'then I can get up on crutches. But I don't want to go home until I'm quite well, Mother will only fuss…' She studied Matilda's face. 'You must have been working awfully hard—you're pale or sad or something.'

Matilda let that pass. 'How are the plans for the wedding going?'

Roseanne launched into a detailed and rather muddled account of the plans; the ten minutes was up but there seemed no way in which to stop her. Matilda was searching in vain for a chance to stem the flow when the door opened and Sister came in and, with her, Mr Scott-Thurlow.

Matilda said, 'Oh, lord,' and then blushed scarlet.

Mr Scott-Thurlow, never a man to dissemble, looked surprised in a manner which appeared genuine, which, considering that he had gone to a good deal of trouble to ensure that he should visit Roseanne when Matilda was with her, did him credit. He had taken a lot of trouble to engineer their meeting, suggesting to Roseanne that since Matilda would be going home that morning it would be nice if she called in. 'I'm sure whoever fetches her won't mind suggesting it,' he had said offhandedly and had left the rest to kindly fate, telling himself that he only wished to see Matilda in order to let her know about Lucy and Theobald.

His 'good morning' was suave; he said politely,

'There is no need to leave the room; I merely wish to tell Roseanne that her latest X-ray is most satisfactory. I think we might start the crutches at the end of next week.'

He waited while Roseanne enjoyed an outburst of delight. 'You'll be here?' she asked anxiously.

'Yes, and I shall bring Dr Bramley with me.' He gave her a kindly smile and looked at Matilda, who was quite pale now. 'You have finished at the school?' he asked blandly.

'Yes.'

His small, mocking smile annoyed her, and she wished that she could think of something clever to say to him but she couldn't. Instead she told Roseanne that she really had to be going. 'Hilary's waiting in the car and they are expecting me at home.' She conjured up a smile. 'I'm so glad you're doing so well.'

'You'll come again?'

'Oh, yes, of course. Goodbye.'

She said goodbye to Sister too and, since there was no way of avoiding Mr Scott-Thurlow's elegant bulk leaning in front of the door, she made her farewells to him too. She looked him in the eye as she did so but most annoyingly he had dropped the lids over his eyes and, since his face still wore its bland, pleasant mask, she was unable to discover what he was thinking. Why am I worrying? she mused as she made her way out to the car. He isn't thinking about me, anyway.

She was wrong of course.

'Mr Scott-Thurlow's here,' Hilary told her unnecessarily as she got into the car.

'Yes, I saw him.' Matilda busied herself with her safety-belt and her sister gave her downbent head

a thoughtful look. There had been a forlorn note in
Matilda's voice. She decided not to pursue the subject
and began to talk about her own forthcoming wedding.

At home, once more, Matilda was engulfed in her
family; the boys were on holiday, so was Esme, and
the house was full. There was no question of a holiday
of course although later on in the autumn, when the
younger ones were back at school, her father and mother
would be going to a small seaside town in Cornwall,
exchanging with the vicar of the parish there for two
weeks, and shortly Hilary would be going to stay with
her future in-laws again.

'Have you any plans?' asked her mother. 'There's
your Aunt Penelope, she would love to have you, and
you've enough money to enjoy yourself there.'

'I'll think about it,' Matilda told her, anxious to put
her parent's mind at rest and not disclose that most of
her cheque had been given to her. 'It's nice just being
at home.'

She was sitting outside the back door stringing beans
with Nelson on her lap. It wasn't very convenient but
he had insisted on climbing up, pleased to see her back
home again.

'Well, dear, you do just what you want—only it's
rather dull for you.'

'Never dull, Mother dear. But I did enjoy that job
at the school and I think I'll see if I can get something
similar for the autumn term. There are dozens of
schools around this part of the world.'

Her mother glanced at her. She was such a lovely
girl, and nice-natured into the bargain; true, she had
a temper when roused and she was impulsive, but her
heart was warm; there must be a man somewhere in

the world who would want her for his wife. A pity the world was such a large place and Abner Magna was so remote. Mrs ffinch cast a mental eye over the village; there wasn't a man around who would do for Matilda. Only Mr Scott-Thurlow, and that was a closed book never to be opened.

Matilda found plenty to do now that she was home again; doing the flowers in the church, taking over a class in Sunday school, driving her father around the parish, which was a scattered one, helping in the house and taking her mother into Sherborne to shop, but there was still time to wander off into the country around, sometimes with Esme but more often than not alone.

Two weeks went by, and Matilda, despite her hidden unhappiness, became nicely tanned, which made her eyes greener than ever and her hair even more fiery. She had a sprinkling of freckles too which did nothing to detract from her prettiness, and only when she was alone did she allow her charming mouth to droop and then not for long. She had plenty of good sense; crying for the moon wasn't going to help but a job would. She went into Sherborne to an agency and put her name on their books, and scanned the local paper each week as well as her father's *Telegraph*. Something would turn up, Esme assured her, coming upon her poring over the vacancies column.

It did, the very next day, in the elegant shape of Mr Scott-Thurlow, getting out of his car with the air of a man who knew what he wanted and intended to get it. Matilda was on her knees, grubbing up weeds from the rose-bed under the drawing-room windows, and since she hadn't intended to go out that day she had tied her hair back with a ribbon and put on a wide cotton skirt and a sleeveless top, neither of them either new or fashionable. All the same she looked delightful.

Esme, perched on the steps outside the french window, saw him first. She went dancing to meet him. 'Look who's here,' she called, 'just in time for coffee.'

Matilda turned to look over her shoulder. Mr Scott-Thurlow was strolling towards her. He had abandoned the drive and was crossing the lawn with Esme skipping beside him. She sat back on her heels and waited until he had paused beside her, looming above her head so that she got to her feet quickly. She had become rather pink in the face but her 'good morning' was cool and faintly questioning.

He smiled down at her. 'Good morning, Matilda. I have come to ask a favour of you. Can you spare the time to listen to me?'

She dusted the earth off her hands. 'Of course. Won't you have some coffee? Mother is indoors...'

She led the way into the house, going through the french window into the drawing-room. 'Do sit down,' she said in what Esme called her hostess voice. 'I'll fetch some coffee and tell Mother.'

'Er—might I not have my coffee in the kitchen, if your mother is busy? What I have to say is for everyone to hear.'

Her already warm cheeks glowed. He had made it sound as though she was expecting to have a tête-à-tête with him. The very last thing she wanted, she reminded herself.

Esme had gone ahead, and Matilda opened the drawing-room door without a word and ushered him through, but he paused in the doorway. 'It would be so much easier if we were on a friendlier footing,' he said blandly, and at her indignant little snort, 'Yes, I know I have not given you reason to be friendly, have I? But if you could believe that what I am going to ask of you is not for myself?'

She looked at him then. He appeared severe and remote, but then he smiled slowly, his eyebrows raised.

'All right,' said Matilda gruffly and opened the kitchen door.

Mrs ffinch had the coffee-mugs on the table; a cake, warm from the oven, sat fragrantly on a plate at its centre and in some mysterious fashion the two boys, her father and Mrs Coffin, unnecessarily busy at the sink, were all there with her mother and Esme. Mr Scott-Thurlow was welcomed with what Matilda considered to be unnecessary warmth, bidden to sit down and offered coffee and a slice of the cake while everyone else arranged themselves around the table. He was allowed to drink some coffee and take a bite of the cake before Mrs ffinch said, 'Esme says you want Matilda to do you a favour. Perhaps you would rather talk to her alone after we have had our coffee.'

'There is no need for that, Mrs ffinch. She may wish to discuss what I have to ask of her with you and it will save time if you are told at the same time.'

'Is there such a hurry?' asked Matilda sharply.

'I am going to see Roseanne, and I should like my answer when I come back, in about an hour.'

'What do you want?'

'Not what I want, Matilda,' he corrected her quietly. 'It is what Lucy wants.' He waited while Mrs ffinch refilled his mug. 'She has the mumps and very severely too. My housekeeper, who was also my nanny, is getting on a bit and although she is wonderfully kind and helpful she is tired. Lucy wants you, Matilda—no one else will do save her mother, and that isn't possible as you know. Would you consider coming for a few weeks? There is very little nursing and you will probably be bored but the child is so unhappy…'

'Well, of course I'll come if she wants me.' Matilda spoke impulsively as she so often did and then had second thoughts. 'But wouldn't your fiancée feel—well, perhaps she would rather be with Lucy?'

His 'no' was decisive and made it difficult to pursue the matter.

'Poor little girl,' said Mrs ffinch, 'of course she misses her mother, though I'm sure you do your best, Mr Scott-Thurlow.'

She glanced at her daughter, who frowned heavily and looked at the faces round the table. They all expected her to accept—somehow he had got them all on his side. She said crossly, 'Oh, very well, I'll come, just until Lucy is feeling better.'

'I wouldn't dream of keeping you a moment longer,' said Mr Scott-Thurlow. 'I know that she will be delighted. Now I must go. Could you be ready in just over an hour?'

'I haven't much choice, have I?' She was being rude and she didn't care.

When he had gone her father said mildly, 'You were rather ungracious, Tilly; he is after all doing his best for the child.'

Her mother added, 'Such a kind man, too.'

'Mother!' said Matilda fiercely, and rushed out of the room.

CHAPTER SEVEN

'I DON'T EVEN know where he lives,' grumbled Matilda, flinging things into her case.

'Well, we can ask when he comes back.' Esme was sitting on the bed eating biscuits out of a tin and advising Matilda on what to pack. 'Don't put that old thing in,' she warned, 'it's only fit for the jumble. Take that flowery skirt and lots of tops. Will you have to do your own washing? I wonder what his house happens to be like. I know he's got a housekeeper, but lots of quite poor people have one—she's his nanny anyway, I dare say she lives there and looks after him in return for a home. She'll have her OAP anyway...'

'How you do run on,' said Matilda, who had been wondering the same thing. 'Shall I take the green dress?'

'Yes—you won't need to dress up if you have your meals with him, but if he has people to dinner or drinks you'll have to look decent. Can't you get another dress? I suppose you gave most of your wages to Mother— she'll let you have them back—'

'Certainly not. I don't expect to lead a social life, love, but I'll pack the green thing if you think I should.' She burrowed into her wardrobe. 'I'd better wear the patterned blouse and skirt.' She glanced at the clock on the mantelpiece. 'Oh, lord, he'll be here in ten minutes. Shut this case for me, there's a dear, and I'll get changed.'

She was thrusting pins into a severe French pleat when Esme asked, 'Do you suppose that Rhoda will be there? In his house…?'

'Probably,' said Matilda thickly through the pins. 'She is going to marry him after all.' It hurt to say that.

'I mean, does she live there?'

Matilda withdrew the pins from her mouth the better to speak clearly. 'I think it is very unlikely. Doctors and the like have to think of their reputations.'

'You'll be living there with him, though,' went on Esme, never one to mince matters.

'I shall be employed by Mr Scott-Thurlow, and that's quite different.'

'Why? I can't see…' Luckily she paused when she heard the car coming up the drive. 'He's here—I'll take your case. Come along, do, you can't keep him waiting.' As they went downstairs she hissed, 'Is he going to pay you?'

'I suppose so.'

'How much?'

Matilda quelled her with a frown and crossed the hall to where Mr Scott-Thurlow stood talking to her father and mother.

'You will want to know where you're going,' he observed in the mildest of tones. 'Lucy is in London with me at present, and as soon as she is well enough I thought you might go, the pair of you, to a cottage I have near Dartmouth-Stoke Fleming—the sea air will do her good.'

It would be more than two hundred miles from London, reflected Matilda. 'It sounds a splendid idea,' she said quietly. 'Whereabouts in London, Mr Scott-Thurlow?'

'Near Piccadilly and Oxford Street. Just off Orchard Street.'

'Isn't that near Wigmore Street?'

'Yes. Fifteen Blenheim Street. Your father has the address and the phone number.'

The rector nodded. 'We shall no doubt hear from Matilda once she has settled in. I hope that she will be of assistance to you and that the little girl will get well quickly.'

Everyone had gathered in the hall by now and Matilda began a round of goodbyes while Mr Scott-Thurlow shook her parents' hands and then waited patiently while she embraced her mother and father.

She twisted round in her seat to wave goodbye as they drove away and said with a snap, 'You're always in such a hurry.' She shot him a cross look and he said gravely, 'I'm sorry about that, Matilda. I promise you that I won't badger you once you are installed and I'll send you down to Stoke Fleming just as soon as Lucy is fit to travel.'

Why not? she thought unhappily, he—and certainly Rhoda—wouldn't want them at his London home. He was doubtless a good godfather and anxious to do his best for the child, but he had his work and more than that he had Rhoda.

He was silent for a while but presently he began to tell her about Lucy. 'She feels wretched, her throat is sore and she is feverish and cross, and above all she misses her father and mother. I'm hoping that you will be able to fill that gap to some extent. She seems very attached.'

The car phone interrupted him and he slowed his speed. He listened for what seemed to Matilda to be a long time, then said, 'I shall be an hour late, Henry. Let Theatre know and if possible get on with that last case yourself. The tendon. How's that boy? Good, I'll see him before I go to Theatre—be around, will you? Goodbye.'

'What boy?' asked Matilda, who liked to know things.

'A nice lad with a fractured spine; he was knocked down by a car last night—'

'Last night? You operated in the night and then drove down here to Roseanne and—and us?'

'Driving is very soothing,' he said smoothly.

'You ought to be in your bed.'

'I don't need a great deal of sleep and I promise I won't doze off over the wheel.'

'I am not in the least nervous, Mr Scott-Thurlow.'

'I suppose it's no use asking you to call me James?'

'No use at all...'

'May I know why?' He was driving fast along the A303 and despite the good weather the traffic was thin.

When she didn't answer he said, 'Ah, well, it is of little consequence.'

He drove on for a time and neither of them spoke. Presently he said, 'I'm afraid there isn't time to stop for lunch on the way—Mavis will have something for you when we get in. You must forgive me if I go straight on to the hospital. Perhaps we can talk this evening when I get home.'

'Very well.' She added impulsively, 'I do hope someone sees that you have something to eat when you get there. You can't work on an empty stomach.'

He forbore from telling her how many times he had done just that and had hardly been aware of it. 'My theatre sister takes good care of me,' he said carelessly.

She sat quietly, watching the countryside flash by now that they were on the motorway, and now and again she stole a glance at his profile, very calm and rather stern, and at his large, well-kept hands resting lightly on the wheel. Her feelings were mixed; she longed for the drive to go on forever and at the same time wished it were over.

He slowed the car as they reached the suburbs, weaving his way through narrow streets until he came out into Millbank, then Whitehall, Trafalgar Square and thence into Pall Mall and St James's Street and so at last to Orchard Street and the narrow street leading off it. Blenheim Street was a cul-de-sac with what looked like mews at its further end. The houses on either side of it were narrow with bow-fronted windows and each had delicate fanlights over their pristine front doors. Early Regency, thought Matilda, peering out of her window, and charming. Mr Scott-Thurlow stopped his car, got out and opened her door and invited her to alight, and at the same time a door was opened and an elderly man, very neatly dressed, came down the few steps to meet them.

'Ah, Twigg, Miss ffinch has come to help us with Lucy. Matilda, this is Twigg, who runs my home with his wife. There's a case in the boot, Twigg; I'll come in for a moment but I must leave within minutes. See that Miss ffinch has lunch, will you?'

As he talked he had ushered her into the house and Twigg put down her case and opened a door in the small square hall. It was charming, red-carpeted, its white walls hung with paintings and lighted by wall brackets, and the room which they entered was just as delightful. It overlooked the street, its bow window draped with chintz curtains patterned in soft dim blues and greens and pinks, colours echoed in the magnificent carpet which covered the parquet floor. The furniture was a nice mingling of delicate rosewood cabinets and tables and comfortable sofas and chairs. Matilda, taking one swift look, approved of it; it was exactly to her taste and despite its elegance it exuded an atmosphere of cosiness.

Mr Scott-Thurlow waved her to a chair. 'I do apologise for rushing you like this. As I said we can have a talk this evening; in the meantime Mavis and Twigg will look after you. But first I will take you up to see Lucy.'

They mounted a graceful curving staircase at the back of the hall to the narrow gallery above. There were several doors here but he turned down a narrow passage leading to the back of the house and opened one of the doors at its end. The room was large and light with a big window overlooking quite a sizeable garden. It was charmingly furnished with white-painted furniture and flower-patterned curtains and quilt and Lucy was sitting up in the bed, her small face rendered grotesque by the mumps, flushed and hot but instantly overjoyed at the sight of them. There were two dogs on the end of the bed, one of which was Theobald, and Matilda hardly recognised him, for he was now well fed and very clean, a happy tongue lolling out of his foxy little face. The other dog was a golden Labrador with a gentle face. They got off the bed and Mr Scott-Thurlow caressed them as he advanced to the bed.

'Your Theobald,' he said to Matilda, 'and this is

Canada.' He bent to kiss the small girl holding her arms out to him.

'Here is our Lucy. Say hello to Matilda, darling; she has come to keep you company.'

Matilda bent to kiss the child and was held in a throttling embrace. 'I knew you'd come—Uncle James said you would. You're the next best thing to my mummy. Will you live here?'

'Well, until you're fit enough to go to school and by then your mummy will soon be home again.'

Mr Scott-Thurlow put a hand on her arm. 'Mavis will be here presently to show you to your room and answer your questions. Then you will have lunch of course.' He bent to kiss Lucy again, disentangling himself gently from her small arms and went to the door, where he paused, turned round and came back again.

'I haven't thanked you,' he told Matilda and bent his handsome head and kissed her too.

Matilda opened an indignant mouth to utter the scathing words on her tongue and then she thought better of it; Lucy was watching. 'Daddy always kisses Mummy when he has to go away,' she remarked.

Matilda conjured up a bright smile and stooped to pat Theobald. She looked composed when she lifted her head just in time to see Mr Scott-Thurlow disappear through the door, Canada at his heels.

'Why Canada?' she asked.

'She's a Labrador,' Lucy explained kindly. 'Didn't you think of that?' and then, 'You won't stay away for long, will you?'

The door opened then and Mrs Twigg came in, a stout elderly woman with small bright eyes in a round cheerful face. 'Welcome, Miss ffinch, and I hope you'll be happy with us. I'll take you to your room if you're ready to see it now and Twigg has laid a nice little lunch for you in the dining-room. Ever so glad we are that Lucy will have you. I've done me best, miss, but I'm not so young any more. She's a dear little girl and no trouble.'

She exchanged a beaming smile with Lucy and Matilda said, 'I won't be long, darling. Do you have a little nap in the afternoons?'

'Sometimes, but I'll read my book and wait until you come back—may I call you Matilda too?'

'Of course you may.'

Matilda was led away but not very far. Her room was in the corridor too, at the side of the house with a window overlooking a corner of the garden. It was just as pretty a room as Lucy's, furnished in some pale wood she thought might be yew. It had fitted cupboards along one wall and a bathroom, tiled in very pale pink and equipped with everything a girl might need.

'I hope there's all you want, miss,' said Mrs Twigg, 'and just you ask if there is anything at all that we can do for you.'

'It's lovely, Mrs Twigg. Would you like me to come down now for lunch? I can unpack later.'

She followed Mrs Twigg downstairs again and into a fair-sized room opposite the drawing-room where Twigg was waiting.

'A glass of sherry, Miss ffinch? You will take soup?'

She lunched with a good appetite; the food was delicious and Mrs Twigg was a splendid cook. Mr Scott-Thurlow might be a very busy man, she reflected, but when he wasn't being busy he had all the creature comforts he could wish for.

She went back presently and found Lucy hot and restless.

'Another nightie?' she suggested. 'And I'll bathe your face and hands, shall I? Then you'll feel cooler.'

Which she did and then shook up the pillows, gave Lucy a drink and suggested that she should read to her. The child looked ill and very feverish, and since there was a thermometer in a little jar on the dressing-table she took her temperature. It was over a hundred and one and after a little muddled arithmetic she decided that was over forty degrees Celsius. A bit high, but Mr Scott-Thurlow would certainly have been keeping a check on that. She settled down close to the bed and opened *The Lion, the Witch and the Wardrobe* and began to read.

Presently Lucy fell asleep and Matilda sat in the quiet room with no other sound but Theobald's gentle snores. After a while she got up silently and went to her room, leaving the doors open, and unpacked the few things she had brought with her and then went back to sit quietly again; when Lucy woke she would probably be cross and hot and thirsty.

She was all of these things and she wanted her mother. Matilda sponged her small swollen face, mopped her tears, gave her a drink and wrapped her in one of the light wool blankets on the bed before sitting her down on her lap.

'You shall tell me all about Mummy and Daddy, and if you want to cry go ahead, darling, and I won't mind a bit.'

Lucy sniffed mightily. 'You really don't mind? Rhoda says I'm a cry-baby.'

'Pooh to Rhoda. Tell me—is your Mummy pretty?'

Lucy embarked on a description of her mother,

pausing for a little weep now and then. She was very hot and Matilda wondered if she should have left her in bed. At least the child was calmer now. She was wondering what was best to be done when there was a knock on the door and Mrs Twigg came in.

'A nice cup of tea,' she said in her soft voice. 'I'll put the tray on this little table so's you can reach it. There's ice-cream for Lucy too. Mr James said as how she could have that.'

'Why doesn't Uncle James come home?' Lucy wanted to know.

'He'll be here in no time, my pretty. Just you let Miss ffinch get her tea while you eat your ice-cream.'

'Her name's Matilda.'

Mrs Twigg looked at Matilda.

'No one ever calls me Miss ffinch...'

'Well, then, Miss Matilda, will that do?'

Lucy nodded a satisfied head and Mrs Twigg trotted off. Matilda longed for a cup of tea; it had been a strange day and she was getting tired. She hadn't phoned her mother yet, her hair was springing loose from its pins and she hadn't even gone round the house to find her way about the place.

Lucy ate her ice-cream and promptly went to sleep, leaving Matilda to clasp her in her arms and watch the teapot, trying to work out a way of reaching it without waking the child up.

The minutes ticked by and all Matilda could think about was how to get a cup of tea; the more she thought about it, the thirstier she became.

Ten minutes passed as slowly as ten weeks, then the door opened and Mr Scott-Thurlow came in. He took in the situation at a glance, and without speaking went to the bed, tidied it, rearranged the pillows, came to Matilda and scooped Lucy off her lap and tucked her into bed. She didn't stir as he took her pulse and felt her head.

'Drink your tea,' he advised Matilda. 'Has it been here long? Would you like a fresh pot?'

'This is quite all right. Do you want some?'

'I had a cup at the hospital.' He sat down in a chair opposite hers. 'How has she been this afternoon?'

'Hot and tearful but she cheered up and ate her ice-cream. She went to sleep all at once before I could get her back into bed.' She added, 'She's feeling wretched, isn't she, poor moppet?'

He leaned forwards and handed her a plate of small sandwiches. She took one and offered them to him. He looked hungry.

He took one and said, 'Now let us go over the routine for you. You will be busy enough for the next few days but by then Lucy will be feeling better and you will have some time to yourself. Mavis will take over from you for an hour in the afternoon—not long, I'm afraid, but you can sit in the garden. Have you phoned your mother?'

She gave him a limpid look. 'No.'

He frowned. 'That was a silly question. Go and do it now as soon as you have had your tea. I'll stay here.'

So she finished her second cup and hurried downstairs and found Twigg to ask where she could phone. There were, it seemed, phones in almost all the rooms; she went into the drawing-room and found Canada lying before the open french window and bent to pat her, wondering when anyone had the time to take the dog walking. Her mother answered her when she rang but she didn't waste time gossiping. 'I'll write,' she promised. 'I must go back to Lucy now. Everything is fine.'

Lucy was still asleep with she went into the room, and Mr Scott-Thurlow was asleep too, lying back untidily in his chair, his long legs stretched out before him so that she had to step over them to get to her chair.

She sat and pondered as to whether she should wake him or not. He had said that he wanted to talk to her, tell her what her duties were; on the other hand he probably needed his sleep. She studied his face lovingly and was suddenly aware that he was watching her from half-closed eyes.

He began without preamble, 'Your duties are vague, I'm afraid—a surrogate mother is the nearest to them and you are, as far as I can make out, the only one whom Lucy fancies in the role.'

'Surely there must be aunts or cousins or—or what about Miss Symes?'

She shouldn't have said that. He said in a voice as bland as his face, 'Her aunts and cousins are scattered far and wide and I don't quite know why you should mention Rhoda.'

'Why shouldn't I mention her?' she snapped. 'She's going to marry you and I should have thought you would have asked her—she knows Lucy.' She gave him a fiercely defiant look, her insides quaking at the expression on his face. Ferocious was the only word for it.

'I do not think that you need to concern yourself with the whys and wherefores, Matilda. If you would be good enough to listen without interrupting, I will give you some idea of what you may expect from day to day while you are here.'

His voice was coolly civil as he outlined her duties. He was brief too and when he had finished he asked, 'Is there anything else you would like to know?' and when she shook her head, 'Then I suggest that you have a breath of air in the garden. I shall be here for half an hour or so.'

So she found her way out of the house through a small side-door and wandered up and down between the flower-beds, feeling miserable. She had been silly to have dragged Rhoda's name into it in the first place, it was none of her business anyway. She would have to apologise…

She went back presently and found Lucy awake and sitting on his knee, sharing one of her picture books with him, but as she went in he popped the child back into her bed.

'I'll be in my study if you should want me. Twigg will let you know when dinner is ready. Lucy has had rather an exciting day; I dare say she will eat her supper and go to sleep very quickly.'

He went to the door and Matilda followed him. 'I'm sorry I was rude,' she said, 'I can't think why I spoke like that.'

He smiled down at her. 'I have always understood that redheads have a habit of speaking before they think. You are no exception.'

After he had gone she busied herself getting Lucy washed and into a fresh nightie before her supper of soup and more ice-cream, and that done she fetched a book and began to read to the child. It was a favourite of Lucy's and of Matilda's too, *The Secret Garden*, and she stopped frequently to talk about it for they both agreed there could be nothing nicer than having a secret place

where one might go, and at Lucy's suggestion Matilda
undertook to accompany her when she was well again
to see if such a place could be found.

'You're really very nice,' said Lucy and fell asleep,
and ten minutes later Mrs Twigg arrived soft-footed.

'Twigg's just about to serve dinner, miss, if you'd
like to go down.'

'Have I time to tidy myself, Mrs Twigg?'

'No need, miss, there b'ain't no guests this evening.'

So she went downstairs, rehearsing in her mind the
kind of conversation she would have with Mr Scott-
Thurlow. The weather was safe enough, and Roseanne's
leg, Theobald and his grandparents—there were plenty
of innocuous subjects.

'In here.' His voice came from the drawing-room and
she went in, surprised to find him in a dinner-jacket.
'You have time for a drink,' he told her and offered her
a chair. 'I'm dining out but Twigg will see that you have
everything you would like.' He poured her a glass of
sherry. 'I dare say you're tired; it has been a busy day
for you.' He sounded uninterested.

'No busier than yours, I should think,' said Matilda,
determined to be polite. 'I expect you have very little
time to yourself.' Her eyes fell upon Theobald and
Canada, sitting side by side, their eyes on their master.
'Whenever do you get time to take the dogs for a walk?'

He smiled a little. 'Before breakfast—Twigg takes
them during the day and I walk them again before I
go to bed.'

She drank her sherry too quickly. 'I expect you want
to go out…'

'As soon as Rhoda arrives. You must stay a moment

and meet her.' His voice held amusement and his eyes gleamed with it when she said,

'Oh, yes, that will be delightful.'

Rhoda came a few minutes later and Matilda, twiddling her empty glass in her hand, wished she hadn't tossed off her sherry quite so quickly.

Rhoda looked lovely, but then she always did. Vivid green satin under an enormous velvet cloak and Italian shoes with gleaming buckles. She pecked Mr Scott-Thurlow's cheek and said, 'Darling, you're actually ready. I'm so glad—the Mathersons' dinners are always such fun and one meets all the right people—prospective patients for you...' She laughed and Matilda watched the look of distaste hidden at once behind that bland mask.

He said, 'Matilda has arrived, you see. Lucy is delighted and so am I to be able to leave the child in such capable hands.'

Rhoda smiled across at Matilda. 'Can you nurse as well as cook?' she wanted to know. 'You really are a paragon.' She didn't hide her scorn.

To which piece of rudeness Matilda could find no answer. It was Mr Scott-Thurlow who spoke. 'Some day some lucky man will make her his wife.' He smiled across the room at Matilda as he said it and she smiled back, dully conscious that she felt suddenly shy, and Rhoda, watching them both, said quite sharply,

'Well, we had better be going, darling. Come back to my place after the Mathersons'—there are so many plans...'

She nodded at Matilda as she went out of the room, but Mr Scott-Thurlow paused by her chair. 'Breakfast is at eight o'clock,' he told her. 'I hope you sleep well. Goodnight, Matilda.'

She ate her solitary dinner presently under the kindly eye of Twigg. The food was delicious but she hardly noticed what she had on her plate. She was entirely occupied with the unsuitability of Rhoda as Mr Scott-Thurlow's wife. She would ruin him, or try to—turn him into a fashionable surgeon when really what he wanted to do was to use his skill upon anyone who needed it, never mind if they could pay or not. That he was a wealthy man was apparent to her now but she had the feeling that it was a matter of little importance to him. She wondered for the hundredth time why on earth he was going to marry Rhoda.

She thanked Twigg for his attentions and went back upstairs to find that Lucy was soundly sleeping and, since she had nothing better to do, she had a leisurely bath and went to bed herself.

She was up soon after six o'clock, roused by Lucy's small unhappy voice demanding a drink, to have her bed made more comfortable and someone to talk to.

Matilda pottered to and fro making the child comfortable, and since it was still so early suggested that she should go on with *The Secret Garden*.

'I'm thirsty,' declared Lucy, 'I'd like a cup of tea.'

Matilda quite fancied one herself. 'All right, why not? I'll pop down to the kitchen and make us some. I'll have to boil a kettle so don't expect me back for about five minutes.'

The house was quiet as she went downstairs, hoping that the dogs, who probably slept in the kitchen, wouldn't bark when they saw her. She went through the baize door at the back of the hall and crept into the kitchen. It was a delightful place with a well-scrubbed table and rows of polished pans on the walls and an old dresser with rows of plates. There was an Aga too but her eye fastened on an electric kettle.

She filled it, switched it on, peered around for the dogs, who were nowhere to be seen, and went in search of a teapot and cups.

She had made the tea, found milk and sugar and a tray and was on her way to the door when it was opened and the dogs came dashing in followed by Mr Scott-Thurlow in elderly trousers and a cotton sweater.

If he was surprised he didn't show it. His 'good morning' was polite and slightly questioning.

'Lucy woke early, she wants a cup of tea.' Matilda was very conscious of her hair all over the place and her dressing-gown, flung on without due regard to her appearance. She looked at the dogs, grinning at her from either side of their master. 'You've been out,' she said foolishly.

'Our usual morning walk. Is there a cup of tea for me?' When she nodded he picked up the tray and, accompanied by the dogs, they went upstairs.

Lucy was delighted. The dogs got on to the bed and settled down beside her and Mr Scott-Thurlow put the tray on a bedside table and sat on the bed too. 'Slept well?' he wanted to know. 'Stick out your tongue…'

Matilda poured the tea and sat down primly in a chair by the window to drink hers. When she was asked she said that yes, she had slept very well and that no, Lucy hadn't wanted anything during the night.

He finished his tea and got up to go. 'Breakfast at eight o'clock sharp,' he reminded her. He wandered over to the door and stood there looking at her. 'Get dressed first,' he said softly.

She dressed with ferocious speed, muttering crossly to herself, and scraped her glorious hair back into a tight French pleat, under a false impression that it made her look severe, whereas it made her look like a little girl whose hair had been pinned up out of the way ready for her bath.

When she went downstairs she went straight to the kitchen for Lucy's tray only to have it taken from her by a respectful Twigg. 'I will see that Lucy has her breakfast, miss—Maisie, here,' he nodded towards a young girl making toast, 'will come with me and stay with her until you have had your own breakfast. Mr Scott-Thurlow is in the dining-room already.'

So she went to the dining-room to find him there at the table, reading the paper. He got up when she went in, seated her and invited her to help herself to whatever she wanted.

'You don't find this too early?' he asked her politely.

'Not at all. Only shouldn't I be with Lucy?'

'No. I've been to see her again. Her temperature is down, which is a good sign, but I must warn you that as she improves she is likely to be peevish. I rely upon you to cope with that.'

He maintained a steady flow of small talk until they had finished the meal; he was, she conceded, a very good host although she found his reserve chilling. He got up to go presently with a word of apology. 'I seldom get home for lunch,' he told her, 'but I should be back rather earlier than usual this afternoon. Remember that you should get out for an hour after lunch. Mrs Twigg will sit with Lucy.'

He laid a hand lightly on her shoulder as he went past her chair. Long after he had gone she could feel the imprint of it there too.

That evening, strolling in the garden after her solitary dinner, she reflected that she had enjoyed her day despite the fact that just as they were sitting down to dinner Mr Scott-Thurlow had been called to the hospital, and now, two hours later, there was still no sign of him. Twigg had told her that this was often the case and there was no knowing when he would return, 'So just you enjoy your dinner, Miss Matilda, and take a turn in the garden; it's a splendid evening.'

She had been kept busy during the day with Lucy, who, just as Mr Scott-Thurlow had predicted, was inclined to be peevish, but she had devised games and read until her throat was dry and the child had settled down for a nap after lunch so that she was able to go for a quick walk in the quiet streets near the house while Mrs Twigg sat and knitted in Lucy's room. When she had returned there was just time to freshen up Lucy before her godfather, true to his promise, came home and they had tea together. He had looked tired, but he had set himself to amuse the child and the little meal was a happy one.

When it was quite dark she went indoors, made sure that Lucy was asleep and took herself off to bed. She was pleasantly tired but she didn't go to sleep—she lay awake listening for Mr Scott-Thurlow's return. It was one o'clock in the morning before she heard his quiet tread on the landing and the gentle closing of his door.

The days slipped easily into each other and by the end of a week Lucy was very nearly her old self again. She had the run of the house and she and Matilda spent a good deal of time playing duets on the piano in a small sitting-room at the back of the house. The child was talented and Matilda played with verve and a great many wrong notes and they enjoyed themselves hugely. They saw very little of Mr Scott-Thurlow for now that Lucy was out of her bed she and Matilda breakfasted after he had left the house. He himself had suggested it in a manner which led her to assume that he didn't wish for their company at that meal, and, since he came rarely to lunch at his own house and when he did dine at home his cool courtesy towards her successfully put a stop to any remarks she might make other than mundane ones about the weather, she rapidly reached the conclusion that he disliked her. If that was so, however, why had he asked her to come and look after Lucy?

Even that melancholy thought couldn't stop her loving him.

The days were warm now and she took Lucy out into the garden where they played clock golf, much hindered by the dogs. Nothing more had been said about their visit to Stoke Fleming and Matilda began to hope that he had decided not to send them away. Perhaps he would take a holiday himself and go somewhere with Lucy and Rhoda, for she herself wouldn't be needed for much longer—an opinion not shared by Rhoda, who arrived one afternoon shortly after Matilda had tucked Lucy up for her rest and then had gone downstairs to sit in the garden.

Her greeting was perfunctory. 'How can you bear to sit in the sun?' she asked, and arranged herself carefully in the shade of some artfully planted silver birch trees. 'Where's that child? Isn't she well yet? It's high time she was sent down to Devon; I absolutely refuse to have her tagging around any longer. James has his nose buried in that wretched hospital all day and half the night and I'm sick of making excuses for him. I'll talk to him and get him to send you both away, then perhaps he will be able to lead a more civilised life again. You can stay down there until she's due back at school…'

Matilda's eyes opened wide. 'Oh, that won't be possible; I came to look after Lucy until she was well again, and she is now, so I am free to go home.' She smiled sweetly. 'Why can she not go on holiday with you? I understood that she had been invited to spend the whole of her summer holidays with Mr Scott-Thurlow.'

'Who cares what you understood?' asked Rhoda rudely. 'He pays you so you'll do what he wants.'

'Perhaps he doesn't want me to go to Stoke Fleming…' Matilda's voice was pure syrup.

Rhoda laughed. 'We'll see about that…'

'What will you see about, Rhoda?' asked Mr Scott-Thurlow from the french window.

'Darling, how you startled me. We were discussing plans. Matilda is looking forward to going down to the cottage with Lucy—'

'No, I'm not,' said Matilda. She spoke pleasantly but her green eyes blazed.

Mr Scott-Thurlow lounged over to where she was sitting so that she felt obliged to look up at him looming over her.

'Now that is a pity,' he said gently, 'for I have arranged for you to go down to Devon in two days' time.'

CHAPTER EIGHT

MR SCOTT-THURLOW HAD an 'I told you so' look on his handsome features. 'I did mention that you would be going to Stoke Fleming as soon as Lucy was well enough and since you raised no objection I went ahead with my plans.'

Rhoda gave a brittle laugh. 'There, did I not say so? How lucky you are getting a holiday for free, Matilda. Darling, I'll cancel my engagements—where shall we go? Will you get tickets? Do be sure that the hotel is a good one-will it be too hot in the Bahamas?'

He had been staring at Matilda and she had been unable to look away for his gaze held hers but now he turned to Rhoda. 'I'm committed to a seminar in Leiden and a couple of lectures in Oslo and I must be back as soon as possible—I have a backlog of urgent cases...'

A speech Matilda heard with satisfaction and Rhoda with ill-concealed temper.

'What am I supposed to do?' she wanted to know. 'Don't think I'm trailing round Europe while you make dreary speeches about bones. The Burches asked me to go to Bangkok; I shall go with them.'

'It sounds delightful; there is no reason why you should get bored while I lecture. Besides, there would be little time to spend together; these sessions carry their quota of dinners and drinks parties and I'm ashamed to say that we all talk shop.'

'I suppose you're going back to that beastly hospital or rooms until midnight or longer. We're supposed to be at dinner with the Burches, or had you forgotten?'

'No, I phoned my excuses half an hour ago. They're expecting you and said they would get another man.'

Matilda, watching Rhoda, saw how her ill temper had made her quite ugly; it was a pity that Mr Scott-Thurlow hadn't seemed to notice that for he was smiling at Rhoda quite charmingly.

'I'm going,' said Rhoda coldly.

He went with her into the house and presently returned to where Matilda was still sitting.

'Have you nothing to say?' he asked. 'I feel sure that you are bottling up a number of searing speeches calculated to put me in my place.'

'Well, I am, but what would be the use?'

'None at all, so swallow your dudgeon and listen to me… You will be kind enough to get your things together tomorrow and Lucy's too, telephone your family by all means—I have already told your mother. I will be here by eight o'clock on the day after tomorrow, so be ready to leave then. We should get to the cottage by lunchtime. There is a housekeeper, my mother's cook, pensioned off—her name is Emma Truscott, and she will have everything ready for you both. Please get Lucy out of doors as much as possible but don't let her get tired. But I don't need to tell you this—you're a sensible young woman. In just over two weeks she must return to school, when your duties will end.'

'Why should I do this?' demanded Matilda. 'You come here without a by your leave—'

'It is my house,' he reminded her blandly.

'You know very well what I mean, Mr Scott-Thurlow; I feel as though I'm being—being trampled underfoot.' She glared at him and looked quite enchanting. 'Do this, do that, go here, go there! I don't know why I put up with it.'

'Yes, you do, Matilda.' He watched the colour flood into her face. 'But when you address me so severely as Mr Scott-Thurlow I realise what a despot I am.'

He sounded so meek that she wanted to laugh and did.

'That's better. Shall we have tea out here? Go and get Lucy and I'll tell Twigg.'

Lucy was enchanted with the idea of going down to Devon. She plied her godfather with questions while they had their tea until he said, 'I must get back to my rooms—I have several patients to see.' He got up and stopped to receive Lucy's hug and kiss. 'Remember to be ready to leave promptly,' he reminded Matilda. He hesitated, staring down at her, smiling wryly, but he didn't say anything, only nodded briefly as he went.

It was Twigg who told her that evening that Mr Scott-Thurlow had gone to Birmingham to operate at one of the hospitals there. 'Some tricky case, I'll be bound, Miss Matilda; he gets called all over the place, so he does.'

They were up early on the day of their departure and went down to breakfast soon after seven o'clock to find Mr Scott-Thurlow already at the table. His 'good morning' was genial and followed by the observation that he was delighted to see them up so promptly.

'Will you stay at the cottage with us?' asked Lucy.

'No, I shall have to come back here this evening; I'm going to Leiden tomorrow.'

'You will come down and see us though?' Lucy persisted.

'Well, we'll have to see about that. Shall we take Canada and Theobald with us?'

Matilda and Lucy chorused, 'Of course,' and two pairs of eyes gave him an indignant look. 'They don't see much of you anyway,' declared Matilda.

His smile was mocking. 'Sometimes I suspect that you would wish to change my life for me, Matilda.'

She choked over her coffee. 'Certainly not.'

She spoke with such vehemence that he laughed. 'You're not much good at telling fibs,' he told her.

They set off in good time with Lucy on the back seat, Theobald on her lap and Canada sitting very erect beside her. Matilda settled into her seat beside Mr Scott-Thurlow and cast about for harmless topics of conversation. She tried the weather, the charm of the country, the pleasure of driving early in the day and so on, then since she had received nothing but grunts and monosyllables in reply, lapsed into silence.

Presently he said, 'You have no need to make small talk with me, Matilda, I am very content to drive with you silent beside me.'

At which remark she drew a long, smouldering breath. 'If you will stop for a moment I will change places with Lucy…'

He answered her seriously, although she suspected that he was laughing to himself. 'No, no that won't be necessary. Have I offended you? I'm sorry; I haven't had much practice with pretty speeches.'

'Well, it's time you had,' said Matilda wrathfully. 'You'll have to change your ways when you get married.'

'I suspect that they will be changed for me.'

She frowned; it had seemed to her that Rhoda would be quite content with a husband who was absorbed in his work and left her free to live the social life she seemed to love. She uttered her thoughts out loud.

'Has she gone to Bangkok?' The words were out before she could stop them, but before she could do anything about it he answered her in an ordinary voice with no surprise in it.

'Yesterday. The Burches were delighted that she could go with them; I imagine that she will enjoy herself enormously.'

Matilda muttered a reply, very red in the face, and he, glancing quickly at her, smiled slowly and then said over his shoulder, 'I thought we'd stop presently, Lucy— would you like that?'

They were north of Salisbury by now, still on the A303, and it was after they had passed Wincanton that he said, 'Your mother suggested that we might stop for coffee,' and turned off on to a side-road. 'We can't stay long but you will have the time to collect anything you may want.'

'Thank you. May Lucy go into the sea?'

'If the day is warm and she stays only a short time. Do you wish to swim?'

'Yes.'

Then they didn't speak again until he drew up outside her home.

The entire ffinch family came out to meet them; Matilda wondered if Mr Scott-Thurlow was comparing the warmth and noise of their reception with the cool and perfect manners of Rhoda. It was impossible to tell from his expression and his own manners were too good to give her a clue. Lucy, instantly made much of, was borne away to the kitchen by Esme to be refreshed with cake and lemonade while the rest of the party strolled after them. The kitchen door was open and the sunlight streamed in to the comfortably shabby room, smelling of freshly ground coffee and newly baked cakes. Matilda saw Mr Scott-Thurlow's splendid nose twitch appreciatively.

'You're in a hurry,' said her mother, 'so I thought it better if we had coffee here—Tilly, you'll want to run upstairs and collect some clothes, I suspect. Hilary put everything out on the bed, ready to pack. If you'll just pick out what you're going to want, my dear.'

'I'll go now, while you're pouring the coffee. Thanks, Hilary…'

She flew upstairs and found the elderly zipper bag they all borrowed in turn in the bedroom and a couple of cotton dresses neatly pressed and folded. Her swimsuit was there too and some old sandals, just right for the beach. She packed the bag, added a thick sweater in case it turned chilly and went back to the kitchen, to find everyone there, some sitting at the table, the younger ones milling around, in and out of the garden.

Mindful of Mr Scott-Thurlow's wishes, she gobbled her cake, swallowed down her coffee and pronounced herself ready to leave, but another ten minutes was wasted while she made her protracted goodbyes and the dogs were rounded up and they were all stowed into the car once more.

'What a pity you can't go and see your grandparents,'

said Matilda at the end of her polite speech of thanks.
'You practically pass their door...'

'No time. I'll call on my way back.' They were
again on the A303 and he sent the Rolls forwards at
the steady maximum speed allowed. They joined the
A30 presently and then turned off on to the motorway
south of Exeter. Here he could travel faster and the big
car shot effortlessly ahead, eating up the miles, and
so on towards Plymouth and to the road over Haldon
and then the long straight stretch to Buckfastleigh and
Totnes and all too soon—from her point of view—they
were on the road to Kingsbridge.

'This is the long way round,' said Mr Scott-Thurlow,
'but it is by far the prettiest road.' At Kingsbridge he
took the road to Torcross and then raced along Slapton
Sands with the beach on one side of them and a
charming lake on the other, and at its end he took the
car smartly up the steep wooded road which led to the
village.

Stoke Fleming rambled on either side of the road;
small white and pink painted cottages with thatched
roofs and gardens bright with flowers, and splendid
views of the beach and sea below. He turned the car
down a narrow lane and in through an open gateway
and stopped before the open door of a traditionally pink-
washed cottage, its thatched roof pierced by small lattice
windows and surrounded by a fair-sized lawn and a
wealth of flower-beds. He leaned over to the back seat
and opened the door for Lucy and the dogs and got out
himself to go round to Matilda's side.

'Why, it's pure heaven!' she told him. 'What a pity
that you can't stay here too—you need a holiday.' She

waved an arm. 'All this space and the view and this darling little house…'

She became aware that he was looking at her and smiling. As usual, she reflected crossly, she was allowing her tongue to chatter on. She looked away from him and said stiffly, 'This seems a charming place; Lucy will love it.'

The child and the dogs had rushed into the house; she could hear Lucy's voice, squeaky with excitement, and a moment later she came running out again, this time with a small round woman, grey-haired and rosy-cheeked.

She went straight to Mr Scott-Thurlow, who hugged her, kissed her soundly and told her in a voice Matilda had never heard before—it was so content—that she was prettier than ever. 'And this is Matilda,' he told her, 'come to keep this imp of mischief out of trouble and keep you company.'

Matilda smiled at the nice kind face as she shook hands; they were going to like each other. She said happily, 'I'm sure we're going to be very happy here.'

'No doubt of it, me love. And as pretty a maid as I seen for many years. Now just you come in and eat your dinners and you, Mr James, must have a nice lay-down before you go back. More's the pity that you have to go.'

She bustled them indoors, through a small hall and into a large, low-ceilinged room with a table set under the far window; the floor was polished and spread with thick rugs and the chairs were comfortable and well cushioned. A matronly cat sat in one of them, washing herself, taking no notice of the dogs pottering to and fro.

'You'll be wanting to tidy yourselves,' said Emma Truscott. 'Up the stairs and the first door on the right—don't be long, I'll be dishing up.' As she trotted off into

the kitchen Matilda heard her telling Mr James to fetch
the cases, do, and take them up to the bedrooms.

When they went downstairs again there was an
old-fashioned soup tureen on the table and Mr Scott-
Thurlow was ladling its contents into deep plates.
Matilda sat Lucy at the table. 'Can I do anything to
help, Miss Truscott?'

'Call me Emma, me love, and sit yourself down.
Watercress soup I made myself and as nice a chicken
as ever I saw to follow.' She cast Matilda an approving
look. 'Enjoy good food, do you? You're a nice healthy
shape—I don't hold with all this fancy eating; I like a
woman to look like one. Don't you agree with me, Mr
James?'

Matilda bent a red face over her plate. Mr Scott-
Thurlow gave a serious reply but she had no doubt that
he was amused.

The chicken was brought in, carved with the
expertise expected of the carver, and eaten with the
appropriate trimmings and followed by raspberries and
clotted cream, while Emma enlarged on the various
small events in the village. All too soon the meal was
over and Mr Scott-Thurlow was preparing to leave.

'You'll not go, Mr James, until you've sat yourself
down for ten minutes, quiet like. Dear knows what your
insides will be like if you get straight into that car of
yours and go dashing off.'

It surprised Matilda that he did as he was told and
went to sit outside in a garden chair with nothing but
the sea in front of him. Lucy climbed on to his lap and
sat quietly while Matilda helped clear the table. At the
end of ten minutes, he got to his feet, hugged the child

and said in a voice which meant what it said that he was leaving.

'Well, if you must, you must,' grumbled Emma, 'but just you take care how you drive.'

He said 'yes' meekly, hugged her fondly, kissed Lucy and nodded to Matilda. However, halfway to the gate he paused and came back to her, put his hands on her shoulders and kissed her. It was a tender, lingering kiss and she thrilled to it, aware that if he had dropped his guard the kiss would have been quite different. She turned her back on good sense and kissed him back, knowing that she would regret it bitterly.

He said nothing at all but turned on his heel, got into his car, and with a wave of his hand, drove himself away.

She turned round to see Emma eyeing her thoughtfully. She said breathlessly, 'I expect he thought I was Rhoda...'

A silly remark which received a tart answer. 'You know and I know that he thought no such thing, love. Now you go and unpack your things and take Lucy down to the beach. There's a path down the cliff to the shore, through the wicket gate at the bottom of the garden.'

The sand was firm and clean, and they strolled along on the edge of the sea, their sandals in their hands, revelling in the warm air and the sound of the water splashing their feet. 'I wish Uncle James was here too,' said Lucy. 'I can't see why he can't have a holiday...?'

'He has to go to Holland, darling—he's a busy man.'

'Do you suppose he'll come and see us while we're here?'

'I don't think so.' Matilda sounded sad; if he had any time at all he would surely spend it with Rhoda.

'Well, I do,' said Lucy, 'he likes me and he likes you too—he kissed you goodbye.'

'Well, that was because he kissed us all, didn't he?'

'He took a lot longer over you,' said Lucy.

They went to bed early, bidden to do so by Emma in her soft West Country voice, so it made sense that they should be up early too, to spend a long day, shopping for Emma, doing a few chores around the house and then going down to the beach, this time with a bucket and spade for Lucy and wearing cheap straw hats to protect them from the sun. All the same Matilda had a sprinkling of freckles across her nose by the evening. She sat at her dressing-table that evening, rubbing them with a cream to remove them and which did no such thing. Not that she minded much; there was no one to see them, and by no one of course she meant Mr Scott-Thurlow. She jumped into bed and inspected her room with pleasure. The cottage was charmingly furnished with the right kind of furniture, pretty chintz curtains and soft rugs. It had been skilfully modernised but it still contrived to look cosy despite the porcelain ornaments scattered around the silver tableware and fine linen. It was, reflected Matilda, a home—a retreat. She wondered how often Mr Scott-Thurlow came to stay in it and if Rhoda had ever been with him. It was a pity that she couldn't ask Emma...

But she had no need; over breakfast the next morning Emma volunteered the information that Mr James, when he came to stay for a few days or a weekend, came alone. 'That Miss Symes he's supposed to wed came to visit one afternoon—she can't a-bear this end of the country; likes the bright lights or foreign parts. Dear knows how they'll sort that out when they marry, if ever they do.'

Matilda murmured vaguely, glad that Lucy had left the table to take the crumbs for the seagulls, and Emma went on chattily, 'You've seen quite a bit of Mr James, I dare say, what with the little dog and his granny and now little Lucy.' She cast a shrewd eye at Matilda. 'He's a good man, is Mr James, as well as being a gentleman born, and you don't often get the two together.' She obviously expected an answer.

'Yes, he's very kind…'

''Andsome too, and then all that money… There's been plenty of young women willing to have him and his money.'

Matilda reflected that she was willing to have him without a single penny piece; she loved him regardless of anything else, but love wasn't enough. She said in a small wooden voice, 'Well, he's found someone he wants to marry…'

She was piling marmalade on to a piece of toast and didn't see Emma's look. 'That he has, me love, and the sooner the better, he's been too long without someone to love him and be loved.' She was suddenly brisk. 'Now, if you'll go, the pair of you, to the butcher's and fetch some of his sausages we'll have toad-in-the-hole for our dinner and there's raspberries to be picked in the garden. You'll be going to the beach presently?'

Matilda got up with a sense of relief. Emma was a darling but her eyes were sharp and she seemed to know a great deal about James—well, of course she would, having been cook to his parents and then joining his grandparents' household until he had installed her as housekeeper in this cottage. He wasn't mentioned again that day and indeed no one mentioned his name during the next few days, which slid with pleasurable slowness into a week, during which the pair of them acquired a glorious tan and Lucy, under Matilda's patient guidance, learned to swim. They also developed healthy appetites. 'I shall get fat,' declared Matilda, helping herself to more clotted cream. They went for gentle strolls in the evenings once the supper had been cleared away and the dishes washed, leaving Emma to sit with her old-fashioned specs perched on the end of her nose, reading the paper, and on Sunday they all went to the village church before going back to Emma's splendid Sunday dinner. Quite perfect, thought Matilda, or almost quite—if James were there it would be...

The lovely weather showed no sign of abating. Matilda got up early while Lucy still slept and got into one of her rather elderly cotton dresses, tied back her hair and went downstairs to give a hand with the weekly wash. There was a washing-machine of course and she had engaged to keep it filled and emptied while Emma got the breakfast. With all the doors and windows open, and the morning already pleasantly warm even at seven o'clock in the morning, she went happily about the task. Emma had put the first load in earlier; Matilda piled the clothes basket, loaded the machine again and went off to where the clothes-line hung out of sight at the bottom of the garden. It was pleasant hanging up sheets and towels and pillowcases with no sound but the waves below, the seagulls on the look-out for breakfast and a car or two on the road, going down the hill to Slapton Sands, intent on finding a vacant parking space before everyone else got there. She finished ramming home the last peg, picked up the basket and went back to the cottage; Emma would have breakfast ready by now.

She put the basket in the scullery ready for the next load and went through the open kitchen door. Mr Scott-Thurlow was leaning against the wall, talking to Emma, frying bacon on the Aga. He was wearing an open-necked shirt and drill trousers and had the air of someone who had been on holiday for some time.

Matilda fetched up short, frowning fiercely because she felt the bright colour flood into her face, but she couldn't stop the happy sparkle in her eyes.

He studied her face for a moment. 'Good morning, Matilda.' His eyes left her face and travelled over her person, giving her time to regret the elderly dress. 'You look well—Emma's cooking, no doubt...'

'If you mean I've got fat—' she began wrathfully.

'No, no, nothing of the sort. You appear to me to be—er—exactly the right shape. And Lucy?'

'Is splendid—she's put on weight too and she looks marvellous.'

'That makes two of you.'

She didn't answer that. 'Have you just got here?' she asked politely.

'I got here about three o'clock this morning.'

'Three o'clock... But you ought to be in bed, you must be tired out.'

'Not a bit of it. I've given myself two days off so I hope that you—and Lucy—will bear with my company.'

She couldn't prevent the wide smile and when he smiled slowly too she actually took a step towards him, wanting to be near him, tell him how happy she was to see him. It was providential that Emma spoke.

'Bacon's done to a turn and there's the tatties fried up how you like 'em. Sit down, do, and eat your breakfasts.'

Matilda dragged her eyes away from Mr Scott-Thurlow's face. 'I'll fetch Lucy.' She flew out of the room and up the little staircase and found the child hanging out of the window. 'I heard some dogs barking, they sounded just like Canada and Theobald, but it's not of course. I was looking to see if there's anyone on the beach...'

'Come down and eat your breakfast, love,' said Matilda, and laughed out loud when she saw the child's delight and surprise when the dogs came to meet them at the kitchen door.

Lucy burst into the room. 'Uncle James, you're here, it was Theobald barking and Canada!' She flung herself at him, talking excitedly, and it took a few minutes before they were all sitting at the table intent on breakfast.

Mr Scott-Thurlow ate an enormous meal, but then he was a very large man and probably he hadn't had his supper or stopped on the way down.

'Are you here for weeks and weeks?' asked Lucy.

'Two days, sweetheart, so tell me what you want to do most and we'll do it.'

He looked across the table at Matilda as he spoke, and because there was something in his face which she found disquieting she said quickly, 'It's going to be a lovely day.'

A silly remark, but he agreed with her, still staring at her until the slow lovely colour crept into her cheeks. He smiled then and looked away and Lucy broke the silence.

'I can swim, Uncle James—can we go down on to

the beach and I'll show you? I do six strokes if Matilda is beside me.'

'I can think of nothing nicer. Emma, have I got some swimming gear somewhere?'

'In the airing cupboard, ready and waiting.' She beamed at him and offered more toast.

'Could we have a picnic lunch in the garden? All of us—sandwiches and so on. Would it upset your plans if we had our dinner in the evening? I'd hate to miss any of this wonderful sun…'

'Anything you say, Mr James,' said Emma. 'It's a treat to have someone in the house. I am going to miss you when you've all gone.'

'I promise you we shall come back again, Emma.'

Matilda, watching Emma's face, knew exactly what she was thinking—if Rhoda were to come she would prefer to be on her own, thank you.

Breakfast over, James astonished Matilda by doing the washing-up while she and Emma cleared the table and set the place to rights again and then went to make the beds.

'Don't be long about it,' he called after them. 'Lucy, feed the dogs, will you? Everything is ready on the garden table.'

So presently, their chores done and leaving Emma to have what she called a nice sit-down, they went down the path to the beach. The tide was on the turn and it was already warm. Matilda sat down against a convenient rock, rammed her wide straw hat over her bright hair and delved into the large straw bag she had brought with her. She had prudently got into her swimsuit and donned her dress on top of it, feeling shy of James, but Lucy's childish bikini was there, and so were three cans of lemonade, a bag of doughnuts, some Dettol cream and some Band-Aids. There was a paperback there too, but she didn't think she would have a chance to read. She hoped she wouldn't.

Her hopes were realised; Mr Scott-Thurlow was transformed from a rather unapproachable consultant surgeon to a godfather willing to do anything within reason. They built a tremendous sand-castle with a channel running down to the water and a moat around it and then they sat eating their doughnuts while the tide came in and washed it all away again.

'Time for a swim,' said Mr Scott-Thurlow and stripped off his shirt and trousers, caught up Lucy in a giggling bundle and waded into the water, leaving Matilda to peel off her dress and follow them.

Lucy had to demonstrate her swimming prowess and, that done, sat happily enough on the beach with the water washing around her feet while Matilda and Mr Scott-Thurlow swam strongly out to sea and back again, and once back they lay, the three of them, with the gentle waves washing over them, soaking up the sun. The tide was coming in, so they got up reluctantly and went to sit out of reach of the water, and presently at Lucy's insistence they built another sand-castle. Matilda, obediently filling buckets of sand and handing it over to the builders, thought what a splendid father he would make and lost herself in a daydream peopled by a horde of little Scott-Thurlows, herself and James, so that she was only aroused by repeated shouts for more sand.

They had their picnic in the garden with Emma and then lay about doing nothing until it was time for tea. After tea, in the cool of the late afternoon, they went walking. Down the hill to Slapton Sands, still packed with day visitors, to walk along the sands, barefooted, splashing along on the very edge of the sea. When they got back to the cottage they showered and changed and sat down to one of Emma's delicious meals. Garlic mushrooms, roast chicken with all the trimmings, a pile of roast potatoes and asparagus, creamed spinach and baby corn, and one of her fruit pies with a crust which melted in the mouth and loaded down with clotted cream.

They sat over the meal until Matilda gathered up Lucy, already half asleep, and bore her off to her bed. When she came down Emma had taken the coffee into the sitting-room and they sat over that too. Presently Mr Scott-Thurlow suggested that a stroll along the sand would be pleasant on such a splendid evening, so Matilda fetched a cardigan and slung it around her shoulders and accompanied him down to the beach once more.

'You really ought to go to bed early,' she told him. 'You shouldn't burn the candle at both ends.'

'Afraid I might let the knife slip? I have never met a girl who was so anxious to order my life for me, Matilda.'

His mocking voice hurt her and wakened her quick temper. 'Don't talk nonsense—I don't imagine there is anyone on this earth who can do that, and if there is it's Rhoda.'

'You are mistaken. Nothing and no one, save one person, will have the power to change my life.'

She had her mouth open to ask who the someone was and then snapped it shut; it wasn't her business, but did it mean that he wasn't going to marry Rhoda? She said in her best social manner, 'What a delightful evening it is; we're having a marvellous summer.'

He answered her with a hint of a laugh in his voice. 'Indeed, yes— of my life.'

Which wasn't quite the answer she had expected; she worked away at her small talk and he politely followed her lead and in a little while they went back to the cottage and said goodnight.

The next day followed the pattern of the previous one only there was no stroll in the evening, for after dinner, eaten a little earlier than usual, Mr Scott-Thurlow prepared to leave.

'Must you go?' asked Lucy tearfully.

'Yes, but I'm taking my two lovely days here back with me, aren't I? And who knows, I may come again before you go back to school. In any case I'll come and fetch you back to London and take you back to Miss Tremble's.'

He swung her up in his great arms and kissed her soundly and then hugged Emma. 'Dear Emma, thank you…' He kissed her pink cheek with affection. Matilda, standing a little apart, wondered if they should shake hands, or would he give her a friendly nod as he went?

He did neither; he put his hands on her shoulders and kissed her too, another gentle, lingering kiss which sent her pulses racing and took her breath, but not quite all of it for she kissed him back, flinging good sense to the winds again, never mind the future, never mind Rhoda, this moment was hers.

Mr Scott-Thurlow straightened his imposing height and then stood looking at her. He said nothing at all but bent once more and kissed her again, this time swift and hard.

They stood at the cottage door waving him goodbye. 'He kissed you twice,' said Lucy. 'I think Uncle James likes you very much, Matilda.'

'Bedtime, love!' said Emma. 'You uncle likes us all and what a lovely time you've had these last two days. Eaten us out of house and home, he has—tomorrow you and Matilda will have to go shopping for me. You can get the bus into Dartmouth.'

She bustled the child upstairs, which gave Matilda a few minutes in which to pull her disordered thoughts together and regret very bitterly that she had returned Mr Scott-Thurlow's kiss. It had been heaven, of course, but now she went scarlet with shame at allowing him to find out her feelings for him, for she had certainly made no secret of them. She frowned; his kisses had been rather more than friendly...

There was a letter from Esme in the morning, full of family news and bits of gossip about the village. One of the maids at the manor-house was going steady with the milkman's son, Lady Fox had a new and quite awful hat, Sir Benjamin had fluffed his lines reading the lesson on Sunday and Nelson the cat had caught a rat at the bottom of the garden. 'And I must tell you,' wrote Esme in her impetuous scrawl, 'who do you suppose came to see Mother the other day? That Rhoda woman who's going to marry our nice Mr Scott-Thurlow; she'd been to see Roseanne, who's almost well—and called in on her way back to London. Said what a lovely time she and he were having—parties and so on—I didn't believe half of it. Said what a pity it was that Roseanne wouldn't be able to be one of the bridesmaids since she and Mr Scott-Thurlow are getting married very shortly. I hate her.'

So do I, thought Matilda bitterly. His kisses hadn't
meant anything, just a last fling before he married. She
hoped that she would never see him again. She looked
at the letter once more. Esme wrote that Rhoda had
actually said that she would send Matilda an invitation
to the wedding because she had been so kind and
capable.

'Pah!' said Matilda with such force that Emma and
Lucy both looked at her with astonishment.

The days, empty of Mr Scott-Thurlow's presence,
went slowly by. They did the same things, went for
the same walks, played the same games and spent a
good deal of time messing about on the beach and in
the water. Matilda made no mention of him and was
outwardly cheerful as usual but Lucy observed a dozen
times a day that she wanted him back.

'You're a very nice person,' she explained to Matilda,
'and so is Emma, but it's not quite the same.' Tears
weren't far off. 'And it's almost time for me to go back
to Miss Tremble's.'

'It's also almost time for your mummy and daddy to
come home, love, only another week or two…'

There was no word from Mr Scott-Thurlow, not until
their very last day when he phoned to say that they
could expect him for lunch on the following day and
they were to be ready to leave in the early afternoon. So
Matilda packed their things and took Lucy down to the
beach for their last morning bathe and, while they were
gone, Emma, listening to Mr Scott-Thurlow's voice on
the phone once again, chuckled comfortably at what
he had to say.

The next day—the last, thought Matilda gloomily,
alternately thrilled at the thought of seeing him again

and still smarting from Esme's letter—they went down to the beach just once more. She had laid their clothes ready for travelling and left enough room to stuff their cotton dresses in at the last minute; she hadn't bothered about make-up either, or her hair, which she had tied back with a handy piece of string from the kitchen.

They were building a sand-castle to end all sand-castles when they heard the dogs—Canada's gruff unhurried bark and Theobald's excited yap. Coming towards them were three people: Mr Scott-Thurlow and a man and a woman.

Lucy flung down her spade. 'Mummy! Daddy!' she bawled, and tore to meet them.

CHAPTER NINE

MATILDA STOOD STILL and watched Mr Scott-Thurlow and the dogs coming towards her; he wasn't hurrying, which gave her time to get over the rapture of seeing him and stoke up her indignation at his behaviour, so that when he reached her she returned his cheerful greeting in a witheringly chilly, calm voice which sent his eyebrows up.

'Surprised you? Matt and Jean got back yesterday, several weeks earlier than they had expected. They'll stay here and keep Lucy with them—Matt has already spoken to Miss Tremble—and they'll take her with them when they go to Berkshire. You're ready to leave? Good. I'll take you back with me and drop you off at Abner Magna—I have to be back in town this evening.'

He didn't wait for her reply, which was just as well. 'Come and meet Jean and Matt...' He stood towering over her, smiling, looking, she reflected, a bit smug. 'I like the string,' he told her.

She gave him a haughty look. 'We weren't expecting you—we came down here for a last hour or two and naturally we couldn't wear the clothes we shall travel in.'

'Lucy won't be travelling. Anyway, I like that chemise thing you're wearing.'

She got rather pink; the white cotton dress she

was wearing was sleeveless and with a scooped-out low neckline—a well-worn garment she had kept for messing around with Lucy, but before she could answer him he was introducing her to Lucy's parents and presently the whole party made their way back to the cottage. Once there, he made no attempt to engage her in conversation but wandered off into the garden, leaving her to gossip gently with Jean while Lucy sat between them bubbling over with happiness.

'We are so grateful to you,' said Jean. 'James says you're marvellous with children, animals and sudden mishaps—you've certainly been a fairy godmother to Lucy. He didn't tell us how pretty you are. No, not pretty—beautiful, and I love your hair.'

'I'm not very tidy, I'm afraid. I'd better go and change; I expect Mr Scott-Thurlow will want to leave directly after lunch and I mustn't keep him waiting. He's giving me a lift home.'

Jean gave her a nice smile. She was tempted to tell this delightful creature in her simple clothes just what James had said about her, but that would never do; besides, they had a long drive before them, ample time for them to talk. 'I'll unpack Lucy's clothes, shall I? I've brought one or two things with me.' She dropped a kiss on her daughter's head. 'Would you like to see them now, darling?'

So the three of them went upstairs and Matilda had a shower and got into the flower-patterned two-piece, stuck her stockinged feet into neat shoes, did her face and brushed her hair into its severe French pleat. Surveying her reflection, she thought that she hadn't looked like that for more than two weeks.

Mr Scott-Thurlow had meant what he said when he

had told her that they would leave immediately after lunch. He stowed her case in the boot, whistled to the dogs, bade everyone a brisk goodbye and then waited with no sign of impatience while Matilda said her own farewells. Prolonged hugs from Lucy and promises to meet again, reiterated thanks from her mother and father and a rather tearful one from Emma, who pressed a dozen brown eggs and a pot of cream on her with the fervent hope that Matilda would come and see her again. A rare pity, she thought as she watched the beautiful Matilda get into the car, that her Mr James hadn't chosen to marry her instead of the haughty creature who, on her one visit, had ignored her completely.

They all waved at the departing car and Emma said, 'Ah, well, it's a nice long drive.'

Jean smilingly agreed; she had only met Rhoda once and she hadn't liked her either. She had no doubt that she and Emma were thinking the same thing.

It was Lucy who put their thoughts into words. 'It would be nice if Matilda and Uncle James got married,' she said.

If they had been in the car they would have had their doubts. Matilda, sustaining a polite flow of small talk in a frosty voice and encouraged to do so by an amused James, was as unapproachable as a bed of stinging nettles. Presently he said, 'We have a long drive ahead of us—could you stop being so polite with your chit-chat and be you?'

She wouldn't look at him. 'I'm sure I don't know what you mean.'

'No? Ah, well—all in good time. Let us continue with our small talk. Did you know that Roseanne is getting married in September? The wedding is to be a very grand affair.'

It was on the tip of her tongue to ask him if his own wedding would be grand too; she couldn't imagine it to be otherwise with Rhoda as the bride. She checked the question just in time and was rewarded by his, 'A wedding should be a family affair with only close friends, do you not agree?'

'Well, yes. Everyone else only comes out of curiosity.'

The car ate up the miles in a well-bred fashion and he kept the talk undemanding, lapsing into long silences which strangely enough left her perfectly at ease with him. They also gave her a chance to think, and her thoughts were sad. This was probably the last time she would be with him; their paths were unlikely to meet in the future, and a good thing too for it was hard to maintain her chilly politeness.

They were nearing Montacute on the A303 and not far from Abner Magna now when he turned off into a side-road.

'You've gone off the road,' said Matilda unnecessarily.

'We are having tea at Grandmother's.' He glanced at his watch. 'It's barely four o'clock—just right. We're expected.'

'But Mother is expecting—'

'Around half-past five or six o'clock.'

Mackrell Cantelo basked in the afternoon sun and the village was quiet as he swept through it and turned in at the stone pillars. As they stopped before the house Slocombe came through the door to meet them.

'A pleasure to see you, Mr James and Miss ffinch. Your grandparents are in the conservatory—I'll bring tea there in a few minutes. Perhaps you would like to freshen up, miss?'

Matilda smoothed her hair, applied more lipstick and tidied her already tidy person and then went back into the hall. Was she supposed to find her way to the conservatory on her own? she wondered. Apparently not; Mr Scott-Thurlow was sitting on the stairs waiting for her. She might have known that he would be; he was so thoughtful of other people. She hoped that Rhoda appreciated that.

His grandparents were sitting in peacock chairs overshadowed by palms, ferns and clinging greenery. The doors to the terrace were open but even then it was warm. The dogs made a beeline for the lawn outside and she envied them as she greeted her hostess and, obedient to Mrs Scott-Thurlow's request, sat down beside her.

'It is delightful to see you again, my dear,' said the old lady. 'Now you must tell me about your stay at Stoke Fleming. Such a dear little cottage, is it not?'

The talk was general and pleasant over tea and presently the old lady said, 'Why don't you two young people have ten minutes in the garden and take a little stroll before you go? My roses are glorious and you really must see them.'

Matilda was surprised when Mr Scott-Thurlow got up. 'A splendid idea—come along, Matilda.'

Her inclination was to refuse, but with the old lady's kindly eyes fixed upon her that would have been impossible. Crossing the lawn with him, the dogs wreathing around them, she said with some asperity, 'I thought you were in a hurry?'

'Oh, I am, but I have found that there is always time for something one wishes to do.'

'Oh, yes, the roses.' They had reached the end of the large garden where the rose-beds made a splash of lovely colours, the beds separated by closely cut turf paths.

He came to a halt, staring down at her with a faint frown. 'What is the matter, Matilda? When I was at the cottage I thought… Well, never mind that now.' He put his hands on her shoulders. 'You have always been frank and outspoken,' he smiled a little, 'too outspoken sometimes, but you are hiding something and I wonder why?'

'I don't know what you're talking about…'

She drew back from him and he let her go at once. 'In that case I'll not say what I wanted to say to you; I should have told you at the cottage.'

She said fiercely, 'Well, I'm glad you didn't for I don't want to know.'

He stared down at her thoughtfully, his face calm and unworried. 'No? If ever you should change your mind, Matilda, you know where to find me.' He smiled suddenly. 'And having admired the roses we had better be on our way.'

They made their farewells and the two old people came to the door with them and watched them drive away, the dogs once more on the back seat, Matilda sitting rather erect beside James.

'A dear girl,' remarked his grandmother. 'She will manage him very well.'

Abner Magna looked peaceful in the late afternoon sunshine and the rectory garden, untidy and a little neglected though it was, was full of colour. Their welcome was warm for everyone was at home and anxious to greet them, but Mr Scott-Thurlow, in a few well-polished sentences, made his excuses, bade them all goodbye and got back into his car, the reluctant dogs climbing in once more. He had said all the right things; Matilda had been of the greatest help and Lucy had grown very fond of her, in fact he was indeed very grateful and hoped that he hadn't hindered her in getting some more congenial job. He had wished her goodbye with a bland smile and eyes as hard as blue steel.

'A pity he couldn't stay for supper,' said her mother, 'but I dare say he wants to get back to town. Did Esme tell you in her letter that Rhoda Symes came here, Tilly? Full of her wedding arrangements, said to be sure and tell you because you'd be interested. I don't like her.'

'Now, now, my dear,' said the rector mildly, 'we must try and like everyone.'

For once his wife disagreed with him. 'You can't like someone you don't like,' she told him with female logic.

THE BUSY, HAPPY life at the rectory was soothing to Matilda. Just for a moment she had felt sudden happiness at the sight of the envelope addressed to her in James's illegible handwriting, which someone had put on her dressing-table. She had opened it with a shaky hand and found a cheque inside and a businesslike slip of paper, typed no doubt by his secretary and signed with his initials. She would have liked to have torn it into little shreds and sent it back to him, but for once good sense had the ascendancy over her red hair. The cheque was for a tidy sum; it meant football boots for the boys, a new hat for her mother, a longed-for book for her father and clothes for Esme, Hilary and herself. She had put it in her purse, sniffed away a great desire to cry and gone downstairs to her supper.

She had been home for a few days when her mother came back from the village. 'I met Lady Fox, Tilly—she had heard that you were back and Roseanne wants you to go and see her.' She glanced at her daughter's beautiful and sad face. 'I hope I did the right thing in saying you would go. She's coming home in a few days now but Bernard has had to go away and she's longing for company. Esme's too young and Hilary doesn't want to talk about anyone else's wedding except her own.'

Matilda rubbed butter into flour, intent on making an apple tart. 'I'll go tomorrow if Father will let me borrow the car.'

It was a quiet morning with the faint haziness of late summer in the air. She drove slowly while she thought. Once the boys were back at school and Esme back at her school, she would get a job, somewhere where there was no chance of meeting James, somewhere where no one knew him so that when he married Rhoda she wouldn't know about it, and then in no time he would become a memory, getting more and more vague until she couldn't remember what he looked like, and that would leave her free to marry some man who wouldn't rock her heart and send her pulses racing. Even as she thought it she knew that the very idea was nonsense; she would never forget him...

Roseanne was sitting outside on the hospital veranda and professed herself delighted to see Matilda, proudly demonstrating the fact that, excepting for a gutter crutch, she was well again.

'Of course, by the time we marry I shall be able to walk without the wretched thing. I must tell you about the wedding...' Something she did at great length; indeed she hadn't finished when she was interrupted—

one of the sisters came through the open door on to the veranda and with her came Mr Scott-Thurlow.

He saw Matilda at once but his face remained impassive. Nothing could have been more polite than his 'good morning', uttered in a pleasant voice before he turned his attention to Roseanne.

'I'll go,' said Matilda, praying feverishly that he would say that she might stay. Only he didn't, merely waited until she bade Roseanne goodbye and then nodded and smiled at her, at his most urbane. The impetuous side of her nature longed to throw something at him but the loving side wept silently at his bland indifference.

The hospital was away from the main road, and Matilda started to drive back to Abner Magna along the network of country roads which would eventually take her home. They were quiet, used mainly by farm vehicles and people who had lost their way, and the villages were few and some miles from each other. The country here was open with splendid views and low, rolling hills. It was halfway up one of these that the engine coughed, laboured on for a few yards, coughed again and stopped.

'Now what?' enquired Matilda of the surrounding quiet and got out and looked under the bonnet—a useless exercise for she had only the vaguest idea as to what was underneath it. It looked the same as usual. She got back into the car and pressed the self-starter; nothing happened, and it was then that she saw that there was no petrol. 'Halfway up a hill, too,' she exclaimed. 'Now what?'

'What' materialised in the shape of a car coming with effortless ease up the hill. It came to a smooth halt a few yards ahead of her and Mr Scott-Thurlow got out. He walked unhurriedly to her car, stuck his head through the window and observed mildly, 'Not a very good place to stop, but no doubt you had your reasons.'

She bristled. 'As though anyone with any sense would stop halfway up a hill...'

He glanced at the dashboard. 'Out of petrol?' He shook his head in a particularly infuriating manner. 'And I thought you were such a sensible girl.'

'I *am* a sensible girl,' she snapped and tossed her fiery head at him. 'Anyone can run out of petrol.'

'Of course,' he said soothingly. 'One only needs to forget to fill up.'

Her eyes gleamed greenly. 'Don't let me keep you—someone will come along presently—or perhaps you would be so kind as to stop at Dunn's garage—it's a mile or so along this road, just before you get to Littlecote-sub-Magna...'

'I will be even kinder—I will put some petrol in your tank for you.' His smile mocked her. 'I carry a spare can or two.'

She might have known that he would; he was a man who was prepared for all eventualities. She watched him go back to his car, fetch the petrol, empty its contents into her tank and return the can to his own boot. He did it without haste and very tidily and then walked back again and opened her door. 'Move over,' he told her.

'Why?'

He glanced at the few yards between the cars. 'I don't want the Rolls to get bashed. So move over, dear girl; much as I would like to waste my time in your company I have to get back to town.'

She moved over. 'You had no need to stop,' she muttered crossly.

'That is one of the silliest remarks I have ever heard; a pity I haven't the time to tell you why.'

He drove her car up to the crest of the hill and stopped. 'Off you go,' he told her as he got out. 'And for heaven's sake drive carefully.'

A remark calculated to send her shooting along the narrow road as fast as she could. All the same, he overtook her at the bottom of the hill and soared away out of sight without even glancing at her as he passed.

She was still seething when she got home and the sight of Lady Fox sitting outside the drawing-room window hardly improved her temper. Her mother was there too and the coffee-tray and both ladies turned to look at her as she crossed the grass.

Lady Fox was all graciousness. 'Matilda—you have just returned from visiting Roseanne? Does she not look well? Such a splendid job Mr Scott-Thurlow has done on her poor leg.' She sighed loudly. 'Though I shudder to think of his bill. Still, one must have the best, must one not?' She took a good look at Matilda. 'I must say you are rather pale; surely you should have more colour after your lovely holiday in Devon? I heard all about it from Rhoda.'

Matilda accepted a cup of coffee from her mother. 'But she wasn't there.'

Lady Fox looked arch. 'Well, no—she dislikes the cottage, I believe, but Mr Scott-Thurlow spent a couple of days there, did he not? And naturally he would have told her all about it.' She added reprovingly, 'They are engaged, after all.'

'I wonder what will happen when they marry?'

mused Matilda out loud. 'Will he spend his holidays at Stoke Fleming and Rhoda carry on with her round of parties?'

Lady Fox's formidable bosom swelled alarmingly. 'Really, Matilda, I don't think that remark is in the best of taste.' She looked away from Matilda's green stare. 'What do you intend to do next?'

'I've no idea, Lady Fox.' She finished her coffee. 'You'll excuse me?' She smiled at her mother. 'I'll get those beans blanched ready for the freezer.'

The two ladies watched her go. 'Such a sensible girl,' said Lady Fox. 'It must be a great worry to you that she is not yet married.'

Mrs ffinch smiled. 'Why should it worry me? Matilda could have married several times over but she is content to wait until she meets the right man.'

'Supposing she doesn't?' asked Lady Fox acidly.

'Oh, but she will, I have no doubt about that.' Mrs ffinch lifted the coffee-pot. 'Will you have another cup?'

Mrs ffinch might have had no doubts about her daughter, but Matilda was a mass of conflicting emotions. She longed to see James again but what good would that do? For when they did meet, she snapped at him and he—he laughed at her even when his face was placid. She must amuse him a good deal and she had been a fool to kiss him. He shouldn't have kissed her in the first place though...

She did her best to settle down into the bosom of her family, undertaking rather more chores than she needed to in and around the parish, helping in the house, cooking and gardening. None of these were enough to stop her thinking. She had been at home for just over a week when she told her mother that she had seen a job in the *Western Gazette* and intended to apply for it. 'Someone wants help with an old lady who has gone a bit dotty, I gather. In the Western Highlands...'

Her mother, beating batter, paused for a second and then went on calmly, 'It sounds a long way away, darling—and an old lady, senile at that—she would be very trying.' She saw the obstinate set of Matilda's gentle mouth and went on quickly. 'But I dare say a change would be pleasant. They say the scenery is magnificent.'

Matilda thought sadly she didn't care a button about the scenery; it was a long way from James. 'I think I'll write anyway,' she announced and drifted away to find pen and paper, sit down at the little desk in the sitting-room and then fall into a daydream where James came in through the door...

Esme came through the door instead. 'I say,' she said excitedly, 'have you seen this?' She waved the *Daily Telegraph* at Matilda.

'How could I have seen it?' Matilda, her daydream interrupted, spoke testily. 'You've got the paper.'

'Well, I'll read it to you. It says, "The marriage arranged between Miss Rhoda Symes and Mr James Scott-Thurlow will not now take place—"'

The paper was whipped out of her hand and Matilda read it for herself, and just to make sure she read it for a second time. He had wanted to tell her something at the cottage and she hadn't let him—he had told her that she would know where to find him if she were to change her mind and yet when he had stopped to give her petrol he hadn't said a word; indeed, he had been at his most tiresome...

'What are you going to do?' asked Esme.

'Do, what should I do? It's no concern of mine.'

Esme gave her a thoughtful look. 'You've been in love with James for a long time, haven't you? The least you can do is tell him.'

Matilda looked at her with horror. 'Tell him? I'd sooner die.'

Which dramatic statement was ignored by her sister. 'Rubbish—you do love him, don't you, Tilly?'

'Yes.' Matilda got up so quickly that paper and envelopes flew in all directions. She darted through the door and into her father's study.

'Father, may I borrow the car? Just to get to Sherborne—I want to catch the London train.'

Her father studied her face, usually so serene, and saw that she was labouring under some strong emotion. 'Certainly you may, Matilda. How long will you be gone? I might need it in the meantime...'

'Oh, I hadn't thought of that. I don't know, I'm going to see James—Mr Scott-Thurlow—if—that is, I might come back later today—it depends.'

The Reverend Mr ffinch pushed his sermon to one side. 'Hilary will be back from Salisbury this afternoon; ask the station-master to tell her to pick the car up from the station yard. She can drive herself back here.' He glanced at the clock on the mantelpiece. 'You had better hurry, my dear.'

She dropped a kiss on to his thatch of grey hair and tore through the house and upstairs to her room, where she began rooting around in her wardrobe. It had become important that she look her best.

A glance at her watch told her that if she was to catch the train fussing around deciding what to wear wasn't

to be considered. She got into the flowered two-piece;
he had seen it often enough, but who cared?

She would have liked to have spent some time on
her face and hair, but as it was they both received
perfunctory attention. She crammed odds and ends into
her handbag; at least she had some money…

Her explanations to her mother were garbled and
vague, leaving that lady to sort them out at her leisure.
She kissed her parent swiftly and ran out to the shed
where the car was kept. Esme was there. 'You're
wearing that again,' she said, 'but of course if James
loves you he won't care if you're wrapped in a sack.'

'I don't know,' said Matilda wildly. 'Sometimes I
thought…and then I was sure that he didn't…'

She got into the car and Esme leaned through the
open window. 'Well, you'll soon know…' She glanced
over her shoulder and luckily Matilda, bent over the
ignition key, didn't see her face, wreathed in a wide
grin. The Rolls was nosing its way through the open
gate and came to a halt. 'Back carefully,' she told
Matilda.

The car started up in a middle-aged fashion and
Matilda began to back it out of the shed; there was
plenty of room to turn at the side of the house. She gave
a perfunctory glance in the mirror, gasped with fright
and braked within a few feet of theRolls, which was
effectively blocking her path.

Mr Scott-Thurlow had got out and so had the dogs.
Esme, regretful that she was about to miss an interesting
situation, whistled to them and took herself off, round
to the back of the house.

Matilda didn't see her go and if Mr Scott-Thurlow
did he gave no sign.

He walked without haste from his car to hers, opened the door and waited while she got out.

'Going somewhere?' he wanted to know.

She was trembling with the excitement of seeing him and the shock of very nearly backing into the Rolls. She said in a shaky little voice, 'I almost backed into your car. I could have damaged it.'

He had taken her hands in his. 'Rolls-Royce motor cars don't damage easily. Were you coming to see me?'

When she nodded he said, 'I thought that you might. You are a very obstinate girl, my darling—that is because of your lovely red hair, of course, but I do hope that, when we are married, you will listen meekly when I have something to say to you. Of course until this moment there has been very little opportunity.'

'Don't you love her?'

'No. And I never did. How delightfully direct you are, dear heart.' He smiled down at her. 'I love you, and deep in your heart you know that. I loved you the moment I saw you in church. I wanted to marry you there and then, but of course that wouldn't have been very practical, and besides I had to end my engagement to Rhoda. All the while I wasn't sure if you loved me.'

'How could you possibly know? I never said a word.'

He smiled slowly. '"There's language in her eye, her cheek, her lip..."'

'Shakespeare, *Troilus and Cressida*,' said Matilda, momentarily diverted. 'Then why didn't you—?'

He bent and kissed her very gently. 'Dear heart, when did you ever give me any encouragement?'

'You don't need encouragement,' she told him flatly. 'You know just what you're doing with your life; you're successful and nothing seems to disturb you—you're so calm.'

'My dear life, I can see that you know nothing about me at all. You will have years in which to discover just what kind of man I am.' He plucked her close and wrapped her in his great arms. 'There is one thing you must learn immediately. I do not care to waste time.' He kissed her then, and there was nothing gentle about it this time.

'Oh, my goodness,' whispered Matilda when she had her breath again. 'What—?'

'Marry me, Matilda. You can ask me anything you want once we are married, but there is one question. Do you love me?'

'Yes, oh, dear James, you have no idea how much.'

'I shall enjoy finding out, my darling heart. We had better tell your family, had we not? But first…'

He pulled her close to kiss her soundly and the ffinch family, watching unashamedly from a variety of windows, sighed their satisfaction. Her father went down to the cellar to fetch up a bottle of champagne he had been saving for some special occasion; her mother, arranging glasses on a tray, reflected with guilty satisfaction that Lady Fox was going to be put out and, as for Esme, she was dreaming up her bridesmaid's dress.

Not that any of these things mattered to the two people standing so close together in the drive; they had found their heaven and they were content.

* * * * *

REQUEST YOUR FREE BOOKS!

2 FREE NOVELS
FROM THE ROMANCE COLLECTION
PLUS 2 FREE GIFTS!

YES! Please send me 2 FREE novels from the Romance Collection and my 2 FREE gifts (gifts are worth about $10). After receiving them, if I don't wish to receive any more books, I can return the shipping statement marked "cancel." If I don't cancel, I will receive 4 brand-new novels every month and be billed just $5.99 per book in the U.S. or $6.49 per book in Canada. That's a saving of at least 25% off the cover price. It's quite a bargain! Shipping and handling is just 50¢ per book in the U.S. and 75¢ per book in Canada.* I understand that accepting the 2 free books and gifts places me under no obligation to buy anything. I can always return a shipment and cancel at any time. Even if I never buy another book, the two free books and gifts are mine to keep forever.

194/394 MDN FELQ

Name	(PLEASE PRINT)

Address	Apt. #

City	State/Prov.	Zip/Postal Code

Signature (if under 18, a parent or guardian must sign)

Mail to the **Reader Service:**
IN U.S.A.: P.O. Box 1867, Buffalo, NY 14240-1867
IN CANADA: P.O. Box 609, Fort Erie, Ontario L2A 5X3

Not valid for current subscribers to the Romance Collection
or the Romance/Suspense Collection.

Want to try two free books from another line?
Call 1-800-873-8635 or visit www.ReaderService.com.

* Terms and prices subject to change without notice. Prices do not include applicable taxes. Sales tax applicable in N.Y. Canadian residents will be charged applicable taxes. Offer not valid in Quebec. This offer is limited to one order per household. All orders subject to credit approval. Credit or debit balances in a customer's account(s) may be offset by any other outstanding balance owed by or to the customer. Please allow 4 to 6 weeks for delivery. Offer available while quantities last.

Your Privacy—The Reader Service is committed to protecting your privacy. Our Privacy Policy is available online at www.ReaderService.com or upon request from the Reader Service.

We make a portion of our mailing list available to reputable third parties that offer products we believe may interest you. If you prefer that we not exchange your name with third parties, or if you wish to clarify or modify your communication preferences, please visit us at www.ReaderService.com/consumerschoice or write to us at Reader Service Preference Service, P.O. Box 9062, Buffalo, NY 14269. Include your complete name and address.

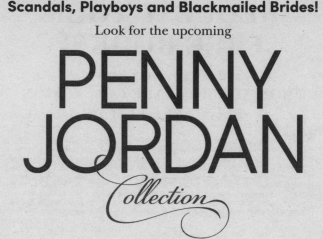

*Harlequin® Romance author **Barbara Wallace** brings you a romantic new tale of finding love unexpectedly in*
MR. RIGHT, NEXT DOOR!

Enjoy this sneak-peek excerpt.

"IT'S TOO BEAUTIFUL A DAY to spend stuck inside. Come with me."

"I can't. I have to work."

"Yes, you can," Grant replied, closing the last couple of steps between them and tucking a finger underneath her chin. "You know you want to."

"So, you're a mind reader now?" The response might have worked better if her jaw weren't quivering from his touch.

"Not a mind reader," he replied. "Eye reader. And yours are saying an awful lot."

His touch was making her insides quiver. She wanted desperately to look away and refuse to make eye contact with him, but pride wouldn't let her. Instead, she forced herself to keep her features as bland as possible so he wouldn't see that a part of her—the very female part—did want to go with him. It also wanted to feel more of his touch, and the common sense part of her was having a hard time forming an opposing argument.

"If so, then no doubt you know they're saying 'remove your hand.'"

He chuckled. Soft and low. *A bedroom laugh.* "Did you know they flash when you're being stubborn?"

Rather than argue, Sophie swallowed her pride and looked to his feet.

"You so don't want me to move my hand, either."

"You're incorrigible. You know that, right?"

"Thank you."

"I still want you to move your hand."

"If you insist…." Suddenly his hands were cupping her cheeks, drawing her parted lips under his. Sophie's gasp was lost in her throat. As she expected, he tasted of peppermint and coffee and…and….

And, oh wow, could he kiss!

It ended and her eyelids fluttered open. Grant's face hovered a breath from hers. Gently, he traced the slope of her nose and smiled.

"Your eyes told me you wanted that, too."

If she had an ounce of working brain matter, Sophie would have turned and stormed out of his apartment then and there. Problem was one, she was trembling and, two, the fact she kissed him back probably wiped out any outrage she'd be trying to convey.

So she did the next best thing. She folded her arms across her chest and presented him with a somewhat flushed but indignant expression. "Do not do that again."

Will Grant convince Sophie to let her guard down long enough to see if he's her MR. RIGHT, NEXT DOOR? Find out in September 2012, from Harlequin® Romance!